PERSON–ENVIRONMENT–BEHAVIOR RESEARCH

PERSON–ENVIRONMENT–BEHAVIOR
RESEARCH

*Investigating Activities and Experiences
in Spaces and Environments*

DOUGLAS AMEDEO
REGINALD G. GOLLEDGE
ROBERT J. STIMSON

THE GUILFORD PRESS
New York   London

© 2009 The Guilford Press
A Division of Guilford Publications, Inc.
72 Spring Street, New York, NY 10012
www.guilford.com

All rights reserved

No part of this book may be reproduced, translated, stored in a retrieval system, or transmitted, in any form or by any means, electronic, mechanical, photocopying, microfilming, recording, or otherwise, without written permission from the Publisher.

Printed in the United States of America

This book is printed on acid-free paper.

Last digit is print number: 9 8 7 6 5 4 3 2 1

Library of Congress Cataloging-in-Publication Data

Amedeo, Douglas.
  Person–environment–behavior research : investigating activities and experiences in spaces and environments / by Douglas Amedeo, Reginald G. Golledge, Robert J. Stimson.
    p. cm.
  Includes bibliographical references and index.
  ISBN 978-1-59385-870-4 (pbk.)—ISBN 978-1-59385-871-1 (hardcover)
  1. Social psychology—Methodology. 2. Environmental psychology. 3. Spatial behavior. 4. Research. I. Golledge, Reginald G., 1937– II. Stimson, R. J. (Robert John) III. Title.
  HM1033.A44 2009
  304.2′3—dc22

2008005433

*To our wives—Pat, Allison, and Geri—
whose support during the extended period
of assembling this volume was invaluable*

Acknowledgments

Producing a book manuscript usually requires the efforts of people in addition to the principal authors. This book is no exception. There are many people to whom we wish to extend our thanks and appreciation. First, we thoroughly appreciated the efforts of the team at The Guilford Press who tried to keep us on track and answered every query with speed and class, and who were instrumental in bringing the book to fruition.

We could not have produced the final manuscript without the intense efforts, support, and dedication of our various support personnel at the University of Nebraska, Lincoln; the University of California, Santa Barbara; and the University of Queensland, Brisbane. In each case, there were many persons involved in reading, interpreting, and word processing almost indecipherable drafts. Others helped with collecting tables and figures, proofing, developing a table of contents, and indexing. All three authors used the support resources in each home base, so we want to jointly acknowledge the substantial efforts of the following people: at Lincoln, Joyce Hurst; at Santa Barbara, Bill Norrington, José Saleta, and Mark Grosch; and at Brisbane, Angela Chau and Vanessa Reid. Jointly, we express our warmest thanks. This book probably would not have been completed without their support and dedication.

Preface

Focusing on Space in Person–Environment–Behavior Relations

This book is about the investigation of person–environment–behavior (P-E-B) relationships. Two facets of the book distinguish it from others of its kind:

1. It explicitly explores the manner in which space and/or environments enter into human activity and experience.
2. It intentionally employs a wide variety of investigative approaches to do so.

This emphasis is deliberately on the *spatial* dimension—whether in a direct sense or, more commonly, as a part of *environmental settings*—and how it influences *human activities* and *experiences*. Too often in social and behavioral circumstances "space" is not given specific attention.

Two basic inquiries underlie any curiosity about the role of space in P-E-B relationships: (1) *Why must spatial influences in such relationships be made explicit?* and (2) *How might one go about making them so?* Of the two, the "how to"—or the more methodological inquiry—demands much more reflection, particularly with regard to issues of appropriateness and of the information produced. This is not unexpected, because research results generated by many of the approaches discussed in this book do not always conform to conventional logic dictated by the assumptions underlying statistical-inference modeling.

But this is not uncommon in human sciences. Weak correspondence between the reasoning employed in statistical-inference modeling and many of the investigative approaches employed in social and behavioral research is the norm. Although this sometimes gets attributed to investigators holding different perspectives about the world, it can probably be equally as well explained by the complexities frequently encountered in these research domains, which preclude meeting the ideal assumptions required for employing this kind of modeling as a research design.

Consider, for example, *some* of the common complexities that arise out of the actual conditions faced by investigators when exploring human issues:

1. Critical processes and characteristics relevant to the study domain are frequently indistinct, fuzzy, or unclear.
2. Plausible empirical counterparts for hypothetical and/or latent constructs are either absent in the study domain or not evident.
3. Model individuals assumed under the research framework are incongruent with the characteristics of real individuals actually observed in the study area.
4. Opportunities are lacking for precisely ascertaining the perceptions of participants, and the meanings, interpretations, and experiences of the principal categories, concepts, and constructs of the study.
5. The population of conceptual relevance is obscure or indeterminable, presenting severe constraints for selecting a stratified random probability sample.
6. Information available in the study domain is not susceptible to measurement employing metrics, such as ordinal, interval, or ratio.
7. Cultural and historical influences on participants in the study area are difficult to identify and/or make concrete.
8. Accumulated and/or previous knowledge is skimpy and unstructured for hypothesis formulation.
9. Conceptualizations or theories in the domain of interest are inconsistent with critical aspects of empirical circumstances.
10. Acquisition of relevant information is severely constrained by the structure of instruments to acquire it and/or by the presumptions about its nature.
11. And, most salient for human research, participants in the study are complex; they feel, act, react, transact, and interact with things and others. As biological entities, they are capable of sensing, perceiving, thinking, constructing, and interpreting; as social beings, they have motivations, beliefs, values, intents, and dispositions. Above all, they are self-oriented. All of these human characteristics—and more—operate in concert!

The concern in actual research is how complexities like these influence the choice of a research framework and how they affect the investigative process itself. Obviously their presence can inhibit what may be inquired about, the information available to handle inquiries, and the methods or approaches that can be used to frame it all for analysis. Some complexities—especially those affecting the determination of populations—might preclude the use of the hypothesis-testing, statistical-inference research design, while a collection of others might prompt the use of a case study format. Others—particularly those affecting measurement and the identification of subject characteristics—could make the meaning content embedded in information difficult to ascertain by conventional methods. It is clear that many of these and other complexities as well impose severe constraints on the attempts by researchers to:

- Represent variables or dimensions in a study area.
- Measure what is being observed.
- Generalize results of an investigation to some larger population.

The point made in this book—by implication and directly—is that the conditions encountered in research investigating human activities and experiences in spaces and environments are not likely to resemble the research-enhancing circumstances that many students are exposed to when first learning how to do research. Those are relatively "ideal" circumstances that are more characteristic of the model situations illustrated in teaching examples than those faced in the actual reality of empirical situations. Investigators involved in research exploring P-E-B relationships must deal with contexts of actuality, and these characteristically have conditions that generate many conceptual and methodological complexities for the investigative process.

The prominence of these complexities tends to be noticeably *amplified* in actual contexts for human activities and companion experiences. Any number of reasons may be cited to account for this intensifying effect, but chief among them would have to be that the contexts of actuality are both constrained and qualified by spatial and/or environmental dimensions. These dimensions *intensify complexities* because of their nearly complete and inextricable immersion into all the other components defining activity contexts.

Although conditions and the complexities they generate are often frustrating when encountered, this does not suggest that researchers should abandon efforts to examine, evaluate, and generally explore. Social and behavioral disciplines are, after all, the inquiring kind. They are faced with many *why* and *how* questions about human issues that need to be entertained in whatever ways are realistically and pragmatically available. Although it is always possible to pretend that all research can be treated, in effect, as closed systems with ideal conditions, researchers must continue to inquire, examine, and explore human issues under whatever conditions are encountered in the "real world." Hence, the discovery of trends, connections, and tendencies, and the continuous ongoing development of *constructs*, are useful in a conceptual sense in order to comprehend or understand domains of human existence. This is what we try to demonstrate throughout this book. Our efforts to do so are reflected in the variety of research questions, approaches, and analyses that are demonstrated within it.

As will become evident, the book describes on occasion a revisiting of that which was presumed to be already known. In examples like these, objectives may be redefined so that a clearer evaluation of individual cases may replace, for example, desires to generalize to populations from results of representative probability samples. They may involve alternative approaches such as emphasizing the development of grounded theory and case studies, or may even be restricted to identifying dimensions of commonality (see, for example, Creswell, 1994, 1998; Patton, 1980). Decisions to adapt these and other alternative approaches to structure one's research often grow out of beliefs about the inappropriateness or shortcomings of conventional approaches to handle evaluative inquiries of interest. It is notable that some authors have challenged the assumptions underlying the commonly used and advocated "statistical-inference" framework. These scholars indicate that such assumptions may be premature for conditions as they are currently understood in many human activity and experience contexts (see, for example, Henkel, 1976; Morrison, 1969; Morrison & Henkel, 1970; Oakes, 1986). In many ways, alternative approaches can be characterized as revisiting conceptual levels or developing more comprehensive descriptions of the phenomena of interest before, say, hypotheses are formed and tested. Many investigators involved in this type of research have devoted their efforts to developing series of "systematic operations" to pragmatically define and measure constructs that seem resistant to fundamental measurement and that, in existence, are only latent or hypothetical.

Thus, conceptual and methodological complexities, their amplification in contexts structured and influenced by spatial and/or environmental dimensions, and the effects augmented complexities might have on the nature of research into aspects of human activities and companion experiences, are the issues of prominence in the book.

Thematic Agenda

In the book we describe how investigators—when faced with conceptual and methodological complexities—have managed to contribute through the use of alternative approaches to the understanding of human activities and experiences in spatially and environmentally structured contexts. The book is organized into seven parts. Since the examples described investigate some aspect of human activities and experiences in actual space and environment contexts, a preliminary discussion of why it makes sense to consider space and/or environments in such circumstances is provided in Chapter 1. It specifically addresses spatial and/or environmental influences on human activities and experiences.

The six chapters in Parts I and II are devoted to detailed discussions about those concerns which are fundamental for researchers, addressing issues that are pretty much generic to all research that is conducted in the scientific or quasi-scientific paradigm. Part I has two chapters on the theme *Comprehending Data Recording and Measurement to Generate Information in Scientific Inquiry*. Part II has four chapters that address a variety of approaches to *Collecting Data and Representing Information*. Those chapters focus on fulfilling information needs in research, as in methods for acquiring information (commonly referred to as data), representing it, sampling to observe and represent it, organizing or recording information, and measuring and defining it.

In Parts III, IV, V, and VI (Chapters 8–18), specific examples of such diverse approaches are provided in which the research orientations and perspectives differ. These research examples are selected to illustrate a variety of research designs and ways in which an aspect of human activity or experience in a spatial or environmental context or setting has been investigated using specific types and sources of information and approaches to measurement involving specific secondary data or specific modes of collecting primary data, and specific analytic tools as appropriate to address the research issues or questions being investigated. The research examples are presented as stand-alone chapters that are arranged sequentially to address the fourfold interrelationships between activities and experiences in spaces and environments. Part III has three chapters giving research examples that address *Activities in Environments*, Part IV has three chapters that address *Activities and Spaces*, Part V has two chapters that address *Experiences and Environments*, and Part VI has three chapters that address *Experiences and Spaces*. We have allocated much space to a discussion of the methodological and conceptual maneuvers that those investigators have employed to deal with the study area or situational complexities they have encountered. Each research example addresses why the researcher proceeded to examine the topic investigated in that particular way. Emphasis is also placed on the analyses employed by the investigator(s) because the selection of methods for examining issues is often reflective of adjustments that needed to be made to deal with complexities encountered.

In Part VII, *Planning Research*, a concluding chapter maps out a strategic plan for organizing one's research investigations as a guide that might help the young and inexperienced researcher to initiate and conduct research that addressed an aspect of human activities and/or experiences in space and environments.

Contents

List of Figures and Tables   xxiii

1. An Overview of Spatial and/or Environmental Influences in Human Activities and Experiences   1
   1.1 Introduction   1
   1.2 Clarifying Terms   2
      1.2.1 Human Activities and Experiences   2
      1.2.2 How to Understand Human Activities and Experiences   3
      1.2.3 Space and/or Spatial Forms in Human Contexts   5
   1.3 Space as a Dimension of Environments for Human Activities and Experiences   9
      1.3.1 Assumptions about Assessing Space in the Human Context   10
      1.3.2 Assumptions Facilitating Further Discussion   12
   1.4 Environments as Contexts and Arenas for Activities and Experiences: A Pragmatic View   20
      1.4.1 Immediate Environments as Contexts and Arenas for Activity   20
      1.4.2 Environmental Information and Behavioral Functioning   21
      1.4.3 The Importance of Memory-Based Environmental Knowledge   22
      1.4.4 Context and Arena Features of Memory-Based Environmental Knowledge   23
      1.4.5 But Why Does This Matter?   24

PART I. Comprehending Data Recording and Measurement to Generate Information in Scientific Inquiry   27

2. Data and Measurement to Generate Information   29
   2.1 Introduction   29
   2.2 Creating Knowledge: Distinguishing between Information and Data   30
   2.3 The Variety of Data Available for Research   32
      2.3.1 Primary versus Secondary Data   32
      2.3.2 Data Sources   32
      2.3.3 Types of Data   33

2.3.4 The Aggregation–Disaggregation Problem 34
2.3.5 The Ecological Fallacy and Other Fallacies 35
2.3.6 The Decision-Making Unit and Its Population 36
2.3.7 The Data Matrix 37
2.4 Measurement Implications for Working with Different Types of Data 38
2.4.1 The Need for Measurement and the Qualities It Requires 38
2.4.2 Levels of Measurement 40
2.4.3 Data Quality Issues 42
2.5 Conclusion 44

3. Collecting Data and Generating Information in a Scientific Mode   45
3.1 Introduction 45
3.2 The Rationale for Data Collection, Measurement, and Analysis in Research 45
3.2.1 Different Degrees to Which Relevant Data Can Be Used Directly or Indirectly in Processed Form 46
3.2.2 Operational Reflectors: Latent Variables 47
3.2.3 Other Difficulties and Complexities 48
3.3 Creating Reflectors or Indicators for Working with Different Forms of Data 48
3.3.1 Concepts and Conceptualizing 49
3.3.2 Attributes and Variables 49
3.4 Diverse Research Formats 52
3.4.1 Qualitative and Quantitative Approaches 52
3.4.2 Survey and Experimental Approaches 52
3.5 The Scientific Approach to Inquiry 53
3.5.1 Modes of Scientific Inquiry 53
3.5.2 Models 57
3.6 Implications for Researching Human Activities and Experiences in Spaces and Environments 61

PART II. Collecting Data and Representing Information   63

4. The Purpose of Collecting and Matching Data and Analysis   65
4.1 Introduction 65
4.2 Approaches to Data Creation 65
4.2.1 Primary Data and Secondary Data 65
4.2.2 Some Definitions 67
4.2.3 Purposes of Data Collection 67
4.3 Matching Data and Analysis 68
4.3.1 Transforming Qualitative Information into Data 68
4.3.2 Spatialization 69
4.4 Roles of Information in Research 70
4.4.1 Research as an Information-Generating Tool 70
4.4.2 Description 70
4.5 The Basic Elements of Geospatial Description 73
4.5.1 Points 73
4.5.2 Lines, Edges, and Boundaries 75
4.5.3 Links and Networks 76
4.5.4 Areas 77
4.6 Explanation 79
4.7 Modes of Collecting Data and Generating Information 79

5. **Qualitative and Survey Approaches to Collecting Data and Generating Information** — 81
   - 5.1 Introduction 81
   - 5.2 Qualitative Methods 81
     - 5.2.1 *The Concern of Qualitative Methods* 81
     - 5.2.2 *The Geographic Tradition* 82
     - 5.2.3 *Objectivity in Qualitative Research* 82
   - 5.3 Theoretical Traditions and Approaches in Qualitative Inquiry 83
     - 5.3.1 *Case Studies* 84
     - 5.3.2 *The Narrative* 86
     - 5.3.3 *Focus Groups* 86
   - 5.4 Using Surveys to Collect Data and Generate Information 87
     - 5.4.1 *The Tasks Involved in Conducting a Survey* 87
     - 5.4.2 *Key Issues to Determine Prior to Conducting a Survey* 88
     - 5.4.3 *Modes for Survey Data Collection* 89
     - 5.4.4 *Relative Advantages and Disadvantages of Survey Modes* 93
   - 5.5 Mixing Quantitative and Qualitative Approaches 93
   - 5.6 Conclusion 95

6. **Collecting Information from Sampled Populations Using Probability and Nonprobability Designs** — 96
   - 6.1 Introduction 96
   - 6.2 When to Use Probability Sampling and Why 96
     - 6.2.1 *Making Inferences and Estimates* 96
     - 6.2.2 *Sample Size, Sample Proportion, and Sampling Error* 97
   - 6.3 Methods of Probability Sampling 99
     - 6.3.1 *Simple Random Sampling* 99
     - 6.3.2 *Systematic Sampling* 99
     - 6.3.3 *Stratification* 100
     - 6.3.4 *Cluster and Multistage Sampling* 100
     - 6.3.5 *Other Probability Sampling Designs* 101
   - 6.4 Nonprobability Sampling Approaches 101
     - 6.4.1 *Haphazard, Convenience, or Accidental Sampling* 102
     - 6.4.2 *Purposive, Judgmental, or Expert Choice Sampling* 102
     - 6.4.3 *Quota Sampling* 102
   - 6.5 Data Sources for Sampling 102
     - 6.5.1 *The Census* 103
     - 6.5.2 *Random-Digit Dialing for Telephone Surveys* 104
     - 6.5.3 *Lists or Directories of Specific Populations* 104
     - 6.5.4 *Sampling When There Is Not a Listing of the Target Population* 104
     - 6.5.5 *Piggybacking onto Existing Surveys* 105
     - 6.5.6 *Automated Data Computer Systems* 105
   - 6.6 Collecting Information from People Using a Survey Instrument 106
     - 6.6.1 *Addressing Sources of Nonsampling Error and Bias* 107
     - 6.6.2 *A Model Conceptualizing the Complexity of the Question–Answer Process* 107
     - 6.6.3 *Instrument Design and Question Construction* 109
   - 6.7 Respondent Behavior 112
     - 6.7.1 *Interviewer Training and Standardizing Interview Behavior* 113
   - 6.8 Conclusion 115

7. **Extrapolating from Controlled Conditions to the Real World** — 116
   7.1 Introduction   116
   7.2 Some Key Issues in Using Controlled Settings to Run Experiments   116
      7.2.1 Maintaining Ecological Validity   116
      7.2.2 Laboratory versus Real-World Experiments   117
   7.3 Ways of Conducting Experiments   118
      7.3.1 Purpose of an Experiment and Evolution of Types of Experiments in Spatial Research   118
      7.3.2 Complexity in Experiments   119
   7.4 Virtual Experiments   121
      7.4.1 Augmented Reality   121
      7.4.2 Desktop Virtual Display   121
      7.4.3 Immersive Virtual Systems   122
   7.5 Simulations   122
      7.5.1 Applications of Simulations   122
      7.5.2 Types of Simulations   123
   7.6 Computational Process Models   123
   7.7 Conclusion   124

PART III. Activities in Environments — 125

8. **Modeling Social-Environmental Factors Associated with Spatial Patterns of Voter Support for Political Parties** — 127
   8.1 Introduction   127
   8.2 Background Context   127
   8.3 Developing the GIS-Enabled Spatial Decision Support System   129
      8.3.1 The Data   129
      8.3.2 Visualizing Electoral Voting Patterns   129
      8.3.3 Integrating the Voting Data with Social-Environmental Data   130
   8.4 Modeling Ecological Relationships: Analysis and Results   130
      8.4.1 Multiple Regression Analysis   133
      8.4.2 Predicting Local Patterns of Voter Support for Political Parties   136
      8.4.3 The Position of the Political Parties in a "Sociopolitical Space"   140
      8.4.4 Accuracy of the Model Predictions   141
   8.5 Discussion   142
   8.6 Acknowledgment   143

9. **Intellectually Challenged People Interacting with Their Environment** — 144
   9.1 Introduction   144
   9.2 Context for the Study of Disability and Activities in Environments   145
      9.2.1 Disadvantage, Disenfranchisement, and Discrimination   145
      9.2.2 Disabling Environments   145
      9.2.3 Activities of Intellectually Challenged Groups Interacting in Their Immediate Environments   146
   9.3 The Experiments   148
      9.3.1 Experiment 1: Determining Knowledge of Environmental Cues   149
      9.3.2 Experiment 2: Sequencing and Distancing of Cues Along Routes   150
      9.3.3 Experiment 3: Examining Configurational Knowledge   151
   9.4 Discussion   153
   9.5 Acknowledgment   155

10. Spatial Competence of Blind and Visually Impaired People   156
    When Performing Activities in Different Spaces
    10.1 Introduction   156
    10.2 Background Context   156
        10.2.1 Difficulties Faced by Blind or Visually Impaired People   157
        10.2.2 Policy Approaches to Creating Accessible Environments
              for Disabled Groups   159
    10.3 An Experimental Approach to Examining Activities in Spaces
         Where Sight Is Absent   160
        10.3.1 The Environmental Setting and Experimental Design   160
        10.3.2 Results   163
    10.4 Using Remote Infrared Auditory Signage   165
        10.4.1 Participants in the Experiment   167
        10.4.2 Procedures   167
        10.4.3 Analysis and Results   168
        10.4.4 Discussion   168
    10.5 Conclusion   169
    10.6 Acknowledgment   169

PART IV. Activities and Spaces   171

11. Decision Process and Choice in the Residential Relocation of Retirees   173
    11.1 Introduction   173
    11.2 Background Context   174
        11.2.1 The Residential Relocation of Retirees   174
        11.2.2 The Retirement Village Alternative   175
    11.3 A Model of Migration and the Residential Relocation Decision
         Choice Process   176
        11.3.1 The Approach   177
        11.3.2 A "Push–Pull" Model Framework   177
    11.4 Methodology and Analysis   180
        11.4.1 Survey Design and Data Collection   180
        11.4.2 Analyzing and Modeling the "Push" Factors   180
        11.4.3 Analyzing and Modeling the "Pull" Factors   182
        11.4.4 What Retirees Are Looking for in a Retirement Village   186
        11.4.5 Satisfaction with the Relocation
              to a Retirement Village   189
        11.4.6 Discussion   189
    11.5 Conclusion   189
    11.6 Acknowledgment   190

12. Sex Roles and the Gendering of Activities and Spaces   191
    12.1 Introduction   191
    12.2 Background Context   192
    12.3 An Experimental Approach to Studying Sex Roles
         in Determining Activities   193
        12.3.1 Participants   193
        12.3.2 Procedures   193
        12.3.3 Analysis and Results   195
        12.3.4 Discussion   196

xviii Contents

    12.4 Investigating the Social Gendering of Spaces and Activities   197
        12.4.1 Procedures   197
        12.4.2 Analysis and Results   199
        12.4.3 Discussion   200
    12.5 Conclusion   201
    12.6 Acknowledgment   201

13. Spatial Structural Influences on Activities in an Elementary Classroom Environment   202

    13.1 Introduction   202
    13.2 Complexities Influencing the Choice of a Research Design   202
    13.3 Details of Amedeo and Dyck's (2003) Case Study   204
        13.3.1 Influences on the Conduct of Teaching and Learning Activities   204
        13.3.2 Activities in the Elementary Classroom and the Significance of "Space"   205
    13.4 Property Perceptions of Classroom Spatial Layout   206
        13.4.1 Exploring Teachers' Property Perceptions of Classroom Spatial Layouts   206
        13.4.2 Teachers' Judgments about Properties of the Five Classroom Spatial Layouts   207
    13.5 Preferences of Classroom Spatial Layouts   211
        13.5.1 Value Implications of Teachers' Preference Rankings   212
        13.5.2 Evaluating the Configuration of the Spatial Layouts in the MDS Conceptual Space   213
        13.5.3 Description and Assessment of the Clusters in the MDS Space of Figure 13.2   214
        13.5.4 Conclusion   222
    13.6 Discussion   223

PART V. Experiences and Environments   **225**

14. Experiences in Everyday Environments   233

    14.1 Introduction   233
        14.1.1 A Search for Norm Influences in Affective Reactions to Everyday Environments   234
    14.2 Examining Participant Responses for Evidence of Affective Norm Influences   236
        14.2.1 Perspective 1: R-Mode Factor Analysis of a Subject–Feeling Array   236
        14.2.2 Perspective 2: Q-Mode Factor Analysis of a Subject–Feeling Array   236
        14.2.3 Integrating the Q- and R-Mode Forms of Factor Information with Original Responses   237
    14.3 Norm Influences on the Affective Responses to the City Street Scene Environment (E1)   237
        14.3.1 Focusing on Salient Feelings Expressed by Subjects for the City Street Scene   239
        14.3.2 Norm Influences on the Affective Responses to the Social Gathering Environment (E2)   240
        14.3.3 Norms in the Affective Responses to the Woodland Setting Scene (E3)   240
    14.4 Overview   243
        14.4.1 Preliminary Remarks about Implications of Results   243

14.5 Affects in Cognitively Oriented P-E-B Frameworks   244
  14.5.1 *Cognitively Oriented P-E-B Frameworks*   244
  14.5.2 *Affect and Cognitive Processes*   245
14.6 Information-Processing Concerns of P-E-B Frameworks   245
  14.6.1 *Conceptually Incorporating "Affect" into P-E-B Frameworks*   246
  14.6.2 *Empirical Association between Affects and Internal Information*   246
  14.6.3 *Integrating Reflections of Affective Norms with Environmental Schemata Indicators*   247
14.7 Discussion   250

15. Aesthetic Experiences in Environments   252
15.1 Introduction   252
15.2 Information-Influencing Perceptions of Scenic Quality   252
  15.2.1 *Understanding the Notion of "Scenicness"*   253
  15.2.2 *Issues Affecting the Comprehension of "Scenic Quality"*   253
15.3 Assessments of Scenic Differences among Scenes   258
  15.3.1 *The Sample and Instrument*   258
  15.3.2 *Format for Eliciting Perceptions of Scenicness*   260
15.4 Versions of Scenic Quality   265
  15.4.1 *Arrangements of Scenes Implied by Versions of Scenic Value Perception*   267
  15.4.2. *Information Influences in Versions of Scenic Quality Perception*   267
15.5 Discussion   275
15.6 Conclusion   278
15.7 Acknowledgment   279

PART VI. Experiences and Spaces   281

16. Deriving Metropolitanwide Spatial Patterns of Perceived Quality-of-Life Dimensions   285
16.1 Introduction   285
16.2 QOL: An Overview   286
  16.2.1 *Defining QOL*   286
  16.2.2 *QOL Measurement*   286
  16.2.3 *A "Domains-of-Life" Approach*   287
16.3 Methodology   288
  16.3.1 *The Study Area*   288
  16.3.2 *Data Collection*   288
  16.3.3 *Measurements*   289
  16.3.4 *Aggregation Techniques*   289
16.4 Results and Analysis   291
  16.4.1 *Descriptive Statistics*   291
  16.4.2 *Aggregation: Results of OWA Operators*   292
  16.4.3 *Interregional Variability*   294
16.5 Discussion   297
16.6 Acknowledgment   298

17. Reflecting the Nature of Cognitive Spaces from Perceived Relations   299
   17.1 Introduction   299
   17.2 Background: The Nature of Cognitive Maps Derived from Perceived Spatial Relations   300
   17.3 The Research Approach   301
      17.3.1 Problem Statement   301
      17.3.2 Hypotheses   302
      17.3.3 Research Design   302
      17.3.4 Collecting Information on Environmental Cues   303
      17.3.5 Pilot Study   305
      17.3.6 Cognitive Mapping   306
   17.4 Analysis and Results   308
      17.4.1 Comparing the Groups Tested   308
      17.4.2 The Analysis of Congruence   310
   17.5 Discussion   311

18. Modeling Group Conservation Perspectives   314
   18.1 Introduction   314
   18.2 Considering Human Perspectives in Environmental Conservation Policy   314
      18.2.1 Perspectives   314
      18.2.2 Latent Constructs   316
      18.2.3 An Example of a Latent Construct in Person–Environment Relations Research   316
   18.3 Context for Modeling "Perspectives on Conservation"   317
      18.3.1 Preliminaries Associated with the Development of Constructs   317
      18.3.2 Environmental Context for the Research   318
      18.3.3 Information for Formulating Environmental Policy   319
      18.3.4 Human Emphasis in Environmental Policy Formulation   319
   18.4 Representing Perspectives on Conservation   320
      18.4.1 Environmental Issues and Their Potential Implications for User Groups   320
   18.5 Steps to Model Group Conservation Perspectives   322
      18.5.1 Step 1: Acquiring Respondents for the Study   322
      18.5.2 Step 2: Using a Sorting Process to Obtain Subject Views on Conservation Issues   322
      18.5.3 Step 3: Respondents' Arrangements of Conservation Statements   324
      18.5.4 Step 4: Making Use of Information Embedded in the Array of Arrangements   326
      18.5.5 Step 5: Similarities and Differences among Respondents' Arrangements   326
      18.5.6 Step 6: Arrangements of Conservation Statements Implied inGroupings   329
   18.6 Group Conservation Perspectives and Respondents' Preferences for Conservation Agencies   334
   18.7 Discussion   336
   18.8 Acknowledgment   337

PART VII. Planning Research: The Common Sense of a Research Proposal — 339

19. Mapping a Strategic Plan for Research — 341
19.1 The Research Plan   341
   19.1.1 Some Issues to Consider   341
   19.1.2 Guides and/or Suggestions for Constructing a Research Proposal   343
19.2 Elaborating on the Sections of a Research Proposal   345
   19.2.1 An Introduction   345
   19.2.2 The "Purpose" of the Study: Research Problem Specification   347
   19.2.3 Review of the Relevant Literature   350
   19.2.4 Research Design   351
   19.2.5 Task Responsibilities, Timetable, and Milestones   357
   19.2.6 Budget and Budget Justification   357
   19.2.7 Likely Outcomes and Contributions to Knowledge   358
19.3 Reporting Research Findings   358
   19.3.1 Means of Communicating Research Results   359
   19.3.2 Target Audiences   359
   19.3.3 Getting Published   359
19.4 Summary   360
19.5 Conclusion   361

References — 363

Index — 379

About the Authors — 389

List of Figures and Tables

Figures

1.1.	Stage 1: Unorganized elements	17
1.2.	Stage 2: Organized elements	18
1.3.	Stage 1: Unorganized elements	18
1.4.	Stage 2: Organized elements	19
2.1.	The data matrix, incorporating a spatial element	37
2.2.	A classification of sources of survey error and bias	44
3.1.	A classification of variables	51
3.2.	Approaches to theory construction and testing	55
3.3.	Logic of scientific research	56
3.4.	From geographic reality to the data matrix	61
4.1.	The process of transforming raw data into information	68
4.2.	Georeferencing to spatialize data and produce spatial information	69
4.3.	Diagrammatic spatialization of data in Table 4.1	70
6.1.	A model of the question–answer process	108
7.1.	Distorted grid maps	120
8.1.	The pattern of voting where the Coalition vote outnumbers the Labor vote and vice versa, overlaid on the distribution of incidence of high-income households: Sydney	132
8.2.	Discrimination between the political parties on Functions 1 and 2 using Z-scores between −2.0 and +2.0	141
9.1a.	Composite error map, experimental group	152
9.1b.	Composite error map, control group	152
9.2.	Control group: Warped grid	154
9.3.	Experimental group: Warped grid	154
10.1.	Plan of the route	160
10.2.	Walking error for all choice points: Interactions between trial and condition	164

10.3.	Walking error for critical choice points: Interactions between trial and condition	165
10.4.	Indoor use of RIAS	166
10.5.	An environmental segment and the track of the experimental subject finding a specific destination by following directions from the RIAS	167
11.1.	Decision and choice factors: The advantages and disadvantages of various housing options for older persons	179
11.2.	Predictor variables explaining which retirees are likely to report the "change in lifestyle" push factor	181
11.3.	Predictor variables explaining which retirees are likely to report the "maintenance" push factor	183
11.4.	Predictor variables explaining which retirees are likely to report the "social isolation" push factor	183
11.5.	Predictor variables explaining which retirees are likely to report the "health and mobility" push factor	183
11.6.	Relative importance of reasons attracting retirees to move to their retirement village	184
11.7.	Predictor variables explaining retirees' reporting of the "built environment and affordability" pull factor	185
11.8.	Predictor variables explaining retirees' reporting of the "location" pull factor	185
11.9.	Predictor variables explaining retirees' reporting of the "maintaining existing lifestyle" pull factor	186
11.10.	Retiree ratings of desirability of services and facilities being provided in a retirement village	187
13.1.	Five spatial layouts	207
13.2.	MDS assessment of teacher preference rankings	212
14.1.	Environment *E1*: An "old city street" scene	235
14.2.	Environment *E2*: A "social gathering" scene	235
14.3.	Environment *E3*: A "woodland setting"	235
14.4.	Graphical example of dataset for a given environment	237
15.1.	Completion of sorting process	261
15.2.	Subjects' arrangements of 56 landscapes according to perceived scenic quality differences	262
15.3.	Nominal illustrations of correlations for all pairs of 407 landscape arrangements	263
15.4.	Nominal illustration of *Q*-mode factor matrix resulting from the alpha factor analysis procedure	264
15.5.	Arrangements of 56 scenes according to their differences in scenicness for each of the three versions	268
16.1.	Variability in QOL using the MAX-OWA operator	295
16.2.	Variability in QOL using the ME-OWA operator	296
17.1.	Cue selection procedure	304
17.2.	Control-group grid	309
18.1.	Panel used for sorting	324
18.2.	Illustration of correlations between sorts	327
18.3.	Three different perspectives on conservation issues in the Sandhills of Nebraska (distribution of conservation statement numbers)	333

Tables

2.1.	Four Levels of Measurement and Some Statistics Appropriate to Each Level	41
2.2.	A Classification of Spatial Data by Level of Measurement and Type of Spatial Object	42
4.1.	An Example of Geographical Data	69
4.2.	The Complexity of Representing Trips	77
5.1.	Theoretical Traditions and Approaches in Qualitative Inquiry	83
5.2.	The Tasks Involved in Conducting a Survey	88
6.1.	The Effect of the Proportionate and Absolute Size of the Sample in the Formula for Estimating the Standard Error	98
8.1.	Variables Derived from the 2001 Census Representing the Demographic and Socioeconomic Characteristics of Polling Booth Catchments	131
8.2.	Results of the Stepwise Regression Modeling: The Most Important Factors Explaining Spatial Variation in the Primary Vote for Political Parties at the 2004 Federal Election	134
8.3.	Descriptive Statistics and the Number of Polling Booths by Favorable Voting Outcomes for Each Political Party and the 2001 and 2004 Federal Elections	138
8.4.	Function Loadings of Predictors on Discriminant Functions 1, 2, and 3	139
8.5.	Predicted and Actual Polling Booth Outcomes: Number of Polling Booths and Percentage of Booths Correctly Predicted by the Model	142
9.1.	Common Environmental Cues in Cities	147
9.2.	Principal Types of Fundamental Cues from Group Home Discussions	147
9.3.	Tasks Completed during Data Collection Sessions	148
9.4.	Familiarity Ratings of 10 Most Familiar Cues	149
9.5.	Skills Needed to Use Mass Transit	150
9.6.	Experimental versus Control Groups: Bidimensional Correlations of Sequencing of Cues	153
10.1.	Technical Aids for Disabilities	158
10.2.	Selected Legislative Acts in the United States, 1961–1990	159
10.3.	Conditions and Participants	163
10.4.	Potential Obstacles to the Development and Acceptance of a Practical Navigation Aid	169
11.1.	Correlations between the "Push" Factors and the "Services and Facilities" Factors	188
12.1.	Spatial Activities Listed by Sex Typing in the Newcombe et al. (1983) Study: 75% or More Agreement among Participants	198
12.2.	Spatial Activities Listed by Sex Typing in the Santa Barbara Community Study: 75% or More Agreement among Participants	200
12.3.	Spatial Activities Listed by Sex Typing in the Student Study: 75% or More Agreement among Participants	201
13.1.	Properties of Classroom Designs	208
13.2.	Classroom Layout Design and Property Characterization by Groups of Teachers	209
13.3.	Preference Rankings of Five Classroom Designs	211
13.4.	Preference Orientations for Educational and Design Issues	215
13.5.	Design Preference Frequencies and Average Scores on Issues for Teachers in MDS	216
14.1.	Characteristics of the Opportunity Sample	234

14.2.	Subject Groups and Their Raw Scores on Feelings Characterizing Emotional Dimensions Being by Yourself in the "Old City Street" Scene	238
14.3.	Subject Groups and Their Raw Scores on Feelings Characterizing Emotional Dimensions Being by Yourself at a Social Gathering	241
14.4.	Subject Groups and Their Raw Scores on Feelings Characterizing Emotional Dimensions Being by Yourself at a Woodland Setting	242
14.5.	City Street Scene: Associations between Affective Norms and Environmental Scenarios	249
14.6.	Social Gathering Scene: Associations between Affective Norms and Environmental Scenarios	250
15.1.	Individuals Selected for the Study: Gender, Age, Places, and Groups	259
15.2.	Subjects' Loading on Dimensions Extracted by Q-Mode Factor Analysis	266
15.3.	Physical Features from 56 Scenes	270
15.4.	Relationships between Physical Features and Perceptual Versions of Scenic Quality	271
15.5a.	Rotated Factor Pattern: R-Mode Factor Analysis of Scene Sortings Produced by Individuals Subscribing to Perceptual Version 1	272
15.5b.	Rotated Factor Pattern: R-Mode Factor Analysis of Scene Sortings Produced by Individuals Subscribing to Perceptual Version 2	273
15.5c.	Rotated Factor Pattern: R-Mode Factor Analysis of Scene Sortings Produced by Individuals Subscribing to Perceptual Version 3	274
15.6.	Comparison of Scenic Spaces Associated with Three Versions (V_i) of Scenic Quality	276
16.1.	Descriptive Statistics for QOL Items	292
16.2.	Transfer of Location-Specific QOL Survey Data into Subregions	293
17.1.	Preliminary Test: Locations in Rank Order	305
17.2.	Cue-Trial Allocations	305
17.3.	Newcomer Stress Statistics over Time	310
17.4.	KYST 3 STRESS Values over Time for the Intermediate Group	311
17.5.	Control Group STRESS Values	312
18.1.	The "Conservation Statements"	323
18.2.	Partial Matrix of Respondents' Arrangements	325
18.3.	Rotated Q-Mode Factor Analysis of Respondents' "Statement Arrangements"	328
18.4.	A Fictitious Example of a Factor	329
18.5.	Devising Weights for Computing a Weighted Average Estimate	330
18.6.	Computing Weighted Conservation Statement Scores to Estimate Sorting Pattern for Example Group in Table 18.5	331
18.7.	Weighted Conservation Scores for the Three Groups and Their Standardized Counterparts	332
18.8.	Dimensions Used to Estimate Respondents' Rankings of Environmental Agencies	335
19.1.	Steps for Preparing a Research Proposal	341

CHAPTER 1

An Overview of Spatial and/or Environmental Influences in Human Activities and Experiences

1.1 Introduction

This book examines approaches employed in research to explore a variety of spatial and environmental influences in *human activities* and *experiences*. Parts I and II focus on information recording and measurement in research and describe various means that may be used to accomplish both. Parts III, IV, V, and VI then provide some detailed examples of actual research projects. Those selected for presentation discuss a variety of spatial manifestations and conditions in human issues and illustrate ways to deal with or rationalize conceptual and methodological complexities encountered in their investigations.

As will be evident in Parts III–VI, spatial conditions in human contexts take a variety of forms. To illustrate that diversity, the research examples chosen for presentation have been selected from a number of topical domains. They focus on a range of issues like wayfinding, voter behavior in a variety of settings, the design of environments for special populations, teaching and learning activities under alternative spatial configurations, affective and aesthetic experiences in and about landscapes, quality-of-life experiences in places, cognition of spatial and/or environmental conditions, and the significance of conservation viewpoints as potential predictors of other environmental perspectives.

This first chapter focuses on the question of *why it is necessary to consider spatial and/ or environmental influences when investigating human-issue topics*. It is evident, when perusing research journals in the social and behavioral sciences, that many investigators proceed with their research without giving consideration to such influences, despite hints that doing so might improve overall comprehension. Admittedly, the inclusion of such influences into an investigation of human issues may often generate severe methodological and conceptual complexities in analysis and/or may aggravate existing complexities implicit in the problem context as well. Nevertheless, the question about the necessity for considering space in research dealing with human activities and experiences is a significant one because it relates heavily to comprehensiveness of understanding. Gradually, this will become quite apparent as additional attention is expended on clarifying notions of human activities and experiences and spatial influences.

1.2 Clarifying Terms

1.2.1 Human Activities and Experiences

There seems to be little further need to elaborate on what human activities mean, for they are said to refer to what people ordinarily do in an everyday sense. Yet, much can be comprehended, even from this broad sense of understanding. Reference to "ordinarily," for example, means they are both *expected* and *typical*, and, from common experience, this makes sense. Given the basic and usual needs of individuals for daily existence, few people can be said to engage in relatively extraordinary activities with any noticeable frequency and, indeed, many can be said to practically never engage in them.

What is also noticeably commonplace about them is the presence of a social–physical–spatial correspondence between activities engaged in and settings or environments within which they are enacted. In American culture, for example, filling one's gas tank takes place in an environment within which gas pumps, among many other related items, are arranged and provided; teaching activity occurs in classroom settings, which in turn are found in school buildings; grocery shopping takes place in supermarkets; dining activity occurs in a restaurant; parking occurs in a parking lot; and so on. It is obvious that, whatever the culture, such regular correspondences between the setting for the activity and the activity's nature are numerous.

This broad interpretation certainly illuminates the essence of *human activities*, but it may also mask aspects of them that stimulate a variety of research curiosities. These include, for example, their specific nature, when and how they are executed, under what circumstances, by whom, at what locations, the length of their duration, their frequency, their effects on other things, the purpose of those activities, their patterns over space and time, and various combinations of these aspects.

Hanson and Hanson (1993), for example, stress that the *geographic patterns of activities in built environments* help us to understand how people use a city. They indicate that the *what*, *where*, and *when* features of such patterns are especially useful information for urban planners because of their concerns for urban land-use trends, responses to environmental changes, and the travel patterns of different groups in cities.

An *activity episode*, or the duration of an activity from its start to its completion, is a complex entity in itself, containing as it does a set of systematically interrelated behavioral components. For some investigators, those components—comprising acts, reacts, transacts, and interacts—may attract more attention than an entire activity as a whole. What is interesting is that an activity simultaneously may be ordinary in the everyday vernacular sense when viewed from its entirety as an episode and, yet, may also be considered extraordinary when examined from its interrelated behavioral-component structure.

There is, however, no standard and universally comprehensive definition of *human activity*. That this should be the case is not surprising. Investigators tend to emphasize different aspects of this construct in their research, and frequently do so in terms of relationships activities have to other issues of interest to them. As an example, if the focus is on the ordinary one of *taking a trip*, some researchers may have an interest in a single aspect of that activity, such as the length of a route traversed in the journey to work. Others, however, might be more curious about the entire activity episode itself, from its initiation to its completion, and that may include questions about its orientation, directional bias, and length; its optimum relative to alternative routes; its temporal features; its effectiveness for meeting a person's objective; the effort and expense required for such a trip; its spatial configuration; and the like. In still other examples, researchers may be essentially curious about *how* an activity proceeds in a particular setting (for example, planners, architects, designers, etc.), and they may be concerned about its appropriateness for that *situation*. With respect to this latter type of emphasis, human activities, in fact, are seldom found to be independent of the *situational context* within which they are expected to occur and/or take part, so that in efforts to develop a comprehensive definition for this construct, such a relationship between the two may need to be taken into consideration (see, for example, Magnusson, 1981); but more about that issue follows later.

1.2.2 How to Understand Human Activities and Experiences

An overwhelming concern in much research about humans is *how to acquire understanding about their activities and experiences*. Should it be gained through attempts to predict and/or explain *participation* in an activity, or acquired mainly by *relating* activity to other human issues having similar priority as the activity itself? This question, of course, is rhetorical, in the sense that no answer to it can be reasonably expected. The likelihood is that both approaches work toward the acquisition of understanding, and neither can ultimately be achieved independently of the other. Yet, one thing is certain: Creating *theory* that would explain and predict participation in a particular activity is, by far, the more complicated way of the two.

Garling and Garvill (1993) refer to *motivational-* and *cognitive-*type approaches frequently used to explain and/or predict *participation* in activity. This seems to make sense, as dimensions like these are expected to be involved in participation. They point out, however, that orientations of this nature typically meet with difficult conceptual and methodological difficulties, especially those associated with attempts to acquire the enormous amount of information likely to be operating in activity participation. Garling and Garvill state that

> explanations of participation in everyday activities based on psychological theories encompass external circumstances (situations, opportunities, constraints, and consequences), personality traits and abilities, motivational states (needs, drives, and goals), and information processing (judgments, evaluations, and decisions). (p. 275)

They also allude to the more common *constraining influences* on activity participation like space and time, biological and psychological needs, power relationships in society, and social-cultural influences in the forms of the expectations, norms, rules, and traditions associated with social systems. It is clear from their discussion that trying to comprehend human participation in activity is, in itself, an extremely involved undertaking, whether a researcher attempts to do so by building a theory about participation or proceeds in some other relatively less-comprehensive manner.

Nevertheless, Garling and Garvill (1993) remain optimistic; they believe, albeit with qualifications, that theory-serving explanations are possible, despite also acknowledging how complicated ordinary human activities are likely to be. Their tentative conclusion is that theories attempting to explain and/or predict participation in activities are likely to be *qualitatively* expressed, and therefore much less precise than more robust quantitatively stated propositions. Their description of the complexities involved in predicting participation in activities is compelling and certainly reflective of actual conditions commonly met in investigations about human issues.

But influences associated with broader sociocultural-level processes need to be given consideration as well. A decision, for example, to engage in a given activity in a particular situational context may, if perceived as inappropriate, evoke curiosity as to *why* that particular choice was made. A choice to participate in an activity, in other words, is not likely to be independent of what is expected and/or what is customary in that particular social situation. Thus, in addition to the constraining influences described by Garling and Garvill (1993), there may also be present, albeit at a more macro level, social influences that, over time, have had an effect on what that choice might eventually be. In well-defined sociocultural systems, for example, social influences (for example, effected through social institutions) are said to operate over time to influence how members develop, perform in different situations, apprehend, and, ultimately, understand (see, for example, Hillier & Hanson, 1984; see also Rapoport, 1982). Indeed, even motivation and cognition, mentioned by Garling and Garvill, as a basis for participation decisions do not go unaffected by such influences. How would a theory about activity decision making, then, take such broader social influences into consideration? What provisions should be made in that theory to predict participation in activities that would deviate from what would be expected under such social influences?

Roger Barker (1968) indirectly provoked a question like this when he suggested that, in a given community, there is likely to be a relatively smaller variance within a particular behavioral activity than across different behavioral activities. Obviously, his observation has implications for understanding variation among activity types based on the necessary relationships they have to the environmental situations in which they are enacted (see also Heft, 2001). What this entire discussion strongly suggests, then, is that the employment of a variety of approaches, having somewhat more modest goals than, say, theory building, may be needed in research to increase comprehension about human activities and their associated experiences.

Here, for example, are some research interests whose focus on human activities is oriented toward the question of how those behaviors may relate to other issues, particularly those in which the *activity, the person, and the situational context appear to be interrelated*:

1. A common interest for *architects, planners*, and *designers* is a concern for the degree to which their proposed schemes for physical-social settings support and facilitate intended *uses* of those settings. Some planners may be curious about the effects particular land-use activities (such as retail, recreation, industrial, public, and residential) have on the living ambiences for residents of some community, whereas others may be concerned with the activity compatibility of mixed land uses in a community.
2. An *environmental psychologist* or a *sociologist* might have an interest in the degree to which place "enters" into people's notion of "self," in terms of its potential significance in activities involving certain levels of face-to-face social exchanges. This, of course, is also an experience-related interest, in the sense of place being looked at as a potential component of identity.
3. A *behaviorally oriented geographer* might be curious about the role environmental schemata or long-term cognitive integrations may play in the activity of wayfinding and/or general spatial orientation issues. This too has something to do with experience as well, since spatial and psychological orientations are likely to be critical in how one experiences the world.

Researchers subscribing to distinctly different emphases may attempt to understand relationships between environmental conditions (for example, pastoral settings, concrete urban slums, climatically extreme places, etc.) and human health activities. Investigators engaged in a mix of objectives may all be concerned with the importance of environmental aesthetics in the conduct of activities (for example, advertisers, marketers, book publishers, designers, etc.). Many disparate interests, despite their differences in perspectives, may seek to understand how children learn space and how learning developmentally affects their activity functioning. The point of importance here is this: *A great variety of interests exists in research that has objectives directed at finding out how human activities and their experiences relate to other significant issues, some of which appear to be based on the assumption that components like person, environment, and behavior likely interrelate.*

The research endeavors illustrated throughout this book emphasize such objectives. One of them, for example, examines the activity of voting, while another looks at elementary teaching and learning activities. The former attempts to understand the importance of socioeconomic and spatial influences in voting behavior, while the latter is curious about the ways the spatial configuration of a classroom affects how teaching and learning are carried out. Neither example of research is directly concerned with prediction and explanation of activity participation, nor do any of the other examples illustrated have that objective in mind. Ultimately, of course, the results obtained in these and other research endeavors will, undoubtedly, affect how theory will develop.

But what of *experience*? In general, the term *experience* is used to refer to either a focused level of cognition activated and reflected on by an individual him- or herself (for example, as in "imaging," "reifying," "representing," etc.) and/or to a particular reaction (for example, "feelings," "emoting," "sensing," "evaluating," etc.) undergone by an individual who may have been aroused or stimulated by some environmental and/or spatially related situation. In almost all cases, the experience examined is treated here as an activity companion or related reaction as, for example, affective and/or aesthetic reactions to surrounding circumstances. But there are at least two cases where it will be demonstrated that the experience exhibited in or with respect to an environmentally structured circumstance has, at the moment of investigation, no direct reference to a specific companion activity.

One thing is clear when attempting to understand an individual's experience in a particular circumstance: The nature of an experience is undoubtedly influenced by the personal attributes (as in beliefs, social and/or cognitive biases, attitudes, previous experiences, dispositions, and the like) of those having it. For an extensive discussion on environmental experiences, see Nasar (1988) and Kaplan and Kaplan (1989).

1.2.3 Space and/or Spatial Forms in Human Contexts

The significance of *space* in the human context is exemplified in many different ways, ranging all the way from its most dominant role as a *structuring dimension* in society to its "presence" as a region of the brain enabling an individual to conceptualize about the world spatially. One need only consult an unabridged *Roget's International Thesaurus* (Chapman, 1977) to comprehend the relative and widespread importance of the use of the term in the English language. "Space" is treated as one of eight major terms in this vernacular, and there are over a hundred categories describing instances of its possible use.

But *spatial terms and expressions*—both simple and complex—permeate all major languages and are essential for comprehending other ideas associated with human experiencing (see Golledge & Stimson, 1997, Ch. 10). Obviously much of the different meanings of space and their connotations cannot be dealt with in this introductory chapter. For this book, we concentrate on space's most dominant expression in the human context, particularly its role as a dimension in *situational surroundings* in which human activities are commonly enacted and experiences are felt.

How, then, might space be construed for this purpose? Composing a response to this question—even a general one—is not a straightforward task. This is because in the human world—particularly with regard to meanings associated with apprehending, experiencing, and functioning in it—space takes on a great number of *forms*. In other words, it is not space as such that matters to individuals, but rather the forms that it takes in activity- and experiential-related circumstances. These forms and their meanings are nearly always dependent on the meanings of other things, contexts, and processes in which space plays a role.

So many diverse forms of space exist in the various realms of the human context that a single classification system of space types would seem to have dubious value for aiding in the comprehension of them. This extensive diversity is confounded further by the different scales at which many of these spatial forms can be apparent in the world and by the potentially large number of individual and group purposes for which they might have meaning. The presence of space in different forms, and its susceptibility to numerous interpretations, creates enormously complex obstacles for constructing a type-oriented theory about its general influence in the human context. It will be noticed, however, throughout this book that it is possible to explicitly refer to some of the more prominent ways space is likely to be apparent in the everyday activity-experience scenarios of society.

1.2.3.1 Space's Manifestation in Social Contexts

To begin with, societies themselves are spatial. This refers not only to their obvious physical outline as a recognizable entity but to their internal makeup as well. The internal presence of space is reflected in their distinctive organizational contexts—as in provinces, counties, states, parishes, districts, and so on—and in their many distributions of populations, routes, settlements, and the like. Whatever else may play a role in their distinctive nature—as in sociocultural influences—these arrangements, dispersions, patterns, and configurations collectively present a potentially recognizable order broadly suggesting something about the internal dynamics of societies. Space's internal presence also suggests its basic participation in the structuring of the things humans transact with and experience in their surroundings.

Space is, in fact, an integral part of movement and communication processes in society, whatever their magnitudes or scales. These processes include all sorts of trip making, migrations, diffusions, transporting, communicating, and the like. Indeed, space, as a fundamental dimension of life, makes occurrences of differentiation inevitable in a society and, through human interpretations of them, movements and communications are generated. Space's most notable influence in movements and communications is a constraining one, which is sometimes characterized as spatial friction. Its significance is translated and interpreted by humans in terms of the allocation of resources, material and otherwise, to deal with its impacts. With each movement and communication type, however, space tends to "take on" distinctive forms, and, thus, often has different implications for other facets that may go to define these processes. It is, in fact, difficult to think of movement and communications without thinking of them in terms of space. It is its extensiveness, its complexity, and the particular ways in which it enters into them that have significant consequences for the impacts it exerts on these processes.

When reflecting on or about societies as distinct entities—particularly in their holistic sense—it would be negligent, at least from the perspective of comprehension, to ignore or avoid contemplating the distinctive ways in which space is reflected in both their external and internal forms. In that sense, space is an inextricable component for the understanding of environments having human and/or social meaning (see Hillier & Hanson, 1984; Peponis & Wineman, 2002). Hillier and Hanson (1984), for example, indicate that buildings and collections of them, as significant elements of a society's internal form, organize and/or arrange spaces and create new ones to facilitate the ongoing interpersonal relating of those using them. The process by which these internal forms of space—namely, built environments—come about over time is, of course, not random; instead, it is likely to be heavily influenced by the social prescripts of societies (traditions or customs about aesthetics and/or styles, planning and construction rules, norms and regulations regarding construction, social values and expectations, etc.) and, in that sense, reflect them.

In their discussion of spatial structure's relevance to environment and behavior relationships, Peponis and Wineman (2002) describe *built space* and its strong ties to social meaning in this way:

> Built space is to be understood as a relational pattern, a pattern of distinctions, separations, interfaces, and connections, a pattern that integrates, segregates, or differentiates its parts in relation to each other. To ask whether space has a "social logic" is to ask how such pattern becomes entailed in everyday behavior, in the structuring of social relationships, and in the way in which society and culture become intelligible through their spatial form. (p. 271)

Still another significant example of the presence of space in social contexts is found in the way it is expressed during social exchange. Sociocultural conventions—as in rules and traditions about spacing—play a fundamental part in interpersonal exchanges that take place between members in societies. Spacing is often a nonverbal reflector of the norms and expectations associated with the roles and relationships inherent in those exchanges. It is frequently expressed in concert with verbal behavior and may embellish or qualify it in some manner. In this way, space appears in a variety of approach–avoidance types of behavior in societies and is manifested in such things as social distances, personal spaces, territories, privacy managements, and the like (see, for example, Altman, 1975; Bechtel, 1997).

And, of course, it is also necessary to point out the importance of space in *processing information* about one's worlds and identifying with manifestations of its presence. People apprehend, think, or cognize spatially; use space as a fundamental dimension of their personal orientation to the rest of their world; and identify with complex manifestations of spaces as they are exemplified in places, regions, homes, landscapes, neighborhoods, revered or sacred locations, and the like.

In short, space is pervasive in numerous processes, patterns, and organizations of things and events throughout a social system; its structural manifestations in the many environments in which human action and experience ordinarily take place; its presence in sociocultural codes associated with human relating and/or exchanging; and its significance in the ways humans image, perceive, and conceptualize their surroundings for orientation and identification. These are a few of the many forms space may take in the world of human issues.

1.2.3.2 Studies about Space in Its Many Forms

The literature discussing the various forms of spatial presence in human contexts is immense, and far too extensive to cover here. In general, it explores how these forms are manifested in interpersonal relationships, in behavior and experience, in human perception and cognition, and in numerous situational circumstances or environments. Some specific topics noticeably focused on in this literature include concerns about:

- Spatially oriented behavior in movement and/or wayfinding
- Spatially influenced experiences as in affective and reactive responses in and to surroundings
- Physical and behavioral expressions of space in sociocultural systems
- Spatial cognition and/or the processes associated with representation in environmental perceptions
- Processes of social exchange and corresponding norms influential in spacing, spatial choice, and decision making
- The role of space in the composition of place formation
- The development of spatial learning
- Spatial economics (for example, location theory).

Among other concerns, these subjects are described extensively in Golledge and Stimson's (1997) discussion on geographic perspectives of spatial behavior, Bechtel's (1997) cross-disciplinary assessment of some of the larger issues contained in the domain of environment and behavior, Pick and Acredolo's (1983) edited collection of research focusing on spatial orientation, and Golledge's (1999) more extended assessment of that issue in a framework that relates spatial cognition to wayfinding.

There are, as well, in this literature a number of works devoted to conceptualizing the nature of *relationships* among persons, environments, and behaviors (P-E-B) that materialize when individuals engage in purposeful transactions with such surroundings. These include a transactional perspective developed by Ittelson, Proshansky, Rivilin, and Winkel (1974); an ecological position described by Wicker (1979) and, then, in more depth, by Heft (2001); a behavioral-geographic approach described by Golledge and Stimson (1987, 1997); and a social-process view developed by Hillier and Hanson (1984). One particular work by Garling and Golledge (1993) presents research emphases from two relatively conventional disciplines in an effort to explore the potential for conceptual intersections between psychological and geographic approaches to behavior and environment.

Still other studies present extensive discussions of various aspects of cognitive processing as they relate to environmental apprehension in general. Examples include an early edited collection of works on environmental knowing by Moore and Golledge (1976); Downs and Stea's (1977) descriptions of the processes associated with cognitive processing and mapping; Moore's (1979) extensive review of research and theory on environmental knowing, a work focusing specifically on cognition and environments by S. Kaplan and R. Kaplan (1982); Spencer, Blades, and Morsley's (1989) discussion on the development of spatial knowledge and cognition; and Devlin's (2001) most recent work relating spatial cognition to environmental behavior.

To these extended considerations of environmental cognition and/or apprehension must be added studies about the closely related issue of *meaning* in built environments. Writers address this issue in various ways. One work is an interdisciplinary collection of papers on various facets of this issue edited by Broadbent, Bunt, and Llorens (1980). Rapoport (1982), on the other hand, develops a theory about the meaning of the built environment using a nonverbal communication approach. And still others, as in the edited collection by Buttimer and Seamon (1980) and a work by Tuan (1974), examine environmental meaning from the perspective of the human experience of place and space (but see also Canter, 1977).

The works briefly mentioned here constitute only a small fraction of what literature is, in fact, available for those interested in these and related issues. Reinforcing them are the many research periodicals within which aspects of these issues are specifically addressed, examined, and explored. A few examples include *Environment and Behavior, Journal of Architectural and Planning Research, Journal of Environmental Psychology, Handbooks of Environmental Psychology, Geography in America at the Dawn of the 21st Century,* 1991 Plenum Series on *Human Behavior and Environment: Advances in Theory and Research, Progress in Human Geography* (1991–92), *EDRA Proceedings* (Environmental Design and Research Association), and *Proceedings for IAPS* (International Association for the Study of People in Their Settings).

1.3 Space as a Dimension of Environments for Human Activities and Experiences

When the focus is specifically on how space relates to physical and social dimensions making up the environments in which human activities are conducted and experiences are felt, a number of *basic* questions come to mind. Here, for example, are three that are commonly raised:

1. Is space important in the assessment of human activity and experience?
2. Why is it necessary to consider space explicitly when investigating human activities and experiences?
3. How is space manifested in environments where the conduct of activities and the having of experiences typically take place?

Responses to questions like these come mainly from *generalized interpretations of what appears to be going on with respect to the role of space in the factual world*. The development of these interpretations is similar to how the conceptualizing of this nature often proceeds in practice in most social and behavioral areas of study, in that they consist of the generalizing and systematizing of trends noticed in past research. A common problem with these interpretations, however, is their poor applicability, particularly in a research-operable sense. In other words, the issue is more than just the conceptual plausibility of these interpretations; in practice, it also lies in determining how to apply them in actual empirical (that is, *factual*) circumstances.

The key to their low potential for applicability is found in the expression *in an operable sense*. A nearly universal difficulty, for example, faced by many engaged in this kind of research is the immense complexity involved in attempting to extricate space from its fixed and intricate interrelationships with physical and social dimensions of an environment for the purpose of examining and observing whatever might be its distinctive influences. The reason for this is that each of the dimensions alone has a distinctive information set associated with it, but when inextricably related, as is the case, to one another in the form of an activity environment, the resulting information tends to be something more than the sum of the three sets. These interrelationships among the dimensions of an environment inhibit, in other words, the setting-aside of space separately to study its effects independently. In the research process itself, this often represents an operational problem that has both methodological and conceptual implications. The ongoing problem, then, is how to translate or match what is suggested by theoretical projections (that is, those generalized interpretations just mentioned) about the influences of space on activities and experiences in environmental circumstances to the practical level of actual research contexts where space as a distinctive determinant is, in practice, difficult to isolate for observation and evaluation.

A large body of literature has, nevertheless, accumulated over time in which the above three questions have been thought about, examined, and debated. It has, however, typically concentrated on broader issues, such as the nature of the unit to be understood in P-E-B relationships; environmental apprehension and its associated cognitive and perceptual processes, combined environments, behaviors, and persons as ecological or behavioral systems; sociocultural processes and their relationships with built environments; and the like. The end product of these discussions has been the development of elaborate conceptualizations, or what is often referred to as *theories* (that is, sets of conceptually coherent generalizations). These have been generated by individuals and groups operating in specializations created in conventional disciplines, as in behavioral geography and environmental psychology, or in clusters that have evolved at the margins or intersections of larger disciplines to form cross-disciplinary associations, such as the Environmental Design Research Association (EDRA) or the International Association for the Study of People in Their Settings (IAPS). Other specialized subgroups much like these have surfaced in areas of human ecology, environmental systems, place studies, environmental health, cognitive studies, and environmental design. These clusters of individuals, having broad interests in P-E-B relations, have been extensively involved in interpreting how space and its many forms enter into a large number of issues concerned with human activities and experiences.

1.3.1 Assumptions about Assessing Space in the Human Context

It is useful to place the *level* of the inquiries inherent in the three basic questions raised above in perspective by noting again the very wide variety of ways space and its forms can be interpreted by individuals engaged in activities and having experiences. In *Roget's Thesaurus* (Chapman, 1977), for example, "space" is shown to be one of eight fundamental terms in the English language and to have at least 145 categories of expressions reflecting the things to which it refers. These expressions occur in mathematical systems; pattern analyses; cartographic projections; orientation systems; distances and separations; assessments of clusters, configurations, arrangements, dispersions, and networks; and numerous other ways for examining things associated with the human world.

Given the many ways, then, that space and its forms can enter into human concerns, it would be beneficial, at this point, to place the focus on everyday, ordinary living scenarios and ask: Do people conceive *space* as independent of other things during processes of *engaging in activities* and *having experiences*? Or do they translate the effects of *space* that they confront into other forms of information specific and relevant to the subject-matter nature of their *activities* and *experiences* as well? From the perspective of how to interpret results obtained when researching human issues, inquiries like these appear to be important.

For example, when discussing perspectives on spatial cognition, S. Cohen and R. Cohen (1985) indicate that there are likely to be two principal approaches to treating the way individuals apprehend the spatial conditions encountered while engaged in activities and/or having experiences:

1. One approach relates it to other information in the activity and experiential context, and views the spatial form in question as a necessary component in terms of its conjunction with these other relevant social/physical factors.
2. Another perspective, however, treats spatial cognitive processing separately from the apprehension of other information.

The authors suggest that these two approaches should be integrated in the development of a more comprehensive spatial cognition theory capable of dealing with all the information constituting the activity and experience context.

In a separate work discussing the role of activity, itself, and its implications for the process of spatial cognition, S. Cohen and R. Cohen (1985; see also Golbeck, 1985) put it this way:

> For the most part, the experimental research has investigated the role of active locomotor movement in space. Given the extant theoretical perspectives on spatial cognition, this was certainly a logical starting point. Yet we would hope that the research presented in the previous section on functional activity will expand the perspectives on activity. Any motor activity in space operates in the service of other cognitive and social concerns. We do not walk (or ride) to a shopping mall in order to walk (or ride). There is a *purpose* to the activity. This purpose provides a *conceptual theme* to the activity, which aids not only in the enactment of the theme but also in the issue of spatial information in the service of the theme. From this broader conceptualisation, we would urge for the consideration of a variety of variables when investigating the role of activity in spatial cognition. (p. 217)

This advice concerning integrating relevant information about social, physical, and personal things when evaluating spatial cognitive processing in human activity and experiencing seems quite relevant and appropriate, especially for the objectives faced here. In any event, it seems implausible to reason that individuals process various facets of the external information they confront separately. It certainly is difficult to deny the importance of physical information in surroundings, for example, when dealing with the perceiving, knowing, and representing involved in cognitive processing. *Perceiving* makes use of directed biological processes in the operation of sensory receptors to detect concrete physical aspects, such as temperatures, the presence of structures, textures, sounds, and odors of the immediate world.

And so too must the sociocultural aspects of surroundings be acknowledged. The presence of these evokes certain interpretative tendencies from individuals because of the role that societal influences have already played in their development and because these aspects are reflective of common traditions, expectations, and norms associated with ongoing ways of construing things and relationships in society. Motivations, purposes, and self-orientations—all intimately related to sociocultural conditions—are also of importance in information processing engaged in while conducting activities and the having of experiences (see Breakwell, 1992; Fiske & Taylor, 1991). Thus, as will be argued shortly, spatial aspects of information are quite significant—often decisively so—in contexts for activities and experiences, *but nearly always in terms of the ways space meshes with other physical, sociocultural, and personal aspects of information in those contexts.*

While it is evident, then, that space exerts significant influences in a great variety of human circumstances, the focus in this book is devoted mainly to comprehending the ways it meshes with those environmentally manifested situations within which people are engaged in regular and/or ordinary activities and are having associated experiences. For most individuals, this daily regimen of activities and experiences is *ordinary* and routine; occurrences of extraordinary instances are relatively rare and, to the extent that they do occur, are likely to have little to do with the human task of functionally facilitating one's existence on a daily basis. Ordinary activities and experiences are concerned with that task. What is important is the nature of that existence for the individual and the circumstances within which it is carried on. Individuals, after all, are members of sociocultural systems: they have purposes and motivations for what they do, and, when individually appropriate, they are conscious of who they are as a person.

1.3.2 Assumptions Facilitating Further Discussion

With thoughts like these in mind, three assumptions are offered now as a basis for elaborating on the questions initially raised when opening this section of the chapter. The first two assumptions are:

1. One reflects on the way space enters into human action and experience and is stated in this way: *Space is not causal in any direct sense of determining human activity and experiencing, but instead exerts significant influences on both through the complex and intricate relationships it has with other important external effects on these aspects of daily human existence.*
2. A second assumption expands on the first one's implications by asserting something about space's *meaning: The meaning of space to humans experiencing its effects in activity and experiential contexts does not depend directly on space's inherent physical properties but rather on translations of those properties by individuals engaged in processing context information in which those properties are an inextricable part.*

These two assumptions merit further discussion before a third is offered to link with them conceptually.

As noted previously, a relatively large number of researchers investigating aspects of human activities and experiences devote little attention to space and the various forms it can take with regard to these issues. Indeed, in some cases, space is totally ignored altogether, even though it is patently obvious that the context under observation has little logical definition without its inclusion. Inattention to the presence of space in these and other instances seems to have a variety of reasons. Sometimes, it is due to an attempt to avoid inevitable conceptual and methodological complications that commonly occur when it is explicitly included in such investigations. At other times, the governing research paradigm itself treats it is as a noncontributing influence in these problem contexts. At still other times, it is simply due to the lack of knowledge that space, in its interacting ways with other external factors, may matter. Whatever the reasons stated or implied, inattention to space seems to go against what is apparent in these human activity and experience situations.

Here, however, we state the obvious: Space, in various forms, is involved in practically everything humans *do and react to*, and in much of what they *imagine*. In this sense of the world that humans know, its pervasiveness is logically apparent and universally widespread. At the more *immediate* action and experiential levels, space is manifested in many different forms in a huge variety of human circumstances.

For this latter reason at least, little is gained to insist on a universal definition of space. Since human activities and experiences vary greatly and are thought of in terms of the situations to which they relate, the role of space is more likely to be interpreted and/or translated in terms of context-specifics and their meanings rather than in terms of some universal definition. At a macro level where such detail focusing is put aside, a universal definition does serve to emphasize time–space's fundamental status in our world. At the practical everyday existence level, however, where numerous environmental situations are encountered daily, a universal definition of space has little utility for promoting comprehension of human activities and experiences.

3. Here, then, is a third assumption that complements the two assumptions just stated: *This meaning referred to in the second assumption is qualified or affected by two fundamental and generic features of space: its structuring and its scaling effects.*

This assumption suggests, in effect, that space exerts *situation-related* influences on human activities and experiences as they are enacted and felt in environmental settings. Structuring influences appearances of external environments, in terms of physical arrangements, configurations, and connectedness, while scaling, from the perspective of stimulus effects related to relative size and/or expanse, influences the way environments are construed and/or apprehended by those who transact with them. Both influences are intrinsic to the basic nature of space itself, and, in that sense, are distinctive from others operating in activity- and experience-related sociophysical contexts (see Montello, 1993; Montello & Golledge, 1999). How both interrelate with other contextual influences in the definition of an environment for activities and experiences is, of course, useful for clearer understanding of them. This issue will be explored by revisiting and addressing in somewhat greater detail the three questions first introduced in this section.

1.3.2.1 Reflecting on the Three Basic Questions

Recall that the first of the three questions previously posed inquires whether *space* is important in the assessment of human activity and experience. In effect, this is asking whether space should be explicitly considered when examining human activities and experiences as they occur in their environmental settings. It has been asserted many times elsewhere and, of course, throughout this chapter that space—in the basic form that it takes in an environment—is essential for *fully* comprehending the nature of that activity or experience. To evaluate the plausibility of that claim, it is useful to now see what some others have stated and/or implied with respect to this question.

Parsons and Tassinary (2002), for example, in their assessment of the relevance of *environmental psychophysiology* in understanding P-E-B relations, quote from Kurt Lewin's work in which he states

> Every scientific psychology must take into account whole situations, i.e., the state of both person and environment. This implies that it is necessary to find ways of representing person and environment in common terms as parts of one situation. We have no expression in psychology that includes both. (p. 2)

Parsons and Tassinary are referring here to Lewin's (1936, p. 12) comments regarding topological psychology. It is clear that Lewin was not just alluding to the larger general meaning of "environment" common to the vernacular to refer to relevant factors, but instead was pointing to the importance of space itself as it interacts with other structural dimensions (that is, social, physical, cultural, etc.) in activity-experience–type settings. Indeed, Lewin then offered the construct "field" when discussing interrelationships among person, behavior, and environments. In his "field theory" he proposed that behavior is some function of the *interaction* of environment with person. But, of course, these were very early comments and much has been thought about since then.

Parsons and Tassinary (2002), however, also quote from Ittelson's (1973b) work on environmental cognition. Ittelson, for example, was much more specific about Lewin's expression "interaction" by stating that person, environment, and behavior mutually interact in their involvement in activity scenarios:

14 An Overview of Spatial and/or Environmental Influences

> In any concrete situation, one does not encounter man and his environment as separate but interacting; instead one finds a total situation which can be analysed in a variety of ways. . . . Rather than defining the situation in terms of its components, the components, including man himself, can be defined only in terms of the situation in which they are encountered. . . . Man is never encountered independent of the situation through which he acts, nor is the environment ever encountered independent of the encountering individual. It is meaningless to speak of either as existing apart from the situation in which it is encountered. The word "transaction" has been used to label such a situation. . . . (p. 18)

Ittelson further clarified this idea of viewing person, environment, and behavior as a unit for understanding human activity and experience throughout his work (1973b) on environmental cognition and also in his 1954 work.

Others besides Lewin and Ittelson have, in various ways, focused on this basic question as well. Urlic Neisser (1976), for example, reflected on its implications for comprehending human transactions with their everyday surroundings in his *Cognition and Reality*. His theme throughout his book was to point out the critical difference between cognition as considered in theory and cognition as it occurs in actual world environments. Neisser's statement below addresses the trend current at that time by theorists to use a computer model to understand cognitive processing:

> This trend can only be reversed, I think, if the study of cognition takes a more "realistic" turn, in several senses of that word. First, cognitive psychologists must make a greater effort to understand cognition as it occurs in the ordinary environment and in the context of natural purposeful activity. . . . Second, it will be necessary to pay attention to the details of the real world in which perceivers and thinkers live, and the fine structure of information which that world makes available to them. (pp. 7–8)

Proshansky (1976) elaborates further on Neisser's expression "real world" in this way:

> There is no physical setting that is not also a social and cultural setting. What this means in effect is that regardless of how focal we make the physical setting in studying the person's relationships to his or her environment, that setting has a social definition and purpose. Indeed its use, function, and consequences are as much a result of these definitions and purposes as they are of its actual physical properties—perhaps even more so. (p. 308)

He adds further:

> The study of how people use space must include not only a description of what space is being used for what purpose but also a description of the broader context of this space including not just its physical properties but its social, organizational, and cultural properties as well. (p. 309)

Statements like these help to clarify the nature of space in terms of its most widespread form, namely, its inclusion as a fundamental presence in the definition of activity environments. They constitute, in effect, responses to the basic question raised of whether space was important in human activities and experiences. It is clear, both intuitively and analytically, that however else environments may be described and labeled, they are fundamentally spatial in nature. In its form via its essential conjunction with the other dimensions of an environment, space in effect helps to differentiate the nature of one environment from others.

Space's presence in this universal and most widespread way emphasizes the importance of its structuring role in environments when it meshes in some way with other dimensions associated with the nature of those settings. Thus, evident in the statements just quoted is the intrinsic or complex relationship that exists among the dimensions that form an environment. Related to that is the contention that, to more fully understand human activities and experiences, it is necessary to observe them as they happen in and with respect to actual environments and to treat person, environment, and behavior as conceptually linked for such an analysis.

It should be noted that the points made and implied in these statements by scholars like Lewin, Ittelson, Neisser, and Proshansky reinforce the reasoning inherent in the first two assumptions mentioned prior to their presentation. To reiterate, the first asserted that space is not *causal* in any direct sense of determining activity and experiencing, but exerts, instead, its generic influences through inextricable conjunctions it has with other important effects in environments, whereas the second asserted that the meaning of space to humans experiencing its effects in activity and experiential contexts does not depend directly on space's inherent properties but, rather, on individual personal and/or sociocultural translations of them. Why, then, is space especially significant in this universal and overwhelming form that it takes in environments?

1.3.2.2 Inherent Effects Specific to Space

The third assumption stated above is especially relevant for responding to this question. It asserts that the meaning of an environment, whether looked at from how it appears in actual external information or as it is construed by an individual engaged in an activity in that environment, is always *qualified* by two fundamental and inherent features of space, its *structuring* and its *scaling effects*. To "qualify," as the term is intended here, means to exert a fundamentally distinct influence on all the features of an environment so as to make apparent, as a result of that influence, a particular configuration and, in that way, exemplify differences in that setting from other coherent surroundings. In effect, as it is present in environments, space exercises *situationally related* influences on human activities and experiences because it exerts, to begin with, *structuring* and *scale* effects on all situations in which it is involved.

Structuring affects the way the external world appears (for example, its organization and/or arrangement) to those experiencing it, while scale influences the ways in which that world is *construed and/or apprehended*. Since both effects influence what gets to be known in an environmental apprehension sense, they need not be independent of one another and are likely not. Structuring and scale effects are, of course, generic across all circumstances in which space plays a significant role. They are intrinsic types of influences emanating from the basic nature of space itself and, in that sense, are distinctive from any other influences arising from particularities associated with sociophysical contexts. Yet, on the other hand, the specific nature of their effects in any particular environment in which activities take place and experiences are felt is usually not immediately apparent from solely a spatial perspective because of intricate and complex relationships they have with other nonspatial structuring effects also present as components of that environment (for example, the physical and the sociocultural).

It is enormously difficult, for example, to explicitly demonstrate what the relationship between scale changes and changes in apprehensions of actual environments is likely to be, without also considering the effects of such things as the presence of other information in such settings, the way that information meshes with space itself, the purposes underlying the need to apprehend the information constituting the setting, and the nature of individuals engaged in this environmental knowing process.

Though such difficulty appears to be fairly well known, there are a number of reasons why the relationship itself has not been completely made explicit and generalized across all environmental situations. One is the lack of enough research results to suggest the particular and common forms of this relationship. Another, which is conceptually the more significant of the two, is the lack of specifics regarding what is meant by *spatial scale in relation to human activities and experiences*. In research on this issue, it is frequently not clear which spaces are being referred to when comparing their scaling effects. Scale effect, when examined from the perspective of its potential influence on the environmental knowing process, would have to refer to something more than just a proportional size-change impact, say, from a smaller or a larger version of that environment, particularly because what might also be varying independently and in conjunction with size is the conceptual relevance to the perceiver of the spaces in question, among other things.

Progressive size changes involved in the series of spaces from rooms, to behavioral settings, to neighborhoods, to cities, to regions, and then to national entities, for example, are not comparable for investigating scale effects on human environmental apprehension. Each space would have a different human purpose behind the need to know information about it. Then, too, scale effects themselves may—and often do—interact with the structuring effects of space, among other things. Yet despite complications like these involved in attempting to explicitly demonstrate such a relationship, it would be implausible to deny that a connection exists between apprehension and spatial scale. This becomes clear when it is noted that apprehension refers to acquiring understanding and/or attributing meaning, and consists of the acquisition of external information; memory activity regarding recall, storage, and transfer; and integration and/or representation processes, among others. The acquisition of external information itself obviously becomes qualified in various ways when directed sensory-receptor transacting of or with surroundings is compromised due to the changing access effects that result from increasing scale of the space involved. This, in turn, feeds into the rest of what constitutes apprehension of the space involved (see Montello, 1993; Montello & Golledge, 1999).

The structuring effect of space—despite it seeming to be ubiquitously apparent in all of the environments in which activities are conducted and experiences are felt—is equally difficult to illustrate explicitly, even though it is more easily imagined than scale effects. Perhaps this is because its presence appears to be more overt to people. Nearly every encounter humans have with the world they sense puts them in contact with the structuring effects of space and, like scale, this is likely to influence what people apprehend about their surroundings.

In the context of environments where activities are conducted and experiences commonly felt, it is possible, utilizing a sort of reflective heuristic device, to demonstrate the structuring effects of space. Peponis and Wineman (2002), for example, describe a "built environment" in this way:

> Built space is to be understood as a relational pattern of distinctions, separations, interfaces, and connections, a pattern that integrates, segregates, or differentiates its parts in relation to each other. (p. 271)

Obviously their comment emphasizes the *structuring effects* of space on a setting. Taking a cue from their statement, illustrations of two built environments, each in two stages, are presented here in Figures 1.1–1.4 to provoke further reflection on the spatial structuring ubiquitously and inextricably present in all environments in which activities and experiences occur. An unstructured rendition of the elements contained in a living room and a kitchen environment is first illustrated, and then a second rendition is presented in which the elements are organized into some relational pattern recognizable to those who commonly transact with such settings.

The first set of illustrations—shown in Figures 1.1 and 1.2—depicts a sketch of a common living-room environment, which has been reproduced here from a two-stage sketch originally created by Jean Mandler (1984, pp. 88–89) to exemplify her discussion about scene schemas (that is, cognitive integrations) and their structural properties.

The second set of illustrations, shown in Figures 1.3 and 1.4, photographed by Jenny Bindrum, a senior student in an upper-level university course, focuses on spatial influences in social systems. Her intention was to examine implications resulting from the decomposition of ordinary environments.

An important point here for both examples is that their structured and unstructured renditions will differ significantly in terms of what they are likely to evoke or stimulate in those confronting and/or transacting with them. The spatially structured rendition of the two, for example, suggests how, in the environmental form, space, in effect, interweaves or meshes with content and relational *meanings* implied by the objects. No such suggestion is implied in the unstructured renditions.

The comments made by Lewin (1936), Ittelson (1973b), Neisser (1976), and Proshansky (1976), which were quoted earlier in this section, particularly stressed the importance of environments for fully apprehending human activities and experiences. Although allusions were also made to the importance of the structuring effects of space (see, for example, Proshansky, 1976) in those settings, they were not quite as compellingly put. Peponis and Wineman (2002) have noticed this general tendency and describe it in this way:

> Studies of environment and behaviour, in the broadest sense, are often stronger on describing behaviour and dealing with intervening social, psychological, cultural, or organisational

FIGURE 1.1. Stage 1: Unorganized elements. From Mandler (1984). Copyright 1984 by Erlbaum. Reprinted by permission.

18   An Overview of Spatial and/or Environmental Influences

FIGURE 1.2. Stage 2: Organized elements. From Mandler (1984). Copyright 1984 by Erlbaum. Reprinted by permission.

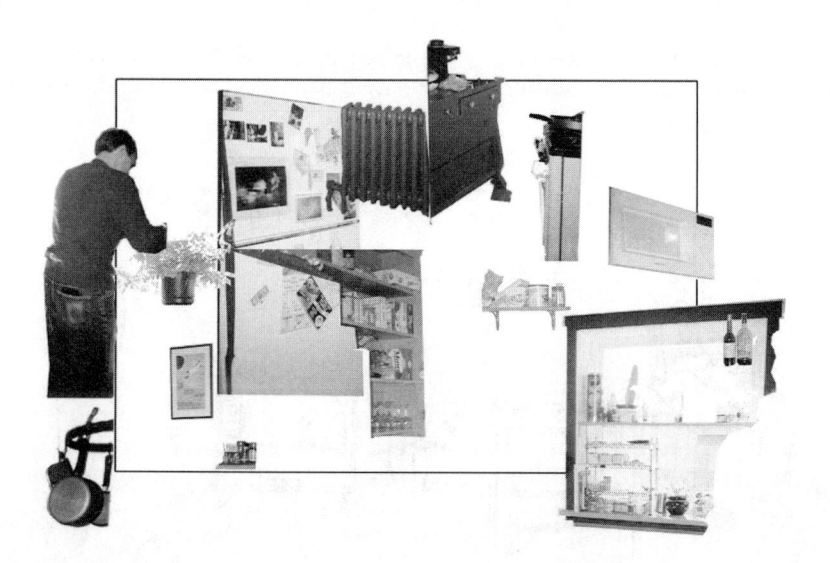

FIGURE 1.3. Stage 1: Unorganized elements. *Source*: Jenny Bindrum, former student of author Amedeo.

FIGURE 1.4. Stage 2: Organized elements. *Source*: Jenny Bindrum, former student of author Amedeo.

variables than they are on describing environment and the spatial structure of environment in particular. (p. 287)

This tendency by investigators to be relatively less emphatic and clear about spatial structuring effects in activity environments can easily be explained by the enormous difficulty involved in trying to demonstrate it conceptually and to illustrate how it operates in conjunction with the other dimensions of a particular environment. The two simple environmental examples just illustrated strongly imply the importance of spatial structuring, but certainly do not demonstrate it. As mentioned previously, this difficulty arises mainly because of the intricate and complex relationship between the fundamental dimensions—spatial, sociocultural, and physical—of an activity environment. None of these dimensions can be investigated independently of the others for comprehension of its role in such environments. What is meant here is that any environment relevant for human activity and experience acquires its significance as a result of that relevance; otherwise, its importance is academic. Hence, this difficulty in describing and assessing spatial structuring in terms of other dimensions of such environments relates, of course, to the relevance referred to here, particularly in regard to its social implications.

When, for example, examining the issue of the social logic of *space* as generally implicated and/or reflected in a specific environment or, better still, in a collection of them in a particular society, Hillier and Hanson (1984) refer to this extricating difficulty as the problem of space. They state:

The aim . . . is to argue for, and to establish, a framework for the redefinition of the problem of space. The common "natural" seeming definition sees it as a matter of finding relations between "social structure" and "spatial structure." However, few descriptions of either type of structure have succeeded in pointing towards lawful relations between the two. The absence of any general models relating spatial structure to social formations it is argued, has its roots in the fundamental way in which the problem is conceptualized . . . , namely as relation between a material realm of physical space, without social content in itself, and an abstract realm of social relations and institutions without a spatial dimension. Not only is it impossible in principle to search for necessary relations between a material and an abstract entity, but also the programme is itself contradictory. Society can only have lawful relation to space if society already possesses its own intrinsic spatial dimension; and likewise space can only be lawfully related to society if it can carry those social dimensions in its very form. The problem definition as it stands has the effect of dissocializing space and despatializing society. To remedy this, two problems of description must be solved. Society must be described in terms of its intrinsic spatiality; space must be described in terms of its intrinsic sociality. (p. 26)

An interesting and related issue is whether spatial effects *matter* in the comprehension of human activities and experiences. This issue is examined in the next discussion by looking at the potential differences in understanding that would be acquired if these effects, as they are present in the nature of environments, were ignored.

1.4 Environments as Contexts and Arenas for Activities and Experiences: A Pragmatic View

Recall that the last of the three *basic* questions raised earlier has not yet been explicitly explored. It inquired about how space was likely to be manifested in those environments where activities are conducted and experiences felt. A *pragmatic*-type argument is constructed throughout this section to respond, at least in a general manner, to that question.

Imagine, to facilitate this argument, the everyday existence of an ordinary individual living in an urbanized area of a particular society. Though this individual's existence might be construed philosophically in any number of ways, the focus here is squarely on its practical side. In that sense, it is, in effect, composed of a daily stream of activities and experiences, most of which are common in their occurrence, others less so, and still others perhaps novel. It is evident that activities are usually conducted and experiences commonly felt in situational-type settings or environments whose configurations, contents, and organizations are generally in accordance with the norms of a given sociocultural system (see the social logic of space in Hillier & Hanson, 1984; further discussion of structure in Peponis & Wineman, 2002; and also the meaning of built environments in Rapoport, 1982).

In this basic sense, then, one might ask, how environments relate to the activity and experience features of an individual's daily regimen. A straightforward response is that such surroundings make available, by their presence, information necessary and useful for both. But this reply, though certainly necessary, is insufficient for generating understanding by itself, for it evokes a number of contingent issues about such things as the kind of information made available by the presence of environments, the manner in which it is acquired and apprehended by individuals, its relationship to other information sources from, say, previous experiences with such settings, and, of course, the role and/or significance of space in that information. All of these need to be addressed as well. The reasoning developed here, then, will attempt to deal with and interrelate these issues, but it will do so in a manner that strives, as much as possible, to stress the more practical implications of them.

1.4.1 Immediate Environments as Contexts and Arenas for Activity

Consider a collection of *activities* that a resident might undertake on a typical day in an urban place in a Western society: "go swimming"; "pick up groceries"; "attend mass"; "work at the office"; "see Marie"; "go to the meeting"; "play tennis"; "have a beer at Duffy's"; "stop at the bank"; "meet Jim for lunch"; "fill the tank with gasoline"; "see the dentist"; "stock the shelves"; "mail package"; "pick up the car"; and the like.

When reflecting on an *activity episode*, reference is to an activity's beginning, its ending, and its duration. It is clear, as mentioned earlier in this chapter, that between these endpoints it consists of a large number of coherently interrelated, purpose-driven, behavioral components made up of, say, "acts," "reacts," "transacts," and "interacts." For that reason, at least, *external* information must be available to serve as a focus and to provide directive orientation for *activity episodes* and, therefore, to facilitate their effective enactment. In this example, then, individuals would typically confront such information in the form of situational-coherent surroundings—such as offices, rooms, theaters, grocery stores, retail establishments, parks, churches, temples, gasoline stations, shopping centers, tennis courts, stadiums, airports, railroads, bus terminals, libraries, restaurants, and lounges, among many others—during their activity episodes. Hence, information needed for the conduct of activities must at least come from these physical–cultural–social surrounds, simply because the intentions or purposes associated with ordinary activities have relevance to such environments.

The nature of some *activities* might require considerable locomotion throughout a setting during their enactment, while the definition and effectiveness of others might be more dependent on both the presence and arrangement of individuals and content in the setting. Of course in practice activities are neither exclusively of one or the other of these types; they are separated here only to bring out the idea that individuals must have access to at least two basic types of external information to begin, continue, and successfully complete the execution of almost all activity in an environment. These include (1) knowledge about the setting's structural aspects, or its *arena facet* and (2) knowledge about its social–cultural–physical makeup, or its *context facet*. The term "facet" is employed here as a heuristic convenience for the purpose of illuminating these two fundamental aspects of the information in environments.

1.4.2 Environmental Information and Behavioral Functioning

It is vital throughout an *activity episode* that an individual be able to continuously monitor and evaluate his or her intended activity for how effectively it is developing within the structural confines of the setting, the degree to which it is fulfilling immediate purposes, whether it is conforming to the cultural–social–physical demands of the setting, and how well it is satisfying any personal aspirations or needs the individual might have about such things as the presentation of "self" in the setting's situational circumstances. From the individual perspective, what is important about context-arena information manifested by immediate environments is that it facilitates effective enactment of intended activities.

But the potential to facilitate activities depends on the relevance of information or its meaning; and meaning, of course, is ultimately determined by people, not by environments. This is not to say that environments play no role in the determination of meaning. The information they make available by their presence—considering how such environments were established to begin with—has the potential to prompt certain inferences, interpretations, and evaluations over others or, equivalently, certain meanings over others. Though meaning is not literally given in the things and relations that make up their information, immediate environments or settings—both in what they contain and in the patterns they exhibit, being products of a cultural–social system—can prompt or cue certain interpretations of their information over others, especially from those that can comprehend the sociocultural codes embedded in them (see Rapoport's, 1982, theorizing on *meaning of built environments*).

This strongly suggests that an additional source of information is needed to interpret external information and, since meaning is ultimately determined by people, this source must be internal to the individual. External information made available by the presence of an environment is neither ordered nor made relevant for a particular activity encounter.

22   An Overview of Spatial and/or Environmental Influences

Its relevance for activity is neither explicitly given, immediately obvious, nor certain. Its amount is likely to be enormous and not all of it relevant for the enactment of an intended activity at the moment. For these reasons and others, there is a need for directed processing of external information if its usefulness for a given activity enactment is to be determined.

1.4.3 The Importance of Memory-Based Environmental Knowledge

That is to say, the "meaning" of external information is an outcome that evolves out of a perceptual-cognitive process engaged in by those carrying on activities in immediate environments. Such processing requires that an individual have both a facility to sense information and an experiential base to interpret its meaning. Hence, perceiving meaning requires not only the presence of external information and its acquisition, but also application (that is, activation) of previous integrated knowledge that can direct information acquisition, encoding, organization, and evaluation. Perceptual guides of that sort are manifested in long-term, memory-based internal information.

A number of writers have examined the importance of internal information in P-E-B transactions (see especially Blumenthal, 1977; Ittelson, 1973b, 1973c; S. Kaplan & R. Kaplan, 1982; G. Mandler, 1985; Moore, 1979; Moore & Golledge, 1976; Neisser, 1976). It is clear from their discussions that activity and experience *in* an environment depend, among other things, on the availability of external information and the way it is processed. Individuals engage in a "knowing" (perceptual-cognitive) process through which they "acquire," "synthesize," and "integrate" environmental information with internal sources of information so as to form, in their perceptions, a *contextual-arena basis* for immediate ongoing behavior. In such a process, internal information or knowledge directs what external information is acquired during environmental knowing and organizes its elaboration to render it informative. The terms "representation," "image," and/or "long-term integration" are all general terms used, sometimes interchangeably, by others to refer to such internal knowledge. An *environmental schema* is a particular type of long-term integration, which refers to memory-based environmental representation knowledge. Vernon (1955) comments on schemas in general, and states that they are

> persistent, deep-rooted, and well-organized classifications of ways of perceiving, thinking, and behaving. They are based upon the individual's knowledge of "what sort of thing to do in, and about, certain kinds of situations." (p. 181)

In her examination and comparison of different types of knowledge structures, Jean Mandler (1984) presents an extensive discussion of a "scene" structure or, what is equivalent, an environmental schema. Her observations regarding these spatially organized cognitive structures are relevant to and illuminate the discussion about internal environmental information. Mandler writes that:

> We not only have an overall schema for a kitchen or bedroom, supermarket or city park, but individual parts of the schema are governed by schemas of their own. (p. 15)

And she goes on to say:

> As in the case of event schemas, the hierarchies organizing scene schemas are collections rather than class-inclusion hierarchies. A dining room contains walls and windows, tables and chairs, but only when these parts are put together into a particular organization does the overall scene emerge. The relations in a scene schema, of course, are spatial, not temporal. (p. 15)

In addition:

> When we first characterized a scene schema . . . we found two factors that were important to the organization of this kind of knowledge. The first was inventory information, that is, what objects typically appear in a scene. . . . The second was spatial-relation information, which describes the typical spatial layout of a scene. (p. 16)

And finally:

> Although . . . there are many commonalities in the processing of events and scenes (i.e., schemas), it is not obvious that spatial relations are exactly comparable to temporal relations. First, there are more spatial connections among items in a scene than there are temporal connections among events. In an ordered event sequence the connections are one-dimensional; in a scene schema the connections form a network of at least two, and typically, three dimensions. . . . In general, one would expect the multiplicity of connections among the parts of a scene schema to allow more complete recall than in the case of an event schema. (pp. 16–17)

Jean Mandler's comments about the spatial nature of the relations in scene schemas exemplify, once again, how space—even in thought processes related to environmental apprehension—structurally integrates with the context of an environment. In later chapters in this book, research designs will be illustrated suggesting *possible* ways to reason about the structural role of space in terms of its relationship to an environment's physical–social context. Aspects of environmental cognitive structures described by Mandler relate in interesting ways to the conduct of human activity itself, as some of the next comments will illustrate.

1.4.4 Context and Arena Features of Memory-Based Environmental Knowledge

Cognitive integrations in the form of environmental schemas are useful for illustrating the apprehension of environments from the perspective of their different facets. As indicated above, one way to *contemplate* an immediate surrounding is from its arena or spatial-structural features. Human activity nearly always involves the negotiation of space, expenditure of motions, moving around to deal with things at various locations, judging or assessing directions and distances, and the like. For that reason, *internal knowledge* to guide ongoing apprehension of immediate environments while transacting with them in those ways would be useful.

Researchers commonly refer to the forming of arena-type environmental schemas as *cognitive mapping* (see Downs & Stea, 1977; Neisser, 1976). This refers to "experience-driven development" over time of long-term memory structures which, in a generalized or schematic way, are believed to "represent" spatial relationships among presumably significant locations in situational settings or environments. Such structures are assumed to direct the acquisition and processing of spatial information during perception and, in that way, are said to facilitate effective spatial or arena functioning in the environment.

As emphasized earlier, however, immediate surroundings or environments also have significance to individuals as contexts, particularly for assessing the "appropriateness" of intended activities. Neisser (1976), for example, indicates:

> In the normal environment most perceptible objects and events are *meaningful*. They afford various possibilities for action, carry implications about what has happened or what will happen, belong coherently to a larger context, and possess an identity that transcends their simple physical properties. These meanings can be, and are perceived. (p. 71)

He states further that "perception of meaning, like the perception of other aspects of the environment, depends on schematic control of information pickup" (p. 72).

This suggests, then, that in addition to *arena features,* there is also a *contextual meaning component* to environmental schemas, one that encompasses what people anticipate and/or expect to be the typical nonspatial attributes of settings.

1.4.5 But Why Does This Matter?

Perhaps the most salient point that can be made in this section is that *activities* are more effectively understood when studied in the setting of the environment of which they are a part and in terms of which they are generally conceived. Despite their apparent substantial social and psychological meaning, it would be incomplete to evaluate activities independent of the *setting* in which they occur. An important reason for this is that too many stimulus effects potentially important to their clarification may be overlooked in the assessment of their nature. The same point, of course, can be made about the occurrences of experiences in environmental contexts.

In general, external information necessary for both the enactment of actions and the onset of experiences ordinarily appears as and is encountered in an environmental configuration. From a definition-of-the-situation perspective, such a configuration is a rather complex gestalt containing information about content and relations, environmental patterning effects on both, and information about properties unique to the patterning itself. *Facets* of environmental information displays such as "arena," "context," and, perhaps, even "ambiance," when viewed *interdependently,* tend to exemplify this gestalt-like character of environments. Hence, since information *external* to individuals is generally manifested as part of environmental arrays and environmental-type schemas are believed to guide and/or to direct apprehension of such arrays, it is reasonable to expect that, in general, the process of perceiving the external world involves apprehending its information in both an ecological and a component manner. In other words, because information external to individuals is usually an inextricable part of a spatial–physical–social setting, comprehension of it is influenced by that mode of its appearance. This suggests that the configuration properties of environmental arrays—such as details about "spacing," "position," "connection," "orientation," "organization," "temporality," and "ambiance"—may, to some extent, qualify how content information such as "social," "physical," and "psychological" details gets to be known in any environmental encounter. Thus, contemplating an activity from the perspective of it being a response to an environment should take into account not only the way in which external information necessary to it normally appears in surroundings, but also any qualifying implications those appearances might have on all aspects of such information. What this amounts to for *cognitively oriented theory about activity* is that different external informational circumstances are encountered when the activity is pictured as happening in environments than when it is not conceived of in that way.

It will be noticed as the reader progresses into the specific research examples presented in Parts III–VI of this book that little of what was discussed in this section is expected to be *directly* applied in particular research projects. The purpose of this chapter was to inform at a broader conceptual level what should be expected with regard to person–environment–behavior *relationships* occurring in the actual and ordinary world of activities and experiences. Researchers face many of the common conceptual and methodological complications described in the preface when actually investigating particular human activities and experiences; these, in effect, routinely preclude applying many of the thoughts developed here. The conceptualization level, in person–environment–behavior paradigms referred to repeatedly throughout this chapter, is commonly more general than the particular level encountered in or characterizing actual research projects. What ultimately matters for readers is an awareness of *person–environment–behavior relationships* involved in their research on human activities and experiences. Hopefully, this awareness can at least serve as a general guide of what is fundamentally governing relationships among P, B, and E, when designing a research approach to investigate a specific problem. We now go on to subsequent chapters to examine other foundation issues involving measurement and information that present complications found in all research.

PART I

Comprehending Data Recording and Measurement to Generate Information in Scientific Inquiry

The process of conducting empirical research involves creating and using data, and analyzing data to generate information about phenomena, events, and situations so as to provide a better understanding of them. The two chapters in this part address the issues of data recording and measurement to generate information. This information is needed for the process of conducting research, particularly for using the scientific mode of inquiry, which we strongly argue in this book is the most appropriate paradigm to use to investigate P-E-B relationships.

Chapter 2 focuses on important issues dealing with the sources and types of data that researchers tap to generate information. There is a discussion of the difference between data and information. In particular, we focus on the complex issue of measurement and its implications for working with different types of data. The chapter discusses the nature of data and information, and the use of both existing secondary data and the collection and use of new primary data in research. The aggregation-disaggregation problem and the issues that arise out of the ecological fallacy, which are so fundamental in research involving a spatial perspective, are discussed. The chapter also examines the nature of the decision-making unit (DMU) in research design for data collection. That then leads to a specific discussion on types and levels of measurement and on issues focusing on data quality.

Chapter 3 discusses the rationale for collecting data to generate information as an essential part of the research process and the different degrees to which relevant data can generate information. That might or might not be directly assessed and discerned through operational reflectors and the creation of latent variables. The chapter discusses important issues regarding the creation of reflectors or indicators for working with different types of data to provide more meaningful information about phenomena, events, and situations. The chapter also discusses the diverse qualitative and quantitative research formats that might be considered as part of this process. Particular attention is given to discussing the creation of information through the use of surveys and

and experiments. In addition, the chapter provides an overview of the scientific mode of inquiry for conducting research, which is the fundamental philosophical paradigm to which we adhere.

Whether qualitatively or quantitatively designed, this scientific mode of inquiry has provided the framework that has been used in our own various research efforts when conducting investigations into aspects of human activities and experiences in spaces and environments as illustrated later in the chapters in Parts III–VI.

CHAPTER 2

Data and Measurement to Generate Information

2.1 Introduction

It is commonly said that we live in the "information age," where modern technologies make it almost possible to use the Internet to gain instantaneous access to an incredible amount of information on virtually anything. In our daily lives we are being bombarded with *information*, and it is not uncommon to hear the comment that we are suffering from "information overload." The trouble is that, despite its ready availability, often it is the case that existing information is insufficient, inadequate, inappropriate, or incomplete. Conversely, too much information may inhibit our comprehension of the issues being investigated.

Research is about the creation of and advancement in *knowledge* to enhance our understanding of human and other phenomena. In the context of P-E-B relations research, investigations with which we are concerned in this book, the research process generates new *information* to improve our understanding about phenomena, events, and situations in P-E-B research and to help *explain*, and even *predict*, their occurrence. To do that we need *data* about those things we are investigating. What we need to ensure is that we have confidence that the data we are using to generate information is *valid* and *reliable*, and that the results of our analysis will be *meaningful* vis-à-vis the research question(s) that are being investigated.

Existing data often cannot be used as the sole source or even *a* source of information to adequately address a research question. If information is to be used, then we may need to recognize the specific limitations of that information and what it can tell us about the research question at hand. It is, then, very likely that researchers will have to generate their own information through the process of data collection, recording, and measurement in order to address their specific research question. Thus, much research has to collect and generate its own data. But even when this is the case, all too frequently the generated information too may suffer from the same deficiencies referred to above.

However, *all* research—whether it is based on the use and analysis of existing data and current information or whether it requires the collection and analysis of new data and the addition of new information through modes appropriate for a given research effort—actually generates new information as a result of the research process itself. That new information—which itself is the output of a research process—provides an addition to the pool of existing information or knowledge.

An important issue to stress is that, in considering data and its use to generate information in research, from the perspective we are taking in this book we are concerned with data creation and use and with the generation of information as a result of the research process to provide an *evidence base* to aid our understanding of phenomena, events, and situations, and in particular human activities and experiences in spaces and environments. That is achieved through the systematic processes of data gathering that involves observing, recording, categorization, measurement, analysis, evaluation, and interpretation to produce information vis-à-vis the phenomenon, event, or situation being investigated. That information needs to be appropriate and explicitly relevant for the research task being undertaken.

In this chapter we explicitly provide an overview of some of the key issues involved—and with respect to which decisions of choice of approach needed to be made—in the matters of data collection, recording, and measurement, highlighting the decisions regarding the choice of approach that the researcher needs to make. We consider the variety of data *sources* and *types* of data and information with which researchers need to be familiar. We also consider issues concerning the creation of *reflectors* or *indicators* for working with different forms of data to generate information. And we address aspects of *measurement* and the implications for working with different types of data.

2.2 Creating Knowledge: Distinguishing between Information and Data

Before proceeding to discuss these important matters, it is necessary first to discuss briefly an issue that can lead to confusion and even misconception, and that is the difficulty that may arise from the rather loose and incorrect way in which researchers sometimes refer to data and information interchangeably.

What is *knowledge*? The *Merriam-Webster Online Dictionary* (www.Merriam-Webster.com) gives these definitions:

> The fact or condition of knowing something with familiarity gained through experience or association . . .
> Acquaintance with or understanding of a science, art, or technique . . .
> The fact or condition of being aware of something . . .
> The range of one's information or understanding . . .
> The circumstances or condition of having information or of being learned . . .
> The sum of what is known . . .
> The body of truth . . .
> A branch of learning information and principles acquired by mankind.

Most important:

> . . . Knowledge applies to facts or ideas acquired by study, investigation, observation, or experience. . . .

—things that are crucial to the research process.

What do we mean by *data* and *information*? The *Concise Oxford Dictionary* (Fowler, Fowler, Della, & Thompson, 1995) defines "information" as follows:

... informing, telling; thing told; knowledge, items of knowledge, news.

The *Merriam-Webster Online Dictionary* elaborates on "information" as follows:

> The communication or reception of knowledge or intelligence ...
> Knowledge obtained from investigation, study, or instruction ...
> Intelligence, news ...
> Facts, data ...
> the attribute inherent in and communicated by one of two or more alternative sequences or arrangements of something ... that produces specific effects
> Signal or character ... representing data ... something (as a message, experimental data, or a picture) which justifies change in a construct (as a plan or theory) that represents physical or mental experience or another construct ...
> A quantitative measure of the content of information ... a numerical quantity that measures the uncertainty in the outcome of an experiment to be performed ...

"Information" thus incorporates a broad range of sources. It involves the passing on of knowledge. It is dynamic. It involves experimentation and measurement. And it is about adding to knowledge by reducing uncertainty.

In the definition of "information," reference is made to *data,* which is a term widely used in research. It can be singular or plural. The *Merriam-Webster Online Dictionary* gives the following definition of "data":

> ... factual information (as measurements or statistics) used as a basis for reasoning, discussion, or calculation ...

It is derived from the term "datum," which *The Concise Oxford Dictionary* (Fowler et al., 1995) defines as:

> ... something known or granted, assumption or premise from which inferences may be drawn; fixed starting point of a scale etc.

The *Merriam-Webster Online Dictionary* indicates it may be given the plural "data" to mean " ... something given or admitted empirically as a basis for reasoning or inference."

Thus, "data" are a specific form of "information" relating to accepted fact, usually measured in numeric statistical terms, and being used as an assumption or premise for inferring an outcome or relationship. Implicit in data is measurement and scientific reasoning, which we discuss later in this chapter. As we will discuss further in Chapter 3, it is helpful to regard information as the output generated from data compilation and analysis; information is the *outcome* of the *transformation* of data.

Where we have collections of information in *digital form,* we refer to that as a *database* or *data file.* Databases tend to contain more than one type of record with information on the linkages or relationship between different types. They contain transparency in that people can gain access to the databases through the information that is given on the format and coding scheme used to record the information in the database. Databases form one of the fundamental components of *geographic information systems* (GIS) where the attributes and locations of phenomena and the connections between them are stored.

In this book we focus on both data and information, regarding both as creative acts to enable the generation of knowledge to enhance our understanding and explanation. However, because of our strong concern for *measurement* in the investigation of human activities and experiences in spaces and environments, we are focused particularly on the collection, creation, and uses of data to generate information to enhance and advance our knowledge of P-E-B relations.

2.3 The Variety of Data Available for Research

A wide variety of data is available to use in research or may be created through the research process that results in the generation of information. Data may come from a similarly wide range of sources and may assume many different forms. And data may relate to different levels or scales of spatial aggregation and disaggregation.

2.3.1 Primary versus Secondary Data

Before proceeding to address some of the detailed considerations involved in the sources of data and its collection, recording, and measurement, it is necessary to make a very important distinction between what we refer to as *primary data* and *secondary data* and information that we alluded to in the beginning of this chapter.

When using existing data and information in research, we are depending on what is called "secondary data," which we then subject to analysis that typically leads to the generation of new but *derived* information from that existing data. A classic example is the high degree of dependence researchers have on secondary data that is available in official data collections such as the census. Such data provide a rich and diverse range of information about the characteristics of people in places at different levels of spatial scale and across a wide range of attributes of people, both at one point in time (*static* data and information) and over time (*dynamic* or *longitudinal* data and information).

Where researchers decide they cannot rely on existing data sources in the form of secondary data to conduct their research investigation, they are faced with the necessity of developing a strategy to generate their own data, which involves choosing a methodology to collect new data designed specifically to generate new information in investigating the research question at hand. In such an instance, researchers must generate "primary data" that subsequently will be analyzed.

Secondary data analysis (see Hakim, 1982, for a comprehensive overview) often uses existing databases that represent the primary data collections undertaken by previous research. When the researcher is using secondary data analysis, typically new information will be derived to augment the existing dataset and to construct new variables derived from that information. This is becoming increasingly common as researchers conduct secondary data analysis on existing survey data collections that are held in survey research repositories, such as the Inter-University Consortium for Political and Social Research (ICPSR) at the University of Michigan, the Australian Social Science Data Archive (ASSDA) at the Australian National University, and the Data Archive at the University of Essex. That further use of data allows for both efficiency in data collection and the conduct of comparative studies across space and time that otherwise would not be possible (Johnston, Gregory, Pratt, & Watts, 2000, p. 730).

2.3.2 Data Sources

There are countless sources of data that we can tap to conduct research. The following is a list indicative of the range and type of data that we typically use in research:

1. *Individual* or *firsthand observation* of a place, people, subjects, or a phenomenon, including field observations and environmental observation.
2. *Individual* or *firsthand experience* of a place, an event, or a situation.
3. *Secondhand accounts* by another person or persons of such observations or experiences, given through *language* in verbal or written form.
4. *Documentary records* or *writings* or *reporting* of or about a place, people, subjects, a phenomenon, an event, or situations, including manuscripts, books, and the printed media such as newspapers, which may include words, symbols, and visual images such as films, pictures, and maps.
5. *Electronic media reporting* of information through, for example, TV, the Internet, and satellite imagery.
6. *Special-purpose numeric and written information* in the form of statistical tabulations and lists compiled by public agencies and private firms, such as census data collections, telephone directories, electoral rolls, business directories, and so on, usually compiled for public access either free of charge or through subscription or fee-for-use.
7. *Specific-purpose collections of information from and on people* about their *views, opinions, attitudes, beliefs,* and *perspectives,* and on *overt behavior* with respect to specific phenomena collected through interview or other survey methods.
8. *Interpretative representations by an individual* of a phenomenon or situation using a specific medium for representation such as paintings by artists; novels, short stories, and poems by writers; and films by directors and producers.

In addition, we may distinguish between data that are about:

- *people* (that is, individuals)
- *groupings of people* (such as households)
- *entities* (such as businesses)
- *institutions* (such as business organizations, nongovernment or nonprofit organizations, and public-sector agencies and governments)
- *objects* (such as buildings)
- *events* (such as an exhibition or festival)
- *places* at different levels of scale (such as towns, cities, regions, and nations)
- *spaces* at different levels of scale (such as rooms, neighborhoods, and districts)
- *landscapes* (which are conceptualizations of and representations of concepts such as industrial landscapes, residential landscapes, rural landscapes, and natural wilderness landscapes).

2.3.3 Types of Data

Not surprisingly, just as there are many *sources* of data, there are also many different *types* of data, and data may assume many forms:

1. Humans—their *activities* and their *environments*—and phenomena, situations, objects, and events may be regarded, noticed, observed, and monitored temporally through comparative statics, cross-sectionally or dynamically, using *continuous data*. This is the difference between static and dynamic analysis.
2. Data and information may also be *place-specific*.

3. In addition, data may involve *subjective* appraisal and/or *objective* categorization, which typically involves recording and/or measurement.
4. Data that is *subjective* may reflect people's *opinions, attitudes, values, beliefs, perceptions,* and *cognitions.*
5. Data that is *factual* reflects the *existence* of a phenomenon and a *categorization* and *measurement* of it.
6. Data may be *simple* or *complex.*
7. Data may be *stated* or *revealed.*
8. And data may be *disaggregated* (individually collected or relating to a singular individual or event) or it may be *aggregated* (relating to groupings of individuals such as populations).

Conducting research requires making decisions about the form in which things will be observed and how to collect data and reorder it in a form reasonable and appropriate for us to analyze. It involves giving due consideration to issues about data form.

2.3.4 The Aggregation–Disaggregation Problem

A significant issue in spatial and environmental research is the *aggregation–disaggregation problem.* When using *spatial scale,* this issue assumes particular importance for the level at which data are recorded, as that restricts the degree to which much official data can be meaningfully used in investigating a particular research question. Take the spatial behavioral activity "migration," where secondary data available from a source such as the census may only permit the aggregate-level analysis of interregional migration between the states or counties of a nation. If a disaggregated or individual-level of analysis of migration behavior is the research objective, then primary data collection using a sample survey approach is likely to be necessary to generate the information required to assist the researcher to understand this phenomenon.

A further aggregation–disaggregation issue relates not specifically to spatial scale but to the degree to which data for a population may be disaggregated into attributes such as gender, household composition, workforce occupational status, income groups, and so on. It relates not only to the degree to which aggregate information is able to be thus disaggregated into such categories or subgroups, but also to the way the researcher may then want to aggregate individual-based data (derived, for example, from a sample survey of individuals in households) into categories or groups to form attribute measures.

This concern, then, gives rise to very important questions regarding:

- *When* do we aggregate or disaggregate?
- *What* do we aggregate or disaggregate?
- *Why* do we aggregate or disaggregate?
- *How* do we aggregate or disaggregate?

To address such questions requires careful thought and planning in the design of a research strategy and in choosing the methodology and mode of data collection and recording to be used vis-à-vis addressing the research question at hand. A fundamental point to remember is that, once collected, individual-level data are then able to be aggregated into groups or broader categories, whereas once data are collected at an aggregate level, it is very difficult if not impossible to then disaggregate it.

The aggregation–disaggregation problem assumes particular significance when we are using secondary sources of information, such as census data, which provides aggregate data on the characteristics of people, households, and dwellings at a base level of spatial disaggregation that is defined by spatial scale of the *areal unit* (such as a census collector's district or census tract or an enumeration district) at which the data were collected from individual people and households but that is only made available in aggregate-level form at that base level of spatial scale. Such information may then be aggregated-up into higher order spatial units (such as counties and states), but the base level of data cannot be further spatially disaggregated.

2.3.5 The Ecological Fallacy and Other Fallacies

The type of situation discussed above gives rise to what is known among geographers and sociologists as the *ecological fallacy*, a problem that arises when we attempt to *infer* the characteristics of individuals from aggregate spatial data by referring to a population of which they are members. As is evident in the census data example, in spatial and environmental research situations often such aggregate-level data are available from a secondary source for defined areal units, and are thus referred to as *ecological data*. The ecological fallacy was highlighted over 50 years ago by Robinson (1950) in a study of U.S. census (aggregate) data in which he observed a high statistical correlation from a regression of the percentage of the population of each state who were illiterate with the percentage of the population of each state who were black. It could be inferred that blacks are more likely to be illiterate than nonblacks. However, Robinson found from a study based on individual-level (disaggregate) data that the same correlation analysis revealed a correlation coefficient that was much lower than it was at the state level. Thus the lesson was that just because blacks were concentrated in the states with the highest levels of illiteracy does not necessarily mean that there was a higher degree of illiteracy among blacks or that individual blacks were illiterate.

A number of other spurious individual-level correlations from aggregate-level data analysis are identified by Alker (1969):

1. *Individual fallacy*, where it is assumed that the "whole" is no more than the "sum of its parts."
2. *Cross-level fallacy*, where it is assumed that a relationship observed on one level of aggregation of a population applies to all others. In a spatial-unit context, this has subsequently been shown to be invalid through research on the *modifiable areal unit problem*.
3. *Universal fallacy*, where it is assumed that the pattern observed across a selection of individuals also holds for the population. This is akin to the *psychological fallacy*, where models of individual-level behavior are extrapolated in an attempt to account for the behavior of aggregate-level populations.
4. *Selective fallacy*, where data from carefully chosen cases are used to "prove" a point.
5. *Cross-sectional fallacy*, where it is assumed that what is observed at one point in time applies to other times.

Great care needs to be taken to avoid committing these fallacies in interpreting the results of studies based on analysis of aggregate-level data and in interpreting the meaning of the information thus generated. While an observed relationship may be consistent with a hypothesis, a causal relationship cannot be assumed in moving from the particular to the general. What we typically do in using the results, for example, of correlation analysis between variables as in spatial analysis at the aggregate level of data for spatial units, is to refer to the existence or not of an *ecological correlation* or *association* between the phenomena in question.

However, as noted above with respect to the "cross-level fallacy," research by geographers (such as Openshaw & Taylor, 1979) has shown that when data are aggregated spatially, the ecological fallacy can be decomposed into two effects:

1. A *scale effect*, where the larger the areal unit of aggregation the larger on average the correlation between two variables.
2. An *aggregation effect*, where, because of the very large number of different ways area units might be grouped together, one can obtain a frequency distribution of the correlation between two variables across the aggregation of units that could cover the full range of possible values from −1.00 to +1.00.

Because spatial boundaries are arbitrary and unrelated to the phenomena being studied, considerable care needs to be given as to how to interpret the results of such correlation analyses. Computer programs are available to assess the extent of this modifiable areal unit problem.

2.3.6 The Decision-Making Unit and Its Population

In conducting research into human activities and experiences in spaces and environments, it is crucial to identify and clearly define the unit for which, from which, and on which data is to be collected and measured. This is usually referred to as the *decision-making unit* (DMU), which is regarded as the *sampling unit* in survey research methods of data collection.

Typically the DMU will be an *individual* person, but it may also be a *collective* or *group*, such as a household. Alternatively, the DMU might be an *entity*, such as a firm, or it might be an *organization* or *institution*, such as a club, an association, a local council, or a state government or one of its agencies. The DMU becomes the focus for generating information and for data recording and measurement. DMUs may be aggregated-up into groups or categories for purposes of analysis. But DMUs cannot be further disaggregated.

The prerequisite to selecting the DMUs that are to be studied in a research project is to define the wider *population* of which the DMU is a part and to which it belongs for the specific purpose of pursuing the research question at hand. This is not as easy as it might seem, because that population needs to be very clearly identified and precisely defined. It needs to be restricted or delineated geographically, such as by the boundary of a suburb or a metropolitan area. That is usually the easy part—and it is important because it sets the geographic scale and context for the study. However, usually the investigation of a research question specifically relates to a particular group or category of people or objects defined by the nature of the research question and the context of which the DMU is a part.

For example, if our interest is in investigating migration and the residential choice made by in-movers to rapidly growing small urban centers in a particular state who are young family households and who have moved from another state in the last 5 years, then defining that *target population* requires explicit specificity. That target population might thus be defined in the following way:

- Small urban centers are those places with populations of less than 10,000 at the latest census
- Rapidly growing small urban centers are those whose population increased at a rate of at least an average of 2% per annum over the decade to that census date
- Young family households are those where the oldest adult is under 40 years and which comprise an adult male and an adult female living as a couple with at least one child living in the household
- Such eligible couples are those who have relocated to an eligible urban center during the period 1997 to 2002 inclusive from an origin in another state.

Such definitions give explicit precision in identifying and precisely defining the target population in which we are interested. However, the next issue is to establish a list of those eligible households in those communities that constitute the DMUs making up the target population—or if one does not exist or cannot be compiled, then to decide on a procedure to produce a random sample of those households, or to obtain a quota number of such eligible households from a random sample of all households in those towns. The number of DMUs to be selected for study needs to be determined. Then the question becomes: From whom do we collect information from within each DMU on the behavior of that DMU vis-à-vis the research question? This is an important point, as a "Household" per se cannot provide information in, say, an interview situation, whereas the individuals or one of them within the household can do so.

We find a similar problem in terms of information collection where entities, groups, organizations, and institutions constitute the DMUs for a study. An individual or specific individuals belonging to or constituting the DMU have to be identified to provide the information we need about the DMU.

2.3.7 The Data Matrix

For purposes of analysis in a research situation, it is usually necessary to transform information into a *data matrix*. In the context of P-E-B relations research, that is likely to incorporate a locational data component in addition to the *variables* on the *attributes* of the *cases* (subjects or places) being investigated. Figure 2.1 illustrates such a data matrix incorporating a spatial element.

Here we let $z_1, z_2, \ldots z_k$ refer to k variables or attributes and s refers to location. The use of the lowercase symbol on z and s denotes an actual data value, while the number inside the parentheses—1, 2, 3, etc.—references the particular case. Attached to a case (*i*) may be

$$\begin{matrix} \text{Data on the } k\text{-variables} & \text{Location} & \\ \begin{bmatrix} z_1(1) & z_2(1) & \ldots & z_k(1) \\ z_2(2) & z_2(2) & \ldots & z_k(2) \\ & & \cdot & \\ & & \cdot & \\ & & \cdot & \\ z_1(n) & z_2(n) & \ldots & z_k(n) \end{bmatrix} & \begin{bmatrix} s(1) \\ s(2) \\ \cdot \\ \cdot \\ \cdot \\ s(n) \end{bmatrix} & \begin{matrix} \text{Case} & 1 \\ \text{Case} & 2 \\ \cdot \\ \cdot \\ \cdot \\ \text{Case} & n \end{matrix} \end{matrix}$$

FIGURE 2.1. The data matrix, incorporating a spatial element. From Haining (2003, p. 10). Copyright 2003 by Cambridge University Press. Adapted by permission.

a location s(*i*). The use of the bold for **s** indicates that this particular case can contain more than one number for identifying a spatial location. For example:

$$s(i) = s_1(i), s_2(i)$$

The equation may be shortened to the form

$$\{z_1(i), z_2(i), \ldots, z_k(i) | s(i)\} \quad i = 1, \ldots, n$$

In addition, data may also have a *temporal* reference, which would give the structure

$$\{z_1(i,t), z_2(i,t), \ldots, z_k(i,t) | s(i), t\} = 1, \ldots, n$$

where *t* denotes time.

The compilation of such a data matrix permits the digital storage of information and its analysis using mathematical and statistical routines and, in the case where spatial information is included, analysis and manipulation in a GIS framework. It also readily permits aggregation-up, both across cases and spatially, as well as over time.

2.4 Measurement Implications for Working with Different Types of Data

In the scientific mode of inquiry, *objectivity* is a major goal. It is concerned with *interpersonal agreement* so that the observations and conclusions by one researcher can be passed on meaningfully to other people. Quantitative methods are employed toward this end and as a means of recording confidence in the *inferences* that are made by manipulating data. That requires *measurement*, which is simply the description of data in terms of *alphanumerics*, generally according to a set of rules. Amedeo and Golledge (1975) note that that "permits accurate, objective, and communicable descriptions that can be readily manipulated in thinking" (p. 96). Specifying the level of measurement of a variable is important as it "specifies" the formal properties and the number system underlying measurement, and it also determines what arithmetic operations are valid, and hence what statistical procedures can be employed (Haining, 2003, p. 50).

2.4.1 The Need for Measurement and the Qualities It Requires

A question frequently asked is *How can we measure those things that do not exist in the form of numbers?* As discussed in the introductory section to this chapter, the answer to that question lies in the idea of an *isomorphism*, which refers to an *equivalence of form* or the *quality relationships* required between what is observed and that which is recorded to generate data. We need to achieve an isomorphism as a necessary and sufficient step to represent what is an empirical situation (one that exists "in reality") with numbers. Sometimes the equivalences between an empirical situation and its numeric representation will be "good," while at other times they will be "rough." For example, we could record the males as "1" and the females as "0" and get a good representation of the sex mix of people living in a city. But if we needed to represent numerically the number of miles people living in a city drive each day in their cars, then we might be satisfied with using a rough equivalence, such as the mean (average) or some other statistic, to give an equivalence to describe that empirical situation.

2.4.1.1 Recorded Observations and Data

In considering measurement, it is useful to distinguish between *recorded observations* and that which is analyzed (that is, data). Recorded observations are a subset of the universe of the potential observations that could be made about an empirical situation. Frequently the recorded observations used to make a description are a small subset of the universe of the things that might describe some phenomenon or situation.

Consider an environment such as a city, which might have an almost infinite number of features or characteristics. We might choose to describe it by focusing on things such as its name, size, area, location, number of functions, and so on. Some of that information might be collected directly by measurement (such as population size or size of an area measured in hectares), but some might have to be transformed to numeric terms before it can become "data." Take its "location," for example, which might be described as east or west of a particular river, or north or south of a border. That is not strictly "data," but it does provide an *interpretative step* to convert the recorded information into a numerical form before it can be regarded as data.

2.4.1.2 Qualities for Data Measurement

The interpretative step of transforming recorded observation into data raises a number of issues. These include the following, which relate to the *qualities* of data for *measurement*:

1. Determining the extent to which a set of numbers in the relation are *unique* and if an *admissible transfer* has been made—that is, one where the numerical system obtained by replacing the empirical situation retains qualities such as *identity, order,* and *additivity.*
2. *Identity preservation* is about the sequencing properties of an observation into *single* or *multiple feature classes,* thus ensuring clarity in the allocation process.
3. *Order preservation* is about the *sequencing properties* of an observation on a temporal, spatial, or qualitative dimension to produce rankings confirming to a chosen monotonic rule set.
4. *Additive* preservation ensures the *manipulative quality* of the observation so that numeric manipulations (+, −) can be undertaken to give results consistent with a linear scale and ensuring that all the fundamental operations can be applied to a set of numbers while retaining internal consistency in the set.

Thus "order" implies a definite sequencing of the numbers, and the order property can be identified even without the use of the numbers (for example, the building is "higher than" another building). "Identity" raises the problem of uniqueness. If both "order" and "additivity" are satisfied, for the most part unique identity is also provided, regardless of whether individual or sets of observations are being dealt with. Mostly "identity" describes the "equivilativeness" between the reality and the number system. In all cases we can argue that the observation-number pair is either identical or different. If they are identical then we may postulate that $a = b$; if they are different, or if making the equivalence violates order and additivity, then we may postulate $a \neq b$. In the first case we have established an identity that will influence the type of model that can be used to analyze data.

2.4.1.3 Types of Measurement

Sometimes it is argued that there are three basic types of measurement. These are:

1. *Fundamental measurements,* which are those that record an existing property of an observation, such as its length or height.
2. *Derived measurements,* which occur in a number of forms but are usually defined on the relations between properties of an observation, such as the distance.
3. *Measurement by fiat,* which depends heavily on the intention of the researcher and may involve producing a single index derived from data to account for a complex variable, such as socioeconomic status.

With respect to "measures by fiat" and the construction of a *composite index* that represents an abstract concept, the values obtained are frequently treated as though they are measured on an interval scale, even if that is not true. The assumption is made that the "distance" as measured on the supposed interval or ratio scale has a meaning, but the problem is that there are usually many ways such an *index* or *scale* can be constructed.

2.4.2 Levels of Measurement

Measurement may be regarded as the construction of "scales" (homomorphous) from empirical relational structures of interest into numerical relational scales that are useful for manufacturing data-using statistics.

2.4.2.1 Measurement Scales

Commonly four *levels of measurement scales* are used:

1. *Nominal,* where each DMU is allocated to one out of two or more mutually exclusive and exhaustive categories (for example, gender categories "male" and "female").
2. *Ordinal,* where either the DMUs or the categories to which they are allocated are rank-ordered on some criterion (for example, A > B > C, which implies there are three classes of phenomena and that A is greater than/comes before B, which in turn is greater than/comes before C; therefore C > A is not possible).
3. *Interval,* where a quantitative assessment is made of the distance between two observations along a predetermined scale where there is an arbitrary zero point (for example, as in a temperature scale °C or °F).
4. *Ratio,* where relative quantitative assessment is made using differences along a scale with zero given a precise meaning that absolutely nothing exists at that point, and that thereafter all the additive properties have a special and powerful meaning (for example, a person's age in years, length of residence at a particular place in months, length of the last holiday taken in days).

Thus, a nominal measurement would say that the population of a city A is 1 million and that of city B is 3 million; an ordinal measurement would say city B has a larger population than city A; an interval measurement would say that city B has 2 million more people than city A; and a ratio measure would say city B has three times the population of city A.

2.4.2.2 Implications of Measurement Scales for Manipulating Data

There are implications in these levels of measurement concerning what one can do to manipulate data:

- *Ratio* measures are needed to +, −, ×, ÷.
- With *interval* measures we can only +, −.
- With *ordinal* measures we cannot +, −, ×, ÷.

One of the simplest forms of nominal measurement is *binary* (nonmetric) representation of data, where only two classes are recognized and a single number (either "0" or "1") is assigned to each class. This form of nominal measure is used to transform nonnumerical binary observations into data; for example, if a survey question is answered by "yes" = 1 and "no" = 0, it can be readily transformed into data.

Table 2.1 provides a useful summary illustration of how the defining relations of each level of measurement become more complex and how increasing degrees of complexity are associated with the statistics suited to each level (Siegel, 1956).

Spatial data have to be classified by the type of spatial object to which a variable refers as well as to the level of measurement of the variable attached to the spatial objectt. Attribute

TABLE 2.1. Four Levels of Measurement and Some Statistics Appropriate to Each Level

Scale	Defining relations	Examples of appropriate statistics	Appropriate statistical tests
Nominal	1. Equivalence	1. Mode 2. Frequency 3. Contingency coefficient 4. Chi-square	1. Nonparametric statistical tests
Ordinal	1. Equivalence 2. Monotonicity	1. Median 2. Percentile 3. Rank correlation 4. Kolmogorov–Smirnov 5. Kruskal–Wallis one-way analysis of variance	1. Nonparametric statistical tests 2. Parametric statistical tests
Interval	1. Equivalence 2. Monotonicity 3. Known ratio of any two intervals	1. Mean 2. Standard deviation 3. Product–moment correlation 4. Probability measures	1. Parametric statistical tests
Ratio	1. Equivalence 2. Monotonicity 3. Known ratio of any two intervals 4. Known ratio of any two scale values	1. Geometric means 2. Coefficient of variation	1. Nonparametric statistical tests 2. Parametric statistical tests

Note. From Siegel (1956). Copyright 1956 by McGraw-Hill. Adapted by permission.

TABLE 2.2. A Classification of Spatial Data by Level of Measurement and Type of Spatial Object

Level of measurement	Spatial representation			
	Point (P)	Line (L)	Area (A)	Surface (S)
Nominal (=)	House: burgled/not	Road: under repair/not	Census tract classified by lifestyle	Land-use type
Ordinal (≥; ≤)	Preference rankings of towns by quality of life	Road classification (motorway, A, B, level roads, etc.)	Census tract assigned to income class	Soil texture (coarse/medium/fine)
Interval (≥; ≤; ±)	SEIFA index for a town	Length using Greenwich Meridian as reference	SEIFA index for neighborhoods	Ground temperature °C
Ratio (≥; ≤; ± ×; /)	Output from a factory p.a.	Freight tonnage p.a.	Regional per capita income	Rainfall (cm); snow depth (cm)

Note. From Haining (2003, p. 52). Copyright 2003 by Cambridge University Press. Adapted by permission.

values may also be attached to the objects themselves, as in area and length of an object. Haining (2003, pp. 51–52) gives some examples that are reproduced in Table 2.2.

2.4.3 Data Quality Issues

It is necessary to give further consideration to data quality issues that go beyond those we discussed earlier concerning the quality of measurement. Here we are concerned with data quality that is affected not only by the way the real world is conceptualized to formulate concepts and to develop models to represent reality, but also by the processes whereby data on variables and attributes are collected.

As Haining (2003, p. 58) points out, it is the overall relationship between the space–(time) attribute data matrix (refer back to Figure 2.1) and the real world it is meant to capture (arguably the most important relationship) that can generate uncertainties because of the complex combination of the stages of model definition and data acquisition through measurement. The concern here is on the importance that must be attached to the *accuracy*—or the lack of error and bias—in the data and *completeness* in the sense of coverage.

2.4.3.1 Key Criteria for Achieving Quality of Measurement

There are three key criteria that are required to be met to achieve quality of measurement. Measurement needs to be characterized by:

1. *Precision,* which refers to the expectedness of the measure used in an observation or description.
2. *Reliability,* which refers to the likelihood that a given measurement procedure will yield the same description of a phenomenon if the measure is repeated.
3. *Validity,* which refers to the extent to which a specific measurement gives data that relate to commonly accepted meanings of a particular concept.

A particular problem is that once data contains *errors* of measurement, then those errors may be propagated through the process of analysis. Thus, it is essential to have valid error models that allow extrapolation of the effects of error propagation. This may be achieved through tests of error magnitude and tests of significance in associations between data variables. Where spatial data are used, it is possible to employ techniques to test for spatial autocorrelation for the effects of outliers on distributions, to test for the effects of choice of scale of analysis, and to conduct areal interpolation. These issues of measurement quality will thus impact on data quality, which, in turn, affects the performance of a dataset vis-à-vis the specifications of a model as it represents reality.

2.4.3.2 Quality and Secondary Data

Data quality is particularly important when there is reliance on secondary data, especially when there are issues concerning such data meeting acceptable scientific standards. Sometimes the use of survey data for secondary analysis will have limitations in modeling as such data may contain too many errors or be too "noisy" to justify the use of rigorous analytic techniques and statistical tests (Haining, 2003, p. 62). In assessing such secondary data and its suitability for use in addressing a specific research situation, the assessment of data quality will need to include both the variable (attribute) values and the spatial objects where relevant.

2.4.3.3 Quality Issues and Spatial Data

In spatial analysis, sometimes the right measurement might be assigned to the wrong location, thus leading to error in counts for areas and in distance measures (Griffith, 1989). Data may also have time coordinates, and error in recording the timing of events can have implications for the quality of datasets. Data quality may also be *spatially heterogeneous,* with its error structure varying across a map. Heterogeneity can also arise from the interaction between processes of measurement and understanding the underlying geography (Haining, 2003, p. 63).

Guptill and Morrison (1995) identify the following six dimensions of *spatial data quality*:

- Data lineage (description of the history of a dataset)
- Positional and attribute accuracy
- Completeness
- Logical consistency
- Temporal specification
- Semantic accuracy (the accuracy with which features, relationships, and attributes are encoded or described given the rules for representation).

In the context of GIS, Veregin and Hargitai (1995) emphasize:

- Data accuracy (the opposite of data error)
- Resolution (or precision) as it relates to data
- Consistency completeness.

However, data quality issues are also of particular concern in primary data collection through surveys. This is seen, for example, in the source of *error* and *bias* in the collection and recording of data and the generation of data variables in survey research. An interesting way of representing that is the concept of *total survey error,* as represented in Figure

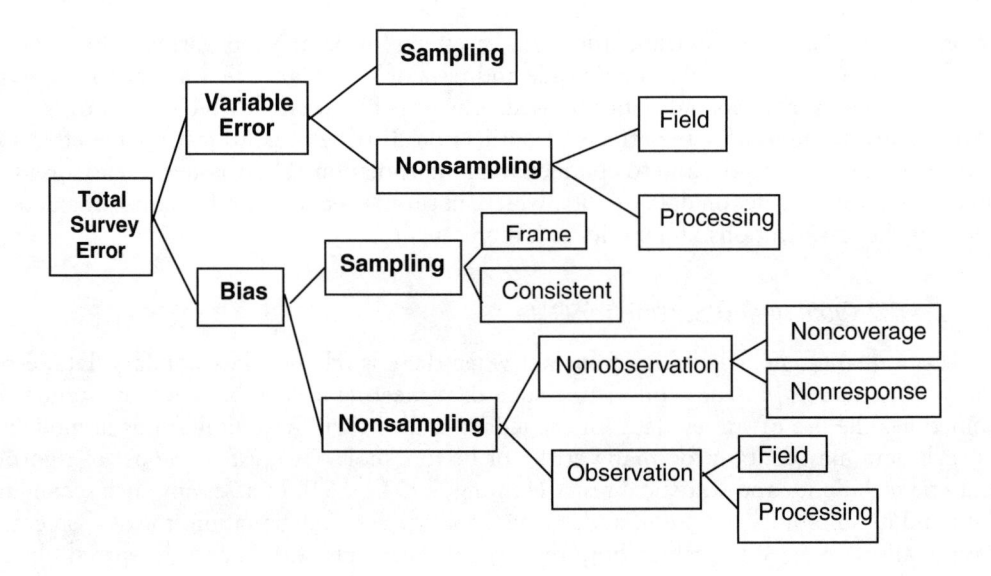

FIGURE 2.2. A classification of sources of survey error and bias. From Kish (1965). Copyright 1965 by John Wiley & Sons, Inc. AAdapted by permssion.

2.2, and developed by Kish (1965). It identifies the specific components and the types of error and bias that affect data quality and that is contributed by the various stages in the survey design and data-collection process. In general, it is recognized that error results from design effects, especially in sampling. But with the use of probability sampling procedures it is possible to statistically estimate the degree and magnitude of such errors. *Bias* has more to do with nonsampling types of problems and arises in particular both from the role of the respondent in not giving full and accurate information in answering questions, and from interviewer behavior as a result of variations in the way questions are asked and how respondents' answers are recorded. Bias also is generated through poor questionnaire design, including ambiguous wordings of questions. Error and bias may also arise through missing data as a result of respondents not answering all questions in a survey. However, a range of *imputation* techniques have been developed to help address that problem (see Kalton & Kasprzyk, 1986).

2.5 Conclusion

This chapter has canvassed a range of important considerations concerning data recording and measurement with which a researcher involved in investigating human activities and experiences in spaces and environments needs to be aware, particularly in the context of conducting research using the scientific mode of inquiry, to which our attention is turned in Chapter 3. The distinction between information and data has been discussed, and reference made to the wide variety of information and types of data available for the researcher, emphasizing specific issues relating to spatial data.

CHAPTER 3

Collecting Data and Generating Information in a Scientific Mode

3.1 Introduction

Essentially the research process is about generating information to further our understanding about phenomena, events, and situations, and to *explain* "why" and "how" those things occur and sometimes even to *predict* future circumstances. As discussed in Chapter 2, conducting research requires data. That may be available in a variety of existing forms and accessible to the researcher, or it might need to be generated by the researcher by design through the research process. As any research endeavor essentially involves guided and systematic analysis of data for its definitions, patterns, trends, relationships, and the like, it was necessary for us to discuss in some detail in Chapter 2 the key issues in data recording and measurement and the different forms that data might take in conducting research.

In this chapter we now turn to consider the broader research process that inevitably involves the researcher in developing a research design that incorporates data collation and/or collection and its analysis to produce information in order to provide insights into the phenomenon, event, or situation of concern to the researcher and possibly to furnish explanation(s) about them.

So that the reader is not left with any misconceptions as to where we are coming from philosophically in this book, it is essential to make it clear that the authors are firmly of the view that the scientific mode of inquiry provides the most appropriate framework to guide the researcher in the design and process of conducting research investigations into the nature of human activities and experiences in spaces and environments. That includes the use of existing and the formulation of new *theories* and the development and use of new *models*. Thus, in this chapter we specifically discuss a range of issues that may guide the researcher toward that end, and we provide a rationale for doing so.

3.2 The Rationale for Data Collection, Measurement, and Analysis in Research

What is crucial with respect to any given distinct information produced by the research effort and generated through the processes of data collection and analysis is the structure of, or characteristics of, the *quantity relationships* in the data that underpin the information that is generated and the insights that are subsequently gleaned through the research process. Those quantity relationships include concepts such as, for example, "distance," "sum," and "product relationships." That requires a thoughtfully conceptualized research framework and the use of carefully selected appropriate methodological tools of analysis to rigorously address the research question(s) specified by the researcher.

3.2.1 Different Degrees to Which Relevant Data Can Be Used Directly or Indirectly in Processed Form

A central tenet of the perspectives we present in this book is that different forms of data facilitate the use of different types of analytical methodological tools to generate information in the search for meaning and to provide explanation in a research project that investigated P-E-B relations. This is central to the scientific mode of investigation.

In the fields of spatial and environmental research and our understanding of the activities and experiences of people in those contexts, we need to be aware of the following:

1. In some cases and for some situations, the *form* of some of the information relevant to addressing specific research questions might be directly accessed and discerned.
2. But in other cases and for some other situations that may not be so.

With respect to the former (1), the chances are high that the *form* or *structure* of that data can be subjected to analytical or logical observations to produce results having corresponding meaning with respect to the conceptual nature of the information itself. Examples of this type of data include conventional spatial concepts such as "distance" and "area" (for example, kilometers, miles, feet, meters, inches, centimeters, acres, and hectares). The structure (that is, the underlying calculus or structure of quantity relationships) of this form of spatial and environmental data is usually fully explicit, systematic, and consistent with the structural characteristics of the relevant interval or ratio scales in our most flexible and precisely descriptive arithmetic. That is to say, data in these forms have consistent relationships throughout their underlying structures that have logical implications for any *quantitative operations* performed on them, as in the calculation of statistical parameters like "averages" and "variances," or in any "product" or "summation" produced by the arithmetic operations performed on them. Such parameters produced by those operations should, then, also have *corresponding meaning* (for example, as in "average distance") with respect to the application in the initial information in a nontrivial human activity (such as the distance moved by a household in a residential relocation) or experience (such as the number of times a place has been visited) relating to a research problem. Hence, an added bonus is that structural characteristics embodied in concepts such as "distance" and "area" and that are exhibited in their empirical counterparts are consistent with the characteristics attributed to them as concepts. In those ways we generate information that provides meaning and understanding about the phenomenon, event, or situation being investigated.

With respect to the latter ((2) above)—that is, where information is *not* able to be directly accessed or discovered—there are many instances in research in which the forms of the available spatial and environmental information lacks explicitness, so that the underlying spatial characteristics of these forms are difficult to discover. Examples of this abound, and include concepts such as "place attachment," "spatial orientation," "environmental schematics," "conservation perspective," and "environmental aesthetics," among others.

Consider the concept *place attachment*, which is not to be easily dismissed, for it is claimed that it might have significant meaning implications for things such as "self-awareness," "adaptation to uncommon environments," "adaptive response in and to environments," and the like. What does it mean to assert that one individual has twice the "place attachment" (or even considerably more or less) for his or her place vis-à-vis another person for his or her place? How is something like this exemplified? How is the "average place attachment" exhibited by a group of individuals for a specific place rationalized, calculated, and then illustrated? How do we measure it for, say, its completeness, accuracy, correspondence to some empirical-type setting, and difference from some other schemata version held by another individual for the same setting? For example, in the case of the "environmental aesthetic," it might focus on the differences between two landscapes or how the aesthetic "scenic quality" is to be calculated.

It is thus evident that there is a relative absence of empirical manifestations for concepts such as those just discussed when compared to manifestations of concepts such as "distance" and "area" referred to earlier. And there will be many instances like these in the realms of human social and behavioral research in the contexts of "spaces" and "environments"—with which geographers, planners, and others are concerned—where the fundamental issue is still one of identifying an empirical instance with its conceptualization. But this is a problem across many disciplines. For example, in economics, where the concept *utility* has facilitated a great deal of theorizing, we find similar dilemmas. To our knowledge, no one has yet to demonstrate an empirical counterpart to "utility" without resorting to the practice of demonstrating an instance of it by inventing still another empirically unanchored conceptualization such as "satisfaction."

3.2.2 Operational Reflectors: Latent Variables

In research involving human beings in particular, it is common for researchers to conceptualize what they believe they are experiencing or noticing while the issue of the empirical existence of what has been conceptualized remains unanswered. While researchers may be able to provide *operational reflectors* of them with *assumed scales*, the actual underlying metrics of these things—if empirical instances exist—remain latent or mute. Hence we have the concept *latent variable* in measurement theory. Further, even when operationalized in some logical way, the resulting scale produced frequently does not fully reveal its structural features, so that structural implications for arithmetic operations, extensions, and modifications of such a scale cannot be fully understood.

The reader needs to bear in mind the many difficulties that will confront researchers in addressing issues to do with data collection, recording, and measurement vis-à-vis the many different forms of spatial and environmental variables that operate on human activities and experiences. Many forms of data—whether empirically grounded or defined observationally—cannot be measured by robust scales having well-developed metrics (for example, in the arithmetic interval or ratio). This is so simply because it is not known whether the characteristics of such robust scales are sufficiently isomorphic to the structural characteristics (that is, quality relationships) of what is being measured. And, in many such situations, even weaker scales (such as the ordinal) also fail to characterize the data that is of interest to the researcher

In some cases, because of the complexity of the existing spatial and/or environmental data and information, a researcher will be compelled to assume the presence of latent variables that "presumably" reflect spatial and/or environmental data, and then to use intercorrelated "items" to develop "usable" scales of those latent data variables (for example, common variance among the items to produce surrogate factors to reflect the latent variable of interest). In still other instances, the needed spatial and/or environmental data may be embedded in secondary (existing) data sources, as in verbal responses about other issues, so that a great deal of extraction, recoding, and qualification becomes necessary in order to comprehend such information. This is fraught with many difficulties of meaning and interpretation, but it may be the only way known to obtain that particular information. Frequently the presence of spatial and environmental influences can only be inferred by looking at variations in nonspatial or nonenvironmental data and information (as in, for example, concepts like "social distance," "proximity," and "institutionalization"). Many other examples dealing with general ignorance of the underlying structures or forms of spatial and environmental information are, no doubt, evident to the reader, and we refer to some later.

Thus, it is important to address issues of measurement in relation to the underlying forms of data prior to discussing the many ways of collecting and working with or representing spatial and environmental information.

3.2.3 Other Difficulties and Complexities

Besides measurement difficulties, there are many other complexities concerning data and information that need to be considered. Commonly encountered ones include the following:

1. The absence of one-to-one empirical counterparts for many concepts and/or constraints created in research.
2. The presence of unanswerable questions; the many difficulties associated with attempts to isolate inferences, effects, and impacts for observation and study.
3. The near impossibility to observe directly and study in detail the workings of many processes (for example, "cognitive" and "affective") and structures (for example, schemas and other memory forms) said to operate in human activity and experience.
4. The practical invisibility, so to speak, of numerous subject motivations, perceptions, and reactions.

An especially prominent complexity commonly faced in human research projects is the presence of *interacting multiple factors* that influence the outcomes of the phenomenon, event, or situation of research interest. Some of these factors may be known, while others cannot be known; some can be identified, measured, and controlled for (in other words *operationalized*) rather easily, while others, though their presence is vaguely understood, cannot be either measured or conceptualized. In addition, it is often the case that both the form and the nature of the *relationships* both *between* and *among* factors are a mystery to the researcher.

Serious researchers are usually aware of the presence of most of such complexities, and for this reason have a more sober understanding of and a careful or even cautious approach to research issues, perspectives, and design.

3.3 Creating Reflectors or Indicators for Working with Different Forms of Data

Capturing data and generating information to represent reality is not a simple task. It involves abstracting reality through generalization and simplification to recover discrete "bits" of information or data on objects, often in a spatial and temporal context. It includes conceptualizing situations to construct concepts and identifying attributes and variables to measure.

3.3.1 Concepts and Conceptualizing

In research, one of the most common things we do is conceptualize things about the real world by constructing *concepts*. That involves the process of refining a general theoretical idea, which is discussed in detail later in this chapter. Defining concepts is often complicated, as they are *abstractions* or *mental images* of a phenomenon or situation. An example of a concept is "poverty," which might be defined and measured in a number of ways. However, over time, it is often the case that widely used and recognized concepts have evolved for which there may also be a standard means of measuring (sometimes, that is called a *benchmark*).

3.3.1.1 Defining Concepts

We need to give definition to concepts. These may be:

1. *Real definitions*, which are statements of the "essential nature" or "essential attributes" of a concept, such as social class.
2. *Nominal definitions*, which are specific definitions that are commonly used or are standard definitions, such as the "workforce," "family," "household," and the like, as defined in data collections such as the census.
3. *Operational definitions*, which involve measurement of a concept in a precisely specified way. For example, in studying the concept "housing financial stress," the operational definition given a way of measuring its incidence might be that the proportion of households in the bottom 40% of the household gross income distribution in which 30% or more of household gross income is allocated to housing costs.

3.3.1.2 Representation

The process of "conceptualizing" extends to the identification of the fundamental properties that are relevant to the situation being investigated. These may relate to both entities and the spatial relationships between them. But, in addition, we need to make decisions that are *representational*, which involve choices concerning scale (individual, aggregates of individuals into groups or categories, and/or level of spatial aggregation/disaggregation), and *category* or *class* to be used to represent entities. As Haining (2003, p. 43) points out, these are the decisions that have to be made about what to include in the data matrix shown previously in Figure 2.1. Of course, in addition, decisions have to be made about how to measure the individual, group, and/or spatial and temporal variables and attributes in the data matrix. These issues are taken up later.

3.3.2 Attributes and Variables

To perform analysis on the data a researcher uses in investigating a research question and to assist one to record data in a form appropriate for analysis, typically the researcher will need to specify the *attributes* and *variables* that he or she is going to use:

1. The term *attribute* refers to an inherent characteristic or quality associated with or belonging to a person or thing that is being investigated. It can ascribe to a quality of that person or thing. For example, attributes of people might be their "height," "social class," "ethnicity," or "race." The attribute of an object might be its "size," "shape," or "location."
2. The term *variable* is the logical grouping of an attribute. It is a quality that may assure any one of a set of values or it may be a symbol representing a variable. For example, for the attribute "gender," the variables are "male" and "female."

3.3.2.1 A Classification System for Variables

It is necessary for a *classification system* to be developed for variables, and it is particularly important that the groups of attributes comprising a variable are both:

1. *Exhaustive:* for example, in talking about age one needs to cover all age groups.
2. *Mutually exclusive:* for example, the age groups would need to be designated, say, into 5-year age groups 0–4 years, 5–9 years, 10–14 years, . . . , 80–84 years, 85–89 years, 95 years and over.

When considering spatial phenomena, attribute characteristics may refer to spatial objects or to entities that are associated with them or that are attached to the spatial objects but are not directly attributed to them.

Thus, conceptualization is about the definition and meaning of an attribute, while that attribute is represented through operationalization into variables in order to enable analysis to be undertaken. From that analysis, information is generated about the research question at hand.

3.3.2.2 Relationship between Attributes and Variables

The relationships between attributes and variables are central to the processes of description and explanation in theorizing and building models in research. Variables may, for example, be divided into either *dependent* or *response* variable or variables (designated Y variable[s] in analysis such as multiple regression) and *independent* (or *explanatory* or *predictor*) variables (designated as $X_1, X_2, \ldots X_n$ variables).

An explanatory variable, when measured at the nominal or ordinal level, may be called a *factor*, and when measured at the interval or ratio level it may be called a *covariate*. The outcome effect might be either an *attribute response* or a *process response*, depending on whether the explanatory variables relate to an underlying process or not. Also, in modeling it may be useful to distinguish between variables that measure individual-level attributes (such as "age" or "gender") and aggregated individual-level attributes (such as combinations of "age groups") in order to assess the *compositional effect* or *exposure effect* on a dependent or response variable.

3.3.2.3 An Indicator or Index

In spatial analysis, it is common for attributes to be attached to areas or locations to refer to area-level or group-level properties, such as represented by an *indicator* or *index*. Examples include the DETR Index of Deprivation used in the United Kingdom and the SEIFA Index of Employment and Income Advantage/Disadvantage used in Australia, both of which are derived from census variables and applied to small-area census tracts or enumeration districts.

Variables that are used to derive such attributes are measuring *area-level contextual attributes*, which may exist at varying levels of spatial scale from the local area or neighborhood up to the citywide or regional-level aggregations of those enumeration districts. A wide variety of such spatial indicators or indexes are derived to measure concepts such as "locational disadvantage," "social exclusion," "social capital," and so on. Such attribute measures are sometimes used to *infer* that individuals or households living in such areas may be exposed to or experience such conditions—in other words, an *ecological association* is inferred. As pointed out by Haining (2003):

> . . . Typically variables that measure such attributes, whilst they might be construed from variables measuring individual-level attributes (derived from the census), involve combining variables into an index which is meant to quantify (or operationalize) a group-level concept. (p. 49)

3.3.2.4 A Scheme for Classifying Variables

Haining (2003) provides a useful schema for *classifying* variables in the context of modeling such attributes, as shown in Figure 3.1. The classification derives from the nature of a model and whether explanatory variables relate to the underlying process or not. Haining (p. 50) gives the example of a regression model to explain variation across a region in

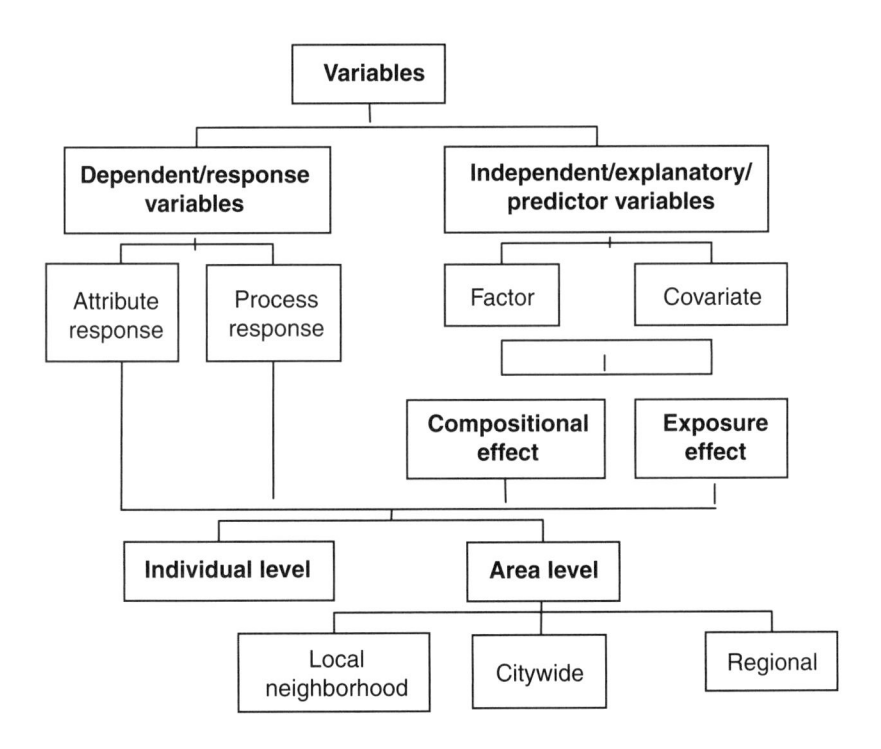

FIGURE 3.1. A classification of variables. From Haining (2003, p. 48). Copyright 2003 by Cambridge University Press. Reprinted by permission.

home prices and whether this is seen in terms of other individual-level and area-level attributes, including housing characteristics and area characteristics.

In the case of an attribute–response model, the analysis focuses on relationships between attributes and is not constructed in terms of processes responsible for determining house prices, which might include market processes and the maximizing behaviors of buyers and sellers. In a process–response model, the explanatory variables would include variables that link directly to the underlying process mechanisms.

3.4 Diverse Research Formats

Acknowledging the complexity of the research process as discussed so far is one thing, but in the actual conduct of research, the researcher will need to give due consideration to the various research formats that are available to collect data and to the analytical methods and tools available to analyze those data to generate information, and how to make appropriate selections to address a specific research question. A significant number of diverse research formats are employed in research into aspects of human activities and experiences in spaces and environments to serve as pragmatic and tentative ways to deal with circumstances in which those complexities are pervasive.

3.4.1 Qualitative and Quantitative Approaches

Sometimes researchers resort to *case studies* to deal with research topics for which description, conceptual development, and theory itself are either nonexistent or in the very immature stages of development. It is not uncommon—particularly when dealing with human activities and experiences—that the question of how to delimit a population so that a *probability sample* can be selected (which is often a preferred approach) is, in some instances, premature because little rational information can actually be provided to assist one in doing that. Researchers sometimes may have to acknowledge the impossibility of identifying and measuring certain factors in their study, but nonetheless still continue with their research.

Other researchers may feel strongly that their observations are—in an interpretative sense—inextricably tied into social contexts, personal beliefs, cultural practices, and so on, and they will judge that a *quantitative* research format involving *hypothesis construction* and *statistical inference* is inadequate to handle what is going on in their domain of interest. Frequently they will thus turn to other frameworks or more *qualitative* approaches, as seen in some ethnographic and perhaps phenomenological studies. Add to this the assertion by many that much sound research dealing with "description" (for example, note the recent mapping of the human genetic code), "pattern recognition," "classifying," and "conceptualizing" frequently arises as a result of not being able to directly come to grips with the complexities we have discussed above and/or many others not mentioned.

Qualitative and quantitative approaches to data collection and information generation are discussed more fully later in Part II (Chapter 5).

3.4.2 Survey and Experimental Approaches

Thus, researchers focusing on aspects of human activity and experience in the context of space and environments have turned to a wide variety of research methodology frameworks in an effort to better understand the information characterizing their research. These include *experimental* and *quasi-experimental designs* and the use of *simulations* and *virtual environments*, in addition to more frequently used traditional research formats widely used by social scientists, which include *survey research* methods (which are discussed in Chapters 6 and 7 in Part II).

The key issue of concern here is to develop a research format and adopt designs and methodologies for information collection, recording, and analysis that are appropriate for the particular research situation at hand, giving due recognition to and admitting the shortcomings that a particular situation has with respect to the type of difficulties and complexities we have been discussing.

In that regard, it is often easy to find agreement that the parameters of people's capacities to "perceive," to "respond," and to "construe" are neither fully understood nor explained by any particular discipline's conceptualization about human behavior and experience. This very observation has implications in terms of what ordinarily *can* be accomplished in research and how the stated objectives *might* be pursued and realized. An excellent model for the conduct of much *science* is the construction of *control-constrained experiments* in which *theory-grounded hypotheses* are *tested* and the results reported. Repeated *replication* of this procedure on random samples drawn from known populations is performed over time, and conclusions are drawn about the changes necessary in existing *theory*, given the results that materialize.

3.5 The Scientific Approach to Inquiry

On numerous occasions throughout this book, mention has been made, and will continue to be made, of the use of *models* to represent reality. The study of human activities and experiences in a spatial and environmental context undertaken by geographers and other social scientists has often adopted what is known as the scientific mode of inquiry that incorporates theorizing and makes use of models. The adoption of this approach reflects a change from what geographers traditionally were largely concerned with, which was the ordering of information. But from the 1960s, during the so-called quantitative revolution in geography (which gathered pace during the 1960s), geographers became more concerned with embracing scientific analysis, which is reflected in research based on testing hypotheses and constructing theories, and that approach is exemplified in the proliferation of literature concerned with geographical analysis and modeling as seen in books such as those by Chorley and Haggett (1967), King (1969), Harvey (1969), and Amedeo and Golledge (1975).

The use of the scientific mode of inquiry in the social sciences such as human geography is often referred to as *quasi-scientific*. It seeks to understand phenomena such as human behavior through the *measurement* of phenomena, discovery of *regularities*, creation of *theories*, and *model formulation* in order to achieve *understanding* about the phenomena and to seek *explanation* for them.

3.5.1 Modes of Scientific Inquiry

Two major modes of scientific inquiry may be distinguished:

1. The *inductive approach*, in which the process of reasoning is from specific observations to the development of general principles.
2. The *deductive approach*, in which the process of reasoning is from general principles to specific instances.

Both approaches involve *specificity* as a key element in the logic of the method in the search for explanation.

3.5.1.1 Exploratory Analysis

Much research is *exploratory* in nature, in which the objective is to become familiar with the phenomenon or situation being investigated as a first stage to inquiry. In exploratory analysis we make relatively few initial assumptions about the expected findings. This is particularly useful where the theoretical basis from which we are working is weak and the empirical expectations are thus fairly imprecise in their goals. Where we are using datasets that have not been collected and recorded specifically for the purpose of theory testing, then exploratory analysis is usefully employed. Johnston and colleagues (2000) write:

> ... Exploratory data analyses, with its emphasis on graphical display, allows researchers to penetrate datasets, appreciate their peculiarity, and draw conclusions which are constrained neither by prior expectations nor by the limitations of inferential techniques. (p. 249)

Exploratory studies generally aim to achieve one or more of the following. They:

- Satisfy curiosity and seek better understanding
- Test the feasibility of undertaking more elaborate and/or extensive investigation
- Develop methodology to use in a more elaborate and/or extensive investigation
- Provide insights.

But rarely does an exploratory study provide satisfactory answers vis-à-vis explanation in answering the research question.

3.5.1.2 Approaches to Theory Development

As discussed in Chapter 1 and in earlier sections of this chapter, an important aspect of scientific inquiry is the description of phenomena, situations, objects, and events that requires careful *observation* and accurate *recording*. Scientific description calls for *measurement*. Attention to these things is necessary in order to be able to *replicate* a study in other situations. The key issue here is that the quality of carefully framed description and accurate recording and measurement results in the *generalizability* of the findings.

Scientific inquiry is also about asking "Why?" questions in order to seek explanation. That usually involves examining simultaneously the many different aspects of a phenomenon, situation, or event—and that has implications for the careful design of the research framework to be used in any study.

A *theory* is a general and more-or-less comprehensive set of statements about the *relational aspects* of a phenomenon or situation. In the deductive approach to scientific inquiry, it is typical to frame a hypothesis (or set of hypotheses) that is a statement specifying the expectations about the nature of things—such as relationships between attributes of situations and variable outcomes—derived from the theory. Typically a model is built to test a hypothesis or set of hypotheses.

Thus, in general terms, one may pursue an *inductive theory construction* or a *deductive theory testing* approach to scientific inquiry, as illustrated in Figure 3.2.

(a) Theory Construction or Inductive

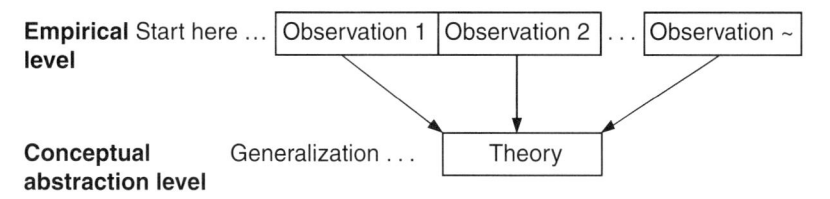

Empirical level: Start here ... Observation 1, Observation 2, ... Observation ~

Conceptual abstraction level: Generalization ... Theory

(b) Theory Testing or Deductive

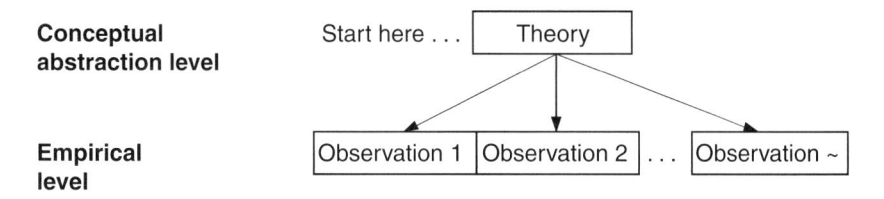

Conceptual abstraction level: Start here ... Theory

Empirical level: Observation 1, Observation 2, ... Observation ~

FIGURE 3.2. Approaches to theory construction and testing.

3.5.1.3 Theory Construction Using the Inductive Approach

The process of theory construction using the *inductive approach* usually begins with the researcher asking a question such as *Is this observation a particular case of some more general factor?* The objectives in this approach are likely to be to:

- Locate the common factor
- Draw on existing theories and concepts as a source of ideas (why reinvent the wheel?)
- Consider the context of the observation (for example, ask questions such as "Is $30,000 per year a reasonable income for a family of two adults and two children where the focus of the study might be families living in poverty?")
- Ask the respondent (that is, the person being questioned in a survey or the person being investigated in a case study) in order to seek clues as to why they believe or think as they do
- Engage in introspection, that is, to put yourself in the role of other people.

In generalizing from this inductive approach, we seek to go beyond particular observations to try to work out what might be a more general factor that the observations represent. In that way, we may make *inferences* that represent possible explanations by moving from the particular to the general, from observation to theory. However, we need to test such explanations because often they are derived ex post facto.

3.5.1.4 The Deductive Approach

The process of theory testing using the deductive approach uses the theory to guide our observations, which should provide a crucial test of the theory. Here the objective is to derive from the theory more limited statements that follow logically from the theory. The key is to derive from statements in such a way that if the theory is true, so will be the derived statement. Information or data on those more limited statements need to be recorded, and the researcher looks at the implications of those data vis-à-vis the initial theory.

Thus, the stages in this approach are to:

- Specify the theory to be tested.
- Derive a set of conceptual propositions; these may be hypotheses.
- Restate conceptual propositions as testable propositions.
- Collect and record the relevant data.
- Analyze the data (typically this involves statistical analysis).
- Assess the validity of the theory.

Often this approach is conducted through what is termed the *hypothetico-deductive* testing of a model.

However, in both the inductive and the deductive approaches, the objective is to develop new or modified theory, as shown in Figure 3.3. This is the dynamic logic of the scientific approach to inquiry in research.

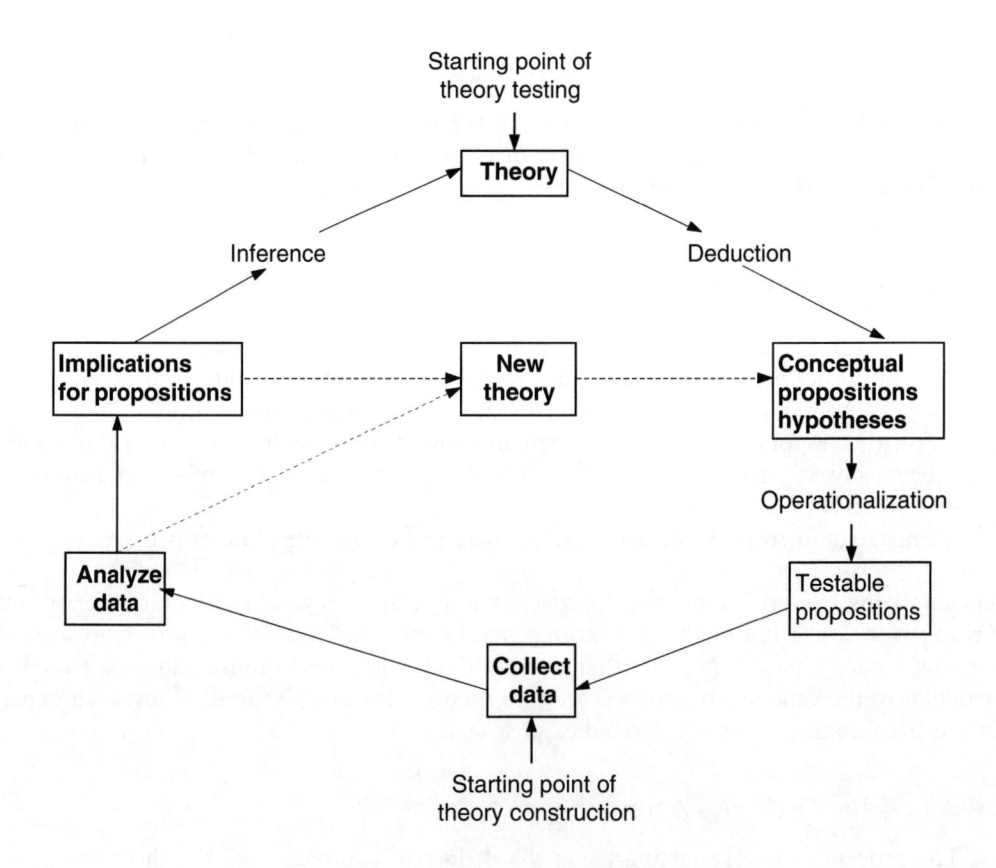

FIGURE 3.3. Logic of scientific research.

3.5.1.5 Restrictions of Theory-Grounded Hypothesis Testing

For many reasons the theory-grounded hypothesis-testing way of proceeding may *not* make sense when dealing with some human activities and experiences. There are many reasons for this, including the following:

- Ignorance of populations
- Difficulties in securing random statistical samples
- A lack of understanding about the distribution of variances throughout a poorly understood population
- The usual and frequent confronting of human responses by the many features associated with being human
- The inability to measure traits of importance
- The difficulties of separating parts of variance
- The difficulty of assessing the importance and interaction of context in any situation of interest
- A general ignorance of processes and representations in cognition
- The impact of the reactive and/or response feedback influences generated by the very act of doing research on humans
- Difficulties encountered in definition in the context of human behavior (for example, as in culture).

Some of those difficulties violate the basic sampling distribution assumptions associated with the use of statistical inference in hypothesis testing. These and many other things all result from working on this enormous complexity called the "human being." The implication of this is that to secure knowledge, no matter how minuscule, researchers have to acknowledge the need to work in many different ways.

3.5.2 Models

Johnston and colleagues (2000) define a model as "an idealized structured representation of the real" (p. 508). A model may be seen as serving the following functions:

1. A model illustrates a theory, and it is a way of summarizing the complex relations that exist in "reality."
2. A model is designed to focus on the relevant or interesting aspects of a theory or a real-world situation and to eliminate incidental information.
3. If a model is a theoretical model, it will have a high degree of abstraction; often this type of model will be referred to as a *conceptual model*.
4. However, models based on empirical rather than theoretical considerations or postulates tend to have a low degree of abstraction; these types of models tend to be referred to as *operational models*.
5. Models tend to apply to a specific real-world situation.

To operationalize a model, it is necessary to develop and use a "data matrix" as shown earlier in Figure 2.1.

3.5.2.1 Objective of Model Building

The overall objective of model building is to make better sense of reality through conceptualizing or depicting a manifestation of situations, processes, or systems of the real world in order to better understand them. Typically, models focus on what are deemed to be principal relationships; often they will "aggregate" variables in an effort to cut down on the complexity of the model; often the functional form of a model is transformed to estimate parameters and/or to avoid working with exponents and operating divisions (as in linear to log transformations); and typically a model will employ selected *assumptions* to make the task of modeling easier.

The term "model" is used rather loosely by researchers to refer to "things" as being models even though the purpose the researcher has in mind may be far more modest than for building or testing a theory. Probably most research is conducted with the purpose being to try to discover the nature of the relationships between phenomena and perhaps to account for the variation in the facts related to a specific problem. But we tend to assume that the longer term objective might be to form theories and bodies of knowledge and, through that process, to come to terms with establishing the validity or otherwise of the relationships among facts, that models are seen to play a significant role. The intent usually is to add to our understanding of the "behavior" of the particular phenomenon being investigated and to explain the nature of the variation that is observed in terms of the relationships between the phenomenon of interest and other phenomena or between the variable of interest and other variables. Attempts to make those relationships explicit are thus the steps toward explaining or accounting for the "behavior" of the phenomenon or situation being investigated. Models can help toward that end.

Thus, a model might be viewed as an approximate representation of the structure of the relationship and of the interrelationships existing in a problem context. In scientific research, models are seen to "grow" out of stated or implied *hypotheses*, which either have been generated through previous knowledge of the real world or are reflected perceptions of it.

The importance of the term "approximation" in models needs to be emphasized, as they are simplified representations of reality; they are implied representations of the "real world" designed to depict only the relevant properties, relationships, or interactions of the reality. However, it is often the case that the researcher starts with a simple model and then builds on that through ongoing research efforts to develop more complex models that are intended to represent fuller and more accurate representations of that reality.

In addition to using models to attempt to isolate the variables that account for or explain the variations in some articulated research problem variable, models are also used to help us to *predict* future situations. Of course this is fraught with difficulties, as over time the context in which the variables specified in the model occur is subject to change. Models thus often tend to propose constant parameters and functional relationships, and these are known as *deterministic models*. However, great advances have been made in developing models in which random processes play a large role or probabilities enter the picture, and these are referred to as *stochastic models*. Progress in this way has been enhanced greatly through the revolution in computational technologies and the proliferation of computational process models (this is discussed in Chapter 7 in Part II).

Because models are approximated or simplified representations of reality, it is important for a model to be subjected to testing and to replication of testing. This is important in order to detect error related to wrong functional forms, incorrect measurement of variables, and the choice of an inadequate analogy to construct a model.

3.5.2.2 Analogue Models

The issue of modeling by analogy is important. *Analogue models* are commonly used in the social sciences. Modeling by analogy involves letting the structure of a relatively well-known single relationship or group of relationships (which do not necessarily constitute a theory) be a model for a not well-known relationship or group of relationships. Suppose a researcher thinks that he or she has recognized some similarities between the structure of the problem situation being investigated and the structural conditions of some other familiar situation that deals with a phenomenon distinct from that situation being considered. Here the researcher utilizes the familiar situation as an aid in building a model about the research situation because the researcher thinks that there are recognizable structural conditions; thus an analogy is being used. Hopefully the structure of the two processes or situations is similar.

An analogy makes the implicit expectation that if certain similar conditions exist, then some other similarities not immediately obvious ought to exist. Attention needs to be given to considering the limits to which such similarities or resemblances are valid. Serious errors can be committed in extending familiar notions to some new situations on the basis of unanalyzed similarities.

3.5.2.3 Skills Needed for Model Building and Steps in Model Building

Unfortunately, a general procedure does not exist that demonstrates step-by-step how to go about building models. Indeed, the vast array of different situations and research questions facing researchers render that nigh impossible. However, Stogdill (1970, p. 10) identifies a number of skills needed for model building:

1. It is about developing a system and its operational characteristics, observing and analyzing real events in order to isolate the determining variable operating in a system of real events.
2. It is about defining each variable or dimension in terms that permit others to identify exactly the same dimension.
3. It is about perceiving or determining the relationships between the different dimensions—that is, determining the structural components.
4. It is about conceptualizing a set of defined concepts and a set of statements about the relationships between the concepts that constitute the model of the system.

Amedeo and Golledge (1975, pp. 92–93) propose the following as the logical sequence of steps in the construction of a model:

1. *Step 1:* Begin the reasoning for the construction of a model with a well-defined research problem. That requires these prerequisites:
   - The problem itself is "recognized" and well understood.
   - The question to be answered in the problem is clear.
   - The domain of the problem is known—that is, there exists knowledge about what phenomena or properties are going to be examined, over what time periods, and for what "area" the problem is to be analyzed.
   - The size of the problem is such that it is capable of being solved by the resources available.

2. *Step 2:* The hypotheses might need to make these assumptions:
   - The hypotheses are statements about what the researcher thinks the principal relationships are in the problem situation.
   - Hypotheses can grow out of existing knowledge about related problems or by induction through observation.
   - Analogous situations may help in hypothesis generation.
   - Assumptions are made as simplifying assertions about certain conditions in the problem so that these may be readily handled.
   - For the given problem, the assumptions are taken as given and only the hypotheses are tested.
   - The assumptions may be questioned and reexamined later on, and the hypotheses to be tested altered.

3. *Step 3:* Provide the rationale for how the model will be constructed. Ask these questions:
   - What can the relationships and/or interactions in reality be that are going to be modeled?
   - Are the variables measurable?
   - Do we need to, and can we, construct surrogates?
   - Can we collect the data for the variables?
   - Are there any variables outside the problem context that appear to affect the variables in the problem?
   - Should the variables be treated in a continuous or a discrete manner?
   - Will time play a role in the model?
   - Which relationships are deterministic and which are nonlinear?
   - Can nonlinear relationships be tracked in a linear manner?
   - How do we represent the structure inherent in the relationships?
   - Are there any elements in the environment that affect the relationships of concern?
   - How can these environmental effects be approximated?

The final shape of the model will depend on the kind of reasoning done in these processes and on the particular nature and content of the research problem.

3.5.2.4 Model Quality

There is, in addition, the issue of *model quality*, which refers to the quality of the representation through which the real world is captured in a model. That involves a combination of the clarity, precision, and completeness with which attribute selection and definition reflects the real world, and it also concerns the consistency with which they are applied. In addition, it concerns the precision with which spatial resolution of representation is achieved, which is affected by the appropriateness of the spatial representation of an object and the level of detail provided (Haining, 2003, pp. 58–59).

Figure 3.4 shows the relationship between the real world and the data matrix, showing how the process of conceptualization and representation leading to the selection of object attributes and their representation in space and time involved in developing a model to represent reality. The figure also indicates what Haining (2003, p. 50) depicts as the uncertainty of the relationship and the influence of both model quality and quantity.

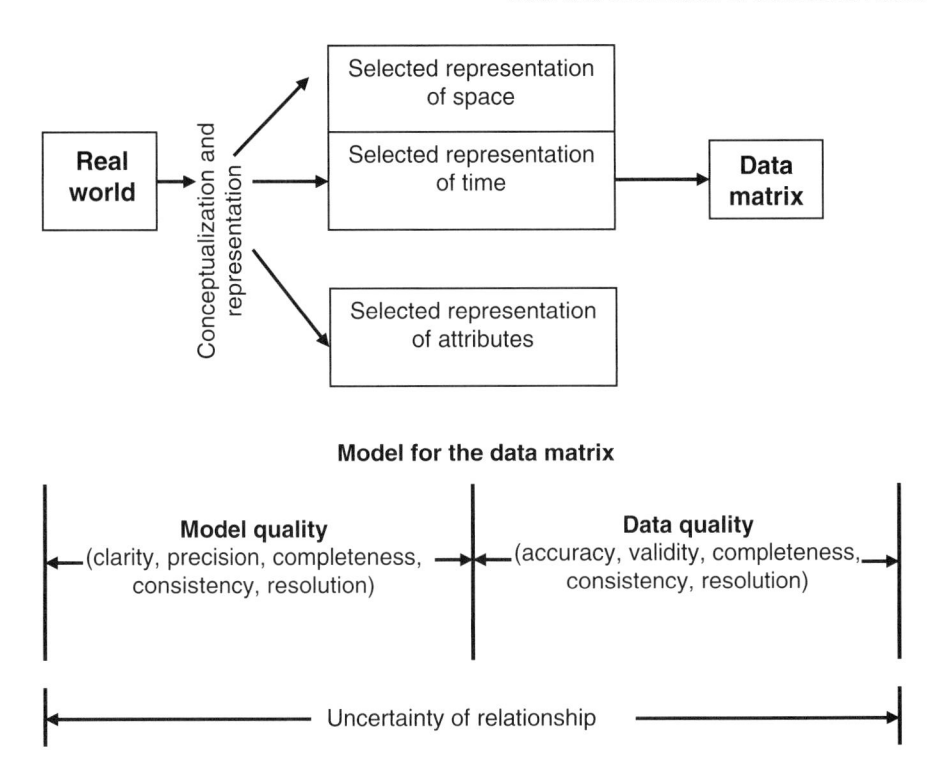

FIGURE 3.4. From geographic reality to the data matrix. Concepts derived from Haining (2003).

3.6 Implications for Researching Human Activities and Experiences in Spaces and Environments

Both Chapter 2 and this chapter canvassed a number of significant issues relating to data collection and information generation, particularly in the context of conducting research into human activities and experiences in spaces and environments. We have discussed using the scientific mode of inquiry to do so. The complexity of the nature of human beings as the subjects from whom and/or about whom researchers need to collect information—along with the explicitly spatial and/or temporal characteristics of the operational environments in which those activities (behaviors) we are interested in occur, and the difficulties of deciding and defining the elements of environments and how people experience them—means that deciding on what data is relevant and needed and how it can be recorded and measured and turned into relevant and useful information is highly problematic in research endeavors in these fields.

Thus, as will be discussed in the four chapters in Part II, there is a need for researchers to consider a wide variety of research formats in the investigation of such matters and to choose carefully one that is pertinent to addressing the research question(s) at hand.

PART II
Collecting Data and Representing Information

The four chapters in this part address a complex set of issues having to do with the modes of collecting data that are widely used to generate information of the type used in research designs that are common in research approaches investigating P-E-B relations.

Chapter 4 focuses on the purpose of collecting and matching data for conducting analysis in research. The distinction is made between primary data collection, in which the researcher has to develop a research design suitable to collect his or her own data, and the use of secondary data that already exists and which the researcher analyzes to address the research problem. The chapter addresses how we need to match data and analysis through the transformation of data into information. The roles of data and information in research—for purposes of description and classification—are discussed, and attention is directed to important considerations concerning data reliability and validity, and to the issue of incomplete information. The chapter provides a discussion of the basic elements of geospatial description, including points, lines, edges and boundaries, links and networks, and areas. There is a discussion of the importance of explanation as an objective in research. The chapter concludes with a reference to the various modes of collecting data and generating information, which are then taken up in detail in the remaining chapters in this part of the book.

Chapter 5 discusses qualitative and survey approaches to collecting data and generating information. It provides an overview of the purpose of qualitative approaches and the important role they have played in the geographic tradition of observing, recording, describing, and classifying. The importance of objectivity in qualitative research is emphasized. The chapter provides an outline of the theoretical traditions and approaches in qualitative inquiry, including the case study and the narrative. The use of surveys to collect data and generate information is discussed, and an overview is provided of the tasks involved in designing and undertaking a survey.

Chapter 6 focuses on collecting data by sampling from a population using probability and nonprobability survey designs. The chapter discusses when to use probability sampling and why that is done where the intent is to generate estimates of population parameters from sample data and to make generalizations about the population from the sample data. There is a discussion of a number of probability and nonprobability sampling designs, including issues for designs that specifically address sampling spatial data. The chapter discusses data sources commonly used for sampling, including the spatial framework provided by census data. The chapter also discusses the complex issues involved in survey instrument design and the data collection process. We discuss the importance of using procedures that seek to minimize not only sampling error but also nonsampling error and bias that arise through the design of the survey instrument or questionnaire, the question-and-answer process, and the behavior of interviewers.

Chapter 7 is concerned with using controlled settings to run experiments to extrapolate from those controlled conditions to the real world. The chapter provides an overview of commonly used approaches to conducting experiments, including virtual experiments and simulations, designs that are becoming increasingly popular and commonplace with the advances in technologies that facilitate the development and use of computational process models to investigate human decision making and behavior in a spatial context.

CHAPTER 4

The Purpose of Collecting and Matching Data and Analysis

4.1 Introduction

This chapter addresses issues concerning the *collection* and *representation* of *data* and *information*. That leads to a further consideration of both the collection and use of *primary data* and also of the use of *secondary data*, as well as to a discussion of the purposes for which data are collected and the transformation of data into information through matching data with analysis to generate new information. The basic elements of *geospatial description* are outlined. The chapter also discusses *explanation* in research. The chapter concludes with a discussion of the *modes* of collecting data to generate information that are commonly used in research investigating P-E-B relations.

4.2 Approaches to Data Creation

4.2.1 Primary Data and Secondary Data

Data are the "raw" unprocessed records from which information may be derived. Data are collected in a variety of ways, but invariably that involves a transformation of parts of reality into a symbolic format (for example, alphanumeric codes). As discussed in Chapter 2, traditionally two broad categories of data are recognized: primary and secondary.

4.2.1.1 Primary Data

Primary data are collected for use by the researcher for the specific purpose of investigating the research question at hand. They include the following:

- *Occurrence counts* (such as present/absent; frequencies)
- *Experiences* in *settings* (such as perceptions and sensing)
- Records of *personal* or *group features* or *characteristics* (including physiological attributes such as skin color)
- *Attitudes, beliefs, values,* and *emotions* that people have about phenomena

65

- *Characteristics* of *overt behavior(s)* in specific *times, spaces,* and/or *situational* contexts
- *Personal descriptions*
- *Experimenter observations*
- *Physical* and *aesthetic* features of environments.

Primary data may be collected from visual observation, personal experience, and direct or indirect communication with data sources, as in various types of surveys. In the collection of primary data through modes such as surveys, typically data are obtained on the demographic and socioeconomic characteristics of the DMU (the subjects of investigation or the respondents to a survey) in addition to the collection of other factual and behavioral data, which may include data on attitudes, opinions, and beliefs, as well as on actual activities undertaken through overt behavior.

It is important to emphasize that, when dealing with primary data, it is the researcher who makes the decision as to the format for collection, the type of data collected, the representation or measurement unit to be used, the categories into which data are allocated, and the extent to which aggregation occurs. It is the researcher who determines the DMU and the specifications of attributes or variables on which data are collected. It is important also to note that, in contrast, for secondary data those decisions have already been made by others—often by a government agency—and only the existing compiled results of the data collection are generally available. There is usually a privacy constraint on the extent to which disaggregated data can be made available.

Traditionally, geographers have relied on primary data *collection*, usually under the concept of *fieldwork*. Geographers have experienced environments and recorded their impressions. Sometimes that was done in colorful descriptive phraseology, sometimes through the use of sketches and diagrams, and sometimes (particularly in the case of physical geographers) by measurements made in the field. Thus geographers often became "regional specialists" in the sense that they focused their attention on specific areas and collected types of data not generally available in a published source. These could include temperature, precipitation, humidity, soil moisture content, river volume and flow rates, and so on. But they also include properties such as land-use types, vegetation types, and urban and rural structures and functions.

4.2.1.2 Secondary Data

Secondary data consists of data compiled for the use of other people as well as for the collection agency itself. Data of this type are often collected and compiled from precisely engineered probability samples, and are then collated and compiled in predetermined categories. Examples include the population census, a census of agricultural production or manufacturing or services, government department statistical reports, World Bank reports, International Health Organization reports, national year books, and annual summaries of local government statistics.

Secondary data are rarely made available in "primary" or "raw" form because of their size and complexity and because of privacy constraints. Thus, secondary data tend to be summarized into well-established categories such as population demographics, Standard Industrial Classification (SIC) classes, gross national product (GNP), disease types, and similar general categories and aggregations. In that way, individual-level information is condensed into *aggregate data* for *spatial units*, as occurs with census data.

However, sometimes primary data collections are made available for secondary data analysis of units of primary data by providing the unit record data files, but incorporating measures to protect the identity of individuals on whom the unit record information is based.

4.2.2 Some Definitions

In collecting and representing information and data, the following terms are widely used. We give them these definitions:

1. *Occurrence:* a unit of phenomena; it can be sensate or insensate and can be defined at any selected scale.
2. *Distribution:* a collection of occurrences usually observed as a set of locations.
3. *Raw data:* unprocessed material collected about objects, places, people, and settings (for example, lists of names, labels).
4. *Processed data:* material collected and represented in symbolic form, usually alphanumeric.
5. *Analysis:* subjection of data to categorization, classification, cumulation, aggregation, association, seriation, and statistical or mathematical manipulation.
6. *Information:* the output from data compilation and analysis.

4.2.3 Purposes of Data Collection

Both humans and inanimate physical objects possess *properties* and *features*. Many of those properties or features are directly observable, while many are not so obvious:

1. Those directly observable (such as "height," "weight," "sex," "color," "shape," "porosity," "solidity") can be recorded immediately by an observer using the human sensory apparatus or using technical aids, such as photography.
2. Not so obvious features and properties might include things such as "tensile strength," "geologic origin," "density" or "frequency of occurrence," "social–economic–political constraints," "beliefs," "values," "attitudes," and "wellness."

In either situation, the entirety of the properties and features present in a situation or setting may not be readily comprehended.

To enable comprehension, data are collected about the presence or absence, the frequency or absence, and the occurrence or nonoccurrence of human and object existence and of the occurrence of properties and features.

The purpose of collecting data is to provide information that contributes to knowledge acquisition. This contribution enables understanding and comprehension of complex settings that might otherwise remain mysterious. The process of transforming "raw stuff" into data and information is summarized in Figure 4.1. Thus data, transformed into information, reduces uncertainty and helps convert chaos into reasoned comprehension. In Chapters 2 and 3 in Part II we discussed various ways or methods of deciding what type of data is relevant to what type of problem or task situation. In the sections of this chapter to follow, we elaborate on experimental designs, data collection engines, and procedures that facilitate analysis and data manipulation to create different types of information.

68 COLLECTING DATA AND REPRESENTING INFORMATION

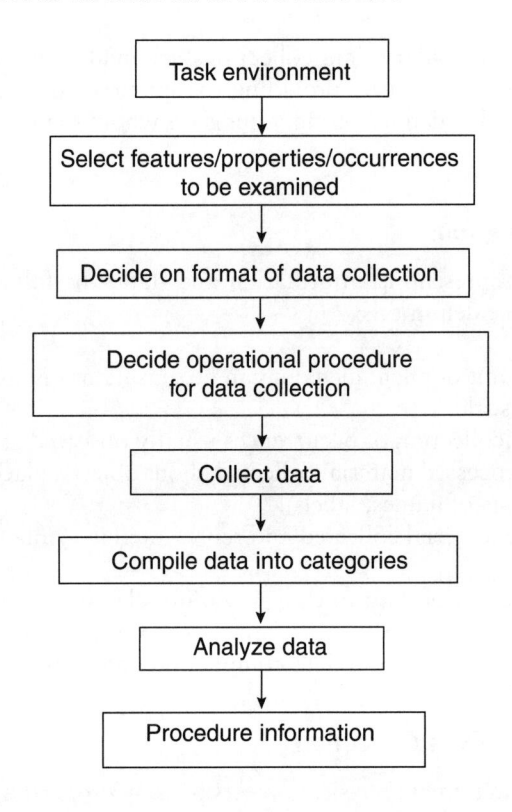

```
Task environment
   ↓
Select features/properties/occurrences
       to be examined
   ↓
Decide on format of data collection
   ↓
Decide operational procedure
    for data collection
   ↓
Collect data
   ↓
Compile data into categories
   ↓
Analyze data
   ↓
Procedure information
```

FIGURE 4.1. The process of transforming raw data into information.

4.3 Matching Data and Analysis

It has been common for *data types* to be specified in a traditional measurement theory mode as *nominal, ordinal, interval*, and *ratio* (see Chapters 2 and 3). At its most basic level, the process of producing *valid* and *reliable* information requires a matching of data type with the nature and power of an analytic technique.

4.3.1 Transforming Qualitative Information into Data

There is, at times, confusion among researchers as to how this matching takes place. Perhaps the most fundamental problem arises with *subjective* (*qualitative*) material that many researchers may say defies transfer into data (for example, emotions, values, attitudes, feelings).

However, in almost every case a simple *binary* record of whether an occurrence, feature, or property is "present" or "absent" (recorded symbolically as 1 = "present" and 0 = "absent") satisfies the minimal requirement for producing data. This *nominal* data may then be analyzed graphically, diagrammatically, or statistically when an appropriate match is made with an analytic procedure (for example, binomial probability, χ^2 [chi-square], or other simple nonparametric evaluation procedures).

Procedural discussions and examples can be found in Denzin and Lincoln's (2000) *Handbook of Qualitative Research*. Texts on spatial statistics (such as those by Clark &

```
Raw Data → Geospatial reference data (coordinate referencing) → Visualization (representation) → Statistical analysis and spatial analysis → Information
```

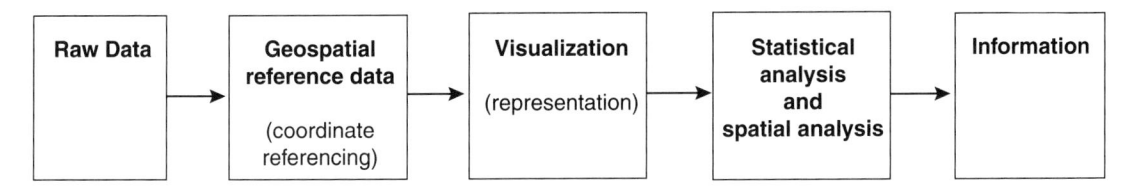

FIGURE 4.2. Georeferencing to spatialize data and produce spatial information.

Hosking, 1986; Haining, 2003) provide well-reasoned examples of this matching process and summarize what properties of data are required by which type of analytic procedure.

4.3.2 Spatialization

Statistical analysis, however, is but one way to convert the data representing a particular set of unprocessed raw material into information. Traditionally, geographers have used diagrammatic and cartographic reasoning to produce information from all types of datasets. The processes used are termed *spatialization,* as depicted through the processes shown in Figure 4.2. The most powerful of these are visualizations represented in graphic, diagrammatic, and map or image formats, while some data are best represented (for some user groups) in tactile, haptic, or auditory form.

Maps are considered to be the most powerful format for representing spatial or spatialized data in such a way that information is readily accessible to both naive and expert users. GIS software has been developed as a powerful tool for data analysis and information representation of spatial and spatialized data. The essential preparatory procedure is to ensure that each bit of data is *georeferenced,* usually in terms of Cartesian coordinates. An example is given in Table 4.1 and in Figure 4.3.

Once data are georeferenced, other georeferenced data can then be used to search for understanding of the spatial distribution of the cow population via processes such as map/graphic overlay to give an immediate visual impression of the degree of association between cows and sets of physical geographic features such as percentage of flat lands or vegetation type, or sets of human factors such as "land values" or "population density." The georeferencing also enables different forms of spatial analyses (such as measures of spatial association) to be calculated. The processes of georeferencing and spatialization then mitigate the nature and power of the information embedded in the original data by facilitating and enabling the appropriate matching of descriptive, representational, and analytical procedures to reveal information embedded (but not immediately obvious) in a set of unprocessed raw data.

TABLE 4.1. An Example of Geographical Data

Location	Milk cows produced (raw data)	Georeferenced county data (x–y coordinates) x y
County 1	22,700	100, 270
County 2	1,500	015, 200
County 3	18,500	075, 120
County 4	11,000	010, 050
County 5	3,100	060, 020

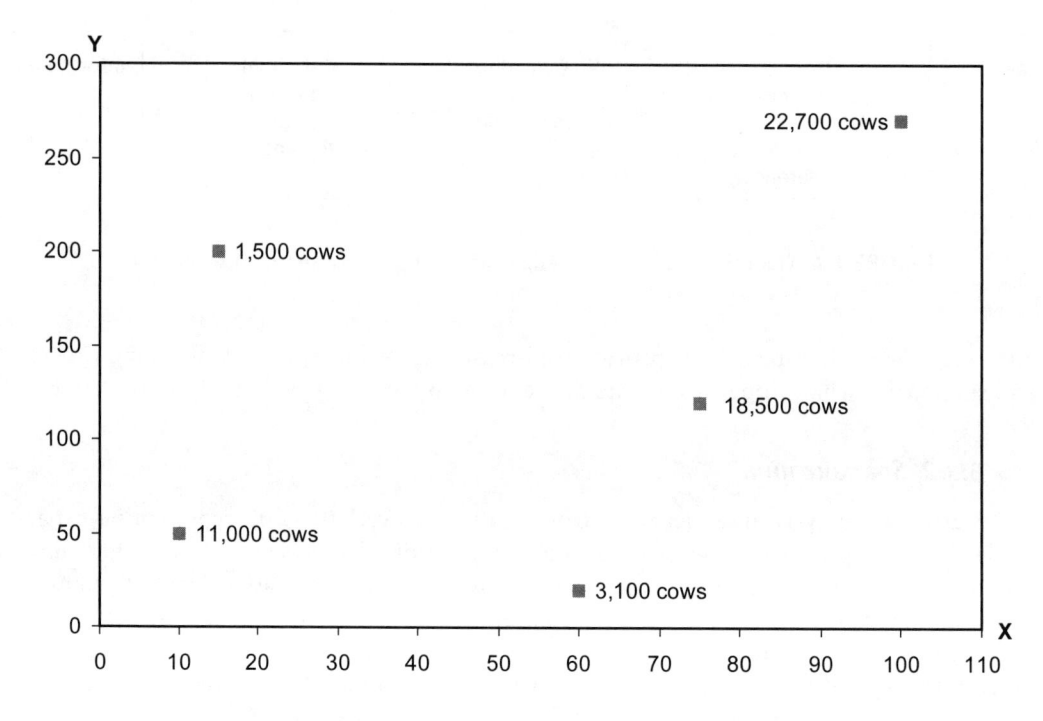

FIGURE 4.3. Diagrammatic spatialization of data in Table 4.1.

4.4 Roles of Information in Research

4.4.1 Research as an Information-Generating Tool

Research is normally *goal-oriented*, that is, it involves the specification of objectives and the testing of hypotheses. When undertaking research, the aim is not to wander at random or chaotically, but to proceed toward an objective. The path may be direct or indirect. Research activities designed to generate information include those concerned with collecting data; testing hypotheses relating to datasets; generating information from data; analyzing data; creating, testing, or evaluating problems; generating, testing, or evaluating theory; understanding interactions; making predictions; and developing policy. While all these are important, nonetheless most successful research involves collecting data; turning data into information; and making use of information to solve problems, help perform tasks, establish policy or procedures, or add to the existing store of knowledge.

4.4.2 Description

Ostensibly, the most "low-tech" and direct way of creating information is to develop *descriptions* of settings or environments. Descriptions may be *auditory* (talk-aloud verbal protocols and/or composed sounds), *written* (novels, poetry, essays), *image-based* (photographs), *artistic representations* (sculpture or painting), *mimed* (obtained from gestures such as pointing), and *haptic* (by feeling, touching, or arranging). All possible combinations of these can create more complete or informative output (for example, combining taste, smell, facial expression, and speech).

Traditionally, much research has focused largely on the most amenable of the above, namely, on "writing," "speech," and "pictorial" or "artistic" representations. While ostensibly these are the simplest and most readily accepted ways of describing, they are *fuzzy* and *inexact*. For example, speech (verbal report or communication) is usually accepted to be the most basic form of description for humans.

But different cultures and societies have different languages. *Language translations* are often inexact and difficult to produce. Many translations bias or subtly alter the original data or messages. Each language has a somewhat different concept lexicon and, at times, different definitional structures. Key concepts for some languages do not exist in others. For example, one language may have many definitions of an elementary concept such as "distance," depending on *scale*, while there may be only a single concept of "distance" in another language.

4.4.2.1 Spatial Language

Spatial language is notoriously *fuzzy*. Different nouns (for example, names) may be given to the same place. Prepositions and prepositional phrases are unclear in the geospatial domain (for example, "along a river," "across a desert," "near a church," "above the park," "close to town") and leave themselves open to numerous interpretations. This gives language (oral or written) great communicative power on one hand (because of its extensive vocabulary), and great complexity and confusion on the other (because of inexact definitions and meanings of terms).

4.4.2.2 Incomplete Information

Descriptions are usually *incomplete*. A perfect description is an explanation, for it would contain everything that is known about the subject. The incompleteness of a description can lead to the generation of false information, as, for example, in a Western thought-based description of primitive tribal activities. Thus, interpretations that are culture-specific may not capture the intent or meaning of customs, values, beliefs, or behaviors in other cultures, even when a superficial similarity exists. Biased observation, recording, or interpretation may result because the data collected lack the necessary recordings that might allow full and unbiased understandings.

Many descriptions *spatialize* their subject matter by using diagrams, graphs, charts, and maps, and by employing constructed images as descriptive tools. For example, an environmental setting that is too spatially extensive to be perceived from any single point on the Earth's surface might be described by producing a map representation of the setting. Though common, this type of description is incomplete and selective, and it generalizes and uses abstract symbols to represent depicted information. Likewise, spatializing data using graphic or diagrammatic description may give unintended or unwarranted emphasis to associations and relations (as was the case with the spurious ecological correlations of environmental determinism).

4.4.2.3 Naive and Expert Description

The purpose of description is to *communicate information*. Descriptions draw on conventions to do this. Conventions are usually differentiated as being either *naive* ("commonsensical") or *expert* ("technical"). This is of great importance for discipline-based information.

In geography and other environmental sciences, naive spatial information results in geobased inconsistencies as, for example, when the distance between place A and place B as opposed to the distance from place B to place A is perceived and recorded differently because A to B is uphill and B to A is downhill. At the macroscale, we usually (naively) align the continents of, say, North and South America along a central meridian and then describe Santiago in Chile (on the west coast of South America) as being west of Miami in Florida (on the east coast of North America), whereas the reverse is geographically true. This conclusion is based on naive understanding of spatial location; geographic fact is modified by an unconscious perceptual alignment process that "shifts" South America to the west. As with written or verbal descriptions, graphic-, map-, and image-based descriptions may be biased, misaligned, or error-prone if they are naively constructed.

The value of a technical language description is that it relies on *formal* and *accepted* definitions. Thus, whereas the use of "north" as a direction in a naively based description may indeed refer to any point of the compass depending on a user's knowledge of orientation and current heading, the same term used in the expert technical sense confines the meaning to a specific directional vector that is exocentric, or independent of a person's heading. And sometimes we are tricked by the naming practices embedded in the built environment. For example, in the United States one well-known case—the coastline near Santa Barbara, California—runs east–west and *not* north–south as many people believe. Streets running geographically east–west are labeled north–south, while streets running geographically north–south are labeled east–west! Here, the naive description is influenced by geographically erroneous naming practices. But this does not prevent residents from following naively given directions and correctly reaching their destinations.

4.4.2.4 Reliability and Validity

Descriptions need not be exact in order for humans to *comprehend* and *use* them. So what is the value of a system developed for experts? Two benefits are obvious: Descriptions become *reliable*, and descriptions become *valid*. In other words, the same terms or concepts used in the same context, even by different people, retain the same meaning. And the same idea or concept can be described in different ways (for example, speech, text, sound, or image) but will yield the same information.

Reliability and validity in descriptions are important for information definition, recognition, retrieval, and processing. In a dataset, if a pattern can be detected and described, then only if the description is reliable and valid will that same pattern be universally accepted as existing. In the absence of those qualities, different observers may see different patterns or no pattern at all. Characteristics such a "beauty," for example, often defy consensus. Our "values," "beliefs," and "emotions" may be critical when recognizing, evaluating, or even discovering whether or not a discernible pattern exists. But even when we—as, say, naive art critics—cannot detect different patterns or meanings in an art form, experts will distinguish originals from fakes, and will classify and accurately describe elemental components because they have reliable and valid procedures for describing a representation.

4.4.2.5 Classification or Categorization

Classification or *categorization* of data is one way of creating information. Classifications may be *simple* (and *univariate*) or *complex* (and *multivariate*):

1. In the *univariate* case, a binary division results; objects or features are either *in* a class or *out* of it. The world is seen in a simple two-valued Aristotelian logic frame. But even then, problems arise: When does "enough" of the one critical factor exist?
2. With a *multivariate* classification, objects or features are able to be assigned to a variety of classes, depending on meeting definition criteria. A common question that arises is: Can an object or feature belong to more than one class or category?

What are the key descriptive factors that facilitate *classification*? Making subsets or categories allows for generalization and reduces the need for exhaustive enumeration or listing. Humans appear to categorize many things in a multilevel dominant/subordinate fashion that produces hierarchies (for example, of "cities," "natural features," "friendship structures," and "environmental cues," such as "landmarks" and "nodes"). Often humans categorize by spatializing by *area*, producing regions.

4.5 The Basic Elements of Geospatial Description

The geospatial domain uses specific terminology that best enables the processes of thinking and reasoning. Whether inspired by naively or expertly defined objectives, there is a spatial concept lexicon and a language ontology that enables *information generation, representation, analysis,* and *interpretation.*

Using a geometrical metaphor, the basic components of geospatial data may be termed *points, lines, edges, boundaries, areas, links, networks, surfaces,* and *volumes*. Whether using speech, text, gesture, imagery, graphics, diagrams, or map representations, the information that is "generated," "stored," "decoded," "manipulated," and "used naively or expertly" usually relies on more and more complex elaborations of these spatial components.

4.5.1 Points

Points are nondimensional phenomena that can be specified in relational or abstract ways. In the geospatial context, they are referred to as locations or places. To be distinguished from the rest of a setting, a *location* is usually given a label or an identity. Location can be specified in a *relative* or an *absolute* way. In the relative sense, points may be described egocentrically (as "to my left" or "ahead") or exocentrically (as "between A and X").

4.5.1.1 Egocentric Specification

Egocentric specification often relies on fuzzy spatial prepositions and a body as a centered frame of reference. An example would be "the tree is ahead and to my right." Terms such as "near," "close to," "far from," "in front of," "behind," "above," and "below" are natural spatial language concepts for specifying location relative to the body of a person. They are general, not "precise" or "accurate," and leave open to interpretation precisely where in an environment an object or feature can be found.

By superimposing a reference frame over a setting, egocentric locations can be made more geospatially precise. For example, one could replace "ahead and to my right" with "at 2 o'clock to my facing direction," thus narrowing the possible location to a body-referenced directional vector. Alternatively, an ego-referenced location could be specified by an angle ("ahead at 45 degrees") or even via a global reference frame ("northeast from my current location"). Where precise point-based location is not needed, the more general concept of "place" location can be used. As before, *places* must be labeled, named, or given an identity before locational information can be made available. Place represents a more general form of "location," and the term is often used when referring to objects or features at scales where those phenomena might be simplified to points for representational purposes (for example, a city may be represented as a point on a state map). The processes of simplifying and generalizing frequently give an aura of accuracy and precision to the specification process designed to produce data. One realizes that phenomena such as cities cover areas, but it is commonsense appreciation that allows places to be reduced to points for purposes of representation and understanding (for example, a location pattern of cities).

4.5.1.2 Exocentric Specification

Exocentric specification of points and places removes the powerful ego structure from location or place specification and enables specification with respect to other phenomena. This is the key to person-independent layout specification.

A point may be *locationally specified* by:

- Referencing it to other points (for example, "between *A* and *C*")
- Referencing it to a reference frame (for example, "at 1612 Elm Street")
- Referencing it with regard to a coordinate system (for example, "latitude 20 degrees South and longitude 119 degrees West")
- Referencing it with respect to proximity (for example, "*A* is *B*'s closest 'nearest' neighbor").

Specifying location exocentrically has enabled the development of numerous data collection devices. These include paired comparison procedures (such as: "Is the spatial separation *A–B* larger than the spatial separation *C–D*?"). Judgments like this can yield proximities, similarities, associations, correlations, linkages, and other information about sets or locations or places by representing them as points. Making judgments based on geospatial data properties, such as "distance," "direction," "connectivity," and "dominance" (or "magnitude") can be obtained. Accurately specifying points geospatially provide ways to measure interpoint and arrangement characteristics.

4.5.1.3 Absolute Location and Relational Location

Absolute location refers to a highly specified location using a globally based referencing system, such as latitude or longitude. Both egocentric and exocentric referencing can be undertaken when using absolute location–based referencing. Egocentrically, one might realize that "object B is located at 21 degrees North and 120 degrees West," and calculate the distance and direction of object B from one's current position, likewise specified in Cartesian coordinates. Given a set of objects with locations specified in such a coordinate system, descriptions and measures of pattern or arrangement can be constructed. Characteristics such as "clustering" or "dispersion," "density," "regularity" or "uniformity," and "departure from randomness" can be constructed.

Point data can provide information about single or multiple locations, characteristics of distributions such as pattern and dispersion, and between-location information such as "proximity," "similarity," "association," "spread," and "density." Data can be less or more precise depending on what frame of reference is used and what information collecting procedure is used. Spatial language—as part of natural speech—provides fuzzy and often inexact renderings of locations and interpoint relations. Measuring techniques based on exocentric referencing frames provide degrees of "precision" and "accuracy" depending on the scale used and the detail being sought.

4.5.2 Lines, Edges, and Boundaries

Lines represent linkages between points. In geospatial environments, they occur as:

1. *Links* between nodes, as in lines of transport
2. *Boundaries*, such as imposed or artificial segments enclosing areas or polygons, as with state or national boundaries
3. *Edges* (or *lines*) that define feature or object limits as with a riverbank, a cliff face, or a shoreline.

The essence of lines is to "connect," "divide," or "surround." They are a means for *partitioning space*. As *edges* or *boundaries*, lines allow data to be collected based on inclusion or exclusion, a simple binary data form. The result is the development of *categorical data*, which can be counted to produce raw scores or frequencies, cumulated or aggregated, or evaluated for proportionality of occurrence.

Data so constructed can be differentiated by *place* or *region* to produce measures, including indices of concentration. If boundary definition produces hierarchical or multilevel classes, statistics can be generated to measure departure from "randomness" (for example, chi-square) or from "uniformity" (binomial probability).

As with points, lines or edges can be "fuzzy" or "precise." The seashore boundary location varies with the tides and results in a *dynamic fuzzy edge* that is differently specified at high tide, at low tide, and at other times in between. This type of edge is time-dependent with a regular and measurable periodicity. Other edges define the *limits* of continents, islands, and physical features (such as rivers, shorelines, cliffs, and the like).

Boundaries arbitrarily or naturally define differentiate space into *subspaces*. Scale plays an important part in boundary need and definition. In geospatial terms and at a global scale, continents are defined by edges such as shorelines, or by arbitrary politically justified lines (as between Europe and Asia). Political boundaries define nation-states. While these are perceived to be well specified (for purposes of controlling international movement and for enforcing national policies), nation-state boundaries are often perceived to be inexact. Consequently, boundary line location may be disputed, as in the Lebanese–Israeli boundary or the boundaries between the Balkan nations.

In a Boolean sense, boundaries define discrete areas so that logical operators—such as "and," "or," "not"—can be applied. They also facilitate exhaustive logical division of spaces and places. Place-based categorization can inform about geospatial occurrences (for example, "the beaches of California" versus "the beaches of Australia") and provides a basis for classification of occurrences and allocation of them to discrete classes.

In everyday language, many boundaries are *inexact*. For example, to define the boundaries of one's neighborhood may require arbitrary definition based on where the majority of residents perceive (or think) they should lie. However, some boundaries are *exact*, but are not generally known or realized—as with a census tract or ZIP code boundary. In some cases, boundaries are deliberately left "vague"—as in many school-district boundaries—whereas in other cases boundaries might not be widely recognized but may be strictly enforced anyway (such as jurisdictional boundaries for law enforcement and policing).

As lines, boundaries generally do not carry a "width" characteristic. This is not necessarily the case with international boundaries, where frontiers often include a "no-man's-land." But, for the most part, as lines, boundaries yield measurable data such as length, direction, and location, while simultaneously *bifurcating* space into subspaces.

4.5.3 Links and Networks

Whereas boundaries often form *links*, and edges terminate with the disappearance of a feature, other lines create structures whose characteristics are *serial* or *network* in nature. A transport line such as a railroad, canal, or highway is a deliberately constructed artifact that is designed to link two or more nodes. *Endpoints* are "point-based," so that even if one discusses the railroad link between Los Angeles and Chicago, the connecting line terminates at specific points or places (railroad terminal stations).

Links can be *single* or *multiple* in nature. A single link joins two points. In doing so, it provides information about distance, direction, and connectivity. Such a link can be represented in flat two-dimensional graphic space, or as a volume in multidimensional space (for example, traffic volume). Descriptively the link can be given *width* to represent volume information, can represent direction of flow by adding an arrowhead to one end, and can be represented via association to show time–space characteristics of connections.

Transport features, such as roads, consist of a *series of links* between locations or places. This seriation yields information such as number of segments, segment lengths, node–connect sequences, the number of choice points, and the number and direction of turn angles. A seriation of nodes and links is called a *path* or *route*. Most of our environmental knowledge is acquired by traversing routes. A connected set of routes becomes a *network*. Networks can be complete (that is, all nodes linked directly to all other nodes) or partial. Most networks are partial. Generally, a small number of nodes stand out as being the most highly and directly connected to other nodes. These anchor a "network" and often gain the status of "landmarks" (for example, within a city).

Spatial knowledge can be acquired by integrating separately experienced or learned routes into a partially connected network. The geospatial route information (that is, the nodes and links) provides access to nearby and visibly distant objects and features, thus producing an understanding of *layout* (or *configuration*) of places in an environment.

Link data can be recorded and stored descriptively or technically. Description usually relies on text, verbal statements, or sketches and diagrams. The information derived from this data is often qualitative or nonmetric. Link sequences can usually be inferred, and one-dimensional arrays of nodes and links can represent what is in the descriptive data. It is often more difficult to construct any but simple, low-connectivity information structures from text or verbal reports, partly because of the inexact nature of the spatial language used (for example, "March Street intercepts Mary Street near Hayward Street"). *Sketches* can be examined to yield information about the sequencing of links, direction of turn, and feature counts, but rarely are able to yield information about distances. Often orientation, frames of reference, direction, and scale are also difficult to determine. This produces the generally accepted nonmetricity of sketch maps and leads to inferences about fragmentation of environmental knowledge, setting distortion, and lack of accuracy and precision in the information that can be obtained from node–link sketches.

In a technical sense, a collection of nodes and links can again use a geometric metaphor and be interpreted as a *graph*. Here we need to differentiate between the concept "graph" as a *network structure* and the concept "graph" as a *spatialization of data*. In the latter case, a graph or diagram may be constructed by plotting the location of the values attributed to pairs of points as projected on two intersecting coordinate axes. The result gives a visualization of trends in the paired scores of data selected for display. The idea of a graph as a "network" is fundamentally a complex interconnected line structure. A collection of nodes without links is called "null," and it is only when links are added that the network graph starts to form.

Technical information that can be obtained from network graphs includes measures of *network connectivity* and designation of the *superordinate nodes* (that is, according to their number of connections). As large numbers of routes can be defined in a network, criteria such as the "shortest path" between any pair of nodes can be calculated. The length of a specified circuit between a pair of nodes can be compared for efficiency or effectiveness with criteria such as the shortest path. But routes can be selected for many different reasons, including shortest path, longest leg first, shortest leg first, most aesthetically pleasing, minimization of turns, avoidance of specified segments, or simply because a traveler has to link specific stops in an order specified by timing criteria rather than spatial criteria.

In transport studies, it is common to analyze trips as links between origins and destinations, with the route followed representing a *path* across a "network." However, trips are complex. Trips may be undertaken for a *single purpose* (for example, to purchase gasoline) or for *multiple purposes* (for example, comparative shopping for appliances). They may include a single stop (for example, of a stand-alone store or to a shopping center) or may constitute a *trip chain* (that is, multiple stops at multiple locations) as represented in Table 4.2.

The nature of connectivity in the network structure can be used in models aimed at predicting human travel behavior. "Convenience travel" is often single-stop, single-purpose. Shopping or variety-seeking behavior produces multiple combinations of stops and purposes.

4.5.4 Areas

The majority of geospatial information is represented in a two-dimensional spatial format—that is, it is presented as a *map*. While there certainly are point-based maps (for example, a "dot map" of the distribution of features), most cartographic representations are made on a real (polygonal) basis. *Areas* can yield data when considered as single units (for example, places such as a city or a neighborhood) or as collections of areas (for example, "regions," "places," "mosaics," "collages," "tessellations").

Single areas can produce data on the quantity of contained phenomena, the size of the area or its "extent," "density of occurrence," "scattering" or "clustering" of internal features, "polygonal shape," and "location." This data can be collected and represented

TABLE 4.2. The Complexity of Representing Trips

Purpose	Number of stops	
	Single	Multiple
Single	One activity One stop	One activity Multiple stops
Multiple	Many activities One stop	Multiple activities Multiple stops

descriptively or technically. Descriptive data (such as "size," "shape," and "location") can be generated by "text," "speech," or "graphic means." For example, one might describe an area as "a narrow elongated valley, stretching in a general north–south direction, with a U-shape, with elevation decreasing from the north."

A selective or comprehensive "oral," "text," and/or "pictorial" representation can yield information on physical properties, human additions (that is, the built environment), specification of activities taking place there, and affective judgments about the area's beauty, safety, friendliness, and so on. For many decades, the mark of a successful and well-trained geographer was the ability to compile an information-rich description of an area (called "regional geography"). Mostly these were factual or declarative statements, and often they were time-sensitive. Getting the "feel" of an area usually involved considerable fieldwork (that is, direct experience).

But some areas exist only in the *imagination* of creative thinkers. Novelists, poets, essayists, and painters all create areas. *Spatial language*—in oral or text format—is the tool of choice for generating the descriptive data that defines the area. In particular, real and imagined landscapes have been generated using creative thinking as the primary methodology.

Areas also act as tools for generating quantitative data. Areas are spatially defined classes or categories, and they give place-based meaning to data. Once defined, an area's shape can be geometrically calculated, boundary length measured, and orientation specified with regard to global frames of reference. Sets of "features," "objects," or "occurrences" can be separately identified and represented in digital form as *layers*. Layers can be mapped separately or overlaid to show spatial associations and relations between or among datasets. Areas can be accurately measured and represented at various scales with different degrees of simplification or generalization.

The areas used in generating geographic data may be *natural* or *artificial*:

1. *Natural* (or bona fide) areas may include continents or islands, river valleys or riverine plains, mountain zones or hilly and undulating land.
2. *Artificial* (or "fiat") areas include arbitrary division of a natural area, as well as the areas enclosed by a multitude of constructed boundaries, including political divisions at various scales, and the subjective boundary of ethnic and cultural neighborhoods, gang turfs, recruitment areas, market and supply areas, and professional or public-service areas.

Descriptions of *multiple areas* are often based on comparative visualizations. Again, experiential data plays an important role. In particular, it complements physical descriptions with sensing of social, cultural, political, religious, economic, or other ambiant features. It is not always a simple matter to determine this type of information or to measure the amount or value or the magnitude present so that similarities or differences between areas can be highlighted. Imprecise geometries are sometimes used (for example, "pear-shaped" or "somewhat circular"), making classification or comparison difficult.

Explicit measurement of areas is part of a scientific approach to creating information about multiple areas. Determining common boundaries (and counting the number of such interfaces), measuring irregular boundaries, defining departures from recognized and measurable shapes, examining the pattern of tessellations, and calculating area *centroids*—all represent attempts to get precise and accurate measurements of, or relating to, area groupings.

4.6 Explanation

A fundamental objective in research that is undertaken using the scientific mode of inquiry is to use data to generate information for the purpose of seeking *explanation* about the situation, event, or phenomena being investigated. Furthermore, the objective may be to make *predictions* from the data about future states relating to these things being investigated. Earlier in this chapter it was suggested that a complete description *was* an explanation. But it was also acknowledged that descriptions are often incomplete, especially when naive thinking and reasoning is involved. So how do we achieve explanation? And what is the basis for prediction?

Explanations are required for *knowledge advancement* (learning), as a *base* for *constructive thinking*, and for *knowledge accumulation*. Explanations are, however, often *incomplete*. Lack of completeness results from an inability to understand a process or the results of its workings, an inadequate understanding of relations embedded in a situation, a lack of concisely defined concepts, and a lack of data that consequently inhibits information generation. Many explanations are not precise, but take the form of hypotheses, theories, or probabilistic statements that may be subjective or objective.

Explanations can be *accurate* without being *precise*. Every day we process data via our senses that is needed to make life-sustaining decisions and choices. We shop for food without knowing precisely what it is going to cost or whether we could get our basket of goods at less cost elsewhere. Human thinking is often inaccurate and imprecise, yet it still serves to keep us alive, solve problems, meet expectations, and satisfy wants and needs.

In lieu of exact information, we make *estimates*. Rather than requiring precise data, we can reason effectively from poor or fragmented data to create the information on which to base decision making and choice behavior. In these circumstances, the process involves estimation, including interpolation. Estimation may be based on superficial and naive processes or on valid and reliable methods. Graphs, diagrams, and statistical methods facilitate estimation with different degrees of confidence.

4.7 Modes of Collecting Data and Generating Information

There are many modes and mechanisms available to researchers through which data is collected and information is generated. These include *qualitative* and *quantitative* methodological approaches. Both of those may incorporate various methodologies and involve choices among a range of modes, all of which require careful attention in order to meet their specific requirements regarding research design and procedures. What needs to be emphasized is that there is rarely just one correct ("right") methodology or mode to use in addressing a particular research issue; rather, it is more a case of choosing an "appropriate" approach. However, in a particular research situation it may well be that a specific mode or methodology is wrong or inappropriate to use vis-à-vis the objective of the research.

Chapters 5, 6, and 7 to follow are devoted to discussing a range of methodologies for generating information and the modes commonly used for collecting data to address research issues in investigating the nature of human activities and experiences in space and environments. Because our concern in this book is to focus on analytical approaches, our emphasis is thus largely on canvassing quantitative approaches to this task and reviewing those modes that traditionally have been used in research as well as new and emerging modes for collecting data. Those quantitative approaches to the generation of information we later consider are:

- Using *surveys*, including both probability and nonprobability sampling approaches
- *Extrapolating* from controlled conditions to the real world, including using laboratory experiments and simulations and creating virtual environments.

However, there is also a role for the use of qualitative approaches, including case studies, to generate information, and often qualitative approaches may be used in conjunction with quantitative approaches, particularly as a prelude to conducting and as a mechanism to inform the design of a survey-based approach to data collection.

CHAPTER 5

Qualitative and Survey Approaches to Collecting Data and Generating Information

5.1 Introduction

As mentioned at the end of Chapter 4, it is usually convenient to distinguish between *qualitative* approaches and *quantitative* approaches to the collection of data and the generation of information, although qualitative methods may be employed to generate quantitative data and quantitative methods may also be used to provide qualitative insights to human behavior and experiences in spaces and environments. In this chapter we provide an overview both of qualitative approaches and of *survey* approaches to collecting data and generating information, focusing on some of the commonly used methodologies employed by researchers. A most useful relatively short book that the reader might wish to consult, one that provides an insightful overview of both qualitative and quantitative approaches in social research, is Bryman (1988). It includes an important discussion on the benefits of combining quantitative and qualitative methods in research.

5.2 Qualitative Methods

In their introduction to a most useful set of short books published by Sage in its Qualitative Research Methods Series, Kirk and Miller (1986) state that, in distinguishing between quantitative and qualitative research, it is best to "think of qualitative methods as procedures for counting to one. Deciding what to count as a unit of analysis is fundamentally an interpretative issue requiring judgment and choice" (p. 5). In qualitative methods, "meanings rather than frequencies assume permanent significance" (p. 5).

5.2.1 The Concern of Qualitative Methods

Qualitative methodologies might be cornered as being considered with the following:

1. *Invention:* particularly in assisting and developing a research design.
2. *Discovering:* particularly through observation and reading, which may also then

lead to the measurement of the associations of the phenomenon, event, or setting being observed.
3. *Interpretation:* particularly through the forms of evaluating situations and information to enhance comprehension and to generate insights.
4. *Explanation:* particularly through enhancing the communication of observed information and the "packaging" of information to enhance understanding.

It is necessary to emphasize the importance of carrying out all four of those phases in undertaking qualitative research because they are the hallmarks of the ethnographic and case study processes that researchers commonly employ in research investigations.

Yin (1990) provides a warning that qualitative approaches like the case study—as with an experiment—do *not* represent a "sample" from which the researcher may then extrapolate the findings to a wider population. Rather, in qualitative approaches to generating information, the goal of the research should be to expand and generalize theories (analytical generalization), not to enumerate frequencies (statistical inference). The researcher is aiming to generalize from "the particular" to a broader theory or postulate that perhaps then needs to be tested through replication of the findings in further case studies or experiments where the theory has specified that the same results should occur.

5.2.2 The Geographic Tradition

Geographers have a long history of using qualitative methodologies. As discussed in Chapter 2 in Part I, geographers have been concerned with *observing, recording, describing*, and *classifying* phenomena, as in *field studies*. Those tasks also involve methodologies such as *participant observation*, usually conducted on human subjects while investigating their behavior.

The *inductive approach* to theory development inevitably involves using qualitative methodologies for information generation. It involves what Zonabend (1992) has referred to as "intrepid subjectivity" in explicitly defining objectively the object of a study. Kirk and Miller (1986) point out how, within the social sciences, qualitative research is a tradition that "fundamentally depends on watching people in their own territory and interacting with them in their own language, on their own terms" (p. 9).

Qualitative methods, then, have a long pedigree. It is essential in research that their use is as refined and as sophisticated as needs to be the case in using quantitative methodologies. In recent times, all too often in geographic research into aspects of human behavior and the conditions in which it takes place, it has become commonplace among the proponents of the postmodernist and humanist ideologies to equate the use of qualitative methods with a break from the positivist tradition (which many postmodernists see as evil). Those views, however, represent a gross ignorance of the historical evolution in the use of both qualitative and quantitative approaches in geographic inquiry (as well as more broadly in the social and behavioral sciences). In addition, too often some contemporary champions of qualitative methodologies fail to recognize and apply the rigor that is implicit in the proper use of such approaches.

5.2.3 Objectivity in Qualitative Research

Kirk and Miller (1986) tell how qualitative research is an "empirical, socially located phenomenon, defined by its own history, not simply a rag-bag comprising all things that are not quantitative" (p. 71). It ranges across analytical introduction, content analysis, semiotics, hermeneutics, elite interviewing, the study of life histories, archival manipulation, computer manipulation, and statistical manipulation. Kirk and Miller stress how important it is to know as much as possible about the "cognitive idiosyncrasies of the observer—which is to say about his or her theories" (p. 51). They include academic commitment, values, behavioral style, and experiences. A particularly important issue is what some consider as the pretense by the social scientist to be a "neutral observer."

But qualitative research should be intended to be *objective*. As Kirk and Miller (1986) say:

> There is a world of experienced reality out there. The way we perceive and understand that world is largely up to us, but the world does not tolerate all understandings of it equally. There is a long-standing intellectual community for which it seems worthwhile to figure out collectively how best to talk about the empirical world, by means of incremental, partial improvements in understanding. Often, the improvements come about by identifying ambiguity in prior, apparently clear views, or by showing that there are cases in which some alternative view works better. (p. 51)

And as Golledge and Stimson (1997) say, "above all, qualitative research and its objectivity must be measured in terms of its validity and reliability" (p. 15).

5.3 Theoretical Traditions and Approaches in Qualitative Inquiry

The theoretical traditions of qualitative approaches to inquiry are many and varied. Patton (1990) sets them out, as reproduced in Table 5.1. Those approaches all involve qualitative empirical observation techniques, but they vary in their conceptualization of what it is that is important to ask and to consider in understanding behavior and situations in the "real world." The approaches use techniques that include field studies, participant observation, nonparticipant observation, oral histories, and case studies.

TABLE 5.1. Theoretical Traditions and Approaches in Qualitative Inquiry

Ethnography: Seeks to understand the culture of a group of people through participant observation.

Phenomenology: Seeks to understand the structure or essence of phenomena or people through participant observation in a shared experience.

Heuristic inquiry: The inquirer shares the intensity of the experience with those being observed through systematic observation, leading to depictions of essential meanings about the structure of experiences.

Ethnomethodology: Seeks to ask how people make sure of their everyday activities so as to behave in acceptable ways, employing qualitative experiments.

Symbolic interactionism: Seeks to identify common sets of symbols and understandings to give meaning to people's interactions using group discussions or interviews with key informants or a panel of experts.

Ecological relationships: Seeks to explore the relationship between human behavior and the environment through nonparticipant observation and quantitative coding of behavior.

Systems theory: Asks how and why a system functions as a whole, employing quantitative and/or qualitative methods through holistic thinking about the system and its component parts.

Hermeneutics: Asks what are the conditions under which a human act takes place or something is produced that makes it possible to interpret its meaning, with investigators reporting from their perspective or standpoints and of the people being studied through a praxis.

Note. From Patton (1990, pp. 66–89). Copyright 1990 by Sage Publications. Adapted by permission.

Wolcott (1990) has warned of the dangers of affixing the label *ethnography* to qualitative methodologies, drawing attention to the need to be aware of the "wide range of alternative terms and approaches" (p. 64). In fact, ethnographic and natural history methodologies represent but a small spectrum of the range of methodologies in the social and behavioral sciences. Although research methodologies in anthropology have relied heavily on ethnographic case studies, many social scientists regard them as having limited scientific or distinguishing value, considering them instead to be forays into unexplored situations or areas of research that are useful more as a systematic means of developing definitions, analysis, and understanding through the use of other methodologies. But case studies are also regarded by many social scientists as having a great deal of scientific or disciplinary value, standing or falling on their own merit.

5.3.1 Case Studies

Case studies are widely used in social and behavioral inquiry. Like laboratory experiments, they require detailed attention to conceptualization and design. Yin (1990) provides an excellent overview of design and methodology issues for conducting case study research.

Hamil, Dufow, and Fortin (1993) point out that the methodological value of the experimental devices in the case study is essentially based on

(a) the quality of the strategies selected in defining the object in study and in the selection of the social unit (or DMU) that makes up the ideal vantage point from which to understand it; as well as
(b) the methodological rigor displayed in the description of this subject in the form of a [sociological] analysis that be understood in action. (p. 40)

5.3.1.1 Evolution of the Case Study Approach

The evolution of the case study approach was influenced greatly by the work of the Chicago school of sociology from the late 19th century and early decades of the 20th century as researchers investigated small local communities and urban neighborhoods where rural and immigrant populations had settled. Those case studies included the investigation of phenomena such as employment, poverty, delinquency and violence. As Hamil and colleagues (1993) remind us, it was the urban sociologist Robert Park in particular who was influential in developing applications of the case study methodology to urban social issues, believing that the case study can "demonstrate a meticulous and a representative approach that was lacking in journalistic accounts" (p. 14). The development of the case study approach in sociology and urban studies was strongly linked to the emergence of the *urban ecology* theoretical perspective of the transformation of small and simple communities to large cities with complex social structures.

The case study was used to help develop an understanding of the processes and the outcomes involved in the evolution of the city and its social characteristics and problems. *Field studies* were also developed using on-site techniques such as observations, open-ended interviews, and collecting documentary evidence. Hamil and colleagues (1993, p. 16) tell how these approaches were used to develop inductive theory about the form and structure of the city. Inherent in the evolution of the case study is the belief that it could provide an understanding of the personal experiences of social actions. As Becker (1970) says:

To understand an individual's behaviour, we must know how he perceives the situation, the obstacles he believes he has to face, the alternatives he saw opening up to him. We cannot understand the effects of the range of possibilities, delinquent subfractures, social norms and other explanations of behaviour which are commonly invoked, unless we consider them from the actor's point of view. (p. 64)

5.3.1.2 Limitations of the Case Study

An issue to emerge from the use of the case study is the degree to which the individual actor's point of view can be incorporated into theory development, and what status is assigned to it in developing understanding and providing explanation. As Hamel and colleagues (1993) point out, one difficulty with the case study involves the extent to which the process produces objective information that "does not result from the social, intellectual and psychological make up of the researcher" (p. 17).

We are given a timely reminder by Hamel and colleagues (1993) that it was in the 1930s and 1940s that the *statistical survey* was developed, largely through the work of researchers at Columbia University in New York, both to provide explanations and to provide a basis for making forecasts. Considerable debate emerged regarding the need for surveys to validate a theoretical idea and how that required researchers to hold their subjective attitudes or feelings in check while conducting their studies. As a result, *deductive* approaches to the development of theory began to incorporate statistical procedures appropriate for testing for accuracy and validity and to generalize. Qualitative methodologies, such as participant observation (see Jorgensen, 1990, for an overview of this as a methodology in human studies), were deemed to be insufficient—or even inappropriate—for such approaches.

Thus, the case study was to become more and more used as an explanatory investigative tool, used primarily as a preliminary study that then would give rise to a statistical survey that could validate or eliminate a theory or a general model (Hamel et al., 1993, p. 21). The limitations of the case study are seen to be (1) its lack of representativeness and (2) its lack of rigor in the collection, construction, and analysis of empirical data bias.

However, as Jacob (1989) points out, there has recently been a considerable revival in interest in the case study. This is so, Jacob claims, because

> there is no scientific method, recipe or algorithm known that will permit scientific discovery. We know of no mechanical means that will generate a hypothesis or theory based on certain facts observed in a finite series of steps. (p. 10)

Jacob argues that all theories are based initially on a particular case or object. This is a particular view, with which many will take exception, and we suggest that such a view is a distorted interpretation of what constitutes the scientific method of inquiry. However, it is certainly the case that methodologies such as the *in-depth interview* case study can be used effectively to elicit theories, the elements of which might or might not be validated by further case studies and/or by a sample survey of a target population. As suggested by Godelier (1982), it is

> the empirical demonstration of such elements which yield good theoretical questions. If they are based on a few factual elements they can pave the way to the discovery of the general structure of some sphere of reality. (p. 25)

If the objective of a research project is to explain the behavior or experiences of actors from the perspectives of their beliefs, attitudes, perceptions, cognitions, and experiences, then the case study approach has real potential as a tool to help develop explanation, particularly through the use of repetitive case studies that confirm or refute verification of postulated explanatory factors. But as Golledge and Stimson (1997) point out, "the issue is not the actual number of case studies but, rather, the suitability of the case for the actual areas of a study and what the cases intend to explain" (p. 18). It is the methodological qualities of the case study or case studies that determine the representative value of the research, and "this determination requires careful and explicit construction of the case study with a theoretical framework" (p. 18). If it is decided that a case being studied is representative of the selected phenomenon, then the scope of the study may prove to be macroscopic through the methodological virtues of the case and the method used. That may permit an in-depth case study to be judged as having explanatory significance (Hamel et al., 1993).

5.3.2 The Narrative

In recent times there has emerged a rush of interest among researchers enraptured by the postmodernist doctrine in human geography in focusing on the product of the case study or the written account of it as an end in its own right. That concern with the *narrative* raises serious issues of a methodological kind concerning the writing up of the results of a qualitative investigation and in particular about ensuring that the textual claims and interpretative properties of the research and the researcher are well illustrated by the data collected.

Wolcott (1990) provides a useful overview of the issues involved in writing up the outcome of qualitative research. A crucial point is that a researcher cannot create ethnography unless he or she has done intensive fieldwork based on rigorous conceptualization of the research problem and the rigorous application of the methodology employed to conduct the study.

5.3.3 Focus Groups

Widely used in market and political research, as well as in other social research situations, are *focus groups*. These involve the assembly of a group of people as participants in a facilitated discussion of a specific topic. Born in the 1930s out of the necessity for social scientists to investigate the values of nondirective individual interviewing as an improved source of information because of doubts about the accuracy of more traditional methods of information gathering, the focus-group method evolved whereby the social scientist would take a less directive and dominating role and the respondent would be able to comment on the areas deemed by the respondent to be of most importance. This was an extension of the nondirective interviewing methods developed by psychologists in the late 1930s, with application to a group situation.

Krueger (1988) provides a comprehensive overview of the process of conducting focus groups and the use of information thus gleaned. Participants in focus groups are usually selected to be relatively homogeneous and unfamiliar with each other. The facilitator or moderator "guides" the discussion among the participants through a focused discussion that generates qualitative data. Often focus groups are used prior to more systematic collection of information through a survey, with the outcomes from the focus group(s) being used as inputs to survey questionnaire design. However, it is common for both quantitative and qualitative information to be gained from focus groups. Highly honed skills are needed for the facilitator/moderator to effectively conduct focus groups.

5.4 Using Surveys to Collect Data and Generate Information

If the researcher has made the decision that it is only through primary data collection (involving collecting new data) that it is possible to address his or her research question, then adopting a *survey approach* to collect that primary data to generate the required information will necessitate giving very explicit attention to the onerous and quite complex tasks that are involved in conducting a survey.

Many excellent books have been published on survey research methods. The reader is encouraged to consult such books in order to become familiar with the intricacies of this very important field of research methodology in the social sciences. A good start might be Moser and Kalton (1971) and de Vaus (1985). Golledge and Stimson (1987, Chap. 2) provide a short summary overview of issues concerned with data collection by survey methods, written as an introduction for students studying behavior in geography. A short book specifically written on survey methods for geographers is Sheskin (1985).

Our aims in this chapter are simply to make the reader familiar with the range of tasks involved in conducting a survey and to draw attention to some of the choices available in deciding on a particular research design involving the collection of data through survey research, and to help the reader to be aware of the many modes that are used to collect data and generate information through surveys. Above all, the concern of the researcher always needs to be to ensure that one uses a methodology and employs a research design that will maximize the chance that the data that is collected is *accurate, reliable*, and *valid*.

5.4.1 The Tasks Involved in Conducting a Survey

Table 5.2 lists the issues that must be addressed if the researcher decides to conduct a survey to collect primary data. Some authorities might combine or further split some of the points listed in the table; our concern is to draw attention to the range of issues that have to be addressed and to propose them in a logical sequence. It is evident that considerable monetary and time resources are involved in undertaking these survey tasks. Moreover, their successful execution requires a team approach encompassing a variety of skills and logistical arrangements. In short, conducting primary data collection through survey research is a specialized field.

The survey process contains many potential pitfalls. Most important, survey research is generally expensive and time-consuming. It is rarely able to be undertaken adequately by an individual working alone. In fact, most researchers are not themselves professionally equipped, in terms of training and experience, to undertake the tasks involved in conducting data collection through surveys and thus they should not attempt to do so alone. Expert assistance is definitely required. A common problem is that, all too often, people think that conducting a survey is something that anyone can do, but it is not! Indeed, we would go as far as suggesting that a survey should only be undertaken as a "last resort" when other sources of information/means of collecting data are inadequate for addressing the research issue at hand. *Nonsurvey* approaches are generally cheaper and less consuming of time. Nevertheless, commonly it is necessary to design and undertake a survey to generate the primary data needed to adequately address the research questions at hand.

If the tasks set out in Table 5.2 are not adequately and properly addressed, then it is almost inevitable (as discussed in Chapters 2 and 3 in Part I) that serious *errors* and *biases* will occur in data collection. That will result in the generation of data that is *incomplete* and *inaccurate*, and the information thus generated will be *unreliable* and *invalid*. It must

TABLE 5.2. The Tasks Involved in Conducting a Survey

1. Define the research questions, including formulating hypotheses for testing.
2. Determine the budget and time constraints for the research.
3. Define the target population from which primary sampling units (PSUs) will be selected.
4. Define parameters.
5. Specify attributes and variables.
6. Decide sampling issues: type of sample, sample frame, sampling fraction, and sample error estimation.
7. Instrument design for data collection: mode of survey; questionnaire design; precoded/open-ended questions; scales; validity, reliability, and variability issues.
8. Administrative procedures: field and office arrangements; training materials and programs (including interview selection and training); monitoring procedures.
9. Pilot survey/pretesting prior to conducting the full survey.
10. Data processing: coding scheme, establishing a clean dataset.
11. Data analysis: dealing with nonresponse and missing data (imputation); cross-tabulation of data variables; creating synthetic data variables; statistical testing and modeling.
12. Report writing, data presentation, and dissemination of survey information/results.

Note. From Golledge and Stimson (1997, p. 20). Copyright 1997 by The Guilford Press. Reprinted by permission.

always be remembered that there are no shortcuts in conducting research involving the collection of primary data through social survey research methods. It is essential that adequate budget and time resources be available if the tasks outlined in Table 5.2 are to be adequately addressed and properly executed. If those resources are not available, then other research designs for collecting data should be used. The tasks involved in conducting social surveys are so onerous and complex that typically the researcher is advised to contract a specialist survey research unit in a university or a commercial survey research firm to undertake the project. Such organizations will have the expertise and infrastructure needed to help the researcher to:

- Plan the survey
- Design the survey instrument (typically a questionnaire)
- Undertake the sampling design and train the interviewers
- Manage a field force of interviewers or provide the CATI (computer-assisted telephone interviewing) system to collect information via telephone interviewing
- Code and process the data collected
- Undertake imputation procedures to account for missing data to produce a "clean" database for statistical analysis and modeling of survey results.

5.4.2 Key Issues to Determine Prior to Conducting a Survey

It is always essential for the researcher to initially direct much time and attention to carefully and precisely defining the research question and to clearly specifying the hypotheses (where relevant) that are to be empirically tested through analysis of the data collected. Specific attention also needs to be given to precisely defining the *target population* from which a sample is to be drawn and to specify precisely the *primary sampling units* (PSUs) on which, and from which, data is to be collected. In addition, it may be necessary to *stratify* the sample according to a need to focus on specific groups in the population and/or to sample from specific geographic areas. Furthermore, decisions have to be made concerning the *sample frame*, the *sampling fraction*, and the *sample size*. Decisions also need to be made about the mode of data collection to be used.

Most importantly, it is essential that all of the decisions are made in the context of the problem and objectives of the research in order to ensure that the research design is appropriate to generate the data that is needed to address the research questions. And, as we repeatedly emphasize, the research design must be rigorous, as must the data collection process, in order to ensure that valid and reliable data is collected and in order that we can accurately estimate the *error* and *bias* due to sampling, and also that we can be relatively confident that *nonsampling errors* and bias are minimized through rigorous instrument design and data collection procedures.

5.4.3 Modes for Survey Data Collection

There are many different modes of survey data collection. The choice of mode will be influenced by a combination of factors, including the budget for the research project, time constraints, the nature of the target population, and the type of information that needs to be collected.

But first, a fundamental decision is whether the survey will seek to collect information from all of the PSUs that form the *target population* by conducting an *enumeration* or whether some form of *sampling* is to be used. For very small populations, often the researcher will decide to conduct an enumeration. More frequently, it is most appropriate to decide on a sampling approach.

Irrespective of whether an enumeration or a sampling approach is used, the researcher will have to choose from one of many modes for surveying data collection. The most commonly used modes are discussed in the sections that follow.

5.4.3.1 Compulsory Registrations

Many public agencies collect information by means of a survey instrument that requires people by compulsion to *register* by filling out a form to provide the requisite information. Examples include motor vehicle registration, applications for social security or other government benefits and support, registration of a business, and registration to vote. Often the requirement for official registration is backed by legislation that may be invoked to enforce people to comply with a registration process. Or it may be that compliance through registration is the only way a person may gain access to a benefit to which he or she may be entitled.

The information collected through compulsory registration is usually used for internal administration purposes by the agency requesting the registration, but sometimes those databanks are accessible to researchers for purposes of secondary data analysis, with the data files being amended to ensure the confidentiality of the individual registrants.

5.4.3.2 Self-Completion Questionnaires

Self-completion forms (or *survey questionnaires*) are a commonly used mode of survey data collection. This is usually a relatively cheap way to collect information. It is usual for someone to deliver or for the respondent to download the form or questionnaire and then to have it picked up or have the respondent mail it back to the data collection agency. Or the form may be mailed out to the respondent who is asked to return it by mail. This method of information collection is widely use in market research. It is also the way in which census data is collected in many countries. Sometimes the person doing the distribution (and possible collection) of the questionnaire might explain to the respondent how to fill in the forms, but basically it is the respondent who is left to his or her own devices to complete the questionnaire unaided.

5.4.3.3 Mail Surveys

The *mail survey* is one of the most commonly used modes for many information collection efforts. This involves self-completion of a survey instrument (typically a questionnaire) by the survey respondents (the PSUs). This might be a straight mail survey where a list of the PSUs by address is obtained and the researcher sends a questionnaire to each address, along with a cover letter telling the respondent how important the survey is, and asking people to participate in it. The researcher hopes that the respondent will return the questionnaire with all the questions described out according to instructions. Usually a reply-paid envelope is supplied for the mail-back of the survey questionnaire. It is best to have a reply-paid registered mail box with the post office rather than to stick stamps on the return envelopes, because about 60–80% of PSUs to whom a questionnaire is sent simply are not likely to return it. Thus the researcher might as well only pay for those that are returned.

Thus, the mail survey is a mode in which there is no contact at all between the people conducting the survey and the potential respondents. The researcher mails the questionnaire out, and hopes the PSUs will cooperate by completing it and mailing it back. But a major problem with the mail survey mode (as with noncompulsory forms of self-completion data collection) is that response rates are low (usually between 20 and 30%). It is thus essential to use a second and a third (or even additional) phase of mailing to increase the response rate. It is typical that each successive mailing results in a return rate that is about half the number returned in the previous mailing phase. In this way, it may be possible to build up response rates to approaching 50%, which is considered good for a mail survey. Specialized mail surveys focusing on an issue of particular interest for a special group have been known to have response rates of up to 70%, but this is rare. It is advisable in conducting mail surveys to also interview a random selection of nonrespondents to a mail survey, as invariably they will display different characteristics from the respondents to mail surveys (see, for example, Ampt & Stimson, 1972).

5.4.3.4 Face-to-Face (or In-House) Interviewing

Face-to-face interviewing is often regarded as the standard mode for collecting survey data. While costly, and requiring the use of skilled, trained interviewers, it is the most flexible and a more reliable methodology in survey research. Here the interviewer goes to the PSU and talks to the chosen person and conducts the interview face-to-face. The interviewer goes through a series of questions that the respondent answers, and the interviewer records those answers. Typically the response rate in face-to-face interview-conducted surveys is in excess of 60%, and often as high as 80% or more.

5.4.3.5 On-Site Interviews

In *on-site interviewing* an investigator goes to the particular site where the activity being investigated is occurring, and the people who are participating in that activity are interviewed face-to-face.

Shopping surveys are a good example of the use of on-site surveys. Developing random selection methods to determine who is selected in the sample poses a difficult problem in on-site surveys. Random selection is difficult and usually is tackled by having a predetermined number of shoppers pass the interview point before the next potential respondent is approached. Furthermore, it is necessary to have some form of procedure for selecting sites at which to station interviews in the shopping center, and to determine—often in accordance with shopper volume variations—the time distribution of interviews.

5.4.3.6 Telephone Interviews

Telephone interviewing techniques have been progressively developed over the last few decades so that now they are one of the most commonly used modes for survey data collection. They often involve intricate designs to generate a random selection of telephone numbers for area-based surveys through techniques such as random-digit dialing. For a detailed discussion on the emergence of CATI methods to enhance the telephone interview survey mode, see Groves and Kahn (1979), which also provides a comparison of that mode with the personal interview mode. A concise overview of telephone survey methods is provided in Lavrakas (1987).

Telephone interviews have become more and more important for a number of reasons:

- They are cheaper to conduct.
- The response rate of face-to-face and in-house surveys has declined quite remarkably over the past 40-odd years, particularly in big cities where there are lots of apartments and security systems and because people are wary of opening their door to a stranger.

Telephone interviews had achieved as high as a 70% response rate. However, a problem is that one cannot cover households without a telephone, and inevitably one will miss out on some part of the population. This became less of a problem because of the widespread nature of telephone ownership, which in many places is now almost universal. But there are some subgroups of the population where telephone ownership is much lower. However, this has dropped somewhat with the proliferation of the cell (mobile) phone. This new technology also represents a further problem because of the difficulty of obtaining access to lists of subscribers to provide a sampling frame, and, particularly in some countries, the difficulty of getting information on the number of subscribers in local exchange areas that is possible with land-line subscribers, in order to have a spatially stratified basis for generating random-digit dialing of telephone subscribers. So one has to be aware of coverage problems, particularly with respect to specific groups of the population, where telephone survey methods are used.

But CATI systems have become more and more sophisticated, incorporating not only random-digit-dialing routines to generate samples, but also with respect to:

- Online information processing for administrating a questionnaire and in coding answers
- The automatic compiling and analysis of data
- The monitoring of interview performance.

There is, however, recent mounting evidence of consumer reaction against participating in telephone survey-based social research because of the proliferation of the telemarketing phenomenon. In some countries (such as Australia), there are new regulations whereby consumers may have their telephone number placed on a register so that telemarketers are banned from contacting them.

5.4.3.7 E-Surveys

While mail, personal interview, and telephone surveys have served researchers well to date, some problems arise. Those include:

- Nonresponse to mailings
- Lack of respondent cooperation with interviewers
- Poor recall ability of respondents
- Difficulties of accessing special groups like the disabled by telephone
- Increasing consumer/respondent resistance to participation.

Such limitations have encouraged surveyors to experiment with electronic surveys designed to overcome many of the response rate problems of traditional paper or telephone surveys.

The attraction of the *e-survey* is in the promise of a "real-time" response to the survey instrument. Such response behaviors are claimed to compensate for poor recall, lack of identification of underreported activities such as trip chains, and underreporting of some short trips such as "visit ATM" or "stop for gas." In practice, however, these goals are not always achieved. Indeed, overcoming reporting problems depends in large part on the length of time between activity and trip occurrence and time of recording the data. Thus, recent innovative e-surveys such as CHASE (the Computerized Household Activity Schedule Elicitor) have been based on using a desktop PC for data entry, storage, and manipulation. While this procedure appears to have improved response rates and the accuracy of trip recording, there are still problems, such as falsely reporting the location of a visited place or the duration of a trip, and participant groups are limited to PC users with either a home PC or access to one. Doherty (2003) reports success rates in terms of responses that, in part, validate the procedure.

Most attempts to build an e-survey have been oriented to using the Internet as the source for finding participants. The potential bias of this approach is evident. Nevertheless, it could produce higher gross returns than more conventional probability sampling–based survey methods. And, when focusing on vehicular travel, for example, data accuracy is usually improved by locating a global positioning system (GPS) in the vehicle. This still has to be activated by a traveler (and sometimes travelers consciously fail to do so). The GPS unit records a trace of the traveler's path and the location of stops. The GPS trace can be matched against participant interview data as a check on the accuracy and completeness of participant's data-recording activities. Thus, Internet-based surveys that elicit trip recall for trips and their purposes, complemented by GPS records of paths followed, tend to give extra dimensionality to survey procedures and to compensate in part for traditional data loss at the input stage.

To enhance these e-survey techniques, author Golledge and his colleagues have been developing a real-time data collection device based on a wearable computer (a pocket PC). This device has extended memory, a GPS chip, and a voice- or stylus-activated interface that relays data in a wireless manner to a nearby server. This device works as follows: the traveler begins by inputting a proposed activity schedule (trip purpose and proposed destination):

- The traveler activates the GPS recorder and begins the day's travel.
- The route followed is tracked by the GPS unit and the first destination is checked

against the proposed activity schedule. If all items agree, the traveler is encouraged to move on.
- If an actual stop does not coincide with a planned stop, the traveler is queried for the reason for such a change, by selecting from a menu of reasons.
- The reasons include change of route, change of destination, change of time for task completion, cancellation of an activity, substitution of an activity, along with reasons such as change in environmental conditions, collaborating with a friend or associate for a particular activity, and so on.
- Any changes (or confirmations) are relayed to the server, which records activity purpose and travel details in a database for immediate or later analysis.

Developments such as the above are making Internet-based e-surveys more common, more economical, and more accurate, reliable, and valid.

5.4.4 Relative Advantages and Disadvantages of Survey Modes

The various modes of collecting survey data discussed above have advantages and disadvantages in terms of cost, efficiency, coverage problems, data validity, and so on. For example:

1. *Mail surveys* have the very great advantage of being quite inexpensive to run, but have the disadvantage of low response rates.
2. *Telephone interviews* are apparently cheaper to run than face-to-face interviews, but they require elaborate computer facilities for random-digit-dialing sampling designs and computer-assisted interviewing systems; they require specialized interviewer training; and they have coverage deficiencies in some contexts.
3. Ideally, one would choose *face-to-face* interviewing to keep nonresponse as low as possible to maintain maximum flexibility in questionnaire design, and to take advantage of techniques of interviewer probing of respondents.
4. Increasingly *e-survey* modes are enabling more cost-effective ways of collecting information from groups of PSUs for generating time–space survey data and for accurately recording locational information relating to human activities using GPS technology.

It is crucial that the researcher be aware of the fact that the mode of survey data collection used will influence the type of questions that can be asked. The mail survey, in particular, restricts the range of question types that can be used.

What has not been discussed above is the mode of collecting data using laboratory testing of *experimental designs*. Increasingly these procedures are being used in many areas of social, behavioral, and spatial research. Laboratory testing may sometimes use subjects that have been selected using probability sampling frames. Those modes of information collection are addressed in Chapter 7.

5.5 Mixing Quantitative and Qualitative Approaches

It is worth reminding the reader that both qualitative and quantitative approaches have vital roles to play in the investigation of activities and experiences in spaces and environments. It is not necessarily a matter of qualitative versus quantitative: rather, it is a matter of choosing the most appropriate methodology—or mix of methodologies—for addressing the research question(s) at hand, taking account of the situational context, and paying attention to pragmatic issues such as the time and funding available for conducting the research. As Bryman (1988) states:

> There are differences between quantitative and qualitative research, in terms of the data that each engenders and the levels of analysis at which each operates. Therefore, each has its own strengths and weaknesses. However, it is important not to minimize the importance of similarities between the two traditions. For example, there does nor seem to be an obvious reason why qualitative research cannot be used in order to test theories in the manner typically associated with the model of the quantitative research process . . . [and] . . . the suggestion that quantitative research is associated with the testing of theories, whilst qualitative research is associated with the generation of theories, can consequently be viewed as a convention that may have little to do with either the practices of many researchers within the two traditions or the potential of the methods of data collection themselves. . . . Rather than the somewhat doctrinaire posturing of a great deal of the literature dealing with the epistemological leanings of quantitative and qualitative research, there should be a greater recognition in discussions of the general aspects of social research methodology of the need to generate good research. This injunction means attending to the full complexity of the social world such that methods are chosen in relation to the research problems posed. (pp. 172–174)

The combining of qualitative and quantitative research approaches is, in fact, quite widespread, and it is not unusual for more than one mode or instrument to be used in the measurement of the main variables in a study through the strategy known as *triangulation of measurement*. Denzin (1970) has described this as an approach in which "multiple observers, theoretical perspectives, sources of data, and methodologies" (p. 130) are combined. That technique enhances the researchers' claims regarding the validity of their conclusions through the potential to demonstrate mutual confirmation.

Furthermore, as discussed by Bryman (1988, pp. 131–156), the mixing of quantitative and qualitative approaches might be undertaken in situations in order to address situations such as the following:

1. Use qualitative methods as a precursor to the formulation of problems and the development of instruments for quantitative research.
2. Use quantitative methods to aid the collection of qualitative data, such as using survey results to identify subjects for subsequent in-depth investigation. Combine quantitative and qualitative methods to fill gaps in research knowledge, particularly in ethnographic research investigating groups, organizations, and communities.
3. Use quantitative tools to establish the existence of structural elements and patterns, while qualitative methods are used to investigate process issues in order to produce an integrated picture of a phenomenon.
4. Use quantitative methods to investigate the specific concerns of the researcher, but use qualitative methods to focus on the perspectives of the subjects in a study. Use quantitative data as a means of establishing the generality of observations derived from qualitative methods.
5. Sometimes qualitative research is viewed (possible erroneously) as being more relevant to the "micro" level of investigation, while quantitative research is more relevant to the larger "macro" scale, with the use of both approaches making it possible to "bridge" the micro/macro gap.

In practice it is possible to envisage a number of *hybrid* designs being appropriate for a given research situation, and there are no "set rules of thumb" for the mixing of quantitative and qualitative approaches in designing and conducting research (Bryman, 1988).

5.6 Conclusion

This chapter has canvassed a range of issues concerning the collection of data and the generation of information through both qualitative and quantitative approaches, including a discussion of case studies, narratives, and survey approaches to the task of collecting data. The importance of ensuring that appropriate measures are taken to ensure the research design and implementation process incorporate the appropriate methodologies was emphasized, noting concern for ensuring that data collection and information generation produce accurate, valid, and reliable data and information.

The complexity of the tasks involved in properly designing and conducting a survey was discussed, including a brief outline of the range of modes researchers use to collect data through surveys. Because of the widespread prevalence of the use of the survey approach to the collection of data in the social and behavioral sciences, Chapter 6 will focus specific and detailed attention on the use of surveys and the design and implementation issues about which researchers must be aware in employing a survey approach for the collection of data.

CHAPTER 6

Collecting Information from Sampled Populations Using Probability and Nonprobability Designs

6.1 Introduction

To generate information through conducting research, in many contexts it is necessary to employ some type of research design that enables us to identify those PSUs from whom, or about which, data are to be collected. That can only be done once we define the *target population* that is the focus for the research. In collecting information to investigate aspects of human behavior—such as activities and experiences in spaces and environments—typically we need to *sample* from the target population, rather than conduct an *enumeration* of the population, and that involves using some form of *probability* or *nonprobability* sampling design. This chapter canvasses the approaches and issues involved in conducting research using such designs, including issues to do with sampling and the sources used to sample, the design of a survey instrument (commonly referred to as a questionnaire), and the sources of error derived from the question and answering process.

6.2 When to Use Probability Sampling and Why

It is important to clearly distinguish between *probability* sampling and *nonprobability* sampling approaches, and to understand when it is "essential" to use probability sampling designs in the collection of data through survey approaches.

6.2.1 Making Inferences and Estimates

The most fundamental point to remember is that probability sampling is an approach where every PSU in a target population is given both a *specified* and an *equal chance* of being selected in the sample. That is important if our requirement is for the sample to be a representational microcosm of the target population. And furthermore, if the objective is to be able to make *inferences* about, or to *estimate* the magnitude of, occurrences of a state or phenomenon in the target population on the basis of measures derived from sample data, then it is absolutely essential to use probability sampling. This is a fundamental difference between probability and nonprobability sampling, as it is *not* possible to generalize to the total population from data collected through nonprobability sampling designs. A probability sampling design *must* be used if the objective is to use statistics derived from a sample to estimate population parameters and to make inferences about the population characteristics on the basis of that sample data.

Probability sampling also means that the probability of each PSU in the target population being chosen in the sample is *known*. And there is a *specified probability* of PSU selection and an *equal probability* of selection over the members of that population, or within each stratum into which the population is divided if a stratified sampling frame design is being used. Another reason for using probability sampling is for *confirmatory analysis*, whereby we need to test whether the result derived from a population-wide survey in one setting may be *replicated* in another setting or other settings.

There exists a copious literature on the effects of sampling on *data quality*. A classic text is Kish (1965). The act of sampling per se means that many members of the target population are excluded from the survey measurement through the selection of a sample subset of the population. How to control for and reduce *sampling error* has become a science in itself, with survey statisticians having developed both simple and complex designs in order to minimize the effects of sampling on survey data quality so as to reduce sampling error to desired levels and to actually measure the resulting error by estimating the *standard error of variation* in sample statistics such as means and totals. Despite the high degree of precision that is possible to build into sampling designs to minimize such errors and to accurately estimate standard errors, amateurish survey practitioners continue to ignorantly violate the principles of proper, rigorous sampling design.

6.2.2 Sample Size, Sample Proportion, and Sampling Error

It is possible to estimate the effect of increasing *sample size* and increasing the *sampling fraction* on sampling error. This is an important consideration, as the researcher can be guided as to what might be an "optimal" size for a sample, as simply continuing to increase the sample size or changing the sample fraction does start to have an effect of diminishing returns vis-à-vis the reduction of sampling error. This has significant implications for containing costs in conducting probability-based survey research.

But the issue of sample size and sample fraction or proportion is not as simple an issue as it might seem vis-à-vis the effect on *sampling error*. It is common sense that sampling error depends primarily on the *proportion* of the sample to the total solution, but it is erroneous to think that, say, a 5% sample will be five times as reliable as a 1% sample, and that a 10% sample will be twice as reliable as a 5% sample, and so on.

Warwick and Lininger (1975, pp. 92–94) provide an example to demonstrate the importance of considering both the *absolute size* and the *proportionate size* of a sample in reducing the *standard error*s of parameter estimates in the population from sample data. They show how an increase in the absolute size of the sample does more to reduce the standard error than does a comparable increase in the proportion that the sample is to the total population. Warwick and Lininger (1975) say, "The practical implication is that in most surveys the absolute size of the sample is of much greater relevance than its proportional size" (p. 93).

That general principle is illustrated in Table 6.1 in the case of simple random sampling. The left half of the table show the values of the corresponding multiplying factors for assenting values of proportionate sample sizes from 0.01 to 0.95. The right half of the table shows

98 COLLECTING DATA AND REPRESENTING INFORMATION

the multiplying factors for absolute sample size ranging from 30 to 25,000. As Warwick and Lininger point out:

> The picture that emerges is clear; even with a sampling fraction up to half, the corresponding multiplying factor does not get below 0.70, while with an absolute sample size as small as 100 cases, the corresponding multiplying factor is 0.10. In other words, the extremely high relative sample size tends to produce a standard error only about 70 per cent of the sample variances, whereas even a small absolute sample size tends to reduce the standard error to 10 per cent of the sample variances. The absolute size clearly carries more weight than does the relative sample size. (p. 93)

Table 6.1 also shows that additions to the absolute sample size have a greater payoff in reducing the standard error than increases in the proportion of the sample in the population. As Warwick and Lininger (1975) show:

> Increasing the sample size from 1 percent to 10 per cent of the population reduces the proportionate size factor only about 5 percentage points, from .99 to .94. By contrast, increasing the absolute sample size from 50 to 250 reduces the corresponding multiplying factor by over half, from .14 to .06. Thus, except for samples from a very small population, it is the absolute size together with the sample variance which have the greatest impact on the size of the standard error of the estimation. (p. 94)

In addition, Table 6.1 also illustrates the principle of diminishing returns with increases in absolute sample size, with the reductions in sampling error decreasing as the absolute size of the sample increases. Warwick and Lininger (1975) also point out that "the standard error

TABLE 6.1. The Effect of the Proportionate and Absolute Size of the Sample in the Formula for Estimating the Standard Error

Sampling fraction f	$\frac{N-n}{N}$ (Proportionate size)	$\sqrt{\frac{N-n}{N}}$	Sample size n	$\frac{1}{n}$ (Absolute size)	$\sqrt{\frac{1}{n}}$
.01	.99	.99	30	.033	.17
.05	.95	.97	50	.02	.14
.10	.90	.94	100	.01	.10
.20	.80	.89	250	.004	.06
.40	.60	.77	500	.002	.04
.50	.50	.70	1,000	.001	.03
.60	.40	.63	2,500	.0004	.02
.80	.20	.44	5,000	.0002	.01
.90	.10	.32	10,000	.0001	.01
.95	.05	.22	25,000	.00004	.01

Note. The formula for estimating standard error ($S_{\bar{x}}$) is

$$S_{\bar{x}} = \sqrt{\frac{N-n}{N} \cdot \frac{s^2}{n}} = \sqrt{\frac{N-n}{N}} = \sqrt{\frac{1}{n}}(s)$$

The three components are (1) a factor representing the influence of relative or *proportional* sample size, $(N-n)/N$; (2) a factor $1/n$ representing the influence of *absolute* sample size; and (3) the square root of the sample variance(s). The standard error of the estimate is the product of the square root of the sample variance multiplied by the factors representing the proportionate and absolute sample sizes. From Warwick and Lininger (1975, p. 93). Copyright 1975 by McGraw-Hill. Reprinted by permission.

is determined in good part by the size of the *group(s)* actually being analyzed, rather than the total sample size" (p. 94).

This is particularly important in large-scale surveys comprising a large sample size. Warwick and Lininger give the example of a hypothetical survey with a sample size of 2,000 conducted across a nation, pointing out that the levels of error are likely to be very acceptable at 0.2 or 0.3 around a percentage for analyses carried out on the entire sample. However, when the analysis is conducted for subgroups of respondents within the sample—for example, age groups, income groups, ethnic groups, or occupational categories, or for geographic areas (subregions)—then the standard error of the estimation for those subgroups depends on the absolute size of the sample for the subgroup. Warwick and Lininger (1975) say that "the more the subgroups to be analyzed, and the smaller the groups, the larger the sample needed to have sufficient cases to keep the sampling error within tolerable limits" (p. 94). Thus, it often becomes necessary in the sampling design to stratify the sample geographically or with respect to particular subgroups for which analysis needs to occur, and to set differential sampling fractions and sample size requirements with respect to those areas or subgroups.

6.3 Methods of Probability Sampling

Detailed discussions of probability sampling designs are available in most survey research textbooks; Kalton (1983) provides an excellent overview. These designs include (1) simple random sampling, (2) systematic sampling, and (3) stratification cluster and multistage sampling, as well as numerous other probability sampling designs. These sampling designs are briefly discussed in the sections that follow.

6.3.1 Simple Random Sampling

By definition, *simple random sampling* implies that every PSU in the target population has the *same* probability of being included in the sample. For example, a sample of 50 households in a 500-household suburb could be drawn by giving a number "001" to "500" to every household, with the sample being selected by drawing 50 numbers out of a hat, or by using three-digit fields in a random numbers table to draw the sample of households. That would generate a simple random sample.

6.3.2 Systematic Sampling

Systematic sampling provides a means of substantially reducing the effort required for sample selection by taking every kth PSU in the target population after selecting a random start, achieved by selecting at random a number within the range defined by the sampling fraction (for example, a 1-in-10 sampling fraction would involve selecting at random a number between "1" and "10," say the number "3") to give the first PSU to be selected in the sample from the list of all PSUs in the target population, with k being the statistical or skip interval, which is the sampling fraction. In the example of drawing a 1 in 10 sample of 50 households in a 500-household suburb, the sample selection would be the households with the numbers 3, 13, 23, 33, . . . , 473, 483, 493. In that way a systematic random sample is drawn.

Often in geographic sampling, and especially in selecting point-located or area samples, the procedure to draw a systematic random sample of points or areas is to place a grid over the space. That way the sample points may be chosen as grid intervals by systematically choosing, say, every fifth grid square or intersection of grids in all directions (N, S, E, and W) from a random starting point or grid.

6.3.3 Stratification

Stratification is commonly used in sample designs whereby the target population is classified into subpopulations, or *strata*, based on supplementary information to categorize the PSUs. The selection of separate samples then occurs from each stratum, using either the same sampling fraction or variable sampling fractions depending on either the need to differentially sample within each stratum in order to weight the selection of PSU for a specific reason (for example, to place greater emphasis on a particular stratum or number of strata) or to provide a minimum number of PSUs in the sample for each stratum when the distribution of PSUs across the specified strata is unequal.

We can use *proportionate* and *disproportionate* stratification:

1. Proportionate stratification is widely used because it produces simple estimators and because it guarantees that the estimators are no less precise than those obtained from a simple random sample of the same size.
2. Disproportionate stratification is used to achieve an allocation that minimizes precision of the estimator of the population mean within the available resources, and the optimal allocation for this purpose is to make the sampling fraction strata proportional to the PSU standard deviation in that stratum and inversely proportional to the square root of the cost of including a PSU in that stratum of the population.

When disproportionate stratification is used it is necessary to set a *quota sample* within each "stratum." Often this is done in order to carry out nonparametric statistical tests to determine the statistical validity of apparent differences in estimates between the strata. This latter approach is often used for investigating differences in behavior (as the *dependent* variable) between subgroups (strata) in the population that are differentiated on the basis of specific independent variable parameters such as age, gender, income, or location of residence (as the *independent variables*). The nonparametric statistical techniques commonly used to test for differences between subgroups of a population thus differentiated often require minimum numbers in the cells of contingency tables that may be quite large when two-way and three-way cross-tabulations between variable parameters are used in testing. Such analytical requirements in research are important to specify up front, as they will have important implications for determining minimum sample design.

6.3.4 Cluster and Multistage Sampling

These approaches are widely used in large-scale population/household surveys, and are of particular interest in research involving spatial sampling. *Cluster sampling* and *multistage sampling* designs are used primarily as a means of producing more efficient and cost-effective survey practice.

In many research situations, the target population can be regarded as being composed of a set of groups or elements—often those are spatial units of different scales or levels of aggregation/disaggregation. As discussed above in Section 6.3.3, such groups may be regarded as strata, and separate samples can be selected from each group.

Another common approach is to treat them as clusters, in which case only a sample of them is included in the sample. If all of the PSUs in the related clusters are included in the sample, the method is known as "cluster sampling." However, if only a sample of the PSUs is taken from each related cluster, the method is known as "two-stage sampling." It is common to use a hierarchy of clusters. This is typically the case in large-scale population surveys conducted on a national or larger area basis, whereby the cluster might be large geographic units that are administrative districts—such as states or counties, their local council areas, and suburb or census tracts within them—with the final selection of PSUs being within the most disaggregated spatial units. That method is known as "multistage sampling."

It is important, however, to remember that both clustering and stratification sampling designs introduce increased sampling error. This is particularly so in clustering, where the greater the degree of clustering, the greater the degree of error.

6.3.5 Other Probability Sampling Designs

There are numerous other probability sampling designs that are also particularly suitable in investigating aspects of human behavior. They include:

1. *Two-phase sampling*, in which certain items of information are collected for an initial or first-phase sample, with further items then being collected for a second phase from a subsample of the initial sampled PSUs.
2. *Replicated sampling*, where the total sample is made up of a set of replicated subsamples, each of which are of identical sample design.
3. *Panel designs*, which are relevant when the survey objective requires data to be collected at two or more points in time.

The literature also refers to other sampling designs, including *block designs* and *network designs*.

Of particular interest in research into human behavior are *panel designs*, especially when the researcher needs to collect configurational travel and activity data in a time–space framework. Panel designs are widely used in market research situations. In panel designs, a sample of PSUs is requested to be reinterviewed over a period of time in what is also referred to as *longitudinal* survey designs.

6.4 Nonprobability Sampling Approaches

In many research investigations, it is difficult—and often not appropriate—to use probability methods of choosing samples. Sometimes we cannot clearly define the PSU or the target population. Often cost constraints will limit the scale of a study and rule out probability sampling. If we are conducting an experimental design approach (discussed in Chapter 7), often it does not matter much if we use a *nonprobability sampling* approach, as the basic concern may be controlling for a whole set of independent variables, and/or we may need to get an adequate number of PSUs with specific characteristics that fall into different groups or types of problem in order that we may be able to directly compare between those vis-à-vis the dependent variable.

Much research has been conducted in the field of spatial behavior—such as consumer behavior and cognitive mapping—using nonprobability sampling designs, particularly when the aim is to test for differences between specific groups of people differentiated on a common set of characteristics. Some commonly used nonprobability sampling methods include (1) *haphazard, convenience,* or *accidental sampling*; (2) *purposive, judgmental,* or *expert choice sampling*; and (3) *quota sampling.* Such nonprobability sampling approaches are widely and validly used for a variety of good reasons, including costs. And they are used in relation to the necessity of having a very strict environmental design in order to compare specific subgroups of a population on a set of specific parameters (Golledge & Stimson, 1987, p. 24).

6.4.1 Haphazard, Convenience, or Accidental Sampling

Here the main aim is to obtain what is supposed to be a cross-section of people or a group of interested people. Many of the surveys on topical issues conducted by the media use this approach, through procedures such as phone-ins (where the respondent is self-selected), or a reporter approaches a "sample" of people in the street for their views. A report on the results of this type of survey will be unclear, haphazard, and marred by the self-selectivity of respondents, and they do not furnish reliable estimates of population views on the topic. It is dangerous, misleading, and fundamentally incorrect to make inferences to the population from the information collected through such approaches. All they do is give an idea of what the people who just happened to take part in the survey thought about an issue, and the results may well reflect the views of a prejudiced group on a particular issue.

6.4.2 Purposive, Judgmental, or Expert Choice Sampling

Here the researcher decides there is a group of people who have a lot of experience or possess much knowledge about the issue being investigated and can thus give an "expert" opinion or view on a topic. It is seminal that such a sample of experts will represent an informed view on the particular issue under investigation. Often relevant research is done in this way, as are surveys into phenomena such as economic conditions or a socioeconomic issue.

6.4.3 Quota Sampling

This involves getting a group—such as 100 people from a particular age category with a specified level of income—who might be thought to share other commonalities of interest or behavior. Much social and behavioral research is based on small-group quota samples, whereby sets of clearly specified groups of 20–40 people are compared to test for differences between those sets with respect to certain behavioral characteristics.

6.5 Data Sources for Sampling

If it is essential to collect information from individual people, households, firms, or some other PSUs, then it is necessary to identify a *target population* that comprises the universe of PSUs from which we wish to sample. That means that we need to have some sort of "list" or another *sample frame* that comprises the target population. Sometimes such a "list" is readily available, but often that will not be the case. And usually research being conducted that requires data collection though some sort of systematic sampling procedure is, in fact, being done so within a geographically bounded area, such as a suburb, a metropolitan city, or a region, but sometimes data needs to be collected from across the whole nation.

6.5.1 The Census

One of the most common sources for sampling in survey research is the *census*. The census is an attempt to enumerate the population, but sometimes—as in the United States—data on the characteristics of people, households, and dwellings is sample-based and not enumeration-derived. It provides data on people, households, and dwellings at a series of different levels of spatial aggregation and disaggregation, from the block level up to the nation. The census does not provide us with an actual list of the households or the members in households living in dwellings from which data was collected in a census. That is forbidden by the strict privacy requirements under which census bureaus operate by legislation. As a result, the census cannot be used strictly as a source from which to draw a sample of a specific group of people, such as divorced persons or females ages 40–60 years who are in the labor force.

Thus, what the census does provide us with is an *aggregate enumeration* of the number of people, households, or dwellings within explicit bounded areas at different levels of spatial scale, which may be as small as blocks or areas with 200–500 dwellings in them.

What we can do is to use such small-area census data to help us draw a random sample of dwellings, and once chosen, to then sample individuals within those dwellings for a general population-wide sample survey. Having this information on a small-area basis—for example, across a town, a region, a city, a county, a state, or the nation—means that we can use census data to enable us to draw a probability random sample of dwellings for the purpose of conducting social surveys. That is typically done using *multistage cluster sampling* (as discussed above in Section 6.3.4).

For example, imagine that we are conducting a survey of adult people in households across a metropolitan city area with a population of 1 million and that we have decided to have a sampling fraction of 1 in 500, which would generate a sample size of 2,000. What we could do is to randomly select census blocks on the basis of selection probability being proportional to the size of their populations relative to the city's population. We would cumulatively list all the blocks, select a random number between 1 and 500 (say, 400). The first block to be drawn would be that one on the list where the cumulative population of 400 falls, and we would then proceed to systematically select blocks with the cumulative populations of 900, 1,300, 1,700 . . . and so on. That way we would then be able to go into the selected blocks and then randomly select a dwelling in each one and then randomly select, from among the adults age 18 years and above, the person to interview. The problem is that that approach means we would have to go into a very large number of blocks across the whole city, go into each block and list the dwellings, and then randomly select one within each block in order to conduct the interviews. That would be expensive and time-consuming, and it would mean that we would have to have people working on block listing across the whole city in order to randomly select the dwellings in which to interview someone.

To avoid such a costly and cumbersome process, typically what happens is that we first *stratify* the city into, say, its local council areas, and randomly select, say, 10 of the 40 such areas, that being done on the basis of selection being proportional to population size. That means we only have to focus our field effort into 10 larger areas across the city. We would then randomly select, say, 10 blocks within each of the 10 council areas—again on a proportionality-to-size basis. That means we would be now focusing on 10 × 10 = 100 blocks. To get our sample of 2,000, we would go into each of the 100 blocks, block-list the dwellings, and draw a sample of dwellings again proportional to size. That would then give us our sample of 2,000 randomly selected dwellings in which we would then choose randomly a person age 18 years and above. That multistage cluster probability sampling approach thus means a spatial concentration of effort in selecting the dwellings and for interviewing respondents. Disaggregated census data is used to enable us to achieve that outcome. An easy to follow illustration of how to design a multistage area sample is given in Warwick and Lininger (1975, Chap. 5), which the reader is urged to consult.

6.5.2 Random-Digit Dialing for Telephone Surveys

An alternative approach to using census data to derive a multistage cluster sample frame is to use *random-digit dialing* in telephone surveying as a mode for collecting social survey data in a general population sample survey. Ideally, telephone directories could be used as an alternative, but, because typically as many as 25–30% of households choose to not have a listed telephone number, using the telephone white pages would give a biased sample. Thus, in our example of the city of 1 million, which may have 450,000 households, we could generate a sample frame through computer-generated random telephone numbers.

We can usually obtain from a telephone company the geographic areas to which the prefix (the first three to four digits) in a telephone number refers. With that information we can then match those telephone prefix districts to aggregations of area blocks and use census data to tell us the number of households in each of the telephone prefix areas. We then know what proportion of the households in our 2,000 sample need to come from each telephone prefix district, again using the proportionality to population/household size rule using census data. That then enables us to determine the "quota" of telephone numbers from which we need to obtain an interview of a person over 18 years of age (again, that person being randomly selected from within each household) in each of the telephone prefix districts. Typically up to five or six randomly generated telephone numbers need to be generated to get a domestic number, as against a business number, and often up to four or five callbacks may be necessary to obtain the interview with the randomly selected person age 18 years and over in that household.

6.5.3 Lists or Directories of Specific Populations

Sometimes it is possible to obtain a list or directory that identifies the PSUs in the target population from which we want to draw a random sample. For example, in the United States there are voter registration lists, and in Australia there are electoral rolls, both of which list people eligible to vote in elections. But such a list excludes non-nationals and, in the case of the United States, those choosing not to register to vote. But if one were conducting a study of voter behavior and attitudes, then such lists could be used to represent the target population sampling frame, and a random sample of voters could be drawn systematically from that list as it relates to the geographic area in which we are interested. Similarly, in studies that might focus on the activities of firms in an industry, it is possible that industry or trade associations will have directories or lists of firms that can form a sampling frame of the target population, and again a sample of PSUs could be drawn.

6.5.4 Sampling When There Is Not a Listing of the Target Population

Unfortunately, more often than not, it is *not* possible to access a listing of the members of the target population being investigated and from which one wants to draw a sample. Much research into human behavior targets a very specific population, such as elderly people, households living below the poverty line, or people with a specific disability. When the focus is on such a specific subgroup of the population, it is absolutely essential to precisely specify the target population in terms of the explicit characteristics of the PSU and conform to that definition. For example, households living in poverty would need to be specified in terms of explicit measures of benchmarked limits of total household weekly/monthly income for specific types of households and possibly also taking account of before and after housing costs.

When the target population is very specifically defined in terms of the characteristics of the PSUs comprising that population, then significant additional costs are involved and more time needed in drawing a sample using data sources such as the census, or when using random-digit dialing, to generate a sample. Our target population may represent only a small proportion, such as 10% of the total population. That then necessitates considerable "oversampling" when using a general population sampling frame, as there will be so much "wastage" of "nonrelevant"/"noneligible" sampling units that do *not* conform to the definition of our PSUs. That may necessitate a "screening interview" approach to eliminate up to 90% of the dwellings/households contacted through a general population sampling frame in order to get the required number of eligible PSUs to form the sample of our target population.

However, when the specific target population is a subset of the total population, as in a census, it is possible to identify, on a small-area basis, where the spatial concentrations of the target population (such as older people) live, as most socioeconomic dimensions of the total population are unevenly distributed across space. Thus, it is often possible to use census data as a device to *stratify* the sample frame in order to focus effort more on those areas where it is known that there are high concentrations of the target population.

6.5.5 Piggybacking onto Existing Surveys

Sometimes it is sensible for the researcher to collect primary data through a survey approach by "piggybacking" onto existing surveys to obtain new perspectives on a topic. That is done by adding new questions to an existing *omnibus survey* or a *periodic survey* and also by phrasing questions in objective terms so that responses can be compared across datasets.

In transportation and travel behavior research, Richardson and Wolf (2001) discuss the need for piggybacking being due to the fact that "larger samples and lengthy questionnaires can often seem as being necessary to capture the variety of travel behaviors . . . and adding to existing surveys may be a more effective way of identifying emerging travel behaviors" (p. 269). For example, in the United States, Pratt (2000) has conducted her travel behavior research by piggybacking onto several major U.S. surveys such as the Nationwide Personal Transportation Survey, American Housing Survey, Current Population Survey, National Longitudinal Surveys of Labor Market Experience, Survey of Income and Program Participation, and Characteristics of Business Owners Survey. Such piggybacking is seen as useful by Pratt in addressing issues such as travel behavior because adding standardized questions to several surveys provides the opportunity for multidimensional data merging. Emerging behaviors can be identified by adding "screening" questions to an existing survey. Adding selected questions to large surveys provides a useful source of information for monitoring trends.

6.5.6 Automated Data Computer Systems

Increasingly it is becoming common to use nonconventional sources of data to assist in the analysis of some aspects of human spatial behavior, and in particular in travel analyses (Richardson & Wolf, 2001). That includes electronic phone books, mobile phones, palm-held computer technology, and the Internet, which, when combined with databases on the geographic distribution of phenomena such as employment, "can provide a good foundation for the mapping of the approaches for use in destination choice modeling" (p. 275).

An overview of the use of automated data computer systems, in the context of metropolitan travel surveys in Atlanta, is given by Wolf, Guensler, Washington, and Frank (2000), who refer to three types of automated data computer: passive in-vehicle GPS systems, electronic travel devices with GPS, and comprehensive in-vehicle data collections systems with both GPS technology and an engine-monitoring device. Asakura and Hato (2000) refer to the possibility of using the positioning function of mobile phones to collect information for travel and activity surveys, describing how that is applied to determine the location of a traveler in time and space. This is seen as an alternative to the use of portable GPS systems, and the mobile phone provides a two-way communication capability during a survey to give the researcher information from respondents.

For investigations into household activity agenda, increasingly the trend is to automate all or part of the in-depth interview task, using a sequence of computer-generated forms and dialogs in order to reduce interview time. But, as Doherty (2003) warns, "the resulting implications for data quality are still relatively unknown" (p. 10).

An example of the retrieval of information over the Internet is the interactive survey technique REACT!, based on the CHASE (Computational Household Activity Scheduling Elicitor) (Lee, Sabetiashraf, Doherty, Rindt, & McNally, 2000). REACT! is designed to allow respondents involved in a survey to collect information on a household's activity agenda to download the CHASE program over the Internet and use their own computers to enter activity choices and then upload them to a server. Palm-top computer technology is also being used to implement a self-completion electronic travel diary in which feedback about recorded travel patterns is given to respondents in an attempt to bring about behavioral change (Thorpe, Law, & Nelson, 2000).

6.6 Collecting Information from People Using a Survey Instrument

Having discussed the issue of sampling from target populations, a further important issue is the design and implementation of an instrument for collecting data from respondents to a survey in order to generate information about the issues with which the researcher is concerned. That involves:

- Designing an appropriate *data collection instrument* (which typically is a survey *questionnaire*) and then going through a process of collecting the required information from the survey *respondents* or *subjects*.
- Considering how to design a survey data collection instrument—such as a questionnaire—and implementing a process through which data is elicited from respondents in order to minimize nonsampling error and bias.

Of course, the mode of survey chosen to collect data will influence how these issues are addressed.

Most of the many standard survey research textbooks provide guidance on survey questionnaire design. Later in this chapter we cite literature that the reader may wish to consult. For an overview of survey interviewing theory and techniques and their applications, see Beed and Stimson (1985) and Lavrakas (1987).

6.6.1 Addressing Sources of Nonsampling Error and Bias

Whatever the mode of data collection used involving a survey, the researcher needs to be aware that any process of asking questions and soliciting answers from people involves a complex set of tasks, and that the process itself—as well as the instrument design—engenders *nonsampling error* and *bias* that affect the *validity* and *reliability* of data generated through the survey process. As we discussed in Chapters 2 and 3 in Part I, the issues of "error" and "bias" are of vital importance. The *sources* of error and bias encountered in use of survey research methods to generate information relate not only to the issues of sampling—as already discussed earlier in this chapter—but also to nonsampling sources that involve error and bias arising from *survey instrument design, interviewer behavior,* and *respondent behavior.*

One of the main causes of nonsampling error and bias is *poor questionnaire design*, so it is vital that the researcher adheres to well-established principles in designing the questions asked in a survey instrument. But errors and bias can also arise due to cognitive difficulties respondents encounter in answering questions asked of them in surveys. Errors and bias arise also from the quality of and variations in interviewer performance. Those errors and biases are sometimes referred to as *observation* or *measurement error*, and have been a source of methodological research inquiry since the 1920s.

6.6.2 A Model Conceptualizing the Complexity of the Question–Answer Process

The complexity of the question–answer situation in survey research has been conceptualized and addressed by Cannell, Miller, and Oksenberg (1981), who proposed the model for this process reproduced as Figure 6.1. What that model does is to set up a "job description" for what a respondent must go through to successfully perform a difficult task. The model indicates how the question–answer process includes a cognitive processing of information and an assessment of what information is needed to give an accurate response. It includes the retrieval of information and its organization in response to the way questions are worded and how they are asked by interviewers. It involves giving a response judged to be accurate by the respondent. The respondent may modify his or her response based on comprehension of the question, cues from the environment, and cues from the respondent's own beliefs and value system. The giving of accurate responses is characterized by conformity, desirability, acquiescence, incompleteness, and other biases.

Thus, responding to questions is a complex process. As shown in Figure 6.1, the model proposed by Cannell and colleagues (1981) conceptualizes five or seven steps (as indicated in the diagram) in the question-answering process. That involves the following tasks for the respondent answering a survey question:

- Comprehending the questionnaire
- Information processing
- Evaluating the response
- Evaluating the response vis-à-vis personal goals extraneous to the survey
- Giving the response perceived to be accurate
- Choosing or modifying the response through reliance on extraneous situational cues
- Giving an inaccurate or incomplete response.

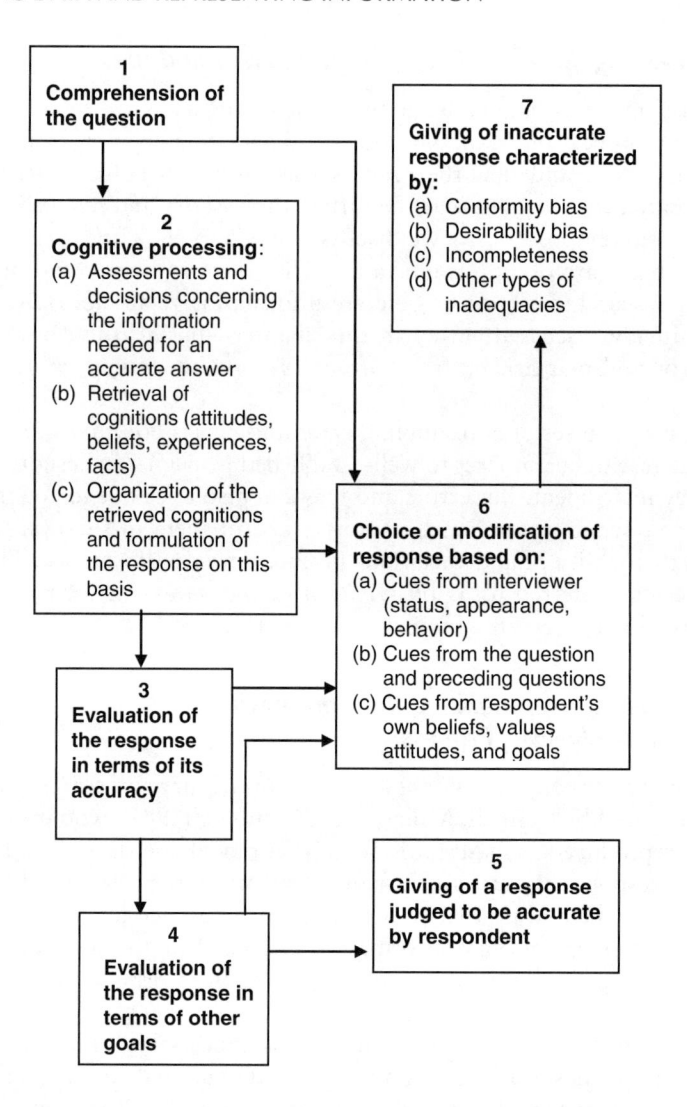

108 COLLECTING DATA AND REPRESENTING INFORMATION

```
┌─────────────────────┐
│ 1                   │
│ Comprehension of    │
│ the question        │
└──────────┬──────────┘
           │
           ▼
┌─────────────────────────┐        ┌──────────────────────────────┐
│ 2                       │        │ 7                            │
│ Cognitive processing:   │        │ Giving of inaccurate         │
│ (a) Assessments and     │        │ response characterized       │
│     decisions concerning│        │ by:                          │
│     the information     │        │ (a) Conformity bias          │
│     needed for an       │        │ (b) Desirability bias        │
│     accurate answer     │        │ (c) Incompleteness           │
│ (b) Retrieval of        │        │ (d) Other types of           │
│     cognitions (attitudes,│      │     inadequacies             │
│     beliefs, experiences,│       └──────────────────────────────┘
│     facts)              │
│ (c) Organization of the │        ┌──────────────────────────────┐
│     retrieved cognitions│        │ 6                            │
│     and formulation of  │        │ Choice or modification of    │
│     the response on this│───────▶│ response based on:           │
│     basis               │        │ (a) Cues from interviewer    │
└──────────┬──────────────┘        │     (status, appearance,     │
           │                       │     behavior)                │
           ▼                       │ (b) Cues from the question   │
┌─────────────────────┐            │     and preceding questions  │
│ 3                   │            │ (c) Cues from respondent's   │
│ Evaluation of       │───────────▶│     own beliefs, values      │
│ the response        │            │     attitudes, and goals     │
│ in terms of its     │            └──────────────────────────────┘
│ accuracy            │
└──────────┬──────────┘            ┌──────────────────────────────┐
           │                       │ 5                            │
           ▼                       │ Giving of a response         │
┌─────────────────────┐            │ judged to be accurate        │
│ 4                   │───────────▶│ by respondent                │
│ Evaluation of       │            └──────────────────────────────┘
│ the response in     │
│ terms of other      │
│ goals               │
└─────────────────────┘
```

FIGURE 6.1. A model of the question–answer process. From Cannell, Miller, and Oksenberg (1981). Copyright 1981 by the American Sociological Association. Reprinted by permission.

Cannell and colleagues saw the process as characterized by *conformity, desirability,* and *acquiescence,* among other issues. They have this to say:

> The cognitive and motivational difficulties in answering the questions are more common and more serious than is generally realized. Questions can often be ambiguous in ways that can have important implications for interpreting survey data. Questions may make excessive demands on the cognitive skills of respondents by making unrealistic demands on respondent's memory or ability to process and integrate retrieved information . . . [and] . . . the psychological implication of providing responses that truly reflect the respondent's beliefs or experiences may lead to suppressing the information or distorting it into a more acceptable response. . . . [The] . . . effect is to distort survey data. That is, the requested information varies from truth in some predictable deviation. (pp. 395–396)

Cannell and colleagues (1981) go on to suggest that failure to report information is the *false negative* and is due to the respondent's failure to retrieve and process information because of memory lapse, carelessness, or unwillingness to make the effort necessary to retrieve the information accurately and fully. This form of inadequate response is frequent in the reporting of past events and behavior. Failure of reporting of events, behavior, and other information is seen as the *false positive*. Frequently, it occurs when time reference is specified in a question, where false reports may reflect faulty recall or be more purposeful.

Experiments run by Cannell, Fisher, and Bakker (1965) and by Sudman and Bradburn (1974) have revealed that the underreporting and nonreporting of events appear to be related to three factors:

- The *time lapse* between events to be reported and the survey interview
- The *salience* of events for respondents
- A respondent's perception of the *social desirability* of the event.

Cannell and colleagues discuss how the *question–answering process* presents a difficult task for the respondents to a survey to undertake. They see that level of difficulty as being "the sum of cognition demands imposed by the requirements of information retrieval and processing and the affective demands imposed by the threat of the information requested" (p. 404). Thus, the quality of the respondent's performance will be a "function of the difficulty of the task and the level of the effort achieved by the respondent" (p. 404).

It is of vital importance for a researcher conducting empirical investigations into the actions and experiences of people in spaces and environments—where typically a medium for information collection and data generation is through the design and use of a survey questionnaire—to be acutely aware of, and be concerned about, the issues of nonsampling survey error and bias that arise from the design of a survey instrument and its use in the question–answering process. It may seem paradoxical that researchers investigating human behavior in spatial contexts have taken considerable care to develop a research paradigm that includes psychological variables, while in practice, in probably the majority of instances, their empirical studies and the data variables needed to investigate their research concerns and to operationalize their models tend to be based on the collection of survey data that is unlikely to have been incorporated in the instrument design and data collection process procedures that adequately address the complexities inherent in the question–answering process as just outlined. If that is the case, then it is evident that much of the data on which much research is based is likely to be fraught with considerable observational and/or measurement errors and biases because of the indeterminate problems of error bias inherent in the question–answering process.

6.6.3 Instrument Design and Question Construction

Collecting data to generate information through a survey can occur through many mediums, the most common being to design and administer a *survey instrument* that is commonly called a *questionnaire*, which consists of a series of structured questions the survey respondent is asked to answer. The business of asking questions to elicit *complete*, *accurate*, and *reliable* information that is required to address the issues with which research is concerned is both an *art* and a *science*. Questionnaire design and question construction need to be approached with caution (even trepidation), and it is important that researchers obtain professional advice for this task. An important early book on the art of asking questions was by Payne (1951). Many survey research textbooks cover this issue in great detail, and classics—such as that by Moser and Kalton (1971)—provide a basic set of "do's" and "don'ts" in designing a questionnaire.

As the questionnaire is often the backbone of the data collection process where it is necessary for primary data to be collected from people who comprise the PSUs in a sample, it is essential that questionnaires are designed so as to minimize bias in reporting and to maximize the likelihood of generating information that is reliable and valid.

6.6.3.1 Types of Information Typically Generated Through Questionnaires

In general it is possible to distinguish between three types of information that are generated through a survey questionnaire:

1. *Facts* such as data for respondents' gender, age, occupation, income, and so on, which is then used to provide information about the socioeconomic and demographic characteristics of respondents.
2. *Opinions* which are responses given by respondents on their views on specific topics or events, such as their assessment of a political leader, their preferred shopping places, and so on.
3. *Attitudes* which are elicited from respondents, usually collected via a procedure asking respondents to rate or rank the importance of a phenomenon or to rate or rank their preference for, say, a set of shopping activities. That rating or ranking is often undertaken using a semantic differential to differentiate between opposites and using a scaling procedure such as a *Likert scale*, whereby the respondent is asked to rate a phenomenon on a scale of 1 to 5, 1 to 7, or such like, thus representing their attitudes to a set of stimuli, such as the attributes of a shopping center.

In using surveys to collect information on the activities and experiences of people in spaces and environments, the emphasis often will be on obtaining data on aspects of overt behavioral acts in a time–space context. That usually involves respondents providing information on past behaviors, and it involves the problem of ex post facto recall.

6.6.3.2 Question Wording

There are a number of basic rules to follow in the design of questionnaires. The researcher needs to constantly remember that poor questionnaire wording is a major source of error and bias in the collection of information through surveys. The following are a set of fundamental principles to follow in questionnaire design and question wording:

- Avoid questions that are insufficiently specific
- Use simple language
- Avoid ambiguity
- Avoid vague words
- Avoid leading questions
- Avoid hypothetical questions
- Avoid personalized questions
- Avoid embarrassing questions
- Avoid questions on periodic behavior
- Avoid questions involving memory recall
- Questions should be relevant

- Short questions are best
- Avoid negative questions
- Avoid biased items and opinions.

Question effects that may induce bias also lead to the necessity of ensuring that one always includes a "don't know" category for all questions, and also ensuring that all categories for potential answers to questions are *mutually exclusive*.

6.6.3.3 Open and Closed Questions

There has been much debate and research on the merits of *open* and *closed questions* and their use in survey questionnaires.

1. In an *open question*, the respondent is given the freedom to decide the aspect, form, detail, and length of his or her answer to the question, and the interviewer must read as much as possible of the respondent's answer. If a self-completion survey instrument (as in a mail survey) is being used, it is entirely up to the respondent as to what written answer is given in response to the open-ended question. But we must remember that the answers to open-ended questions do eventually need to be coded into categories or classes in order to conduct analyses of the responses, and in particular to cross-tabulate the responses or an aspect of the responses to an open-ended question against other data variables, such as the gender, age, income level, and so on, of respondents. Respondent responses to open-ended questions might also be analyzed through procedures such as *content analysis*, which also leads to a degree of categorization. In addition, responses to open-ended questions may also be used in survey reporting to illustrate a point by quoting from one or a number of the answers given by respondents to the question.

2. In a *closed* or *precoded* question, either the respondent is given a limited number of answers from which to choose his or her answer, or the question is asked by the interviewer as an open-ended question with the interviewer then allocating the answer to the appropriate predetermined category or categories. The latter may offer two or more relevant answers, in which they are *dichotomous* or *multichoice* questions. One risk involved in using the precoded question is that it may force respondents into a category in which they do not belong. However, for reasons relating to cost and time, using precoded questions is usually preferable. The presurvey *pilot testing* of open-ended questions can enable the researcher to categorize the range of answers relevant for the purpose of the research so that closed questions are used in the instrument for the survey proper. *Closed questions are* also used extensively in survey instruments where respondents are asked to respond to a question rating the degree to which they agree/disagree with a statement or proposition or how they might rate something on a *Likert Scale* of 5, 7, or more points. Such scaling is used extensively to collect information on people's attitudes toward phenomena.

6.6.3.4 The Ordering of Questions

It is important to be aware that the order in which questions are asked will affect the answers respondents give, as well as the refusal rate to answer questions. Thus, it is best to begin with questions that will set the respondent at ease and to build rapport between the interviewer and the respondent. The early questions asked in a questionnaire need to ensure that the respondent's interest is captured so as to get the respondent to commit to completing the task. After these preliminaries, questions may proceed in a *logical sequence*, so as to move from topic to topic in such a way as to indicate to the respondent the relationship between the questions. When a break occurs, the interviewer should explain the shift from one topic to the next. In a self-completion questionnaire, the written interactions should achieve that.

An important issue in questionnaire design and question construction is the use of *funneling* and *filtering sequences*. Start with a general broad question about the topic, then narrow down into the more detailed specification (funneling). Depending on the answer given to a question in a sequence of questions, the respondent may need to skip to an item later in the questionnaire (filtering).

A further consideration that comes in questionnaire design is the use of *randomizing* to vary the order of the questions from one respondent to the next when respondents are asked about different aspects of a particular phenomenon or belief. Randomizing the order of questions overcomes the problem of one answer influencing a later answer. One can randomize the order in which, for example, a series of attitude-scale items are being asked of respondents so that the ordering of items on the scale will be different for each respondent.

One also needs to be aware that *respondent fatigue* can occur when dealing with a long list of items. One way of addressing the bias effect of that problem is to randomize the sequencing of questions among respondents.

6.6.3.5 Other Issues in Questionnaire Design

There are many other issues in this extremely complex area of survey instrument and questionnaire design that can affect error and bias in survey data generation. They include:

- The *formats* for responses
- The use of *contingency* questions
- The use of *matrix* questions
- The use of *sketches* and/or *pictures* in the pursuit of symbolic responses
- The use of *flashcards* by the interviewer
- The complex use of *interviewer instructions* and/or *written instructions to the respondent* in self-completion questionnaires.

Questionnaire design and question-wording issues become particularly important in self-completion survey information collection modes where the opportunity for interviewer–respondent interaction is not feasible. In self-completion modes, the respondent is totally dependent on the format of the questionnaire and the written form of each question in providing interpretability in guiding him or her through the process of answering each question in the sequence as presented in the questionnaire. Detailed *pretesting* or *pilot testing* of the survey instrument is thus crucial in overcoming many of the pitfalls and in avoiding the many common deficiencies in survey instrument design.

6.7 Respondent Behavior

The complexities involved in the model of the question-and-answer process identified in the Cannell and colleagues (1981) model (refer back to Figure 6.1) places considerable emphasis on the *motivational* and *social desirability* effects for the survey respondent, on one hand, and on the *cognitive demands* of answering questions, on the other hand.

Bradburn, Sudman, and Associates (1979), and earlier work by Warner (1965), provide perspectives on the motivational effects and of the social desirability effects of the interview process for survey respondents. As discussed earlier, respondents may fail to report information (the false negative) due to memory lapse, carelessness, or unwillingness to make the effort to retrieve information. And respondents may fail to report events, behavior, and other information (the false positive) as a result of lapsed time, the salience of an event, and the respondent's perception of the social desirability of an event. As outlined by Groves (1987), considerable efforts have been directed toward developing techniques to be employed in the interview process to increase positive feedback and establish rapport with the respondent to motivate him or her to diligently attend to the demands of questions and to give accurate answers. Much attention has also been directed to finding ways to limit the deleterious impacts of the perceived social desirability effects of questions through the use of open-ended questions and processing techniques.

Work by Cannell and Fowler (1963), Neter and Waksberg (1964), and Biderman and Lynch (1981) pioneered research into the problem of *recall* of events in the question–answering process, promoting the notion that there needs to be incorporated into the interview process means of cueing the retrieval of memories of past events and behaviors by finding *temporal landmarks* that are useful to remind respondents of the time (and place) of occurrences of such things. Investigations have also focused on the effects of present mental states of respondents on measures of their past mental states, on mechanisms by which content effects come about, and on the nature of representation of past events for reporting them in an interview situation. Survey design approaches to address such issues have sought to reduce measurement error through the use of questions that prompt memory retrieval more efficiently.

6.7.1 Interviewer Training and Standardizing Interview Behavior

It is good survey practice to ensure that in the face-to-face and telephone-interviewing modes of survey data collection, interviewers are thoroughly briefed and put through a training session to adequately prepare them to do an effective job in administering the survey instrument and to collect and record respondent answers to the survey questions. And it is important that the survey administrative and management arrangements that are implemented are such to ensure the effective monitoring of how diligently interviewers perform their task.

The concern over the effect of interviewers on responses to surveys and on data quality has been a fertile field for methodological research and analysis since the 1920s. In a pioneering study Rice (1929) investigated the causes of destitution in the United States. Two different interviewers were used in the collection of primary data, and they produced materially different data. The first interviewer was a prohibitionist, and respondents that the interviewer interviewed were found to be destitute because of overindulgence in alcohol as the main reason. The second interviewer was a socialist, and that person's respondents were found in the main to be destitute due to social and economic circumstances. With the rise of opinion polling in the late 1940s, a number of studies documented a major concern over interviewer-induced bias, particularly in pre-election polling (Caholun, Tamulonis, & Verner, 1947; Cantrill, 1947). Later, in a study conducted by the National Opinion Research Center into the effects of interviewers on survey results, Hyman and colleagues (1954) found that three kinds of interviewer expectations produced bias. Those interviewer expectations are:

1. *Role expectation*, whereby certain responses from a respondent are expected on the basis of their belonging to a particular group, such as women, businessmen, or blacks, which is a stereotyping of respondents by the interviewer.
2. *Attitude structure expectations*, whereby an interviewer expects a respondent's views to be internally consistent.
3. *Probability expectations*, whereby the interviewer expects certain responses because of his or her beliefs about sentiments prevailing in the population at the time of the survey.

By the late 1960s, a lot of research had been conducted using laboratory and other experimental designs to investigate and measure interview effects on survey data. For example, Rosenthal (1966) and Rosenthal and Rosnow (1969) found that interviewer effects related both to their own opinions and to their expectations for the respondent. Schuman and Converse (1971) demonstrated that the characteristics of interviewers (for example, race) influenced their reporting of racial attitudes by respondents who were black. Sudman, Bradburn, Blair, and Stocking (1977) found that interviewer training and the resultant standardization of interviewer behavior helped reduce bias and control for interview efforts. That included:

- Stressing the importance both of appearing neutral and of being accepting toward all responses.
- Standardizing questionnaire wording and the administration of the questionnaire.
- Standardizing the nondirective probing procedures used by interviewers.

During the 1970s, the Survey Research Center in the Institute of Social Research at the University of Michigan conducted a series of experimental studies to develop good working techniques for interviewers following the evaluation of interviewer performance (Cannell, Fowler, & Marquis, 1968; Cannell, Lawson, & Hausser, 1975; Cannell, Marquis, & Laurent, 1977; Mathiowetz & Cannell, 1980).

Prescriptive procedures for controlling interviewer performance were developed, the goal being to minimize and even eliminate nonsampling error and bias. They include approaches such as:

1. Randomization of interviewer assignments.
2. Monitoring interviewer performance, made much easier with the advent of CATI systems.
3. The development and implementation of standardized procedures for the interviewer with respect to interviewer behavior in:
   - Asking questions
   - Repeating questions
   - Defining/clarifying issues raised by the respondent vis-à-vis a question
   - Giving feedback to the respondent
   - Spacing/timing the asking of questions; and the clarity with which a question is asked, including speech inflection
   - Giving the respondent positive feedback and eliminating negative feedback.

The purpose of such interventions to manage interviewer behavior and to standardize the interviewing process is to minimize variation in interviewer behavior.

Interviewer procedures need to take into account the difficulty of the task, as outlined earlier in the Cannell and colleagues (1981) model of the intricacies involved in the question–answering process (as depicted in Figure 6.1). Cannell and colleagues (p. 405) suggest that in order to improve the validity of the survey responses, techniques and standards of measurement need to be employed that are aimed at:

- Teaching the respondent what is expected of him or her in general in order to perform a task properly
- Informing the respondent and providing cues as to how to be most efficient in answering specific questions
- Encouraging the respondent to work diligently to recall and organize information and to report even potentially embarrassing and personal information
- Ensuring standard techniques for delivering the questionnaire by all interviewers to achieve greater comparability of interviewer behavior.

6.8 Conclusion

This chapter has canvassed the wide range of issues that researchers have to address in undertaking the collection of data to generate information using a survey research approach. That involves making multiple decisions in choosing an appropriate survey mode, making choices regarding sampling and sample design, and addressing nonsampling procedures and aspects of survey instrument design and administration to respondents. We have looked at both nonprobability and probability survey designs. And most importantly, we have emphasized how it is necessary to use a probability sampling design if the intention of the research is to use the sample data to generate estimates of the population parameters and if the intent is to make inferences about the prevalence and magnitude of a phenomenon in the target population from which the researcher has sampled.

The chapter has discussed in some detail those important issues concerning sampling and questionnaire design, and has also provided an overview of the need to adequately address the issue of interviewer training and behavior standardization. In particular, the discussion highlights the necessity of the researcher to be cognizant of the measures that are both necessary and appropriate to address in the design and the conduct of a survey. These issues are vital and are crucial to address in order to collect data that is accurate and to generate information that is valid and reliable. In short, the researcher must be aware of the concept of *total survey error* as set out in the framework in Figure 2.2 in Chapter 2 in Part I. The objective must be to use best practice survey design and management procedures in order to properly address both sampling and nonsampling in order to minimize total survey error and bias. These issues may also be important for the researcher to address in collection of data through other approaches, such as experiments, which are discussed in Chapter 7.

CHAPTER 7

Extrapolating from Controlled Conditions to the Real World

7.1 Introduction

Increasingly it is common for researchers to use *controlled settings* to run *experiments*, free from confounding influences, in order both to develop and implement models and to test theories that have sets of assumptions that act as constraints to give insights into how processes work in natural and tightly controlled situations, and to enable exploratory renderings and manipulations of constructs and structures prior to engaging in carefully designed experimentation. *Experimental designs* are being widely used in research investigating human behavior in spatial settings, and in particular to investigate phenomena such as the cognition of space and how people acquire spatial knowledge.

This chapter discusses some of the issues researchers need to be aware of in designing experiments. It looks at a number of ways to conduct experiments, including *virtual experiments* and *simulations*. In particular we discuss *computational process model approaches*.

7.2 Some Key Issues in Using Controlled Settings to Run Experiments

There are a number of issues about which researchers need to be aware in using controlled settings to run experiments. Two in particular are important: (1) how to maintain *ecological validity* and the issue of *extrapolating* from the results of an experiment, and (2) how the *laboratory* can be used to *represent* "real-world" situations. These are discussed in the sections that follow.

7.2.1 Maintaining Ecological Validity

The most critical problem faced when engaged in *experimental procedures* is to ensure—as much as possible—that ecological validity is maintained. Doing so implies that an activity or experiment conducted in the *controlled setting* has some "validity" when the results are interpreted in relation to the "real world," or that extrapolation of experimental results to the real world can be done so with confidence. For the most part, this problem of ecological validity is handled through the different research designs, including sampling procedures, discussed in previous chapters in Part II of this book.

Probability sampling ensures the greatest confidence in extrapolating from controlled conditions (the sample) to the real world (the relevant target population). But much research does not use probability-sampling procedures. This is often the case with pilot experiments, case studies, or small-sample probability and nonprobability design studies, particularly where the intent is to explore whether a hypothesized relation differs (or not) from chance. Many individually based behavioral experiments fall into this category, usually because the time taken for the experiment (response times), the amount of supervision required for data collection, and concerns for the wellness of participants (for example, relating to fatigue or boredom) all mitigate against the use of large numbers of participants. Both time and cost are important constraints under these circumstances. The experimenter is often left only with the option of evaluating whether or not the data collected in an experiment differs from randomness. The results of these studies suggest outcomes that might be relevant to evaluating concepts or hypotheses, but are not usually extrapolated to make assertions about entire populations (or even subsamples of those populations).

Extrapolations from controlled experimental situations are least effective or valid when *surrogates* for real-world actions are used in the controlled experiments. An example is the use of paper-and-pencil testing of people's spatial abilities (as in standard psychometric test formats) to evaluate geoscale human spatial behaviors. Although such tests have long considered to be valid indicators of the capacity of people to perform geoscale tasks, over the last few decades researchers using such tests have produced more and more evidence that such tests are not good surrogates for many human spatial behaviors.

7.2.2 Laboratory versus Real-World Experiments

Conducting experiments in the real world can be a hazardous business. Apart from situations such as changing weather conditions, it is difficult to control for ambient noise, for unexpected intrusions into the experimental setting, and for somewhat different environmental conditions. *Laboratory experiments* are usually carried out under *controlled conditions* and usually do not suffer from the intrusions typical of real-world activities. However, while allowing the experimenter to focus only on a set of hypothesized relevant factors, the controlled laboratory setting sometimes does not allow for interactions that may be part of the real-world phenomena.

Scale also is an important factor. Thus, a set of relations that are expected to hold in the lab situation may become less relevant with a change to uncontrolled real-world (large-scale) settings. For example, distance or directional tasks may be successfully completed at the perceptual ("vista") scale, but may be much harder to determine at the large-distance geographic spaces of geocognitive examination. The reverse may be true for some "special" populations. For example, a moderately intellectually disadvantaged person may find it easy to recognize a real three-dimensional clock object in the real world, but may have difficulty recognizing an abstract two-dimensional pictorial representation of a clock object in a laboratory setting.

As researchers deal more and more with real-world settings, it has become apparent that there need not be a perfect match between results of laboratory experiments and the occurrence of equivalent objects and relations in large geocognitive environments. Nevertheless, at times, the only way a task can be confronted and a problem solved is to experiment in the controlled laboratory setting.

7.3 Ways of Conducting Experiments

Experiments can be conducted in a variety of ways, including the following:

- Laboratory experiments with different degrees of control
- Uncontrolled field experiments
- Experiments to test hypotheses
- Experiments to test theories
- Experiments to define model components
- Experiments to estimate and calibrate model parameters
- Experiments with human components
- Experiments in the physical domain
- Experiments to define relevant types of data or to build and/or manage databases
- Experiments using different age/sex/ethnic/cultural cohorts
- Experiments conducted in augmented or virtual realities.

Regardless of the type of experiment, all are deliberately designed to help solve problems, attack tasks, or help define policy. In the latter case, experiments may involve iteratively looking at scenarios and, via simulation procedures, displaying data and solving problems. Currently there is an interesting controversy over the value of conducting experiments in *virtual*—as opposed to *real*—environmental settings. The value of experimentation in a "virtual system" is in the ability to define, test, and evaluate scenarios driven by different combinations of variables that cannot be so manipulated in the real world—for example, changing building heights or adding/deleting traffic lanes, thus enabling the production of alternative scenarios for decision makers to examine.

7.3.1 Purpose of an Experiment and Evolution of Types of Experiments in Spatial Research

Types of experiments differ depending on the purpose of action. In the use of experiments to investigate aspects of human activities and experiences in spaces and environments, geographers and planners have used a number of experimental designs, including simple approaches such as getting subjects to draw sketch maps, and more complex designs involving the use of specially developed instruments and analytical procedures to collect information on people's cognitive images of large-scale environments and to represent them in diagrammatic form, and experiments using simulation procedures to investigate spatial decision choices and behavior.

For example, in a classic study that sought to define and investigate the cities of Boston, Jersey City, and Los Angeles, the planner Kevin Lynch (1960) simply asked people to draw a *sketch* of the cities in question. Participants were given a sheet of paper and a pencil, and were allocated a time interval during which they recorded locations of objects and places at perceived sites. Examination of the sketches revealed that they could be analyzed by counting and recording the frequency with which objects and places were found on the sketches. By recognizing that *sketch map* features could be recorded as "nodes," "landmarks," "paths," "edges," and "districts," a generalized city image could be produced that included only those objects and places that were designated on a significant proportion of the maps. Lynch's experiment used a nonprobability sampling design, created descriptive statistics related to feature/object/place counts, and illustrated the perceived nature of human knowledge about cities.

Another experiment aiming to conduct a similar type of study, but using a different experimental design, was that undertaken by a research team at Ohio State University in the late 1960s (Golledge, Briggs, & Demko, 1969). Whereas Lynch (1960) focused on recall of locations and labels (object names and place names), Golledge and colleagues (1969) aimed at getting geospatial information from sample participants by accessing latent information stored in the brain. Essentially, participants were queried via a *paired comparisons* strategy (for example, "Is the distance between *A* and *B* longer/shorter than the distance from *C* to *D*?"). Proximity/similarity matrices of the results of this procedure were analyzed by nonmetric multidimensional scaling procedures—for example, Kruskal's MDSCAL, later replaced by Kruskal, Young, and Seery's (1976) KYST—and a solution space was generated (that is, a space of minimal dimensionality) in which individual features were placed. A more powerful method than the earlier multidimensional scaling procedure MDSCAL, KYST uses an iterative process and steepest descent solution procedure to search for the minimal dimensioned configuration. Golledge and colleagues assumed that, by obtaining spatial relational information in this indirect way, concerns about reliability and validity of the responses could be ameliorated. Configurations so produced showed that cognitive maps were incomplete, fuzzy, in parts folded, or otherwise metrically or topologically distorted (see Figure 7.1).

Many researchers have taken a different perspective when designing experiments. Illustrating growth, change, and development over time, the evolution of experimental designs eventually led to the use of *simulation procedures* to show how constancy or change occurred in spatial distributions. For example, many geography researchers in the 1960s and 1970s evinced an interest in migration and mobility. To examine these processes, data were collected to show changes in the spatial distribution of people over time. Urban growth and change likewise was a focus of these experimental designs (Tobler, 1968). Usually spread took place via a nearest neighbor diffusion process, but much research also focused on randomized growth processes using a mean information field, a random number generator, and a negative exponential function that conditioned how spatial spread occurred (Hägerstrand, 1970). Classic simulations included those by Hägerstrand (1952, 1953) on migration fields and innovation diffusion, Morrill (1965) on the expansion of a black ghetto, and Brown (1968) on the diffusion of innovative ideas.

7.3.2 Complexity in Experiments

Experimental procedures with human participants are very time-consuming and require resources and close supervision. These factors have been emphasized through controls exerted by human subject/ethics committees whose aims include protecting participants from risk or harm. Consequently, it is very time-consuming and expensive for investigators to conduct research involving human subject experiments. Many experimental designs are *factorial* in nature, and many tasks involve *multiple trials* and/or *repetitive procedures*. This could mean 1–2 hours per person in a sample of subjects participating in an experiment. Given some scheduling restrictions, changing weather, and unexpected conditions (for example, freeway congestion), it may be difficult to run more than two people per day through the experiment. Even for participant sample sizes as small as 30–35 members, pro-

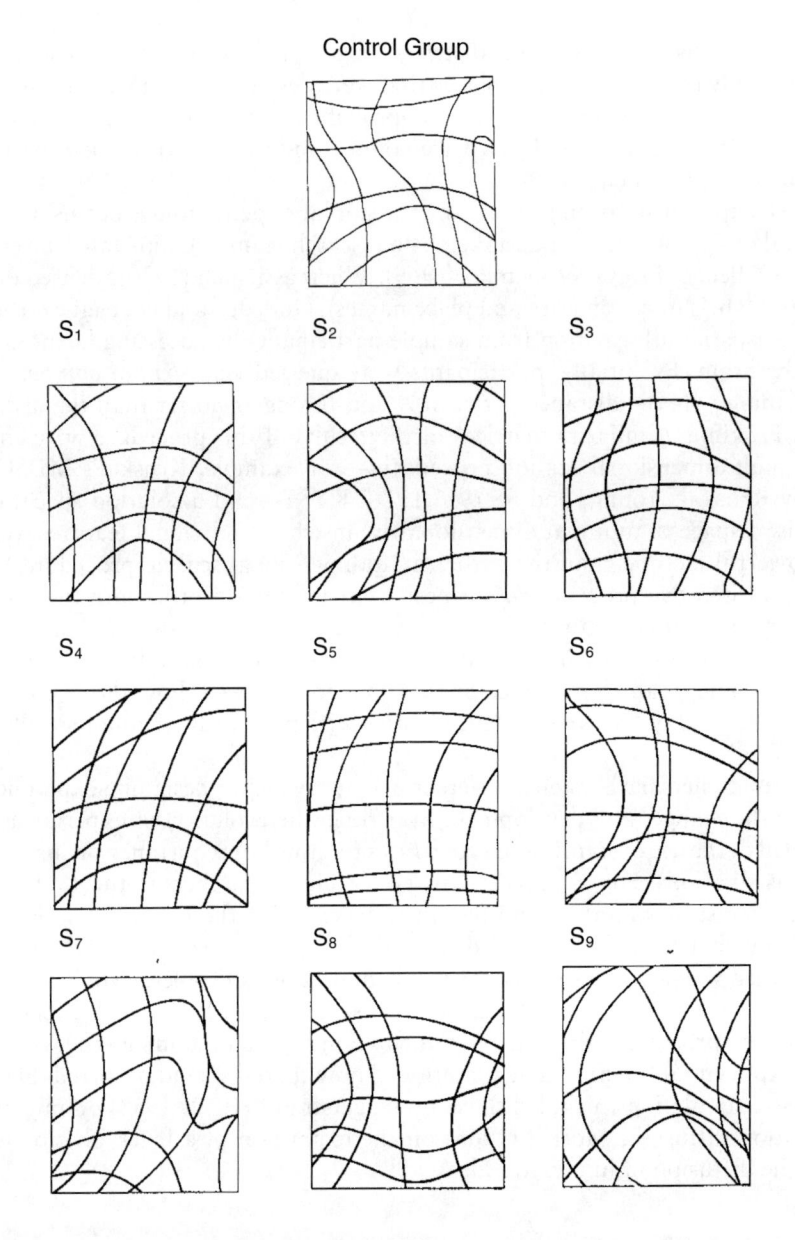

120 COLLECTING DATA AND REPRESENTING INFORMATION

FIGURE 7.1. Distorted grid maps. From Golledge (1974).

cedures could take several months to complete. This problem is not as severe in the laboratory as it is in the real environment, where interruptions and distractions beyond the control of the experimenter often occur.

A number of common approaches to conducting experiments, including virtual experiments, in the investigation of human activities and experiences in spaces and environments are discussed in the sections to follow.

7.4 Virtual Experiments

The most recent experimental settings that have attracted attention include *augmented reality*, *desktop virtual worlds*, and *immersive virtual systems*.

7.4.1 Augmented Reality

Augmented reality experimentation implies that a user superimposes a structure on a real-world setting or a representation of such a setting to "augment" one's sensing of what is "out there." A case in point might be a scenario where a participant wears special eyeglasses and carries a wearable computer. For example, in a wayfinding setting, the computer might be instructed to embed linear representation of a path through the environment using the eyeglasses worn by a traveler as an LCD screen. The traveler turns his head until the first path segment projected on the glasses would overlie a particular real-world route segment ahead of the traveler. As movement along a path occurs, relevant screen-based information keeps the traveler from veering off-path.

7.4.2 Desktop Virtual Display

A *desktop virtual display* could also be used for wayfinding and route-based learning of an environment. For example, Golledge, Dougherty, and Bell (1995) have developed a desktop virtual system that was used in environmental layout learning:

1. A simple five-by-five grid was developed as a representation of the ground floor of a building.
2. Corridors were defined along grid lines, and objects (colored shapes) were located along two prespecified routes and along neighboring corridors or end walls.
3. A participant sat in front of a computer screen and was instructed in the use of the joystick to monitor rate of travel and direction of movement. Options for rate of travel were "slow," "normal," or "fast" walking speeds.
4. The task was to successfully navigate over two partially overlapping routes. On the way, participants rotated their heads at corridor intersections, looking down each segment to observe features on the floors or walls of such corridors. Moving the joystick gave the distinct impression of traveling with an avatar that was walking along the corridor.
5. Experimental tasks included drawing route maps, locating target features, and estimating distances and directions among target features. The results were compared with the actions of a control group who learned the layout from two-dimensional maps of the environment. Results favored the virtual travelers, whose response times were quicker and whose locational recognition of objects was more accurate.

7.4.3 Immersive Virtual Systems

A more comprehensive procedure is to build a virtual world in which a person can be immersed. This is usually accomplished by wearing a head-mounted display. A simple experiment (Waller, Loomis, Golledge, & Beall, 2002) might involve:

- Designing a featureless environment
- Inserting a series of colored poles at the same height and width at specific locations
- Having participants immerse themselves in the environment by wearing a helmet with a display screen and walking to each differently colored pole in turn so that both egocentric (polar coordinate) and exocentric (Cartesian coordinate) information can be obtained.

Theoretically this should allow the experimental subject to learn feature layout and to find a path between any pairs of poles. After completing this exploratory experience, the participant is "removed" from the virtual scene and is readmitted through the same (or a new) entrance. In the meantime, all the colored poles have been removed from the setting, and the task is for the participant to walk to the location of each previously experienced pole, relying solely on locational recall to complete the task. The distance between the originally occupied locations and where the test subject walked gives an indicator of accuracy of remembered locations.

7.5 Simulations

When data provide an incomplete rendering of a setting, or when it is desirable to extend beyond the spatial or temporal confines of a dataset, *simulations* are often performed by the researcher. A *simulation* of a situation is a re-creation of the situation based on sets of premises and assumptions concerning the spatial and/or temporal processes that have been hypothesized (or found) to be signifiers of the real-world situation.

7.5.1 Applications of Simulations

Simulations are used for a variety of purposes, including the following:

1. Estimate missing data (imputation, interpolation, and the like).
2. Test hypotheses relating to the nature of the structure or function of a system (for example, political redistricting).
3. Project spatially or temporally beyond a database given information embedded in the database itself and hypothesized reasons for extrapolating beyond the database limits (for example, simulating the spread of an infectious disease, given some knowledge of how it is transmitted).
4. Reproduce scenarios so that knowledge of their function and structure can be extended (for example, simulating the evacuation process of a population exposed to a hazard).
5. Predict future (or past) trends that seem related to a given database (for example, simulating population spread over space and time).
6. Build hypothetical situations that are presumed to reflect actual conditions about

which no data is available (for example, simulating hypothesized conditions on other planets or in inaccessible areas such as the ocean floor).
7. Enable testing of dynamic processes, either hypothesized or real (such as simulating economic growth of an emerging economy).
8. Test and evaluate models that offer to explain or predict given situations (such as using simulation to predict different types of criminal activity).
9. Facilitate transformations of static or cross-sectional information into dynamic or longitudinal information (such as constructing episodic activity patterns from a set of cross-sectional travel surveys).

7.5.2 Types of Simulations

Simulations can be generalized into categories such as:

- Computer-based visualizations using different agent-based structures
- Symbolic model–based reproductions or predictions
- Action simulations (for example, driving, flying)
- Interactive simulations (for example, games)
- Computational process models (CPMs).

Examples of these abound in the research literature, but perhaps least is known about CPMs.

7.6 Computational Process Models

A CPM is a set of operational computer programs. The purpose of building such a system is to model and predict spatial behavior, usually at the individual level. The process relies on an assumption that human decision making and choice behavior depends on information stored in long-term memory (that is, cognitive maps), and this is defined as the basic *knowledge structure* that ultimately determines individual behavior. CPMs have three fundamental components: (1) a knowledge structure (KS), (2) processes by which the KS is accessed and modified, and (3) cognitive architectures. These essential components of a CPM are outlined by Smith, Pellegrino, and Golledge (1982).

The focus first is on the idea of a knowledge structure. The KS is assumed to include two fundamental knowledge types:

1. *Declarative knowledge*, which consists of facts and fundamental operations that can be implemented on them.
2. *Procedural knowledge*, which consists of the logical structures that tie bits of knowledge together and are often manifest in "if X, then Y"–type statements. These determine the actions a person undertakes.

The second component consists of the concepts and techniques that relate to the *processes* by which KSs become organized, accessed, and modified, including pattern matching and activation spread. The third component relates to the governing *cognitive architecture*. That includes the manner in which a KS is organized with regard to information processing in a cognitive system, often operationalized as a production system.

A classic example of a CPM is provided by Kupiers (1978), who modeled the wayfinding behavior of an individual in a novel environment. The KS was defined as containing perceptions of environmental features, a current state represented by location within an environment, and a set of inference rules used in wayfinding and updating the representation of the environment. The traveler is presumed to perceive the environment in terms of the five basic components identified by Lynch (1960), namely, "landmarks," "nodes," "edges," "paths," and "districts." The current relation between traveler and environment is represented as a state in short-term memory, and consists of a number of descriptors of the traveler's current location. The traveler perceives the environment, and a series of procedural statements is constructed. Using these constructions, the CPM models the behavior of the traveler as he or she makes his or her way through the environment to a prespecified destination. Movement is thus controlled by procedural rules and implemented as a change of location status at different iterations (time periods).

7.7 Conclusion

This chapter has provided an overview of a number of commonly used experimental approaches to the collection of data to provide information about human behavior in spatial contexts and environmental settings that are typically controlled. These experimental approaches are becoming more widely used. The use of experiments in itself raises explicit issues of design and implementation and will have implications for the type of data that is generated and for the degree to which the results of analysis conducted using information generated from the experiment may be interpreted and used in a wider context.

Nonetheless, experiments have an increasingly important role as an approach to investigating a wide variety of social and behavioral questions. And the use of experiments does not necessarily mean that the researcher can disregard the crucial issues concerning the recording and measurement of information and the collection of data and the representation of information that we have discussed in the chapters in Parts I and II of this book. In fact, the use of an experimental approach typically raises explicit issues of research design and data validity and reliability that the researcher must address.

PART III
Activities in Environments

This part provides three cases of research designed and conducted to investigate contrasting aspects of human behavior when undertaking different types of *activities* in *environments* at different levels of scale. The research examples are chosen to illustrate a variety of research designs that involve quite different approaches to data collection and analysis to generate information that provides insights about the nature of the human activity being investigated in its particular environmental context.

Chapter 8 provides an example of research conducted by author Stimson and his colleagues based on secondary data analysis. It uses multivariate statistical tools, such as multiple regression and multiple discriminant analysis, to investigate the nature of an activity (or behavior) for population aggregates. It models the ecological relationships between an activity outcome and the social environmental factors at the local scale. It is an example of a large-scale study conducted across a nation but involving spatially disaggregated analysis down to the local level. The assembly of large datasets is involved. The study uses a geographic information systems (GIS)–enabled Spatial Decision Support System (SDSS) to produce an online accessible electoral geography for a nation visualizing spatial patterns of voter support for political parties. It runs a model to identify socioeconomic factors that might account for variations in those local patterns of voter support for political parties.

In **Chapters 9 and 10,** specific attention is given to a series of research studies, conducted over the years by author Golledge and his colleagues, that focus on investigating aspects of activities in environments undertaken by "special groups" (in this instance disabled people) in society. These studies use complex research designs to observe behavior and to collect information from individuals to test propositions about the behavior of those special groups and the difficulties they face in undertaking spatial activities—such as "wayfinding" and "travel"—in particular environmental settings. The research approaches discussed incorporate the design and conduct of experiments, both in field and in laboratory settings.

While in general there are two different ways of looking at disability—either as a physical limitation or as a limitation in performing social roles—the focus taken is on the former, with the studies examining the interaction between members of a selection of disabled groups and their physical environment. The emphasis is, therefore, empirical more than theoretical in approach, a path that might be followed by a social theorist who may focus on how society as a whole deals with "the other" and what changes may have to be made to attitudes, opinions, policies, and decisions in the future to remove stigmatism from such groups.

In **Chapter 9** the focus is on the activities of individuals comprising two "special groups" in society—the intellectually challenged and the visually impaired—and in particular on their wayfinding capabilities in a particular environmental setting. A series of experiments are undertaken in both laboratory and real-world field settings, using both experimental groups and contrast (or control) groups of participants. Unique empirical designs are required to allow studies at the geospatial scale. Analysis is both qualitative and quantitative, using pilot studies, nonprobability samples, and (where possible) quantitative analysis such as Likert scaling, multidimensional scaling, two-way analysis of variance, and graphic and cartographic representation and analysis.

Chapter 10 examines cases of P-E-B relations of visually impaired people. It focuses attention on their geospatial abilities to use wayfinding strategies to learn routes and landmarks in a localized field environment. Experiments conducted involve carrying out a variety of task designed to help wayfinding to evaluate which aid might be deemed to be useful to assist with this everyday task. Use is made of special technologies that change environments and influence activities and behaviors. The chapter discusses four technical systems that might act as guidance tools for wayfinding by sighted or by visually impaired people. Both qualitative and quantitative experiments are used. The focus is on how travelers may use these devices to help them to solve wayfinding problems.

CHAPTER 8

Modeling Social-Environmental Factors Associated with Spatial Patterns of Voter Support for Political Parties

8.1 Introduction

The example of research investigating a human activity in an environmental context discussed in this chapter is taken from work conducted by author Stimson and his colleagues in the Centre for Social Research at the University of Queensland (Stimson, Chhetri, & Shyy, 2006; Stimson, McCrea, & Shyy, 2006). That research has developed an online GIS-enabled Spatial Decision Support System (SDSS) for a national electoral geography of Australia to map and analyze patterns of voting activity at a national election (see *www.siss.edu.au*, go to Shared Research Resources directory). The research involved modeling the social-environmental factors associated with spatial variations in voter support for political parties.

This research is an example of *secondary data analysis* investigating an *aggregate behavior* of populations at a disaggregated local spatial scale. The research design uses GIS technology to integrate diverse spatial databases containing information about population aggregates at the local level of scale across the nation. It uses multivariate statistical modeling tools to investigate *ecological relationships* between local levels of voter support and the demographic and socioeconomic characteristics of local populations. Multivariate statistical analytic tools including *stepwise multiple regression analysis* and *multiple discriminant analysis* are used to model the relationship between the spatial patterns of voter support for political parties at the 2001 federal election and the local social environments where voters live. The modeling conducted permits the development of a *typology* of polling booths according to the propensity of local voters to vote for a particular political party at a specified level of support by voters.

8.2 Background Context

One of the most fundamental principles of a democratic society is the right of adult citizens to vote. Typically, voting occurs at regular intervals in time in accordance with the cycle for electing representatives of the people to a legislative body—such as a parliament or a council—at the national, state, and local levels. Often it is the case that voting occurs to elect a local member to a legislature to represent the people from a geographically defined area that might be known, for example, as an electorate, a congressional district, or a council ward or district. In national and state elections it is common for a legislative body—such as a parliament or congress—to comprise the representatives from many seats, districts, or electorates from across the whole nation or state.

Elections usually involve people voting to select a representative from among a number of candidates who are usually standing for election to represent a particular political party or interest group, but sometimes a candidate might be standing as an independent person. Not surprisingly, there are many variations across nations, and even within them, in the nature and type of electoral systems and legislatures. However, a common characteristic of electoral systems and of voting outcomes tends to be that there is considerable spatial variation in the patterns of voting support for candidates from the different political parties that constitute a legislature.

In the research discussed here, the macroenvironmental context is the national electoral system in Australia, where voting is compulsory for Australian citizens or British subjects ages 18 years and over. The vast majority of people vote at their local polling booth. In the research discussed here, the patterns of voting for candidates within and across the 150 electorates that constituted the House of Representatives at the 2004 federal election were analyzed by Stimson, McCrea, and Shyy (2006) and Stimson, Chhetri, and Shyy (2006) to investigate the spatial patterns of voter support for the various political parties contesting a federal election. It provides an example of how a GIS framework may be used to visualize the spatial patterns of voting for the various political parties and how sociospatial multivariate analytic tools may be applied to explain how local demographic and socioeconomic characteristics of the places where voters live across a nation might account for variations across those local places in the level of voter support for the various political parties.

Relatively little has been published in Australia on its electoral geography. A number of earlier studies had analyzed spatially disaggregated patterns of voting behavior in federal or state elections (see, for example, Davis & Stimson, 1998, 2000; Forrest, 1996; Forrest, Alston, Medlin, & Amri, 2001; Walmsley, 1997). The Australian Electoral Commission (AEC/IRS, 1998) produces electoral atlases for Australia. However, much of the research by political scientists analyzing voting patterns and trends (for example, Bean, Simms, Bennett, & Wahurst, 1997; Manne, 1998) tend not to incorporate contributions providing either a spatial analysis of voting or statistical modeling of socioeconomic variables to identify the determinants of voter behavior and trends. Some studies—such as that by Bean, Gow, and McAllister (1999)—have provided a guide for using machine-readable data files to analyze voting at elections.

In the Netherlands, for example, Schram (1992) has analyzed voting behavior in elections using predictive multinominal logit models to project results using survey data variables. Some attempts have been made in Australia to compare patterns of socioeconomic variables with the voting behavior of people (for example, Jones, McAllister, & Gow, 1996; Singleton, Martyn, & Ward, 1998). Shyy, Stimson, and Murray (2003) demonstrate how GIS provides capabilities for presenting spatial data in a form that is understandable for most audiences through the thematic mapping of socioeconomic variables and integrating spatial databases at different levels of scale. Two- and three-dimensional display models may enhance understanding of spatial distributions and patterns of change. These technologies, along with the use of statistical and spatial modeling tools, make it possible (as demonstrated by Davis & Stimson, 1998, 2000; Stimson, Chhetri, & Shyy, 2006; Stimson, McCrea, & Shyy, 2006) to conduct spatially disaggregated analysis of voting patterns at an election. Such data is available from the Australian Electoral Commission (AEC). Multivariate statistical analytic tools may be used to identify the key demographic, socioeconomic, and spatial variables that may explain variations in the level of support for a political party at an election across the voter catchments surrounding polling booths. The results of such modeling approaches may then be used in a predictive context to model the potential level of voter support that might be expected to occur for a political party at a future election in response to particular policies that are oriented to specific demographic and socioeconomic groups. Such an attempt has been made by Davis and Stimson (2000).

8.3 Developing the GIS-Enabled Spatial Decision Support System
8.3.1 *The Data*

The GIS applications developed to visualize and analyze patterns of voting at federal elections in Australia (Stimson, Chhetri, & Shyy, 2006; Stimson, McCrea, & Shyy, 2006) were achieved through the following processes using the database for recent federal elections provided by the AEC:

1. All 7,567 electoral booths across Australia were geocoded in a GIS across all of the 150 House of Representative electoral divisions for the 2004 federal election database.
2. The AEC supplied an electronic database on the number of votes cast at all polling booths across Australia for each candidate standing for the House of Representatives at the 2001 and 2004 federal elections. That raw data was rearranged to create a table giving the number and the proportion of total votes cast for each political party for each electoral division in each state/territory. Those tables were then joined to the polling booth file for all electoral divisions.
3. Overlaid on the polling booth locations are electoral division CD, SLA, and LGA boundaries from the 2001 census; and the 1:1 million scale main road layer available from Geoscience Australia.
4. Data derived from the 1996 and 2001 censuses at the above disaggregated or aggregated levels of spatial scale is overlaid on the polling booth voting data.
5. For the metropolitan city regions of Sydney, Melbourne, Brisbane, Perth, and Adelaide, a 5-kilometer zonal and a 45° sectoral axial pattern is overlaid on the polling booth and census data, using an origin point in the CBD of those cities. This enhances visualization of the geographic pattern of voting and of demographic and socioeconomic data distribution across the large metropolitan city regions.
6. Using the digital boundary databases available from the Australian Bureau of Statistics (ABS) for the 2001 census, state/territory census collector district (CCD) layers are merged into one Australia CD layer. Those CCDs are then spatially allocated to a nearest polling booth location to form *polling booth catchments* enabling the modeling of the relationships between voting patterns and demographic and socioeconomic characteristics of the residents within those polling booth catchments using variables derived from the 2001 census databases.

8.3.2 *Visualizing Electoral Voting Patterns*

The spatial patterns of both voting at an election and the distribution of demographic and socioeconomic data from the census can be accessed online to produce the following types of displays in a GIS:

1. Voting patterns at the level of polling booths may be displayed from the aggregate national to the disaggregated local scale using the *Zoom In, Zoom Out, Pan, Identify*, and *Classification* functionalities available on ArcView GIS. These functionalities are useful to show the pattern and level of voter support for a political party received through the primary votes cast for candidates standing for a party.
2. Voting patterns for polling booths may be displayed as a dot distribution pattern in a 2-D space across Australia as a whole or at any level of spatial scale.
3. Voting patterns at the polling-booth level may also be analyzed and interactively displayed in a three-dimensional space in the ArcView extension 3-D analyst environment.

8.3.3 Integrating the Voting Data with Social-Environmental Data

To address the objective of analyzing and modeling the relationships between spatial variations in the patterns of local support for political parties and the social-environmental characteristics of local areas, Stimson, Chhetri, and Shyy (2006) found it necessary to integrate the disaggregated voting database for polling booths with disaggregated census data for polling booth catchments. Thus, the GIS-enabled SDSS developed by the researchers comprised the following two matrices of information:

- A matrix of point locations that are the polling booth locations (the rows) × the percentages of primary votes cast at each polling booth for all political parties (the columns).
- A matrix of areas that are the polling booth catchments (the rows) × the incidence of demographic and socioeconomic phenomena as measured by 46 variables listed in Table 8.1 (the columns).

These data matrices may then be merged.

The geographic distribution of both the point data (that is, the polling booth locations showing levels of voter support for a particular political party) and the area data (that is, the polling booth catchments showing scores on a variable derived from the census data) may be integrated within a map display. Thus, the point data and the area data patterns may be overlaid one on the other in the GIS. That permits a user to also overlay across those patterns of voting at polling booths a choropleth map (that may be classified by natural breaks, equal intervals, or quantiles) in ArcView GIS showing patterns of distribution of the 46 selected demographic and socioeconomics variables derived from the census. Figure 8.1 provides an example for Sydney, where the spatial patterns of voting for the governing Coalition parties outnumber those for the opposition Labor Party, and vice versa. Both are overlaid on the spatial pattern of distribution of the incidence of high-income households.

8.4 Modeling Ecological Relationships: Analysis and Results

An important objective guiding the research design developed and implemented by Stimson, McCrea, and Shyy (2006) and Stimson, Chhetri, and Shyy (2006) was to be able to say something more definitive about those factors that potentially may help "explain" the spatial variations that are clearly evident across the cities and regions of Australia at the local level of the primary vote for political parties and their candidates for the House of Representatives seats at a federal election in Australia. That involved using multivariate

TABLE 8.1. Variables Derived from the 2001 Census Representing the Demographic and Socioeconomic Characteristics of Polling Booth Catchments

Age and sex
  % population males MALES
  % population age 0–17 years YOUTH
  % population age 18–29 years GENY
  % population age 30–39 years GENX
  % population age 40–54 years BOOMERS
  % population age 55–69 years (Post-Depression Wartime Generation) WW2GEN
  % population age 70+ years (Pre-Depression Generation) DEPGEN

Family and household structure
  % single-person households SINGLES
  % couple without children households COUPLES
  % one-parent family households ONEPARENT
  % couples with children households COUPCHILD

Housing tenure
  % households that are homeowners HOMEOWN
  % households that are home purchasers MORTGAGEES
  % households that are private renters RENTERS
  % households that are public housing tenants PUBHOUS

Ethnicity/race
  % population indigenous persons INDIG
  % population born overseas IMMIG
  % population born in UK and Ireland UK
  % population born in Southern and Eastern Europe SEEUROPE
  % population born in Middle East MIDEAST
  % population born in Asia ASIA

Religious affiliation
  % population Catholic CATH
  % population Anglican ANG
  % population Pentecostal PENT
  % population other Christian OTHCRIST
  % population Islamic ISLAM
  % population other non-Christian religion ONCHREL
  % population with no religion NORELIG

Residential stability/mobility
  % of population at the same address 5 years ago RESSTABLE

Digital divide
  % population using computer DIGCON

Engagement in work
  Labor force participation rate INWORK
  Unemployment rate UNEMPLOY

Industry of work
  % labor force employed in extractive industries EXTRACT
  % labor force employed in transformative industries TRANSFORM
  % labor force employed in distributive services DISTRIB
  % labor force employed in producer/business services BISSERV
  % labor force employed in social services SOCSERV
  % labor force employed in hospitality industries HOSPTOUR

(continued)

132 ACTIVITIES IN ENVIRONMENTS

TABLE 8.1. *(continued)*

Occupation (Robert Reich's categories)
  % labor force in "routine production worker" occupations ROUTPROD
  % labor force in "in-person service workers" occupations INPERS
  % labor force in "symbolic analyst" occupations SYMBA

Human capital
  % persons age 15 years and over with a degree or higher qualification UNIVED
  % persons age 15 and over with a certificate, diploma, or advanced diploma TECH

Income
  % households in the lowest quintile for household income (less than $600 per week) LOWINC
  % households in the middle three quintiles for household income ($600–$1,499 per week) MIDINC
  % households in the highest quintile for household income ($1,500 and over per week) HIGHINC

Note. From Stimson, Chhetri, and Shyy (2006).

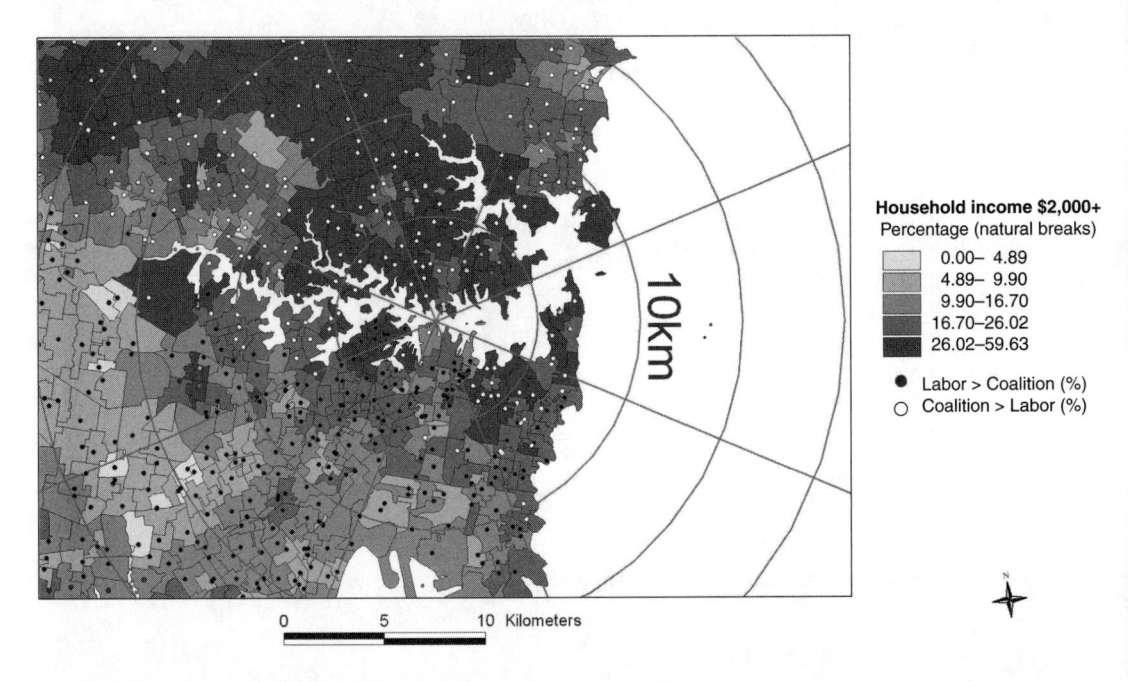

FIGURE 8.1. The pattern of voting where the Coalition vote outnumbers the Labor vote and vice versa, overlaid on the distribution of incidence of high-income households: Sydney. From Stimson, Chhetri, and Shyy (2006).

statistical analysis and modeling tools to investigate the ecological associations between those local levels of voter support for a political party and the local social environment as measured by the demographic and socioeconomic variables listed in Table 8.1 relating to the characteristics of polling booth catchments, and then to develop a typology of polling booth support for political parties.

8.4.1 Multiple Regression Analysis

The variables listed in Table 8.1 were used to run a *stepwise multiple regression model* on the primary vote for all of the political parties at the 2004 election in order to identify the most important demographic and socioeconomic factors that are associated with the variation in the spatial pattern of the level of voter support for a political party. This type of modeling identifies the amount of variation in a *dependent variable*—in this case the level of the primary votes for a political party across the polling booths at the 2004 federal election—that is explained by a set of *independent variables*—in this case the variables measuring the demographic and socioeconomic characteristics of the people living in the polling booth catchments.

The results of a regression analysis produce a set of statistics including what is known as the R^2 statistic that ranges from zero up to 1.00 (or 100%). This statistic tells us what proportion of the total variance in the distribution of the dependent variable is explained by the independent variables used in the modeling. The statistics produced also provide us with beta coefficients for each of the independent variables, which are a measure of the importance of a variable in explaining the variation in the dependent variable. An R^2 that is greater than 0.40 is regarded as providing a reasonable level of explanation, while an R^2 of greater than 0.80 provides an exceptionally high level of explanation. What a stepwise regression model does is run a series of model iterations to progressively identify additional independent variables that provide a diminishing additional contribution to the R^2 value derived from the regression procedure. The idea is to be able to identify in descending order of importance those variables that account for as much of the variation in the dependent variable as possible.

8.4.1.1 Model Results

The results of the modeling analyzing spatial variation in the level of the primary vote for the major and the minor political parties at the 2004 federal election in Australia are summarized in Table 8.2. Because the Country Liberal Party operates only in the Northern Territory, the model was not run for that party's vote.

The number of model iterations run for the stepwise regression analysis varied for each political party. That is because the iterations needed to get "meaningfully interpreted" results with a sufficient number of variables identified to provide a reasonable R^2 value. Full statistical details of the results of the stepwise regression models run by Stimson, Chhetri, and Shyy (2006) are not given in Table 8.2. Rather, a summary of the results is provided, listing, in order of importance, those demographic and socioeconomic factors from the list of independent variables used in the analyses that are most important in explaining the variation in the dependent variable, namely, the variation across the polling booth in the level of the primary vote for a political party. The standardized beta coefficients indicate not only the relative importance of the variable as an explanatory factor in the model but also the direction—positive or negative—of the effect of the variable in terms of its association with the level of the primary vote for a political party. The adjusted R^2 statistics are also included in the table.

TABLE 8.2. Results of the Stepwise Regression Modeling: The Most Important Factors Explaining Spatial Variation in the Primary Vote for Political Parties at the 2004 Federal Election

Coalition Parties ($R^2 = 0.54$)		Liberal Party ($R^2 = 0.30$)		National Party ($R^2 = 0.32$)		Labor Party ($R^2 = 0.53$)		Australian Greens Party ($R^2 = 0.50$)		Family First Party ($R^2 = 0.29$)	
ONEPARENT	–.10	DIGCON	+.34	EXTRACT	+.28	EXTRACT	–.23	UNIVED	+.68	UNIVED	–.47
SEEUROPE	–.19	UK	+.17	NOREL	–.26	DIGCON	–.01	NOREL	+.25	CATH	–.29
HOMEOWN	+.13	UNEMPLOY	–.23	IMMIG	–.28	ANG	–.08	UNEMPLOY	+.25	ANG	–.37
UNEMPLOY	–.22	TRANSFORM	+.17	UNEMPLOY	+.15	IMMIG	+.08	HOSPTOUR	+.10	ONCHREL	+.24
SOCSERV	–.09	WWGEN	+.13	INDIG	–.18	COUPLES	+.18	RESSTABLE	–.17	PENT	+.11
SYMBA	+.39	CATH	–.03	TRANSFORM	–.13	NOREL	+.13	TECH	+.24	DIGCON	+.27
UNIVED	–.51	ANG	–.03			DISTRIB	–.13	DIGCON	–.26	RENTERS	–.14
RESSTABLE	+.16	UNIVED	–.24			SYMBA	–.22	WW2GEN	–.14		
DIGCON	+.28	BUSSERV	+.14			SEEUROPE	+.14				
BOOMERS	+.15	SYMBA	+.14			GENY	+.03				
		BOOMERS	–.07			INWORK	–.12				
		PENT	+.06			GENX	+.10				
						INDIG	+.21				
						YOUTH	–.17				
						ISLAM	+.08				
						UNEMPLOY	+.09				

Note. From Stimson, Chhetri, and Shyy (2006).

From the results summarized in Table 8.2, the following conclusions may be drawn:

1. Quite high R^2 values that are greater than 0.50 were derived in the modeling of the primary votes for the combined Coalition parties and for the Labor Party, and this is also the case for the Greens. Thus, the models explain more than 50% of the variance in the spatial pattern of the primary vote for these parties. However, relatively low R^2s of less than 0.35 are achieved when the models of the primary vote are considered separately for the Liberal Party and the National Party, and this is also the case for the Family First Party. Thus, the models explain only about one-third of the primary vote for those parties. The primary vote for the Australian Democrats is not modeled.

2. The model explains 53% of the pattern of the primary vote for the Labor Party after 16 iterations. Those demographic and socioeconomic factors associated with a stronger primary vote for Labor at the 2004 federal election are the presence of relatively high concentrations of immigrants (including people born in southern and eastern Europe), couples, generation Xers and generation Yers, indigenous people, unemployed persons, people with no religion, and people following Islam. Conversely, places with a strong primary vote for Labor tend to have a relatively lower incidence of workers in both the extractive and the distributive industries, fewer people in symbolic analyst occupations, people who are less likely to be digitally connected (nonusers of computers), people who have fewer children, fewer youths, and fewer people who are Anglicans.

3. The model explains 54% of the variation in the primary vote for the Coalition parties after 10 iterations. Higher levels of primary votes for the Coalition parties are associated with places that have a higher incidence of homeowners, people working in symbolic analyst occupations, and people who are digitally connected. They tend to have populations that are residentially stable (not as many movers), and they have a relatively high incidence of baby boomers. But the places with higher levels of support for the Coalition parties have a lesser incidence of one-parent families, people who are unemployed, and people born in southern and eastern Europe; fewer university-educated people; and a lower incidence of workers in the social service industries.

4. When considering the Liberal Party vote separately, after 12 iterations the model accounts for only 30% of the variation in the primary vote for the Liberal Party. Places where the Liberal vote is higher tend to have a relatively higher incidence of people who are digitally connected, and workers in the symbolic analyst occupations, the business services industries, and the transformative industries. They have relatively higher concentrations of people born in the United Kingdom, people from the Depression to the end of World War II generation and baby boomers as well, and a higher incidence of people who are Pentecostals. However, the places with higher levels of voter support for the Liberals tend to have fewer people who are unemployed, fewer university-educated people, fewer Anglicans and Catholics, and fewer renters.

5. The model explains 32% of the variation in the level of the primary vote for the National Party after six iterations (with virtually nothing much being added in way of explanation after further iterations). Not surprisingly, those places where the level of primary votes for the Nationals was higher tend to be characterized by people working in the extractive industries (which includes farmers and pastoralists). But these places also tend to have a greater incidence of unemployed persons, confirming the concentration of some structural unemployment in rural and regional Australia. However, a higher incidence of voting support for the Nationals is also associated with places characterized by a low incidence of indigenous populations, immigrants, people with no religion, and workers in the transformative industries.

6. The model explains 50% of the variation in the level of the primary vote for the Australian Greens Party after eight iterations. Those places with higher levels of voting support for the Greens tend to have higher concentrations of university-educated people, people with technical qualifications, people with no religion, people working in the hospitality and tourism industries, and unemployed persons. And those places also seem to be likely to have more mobile populations. However, the places with higher levels of voter support for the Greens also tend to have populations that have fewer people from the Depression to World War II generation and a lower incidence of digitally connected people.

7. The model explains only 29% of the variation in the incidence of voter support for the Family First Party. The vote for that party was relatively low at the 2004 federal election. Places with a higher level of primary votes for the Family First Party tend to be characterized by a higher incidence of people from the Pentecostal religion, people who belong to non-Christian religions, and digitally connected people. However, those places with higher levels of primary votes for the Family First Party seem not to have many renters, a lesser incidence of university-educated people, and a lower incidence of Catholics and Anglicans.

8.4.1.2 What May Be Concluded from the Regression Model Results?

Caution needs to be exercised in drawing firm conclusions from the results of the regression modeling reported here. However, it is clear that there is a statistically significant association between the levels of primary votes cast at the 2004 federal election for political parties at the disaggregated local level of polling booths and the demographic and socioeconomic characteristics of the people living in polling booth catchments across Australia.

It is evident from the modeling that there is a differentiation between the political parties in the type of people and households they attract. This is, of course, well known and has received much comment in the media for many years as well as attention in research by political scientists. However, following on from the research conducted by Stimson, McCrea, and Shyy (2006) analyzing the 2001 federal election, the analysis of the 2004 federal election discussed here and undertaken by (Stimson, Chhetri, & Shyy, 2006) demonstrates that this type of analysis and modeling may be conducted at such a spatially disaggregated level of scale using an explanatory modeling approach to measure the relationships between the primary vote for political parties and local characteristics of people and households.

The models do provide explanation—in statistical terms—for a relatively high degree of the variance in the vote for the Coalition parties and for the Labor Party and for the Greens Party across the thousands of polling booths where the large majority of people ages 18 years and over voted at the 2004 federal election in Australia. And the modeling does provide statistically reliable identification of some of the key socioeconomic characteristics of local areas that seem to be important explanatory factors that differentiate the patterns of primary voting support for those political parties. But the models have considerably less explanatory power when votes for the Liberal and National parties are considered separately. The explanatory power of the model is also relatively low for the Family First vote.

Of course, in all the models there remains much of the variation in the spatial pattern of the primary vote for all of the political parties at the 2004 federal election. Other spatial and other local variables might need to be incorporated into the models as additional independent variables. Those factors might, for example, be measures such as the location characteristic of polling booth catchments within the Australian settlement system and levels of voter support for a political party at previous elections.

8.4.2 Predicting Local Patterns of Voter Support for Political Parties

Multivariate statistical methodologies were also used by Stimson, Chhetri, and Shyy (2006) to develop a model that seeks to predict the distribution of voting outcomes across polling booths by analyzing the relationship between voter support for political parties and the demographic and socioeconomic characteristics of the population living in polling booth catchments. The results of such a predictive model may be compared with the actual results of voting at the 2004 federal election.

8.4.2.1 Discriminant Analysis

Stimson, Chhetri, and Shyy (2006) use *discriminant analysis*—the same methodology employed earlier by Stimson, McCrea, and Shyy (2006) in a study of voting patterns at the 2001 federal election—to analyze the relationship between voting outcomes at polling booths across Australia at the 2004 federal election and the demographic and socioeconomic characteristics of people living in polling booth catchments using the GIS-enabled databases described earlier.

While relationships between booth voting outcomes and various demographic and socioeconomic variables can be seen visually using a GIS, discriminant analysis (see Tabachnick & Fidell, 2001) is a tool specifically designed to detect differences between two or more groups, and it can accommodate many variables in a multivariate approach such as that used by Stimson, Chhetri, and Shyy (2006). Moreover, it is a tool that simplifies the interpretation of a large set of variables by combining them into a small number of functions that explain much of the variation in the dataset used. In addition, discriminant analysis simplifies the interpretation of a large number of variables by combining them into a small number of functions (in a similar way that "factors" are derived in factor analysis). Thus, in this study, discriminant analysis provides a powerful tool used to establish the extent to which polling booth voting outcomes (dependent variable) and the local social-environmental characteristics variables listed in Table 8.1 (the independent variables) are statistically related, and to distinguish between patterns of voting for political parties across the nation's polling booths according to the demographic and socioeconomic characteristics of the polling booth catchments as measured by those local social-environmental phenomena variables.

8.4.2.2 Classifying Polling Booths into "Groups" According to Voter Support for Political Parties

The analysis conducted by Stimson, Chhetri, and Shyy (2006) resulted in the polling booths across Australia being classified into the seven *groups* listed in Table 8.3. These groups are made up of polling booths that are characterized by particular levels of voting for a political party:

1. Groups 1, 2, and 3 in the table comprise polling booths with favorable voting outcomes—"most votes"—for the major political parties, namely the Labor Party, the Liberal Party, and the National Party. The fourth group relates to polling booths with favorable outcomes for the Country Liberal Party in the Northern Territory.
2. There are also three further groups identified comprising those polling booths where there was a voting outcome favorable to a minor political party where the primary vote exceeded 20%.
3. Group 5 comprises 217 polling booths where the primary vote for the Greens party reached 20% or more, and this was an increase of 136 polling booths on 2001.
4. Group 6 comprises only one such polling booth in 2004 for the Australian Democrats, down from 24 polling booths at the 2001 election. Compared to the 2001 election, in 2004 there was a decline of 23 in the number of polling booths where the Democrats gained over 20% of the primary vote.
5. Group 7 comprises only one polling booth where the Family First Party, contesting its first federal election, exceeded the 20% primary vote level.

(Note that the One Nation Party dropped out of the analysis in 2004 because there was a dramatic decline in its primary vote, whereas at the 2001 election there were 97 polling booths where it gained 20% or more of the primary vote, which is an arbitrary figure.)

8.4.2.3 Discriminating between the Groups

The 46 demographic and socioeconomic variables listed in Table 8.1 were used as "predictors" of voting behavior in the discriminant analysis model run by Stimson, Chhetri, and Shyy (2006) to derive a small number of "functions" that explain the large majority of the differences between the seven groups of polling booths listed in Table 8.3.

Three *discriminant functions* emerged as being significant, as shown in Table 8.4, and between them they explain 96.7% of the between-group variance across the groups of voter support for the political parties that are listed in Table 8.3. In Table 8.4, those variables among the 46 variables listed in Table 8.1 that have a significant loading on one of the first three most important discriminant functions are listed. The information in Table 8.4 may be interpreted as follows:

- The figures in bold type indicate where a variable is significant for a discriminant function
- In that way, a variable is judged as being an important *predictor* of voting behavior in discriminating between the groups listed in Table 8.3

TABLE 8.3. Descriptive Statistics and the Number of Polling Booths by Favorable Voting Outcomes for Each Political Party and the 2001 and 2004 Federal Elections

Polling booth groups vis-à-vis nature of voter support for a political party	Mean vote (%)	SD (%)	No. of polling booths 2001 election	No. of polling booths 2004 election	Change between 2001 and 2004 elections
1. Labor Party—most primary votes	34.03%	17.56	2,568	2,227	−341
2. Liberal Party—most primary votes	37.56%	22.60	3,421	3,879	+458
3. National Party—most primary votes	10.02%	21.21	1,039	1,199	+160
4. Country Liberal Party—most primary votes	0.59%	4.54	29	32	+3
5. Australian Greens Party—20%+ primary vote	6.71%	5.17	81	217	+136
6. Australian Democrats Party—20%+ primary vote	1.09%	1.07	24	1	−23
7. Family First Party—20%+ primary vote	1.89%	1.96		1	
One Nation Party—20%+ primary vote (not used in the 2004 election analysis)			97		
Total			7,259	7,556[a]	

[a]Nineteen voting booths could not be allocated to a party on the criterion as two parties hold equal percentages of primary votes in those voting booths.

Note. From Stimson, Chhetri, and Shyy (2006).

- The combination of those variables with significant loadings on a discriminant function in Table 8.4 is then used to develop descriptive interpretation of what a function means.

The three discriminant functions are discussed below:

1. The *first function* derived from the discriminant analysis accounts for much of the between-group difference, explaining 54.7% of the variance, with 15 variables having significant loadings on the function. The function may be interpreted as one that differentiates between places (polling booth catchments) on the basis of their degree of monoculturalism and older generation populations and with people employed in extractive industries (especially farming), as indicated by the variables with a significant positive loading, versus their degree of multiculturalism, population by generation Yers, characterization by some disadvantage, and with people working in social service industries (as indicated by the variables with a significant negative loading). This is labeled a *monocultural older/multicultural younger discriminant function*.

2. The *second function* derived from the discriminant analysis accounts for 28.9% of the variance, with 19 variables having a significant loading on the function. This function might be described as differentiating between places that are characterized by disadvantage with low-income households, unemployed people, and routine production workers (as indicated by the variables with a significant positive loading) versus places that are characterized by advantage, home purchasers, higher income households, digitally connected people with high human capital, and people working in business services (as indicated by the variables with a significant negative loading). This is labeled a *disadvantage/advantage discriminant function*.

3. The *third function* derived from the discriminant analysis accounts for a further 13.2% of the variance, with six variables having a significant loading on this function. The function may be interpreted as differentiating between places that are characterized by couples with no religious affiliation, high human capital symbolic analyst occupation workers, and people working in the transformative industry sectors (as indicated by the variables with a significant negative loading) versus places characterized by families with children and workers in routine production occupations (as indicated by the variables with a significant negative loading). To some extent, this discriminant function is similar to the second function, and, in the case of four of the eight variables with significant loadings on this third function, there is a commonality of variables that are significant as well on the second discriminant function. Because of the much smaller amount of the total variance accounted for by this discriminant function, this function is not used further in the analysis that follows.

TABLE 8.4. Function Loadings of Predictors on Discriminant Functions 1, 2, and 3

Predictors	Function 1	Function 2	Function 3
IMMIG	–.512	–.243	–.097
EXTRACT	+.475	+.322	+.108
SEEUROPE	–.464	+.053	–.079
ONEPARENT	–.461	+.24	–.006
GENY	–.455	–.061	+.166
HOMEOWN	+.452	+.028	–.104
ANG	+.421	+.175	–.017
RENT	–.418	+.161	+.174
ONCHREL	–.417	+.057	–.041
ASIA	–.393	–.022	–.064
ISLAM	–.358	+.147	–0.11
PUBHOUS	–.342	+.164	–.053
MIDEAST	–.322	+.103	–.111
WW2GEN	+.321	+.132	–.017
SOCSERV	–.310	–.131	–.28
DIGCON	+.185	–.644	+.021
UK	–.035	–.546	–.094
NORELIG	–.089	–0.55	+.398
HIGHINC	–.037	–.494	+.043
BUSSERV	–.245	–.460	+.118
LOWINC	+.059	+.446	+.092
MORTGAGEES	+.006	–.369	–.215
INWORK	+.123	–.352	+.165
UNEMPLOY	–.208	+.348	+.167
UNIVED	–.107	–.471	+.461
SYMBA	+.384	–.192	+.451
TRANSFORM	–.264	–.117	–.372
ROUTPROD	–.228	+.342	–.351
COUPCHILD	+.046	–.073	–.343
COUPLES	+.318	–.082	+.339

Note. The table includes only those variables with a loading of ≥ ± .300 (in **bold**) on at least one of the first three functions. From Stimson, Chhetri, and Shyy (2006).

8.4.3 The Position of the Political Parties in a "Sociopolitical Space"

8.4.3.1 The Method

It is the first two of these "discriminant functions" that are identified from the discriminant analysis and that are described in the previous section. These were of most interest to Stimson, Chhetri, and Shyy (2006), as combined they account for 83.5% of the total variance. Thus, the Z-scores for political parties were calculated on both of these functions for all the polling booths having a favorable outcome for a party. To calculate the Z-score for a particular booth, the following discriminant function is used:

$$Z_i = d_{i1}p_1 + d_{i2}p_2 + \ldots + d_{ip}z_p$$

where Z_i is the Z-score on the ith function for the booth, d_i is the standardized discriminant function coefficient for the ith function, and p is the standardized score on each predictor for the booth.

8.4.3.2 Plotting the "Sociopolitical Space"

Stimson, Chhetri, and Shyy (2006) were able to compile a diagram whereby the position of each polling booth categorized according to the political party voting group to which it belongs could be plotted using the first two discriminant functions as the axes in the resultant graph. That results in more than 7,500 points (representing the polling booths) being plotted, which makes the graph indecipherable. Thus, what is involved in the compilation of Figure 8.2 is a representation of the "centroid" of the plot of the scores for all the polling booths associated with the groups for each of the political parties on the first two discriminant functions.

Figure 8.2 indicates the centroid position of the Liberal, National, Country Liberal, Labor, and Australian Greens parties on the first two discriminant functions. Because of the minuscule number of polling booths associated in the groups defined by the Family First Party, and because there were no polling booths identified in the model associated with the Australian Democrats, Figure 8.2 does not include a plot for those minor political parties. In that figure the horizontal axis on the graph is the *monocultural older/multicultural younger* discriminant function, and the vertical axis on the graph is the *disadvantage/advantage* discriminant function.

In this way, a visual representation is provided of the differentiation between the seven groups of polling booths distinguished by the predominance of the vote for a political party and the relationship of those polling booths vis-à-vis the demographic and socioeconomic characteristics of polling booth catchments as represented by scores on the first two discriminant functions. This figure may be interpreted as representing a type of "sociopolitical space" for voting at the 2004 federal election for the House of Representatives.

From the plot in Figure 8.2, Stimson, Chhetri, and Shyy (2006) were able to draw the following conclusions:

1. The Labor Party is clearly separated from the other political parties, being located within the *multicultural/younger–disadvantaged* quadrant of the graph.
2. In contrast, the Liberal Party is located within the opposite *monocultural/older–advantaged* quadrant of the graph.
3. The *National Party* is located in the *monocultural/older—disadvantaged* quadrant of the graph.

Disacvantaged

```
                        2.0
                         |
                         |        National Party
                         |            •
         Labor Party     |
             •       Function 1
Multicultural/           |                    Monocultural/
Younger ─────────────────┼──────────────────── Older
  -2.0                   0    Function 2    2.0
         Country Liberal |
         Party  •        |   •
                         | Liberal Party
              •          |
         Australian      |
         Greens          |
         Party           |
                         |
                       -2.0
                      Advantaged
```

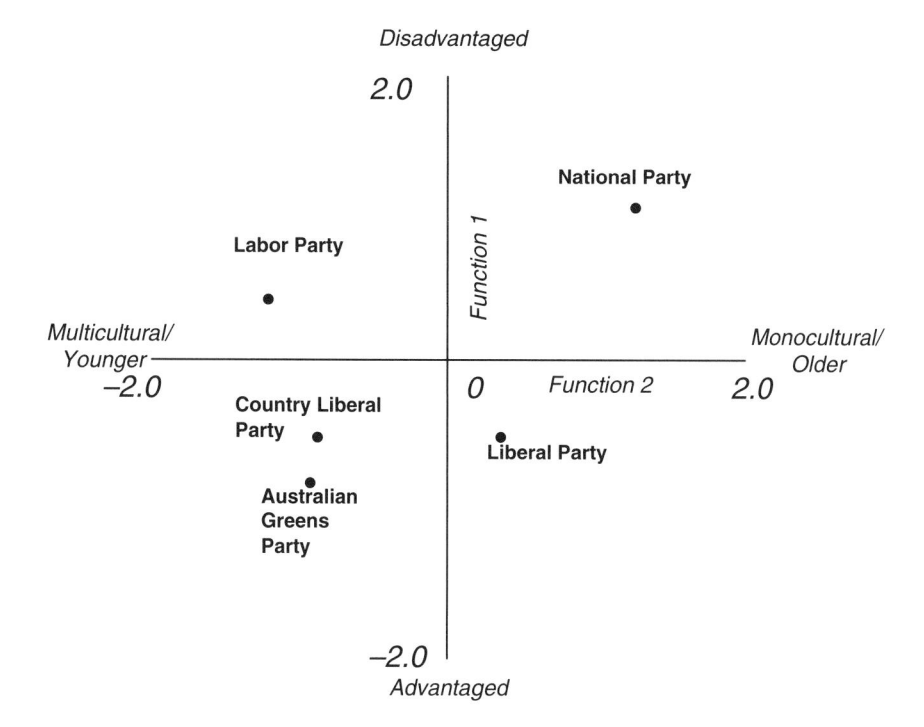

FIGURE 8.2. Discrimination between the political parties on Functions 1 and 2 using Z-scores between –2.0 and +2.0. From Stimson, Chhetri, and Shyy (2006).

4. The Australian Greens Party and the County Liberal Party are both located in the *multicultural/younger—advantaged* quadrant of the graph.
5. The widest separation is between the Nationals and the Greens.
6. There is a wide separation between the Nationals and the Liberals within the Coalition, with the results from the discriminant analysis modeling a demonstration of just how much the voting constituencies for these Coalition partners are differentiated.

8.4.4 Accuracy of the Model Predictions

The predictive accuracy of the discriminant analysis model developed and run by Stimson, Chhetri, and Shyy (2006) is quite high, as shown by the figures in Table 8.5. The overall predictive accuracy is 67.2%. However, the predictive accuracy of the model does vary for each of the voting outcomes for the groups that relate to the main political parties.

In Table 8.5, the data in the final column shows the actual voting outcomes for polling booths at the 2004 federal election for the House of Representatives seats, where the voting outcomes were "most primary votes" in the case of the Coalition parties and the Labor Party, and "20 percent or more of the primary votes" outcome in the case of the Greens Party. The data in each row of the table indicate for a political party the number of polling booths that were predicted by the model to give that voting outcome supporting a party. The level of model predictive accuracy does vary considerable with respect to the various political parties.

TABLE 8.5. Predicted and Actual Polling Booth Outcomes: Number of Polling Booths and Percentage of Booths Correctly Predicted by the Model

	\multicolumn{5}{c}{Outcome predicted by model (no. of polling booths and % correctly predicted)}	Actual outcome
	Liberal	National	CLP	Labour	Greens	
Liberal Party—most primary votes	2,507 (64.6%)	677 (17.5%)	79 (2%)	362 (9.3%)	254 (6.5%)	3,879
National Party—most primary votes	145 (12.1%)	1,006 (83.9%)	6 (0.5%)	24 (2.0%)	18 (1.5%)	1,199
Country Liberal Party—most primary votes	0 (0%)	0 (0%)	32 (100%)	0 (0%)	0 (0%)	32
Labour Party—most primary votes	368 (16.6%)	176 (8.0%)	101 (4.6%)	1,352 (61.2%)	213 (9.6%)	2,210
Australian Greens Party—20%+ primary vote	28 (12.9%)	8 (3.7%)	2 (0.9%)	14 (6.5%)	165 (76.0%)	217

Note. From Stimson, Chhetri, and Shyy (2006).

8.5 Discussion

The study undertaken by Stimson, McCrea, and Shyy (2006) and extended by Stimson, Chhetri, and Shyy (2006) discussed in this chapter demonstrates how GIS-enabled statistical and spatial analysis, modeling, and the associated visualization of data may be applied to:

- Investigate the pattern—at a spatially disaggregated level of scale—of variations in the level of voter support for political parties at a federal election
- Identify those local demographic and socioeconomic factors that are associated with, and which may help explain, variations across Australia in the level of voter support for political parties at the level of the polling booth.

The research design used enabled the researchers to identify and map at a highly disaggregated level of spatial scale patterns of "political landscapes," both nationally and within the large metropolitan city regions.

The multivariate statistical modeling provides new insight that enhances our understanding of the ecological relationships between voter support for political parties and local social-environmental conditions. The research demonstrates how a multiple regression model may be used to identify the social-environmental characteristics relating to the demographic and socioeconomic characteristics of local populations that are statistically significant is helping explain variations in the level of voter support for a political party. And the predictive model developed to identify groupings of local polling booths that would be likely to produce primary votes at a particular level for a political party at the 2004 federal election has considerable potential as a predictive tool. That modeling approach enabled the identification of a small number of key functions that differentiate between groupings of polling booths where the primary vote support for a particular political party is at a specified level, and subsequently for the position of the political parties on a two-dimensional "sociopolitical space" to be plotted. That enabled the placement of the political parties on the axes that define that "sociopolitical space" to be compared.

The analysis of demographic and socioeconomic characteristics of the populations living in the polling booth catchments that were included in the analysis and modeling conducted so far only uses variables derived from the data available on CD-ROM census data files. It would be important to experiment with a wider set of variables that may be derived from special runs of the census data where cross-tabulated variables are produced, such as the generational age breakdown of household family types and the income level of those generational household types. In addition, it would be interesting to include synthetic data variables, derived through microsimulation, such as levels of wealth, dependence on income support payments, child and family support payments, and so on. Additionally, spatial variables might be included as dummy variables in the modeling, to indicate, for example, the location of polling booths and polling booth catchments within a settlement system of Australia (for example, inner city, middle suburbs, outer suburbs, large regional center, small town, rural). Also, it needs to be pointed out that statistical and spatial analysis, modeling, and visualization of the type carried out by the researchers can only go so far in adding to our understanding of the nature of patterns of voting for political parties in Australia and the relationship between voting patterns and local demographic and socioeconomic—and other local—phenomena.

Finally, it is important to realize that studies such as the research reported here—which uses secondary data analysis of aggregate behavior for populations in local spatial units, and which relates that behavior to local social-environmental phenomena—simply investigates the spatial incidence of the relationships between aggregate individual behaviors and similarly aggregated spatial objective information. As stated at the beginning of the chapter, such an approach is concerned with looking at "ecological associations," and it is important that the researcher and the reader of the results of the research do not fall into the trap of the "ecological fallacy" that was discussed in Section 2.3 of Chapter 2 in Part I. From such data and its analysis and modeling, it is *not* possible to understand the basis of the underlying motivation for the behavior choices being made by individuals or groups of people regarding the activity being investigated—in this case the voting of people for a political party at an election. To do so would require the collection of primary data through a survey of voters across the polling booths studied in the case study presented here.

8.6 Acknowledgment

The research reported in this chapter draws on research funded by grants to author Stimson from the University of Queensland and from the Australian Research Council Discovery Scheme, Grant No. DP0558277. The contribution of author Stimson's colleagues Rod McCrea, Prem Chhetri, and T.-K. (Paul) Shyy to the research discussed in this chapter is gratefully acknowledged. The tables and figures in this chapter are reproduced from a 2006 conference paper jointly authored by Robert Stimson, Prem Chhetri, and T.-K. Shyy presented at the ARC Research Network conference, Melbourne, Australia.

CHAPTER 9
Intellectually Challenged People Interacting with Their Environment

9.1 Introduction

In this chapter the focus is on the study of *microbehavior* at the level of the individual, with the participants being chosen from within a "special group" in society defined by a particular characteristic, namely, people who are *intellectually challenged*. The study, undertaken by author Golledge and his collaborators, examines the *activities* of a *deinstitutionalized intellectually challenged* group by conducting "daily living" types of experiments in environments that are well known to the group and in laboratory experiments using slides taken from that environment.

The study is an example of how an *experimental design* may be developed and implemented specifically to investigate differences between the activity behavior of the "target" or "experimental group" and that of a "control group" (or a "contrast group"). It investigates the group members undertaking a number of tasks in a specific environmental setting. The selection of participants in the study was dependent on volunteers from among the target or "experimental" groups who met the required criteria for selection for both the experimental and the "control" groups who were living in that specified environmental setting. Thus, small-size *nonrandom samples* are used for both the experimental and the control groups.

The three experimental studies discussed here were conducted in the 1980s at the University of California, Santa Barbara, and at Ohio State University in Columbus, Ohio (Golledge, Richardson, Rayner, & Parnicky, 1983). The experiments were conducted in a neighborhood in those cities.

1. The first experiment was designed to determine the nature of any difference between the experimental and control groups with respect to the participants' *declarative knowledge* of both the larger city and the local neighborhood where they lived.
2. The second experiment had the participants define routes in terms of a *sequence of places* along commonly traveled *paths*.
3. The third experiment sought to assess the degree of *configurational knowledge* or understanding typically found in the experimental and the control groups.

9.2 Context for the Study of Disability and Activities in Environments

9.2.1 Disadvantage, Disenfranchisement, and Discrimination

"Disadvantage," "disenfranchisement," and "discrimination" occur implicitly and explicitly with respect to *disabled people* in all societies (Golledge, 2004). This is inevitable considering that a basic dictum of society is that the good of the many should outweigh the good of the few. It is important for us to have a better understanding of the capabilities of disabled people to undertake spatial activities and the limitations they face in particular environmental settings.

A person is labeled "disabled" if he or she is unable to perform activities and functions that are generally considered to be part and parcel of the everyday life of able-bodied people. On one hand, historically, the health professions have regarded such individuals as "impaired," "abnormal," or "disabled." Some social scientists, on the other hand, focus on situations where a person is considered disabled if there is an inability to engage in actions and activities that are perceived to be "norms" in a given society, economy, or culture. Nontraditional activities and behaviors are often interpreted in terms of "disenfranchisement" and "discrimination." Impairments, however, are often linked with abnormalities of body structure, organ, or system function and appearance (that is, they usually are perceived as having a physical base or, if mental in nature, are reflected by types of behaviors). Disabilities usually reflect the consequences of impairments in terms of functional performance; that is, a person is regarded as disabled when he or she is unable to perform or mimic a variety of actions or activities that are usually undertaken by the rest of a population. As a bridging term, "handicapped" is often designated as being associated with the disadvantages experienced as a result of impairment and disability, and the interaction of an individual with his or her surroundings. But this term has become politically incorrect, and is used less frequently in today's societies and cultures.

This raises the fundamental question concerning who are "the disabled." Increasingly, as a group disabled people are referred to as "the other," a term that has been coined to cover groups who suffer a loss of freedom or a loss of independence for one reason or another. The reasons may be physical, mental, social, economic, political, or religious in nature, or may be caused by other factors that repress, disenfranchise, or discriminate. For some groups, such as "the poor," "the indigent," and "racial," "ethnic," or "cultural" groups, the disabling factors are usually bound up in the structure of the society. Discrimination against women, ethnic groups, and groups with distinct sexual preferences has occupied the attention of many social scientists. Traditionally, less attention has been given to those who suffer disability largely because of a physical or mental impairment. In this chapter, and in Chapter 10 to follow, we focus primarily on this latter group.

9.2.2 Disabling Environments

Most cultures inherit their environments together with modifications made to both natural and built environments by their predecessors. Architectural styles of previous centuries may still dominate the building structure and spaces of large proportions of today's cities. Entrances and exits to buildings are likewise usually inherited, with combinations of architecture, design, artistic quality, or simply convenience as critical controlling factors. Thus, doors requiring round handles that have to be turned in order to open them historically discriminate against people with crippling arthritis or others with similar limited hand-functioning ability. Such a condition has not prevented the continued use of building doors with round doorknobs. But, as we will see later, over the last few decades there has been increasing pressure to address the problem of environmental discrimination by producing barrier-free environments. In such cases, architectural and design modifications have been made, but usually only to a very small part of any total built environment.

Disabling environments are not restricted to buildings and their uses, however; different forms of transportation, the important element that enables freedom of movement from place to place, likewise have traditionally incorporated limitations that are not easily overcome by many disabled groups. Many of the current and ongoing environmental changes are directed toward removal of both physical and social barriers facing disabled people. For example, for many years blind individuals who relied on a guide dog for travel assistance were not allowed to take the dog on public transit or into common restaurant spaces. Those confined to wheelchairs had difficulty using mass transit such as buses or trains that left gaps between the vehicle interior and the edge of the platform or required the ability to climb steps to enter or leave a vehicle. And today, computers that were designed with interfaces requiring nimble fingers for keyboard input or vision for mouse or joystick input are being modified for voice control at both the input and output phases.

9.2.3 Activities of Intellectually Challenged Groups Interacting in Their Immediate Environments

We now turn to an examination of activity and activity spaces associated with some disabled groups. Until a few decades ago, they rarely were able to venture beyond institutional walls. Now ensconced in group homes or private institutions that have relaxed the rigid confinement codes of yesteryear, some intellectually challenged people have more freedom to interact with ordinary environments.

Intellectually challenged groups—and more particularly those traditionally referred to as mildly, moderately, or severely challenged individuals—are limited in their ability to accumulate spatial knowledge, store it, and use it in traditional ways. These limitations are the result of impaired information processing and sensing abilities resulting in an inability to comprehend the nature of large-scale macrospaces or functionally complex environments. The same limitations can be found when group members face the task of using two-dimensional abstract representations of large-scale environments—that is, *maps*. These situations are some of the results of selective physiological impairment, including localized brain damage; rotation or reflection problems, such as might be found in those suffering from dyslexia or loss (or lack) of development of spatial memory capacity; and limited problem-solving ability. Given these constraints, it seems inevitable that members of this population would have difficulty understanding the many different nuances of today's complex environmental systems, such as today's cities.

In all cities, buildings are usually classifiable based on functional differences (see Table 9.1). For example, for members of these groups, locations may not be easily understood (that is, unless labels and signifiers are clear, such as McDonald's hamburgers and the "Golden Arches"). But additional even fundamental spatial concepts (such as indirect connectivity, density, arrangement, pattern, shape, regions, spatial association, and so on) are not readily comprehended. For example, it may not be perceived by members of this group that different buses passing the same bus stop location day after day may be headed for quite different destinations. Location can become clouded by multiple identities, for example, by referring to a single place by multiple names such as "the corner of State and High," "Olson's corner," "bank corner," and so on. The size or magnitude dimensions or function of a place also may

TABLE 9.1. Common Environmental Cues in Cities

1. Shopping centers
2. Railroad crossings
3. Direction signs
4. School buildings
5. Banks
6. Churches
7. Movie theaters
8. Restaurants
9. Open areas such as parks or green spaces
10. Speed limit signs
11. The city skyline
12. Traffic congestion
13. Traffic lights
14. Street-width changes
15. Billboards
16. Figures
17. Neon lights in business areas
18. Rivers, streams, or other water bodies
19. Hills
20. Any freeway system
21. Number and spacing of freeway exits
22. Individual buildings (architectural style)
23. Public buildings (functional characteristics)
24. Residential-quality changes (housing submarket changes)
25. Residential-density changes (housing spacing)
26. Smog
27. Increased density of buildings in low-type situations
28. Major department stores
29. Slums
30. Construction work

have little meaning beyond a simple relational statement of "bigger than" or "smaller than." Time may not be regarded in a traditionally measured way. Consequently, *activity patterns* may be few in number, uncomplicated, and with very low periodicity or repetition ratios. Preliminary discussions with members of several group homes elicited only three general classes of city functions (see Table 9.2).

Movement problems are usually solved only in one dimension (that is, by comprehending cue or route segment sequencing), and concepts of *network integration* and *connectivity* are invariably poorly understood. Complex or continuous decision making and choice behavior may be too difficult to handle as a problem-solving device and movements may be restricted among a limited number of habitually patronized places. *Search* and *exploration* may be substantially limited. Freedom of movement may be necessarily controlled by the need for some guide or supervisory person to be present at all times.

Thus, given a constrained ability to comprehend even elementary components of a complex built environment, we may conclude that the environment as perceived, stored in long-term memory, recalled, and used on the part of those who are intellectually challenged may be substantially different in terms of complexity and comprehension from those same perceptual encodings that would be typical of able-bodied persons in a given population. The difference may not only consist of a severely limited set of encoded and stored memories of objects, their functions, and their uses, but also in terms of an ability to link activities with environments. For example, if one is unable to recognize a particular storefront as a pharmacy as opposed to a theater, appropriate behaviors that are outside the range of acceptability may be initiated and the result may prohibit goal achievement.

Given this background material, the discussion now turns to describing a set of experiments that could be undertaken to provide empirical evidence of the capacity to use environments by members of this particular disabled group.

TABLE 9.2. Principal Types of Fundamental Cues from Group Home Discussions

Shopping centers	15
Intersections	15
Landmarks	20

9.3 The Experiments

The purpose of the research by author Golledge and his collaborators that is discussed in the sections that follow was to design experiments to compare the activity behavior of a group of deinstitutionalized moderately intellectually challenged individuals with those behaviors and activities found in a socioeconomically deprived population living in the same space (namely, a neighborhood). In this case, the disabled group will be called an *experimental* group, and the selected participants from the surrounding area will be called a *control* group (sometimes referred to as a *contrast* group). The set of tasks undertaken in the data collection phase are given in Table 9.3.

TABLE 9.3. Tasks Completed during Data Collection Sessions

A. Experimental subgroups

Session I

1. Naming places
2. Identifying slides of 20 places
3. Preliminary map board responses
4. Plotting pictures of places in neighborhood area on map board
5. Naming what one sees in city, suburban, country areas
6. Identifying slides of places in city, suburban, country areas

Session II

1. Personal characteristics
2. Educational data
3. Occupational data
4. Income and expenses
5. Family information
6. Recorded test scores
7. Residential information
8. Mobility information
9. Knowledge of community resources
10. Familiarity with city at large

Session III

1. Wide Range Achievement Test
   a. Spelling
   b. Reading
   c. Arithmetic
2. AAMD Adaptive Behavior Scale
   a. Social Skills
   b. Deviant Behaviors

Session IV

1. Places on/off routes
   a. to grocery store
   b. to workshop
   c. to shopping mall
   d. to downtown department store
2. Sequence places along routes
   a. to grocery store
   b. to workshop
   c. to downtown department store
   d. to neighborhood movie

Session V

1. Bicycle or walk to and from
   a. neighborhood food shop
   b. neighborhood movie
2. GQ in auto to and from
   a. workshop
   b. shopping mall
3. Go in bus or auto to and from downtown department store

B. Contrast groups

1. Naming places
2. Identifying 20 slides of places
3. Preliminary map board responses
4. Plotting pictures of places in neighborhood on map board
5. Naming what one sees in city, suburban, country areas
6. Identifying slides of places in city, suburban, country areas
7. Sequencing places along routes
8. Personal background information

Note. From Pick and Acredolo (1983). Adapted by permission of first author.

9.3.1 Experiment 1: Determining Knowledge of Environmental Cues

9.3.1.1 Procedure

In this experiment, an attempt was made to determine the nature of any difference between *declarative knowledge* of both the larger city and the local neighborhood between the experimental and control groups. A simple qualitative approach based on listings of recalled cues was used. In the experiment:

1. Each individual participating in the experiment was asked to list the features, characteristics, and places they knew best in the study area.
2. From these lists, sets of commonly recognized environmental cues were established.
3. To check on the degree of familiarity and recognition capability of these cue sets, participants were asked to identify photographs of the cues (the *scene recognition* task). This allowed a further refinement of cue sets to define those common cues rated highly familiar and recognizable by all members of the participant groups. Sixteen such cues were identified (see Table 9.4 for the 10 most familiar ones). Cues were spatially scattered throughout the environment, although a slight concentration of cues in the vicinity of the home area of both groups occurred (as any geographer would expect).

9.3.1.2 Results

Results of this preliminary experiment, however, indicated there were *no* significant differences between the recognition capability regarding these final cue sets between the experimental and the control groups. This result by itself indicated that members of the experimental group, despite the fact that they were intellectually challenged, acquired a declarative knowledge base of both the large-scale city-wide complex environment in which they lived and of their local neighborhood. This was evident in terms of being able to identify major landmarks or locally important environmental features.

No attempt was made at this stage to determine a more complete knowledge structure of either neighborhood or city for the different groups, partially because the standard procedures used to elicit such information (such as extended verbal protocols, sketch maps, and so on) appeared to severely task the capabilities of the experimental group.

TABLE 9.4. Familiarity Ratings of 10 Most Familiar Cues

Locations	Familiarity ratio
1	.866
2	.810
3	.795
4	.785
5	.754
6	.741
7	.733
8	.732
9	.730
10	.674

Note. From Golledge (1974, p. 118).

9.3.2 Experiment 2: Sequencing and Distancing of Cues Along Routes

9.3.2.1 Procedure

In the second experiment, an attempt was made to have participants define routes in terms of a sequence of places along commonly traveled paths:

1. The procedures used tested abilities to recall one sequence and to estimate (metrically or nonmetrically) the distance apart of adjacent cues.
2. All routes had a common origin (the location of the group home for the experimental group).
3. The destinations for the routes were repeatedly patronized and well-recognized places such as sheltered workshops, supermarkets, discount stores, department stores, and cinemas.

Although this task seems simple, sequential knowledge is important for pedestrian *wayfinding* and *transit riding*. As shown in research by Hunter-Zaworski and Hron (1993), the sequence of skills needed to correctly catch and ride a bus to a destination included the nine skills listed in Table 9.5.

The "real-world" task involved a procedure requiring the participants to reconstruct the *order* and *relative distance apart* of a small set ($n = 6$) of highly recognizable *cues* encountered along each route. Along with the origin and destination, four other cues were selected to make up this number along each route. Each cue was associated with a major choice or decision point along the route (Smith et al., 1982). Although routes were commonly traveled by participants from both groups, the routes were generally more familiar

---

TABLE 9.5. Skills Needed to Use Mass Transit

1. Understanding and performing the tasks needed to ride the system such as accessing the correct vehicle, entering the vehicle, traveling on the vehicle, departing it, and exiting the stop or terminal.
2. Identifying the potential origin and destination of the transit trip.
3. Identifying special services that might be required to allow the trip to take place such as wheelchair lifts, kneeling buses, low-floor buses, ramps, special routes, door-to-door pickup and delivery, or assistance in transferring between modes.
4. Acquiring information necessary to allow use of the transit vehicle. That may be via a telephone information service or through printed schedules.
5. Determining which part of the system will be used, including definition of specific routes, when to request for and how to use transfers, how to resolve fare payment problems, understanding fare media (for example, tickets versus tokens, cards versus cash).
6. To initiate the trip the correct pickup point must be identified, and if more than one class of vehicle uses that stop, the potential rider must be able to differentiate between those alternate users (for example, buses that eventually diverge to different routes).
7. The traveler must be able to enter a vehicle in the time allocated (for example, light rail), or be able to use the lift or stairs and negotiate gaps between cars or between curb and vehicle or platform and vehicle.
8. The potential rider must be able to adjust to the start, stops, motion, or noise of the vehicle and be able to comprehend announcements relating to stops or emergency actions.
9. The potential rider must have the skills needed to depart the vehicle.

Note. From Hunter-Zaworski and Hron (1993).

(that is, experimentally biased toward) the members of the experimental group. The task required participants to do two things: (1) reconstruct *cue order* and (2) reveal the *relative distances apart* of each of the *cue pairs*. This was undertaken after members of both the experimental groups and the control groups had walked over each route a number of times guided by an experimenter.

To complement the *field task*, a *laboratory-based procedural task* tested recall and cognition rather than immediate visual perception of the surrounding (local) environment:

1. The first step was to arrange markers representing *cues* along a straight line representing the *learned routes*. First the order of the cues was examined.
2. A second task required participants to place the cues at their *relative locations*, thus giving a relative indication of their distance apart. It was hypothesized that each group would deal adequately with the sequencing task, but that the control group would better perform the relative distance task (because of a higher level of comprehension of metricity).

9.3.2.2 Results

Results indicated the following:

1. Although selected individuals in both experimental and control groups performed the sequencing correctly, a greater proportion of the contrast group in each environment produced perfect ordering.
2. Both control and experimental groups consistently produced significant correlations regarding subjective and objective orderings, indicating a common ability to recognize order and sequencing properties along routes.
3. As hypothesized, the distancing component produced indicators of difference in terms of spatial comprehension. Members of the experimental group performed poorly on this task, whereas most members of the control group successfully performed it. This suggested that metric relations might not be well understood by members of the experimental group, even when those metric relations were confined to a one-dimensional problem.

9.3.3 Experiment 3: Examining Configurational Knowledge

9.3.3.1 Procedure

The third experiment attempted to assess the degree of *configurational knowledge* or understanding typically found in each group. Again, this task was completed in a laboratory setting, relying on memory and cognition. The experiment involved the following:

1. The task environment consisted of a *map board* representing a scaled-down version of the experimental neighborhood. Tapes placed along the edge of the board were identified as the major streets bounding the task area, and additional tapes represented the main north–south and east–west streets within this environment. The streets were also named. A single location—the origin of a group home—was indicated on the map board and identified by a photograph of the actual scene.
2. Participants were shown photographs of cues along a selection of familiar routes. The photographs were 3″ × 2½″ and were mounted on small napkin holders.

3. In turn, each participant was shown a set of randomly mixed mounted photographs of the *cues* used in the declarative knowledge experiment.
4. The *scene recognition ability* was checked, ensuring that each cue was familiar and was recognized with ease by all members of the participant populations.
5. Instructions were given to place each photograph at a location on the map board that best represented its relative location in the real world. During placement, participants were allowed to alter locations at will until they were satisfied with the final configuration.

This experiment was designed to test the ability to recreate a two-dimensional arrangement of well-known places at a reduced scale.

9.3.3.2 Results

Successful completion of the task would involve translating the various distances and locational components of the declarative knowledge base into a two-dimensional configurational format. This involved metric representation of geolocations scaled proportionally to represent their arrangement in the real world. Figure 9.1 provides samples of configurational accuracy expressed in terms of error ellipses associated with each point. Figure 9.1a represents the experimental group member; Figure 9.1b represents control group configuration (Gale, 1980; Tobler, 1976).

This task showed that there was substantial variance in performance within both participant groups. However, there was also interesting evidence that the bulk of the control group were able to perform the experiment with a statistically significant correlation between their subjective configuration and an objective configuration of the real location of the cues (Table 9.6). There appeared to be a fundamental problem of handling the scaling, abstraction, and configurational component of the task by most members of the experimental group.

Figures 9.2 and 9.3 are simplified illustrations of the *degrees of distortion* by selected members of the experimental and contrast groups represented as regular grids warped to fit

FIGURE 9.1a. Composite error map, experimental group.

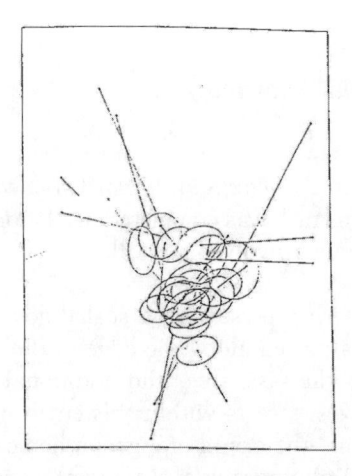

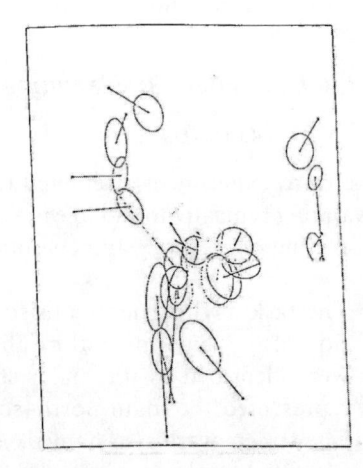

FIGURE 9.1b. Composite error map, control group.

TABLE 9.6. Experimental versus Control Groups: Bidimensional Correlations of Sequencing of Cues

Columbus subjects			
Mentally challenged subjects		Control subjects	
Subject ID number	Bidimensional correlation	Subject ID number	Bidimensional correlation
002	0.268	102	0.877
003	0.395	103	0.548
004	0.385	104	0.743
005	0.274	105	0.441
006	0.135	106	0.791
007	0.409	107	0.457
008	0.263	109	0.442
009	0.236	110	0.855
010	0.716	112	0.552
011	0.071	113	0.833
012	0.319	114	0.952
013	0.161	115	0.424
014	0.460	116	0.793
015	0.332	117	0.755
016	0.292	118	0.595
		119	0.375
		120	0.674
		121	0.187
		122	0.510
		123	0.550
		124	0.827
		125	0.940
		126	0.868
		127	0.517
		128	0.786
		129	0.240
		130	0.586
		131	0.335
		132	0.239

Note. From Golledge, Richardson, Rayner, and Parnicky (1983).

their subjective configurations (Golledge, 1977; Tobler, 1976). Although both groups have some warping, distortion, and folding, in general the configurations produced by the control group showed a reasonable degree of bidimensional correlation (Tobler, 1978) with the real-world configuration, whereas those of the experimental group were substantially distorted.

Following these experiments, information was collected on the personal characteristics of each participant. Some psychometric test scores and other background data were made available from state agencies on condition of strict anonymity. During the experiments, all supervision was under the control of licensed psychologists and social workers.

9.4 Discussion

The results of the three *experiments* discussed in this chapter provide some substantial insights into the relationship between the abilities of our chosen *experimental group* with respect to *knowing* and (potentially) *using* the environments within which they have to survive:

154 ACTIVITIES IN ENVIRONMENTS

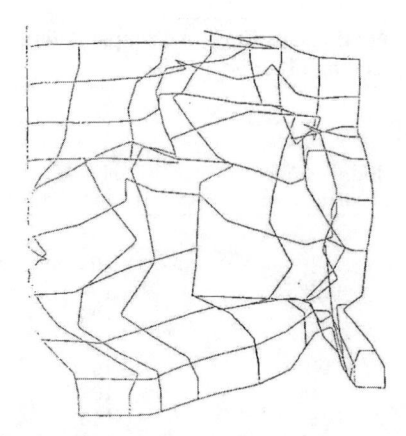

FIGURE 9.2. Control group: Warped grid.

1. There is convincing evidence that one-dimensional knowledge (for example, route sequencing) is well understood by members of this disabled group.
2. Similarly, the disabled group had significant place recognition capabilities, particularly of significant global and local environmental cues.

These two abilities are apparently sufficient to enable members of this disabled group to interact constructively with their local environment, regardless of its complexity. What also becomes evident, however, is that knowledge or awareness of spatial properties, even elementary ones such as distance, direction, and orientation, are less evident in the behavioral responses of the experimental group.

In the control (or contrast) group (that is, those socioeconomically disadvantaged members of a relatively poor section of the city's population), there appears to be no truncation of what might be expected to be a reasonable spatial ability that can be translated into successful dealings with the environment in terms of place identification, destination selection, route following, and configurational understanding.

Thus, while there is convincing evidence that members of the contrast group were able to perform all experiments at a statistically significant level with a satisfactory degree of cor-

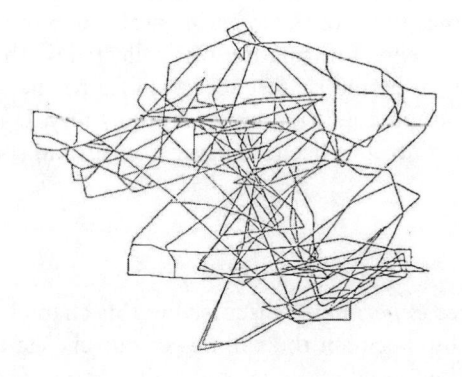

FIGURE 9.3. Experimental group: Warped grid.

relation between subjective and objective configurations (one- and two-dimensional), few members of the experimental group were able to perform at a similar level. Scaling, abstraction, and spatial relations all were done poorly by members of the experimental group. What this implies is that in some situations, such as might be the case where the deinstitutionalization of an intellectually challenged person is being considered, some effort should be made to learn the sequencing, destination choice, and cue recognition capabilities of the person about to be released into the world at large.

There was no opportunity to see if members of the *experimental group* would respond to teaching situations aimed at improving their understanding of two-dimensional configurational relations and spatial relations generally. Further experiments along these lines may shed light on such a practice, and by so doing, may limit the degree of confusion and uncertainty that a deinstitutionalized intellectually challenged person might face when being sent to exist independently in a complex real-world setting. In other words, this may be a procedure undertaken in addition to the testing and evaluation that sociologists or other behavioral scientists undertake with respect to those groups prior to deinstitutionalization (for example, walking up stairs one at a time, tying one's shoes). A different sort of spatially related testing should be undertaken as a way of assessing the potential capability of a person to exist independently or with some group home assistance in a complex real-world setting.

The results of these experiments would indicate that some attention has to be paid to assessing the geospatial competence of such individuals. At an absolute minimum, that should include the ability to function in a one-dimensional environment, such as:

- Recognizing environmental cues
- Understanding the different functions represented by different types of cues
- Linking cues in sequence to solve decision making and choice problems in defining paths between origins and destinations.

And it may be advisable—or even required—for those abilities to be tested and taught.

Other ways of examining this problem could be developed for both laboratory and field conditions. Some further understanding of spatial relations—such as distance, direction, orientation, layout, and so on—should be evaluated using either verbal tests or simple graphic tests such as sketching or scene identification tasks. The results of such a program should be the development of a markedly geospatially improved deinstitutionalized client.

9.5 Acknowledgment

The research undertaken by author Golledge and his colleagues Parnicky and Rayner and their students reported in this chapter was funded through grants from the U.S. National Science Foundation.

CHAPTER 10

Spatial Competence of Blind and Visually Impaired People When Performing Activities in Different Spaces

10.1 Introduction

This chapter focuses attention on another subgroup in the population that is disabled, namely, those who are *blind or visually impaired*. Again the activity emphasized is *wayfinding*, but this time *wayfinding without the use of sight*. The *environment* in which that activity was researched is a college campus in which learning the environment was reinforced by different practices. The main aim of the study—conducted by author Golledge and an international group of researchers—was to find which practice contributed most to successful wayfinding (Blades, Lippa, Golledge, Jacobson, & Kitchin, 2002; Golledge, Jacobson, Kitchin, & Blades, 2000).

The study design involved the selection of four *task groups*—in all a total of 38 participants—who undertook *experiments* that were conducted on campus at the University of California, Santa Barbara. Three *experimental groups* undertook specific tasks to test their wayfinding abilities. That involved them learning a route to traverse. There was a fourth *control group* that traversed the route without added aids apart from their normal orientation and mobility skills. The experiments were designed to test specific *hypotheses*.

10.2 Background Context

While it is true that some environmental modifications have been made for some disabled groups, such as the mobility-disabled, technological advances for other disabled groups have not been as readily incorporated into the everyday environment. Thus, free and independent travel has not been substantially enabled. Successful technological modifications include vehicles that can be operated using hands only, dedicated paratransit for those confined to wheelchairs, and terminally and route-elastic group transportation devices (such as scooters or electric carts) for those who have difficulty walking. However, even given these advances, episodic movement patterns representing the activities of some disabled groups are quite dependent on the assistance of other people, either as guides or operators. For example, in many cases the choice of outdoor recreation used by a sight-disabled person requires the assistance of a sighted guide. It is true, however, that there are a limited number of places where environmental modifications such as talking signs, environmental sounds, and specially prepared surfaces give an increased degree of mobility and travel independence to some disabled groups.

10.2.1 Difficulties Faced by Blind or Visually Impaired People

With respect to the sight-impaired population, successful travel is often constrained by the inability to preview and preprocess information needed for travel. Garling and Golledge (1993) discuss how previewing (creating a travel plan) allows a potential traveler to develop a heuristic for selecting a destination and a path for getting to that destination. While a sighted person can use a map together with the reading of environmental signs (including distant landmarks) for obtaining information prior to and during travel, the sight-disabled person must rely on the sighted guide (as a passive traveler), must be able to interpret verbal directions (usually given in natural rather than in technical language and consequently often spatially fuzzy), or must be amenable to using some of the personal technical aids that are slowly being developed and distributed (Table 10.1). In each of these cases, understanding fundamental geographic concepts and geospatial relations is important. These include orientation, direction, bearing, distance, proximity, linkage, and geographic association, and understanding the configuration or layout understanding of environmental cues.

The potential *traveler* must be able to develop and comprehend the local frame of reference (for example, understand the structure of a local street system) or be able to comprehend verbal interchanges that may use unique relational systems (for example, relating current location to specific landmarks) as opposed to what a sight-enabled individual might use, such as globally georeferenced location systems, textual signage, and distant environmental features.

For those who are sight-disabled, touch and sound must substitute for vision (smell may also be considered a substitute in some circumstances). But even with this type of sensory substitution, the ability to preprocess information prior to movement (that is, prepare a travel plan) may be limited if the simple processes of orientation, alignment, and establishing a frame of reference cannot be carried out successfully.

Some of the most pressing problems facing all disabled groups relate to *information accessibility* (Foulke, 1983; Marston & Golledge, 1998). The wheelchair-bound person may need to know if there are curb cuts along a potential route that will allow crossing of a street. A blind person may need to know what type of traffic control exists at intersections and whether or not there are auditory prompts that will help decide when to cross (Brabyn & Brabyn, 1983). In most of today's environments, it is still difficult to clearly integrate disabled people into ordinary environmental situations; these include vocational environments and the environments of recreation, employment, and transportation. There are also less obvious problems other than the physical ones in integrating members of disabled groups into societies where inherited attitudes and social inertia may still dominate with respect to relations between the mass of the able-bodied and "the other" (Golledge, 2004).

The movement of disabled people when using technical aids evolves only after learning about the technology, experiencing it, and beginning to feel comfortable about its operation in terms of handling some previously experienced environmental barriers. This means that an individual needs to be able to use the aid to help sense, absorb, store, and use bits of information that might otherwise be unavailable to his or her operating senses. Even when using a technical aid in a confidential manner, a visually impaired person's movement through an environment is often slower, more cautious, less graceful, and perhaps less effec-

TABLE 10.1. Technical Aids for Disabilities

Vision

Long cane
Guide dog
People (assistance)
Laser cane
Mowat sensor
Sonic guide
Nottingham obstacle sensor
Opticon (OCR)
Reading machine VOICE
Synthesizers
Tactile maps/arrays
NOMAD
Personal guidance system
Braille
Voice-operated computers
Bar code readers
Beacons
Vision-enhancing devices
Infrared detectors

Physical/ambulatory

Wheelchair (manual/motorized)
Crutches
Canes
Walkers
Prosthetics (limbs/joints)
Paratransit
Flatbed roller
Modified/refitted vehicles
Grabber
Elevator/escalator
Environmental modification
Stationary/moving ramps
Moving sidewalks
Curb cuts

Hearing

Hearing aids
Sign language
Close captioning
Modified telephones

Hearing (cont.)

Internet
Flasher warning systems
Hearing-enhancing devices (parabolic mikes)

Touch

Digitized/synthesized speech
Tape recorders
Video
Operating lights/sound
Grabber
Clapper
Chordic keyboard
Talking signs
Auditory beacons
Electronic strips
Motion detectors
Pressure detectors

Speech/sound

Sign language
Computer communication
Written aids
Artificial larynx
Prerecorded speech
"Screamer"
Nonspeech sounds/tones
Music
Pounding

Reading

Scanning devices
Digitized/synthesized speech
Kurzweil reader
Opticon
Talking signs/maps
Video/TV/radio (mass communication)
Icons/earcons
People—readers
Glasses/contacts
Inverting lenses

Note. From Golledge and Stimson (1997, p. 499). Copyright 1997 by The Guilford Press. Reprinted by permission.

tive or efficient than is the movement undertaken by a person with sight. There is also the possibility that the aid will not provide appropriate information when bypassing significant cues, modifying veering tendencies, helping with spatial updating of locations, or facilitating shortcutting procedures.

While each of these is part of the *wayfinding activities* of able-bodied people, in general they have to be facilitated and learned among sight-impaired or blind groups. Without prior knowledge of a route to be followed, for example, successful *navigation* by a blind traveler might take place, but the route might be extremely inefficient when compared to the one selected using sight.

What do theories tell us about these problems?

1. *Deficiency theory* suggests that the lack of sight or a condition of partial sight would produce distortions and errors when encoding sensed information.
2. *Inefficiency theory* argues that lack of sight does not mean a person lacks spatial abilities, but that such a person would have to substitute other senses for sight and these are less effective and less comprehensive than is sight in the spatial domain. For example, sight can deal with distant landscapes; absence of sight might imply that hearing (a less robust sense when dealing with large areas) may have to substitute, making a person more inefficient at recognizing cues, layouts, and spatial relations generally.

10.2.2 Policy Approaches to Creating Accessible Environments for Disabled Groups

Creating accessible environments for different disabled groups has become a matter of significance in the national policy domain in many countries (Table 10.2). Often labeled a "barrier-free movement," this involves the collaboration of groups of planners, engineers, designers, architects, geographers, politicians, and others interested in the built environment.

Recommendations being implemented in many countries include:

- Providing ramps for wheelchair access where steps or stairs previously inhibited access
- Providing wheelchair- and aged-person accessible toilets
- Widening doors to allow ease of wheelchair access
- Altering round door latches to lever-type latches
- Providing curb cuts for easier access at street crossings
- Installing tiled or scored concrete warning patches at hazardous places such as curbs, bicycle lanes, stairwells, and so on
- Lowering some public telephones for ease of access by people in wheelchairs
- Developing wheelchair lift capabilities in public transport
- Installing *remote infrared auditory signage* (RIAS) on mass transit vehicles (bus and train) and in congested areas such as shopping centers and airports.

TABLE 10.2. Selected Legislative Acts in the United States, 1961–1990

1. American Standard Specifications for Making Buildings and Facilities Accessible to and Used by the Physically Handicapped, U.S. Congress, 1961 (Revised 1980).
2. Canadian Building Standards for the Handicapped, 1965.
3. Access for the Disabled to Buildings, United Kingdom, 1967.
4. Design for Access for Handicapped Persons, Australia, 1968.
5. Regulations for Access for the Disabled to Buildings, Sweden, 1969.
6. Policy Document: National Commission on Architectural Barriers to Rehabilitation of the Handicapped, Designed for all Americans, United States Rehabilitation Services Administration, 1967.
7. Architectural and Transportation Barriers Compliance Board, United States, 1981.
8. Americans with Disabilities Act, United States, 1990.
9. Chronically Sick and Disabled Persons Act, United Kingdom, 1970.
10. Disabled Persons Act, United Kingdom, 1981.
11. Amendment to the Urban Mass Transportation Act, United States, 1970.

160 ACTIVITIES IN ENVIRONMENTS

Most of these efforts are the result of innovative thinking by concerned able-bodied persons.

10.3 An Experimental Approach to Examining Activities in Spaces Where Sight Is Absent

An examination of the literature reveals there is inadequate evaluation of what different user groups among the disabled either need or would prefer in order to assist them in knowing their environments and interacting with them. The experiments in the study reported in this chapter were designed specifically to find the most effective and most convenient ways for sight-disabled people to learn about the complex urban environments in which the bulk of them live and perform their daily activities. For this purpose we draw on the work of Blades and colleagues (2002) and Golledge and colleagues (2000).

10.3.1 The Environmental Setting and Experimental Design

In these *experiments*, people with visual impairments learned a 483-meter route through a university campus (Figure 10.1). To examine different ways of learning the route, four groups were defined:

- A group focusing on *verbalization*
- A group where the *travelers built table models of the routes they had covered* in order to formalize their knowledge structures and pass information on to others

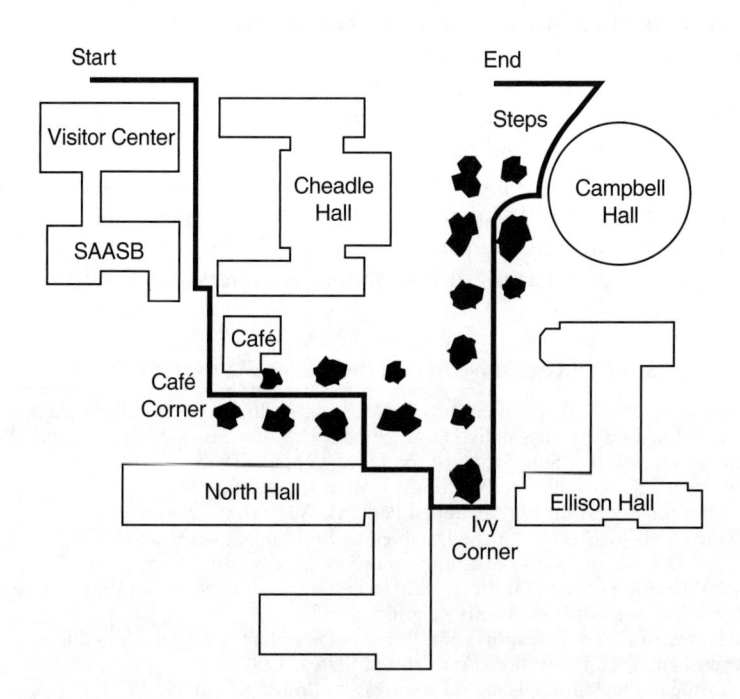

FIGURE 10.1. Plan of the route. From Blades, Lippa, Golledge, Jacobson, and Kitchin (2002, p. 412). Copyright 2002 by the American Foundation for the Blind. Reprinted by permission.

- A group who performed *pointing tasks* at various locations on route to verify their knowledge of the layout of key route-related landmarks
- A *control group* that had no added aids apart from their normal orientation and mobility skills.

Route-learning experiments were carried out on the campus of the University of California, Santa Barbara. The aim of the experiments undertaken in this study was to find out the extent to which spatial tasks such as pointing, verbally describing, and modeling experienced routes facilitated environmental learning and to determine if any one of these spatial processes was more effective than the others when pursuing this learning task.

10.3.1.1 Participants in the Experiment

Thirty-eight participants undertook the study. They were all blind or legally blind. The primary task was to learn an unfamiliar route through a university campus by walking the route several times. Initially each participant had a guided experience of the route. They then walked it three times without being guided.

10.3.1.2 Four Task Groups

Procedures differed somewhat among the four task groups identified above.

1. The *pointing group* were asked, on trials after the guided trial, to stop at specific landmarks and point to where they thought other previously identified on-route landmarks were located.
2. The *verbal description group* was required, after completing their own unguided traverses, to describe the route verbally in such a way that a companion could then follow the route without error.
3. A third group performed a *modeling task* at the end of each unsupervised trial. The modeling task used a magnetic board with pieces that represented the route segments and landmarks that could be arranged on the board to represent the route that was being learned.
4. The fourth or *control group* learned the route without carrying out any tasks during the walk or immediately thereafter.

10.3.1.3 The Experiments

Prior to carrying out the experiments, each participant met with an experimenter and received instructions in an office located some distance from the route. They were then blindfolded and guided to the start of the route, to ensure that no indicators of environmental familiarity were picked up on the way to the starting location. At the origin, blindfolds were removed. The experimenter then guided the participant along the *route* (referred to as the "learning trial"). On this trial, distinct characteristics of starting point, intermediate points, and changes of direction were made clear to the traveler. In the "learning trial," participants were guided along the route by verbal instructions given by an experimenter who walked closely behind the participant and monitored his or her safety. The experimenter also helped on this first trial by indicating where the use of techniques such as "shorelining" (that is, following the edge of a sidewalk, curb, grass verge, or the base of buildings) could be used to facilitate travel. Participants had to remember the number of route segments and changes in directions along the route. Each segment was described and guided in a like manner. At the end of the walking task, a short break was offered and the participant was blindfolded and guided back to the start of the route by a circuitous path.

On subsequent trials, the participants were required to retrace the route by themselves and to stop and name each landmark as they made contact with it. Travelers were given a constant assurance that an experimenter was following close behind them to ensure their safety in case they wandered off the path or advanced toward a hazardous obstacle. The behavior of each participant was videotaped. If the participant moved more than 6 meters in an incorrect direction he or she was stopped and taken back to the point of departure.

In the *control* condition, participants simply retraced the route after the initial guiding trial. After reaching and naming a landmark, they continued along the route until completing it. Performance was measured initially by the *response time* (RT) taken to complete each of the spatial tasks. Participants were not given any feedback on their performance.

Performance was measured in two ways: (1) the number of errors made while walking the route and (2) the time taken to complete the route. Errors included wrong turns, wrong direction of turn, wrong place of turn, incorrect identification of landmark, and so on.

The experimenters identified 28 choice points along the route where it was required to go straight, to turn, or to stop. Errors were recorded at each of these 28 choice points. At each point, a grade was given defining:

1. Successful navigation
2. Hesitation or deviation from the route that was self-corrected
3. Deviation that needed guidance for correction
4. Being lost (that is, when the participant had no idea where he or she was or how to get back to the route from which he or she had departed).

The principal *hypotheses* were that there would be no difference between the four groups in terms of their success in recalling the route the first time after walking it on their own, but that if the tasks did contribute to learning, then each of the experimental groups should, after subsequent trials, perform the recall task better than the control group (that is, the group that was given no such opportunity to assess and communicate their knowledge after each trial).

Prior to undertaking any experiment, the volunteer participants (who were paid an honorarium for their efforts) completed a survey about the extent of their sight and were asked to what extent they could see environmental features such as trees, sidewalks, or buildings. Those replying "no" in each instance were classified as severely visually impaired, and those who could see part or some of these items were classified as moderately visually impaired. Before undertaking any task, participants were also asked to rate their confidence in traveling independently. Scale values varied from 1 to 5 and included the categories "very unsure," "unsure," "undecided," "confident," and "very confident." They repeated this scaling task for a number of different environmental contexts such as being at home, on local streets, on busy roads, at traffic lights, at non-light-controlled intersections, in new environments, when detouring around unknown hazards, and when exploring unfamiliar territory. Those whose self-rating of confidence was 2.5 or higher were classed as having high travel confidence, and those whose self-rating was less than 2.5 were grouped into a low confidence class. Participants were also asked to provide information on how much mobility instruction they had received, choosing one of four options: none, little, partial, or extensive.

10.3.1.4 Participants in the Task Groups

The mean age of the participants was 54.4 years (range: 18–82 years). The mean number of years of visual impairment was 26 (range: 1–73 years). Ten of the 38 were congenitally impaired (that is, blind at birth or before the age of 2) and 28 were adventitiously impaired (that is, sight loss later in life) (see Table 10.3).

Ten individuals were placed in each of the modeling and verbalization groups, and nine were placed in each of the pointing and control groups. Age differences were carefully considered in dividing people among the four conditions and no significant mean age difference among them was found; likewise no difference was found in the average number of years of visual impairment. In each group half of the participants were men and half were women. Also, half the participants were severely impaired and half were moderately impaired. Each group had the same proportion of high- and low-confidence participants and the same proportion with respect to the amount of mobility instruction. Thirty-five of the participants used long canes as their primary assisting device, but six also used dogs. There were no more than two dog users in any condition.

10.3.1.5 The Experimental Environment

The task environment consisted of a 483-meter route (shown in Figure 10.1). It followed a path between buildings and groups of natural and artificial vegetation. Apart from the origin and destination landmarks, three others were identified along the route: Café Corner, Ivy Corner, and Steps.

10.3.2 Results

Results were assessed in terms of the number of walking errors and by the time taken to complete the route. With respect to walking errors, a 4-condition (control, verbalization, modeling, and pointing) × 3 (trials) × 2 (sight conditions) analysis of variance (ANOVA) was conducted. There was a distinct effect of trial indicating that learning was taking place. In particular, participants scored better on trial 3 than on trial 2 and better on trial 2 than on trial 1 (Figure 10.2). There was also an effect for type of sight, with moderately impaired participants scoring better than those who were severely impaired. Thus, obviously some sight helped in the recall of information (however little) about the environment and apparently influenced the ability to recall and/or represent it. Surprisingly, there was no effect for condition.

Examination of errors at the 28 choice points did indicate that some places were less or more error-prone than others. To mitigate the effect of choice point learning in early trials,

TABLE 10.3. Conditions and Participants

	Modeling	Verbalization	Pointing	Control
n	10	10	9	9
Males	5	5	5	4
Females	5	5	4	5
Severely impaired	5	5	5	4
Moderately impaired	5	5	4	5

seven choice points where performance was poorest were chosen for more detailed analysis. Statistical analysis showed that the pattern of performance in these poor empirical choice points was the same as the pattern found in the total analysis, thus indicating conclusively that the participants' performance improved across the three trials (see Figure 10.3).

When considering response times, the verbalization condition showed a significant reduction between trials 1 and 3 in terms of the time it took a participant to describe the route just completed. There was also significant improvement in the accuracy of the descriptions. Similarly, in the modeling condition, participants became more efficient and quicker at laying out the model of the route between trials 1 and 3. Models were also analyzed for accuracy of topological structure and via bidimensional analysis (Kitchin, 1994; Tobler, 1978) to measure the goodness of fit between the model and the real world. Interestingly enough, there was a significant change in the fit of the models for the severely impaired group but not for the moderately impaired group.

In the pointing condition, once again the time to complete the pointing task declined significantly between trials 1 and 3. Evaluations of the difference between estimated and true bearings (that is, the pointing error) was calculated and converted into percentages. There was no significant difference in the mean error between trials, but this was attributed to the fact that the pointing task was reasonably accurate even on the first trial. The clearest difference was found between measures of performance developed in each condition and in deviation from a measure of performance derived from the control group (refer back to Table 10.1).

The control group showed little improvement between the first and second trials, whereas other groups showed significant improvements. The modeling group showed the largest improvement and provided the greatest difference between control and experimental

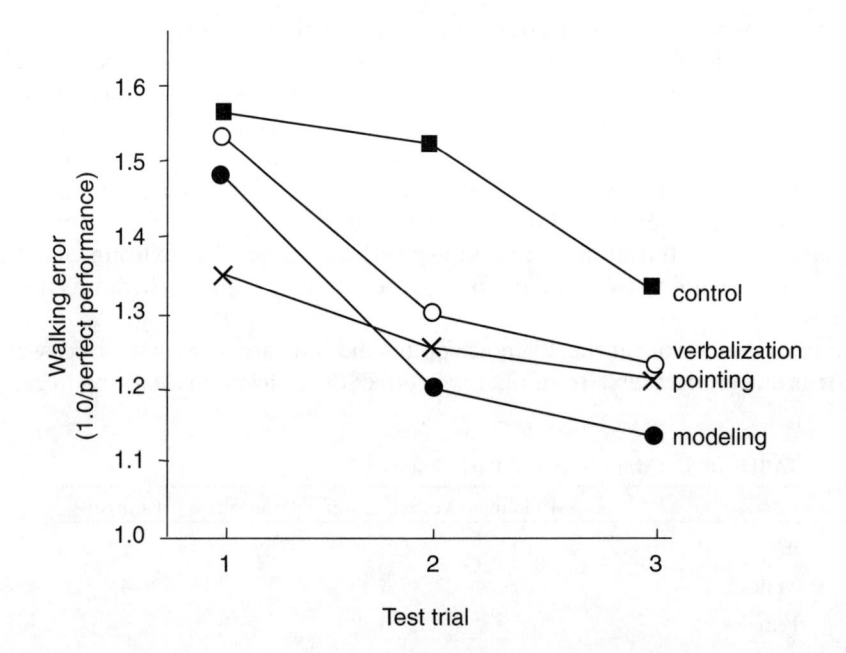

FIGURE 10.2. Walking error for all choice points: Interactions between trial and condition. From Blades, Lippa, Golledge, Jacobson, and Kitchin (2002, p. 415). Copyright 2002 by the American Foundation for the Blind. Reprinted by permission.

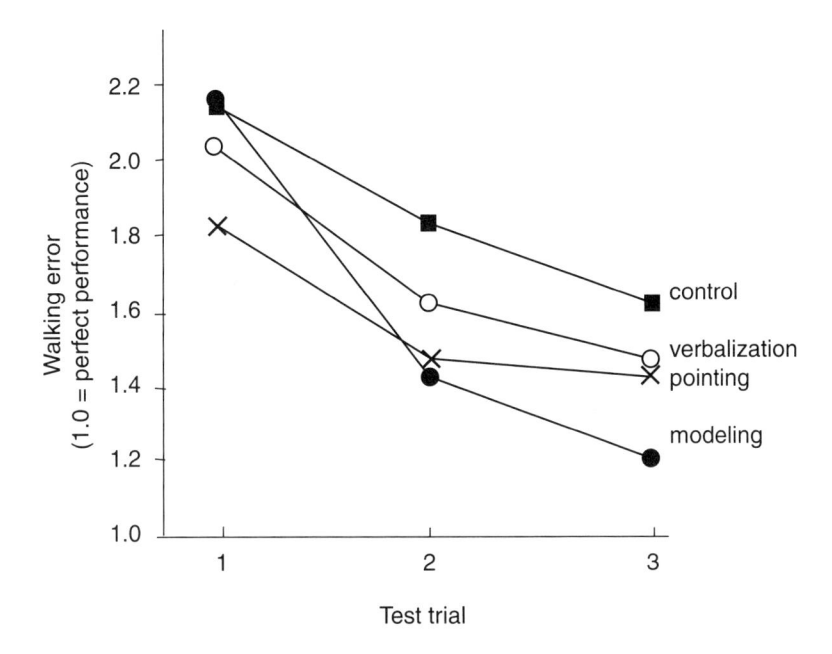

FIGURE 10.3. Walking error for critical choice points: Interactions between trial and condition. From Blades, Lippa, Golledge, Jacobson, and Kitchin (2002, p. 416). Copyright 2002 by the American Foundation for the Blind. Reprinted by permission.

group. On examining differences after the third trial, the modeling group again showed the greatest degree of difference from the control group (Figure 10.4).

10.4 Using Remote Infrared Auditory Signage

The research reported here was undertaken in the late 1990s (Loomis, Lippa, Klatzky, & Golledge, 2002; Marston, 2002), with the experiments being conducted in a specially selected study environment in San Francisco. The intent was to explore the complex *activity of wayfinding* and the *difficulties experienced by blind and visually impaired people*. A first experiment examines what happens when a travel-mode change is required. A second experiment then examines the activity of spatial updating during travel. A third experiment describes a self-contained device worn by a pedestrian to help choose a path through a complex environment.

A recently developed technical aid for blind travelers is that of RIAS. Developed by researchers at the Smith–Kettlewell Eye Research Institute in San Francisco (Crandall, Bentzen, & Meyers, 1988), this type of informational and guidance device is epitomized by a commercial product, Talking Signs®.

For this product, an infrared transmitter containing a text message of a particular duration is installed at appropriate sites within an environment. Talking Signs may be on the outside of buildings (so as to indicate street names or the type of business conducted therein) or can be installed indoors to specify and label the place of features such as stairwells, elevators, kiosks, toilets, or even specific sections within a library (for example, the public library in San Francisco is thus auditorily documented).

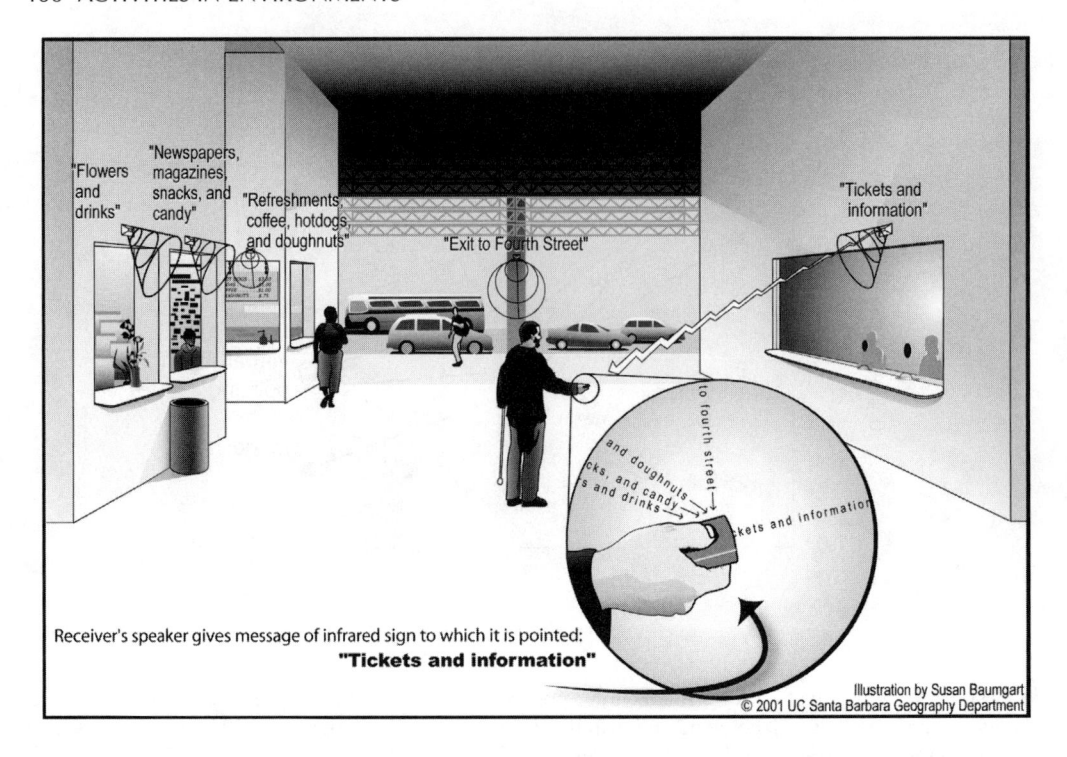

FIGURE 10.4. Indoor use of RIAS. From Department of Geography, University of California, Santa Barbara.

Label or *location information* is transmitted over a limited distance and within a specified vector (see Figure 10.4). Infrared is used so that no conflict occurs with traditional wireless messaging.

The traveler carries a handheld receiver that, when entering the vector of the transmitted message, translates the electric code to a verbal message and relays it to the traveler. In addition, the traveler can explore the limits of the message vector, bisect it, and walk directly to the origin of the message. This is particularly useful for finding specific locations such as entranceways, doors, or specific meeting places. This type of device can be programmed in a variety of languages and can be used as a place locator, as an indicator of the presence of specific types of goods or services, or as the basis for locating oneself on a street or within a larger environment. They have already been installed in many nations including the United States, Canada, Japan, Norway, France, and Australia. They provide a convenient source of information for travelers who do not read signage, cannot see specific environmental cues, do not speak or read a specific language, or are intellectually challenged to the extent that they do not read text but understand speech.

An example of an experiment that proves the usefulness of devices such as those mentioned above was undertaken by Marston and Golledge (1998). They undertook experiments at a location in San Francisco where there was a confluence of suburban rail, light rail, and bus and taxi services. With the technical assistance of researchers from the San Francisco–based Smith–Kettlewell Eye Research Institute, RIAS was installed throughout a suburban train station, at the nearby light rail station, at a major street intersection, and at nearby bus and taxi stops (see Marston, 2002).

10.4.1 Participants in the Experiment

A selection of competent blind or vision-impaired travelers from the San Francisco area volunteered to help in the experiment (approximately 40). Individuals were trained in the use of Talking Signs receivers. They were then split into two groups, one of which used Talking Signs receivers initially to perform some tasks, then followed that up by attempting to redo the tasks without the use of Talking Signs, and a second group that used their normal mobility aid initially and then used Talking Signs secondarily.

10.4.2 Procedures

The tasks developed by Marston (2002) were to imagine that one had just departed from an incoming train and wished to proceed further into the city either using the light rail, bus, or taxi service. As the individuals exited the platform, they were able to pick up RIAS-based locator information in the station, including side entrance, waiting area, toilets (male and female), drinking fountains, stores where food or drink could be purchased, and a ticket booth (see Figure 10.5). Remote signage was attached to the inside and outside of entrances, at street corners tuned to traffic lights, at the entrance to the light rail station where electronic tickets had to be purchased, and at locations along the light rail station where doors would open. Across the street remote signage was placed at a bus shelter, and outside the station on a nearby street such signage was placed at a taxi stand.

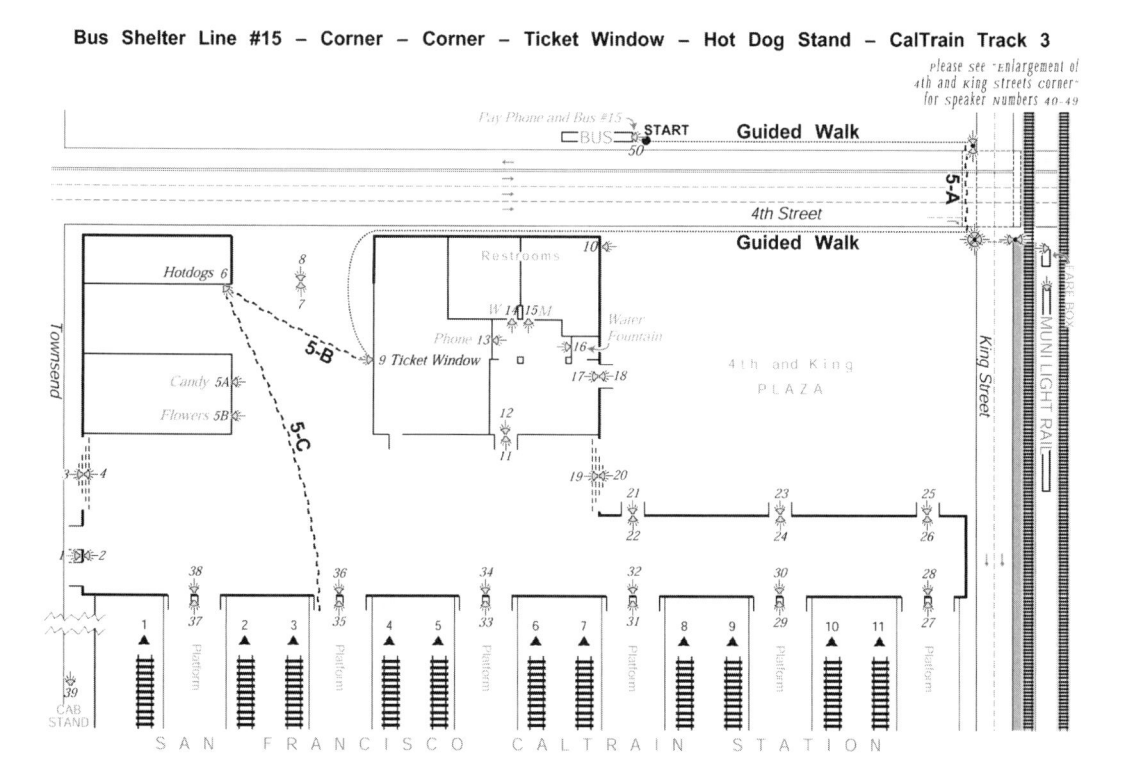

FIGURE 10.5. An environmental segment and the track of the experimental subject finding a specific destination by following directions from the RIAS. From Marston (2002).

Individuals were required to travel through the rail terminal, identifying sets of facilities, then find and simulate boarding light rail, bus, or taxi transportation. The latter task involved crossing a busy four-lane street and a busy two-lane street, each with central dividers. The remote signage was tied to the traffic signals to coincide with Walk and Don't Walk designations.

Participants reported individually to the experimenter and were closely monitored on their travel tasks. The experimenter in particular watched out for their safety, especially when faced with the task of crossing the busy streets. Participants were also asked a series of questions before undertaking any trip and were debriefed with a similar set of questions after completing the tasks.

10.4.3 Analysis and Results

The results were most revealing of the potential contribution of this type of technical aid to inner-city travelers. First, those using Talking Signs were able to complete all the required tasks. They also completed them in a reasonable time. The experimenters had determined a maximum time for each segment of the task. This was done by allowing a participant to experiment with different strategies that might help to complete the task segment. All the users of remote signage completed all the tasks well within the designated maximum times. However, for those participants using their usual mobility aid, response times were up to ten times longer, and, in many cases, participants were not able to complete a task segment within the maximum allowable time. This was particularly true when faced with the problem of crossing the busy streets at the lighted intersections. Four individuals refused to undertake this task at all, saying it was too dangerous because they could not estimate when the lights indicated that it was safe to walk. This is because of a constant stream of turning traffic that failed to stop and give way to potential pedestrians even when the Walk sign gave pedestrians the right of way.

The advantage of RIAS was manifested in terms of the value of technical assistance to help potential travelers perform tasks given this complex system of modal transfer. They had to do this while dealing with high-volume street traffic. The pre- and postreactions of both participant groups were even more remarkable. All participants, regardless of whether or not they indicated some hesitation in assigning value to the remote signage device before undertaking the experiments, uniformly agreed on its significant positive value to trip completion, safety, and the lowering of stress and fear. This emphatically indicated the value of the technical aid in helping to overcome very obvious and significant environmental and hazardous obstacles. Despite the presence of significant obstacles to traversing such spaces, without exception individuals said that if these devices were more widespread throughout the city, they would travel more frequently, more independently, and with less emotional involvement including stress and fear for safety, than they were doing currently (Table 10.4). They also indicated they would be prepared to travel more frequently, undertake more surface exploration, be prepared to explore unfamiliar areas, and be more active searching for employment given access to the environmentally friendly RIAS-enabled system (Marston & Golledge, 1998).

10.4.4 Discussion

In this particular domain, therefore, there is clear evidence that a technical aid can make an environment become friendly for blind or visually impaired travelers without having to undertake extensive environmental changes, or to change the social or economic

TABLE 10.4. Potential Obstacles to the Development and Acceptance of a Practical Navigation Aid

- No satisfactory means of determining traveler position and orientation
- Paucity of spatial databases suitable for the blind traveler
- Auditory distance perception inadequate for effective use of virtual display
- High cost
- Cosmetic unacceptability
- Hardware unreliability under extreme environmental conditions
- Errors in spatial database (for example, resulting from failure to update database as environment changes)
- Potential liability associated with system failure

attitudes of society and its decision makers. Marston (2002) was able to show that the investment of the City of San Francisco in providing widespread remote infrared signage, although involving a substantial cost, could be more than balanced by the monetary savings when not having to provide disabled people with free transit passes. Social benefits also follow when members of such groups search for and gain means of economic support other than federal- or city-based welfare systems.

10.5 Conclusion

The results from the experiments discussed in this chapter suggest that building a model of a task environment after experiencing it provided the best practice for enabling environmental learning, route learning, cue location, and comprehending spatial relations among cues.

Each of the *re-enforcing practices* partially *enabled wayfinding and layout learning*. All *experimental* groups performed better than the *control* groups. Multitasking experiments might have significant interaction effects. Given the researchers' comprehensive design, implementation, and analysis, and the fact that both quantitative and qualitative information was generated, there is little need to suggest other ways to examine this wayfinding problem. The design and the results are robust and meaningful.

10.6 Acknowledgment

The research undertaken by author Golledge and his collaborators reported in this chapter was funded by the U.S. National Science Foundation.

PART IV
Activities and Spaces

In the three chapters in this part we discuss examples of different approaches to research that investigate specific aspects of P-E-B interactions, in particular the *interactive activities* by selected *population groups* and the specific *spaces* in which a particular activity take place. The studies have been conducted at a range of spatial scales. They provide examples of data collection through a variety of approaches using research designs ranging from *large-scale probability sample surveys*, to *case studies*, to the conduct of research using *experiments*. In addition, the spatial scale of the research setting varies from a *macro*spatial context of the nation or a city to a *micro*spatial context at the scale of a space within a building. The research designs used generate a wide variety of overt behavioral, perceptual, and evaluative information and the data are analyzed using a variety of quantitative analytical methods—both univariate and multivariate statistical analysis and modeling tools—to test hypotheses using laboratory experiments, to develop behavioral activity typologies, and to derive population estimates from probability samples.

Chapter 11 provides an example of how a research design incorporating probability sampling and a structured survey questionnaire, designed specifically to generate data to operationalize a model framework derived from the literature, investigates a specific spatial activity behavior using statistical modeling tools to test a model and develop typologies of decision makers. It demonstrates how such research can provide a practical evidence base for use in a policy or business context. The study was undertaken by author Stimson and his collaborators. It investigates and models the *residential relocation decision process and choice* (as a deliberative act), which is an important *activity* that individuals and households undertake usually numerous times during their life. Here the focus is on the decision of retirees to move to a retirement community. It uses a disaggregated "push–pull" migration model framework. To undertake such an investigation requires the collection of primary data from decision-making units through a *probability sample survey* approach to collect the required data to operationalize the model framework being used.

Chapter 12 examines the influence of sex differences on human spatial activities and how spaces are used. It discusses the research designs and outcomes of a series of related studies conducted by author Golledge and his collaborators that set out specifically to test some of the key postulates that may be derived from this background research. The focus is on exploring *how changes in society's views on sex roles in turn influence how people categorize spatial activities*. The suite of interrelated studies employ a mixture of research designs, including a probability sample survey to generate population estimates of sex differences in household activity patterns in an urban setting case study. A subsample of males and females from that sample was then chosen and those people participated in *experiments* involving group sessions in which participants completed psychometric tests and several tasks related to spatial abilities. A parallel study involves a group of student volunteers who were tested to determine sex biases in spatial activities, with participants completing a survey instrument that asked them to indicate their participation in a long list of spatial activities and to rate them on a scale as being "masculine" or "feminine." Both univariate and multivariate statistical tools are used to analyze the data collected in these studies and to test hypotheses about sex stereotypes and sex roles in how people categorize spatial activities.

Chapter 13 examines how the *spatial structure of an environment* might influence the *conduct of activities* in that setting. The investigation focuses on the influence of spatial structuring on the activities of teaching and learning conducted in the *microscale environment* of an *elementary classroom*. The research, conducted by Amedeo and his colleagues, illuminates explicit research concerns involving P-E-B relationships in which spatial influences are central concerns, discussing constraints that arise in the design of research when methodological and conceptual complexities are encountered. The research discussed in Chapter 13 might be categorized as a *case study*, collecting data through an approach involving interviews to collect information through open-ended questions asked of a nonprobability sample of teachers (who are the subjects) in a small number of elementary schools. The subjects undertook a complex procedure to generate information on preferences for alternative classroom spatial configurations. An assessment of the impact of different classroom spatial layouts with respect to a set of design properties was derived using a variety of multivariate analytic tools, including multidimensional scaling, to derive clusters of the subjects and to determined how the properties of the alternative settings affect their preferences for those alternatives and their assessments of impacts on the teaching and learning activities that take place within them.

CHAPTER 11

Decision Process and Choice in the Residential Relocation of Retirees

11.1 Introduction

This chapter discusses an important *activity decision process* and *choice* that people typically experience and make a number of times during their lives. That involves the decision to change their place of residence and to relocate to another dwelling at another residential location that they choose. Thus, it is an activity that occurs in a spatial context. The research reported here was undertaken by author Stimson and his colleague Rod McCrea and others at the Center for Research into Sustainable Urban and Regional Futures at the University of Queensland in the early 2000s (Stimson, 2002; Stimson & McCrea, 2004). The objective was to investigate and model the decision process and choice by retirees in Australia in moving into a retirement village.

The study involved the collection of *primary data* through a *self-complete questionnaire* using a *probability sample survey* design. The study sought to find out the reasons why they had made that residential relocation decision and why they chose to move to a living space and environment especially designed and developed to cater to retirees as provided by retirement villages. The study analyzed a wide range of data variables generated through the survey, and it undertook *multivariate statistical modeling* that incorporates *factor analysis* and *path analysis* to develop *typologies* of retirees who had decided to relocate to a retirement village, and to investigate the factors that attract them to that form of residential space.

The study is an example of how a research design incorporating probability sampling and a structured survey questionnaire—designed specifically to generate data to operationalize a model framework derived from the literature to investigate a specific spatial activity behavior—along with sophisticated statistical modeling of the survey data can provide a practical evidence base for use in a policy or business context. The results of the study (Stimson, 2002) have been widely used in Australia by the retirement village industry.

11.2 Background Context

The residential relocation decision process and choice is complex and has been extensively investigated by social scientists, including geographers. It involves a decision-making unit (DMU) that is the household. People tend to move numerous times during their lives, and those residential relocations are often associated with life-cycle transition events, such as leaving the parental home, going to college, finding a job, getting married, having children, being divorced, remarriage, changing a job, one's children leaving home, retirement, deteriorating health and impaired mobility, and the death of a spouse. The decision to move is thus in response to one or many factors that may trigger a discretionary or a nondiscretionary response by the DMU. That leads to a process that involves finding out about feasible and desired alternative residential locations and types of housing alternatives from which to choose a new place to live. The move may be over a short distance within the same suburb or town or within the same city, or it may involve long-distance migration from one city to another in another state.

Golledge and Stimson (1997, Chaps. 12 and 13) point out that investigating the moves people make may be conducted at the *aggregate* or *macrolevel* by using census and other *secondary data*. But that only tells us about the type and number of people or households that ove from one location to another over a specified period of time. Such approaches to the study of interregional migration are important in enabling researchers to understand and model the spatial dynamics of migration and the propensity of particular groups of people and types of households to move. But such investigations tell us nothing about the *behavioral* process involved in the decision to move, and in particular of the motivations underlying such moves and the decision process and choices made by individuals and households in deciding where to live. That necessitates a *disaggregated* or *microlevel* approach that typically involves collecting *primary data* through *survey research*.

11.2.1 The Residential Relocation of Retirees

While the big majority of older people in Australia prefer to "age-in-place," many do relocate, with a small proportion choosing to move to a retirement village that provides a purpose-designed and purpose-built residential and lifestyle environment. A multibillion-dollar industry has evolved to provide that housing and lifestyle alternative for retirees. However, relatively little is known about the residential relocation decision choice process of retirees who make the move to a retirement village.

11.2.1.1 The Propensity of Older People to Move

Secondary analysis of census data reveals that only between 1 in 5 and 1 in 4 older people in Australia change their place of residence. Most moves are made within the same geographic region. The propensity of older people to move increases with advancing age, and especially after people reach their mid-70s. A move may involve downsizing to a flat, apartment, or townhouse. Over 90% of older-person (ages 65 years and over) households in Australia continue to occupy housing types where they can live independently and with autonomy. That proportion declines to 66% for those ages 85 years and over, with one-third of that "old-old" age cohort having to move to an environment where they receive care and ongoing support with reduced or no autonomy. However, only about 3% of those ages 65 years and over choose to move to a retirement village. Because the large majority of older people in Australia choose to retire and continue to live in their home by "aging-in-place," it seems that *rootedness* drives many retirees to stay put.

It has been suggested that migration can heighten enjoyment in one's retirement years (McDonald, 1986), a notion reflected in the "sun belt" migration of some retirees attracted to places noted for residential environments and lifestyle opportunities oriented to the aspirations of retirees, such as the Florida and Arizona in the United States and the Gold Coast in Australia. In general, research has shown that the movement of older people is mainly in response to changing circumstances as a consequence of transitions in the life cycle (Rowland, 1996).

Previous research has revealed that a number of individual and household characteristics seem to contribute to the decision of older people to move (Golant, 1989; Golant, Rowles, & Meyer, 1988; Loomis, Source, & Tyler, 1989; Rowland, 1996), including:

- Family ties and the location of friends
- Previous mobility experience
- The need for assistance due to deteriorating health
- The need to reduce living costs
- Previous residential ties
- Deterioration in the condition of the present dwelling and/or cost of upkeep
- The death of a spouse or close friend
- Fear of crime and the desire for safety and security
- Attraction to high-amenity locations
- A change or an anticipated change in health, finances, or social activity.

Not surprisingly, considerable variations exist between individuals and households in the relevance of those factors in the decision choices of older people to move. For example, younger retirees may choose to relocate to an amenity location, whereas an older retiree may be more likely to relocate due to deteriorating health status, the loss of a spouse, or the fear of crime.

11.2.2 The Retirement Village Alternative

The retirement village or community is a relatively recent phenomenon of the post-1950s era, but worldwide it is gathering momentum. However, it has attracted little research interest compared to other aspects of housing and residential relocation choice.

Early work in the United States suggested a segmentation of retirement relocation into three subgroups (Warner, 1983):

- The *recreation and amenity market*, where the primary motivation for moving is family and friends who have relocated to an area
- The *metropolitan convenience market*, where the motivation is a desire to maintain home ownership, especially for single older females and couples in deteriorating health
- The *supported independent market*, where the motivation is for older people to seek on-site support and care services as well as stability.

Marans, Hunt, and Vakalo (1984) classify retirement communities according to scale, population characteristics, levels of service, and sponsorship, proposing a five-category typology.

In Australia there is not yet such a wide diversity, but the industry is evolving to incorporate a range of housing and lifestyle environments offering a variety of services, including support and high-care facilities. The industry is dominated by resident-funded villages, operated by both not-for-profit church and charitable organizations and "for-profit" commercial entities. Retirees pay an entry contribution and an ongoing service fee, with a deferred management fee being deducted from the market price gained on exit. Few operators focus on rental accommodation aimed at catering for retirees eligible for social housing rent support.

In the United States, in the 1980s, Loomis and colleagues (1989) investigated why older people move to a retirement village, suggesting that the decision relates strongly to lifestyle issues. In Australia, a Commission for the Future (1992) study claims that many moves to villages are related to declining health, declining access to amenities and friends, increasing worries about home maintenance, and increased crowding in the neighborhood. Both anecdotal and survey-based information on resident attitudes to life in a retirement village suggests physical and psychological well-being is predicated on the kind of lifestyle being experienced, the prevailing sense of community, maintaining friends and relationships outside the village, and the level and type of support provided (Commission of Inquiry, 1984; Legge, 1984, 1986, 1987).

In the United States, Parmlee and Lawton (1990) suggested that a complex relationship exists between older people and their residential environments, with *effectance* (that is, the need to be competent in transactions in one's environment) being a central motivating force. "Autonomy" and "personal mastery" with respect to the environment are important in maintaining older people's morale and life satisfaction (Saup, 1986). Visual orientation, reduced risk of accidents, environmental familiarity, and neighborhood interaction are significant contributors to well-being (Regnier, 1987). Retirement communities designed and developed to enhance a *person–environment–congruence fit* can impact those physical and psychological outcomes and enhance resident well-being (Kahana, 1982; Marans, Feldt, Pastalan, Hunt, & Vakalo, 1983; Marans et al., 1984; Scott & Albany, 1997).

In Australia, Gardner (1996) found that some retirees gain advantages by selling their assets (which is usually their home) to purchase access to accommodation more suitable to their needs and lifestyle. He identifies two groups of movers to retirement villages:

1. The *planners*, who indicate future health conditions as a major consideration, along with personal security, home maintenance, isolation, and the need to be independent of family members. These retirees are proactive in laying out their future lifestyle.
2. The *reactors*, who move because of the onset of ill health and believe they are experiencing isolation or loneliness, or neighborhood change, or are having problems maintaining their home. They are more likely to be older than the planners.

11.3 A Model of Migration and the Residential Relocation Decision Choice Process

Established theoretical and methodological approaches in the study of migration and the residential relocation process and choice provide insights for investigating why retirees move to a retirement village. The published work referred to above has not developed an analytical modeling approach to investigate this phenomenon. That is what the study reported here set out to do (Stimson, 2002; Stimson & McCrea, 2004).

11.3.1 The Approach

In an overview of the migration and decision choice literature, Golledge and Stimson (1997, pp. 424–488) distinguished between two approaches:

1. The *macro-* or *aggregated* analysis and modeling of migration flows between places using *secondary* data.
2. The *micro-* or *disaggregated* analysis and modeling of migration and the residential relocation decision choice using *primary* data collected through surveys.

The *micro*approach is further categorized into:

- A *functionalist* approach, taking the view that social interactions are undertaken according to principles of utility maximization, with the decision to move being in response to structural elements in society, such as labor market differentials
- A *behavioralist* approach, focusing on overt behavior and asserting the underlying motivation of that act is goal-oriented, the assumption being that people gain knowledge about places and evaluate that information to make a decision to achieve a specific outcome.

That latter approach is readily extended to take account of cognitive processes and the judgments people make with respect to *attributes* of their current and potential future housing circumstances, encompassing both dwelling-specific and location-specific factors.

The earlier discussion of why retirees move to a retirement village points to many reasons. Fundamentally, retirees face a choice between either:

- Deciding to *age in place* or not to move from where they live; or
- Deciding to *relocate* to another place of residence either within the city or region where they live (that is, a short-distance move) or to another place in a different region (that is, long-distance migration).

In addition, at the location chosen there will be a further choice that needs to be made, and that is choosing a particular form of housing, including the retirement village alternative.

11.3.2 A "Push–Pull" Model Framework

A widely used framework to investigate migration and the residential relocation decision choice framework is the *push–pull* approach (Bogue, 1969). That early work and subsequent research (for example, Bonner, 1979; Fielding, 1992; Lewis, 1982; Warnes, 1992) proposes a range of both place-based and people-based socioeconomic, life-cycle, and locational attributes constituting factors which:

- On one hand, act to *push* people away from and thus cause them to decide to leave a place (often referred to as *stressors*)
- On the other hand, act as factors that *pull* people to a place and thus cause them to relocate/migrate (often referred to as *attractors*).

That framework is applicable to investigate the relocation of older people to a retirement village.

Over the years such modeling frameworks have progressed from being somewhat deterministic and structuralist to becoming less deterministic and more behavioralist in nature to focus explicitly on the residential relocation decision choice process. Newer frameworks place emphasis on stressors, space preference, information sources, spatial search behavior, and the trade-offs people make to achieve a satisfactory outcome (see, for example, Brown & More, 1970; Cadwallader, 1979; Clark, 1993; Clark & Cadwallader, 1973; Huff, 1986; Huff & Clarke, 1978; Michelson, 1979; Ritchey, 1976; Short, 1978; Taylor, 1979).

The migration literature also refers to *anchors* and *moorings*, which assume particular significance for the decision of retirees to relocate:

1. *Moorings* are factors attaching a person or household to a locality. They have to be "untied" if migration is to occur. Moorings emphasize social networks and reference groups, representing the relational group factors that influence a person's decision to move or not to move, particularly over a long distance (Longino, 1992).
2. *Anchors* represent a reverse concept, being conditions or circumstances that can be "pulled up" at one location and "set down" in another to provide stability. They include things like club membership, occupational and business skills, and the transfer ability from place to place of transfer payments and support services. Anchors may operate to provide stability in life circumstances for older people while being able to move readily from place to place (Manicaros & Stimson, 1999, p. 25).

Further light is shed on the propensity of retirees to relocate by the concept *habitas* (Bourdieu, 1984), which refers to a cultural process that may affect migration decisions (Fielding, 1992; Halfacre & Boyle, 1993). Shared ideals, beliefs, values, and knowledge that contribute to the societal basis of socialization may bring about a propensity to move or not to move, and may relate, for example, to disengagement with respect to a reference group (such as retiring from work) or marginalization (such as the influx of new and different people into the neighborhood) causing dislocation.

Thus, a diverse set of postulates potentially may be proposed to develop plausible frameworks to investigate why and how retirees might decide to move and to choose the retirement village housing and lifestyle alternative. In the study reported in this chapter, a generalized *push–pull model framework* has been employed to analyze that decision choice process, as conceptualized in Figure 11.1.

The objective of the research by Stimson (2002) and Stimson and McCrea (2004) was to test the propositions in that model framework with respect to the process that led retirees to decide to leave their last permanent place of residence and to choose to move to their retirement village. This was done by modeling data collected through a sample survey of village residents. While there are deficiencies in the ex post facto recall method of collecting information requiring people to give reasons for a past behavioral act, and while such an approach eliminates the possibility of investigating the decision process of retirees who might or might not have considered the retirement village alternative in contemplating and making a residential relocation to another form of housing or who decided to stay put, nonetheless the survey approach used does enable the push–pull model framework to be empirically tested.

The framework incorporates the following contentions:

1. *Push factors* underlying the decision of retirees to move from their last place of residence are likely to relate to a mixture of reasons, including changing life circumstances (deteriorating health status, difficulties in coping with maintenance of the

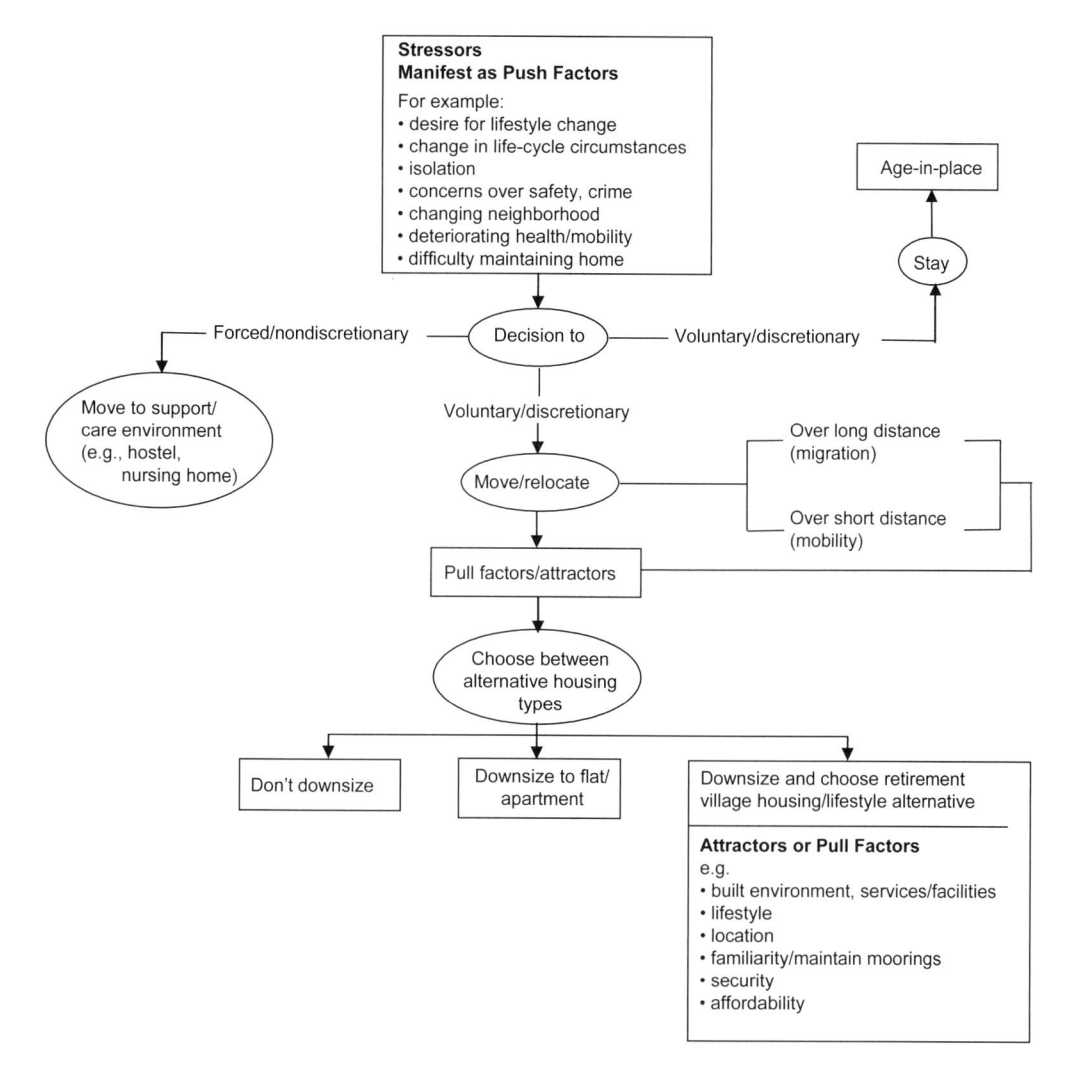

```
                    Stressors
                    Manifest as Push Factors
                    For example:
                    • desire for lifestyle change
                    • change in life-cycle circumstances
                    • isolation                                    ┌─────────────┐
                    • concerns over safety, crime                  │ Age-in-place│
                    • changing neighborhood                        └─────────────┘
                    • deteriorating health/mobility                       ▲
                    • difficulty maintaining home                    ( Stay )
                                    │                                    ▲
      ┌─── Forced/nondiscretionary ──( Decision to )── Voluntary/discretionary ──┘
      ▼                                    │
 ( Move to support/             Voluntary/discretionary
   care environment                        │                    Over long distance
   (e.g., hostel,                          ▼                    (migration)
   nursing home) )                   ( Move/relocate ) ─────┤
                                           │                    Over short distance
                                           ▼                    (mobility)
                                  Pull factors/attractors ◄─────┘
                                           │
                                           ▼
                                  ( Choose between
                                    alternative housing
                                    types )
                          ┌────────────────┼────────────────────┐
                          ▼                ▼                    ▼
                   ┌─────────────┐  ┌─────────────┐   ┌──────────────────────────┐
                   │Don't downsize│  │Downsize to  │   │Downsize and choose       │
                   └─────────────┘  │flat/apartment│   │retirement village        │
                                    └─────────────┘   │housing/lifestyle alternative│
                                                      ├──────────────────────────┤
                                                      │Attractors or Pull Factors│
                                                      │e.g.                      │
                                                      │• built environment, services/facilities│
                                                      │• lifestyle               │
                                                      │• location                │
                                                      │• familiarity/maintain moorings│
                                                      │• security                │
                                                      │• affordability           │
                                                      └──────────────────────────┘
```

FIGURE 11.1. Decision and choice factors: The advantages and disadvantages of various housing options for older persons. From Stimson and McCrea (2004). Copyright 2004 by Pion Limited, London. Reprinted with permission.

dwelling) and the desire for a lifestyle change, and that stressors precipitating the desire to move might also be related to feelings of security and safety and aspects of neighborhood change.

2. *Pull factors* attracting retirees to a retirement village will likely relate to a mixture of reasons and attributes, including the maintenance of existing social and other networks to maintain moorings, access to a new lifestyle, and the provision of a living environment that enhances *effectance*.

Modeling the push-and-pull factors is likely to identify a symbiotic relationship between them. For example, the push factor of deteriorating health status might be expected to manifest in a pull factor relating to a village providing a secure and supportive environment,

180 ACTIVITIES AND SPACES

while a push factor relating to a desire for a lifestyle change and recreation amenity might be expected to manifest in a pull factor relating to a village providing sporting facilities and healthy lifestyle opportunities in a resort-style environmental setting.

11.4 Methodology and Analysis

11.4.1 Survey Design and Data Collection

Data was collected through a survey of current residents of retirement villages across Australia using a self-completion questionnaire. The *sample frame* was the member villages of the Retirement Village Association, Australia. A *systematic sampling* procedure and a *structured survey questionnaire* were used. A probability sampling design was employed because an objective was to *estimate* some *population parameters* of retirees who had made the move to live in a retirement village. The survey covered 208 member villages of the Retirement Village Association Australia. Managers were given questionnaires for distribution to village residents, along with instructions for a random selection of units using a sampling fraction of 1 in 7. A total of 111 villages participated in the survey. The response rate was 37%, reasonable for a self-complete mail survey, with 985 respondents completing questionnaires. Data collected from 74 respondents to an earlier pilot study (Manicaros & Stimson, 1999) of four villages were added to the database to give a sample of $n = 1,069$ for data analysis.

The survey consisted of 55 questions. In addition to demographic and socioeconomic information, a range of attitudinal and behavioral information was collected relating to the decision of retirees to leave their home (the *push factors*) and to choose to move to a village (the *pull factors*), and of their evaluation of services and facilities and their assessment of satisfaction with life in their village.

Multivariate statistical analytic tools—including *factor analysis* and *path analysis*—were used to model the relationships between both push and pull factors and the demographic and socioeconomic attributes of retirees, as well as the attributes of the home they left and the retirement village to which they moved.

11.4.2 Analyzing and Modeling the "Push" Factors

11.4.2.1 The Main Reasons Why Retirees Decided to Move

Stimson (2002) and Stimson and McCrea (2004) list why retirees decided to leave where they had been living and seek an alternative residential dwelling and location. In order of importance, those reasons relate to health issues and the need for assistance, death of a spouse or partner, problems maintaining the home, need for a lifestyle change, and a desire to be close to family. Those findings reaffirm earlier research in the United States (for example, see Loomis et al., 1989) and is commensurate with those in much of the literature cited earlier. The findings also reflect the role of moorings.

11.4.2.2 Factor Analysis: Summary Dimensions for the "Push" Factors

To investigate more explicitly the decision of retirees to leave their homes and move to retirement villages, the researchers (Stimson, 2002; Stimson & McCrea, 2004) used two multivariate analytic tools. Initially *factor analysis* was used to identify underlying factors that explain common variation in the reasons for leaving home. This identified four *push factors* explaining 57% of the total variance. In order of importance, those factors are:

1. *Change in lifestyle*, which relates to wanting more free time, more time to spend with other people (related to moorings), and wanting a lifestyle change. That reflects the proposition by McDonald (1986) that some retirees seek heightened enjoyment relating to amenities and activity.
2. *Maintenance*, which relates to the difficulty and cost of maintaining a home and garden, wanting a smaller home, wanting more free time, and having others move out of home. That reflects a difficulty of coping with the dwelling environment as identified in much of the existing research cited earlier.
3. *Social isolation*, which relates to the death of a spouse or partner, being lonely, and wanting to spend more time with people. That reflects a disruption of moorings.
4. *Health and mobility*, which relates to deteriorating health, the need for assistance, and no longer being able to drive a car. That reflects a commonly found reason for older people deciding to move reflected in much of the literature citied earlier.

The four factors explaining the "push" component of the model framework confirmed the general proposition that decisions of older people to move are driven by a mix of life events, coping, and lifestyle-related reasons (Golant et al., 1988; Loomis et al., 1989; Rowland, 1996).

11.4.2.3 Path Analysis: Modeling Determinants of the "Push" Dimensions

Path analysis was then used (Stimson, 2002; Stimson & McCrea, 2004) to model the *intervening* variables that might explain the characteristics of retirees who decided to move because of the dominant effect of each of the four push dimensions identified through the factor analysis discussed above.

1. The *change in lifestyle push factor* is modeled in Figure 11.2. Those retiring at a younger age, and those moving into a village at a younger age, are more likely to be

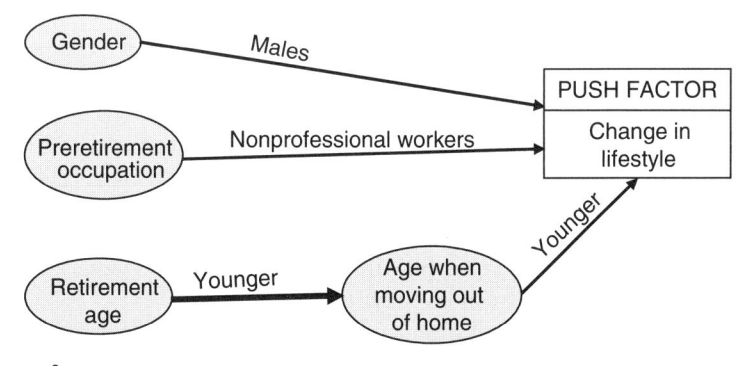

$\chi^2(3, N = 985) = 3.67; p = .30;$ AGFI = 1.00, RMR = .02; RMSEA = .02.

FIGURE 11.2. Predictor variables explaining which retirees are likely to report the "change in lifestyle" push factor. From Stimson and McCrea (2004). Copyright 2004 by Pion Limited, London. Reprinted by permission.

seeking a lifestyle change. That confirms findings by McDonald (1986). These movers equate to Gardner's (1996) proactive *planners*. Males and nonprofessionals are also more likely to report moving for lifestyle-change reasons.
2. Modeling the *maintenance push factor* (Figure 11.3) shows the most important predictors are living in a separate house and working in a nonprofessional occupation. The impact of relationship status is both direct and indirect. Singles experience this push factor directly because maintaining a home and garden is more difficult when living alone. Couples experience this push factor indirectly by being more likely to live in a house than in a smaller dwelling. Singles experiencing this push factor are more likely to be female or older males.
3. The *social isolation push factor* modeled in Figure 11.4 shows that being single is the most important predictor. These retirees are often female and older. Retirees deciding to move at a younger age are also more likely to experience social isolation, perhaps due to leaving work, as are retirees from nonprofessional work backgrounds. But these predictors are less important than being single.
4. Modeling the *health and mobility factor* (Figure 11.5) shows three main predictors of equal importance: age when moving, gender, and former dwelling type. Older retirees are more likely to be pushed by poor health and mobility impairment; males more than females cite this push factor. While most residents of villages (80%) previously lived in a separate house, if retirees had lived in a flat or apartment they are more likely to move for reasons associated with health and mobility. These findings support Gardner's (1996) notion of older *reactor* movers.

11.4.3 Analyzing and Modeling the "Pull" Factors

11.4.3.1 The Main Attributes Attracting Retirees to a Retirement Village

Turning to the *pull factors* associated with the move to a retirement village, in the research (Stimson, 2002; Stimson & McCrea, 2004) respondents were asked to select and rank five reasons from a list of 17 that might be associated with their village. The top-ranked reasons were given a value of 5 through to the fifth-ranked reasons being given a value of 1, thus producing weighted frequency scores for each reason. Figure 11.6 shows the relative importance of each reason. For ease of interpretation, the reasons are grouped into three categories derived from a factor analysis of the weighted frequency scores.

The three *pull factors* identified are:

1. *Built environment and affordability pull factor*, relating to a range of village attributes, including design and layout, site and size, services and facilities provided, staff and management, and affordability. These may relate to "effectance" proposed by Parmlee and Lawton (1990).
2. *Location pull factor*, relating to access to public transport, proximity to social activities and recreational facilities, proximity to the coast or water, the climate, and familiarity with the area from holidaying there.
3. *Maintaining existing lifestyle and familiarity pull factor*, relating to the village being located close to friends and family, close to services being used before relocating, and familiarity with the area from having lived there. These relate to moorings, and are about maintaining stability in one's activity space.

$\chi^2 (7, N = 985) = 2.77; p = .91;$ AGFI = 1.00, RMR = .02; RMSEA = .01.

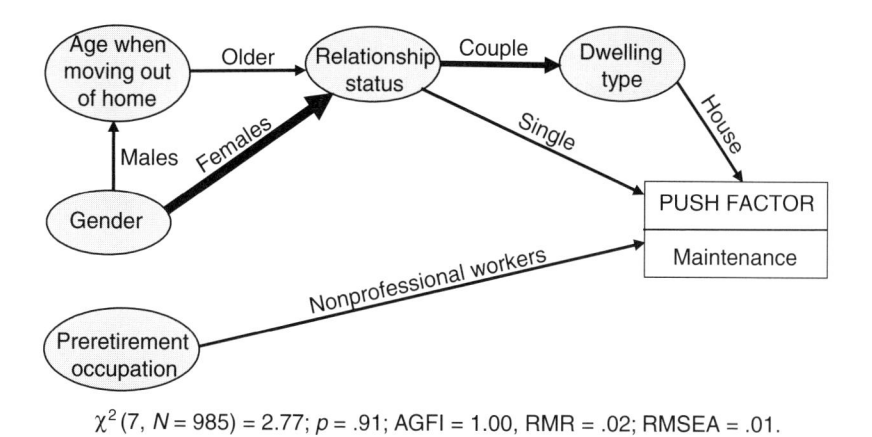

FIGURE 11.3. Predictor variables explaining which retirees are likely to report the "maintenance" push factor. From Stimson and McCrea (2004). Copyright by Pion Limited, London. Reprinted by permission.

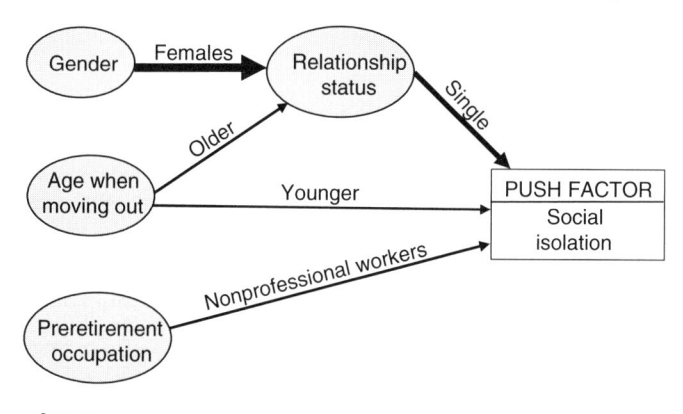

$\chi^2 (2, N = 985) = 1.70; p = .43;$ AGFI = 1.00, RMR = .01; RMSEA = .01.

FIGURE 11.4. Predictor variables explaining which retirees are likely to report the "social isolation" push factor. From Stimson and McCrea (2004). Copyright by Pion Limited, London. Reprinted by permission.

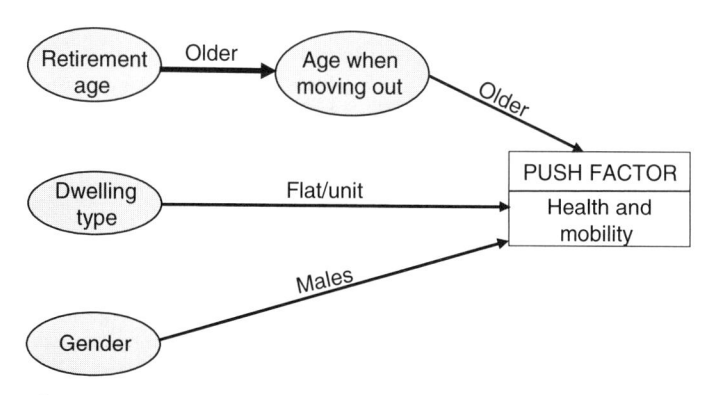

$\chi^2 (3, N = 985) = 3.34; p = .34;$ AGFI = 1.00, RMR = .02; RMSEA = .01.

FIGURE 11.5. Predictor variables explaining which retirees are likely to report the "health and mobility" push factor. From Stimson and McCrea (2004). Copyright by Pion Limited, London. Reprinted by permission.

184　ACTIVITIES AND SPACES

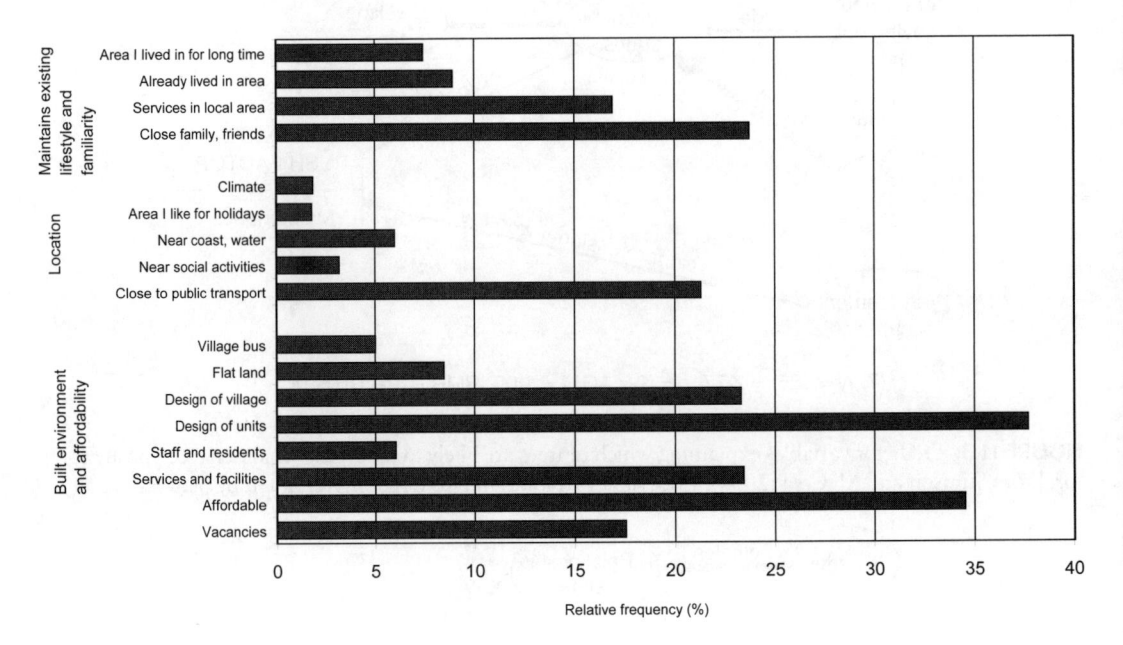

FIGURE 11.6. Relative importance of reasons attracting retirees to move to their retirement village. From Stimson and McCrea (2004). Copyright 2004 by Pion Limited, London. Reprinted by permission.

11.4.3.2 Path Analysis: Modeling Determinants of the "Pull" Factors

Path analysis was then used by the researchers (Stimson, 2002; Stimson & McCrea, 2004) to model the relationships between residents' socioeconomic and other attributes and these three pull factors. Figures 11.7 to 11.9 show the results:

1. Figure 11.7 models the *built environment and affordability pull factor.* Having visited a village previously and finding it appealing is both a direct and an indirect predictor. In other words, retirees are more likely to be attracted by the village grounds, unit design, staff, management, and affordability if they had previously visited it. Retirees are also more likely to relocate over longer distances if they had previously visited the village. Other important variables predicting this pull factor are the influence of advertising, gender, and relationship status. Couples are more influenced by the built environment and affordability pull factor than are singles, and couples are more willing to relocate over a long distances. However, male retirees are more attracted by this factor than females. The relatively strong importance of this pull factor lends weight to the *effectance* factor as a motivational force (Parmlee & Lawton, 1990) and it also suggests that the "person–environment–congruence fit" proposed by Marans and colleagues (1983, 1984) is important for many retirees.

2. The *location pull factor* modeled in Figure 11.8 shows that the distance from the previous home to the retirement village is the most important predictor variable. Presumably, retirees relocate over longer distances if the retirement village has favorable locational qualities. Those retirees moving longer distances are also more likely to be influenced by word of mouth, having friends or family living in the village, and having previously visited the village. Thus, the locational pull factor is associated not only with the geographical advantages of the village but also with the social advantages of the village. The latter finding

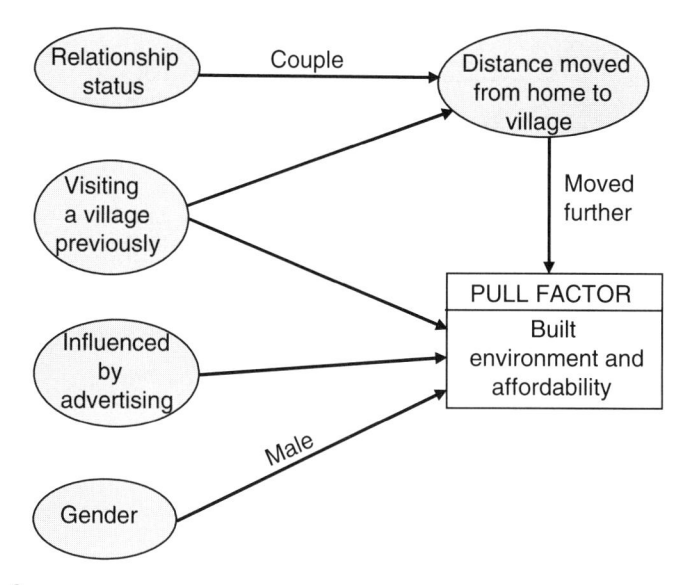

$\chi^2(3, N = 911) = 3.80; p = .28;$ AGFI = 1.00, RMR = .01; RMSEA = .02.

FIGURE 11.7. Predictor variables explaining retirees' reporting of the "built environment and affordability" pull factor. From Stimson and McCrea (2004). Copyright 2004 by Pion Limited, London. Reprinted by permission.

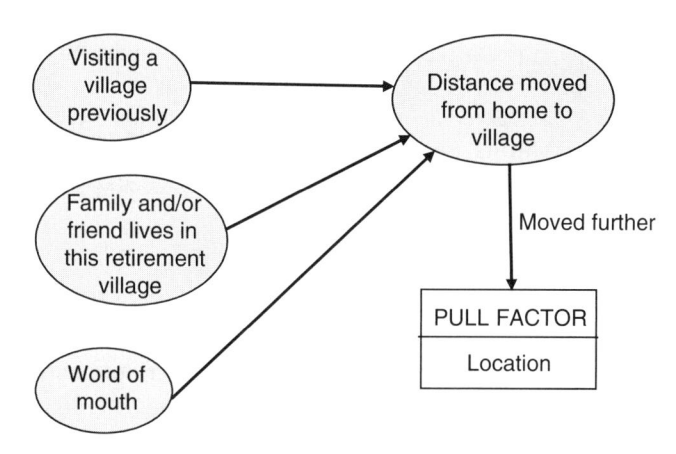

$\chi^2(3, N = 911) = 3.77; p = .29;$ AGFI = 1.00, RMR = .01; RMSEA = .02.

FIGURE 11.8. Predictor variables explaining retirees' reporting of the "location" pull factor. From Stimson and McCrea (2004). Copyright 2004 by Pion Limited, London. Reprinted by permission.

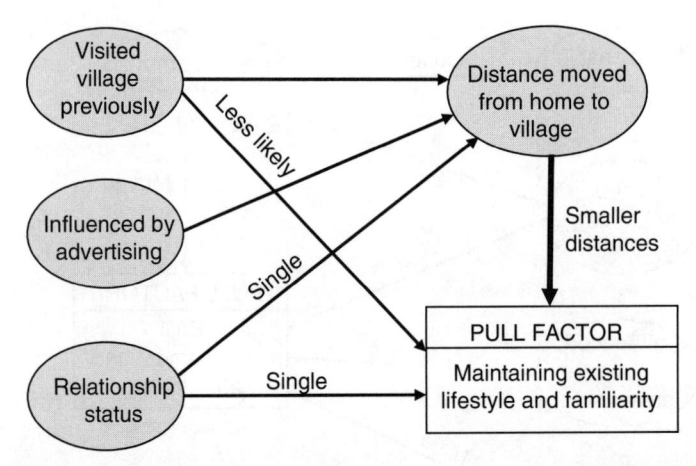

186 ACTIVITIES AND SPACES

$\chi^2(3, N = 911) = 3.77; p = .29;$ AGFI = 1.00, RMR = .01; RMSEA = .02.

FIGURE 11.9. Predictor variables explaining retirees' reporting of the "maintaining existing lifestyle and familiarity" pull factor. From Stimson and McCrea (2004). Copyright 2004 by Pion Limited, London. Reprinted by permission.

supports McDonald's (1986) contention that for many retirees a move to a retirement village can renew engagement.

3. The *maintaining existing lifestyle and familiarity pull factor* modeled in Figure 11.9 shows that the key predictor is distance moved to the village. Retirees strongly attracted by this factor relocate to a village close by. This finding suggests the importance of moorings (Longino, 1992) for many retirees who are also less influenced by having visited the village previously or by advertising. Singles are less likely to move over longer distances and are more likely to be attracted to a nearby village enabling them to maintain their existing lifestyle and area familiarity. Conversely, couples are more willing to move over longer distances and may have a lesser need to maintain their existing lifestyle and area familiarity.

11.4.4 What Retirees Are Looking for in a Retirement Village

The survey conducted by the researchers (Stimson, 2002; Stimson & McCrea, 2004) also collected data on the importance/desirability of village services and facilities and how often residents use them.

11.4.4.1 Most Important/Desirable Attributes of a Village

Figure 11.10 shows the most important/desirable service or facility (as rated on a 5-point scale) is a 24-hour emergency call system. That finding reaffirms the notion that older people place great importance on issues of security and psychological well-being as suggested by Regnier (1987) and Carp (1987). Next in importance are reputable management and staff, a community center, social activities, a village bus, a library, a lock-up garage, serviced apartments, a games room, a barbeque area, and an on-site nursing home and hostel for later care. Those services and facilities are rated as very desirable or desirable by over 60% of respondents. Services and facilities rated as very undesirable, not desirable, or neutral by

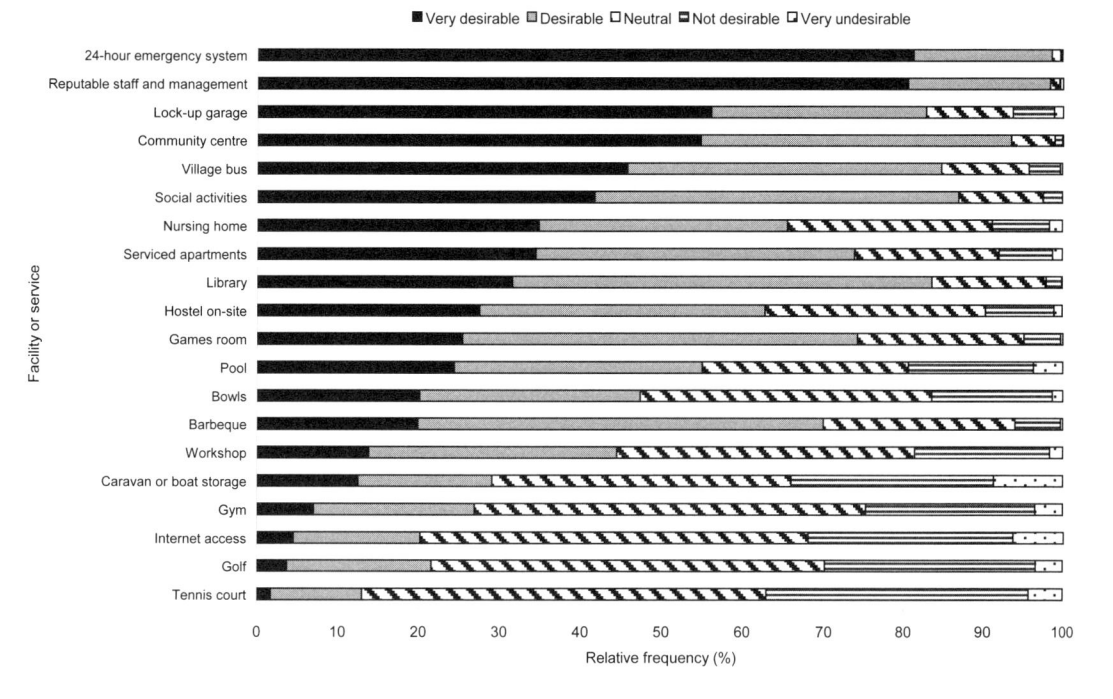

FIGURE 11.10. Retiree ratings of desirability of services and facilities being provided in a retirement village. From Stimson and McCrea (2004). Copyright 2004 by Pion Limited, London. Reprinted by permission.

more than 25% of respondents are a gymnasium, a golf course, a tennis court, storage for a caravan and/or boat, and access to the Internet.

11.4.4.2 Factor Analysis

To investigate further those 20 services and facilities, Stimson (2002) and Stimson and McCrea (2004) conducted a factor analysis of the desirability ratings identified. Three factors explained 44% of total variance in the ratings. Those factors identified are:

1. An *active lifestyle factor* defined by desirability of sporting facilities, Internet access, a workshop, and car/boat storage. This lends support to the finding by Loomis and colleagues (1989) that lifestyle issues are important for many retirees in moving to a retirement community.
2. A *social factor*, defined by desirability of a community center, games room, social activities, library, and barbeque area. This supports the Commission for the Future (1992) study and also that the notion that *habitas* is important.
3. A *care factor*, defined by the desirability of a hostel, nursing home, serviced apartments, and a village bus. This reflects the findings by much of the research cited in this chapter that many older people are concerned about gaining access to support services that might be needed with deteriorating health and a reduction in personal autonomy (Rowland, 1996).

While a 24-hour emergency call system and lock-up garages do not relate specifically to any of these desirability factors, nonetheless nearly all residents rate them as highly desirable or desirable.

11.4.4.3 Correlation between the "Push" Factors and the "Service and Facility" Factors

The *push factors* and the *pull factors* discussed previously were related to these desirability factors. The next step involved the researchers (Stimson, 2002; Stimson & McCrea, 2004) conducting a correlation analysis to investigate the relationship between the *push factors* and the *desirability factors*.

The results are given in Table 11.1. These suggest that those retirees moving from their home for lifestyle reasons are more likely to find social services and facilities desirable. One might expect there to be a significant correlation between the *active lifestyle* and the *activity* factors. However, it seems that retirees moving for lifestyle reasons prefer *social* rather than *active lifestyle* services and facilities that enhance their social interactions. The *active lifestyle* factor does not correlate significantly with the *care factor*, presumably because retirees moving for lifestyle reasons tend to be younger. Retirees moving for *health and mobility* reasons are likely to desire the *care* services as well as *social* facilities, but they are *not* likely to seek active lifestyle facilities.

The *social isolation* push factor does *not* significantly correlate with the *social* factor, but it *is* correlated with the *active lifestyle* factor. This is perhaps a surprising finding. However, many retirees experiencing social isolation are younger, and maybe these retirees are more active and use such activities to interact with others.

The *maintenance* push factor does *not* significantly correlate with any of the desirability factors, which may mean that those retirees experiencing this push factor are *not* attracted by any particular services or facilities. However, the correlations are all negative, implying that retirees experiencing the maintenance push factor place less emphasis on services and facilities when choosing a village than do residents pushed by other factors.

None of the three *pull factors* significantly correlate with any of the desirability factors. It seems that retirees attracted by village location, the opportunity to maintain their existing lifestyle and familiarity, or the built environment are *not* influenced by any particular set of services and facilities in a retirement village. However, village services and facilities are important in defining the *built environment* and *affordability* pull factor. Thus, it is surprising that retirees attracted by the *built environment and affordability* pull factor are *not* more likely to find the *active lifestyle, social*, or *care* factors desirable. This finding is

TABLE 11.1. Correlations between the "Push" Factors and the "Services and Facilities" Factors

Push factors	Services and facilities factors		
	Active	Social	Care
Lifestyle	.08	.23[a]	.06
Health and mobility	.03	.11[a]	.13[a]
Social isolation	.20[a]	.09	.06
Maintenance	−.05	−.10	−.02

Note. From Stimson (2002, p. 77).

[a]Significant correlation ($p \leq .05$).

perhaps because the design of both the village and the living unit are seen to be more important in defining the factor than the services and facilities provided on-site.

11.4.5 Satisfaction with the Relocation to a Retirement Village

In the survey conducted by Stimson (2002) and Stimson and McCrea (2004), the respondents were asked to indicate their *level of satisfaction* with their move to a retirement village. Overall, the level of resident satisfaction of survey respondents with their retirement village and with village life is high. Over three-quarters say it meets their expectations, and 17% say it exceeds their expectations. It was found that:

- "Built environment" attributes are important, with 40% of residents saying that either the unit design and the size or the village design is the most important reason in determining whether their expectations have been met
- "Social atmosphere" is also important, as are "village management," the "services and facilities provided," and the "other residents"
- Issues not considered to be important in influencing satisfaction of residents are the "number of units (village size)" and the "level of the ongoing service fees."

11.4.6 Discussion

The study discussed in this chapter found that four push factors ("change in lifestyle," "maintenance," "social isolation," and "health and mobility") explained most of the variation in reasons why retirees leave their home and move to a retirement village. Three pull factors ("built environment and affordability," "location," and "maintaining existing lifestyle and familiarity") identify the underlying reasons retirees are attracted to their village. Some push factors are associated with finding particular types of services and facilities more desirable while others were not.

Modeling the push–pull factors underlying decisions of retirees to relocate to a retirement village provides a more comprehensive picture of complex interrelationships between the attributes of retirees and their previous home, attributes of retirement villages, and the distance between the latter two. Such information is valuable to the industry for long-term planning, developing products, and implementing retirement village plans at specific locations.

11.5 Conclusion

The retirement village industry in Australia is a growing niche market in the retirement housing and lifestyle sector, but currently older people continue to exhibit a strong preference to age in place, with fewer than 3% of those ages 65 years and over living in a retirement village, a proportion less than half that in the United States. The aging of the baby boomers and increasing life expectancy will result in a dramatic increase in the number of retirees and in particular of retirees living to older ages. According to Stimson (2002), that will create circumstances for an increase in demand for a wider range of goods and services and for facilities oriented to meet the needs and fulfill the aspirations of an increasingly sophisticated and diverse market of retirees. That will likely translate into a significant expansion in new opportunities for investors, developers, and operators involved in the retirement village industry. A challenge will be to provide the product mix to ensure affordability of access so as to make retirement village living a desirable and feasible choice for the full socioeconomic spectrum of retirees, while providing a sufficient level of return to make investment in the development of the industry attractive.

The large-scale probability survey approach used in the study discussed in this chapter, and the results of the push–pull framework modeling of the relocation decision choice process of retirees who have made the move to a retirement village using the data variables generated from the structures survey questionnaire, provided a powerful *evidence base* that gives both researchers and actors in the retirement village industry a better understanding of what particular groups of retirees may be attracted to different types of retirement village services and facilities. That information has received wide media coverage in Australia and has been widely used in the industry to help it better understand its potential client base and to plan village products that are likely to attract retirees to relocate.

11.6 Acknowledgment

The research by Stimson (2002) and Stimson and McCrea (2004) discussed in this chapter was funded through the Australian Research Council SPIRT program (Project No. C79937006) and by the Retirement Village Association, Australia, as the industry partner. The material has been published in Stimson (2002) and Stimson and McCrea (2004). Text, figures, and tables are reproduced by permission of Pion Limited, London.

CHAPTER 12
Sex Roles and the Gendering of Activities and Spaces

12.1 Introduction

In this chapter the focus is on exploring how changes in society's views of *sex roles* in turn influence how people *categorize spatial activities*. The research discussed here draws on a number of studies conducted by author Golledge and his colleagues and graduate students at the University of California, Santa Barbara, in the 1990s (Montello, Lovelace, Golledge, & Self, 1999; Self & Golledge, 1994; Self, Golledge, Montello, & Lovelace, 1997).

The research design involved three separate approaches:

1. First, a large *probability sample survey* of residents in the Santa Barbara area of California completed a *mail questionnaire* to provide general background information on *household activities over time.*
2. Second, a *subset* of both *male* and *female* respondents to that *survey* were selected for further study (81 were selected). These participants were then involved in *experiments* that were designed to test for gender differences in the participants undertaking a number of specific tasks. *Group sessions* were conducted in which participants completed psychometric tests. Several tasks related to spatial abilities. *Univariate statistical analysis* was conducted on the results of the psychometric test, and the other task results were analyzed using *multiple discriminant analysis*. Comparisons were made over time to show how society's gendering ideas influence what is acceptable activity for males and females and how this has changed in recent decades.
3. In a parallel study conducted by Self and Golledge (2000), a group of student *volunteers* were tested to determine *sex biases in spatial activities*. Respondents were administered a survey instrument that asked them to indicate their participation in a long list of spatial activities and to *rate* them on a *scale* as being "masculine" or "feminine."

These studies were designed specifically to identify *changes over time* in *gendering* (as a social process) in *spatial activities*.

12.2 Background Context

There has been a considerable amount of research conducted that aims at exploring sex differences in spatial learning and differences in abilities to undertake specific spatial activity tasks. Research experiments conducted during the late 1990s (for example, Roskos-Ewoldson, McNamara, Shelten, & Carr, 1998) explored the difference between spatial knowledge gained from maps and the knowledge gained via real-world *route learning*. Those approaches were designed to explore alignment effects in both large- and small-scale spatial layouts and whether or not the viewing of maps was orientation-free or orientation-dependent. One by-product of the research was that women were found to be *less* accurate in judgments of relative direction than were men. These and other similar results tended to support a belief that men more accurately and more effectively use geospatial knowledge in their commerce with large-scale environments.

Similarly, a number of studies have explored sex-related differences in *wayfinding skills*. For example, research by Montello and Pick (1993) and Sadalla and Montello (1989) focused on investigating the accuracy of pointing to landmarks. Others, such as Beaumont, Gray, Moore, and Robinson (1984), focused on the wayfinding actions of visitors to an office building. Work by Passini (1992) focused on wayfinding by the blind. Such studies offered the conclusion that men were more accurate than women in geographic placement of buildings on a map, in locating the direction of landmarks, in estimating travel distances, and in using cardinal reference points to give directions. Other researchers found that men made fewer errors in a computer simulation of wayfinding tasks (Devlin & Bernstein, 1995), and that men made fewer errors and required fewer trials to learn a novel route through an unfamiliar environment than did females (Galea & Kimura, 1993). The latter found a positive correlation between "route learning" and "mental rotation tasks."

Several studies have indicated that men perform better on mental rotation tasks than women, and that women are more likely than men to refer to "landmarks" when giving directions. With respect to wayfinding, it is generally suggested that women express a preference for step-by-step instructions about a route, with each step being anchored firmly to a landmark. Thus, it is suggested that "women" in general prefer a wayfinding approach based on *piloting*, and that "men" in general prefer an approach based on *path integration* or *dead reckoning*. Examination of teenage and preteenage boys' and girls' maze-walking activities (Schmitz, 1997) showed that differences occurred between the way in which male and female participants undertook the task. Females showed more task anxiety and task-specific fear; boys moved through the maze more quickly than girls; girls described themselves as being more anxious and fearful than boys; and boys used more technical terms in describing routes, while girls used more natural language terms. However, the final conclusion was that there was greater variability within the sex groups than there was between them.

With respect to geographic knowledge, particularly relating to large areas beyond the immediate perceptual domain—such as a large-scale urban environment—Henrie, Aron, Nelson, and Poole (1997) have developed an *experimental design* to test male and female participants on their knowledge of physical, human, and regional geography, and in their map skills. A 60-item test was developed, consisting of questions on each of these four subareas. The experimental design also divided participants into five groups: junior high, senior high, college education/psychology, college/introductory geography, and upper-division geography. Sex differences were found with regard to geographic knowledge. Males scored on average 13% higher than females. Male–female differences were most pronounced in the introductory and advanced geography groups. The best predictors of performance found in this study were hours of reading, number of sisters, scores, and sex. The authors did note, however, that in contrast to their experimental tests, analysis of final course grades showed no significant differences between males and females (as a group) in terms of their classroom performances. Golledge, Gale, Pellegrino, and Doherty (1992) and Golledge, Dougherty, and Bell (1995) have also conducted studies involving male and female geographers and nongeographers who had to perform tasks such as route learning, distance estimation, and angle estimation. In these experiments, female geographers outperformed all other groups.

The outcomes of the studies referred to above seem to indicate a possible male–female difference in spatial ability, but the statistical evidence is not overpowering.

12.3 An Experimental Approach to Studying Sex Roles in Determining Activities

To explore more completely the nature of any sex differences (that is, whether they were a product of the particular experimental design or were more general), a large comprehensive study was undertaken in the Santa Barbara area in California by Golledge and his collaborators. The results of the first part of this study are summarized in Montello and colleagues (1999).

12.3.1 Participants

Participants were drawn from a pool of about 450 residents from the Santa Barbara area who had responded to a 2% *probability random sample* using a *mail survey mode* to collect information via a questionnaire that generated data about their *spatial activities and experiences.*

A *subset* of 81 people from that original "experimental" group was solicited to undertake further testing, and attempts were made to balance the age composition of the sample between males and females. The 81 participants began the study, but two were dropped because of lack of completion of data collection sessions. Participants were paid for their time in completing the *experiments.* They ranged in age from 19 to 76 years of age, with a mean equal to 47. Participants had a median income level between US$40,000 and $60,000 per year, and a median educational level of 4 years of college.

12.3.2 Procedures

A set of tasks were administered to each participant. They included the following:

1. *Psychometric testing.* The Hidden Patterns Test, the Card Rotations Test, and the Vandenburg Mental Rotations Test were used. These tests are visualization and orientation tests in two-dimensional and three-dimensional spaces (see Eliot & McFarlane-Smith, 1983).
2. *Route learning on campus.* For this task, participants were taken on a 420-meter *guided walk* through an area of campus. The walk required about 5 minutes to complete and meandered around sets of buildings. The initial walk constituted an independent learning trial, and no instructions were given to participants, except those needed to follow the researcher. Consequently, participants, after completing the walk, were sat on a bench and

asked to draw a *sketch map* of the route on a 8.5-inch × 11-inch piece of paper. The paper was blank, except for the initial start segment of the route, which was 55 meters in length in the real world. The line representing this on the paper provided some idea of scale for the sketches. Eight *landmarks* were pointed out during the trials and were named by the trail guide during the second and third trials. Participants were asked to remember the names and locations of the landmarks. When drawing *sketch maps*, an alphabetically ordered list of landmark names was given to the participants so that all sketches would at least contain the same number of marked locations for landmarks.

3. *Map learning.* In this task, individuals were given two *hypothetical maps* and were required to learn information from them. The first was a map of an amusement park. Individuals were asked to perform a *route-learning task* from this map. The route shape was exactly the same as that previously used in the campus experiment and also had eight landmarks in the same locations with respect to the route, as were the target locations in the campus map. The second map was a map of Grand Forks, North Dakota (this was, again, presented as a fictitious map). This map was constructed from a simplified line map of the city of Santa Barbara, with the names of target landmarks and other features changed. Participants were given 2 minutes to study the map and to learn the nature of the *route* and the eight target *landmarks*. After that, they were asked to draw a sketch of the city, including as many of the landmarks and their names as they could remember. The map study and drawing cycle were repeated after each trial. After completing the sketch maps, the participants were asked to perform estimates of the Euclidean distance between pairs of the eight landmarks. The instruction given was to establish a scale of 100 units between a particular pair of landmarks and then have participants do *ratio scaling*, using this as the base for all other landmark pairs.

4. *Extant geographic knowledge.* This set of tasks was four in number and required participants to answer questions about local, national, and international *place locations*. They included distances between places in Santa Barbara, determining which of a pair of cities was farther north or farther east (such as: "Which is farther north: Washington, D.C., or Paris, France?"). The next task in this area was *ordinal distance estimation* using city–state combinations. The questions were of the type: "Which city is closer to New Orleans: Miami or St. Louis?" The last task in this segment was *city placement*. Here, participants were given an outline Mercator projection map of the world and a list of 15 cities and the countries in which they were located. The task was to locate a small dot on the map that would be the best guess of the location of each city.

5. *Object location memory.* This was a replication of the Silverman and Eals (1992) task, where participants were taken to a curtained-off corner of a room that contained two tables. Thirty-five items were placed on the tables, on the walls above the tables, and on the floor beneath them. Participants were given 2 minutes to study the items and were told to try to memorize the identities of everything. Locations were learned incidentally. After 2 minutes, participants were taken to a different table where they were given a perspective drawing of the corner of the room and a list of the 35 items. They were then asked to place a numerical label of each of the 35 items on the drawing of the setting they had previously seen.

6. *Global spatial descriptions.* This was performed as part of the *route-learning task* on campus. After walking around and sketching it, participants were asked to describe a route into a tape recorder in such a way that someone else would be able to follow the route, based on their instructions.

7. *Self-report measures.* Finally, participants gave demographic information about themselves, including residential histories, income levels, education, age, sex, occupation,

and so on. Self-evaluations of *familiarity* with the campus, the city, the United States, and world cities were expressed in 5- and 7-point *scales*. Participants were asked also to evaluate 10 statements relating to sense of direction, spatial ability, spatial preference, and spatial anxiety. These were expressed on a 7-point scale, where 1 was labeled "strongly agree" and 7 was labeled "strongly disagree."

Tasks were administered in two sessions: (1) a group session that lasted about 2½ hours and (2) an individual session lasting approximately 1½ hours. The sessions were scheduled approximately 2 weeks apart in counterbalanced order. The assignments to sessions were made on the basis of sex and age groups.

The group session consisted of psychometric tests, the map-learning task, and the extant geographic knowledge trials. Individual sessions consisted of route learning and object location tasks, while the self-report questions were administered either at the beginning or the end of the route-learning task.

12.3.3 Analysis and Results

Two major types of analysis were undertaken: (1) a univariate analysis of the psychometric tests and (2) a multivariate discriminate analysis of the other tasks.

12.3.3.1 Univariate Analysis

With respect to the *psychometric tests*, mean scores were calculated and showed that males had statistically significantly higher scores than females. For example:

- On the Mental Rotation Test, the males averaged 16.6, while females averaged 11.8.
- On the Hidden Patterns Test, males averaged 191.4 and females averaged 177.3.
- On the Card Rotation Test, males averaged 100.7 and females 93.9.
- The difference between males and females on the Mental Rotation Test was significant at the level of $p \leq .001$.
- Despite the appearance of male–female differences in the other two tasks, nonsignificant differences occurred on the Hidden Patterns and Card Rotation Tests.

With respect to the other tasks, the following results were derived:

1. With the *route-learning task*, data was collected on errors such as turning, including extra turns; omitting turns; wrong direction turns; and landmark errors, including landmarks on the wrong route segment and skipped landmarks. Data was also collected on route distance error and straight-line distance error, as well as straight-line direction error. It was suggested that the first set of these measures related to route knowledge, while the latter related to survey knowledge. Route distance error was significantly lower for males than females (t (77) = 2.55, $p \leq .01$).

2. The *survey direction task* likewise showed a significant male/female difference (t (77) = 3.04, $p \leq .01$). On the other hand, females made fewer route landmark errors (t (77) = –1.92, $p \leq .05$). Neither route turners nor survey distance errors showed any significant difference between males and females.

3. On *map-learning tasks*, males and females did not significantly differ on any variables for the Grand Forks map. The only measure was mean error on the pairwise distance

estimation task involving the eight landmarks found on the map. Females scored better than males, but the difference was not statistically significant.

4. On the *extant geographic knowledge tasks*, on the first task—landmarks in Santa Barbara—males and females performed similarly, although again the raw scores of females were marginally better.

5. On the *city cardinal location task* ("Which is farther north?"), again no significant statistical difference was found between males and females as were responses on the city/state ordinal distance task. On the city placement task, the mean error (in miles) was significantly greater for females than for males.

6. For the *object location task* (the Silverman and Eals Task), males significantly misplaced more objects than did females. In location tasks where interpoint distances again were the prime measures, males had greater errors than did females ($t(77) = -2.49, p \leq .01$).

7. On the *verbal spatial description task*, measures included the total number of words used, the total amount of filler material and repeated words, pauses and irrelevant asides, total number of turns mentioned, total number of correctly mentioned turns, total number of "landmarks" mentioned, total number of movement statistics, total number of nonmetric distance terms such as "next" or "beyond," total number of fuzzy and imprecise metric distance terms such as "quite a ways" versus "about 50 feet," and the number of times that cardinal directions were referred. When examining these it was found that females referred to cardinal directions less frequently than males ($t(77) = -4.04$). Females also used marginally more nonmetric distance terms and largely fewer metric distance terms. None of the other measures approached statistical significance.

8. Finally, on the *self-report measures*, greater variation within the male and female subgroups was found than between them. Overall, however, males rated themselves significantly better at judging distances and in terms of thinking about cardinal directions. No other significant differences were found.

12.3.3.2 Multivariate Analysis

Montello and colleagues (1999) then performed a *multivariate discriminate analysis* to determine if some linear combination or composite of measures can reliably distinguish "males" from "females" based on a selection of the previously given task situations:

- The answer appears to be "yes," as 40 females were distinguished from the 36 males ($F(33,42) = 2.70, p \leq .001$).
- The squared mathematical correlation indicated that the shared variance between sex and linear combination of spatial measures is 67.9%.
- Overall, it was found that given an individual's performance on this set of spatial tasks, a discriminant function would satisfactorily predict his or her sex with only about 8% probability of error.
- This is much better than a simple guess, where approximate error would be 50% of the time.

12.3.4 Discussion

Overall, these series of tests indicate the possibility of differentiating between the male and female sexes on the basis of their performance on sets of spatial tasks. On some tasks (for example, mental rotation), males performed at a superior level. On other occasions (for example, the Silverman and Eals Task), females performed significantly better.

While sex differences can be found while undertaking univariate testing based on each separate task, it was found that the overall multivariate discriminate analysis indicated that the combined set of tasks would allow them to differentiate between a male and a female performer with a very high degree of reliability. This seems to indicate that the set of tasks overall showed that males and females interacted with, memorized, recalled, and used environmental information in somewhat different ways. The question raised by the earlier experiments reported in this section, however, relate to whether this is a sound distinctive generalization or whether the continued *processes of gendering* by society would also be reflected in the gendering of environments such that future studies may or may not confirm the details of the Montello and colleagues (1999) experimental procedures. To explore this possibility, another self-report study was undertaken, and is discussed below.

12.4 Investigating the Social Gendering of Spaces and Activities

The rapidly growing literature on *feminist roles* has generated a need to distinguish between two dominant terms, *sex* and *gender*:

- *Sex* differences are "biologically based"
- *Gendering* appears to be a "social concept."

To investigate this, Golledge and his collaborators use *samples stratified by sex* to examine how, over time, *changing social attitudes and social roles* have changed the image of what activities are perceived to be appropriate for "females" and for "males." This changing of social attitudes over time is one of the aspects of *gendering*.

12.4.1 Procedures

Self and Golledge (1994) devised a *pilot study* to examine *changing attitudes toward participation in spatial activities by males and females over time*. This was undertaken because of the substantial influence that feminist activism has had on activities, actions, and perceptions of the sex-based appropriateness of different types of behaviors. The pilot study compared how people classified spatial activities by *sex* by comparing two different time periods.

In an earlier study, Newcombe, Bandura, and Taylor (1983) had published a scale to measure the spatial experience of adolescents. They specifically focused on spatial activities as a way of evaluating theories of differentiated experiences based on sex. Newcombe and colleagues compiled a list of 231 activities. In their initial study, a group of 45 "male" and 61 "female" undergraduate students was selected. The students rated each activity according to whether it involved spatial ability. Participants were also asked to classify activities as traditionally masculine or feminine and to indicate whether or not they had participated in each activity. The raters were required to complete two examples and five problems from the spatial relations subtest of the Differential Aptitudes Test (DAT), which is a paper-folding test. The result was that 81 activities were selected as spatial; 61 of those were chosen as primarily masculine or feminine. An activity was classified as masculine or feminine when 75% or more of the participants labeled it (M) or (F) respectively. This dichotomous forced-choice situation resulted in agreement on 61 out of the 81 activities. However, 20 activities were not differentiated by sex sufficiently to reach the 75% rate of agreement criteria (see Table 12.1).

TABLE 12.1. Spatial Activities Listed by Sex Typing in the Newcombe et al. (1983) Study: 75% or More Agreement among Participants

Masculine	Feminine	Activities not meeting the 75% agreement criteria for masculine or feminine categorization
Touch football	Figure skating	Bowling
Tackle football	Field hockey	Softball
Baseball	Baton twirling (toss in air)	Advanced tennis
Basketball	Baton twirling (> 1 baton)	Ping-pong
Ice hockey	Water ballet	Volleyball
Advanced racquetball	Gymnastics	Beginning racquetball
Soccer	Ballet (pirouettes)	Dodgeball
Squash	Ballet (choreography)	Jumping horses
Darts	Tap dance (own routine)	Diving
Horseshoes	Disco dancing (with falls)	Frisbee
Archery	Pottery (wheel)	Jewelry (mount stones)
Golf	Embroidery (no pattern)	Drawing (3-D)
Hunting	Crochet (with seams)	Painting (3-D)
Target shooting	Knitting (with seams)	Leatherwork (with seams)
Rock climbing	Knitting (multicolor)	Sculpting
Canoeing (shooting rapids)	Quilting	Weaving (design own warp)
Sledding (around obstacles)	Tailoring	Photography (adjusting focus)
Skiing (slalom)	Arranging furniture	Navigate in car
Skiing (jumping)	Touch typing	Layout for newspaper, yearbook
Skateboarding	Interior decorating	Marching band
Fencing	Sketch clothes designs	
High jumping		
Pole vaulting		
Shooting pool		
Foosball		
Air hockey		
Glass blowing		
Building model planes		
Building train or race car sets		
Building go-carts		
Juggling		
Mechanical drawing		
Car repair		
Electrical circuitry		
Plumbing		
Carpentry		
Make/fix radios, stereos		
Sketch auto designs		
Sketch house plans		
Using compass		

Note. From Newcombe, Bandura, and Taylor (1983, p. 381). Copyright 1983 by Springer. Reprinted by permission.

In a second study, 22 "male" and 23 "female" undergraduates were administered the DAT and were given a list of the 81 spatial activities generated previously. They were asked to indicate on a 6-point scale their level of personal participation in the activities. Not surprisingly, males were found to have participated in more activities labeled as "male," while females participated more in activities judged as "feminine."

Self and Golledge (1994) undertook a follow-up test about a decade later. Specifically the question pursued was whether a decade or so of evolving social forces that emphasized the changing roles of women in society, and national trends in legislation in producing equal opportunities in many behaviors including sports (for example, Title 9 Legislation in the United States), had had any appreciable effect on the sex typing of activities. A comparison was to be made between the new data and the results from the Newcombe and colleagues (1993) experiment so the same 81 activities were used. The *pilot study* revealed significant attitudinal change regarding the sex typing of spatial activities.

Consequently a more comprehensive pair of studies was initiated. Participants in the first study were obtained from the 2% random sample of registered voters in the Santa Barbara/Goleta/Carpinteria area of California that were also used in the Montello and colleagues (1999) study discussed earlier in this chapter. Among other things, respondents completed a task involving sex typing a list of 84 activities (three additional ones were added to the Newcombe et al. set of 81).

The final pool of participants was $n = 422$. There were 257 females and 165 males. The age range of the respondents was from 19 to 94 years, with a mean of 51 years; and 92% of the respondents self-identified as Caucasian, 5% as Hispanic, and 3% as Asian.

Procedurally, respondents were given a list of 84 *activities* having a spatial component and asked to sex type them as traditionally male or female. In this task, however, the Newcombe and colleagues (1993) forced-choice dichotomous task was enlarged to be a *forced-choice trichotomous task* by adding a third category of neutral (N). Again, respondents were asked to indicate their *level of participation* in each activity.

12.4.2 Analysis and Results

The results set out in Table 12.2 were reported separated by male and female respondents (Self, Golledge, Montello, & Lovelace, 1997). Using the previous criteria of 75% agreement and a three-category classification as "male," "female," or "neutral," only six activities were sex-typed by the 425 community participants (three masculine, three feminine). This compared to the 40 and 21 respectively classified in the Newcombe and colleagues study. Forty activities were rated by the Santa Barbara participants as "neutral."

Although the participants in the Newcombe and colleagues (1993) did not have the opportunity to classify activities as "neutral," the results (at least on the surface) indicate a significant change of attitude toward the sex bias of a large range of spatial activities:

- Only "tackle football," "ice hockey," and "building go-carts" were seen by the bulk of people to be predominantly "masculine."
- "Quilting," "embroidery," and "water ballet" were seen by 75% of respondents to be predominantly "feminine."
- Most other spatial activities were seen as "neutral."

Considering that the Newcombe and colleagues (1993) participants were students and the Self and Golledge participants were community members, a third study focusing on students at the University of California, Santa Barbara, was undertaken. In this final study, 119 undergraduate students participated. They came from a pool of students in an introductory geography class but most of them were not geography majors; 73% self-identified as Caucasian, 18% as Asian, 7% as Hispanic, and 3% as black.

Procedurally, participants completed the one-page activity sex-typing survey in the classroom using the same instructions as those given to the previous groups. The undergraduate students sex-typed 20 activities using the same criteria of 75% or more agreement (Table 12.3). On average, for the undergraduate students, 48.9% of activities were sex-

TABLE 12.2. Spatial Activities Listed by Sex Typing in the Santa Barbara Community Study: 75% or More Agreement among Participants

Masculine	Neutral		Feminine
Tackle football	Bike riding	Frisbee	Quilting
Ice hockey	Volleyball	Navigate in car	Embroidery
Building go-carts	Advanced tennis	Disco dancing with falls	Water ballet
	Roller skating	Leatherwork with seams	
	Bowling	Archery	
	Checkers/chess/board games	Dodgeball	
	Marching band	Tap dance own routine	
	Layout for newspaper, yearbook	Jewelry mount stones	
	Painting (3-D)	Jumping horses	
	Sculpting	Beginning racquetball	
	Diving	Figure skating	
	Photography (adj. focus)	Glass blowing	
	Drawing (3-D)	Using compass	
	Ping-pong	Canoeing	
	Golf	Sketch house plans	
	Softball	Juggling	
	Pottery	Tailoring	
	Ski slalom	Rock climbing	
	Gymnastics	Basketball	
		Videogames	
		Touch typing	

Note. From Self, Golledge, Montello, and Lovelace (1997).

typed, compared with 33.9% in the larger community sample. Again, males sex-typed significantly more activities than did females, and again, as expected, males participated more in the 13 activities sex-typed as masculine than did the females participate in the activities sex-typed as feminine (52% and 20%, respectively).

12.4.3 Discussion

The conclusion of this University of California, Santa Barbara, study by Self and Golledge (1994) was that *sex typing of activities* differed significantly between the community mixed-age group and the undergraduate student sample, and that both of these differed significantly from the college student sample collected a decade earlier in the Newcombe and colleagues (1993) study that was conducted in the eastern United States. In the Santa Barbara study it is evident that male college students significantly sex-typed more activities than did female students, particularly with respect to activities judged to be masculine, and the participants in the study were found to sex-type almost twice as many activities as "masculine" than as "feminine." In general, the participants engaged more than once in several of the activities specified on the list, and there was no disagreement that activities on the list represented those that needed some form of spatial ability to complete.

Consequently, it was concluded that the increased emphasis on equal opportunity and feminist roles in society that had occurred during the intervening decade and a half had produced a *change of attitude and perceptions* toward "masculine" and "feminine" participation in activities. This was hypothesized to be a *degendering effect* in that many more activities were classified as "neutral," males participated in more traditional "female activities," and females participated in more traditional "male activities" than had been indicated by the earlier studies.

TABLE 12.3. Spatial Activities Listed by Sex Typing in the Student Study: 75% or More Agreement among Participants

Masculine	Neutral	Feminine
Tackle football	Tennis	Water ballet
Car repair	Volleyball	Quilting
Building go-carts	Checkers/chess/board games	Knitting
Ice hockey	Drawing (3-D)	Embroidery
Hunting	Marching band	Baton twirling (toss in air)
Plumbing	Bowling	Baton twirling (>1 baton)
Building model planes	Painting (3-D)	Weaving—design own warp
Building trains/race cars	Bike riding	
Sketch auto designs	Sculpting	
Make/fix stereos/radios	Disco dancing with falls	
Carpentry	Diving	
Electrical circuitry	Ping-pong	
Skateboarding	Layout for newspaper/yearbook	
	Photography	
	Frisbee	
	Roller skating	
	Soccer	

Note. From Self, Golledge, Montello, and Lovelace (1997).

12.5 Conclusion

All the experiments conducted by author Golledge and his collaborators reported in this chapter identified differing spatial abilities between males and females, but also indicated that no sweeping or all-encompassing generalization about one sex being "superior" in spatial ability could be supported. There was, however, an indication that different spatial abilities produce better or worse preference between males and females. The final study also appeared to indicate that what, in the 1980s, seemed to be a marked gendering of spatial activities had, by the 1990s, been somewhat defused or degendered. Societal attitudes toward accepting different activities as most appropriately undertaken by one sex or the other appeared to have almost disappeared in that formerly sex-typed activities were largely classified as neutral. The variety of experimental tasks—ranging from pilots, to self-ratings and to categorizations, to completing standard psychometric tests and evaluating extant geospatial knowledge at varying scales—gives credence to the separate and joint results of the various tasks and mix of the qualitative and quantitative analyses.

12.6 Acknowledgment

The studies conducted by author Golledge and his collaborators discussed in this chapter were funded by the U.S. National Science Foundation.

CHAPTER 13
Spatial Structural Influences on Activities in an Elementary Classroom Environment

13.1 Introduction

The broad interest in this chapter is a curiosity about how spatial structures of built environments influence the activities conducted in such settings. Amedeo and Dyck (2003) illustrate a specific case within this interest in which they explore how space is perceived to affect activities of teaching and learning as they take place in an elementary classroom environment. In their exploration, they express what must be the mutual interplays of persons, environments, and behaviors, but also emphasize the conceptual and methodological complexities inevitably encountered when attempting to work with them.

Here, then, are some of the main inquiries they try to address in their research:

- Do elementary teachers perceive classroom spatial layouts as being significant in the conduct of teaching and learning activities?
- Do they believe there are differences among spatial layout types in that regard?
- Is there one or a number of optimal spatial layouts for teaching and learning activities in an elementary classroom environment?
- In what ways do teachers' views about quality teaching and effective learning influence their perceptions about the "goodness" of classroom spatial layout types?

13.2 Complexities Influencing the Choice of a Research Design

Amedeo and Dyck (2003) realized that the lack of "theory" in the literature addressing their interests would have considerable constraining implications for how they might design their investigation. In the usual situation, well-formed theoretical conceptualizations contain construct definitions, assumptions about interrelationships among the constructs, and a logical coherence linking them together. The absence of a knowledge base of this sort affects the way any study can be approached and conducted.

Consider, for example, the authors' need for a viable definition of an elementary classroom. What such an environment includes and excludes is not clear; diverse settings, such as learning centers, preschool institutions, and child development centers, among others, are occasionally viewed as functionally equivalent to this setting. Although it seems reasonable to expect substantial commonality of meaning among instances like these at some broader level, no definition is available that might encompass them all. Without theory providing a standard definition, the opportunity for delimiting a well-defined *population* of elementary classroom environments for the study contemplated by Amedeo and Dyck (2003) was nonexistent.

In fact, Amedeo and Dyck (2003) faced a number of conceptual and methodological complications arising because of the absence of theory. These included insufficient information about the precise nature, types, and extent of this type of environment; absence, therefore, of an opportunity to select a plausible random sample; and the lack of robust theoretical groundings to serve as a basis for hypotheses. In sum, the opportunity for employing a statistical-inference, hypothesis-testing framework for pursuing their investigation was nonexistent for the authors' research interests, despite the many advantages that might accrue from using such an approach. (For a discussion of statistical inference, see Henkel, 1976; Morrison, 1969; Morrison & Henkel, 1970; Oakes, 1986; Siegel, 1956.)

One complexity, in particular, helps to explain in part the authors' choice to focus only on a particular activity-setting association. In the actual everyday world, a great variety of activity types are, of course, present in a social system, and each is typically conducted in an environment whose situational context is likely to be socially congruent to it. That is to say, environments tend to be associated with types of activities in socially distinctive ways. In the United States, for example, instances of such associations include fueling cars in gas stations, grocery shopping in supermarkets, playing tennis on tennis courts, dining in restaurants, teaching and learning in classrooms, shopping in malls, and, of course, numerous other activity–environment associations. Indeed, social pairings between activities and environments in which they are enacted are likely to be the pattern for just about any sociocultural system, the distinguishing details conforming to the ways of the particular system. Theorists such as Lewin (1951), Wicker (1979), and Heft (2001) have made reference to such congruencies between environments and activity types, emphasizing, in the process, their coherence significance in an ecological sense. Roger Barker (1963, 1968) as well reflects on this social accordance between the two with his use of the construct "behavior setting" to refer to an activity–environment association. It is its particular social-accordance sense by which an activity–environment association is known and distinguished from other such associations in society. That is because each instance of that accordance is based on sociocultural characteristics specific to its situational definition. Hence, for the authors to employ a research design that would attempt to generalize about spatial structural effects across all human activities and such distinctions would be a difficult if not impossible undertaking. Amedeo and Dyck's decision, then, to focus on teaching and learning activities in elementary classroom environments was clearly constrained by this complexity as well.

Ittelson, Proshansky, Rivlin, and Winkel (1974) were especially aware of this complexity when they reflected on the sociocultural significance of activity–environment associations:

> there is no physical environment that is not embedded in and inextricably related to a social system. We cannot respond to an environment independently of our role as social beings. . . . The nature of an environment will affect the functioning of groups, whether this environment be a city or a schoolroom. The arrangement of space makes possible certain types of relationships and inhibits others. (p. 13)

Thus, efforts to build systems of generalizations to account for the structuring effects of space on human activity would—at the very least—have to search for underlying commonalities among these distinctions exemplified by activity–environment, social-accordance relationships. Currently the commonalities that would make such generalizations plausible and coherent are not well understood, and, hence, not operationally useful. It is for reasons such as these that case studies, much like this one by Amedeo and Dyck (2003), which focus on a specific activity–environment association using opportunity samples as a base, still need to be undertaken.

13.3 Details of Amedeo and Dyck's (2003) Case Study
13.3.1 Influences on the Conduct of Teaching and Learning Activities

Curiosity about factors affecting the performance of teaching and learning activities in elementary classroom settings is widespread among interests in education and architectural design. The latter interest is a particularly challenging one because efforts to design the spatial layouts of classrooms that effectively facilitate teaching and learning repeatedly confront differences in educational philosophies. Financial resources, curricula structure, teaching competence, administrative support, organizational efficiencies, student characteristics, classroom management, and instructional strategies, for example, have long been thought important to teaching and learning activities (see discussions, for example, by Charles, Senter, & Barr, 1996; Delmamont, 1984; Denscombe, 1985; Emihovich, 1989; Evertson, Emmer, Clements, Sanford, & Worsham, 1994; Schwartz & Pollishuke, 1991). Selected features of various learning-type environments also have been singled out for detailed assessments in investigations of class size by Glass, Cohen, Smith, and Filby (1982) and Montello (1988), and classroom seating in relationship to student achievements by Moore and Glynn (1984). (See also King & Marans, 1979, and Spencer, Blades, & Morsley, 1989.)

Few investigators, however, have examined impacts on these activities as they might be exerted by entire facets, as in its arena and context, of a classroom environment. A notable exception, however, is Bloom's (1989) thoughtful characterization of the overall sociocultural process involved in student–teacher exchanges taking place in this environment. His extensive description of that process clearly reflects the importance of *context* on teaching and learning activities, but it suggests little about how the classroom's arena or, essentially, its spatial layout might qualify the nature of those contextual influences.

In their study, Amedeo and Dyck focus on spatial structural effects on these activities in an *elementary classroom environment,* but not without awareness that the effects of *space* itself cannot be understood independent of this environment's context. In other words, arena and context are two *facets* of an environment inextricably related to one another. Hence, they initiate their investigation by utilizing indications of spatial layouts to reflect a classroom's arena, but, then, rely on the teachers' *assessments* of layout alternatives to illuminate how alternative spatial layouts relate to this setting's context. Since teachers direct and control the daily activities taking place in this environment, it made sense to consult them for information about the way the arena facet of this surrounding connects with its context. It will become evident, however, that eliciting the teachers' *perceptions* is one thing; getting *agreement* among them is another. In this way, Amedeo and Dyck focused on inquiring into whether the spatial layout of an elementary classroom qualifies, enhances, or compromises activities conducted in that setting.

Spatial layouts or configurations of activity environments matter in the actual design of an elementary classroom, as they do in all activity settings. Differences that would result in activity-facilitating effectiveness from spatial configuration possibilities are, of course, a major concern of the designer. Sanoff (1994), for example, discussed the importance of the physical, intellectual, and affective aspects of child development and illustrated ways to relate behavioral objectives to spatial needs, while Moore (1986) emphasized the importance of the "spatial definitions" of settings—a distinctive and salient feature of arenas—in terms of their influence on cognitive and social behaviors in childcare centers.

In choosing a way to approach their research, Amedeo and Dyck sought to minimize inevitable constraints exerted by the more severe complexities they encountered by adopting a design that seemed least affected by them. With that as their strategy, they examined *beliefs* teachers possessed about the impacts classroom layouts had on the conduct of teaching and learning activities by employing a combination of structured and open-ended interviewing. They utilized as many teacher beliefs or perceptions as could be secured by sampling from multiple elementary schools in a larger region of study. They incorporated into their reasoning the idea that elementary school teachers are likely to differ in their educational philosophies about effective teaching and learning principles by using their perspectives as qualifiers of the responses they made to other inquiries in the study. As more of the details of their procedures are presented, it will become evident that they found it necessary to repeatedly make adjustments to their research design to address these inquiries because of the complexities encountered. Such compromises are not unusual, however. In social and behavioral research in general, *preferred* research approaches, frameworks, or designs seldom get completely—and, it should be mentioned, appropriately—employed because of such complications. The way these authors treated the activities of interest to them, and the reasoning they employed to describe their expectations about spatial structuring effects, will illustrate that point vividly.

13.3.2 Activities in the Elementary Classroom and the Significance of "Space"

Amedeo and Dyck do not distinguish between teaching and learning activities as if they would take place separately in the elementary classroom environment. They point out that they are so entwined into this setting's overall objectives that the execution of either is likely to depend on the level achieved by the other. Hence, given that those activities relate in a way that teaching fosters learning, the level attained in learning itself can act as a feedback to the ongoing performance of teaching to prompt adjustments needed to reach a given learning objective. Emphasis in their study, then, is placed \on the *activity of teaching*, which—if executed effectively—would drive the development of the *learning activity* that takes place. This emphasis was supported further by their idea that, in the elementary classroom, teachers have relatively more control over the teaching segment of these intricately related activities.

Amedeo and Dyck were certainly aware that an activity episode, or the duration of an activity from start to finish, is a time-oriented entity containing an ordered set of systematically interrelated behavioral components that may—for convenience—be referred to as *acts, interacts, transacts*, and *reacts*. Depending on the research objectives, selected components or specific combinations of them can attract relatively more investigative attention than the entire activity episode itself. However, in this research "component focusing" is not directly pursued; rather, the entire activity—as in *teaching*—is the interest of these researchers.

As they suggested earlier, there are at least two prominent reasons why it is useful to investigate the relationship of classroom spatial layouts to activities conducted in that setting. One is the general need for more information about the congruencies between designer-intended space *uses* in a setting, and *user*-intended *uses* of such spaces. Smith and Keith (1984), for example, assess the reasons for the failure of a notable school design;

Gump (1987) evaluates the controversial open-plan educational configuration; and Seidel (1994) comments on the state of design in general. A more immediate reason, however, pertains to the need for far more knowledge about how the spatial layout of a setting relates to the dynamics of activities conducted in it. Consider, for example, the implications of the spatial configuration of an elementary classroom for the person charged with directing this setting's primary process:

- Teachers may move about while describing, explaining, illustrating, and attempting to stimulate groups of students.
- They may spatially innovate by rearranging student activities into distinct groups or clusters.
- They certainly define and set interpersonal spatial relationships by allocating and maintaining "appropriate" spaces among students, and between themselves and students, for such purposes as avoiding crowding, reducing distractions, and maintaining prevailing social norms.
- Teachers make use of the opportunities and limitations in the spatial layout of their classrooms to fix attention and establish effective stimulus and/or information flow routes throughout a teaching episode.

In other words, movements, motions, orientations, positions, interactions, and arrangements are all part of the activity dynamics in the classroom. In this sense, the spatial layout of a classroom setting, because it is the arena for such behavioral dynamics, should have considerable significance for the conduct of its activities. But how did Amedeo and Dyck actually elicit the views of the principal and the most effective users of the classrooms—that is, the *teachers*—to see whether, in their perceptions, the spatial layouts do have such general and immediate implications in the conduct of activities? How they did so is outlined in the next sections.

13.4 Property Perceptions of Classroom Spatial Layout

To compare perceptions of alternative spatial layout possibilities for the elementary classroom, Amedeo and Dyck formulated their working research question in this way: *From the perspective of enhancing teaching and learning activities, what differences do teachers perceive among a collection of five alternative classroom spatial layouts?*

Information acquired from working with that question assisted in dealing with the four objectives listed at the beginning of this chapter. Seventy-nine teachers from four elementary schools were asked to respond to an interview containing inquiries related to this question. Forty-eight of these were chosen from three elementary schools in the city of Lincoln, Nebraska, and 31 from an elementary school in the city of York 50 miles away. "Chosen" is used here advisedly; it means acquiring an *opportunity* sample. It was difficult to design other types of samples because teachers had trouble finding time slots available to respond to interviews in their busy schedules.

13.4.1 Exploring Teachers' Property Perceptions of Classroom Spatial Layouts

The open-ended interview used in Amedeo and Dyck's study was designed to address a variety of issues about the five possible spatial-layout types illustrated in Figure 13.1.

An Elementary Classroom Environment 207

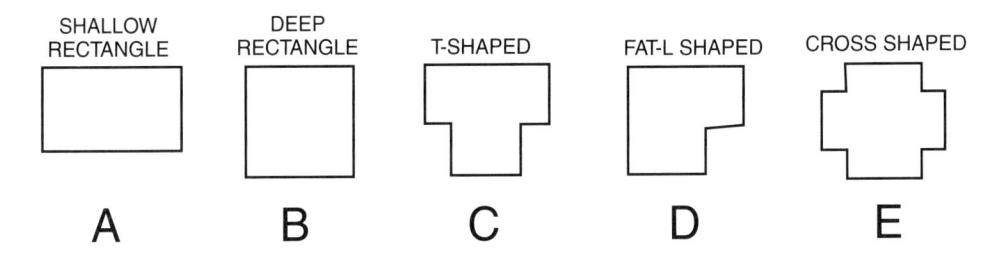

FIGURE 13.1. Five spatial layouts.

These alternative classroom configurations, along with their identification letters A–E, were presented to the teachers in order to assess their reactions to them from a variety of perspectives. The *labels* above the layouts were used only for reference and were not, in any event, available to the teachers throughout the study.

The labels, however, do try to reflect, in a broad way, the presence of noticeable classroom design trends over time. They include, for example, the two rectangular spatial configuration types of A and B commonly found throughout older elementary classrooms, which facilitate row-and-column student arrangements with teachers holding forth at the head of the room. They also include deviations from the rectangular in the shapes of C, D, and E, or those referred to as the T-shaped layout, fat-L layout, and the cross-shaped configuration, respectively. The literature suggests that these three layouts were designed to accommodate "innovative" approaches in the conduct of teaching and learning activities.

Eliciting *perceptions* of something as complex as a classroom spatial configuration requires that multiple information sources be exploited. With that in mind, teachers were asked to relate what comes to their mind when thinking about each of these five layouts, their "beliefs" about whether each layout design "had" specific properties related to teaching and learning activities, and their relative preferences for the five different classroom spatial layouts. What follows is a description of how these segments of information were combined. Property judgments are first joined with preferences, and, then, thoughts characterizing layouts are brought into these assessments in order to explore the presence of distinctive teacher perspectives.

13.4.2 Teachers' Judgments about Properties of the Five Classroom Spatial Layouts

Table 13.1 illustrates the 14 design properties chosen for consideration in Amedeo and Dyck's study. Past research suggests such properties are likely to have impacts on teaching and learning activities conducted in elementary classrooms.

As is evident in this table's instructions, teachers were asked to focus on the five alternative spatial layouts, *each in its turn,* and indicate whether the listed property items did or did not describe them. In this way, the teachers evaluated the spatial layouts for presence or absence of the 14 properties. An index measuring similarity in responses (that is, agreement responses ÷ total possible response) was then used to compare property judgments between any two of the teachers for all distinct pairings of them. This index ranges in value from an upper limit of 1 for identical judgments between two teachers to a lower limit of 0 for no similarity in judgments.

TABLE 13.1. Properties of Classroom Designs

We now want you to examine these classroom designs one at a time. We want you to tell us, in your opinion, whether each feature in the ITEM TABLE below describes a property of the design you are observing. If you believe a specific item describes a property of the design you are examining, then give the item a check ✓. If you believe it does not, then ignore that item and go on to the next one in the table. Please go through the entire table of items when examining each classroom design. Begin with classroom design A.

Design A

ITEM TABLE

☐ 1. This classroom design is nonstandard in shape.

☐ 2. This design facilitates the enactment of supervision and vigilance in the classroom.

☐ 3. The design mainly encourages single-group coordinated activity in the classroom.

☐ 4. This design primarily encourages fixed time-scheduling of classroom activities.

☐ 5. This classroom design supports directed focusing of student activity.

☐ 6. This classroom design facilitates front-facing orientation of students.

☐ 7. This design makes possible multiple and diverse activity in the classroom.

☐ 8. This design is essentially a compact one and enhances unified spatial layout of activities.

☐ 9. This design fosters flexible time-scheduling of activities.

☐ 10. This design makes separation of classroom activity possible and enhances privacy among activities.

☐ 11. This design makes possible multiple orientations of student activity.

☐ 12. This design is the standard institutional shape.

☐ 13. This design facilitates multiple focusing of classroom activities.

☐ 14. This classroom design promotes the creation of multiple space-uses and enhances flow potentials between them.

These similarity comparisons among teachers' *property judgments* were then calculated for all possible pairings of the teachers, and for each of the five spatial layout designs under consideration. This resulted in five arrays, one for each spatial layout, containing the calculated similarity values. Each of these were, then, factor-analyzed to search for the presence of teacher groupings, based on commonalities among property judgments. Table 13.2 illustrates the more prominent groupings that emerged from this analysis for each of the five spatial layouts.

13.4.2.1 Implications of Property Characterizations of Spatial Layouts by Groups of Teachers

Some inferences, tentative in nature, may be drawn from comparing how *groupings* of teachers characterized the five spatial layouts. For example, with regard to classroom spatial layout of the *shallow rectangular configuration* (Type A), Table 13.2 illustrates that teacher Groups 1 and 3 have similar perceptions for all 14 properties except one. Both groups perceive the shallow rectangle to be a standard design, one that facilitates supervision and vigilance; encourages single-group, coordinated activity and fixed time-scheduling; supports directed focusing of student activity; and is mainly a front-facing orientation design. Both also believe that the shallow rectangle is standard in shape, makes difficult a variety of orientations, does not facilitate multiple focusing, and does not support multiple space uses. The property that distinguishes these two groupings from one another is number 8. The 19 teachers in Group 3 believe that this shallow rectangular layout is essentially a compact one

An Elementary Classroom Environment 209

TABLE 13.2. Classroom Layout Design and Property Characterization by Groups of Teachers

Group #	Teachers in group	Classroom design		1 Shape is nonstandard	2 Facilitates supervision and vigilance	3 Encourages single-group coordinated activity	4 Encourages fixed time-scheduling of activities	5 Supports directed focusing of student activity	6 Facilitates front-facing orientation	7 Makes possible multiple and diverse activity	8 Compact; enhances unified spatial layout of activities	9 Fosters flexible time-scheduling of activities	10 Makes separation of activity possible and enhances privacy among activities	11 Makes possible multiple orientations of student activity	12 Standard institutional shape	13 Facilitates multiple focusing of activities	14 Promotes creation of multiple space uses and enhances flows between them
1	24	A	Property present	1	24	24	18	20	23	0	0	0	0	0	24	1	1
			Not present	23	0	0	6	4	1	24	24	24	24	24	0	23	23
3	19	A	Property present	0	19	19	17	19	17	0	19	0	0	0	18	0	0
			Not present	19	0	0	2	0	2	19	0	19	19	19	1	19	19
1	23	B	Property present	0	22	23	23	17	22	0	0	0	0	1	22	0	0
			Not present	23	1	0	0	6	1	23	23	23	23	22	1	23	23
3	18	B	Property present	0	18	18	18	17	18	0	18	0	0	0	18	0	0
			Not present	18	0	0	0	1	0	18	0	18	18	18	0	18	18
1	25	C	Property present	24	0	1	0	0	1	25	2	22	25	25	0	25	23
			Not present	1	25	24	25	25	24	0	23	3	0	0	25	0	2
2	7	C	Property present	7	7	0	0	4	0	7	7	7	7	7	0	7	7
			Not present	0	0	7	7	3	7	0	0	0	0	7	0	0	0
4	9	C	Property present	9	9	0	0	9	2	9	0	9	9	9	0	9	9
			Not present	0	0	9	9	0	7	0	9	0	0	0	9	0	0
1	32	D	Property present	28	7	1	0	1	2	32	10	27	32	32	2	31	31
			Not present	4	25	31	32	31	30	0	22	5	0	0	30	1	1
2	8	D	Property present	7	8	0	0	8	8	8	5	6	8	8	0	8	8
			Not present	1	0	8	8	0	0	0	3	2	0	0	8	0	0
1	28	E	Property present	28	0	0	0	0	0	28	0	28	28	28	0	26	28
			Not present	0	28	28	28	28	28	0	28	0	0	0	28	2	0
2	17	E	Property present	17	2	0	0	8	3	17	0	13	17	15	0	15	16
			Not present	0	15	17	17	9	14	0	17	4	0	2	17	2	1

and enhances a unified spatial layout of activities, while the 24 teachers in Group 1 apparently believe just the opposite with respect to this property.

Table 13.2 shows that property 8 also provides the distinction between the two groups that emerged from the responses to the *deep rectangular-shaped layout* (Type B). For example, Groups 1 and 3 agree on the presence and absence of all the properties listed in the table, except again property 8. Perhaps this result is to be expected because layouts A and B appear to be similar spatial configurations.

In the property characterizations of *T-shaped design* (Type C), on the other hand, distinctions among the three groups illustrated lie in different beliefs about the presence or absence of properties 2, 5, and 8. Teachers in Group 1, for example, felt that this T-shaped layout did not facilitate supervision and vigilance in the classroom, nor does it support directed focusing of student activity. Yet, Groups 2 and 4 characterize this T-shaped configuration as supporting directed focusing. There is also perceptual disagreement about whether this layout design is a compact one that enhances the unified spatial layout of activities. Groups 1 and 4, for example, believed it is not, whereas all the teachers in Group 2 felt that it does exhibit that property.

Differences in the "present–absent" responses to properties 5 and 6 were found to account for the distinction between the two teacher groups that emerged from the perceptions of the *fat-L spatial layout* (Type D). Group 1, for example, saw the fat-L layout as not supporting the direct focusing of student activity and as not facilitating a front-facing orientation of students. But Group 2 perceived this layout in just the opposite way with regard to those two properties.

In reference to the last of the five classroom spatial layouts, teachers in the larger of the two groups overwhelmingly perceived the *cross-shaped configuration* (Type E) as one that does not support directed focusing of student activity, nor does it allow for front-facing orientation. Instead, they believed that this spatial layout makes possible multiple and diverse activity, fosters flexible time-scheduling, makes separation of activity in the classroom possible, enhances privacy among group activities, and allows for multiple orientations. The second teacher group perceived this cross-shaped design in much the same way in that they largely agree that these properties are its features. Some divergence, however, is noticeable between the two groups of teachers in the sense that the teachers in this second group were split down the middle as to whether this layout supports directed focusing of student activity and are also not unanimous about the presence and absence of properties 6 and 9.

13.4.2.2 Observations about Perceptions of Spatial Layout Properties

Comparing these beliefs exhibited in Table 13.2 about alternative designs of classroom spatial layouts reveals that teachers divide into different groupings with regard to the properties they perceive to be present in each of the classroom spatial layouts. This leads to a number of observations. One is that there is no unanimous property perception of any of the five designs; instead, multiple but distinct perceptions of the same layout design emerge. Another is that the five designs seem to fall into two broad classes, with designs A and B in one class, and designs C, D, and E in the other. The latter layouts seem to be perceived as more flexible for innovative teaching than the first set, but the properties perceived as characterizing the two rectangular configurations (Types A and B) in this first class appear to be those that facilitate control and focus in teaching and learning activities, and such features may not reflect trivial or traditional needs.

Amedeo and Dyck conclude that, in retrospect, although these results are to some degree informative and in some cases even unexpected, asking teachers to indicate which of 14 properties "do" and "do not" characterize each of five classroom spatial layouts may be somewhat restrictive, in the sense that no opportunity is provided for teachers to entertain properties not present in Figure 13.2 or Table 13.1. Furthermore, a check-off directive like this evokes little more than a nominal response from a teacher, which because of its nature provides few opportunities for further elaborating about possible extended implications of that response. Limitations such as these tend to inhibit attempts to more fully understand the perceived importance of classroom spatial layouts in the conduct of teaching and learning activities. With thoughts like these in mind and a desire to enlarge on implications potentially inherent in these property beliefs, *additional facets of perception*, such as *teacher layout preferences* and *teacher thoughts about these layouts*, were examined.

13.5 Preferences of Classroom Spatial Layouts

Classroom spatial layout preferences were obtained by asking teachers to rank-order which of the five configurations (Types A to E) would "best support their beliefs about teaching and learning activities," which configuration would "next best support them," and so on, to a final inquiry of which would "least support their beliefs about those activities." Table 13.3 illustrates how each of the teachers ranked the five layouts in response to this request.

Presumably, the implicit information in these rankings could reveal much about differences perceived among the five classroom spatial layouts, criteria employed to *discriminate* among the layouts, and *similarities* and *dissimilarities* perceived to be present among them. Information of that variety, however, cannot be acquired by visualizing the raw rankings themselves. Instead, some procedure like a nonmetric, *multidimensional scaling analysis* (MDS) needs to be performed on these preference rankings in order to extract cues inherent in them about this information. This quest for such information explains the authors' use of MDS in their study.

Amedeo and Dyck assume that teachers—equipped with distinctive beliefs about teaching and learning activities—ranked the five classroom layouts according to preferences consistent with their beliefs. Ranking involves discriminating among the things being ranked. Those doing the ranking typically mull over the things to be ranked in terms of the differences in values they are perceived to have on some property or characteristic of interest.

TABLE 13.3. Preference Rankings of Five Classroom Designs

TCHRS	A	B	C	D	E	TCHRS	A	B	C	D	E	TCHRS	A	B	C	D	E
c1f	3	5	2	1	4	m13f	3	4	2	5	1	y6f	4	5	2	3	1
c2f	4	5	2	3	1	h1f	4	5	2	3	1	y7f	3	5	2	1	4
c3f	4.5	4.5	1	3	2	h2f	4	3	1	5	2	y8f	4	5	2	1	3
c4m	5	4	2	3	1	h3f	2	3	4	5	1	y9f	5	4	3	2	1
c5f	4	3	2	5	1	h4f	3	4	1.5	5	1.5	y10f	2	3	4	1	5
c6f	4	5	3	2	1	h5f	2	1	4	3	5	y11f	4	5	2	1	3
c7f	5	4	3	2	1	h6m	5	4	2	3	1	y12f	4	5	2	3	1
c8f	4	5	2	3	1	h7f	1	2	3	4	5	y13f	5	4	1	2	3
c9f	4	3	1	2	5	h8f	2	1	4	3	5	y14f	3	2	5	4	1
c10f	4	5	3	2	1	h9f	3	2	4	5	1	y15f	5	3	4	2	1
c11f	4	5	2	1	3	h10f	1	3	4	2	5	y16f	1	3	4	2	5
c12f	1	5	4	2	3	h11f	3	2	1	5	4	y17f	5	4	3	1	2
c14m	1	2	3	5	4	h12f	4	5	2	3	1	y18f	3	4	1	2	5
c15f	5	4	2	3	1	h13f	5	4	1	3	2	y19f	5	1	4	2	3
m1f	4.5	4.5	1	2	3	h14m	5	4	3	2	1	y21f	5	4	3	1	2
m2f	5	4	1	2	3	h15f	5	4	2	3	1	y22f	2	2	5	2	4
m3f	2	1	4	5	3	h16f	5	4	3	2	1	y23f	4	3	1	2	5
m4f	5	4	2	3	1	h17f	4	5	2	3	1	y24f	5	1	4	3	2
m5f	5	4	3	2	1	h18f	5	4	2	3	1	y25f	4	5	2	3	1
m6f	5	4	2	3	1	h19m	5	4	2	3	1	y26f	5	4	3	1	2
m7f	5	4	2	3	1	h20m	1	2	4	3	5	y27f	4	5	2	1	3
m8f	5	4	1	3	2	y1f	1	5	3	2	4	y28f	2	3	4	1	5
m9f	3	4	5	1	2	y2f	4	3	2	1	5	y29f	4	5	2	3	1
m10f	4	5	2	1	3	y3f	5	1	4	2	3	y30f	3	2	4	5	1
m11f	4	5	2	3	1	y4f	4	5	2	1	3	y31f	4	5	3	2	1
m12f	5	4	2	3	1	y5f	5	4	3	1	2						

212   ACTIVITIES AND SPACES

Because of the presence of personal idiosyncrasies, however, unique ways of assessing value will also play a role in such discriminations. For that reason, the metric underlying the separation between things in any ranking frequently remains only nominally understood. Hence, little can be assumed about its quantity characteristics except the obvious intended ordinal relations such as things are greater than, less than, or equal to other things. Nevertheless, significant value information may be so apparent in some rankings that it is possible to exemplify it in some broad or general way. The *nonmetric* MDS procedure used by the authors accomplishes just that.

13.5.1 Value Implications of Teachers' Preference Rankings

When, in research, rankings of things are taken to reflect discriminations, MDS will make use of their quantity characteristics to estimate a "conceptual space" that displays the relative separations of things implied by the rankings. This space contains not only estimates of the relative separations among the things being ranked but also estimates of differences among the perspectives of the rankers as well (see the statistical package SPSS). Figure 13.2 illustrates the conceptual space obtained by Amedeo and Dyck from their analysis of teachers' preference rankings of the five spatial layouts of classrooms.

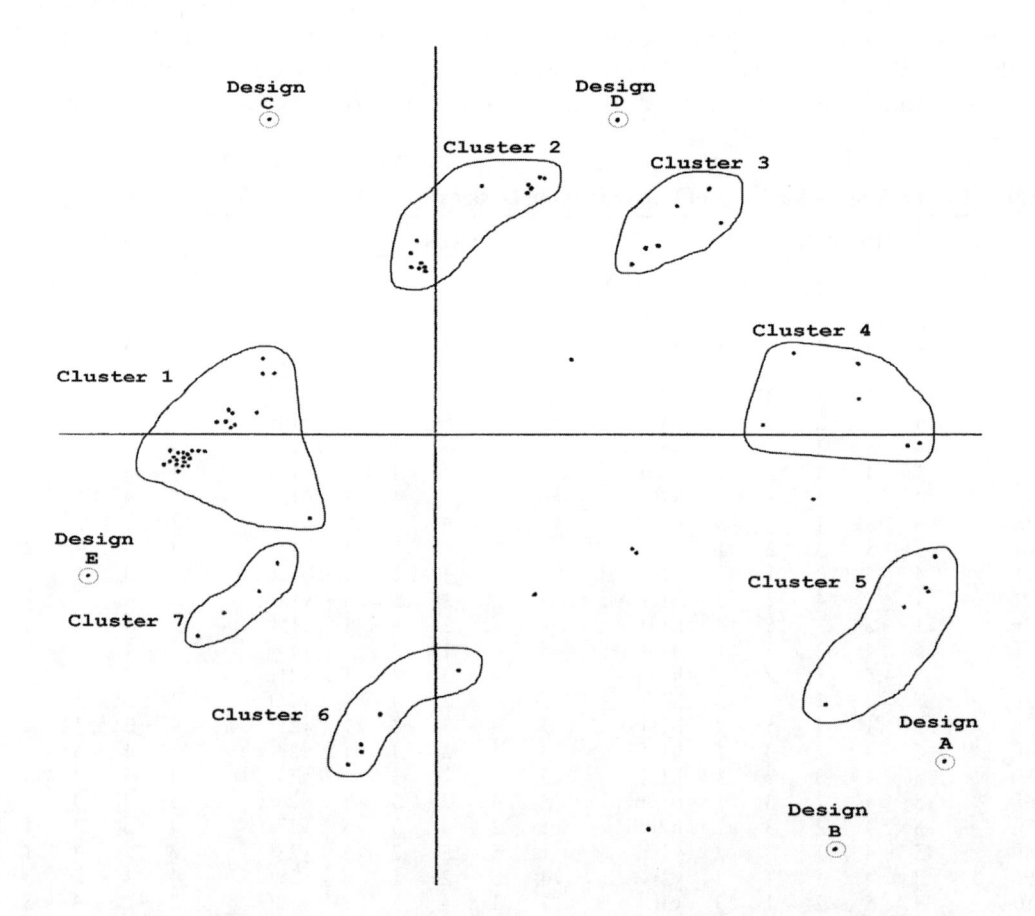

FIGURE 13.2. MDS assessment of teacher preference rankings. Letters "A" to "E" refer to the five spatial layouts; dots, teachers; and outlines, clusters of teachers. From Amedeo and Dyck (2003).

13.5.2 Evaluating the Configuration of the Spatial Layouts in the MDS Conceptual Space

The relative position of the five classroom spatial layouts—Types A–E—in the two-dimensional MDS space of Figure 13.2 suggests a number of things about the way the teachers have conceptualized those layout designs when expressing their preferences. In general, teachers seemed to perceive the T-shaped configuration (C) and the fat-L layout (D) as being very much alike, so that they are near to one another in this MDS space. The same appears to be the case for the two rectangular configurations, A and B. Yet, in comparing the positions of these two pairs in the MDS space, it is clear that the teachers perceive the first layout pair, C and D, as being quite different from the second pair, A and B. The cross-shaped design (E) is viewed as being somewhat distinctive in itself relative to either of the two pairs; although based on its location, it is probably conceived as more like the T-shaped and fat-L layouts than like the two rectangular designs.

The remaining dots shown in the MDS space of Figure 13.2 reflect the positions of the teachers, as influenced or dictated by the relative preferences they expressed for the five different spatial designs. Teachers preferring any one of the five classroom spatial layouts as "best" are generally closer to that design in the space than to others. Their actual locations, however, are also influenced by their preference choices for the remaining four layouts. In addition, teachers preferring the same layout as "best" are closer together in the space, their *actual* separation being influenced by their other four choices as well.

Focusing on the directional trends of the spatial layouts, the two-dimensional configuration of this MDS space suggests that, collectively, teachers used at least two fundamentals when they discriminated among the five designs to express their preferences. The vertical dimension—having rectangular classroom spatial layouts A and B on one end, with C and D positioned on the other end—suggests that they made something like a *traditional–nontraditional distinction* when discriminating among the designs. The horizontal orientation of the MDS space—having A and B on one end and E on the other—implies that the teachers also used a *spatially complex–spatially simple* distinction as a second criterion when mulling over their preferences. If an imaginary southwest–northeast diagonal is passed through this preference space just below its center intersection, an impression is gained that teachers perceived classroom layouts as either more spatially complex (for example, as in E, C, and D) or spatially elementary and compact (for example, as in A and B).

On further inspection of the MDS space in Figure 13.2, it is also evident that this scaling assessment of preferences reveals additional information about teacher perceptions of classroom spatial layouts. For example, the scattered distribution of the teachers in the MDS space indicates that not all of them perceived the layouts in the same way. Might these perceptual differences be products of differences in educational perspectives?

13.5.2.1 Relating Spatial Layout Preferences to Educational Perspectives

Figure 13.2 illustrates the presence of several *clusters* in the MDS space, suggesting that, in a number of instances, teachers expressed similar spatial layout preferences. It is evident that some clusters contain many teachers bunched closely together, while others contain fewer and are more loosely spaced. The closer the teachers are in a cluster, the more similar their layout preferences are likely to be. But what accounts for these particular clusters and their distinctiveness?

The initial expectation in this study was that the teachers' *views on teaching and learning issues* relating to the conduct of activities in the classroom should influence, in some consistent manner, the ways teachers express their preferences for the five classroom spatial layouts. Hence, *prior* to the request that they rank their layout preferences from best to worst, teachers were asked to indicate their inclinations toward such educational issues and also toward closely related design items by responding to the scales illustrated in Table 13.4.

Instructions directed the teachers to mark an X on each of the scales in this table at a location that best reflected their views on the corresponding issues. Their responses were then coded from 1 to 5, where a larger number meant that it was made closer to the right end of the scale and a smaller number meant that it was made closer to the left end. It was after this task was completed that the teachers were then asked to rank-order their classroom spatial layout preferences. The reason for employing this sequence in the interviewing process was to keep these two tasks cognitively proximate to one another, but in that particular order. Table 13.5 combines the teachers' responses to these issues with their preference rankings of the five classroom spatial layouts for the purpose of describing and contrasting the larger clusters present in the MDS space of Figure 13.2.

13.5.3 Description and Assessment of the Clusters in the MDS Space of Figure 13.2

13.5.3.1. Cluster 1

Most of the 32 teachers in cluster 1, when expressing their inclinations toward teaching and learning issues, registered their responses closer to the right or high end of the E and H scales illustrated in the center section of Table 13.5. These issues reflect student learning themes and are the most important for teachers in this cluster. However, this cluster of teachers also responded closer to the high ends of teaching and learning scales C, I, and K as well.

Given such responses, it is plausible to describe the educational perspectives of the teachers in Cluster 1 as those that emphasize, in the conduct of teaching and learning activities, exploration, examination, inquiry, hands-on involvement, independence and spontaneity, a small-group and/or individualized curriculum, and class development emerging out of activities. Table 13.5 illustrates that 91% of the teachers in this cluster declared that the cross-shaped configuration (Type E) would best facilitate the exercising of these views in the classroom and that the rectangular-shaped layouts, either Type A or B, would least support them.

Their high-end responses to the design issues B, C, E, F, and G, illustrated at the bottom section of Table 13.5, suggest that these teachers perceive this cross-shaped layout (Type E) as one that is nonstandard in shape, is adaptable for a variety of student orientations, promotes the conduct of diverse activity, and permits multiple space uses with flow potentials between them. Here is how they rationalized their selection of this classroom layout as their most preferred one:

> "There are multiple options for varying instructional grouping and team teaching."
> "It looks like the arrangement would lend itself to the use of learning centers and small-group activities."
> "Large-group activity center with smaller activity centers on wings."
> "Lots of corners for centers with a certain amount of 'semiprivacy.'"
> "Options for placing centers around the room to explore."

TABLE 13.4. Preference Orientations for Educational and Design Issues

Teaching and Learning Issues

Please express your preferences regarding these teaching and learning issues by marking an X on each scale A through K at a location that best reflects your views and their intensity.

Arrangements of Classroom Activities

A. Fixed Time Scheduling _____ Alterable Time Scheduling

B. Entire Class or Large Groups _____ Small Groups or Individual

Student Expression and Response

C. Directed, Controlled, and Planned _____ Independence and Spontaneity Encouraged

D. Complying/Conforming _____ Nonconforming and Spontaneous

Student Learning

E. Drill, Practice, Rehearse _____ Explore, Examine, Inquire

F. Group Learning _____ Individual Learning

G. Teacher Directed _____ Learner Generated

H. Listening and Observing _____ Hands-On Involvement

Course or Class Materials

I. Class Curriculum _____ Small-Group and/or Individualized Curriculum

J. Core Curriculum for Class Level _____ Curriculum Geared to Circumstances

Class Direction and Development

K. Teacher-Centered _____ Emerge from Student Activities

Classroom Design Issues

Please express your preferences regarding these classroom design issues by marking an X on each scale A through G at a location that best reflects your views and their intensity.

A. Fixed Spatial Arrangement of Student Working Facilities _____ Alterable Spatial Arrangement of Student Working Facilities

B. Classroom Design Having Single Front-Facing Orientation of Students _____ Classroom Design Adaptable for Multiple Orientations of Students

C. Classroom Layout Promoting Single-Group Coordinated Activity _____ Classroom Layout Promoting Multiple and Diverse Activity

D. Classroom Design Facilitates Supervision and Vigilance _____ Classroom Design Facilitates Separation and Privacy

E. Classroom Designed Mainly for Directed Focusing _____ Classroom Designed for Multiple Focusing Potential

F. Classroom Design is Compact for Unified Spatial Layout _____ Classroom Design is for Multiple Space Use with Flow Potentials

G. Classroom Design is Standard Institutional Shape _____ Classroom Design is Nonstandard in Shape

216 ACTIVITIES AND SPACES

TABLE 13.5. Design Preference Frequencies and Average Scores on Issues for Teachers in MDS

			C1	C2	C3	C4	C5
	Cluster numbers:						
	Teachers in cluster:		32	13	6	6	5
SPATIAL LAYOUT DESIGNS			\multicolumn{5}{c}{PERCENTAGE OF BEST/WORST}				
Shallow rectangle / Design "A"		BEST				67	60
		WORST	59	54			
Deep rectangle / Design "B"		BEST					40
		WORST	41	46	33	33	
T-shaped / Design "C"		BEST	9	23	50		
		WORST					
Fat-L-shaped / Design "D"		BEST		77	50	33	
		WORST					20
Cross-shaped / Design "E"		BEST	91				
		WORST			67	67	80
TEACHING AND LEARNING ISSUES			\multicolumn{5}{c}{AVERAGE SCORE ON SCALES}				
A. Fixed time ..... alterable time scheduling			2.98	3.04	3.10	3.25	2.37
B. Large group ..... small groups or individuals			3.34	2.36	3.28	3.18	2.53
C. Directed and controlled ..... independence and spontaneity			3.63	3.10	3.10	2.82	3.21
D. Complying/conforming ..... nonconforming/spontaneous			3.15	2.58	2.54	2.57	2.30
E. Drill, practice, rehearse ..... explore, examine, inquire			3.83	3.43	3.99	2.65	3.52
F. Group learning ..... individual learning			3.27	2.75	3.18	2.54	2.96
G. Teacher-directed ..... learner-generated			3.46	3.07	2.88	2.73	3.03
H. Listening and observing ..... hands-on involvement			3.88	3.66	3.71	3.57	3.57
I. Class curriculum (CU) ..... individualized/small group CU			3.30	2.40	2.62	2.38	2.73
J. Class level core CU ..... circumstances geared CU			3.15	2.37	2.17	1.83	3.09
K. Teacher-centered ..... emerge from student activities			3.37	3.17	2.40	2.14	2.99
CLASSROOM DESIGN ISSUES			\multicolumn{5}{c}{AVERAGE SCORE ON SCALES}				
A. Fixed-facilities arrangement ..... alterable arrangement			3.99	3.55	3.91	3.15	3.23
B. Single front orientation ..... adaptable/multiple orientation			4.30	3.68	3.46	3.29	3.39
C. Single-group coordination ..... promoting multiple activity			4.20	3.75	4.04	3.23	3.51
D. Supervision and vigilance ..... facilitates separation and privacy			3.01	3.02	3.21	1.95	2.14
E. Designed for directed focusing ..... for multiple focusing potential			3.98	3.34	4.07	2.39	2.71
F. Compact design/unified layout ..... multiple use/flow potentials			4.17	3.70	4.11	2.80	3.28
G. Standard institutional shape ..... nonstandard in shape			3.95	3.80	3.68	2.30	2.76

"Multiple possibilities."
"Would have room for large-group instruction but still have areas for individuals and small groups."
"Available space for a multitude of different activities with space as a buffer."
"Whole-group area yet separate areas for kids to do individual or small-group activities."
"Corners provide many options for room (table, materials, etc.)."
"Lots of spaces for small groups with direct supervision."
"Spaces, different areas to go to."
"Teacher can still see everyone if located correctly."
"Many different activities."
"This option provides space to explore without disrupting other groups, yet a space to come together as a whole class."

It is clear that these teachers view the cross-shaped layout (Type E) as one offering much potential for establishing multiple instructional groupings. They see it as a design configuration that affords space for the usual large classroom group, while simultaneously allowing for smaller interest and learning groups requiring relatively more privacy. In that sense the cross-shaped configuration (Type E) is perceived as a rather flexible spatial layout, facilitating much innovation in the arrangement of students for a variety of instructional and participation purposes. The remaining 9% of the teachers in this cluster, who chose the T-shaped layout (Type C) as most supportive, focused on this same message.

Teachers in Cluster 1 offer these comments as to why the rectangular layouts (Types A or B) have been designated by them as least supportive of their educational perspectives:

"Rows."
"Traditional classroom setting with the students facing one direction being instructed, not much space for small groups or regrouping."
"Boring, little room for creativity."
"Too balanced; difficult to break into areas."
"Very stagnate—no nook areas."
"Too constricting—everything is squished."
"One-room schoolhouse."
"Too long—lose unity."
"Not flexible—no areas for small-group instruction."
"Set up for teacher-directed instruction."
"Long and narrow limits usage of space."
"Not very flexible."
"Teacher-directed, traditional, less child-centered."
"Boring—institutional—straight rows."
"Wide open with no privacy."
"Too square and makes it seem like the teacher is the center of instruction."
"Too controlled."
"One large space—hard to separate off part of the room."
"Best designed for large-group instruction."

Obviously the main sense of their comments about the rectangular designs is the inverse of what they said about the T-shaped and the cross-shaped layouts (Types C and E). They per-

218 ACTIVITIES AND SPACES

ceive these rectangular configurations (Types A and B) as inflexible and constraining with respect to facilitating innovative and/or creative arrangements of students for instruction and participation. Note that their use of the term "traditional" is an expression that seems to be well mirrored in the configuration of the MDS space.

13.5.3.2 Cluster 2

The second cluster of teachers, located in the upper part of the MDS space of Figure 13.2, is also fairly sizable, containing 13 teachers, or 17% of the sample. Table 13.5 illustrates that most of the teachers in this cluster preferred the fat-L classroom spatial layout (Type D) as most supportive of their educational perspectives, while the remaining teachers preferred the T-shaped layout (Type C) for that purpose. All of the teachers in this cluster, however, selected one of the two rectangular layouts (Types A or B) as the configuration that least supports their views about teaching and learning activities.

As is evident in Table 13.2, the educational viewpoints of the teachers in Cluster 2 resemble rather closely those in Cluster 1. For example, with regard to the teaching and learning issues E and H, nearly all of those in this second cluster responded to the high or right end of these scales. This finding indicates that this cluster of teachers, like those in Cluster 1, also favor exploring, examining, and inquiring activities in the classroom, together with a hands-on approach to student learning activities. It is also clear, as suggested by their responses to the design issues C, F, and G in the third part of Table 13.5, that the teachers in this second cluster would ordinarily prefer a classroom spatial layout that was adaptable for a variety of student activity orientations, one that permitted multiple space uses with flow potentials between them, and one that was nonstandard in shape. Even in the case of layout features, then, their aspirations resemble those of Cluster 1.

Given their most preferred selections, however, the teachers in Cluster 2 did not choose the cross-shaped configuration (Type E) as their "best." Rather, they perceived that the fat-L configuration (Type D) and, to a lesser degree, the T-shaped layouts best fulfilled their teaching and learning objectives about classroom activities and were perceived to have the complementary design properties to do so. The rectangular designs were perceived as inadequate in both regards. Here are the reasons the teachers in Cluster 2 give for choosing these layout designs as most supportive of their educational views:

For the fat-L (Type D) layout:

"Nice area for students to come together to listen or play together."
"It seems to work well with all types of instruction—both exploratory as well as direct."
"Multigroup arrangement. Either large-group/small-group interaction can take place."
"Lots of choices for teaching."
"Students able to move to own area but can still be easily supervised."
"A separate place for sand/water, paint, and playhouse."
"Wide open with area of individual work."
"Areas for small groups, areas for large groups, and wall space for visuals and furniture."
"It is possible to have a small group working relatively secluded while a larger group is involved in an activity."
"Diversity."

<u>For the T-shaped (Type C) layout:</u>

"Large-group and small-group space. There may be room to have activities at the end and students could be seen and/or gather as a group without furniture in the way. Sit in a circle, etc."

"Large area—small-group corner(s)."

"Large group working and others away from them doing individual activities."

As to why the rectangular layouts (Types A or B) were perceived as least supportive of their educational perspectives, the teachers in this second cluster describe them in this way:

"Too square. No quiet areas.

"It's boring—there are no 'nooks' or areas to have small groups learning together."

"Limits arrangements—very traditional."

"No choices."

"It is very confining."

"No specific areas for centers."

"Only for large-group use."

"Too long and narrow—no place for individual or group work without everyone involved."

"Not much available for diverse room settings unless classroom furnishings were such that room could be partitioned off."

A classroom configuration that makes it possible to establish multiple arrangements of students for teaching and participation purposes, then, is one that matters for these teachers in cluster 2. According to their layout preferences, the spaces of the fat-L configuration (Type D) and the T-shaped configuration (Type C) facilitate the distributing of students in a variety of ways during a class period, but the rectangular configurations (Types A and B) do not.

Figure 13.2 does show the presence of still additional clusters of similarity among teachers in their classroom spatial layout preferences. These, however, are smaller than are the two larger of the Clusters 1 and 2 just described. As such, they may hint at the presence of minority views about spatial layouts among teachers, but this cannot be substantiated with the sample size employed in this study. Nevertheless, three of these smaller clusters display enough characteristics to merit brief descriptions here.

13.5.3.3 Cluster 3

All six of the teachers in Cluster 3 in the MDS space in Figure 13.2 selected either the fat-L configuration (Type D) or the T-shaped configuration (Type C) for classroom spatial layouts as being the "best" supporting designs (see Table 13.5). Two teachers chose the deep rectangular layout (Type B) as being the "least" supportive, while the remaining four chose the cross-shaped (Type E) configuration for that designation. This latter choice suggests that those teachers perceived the cross-shaped layout (Type E) quite differently than did the teachers in other clusters. (Their comments below about a need for a "balanced approach" help to explain why they do.)

The high average scores of teachers in Cluster 3 on the teaching and learning scales E, H, and B in Table 13.5 indicate that these teachers prefer independence and spontane-

220 ACTIVITIES AND SPACES

ity in student expression; the use of exploration, examination, and inquiry in instruction; and a hands-on approach in student learning. Likewise, their high average scores on all design issue scales suggest a preference for a classroom that is adaptable for multiple and diverse student activities, supports alternate spatial arrangements of student working facilities, and allows for separation of activities with privacy. For the teachers in Cluster 3, then, the T-shaped (Type C) and the fat-L (Type D) layouts are perceived as configurations that fulfill their design preferences and support their views about teaching and learning activities, while the cross-shaped and, to a lesser extent, the deep rectangular (Type B) layout are perceived as configurations that do not. Here are the comments they offer to explain their selections of the T-shaped and fat-L layouts as being "best" and the deep rectangular and the cross-shaped designs as being "least" supportive, respectively:

"A separate nook area for privacy, different activity."
"Since I am a believer of balance—I think I can go smoothly [with this structure] in and out of different settings—sometimes using the teacher-directed mode and sometimes using student-centered mode. This room gives me the option."
"Area to place big tables."
"Whole-group area, but also space for different centers."
"Interesting."
"It has shape and it is not the standard room."
"No special little places for students to go."
"In E—there is no balance—it seems totally student-oriented—which I do not promote. I believe kids need both direction and a chance to explore."
"Too busy, hard to work with so many corners."
"Too chopped up but could be fun."
"It might make it too difficult to arrange the room."

13.5.3.4 Clusters 4 and 5

The teachers in Clusters 4 and 5 in the MDS space in Figure 13.2 have layout preferences which are noticeably different from those in the previous three clusters discussed above. Table 13.5 illustrates that nine of the 11 teachers in these two clusters combined have selected a rectangular layout (Types A and B) as being "best" for supporting their teaching and learning views. No other teacher from any of the three previous clusters chose a rectangular configuration for that purpose. Furthermore, eight of these 11 teachers designated the cross-shaped layout (Type E) as being "least" supportive for their educational views about the conduct of activities in the classroom. This contrasts sharply, for example, with the 91% of teachers in Cluster 1 who chose this classroom spatial layout as being "best."

In terms of classroom spatial layout preferences, then, these teachers in Clusters 4 and 5 are quite unlike those in the first cluster and noticeably unlike those in the second; their choices of "best" and "least" supportive are, for the most part, the reverse of the teachers in Clusters 1 and 2. For want of a larger sample, these observations should certainly be treated as tentative; yet, combined, teachers in Clusters 4 and 5 constitute 14% of the total sample employed in this study.

Given these differences in design preferences from the previous clusters, it might be tempting to reason that the teaching and learning views of the teachers in these two groupings should be the reverse of those in Clusters 1 and 2. As the middle section of Table 13.5 illustrates, this is simply not the case. Hence, the pattern emerging in this research is that there exist different perceptions of which classroom spatial layout designs would be most supportive and which would be least supportive of essentially similar educational perspectives about teaching and learning activities in the classroom.

Teachers in the last two clusters did, however, have a much lower average response to the design issue D than those in the other three clusters (see the last section of Table 13.5), thus suggesting a greater concern for a layout that facilitates supervision and observation of students in the class. This helps to explain that, for the teachers composing Clusters 4 and 5, the most supportive layout designs are likely to be the rectangular-shaped configurations (Types A and B) and possibly even the flat-L (Type D) configuration, but certainly not the cross-shaped (Type E) configuration!

Their comments rationalizing their choices of the rectangular designs (Types A and B) or even the fat-L layout (Type D) as being "best" supportive are:

For fat-L (Type D):

"It's like what we have. I like it."
"Having a large area for whole-group/teacher-directed lessons, and spaces for small or individual work areas."

And for rectangular shallow (Type A):

"It resembles the way my class is set up right now. Students can work in different places but I can keep an eye on them to supervise learning."
"Desk arrangement is freer and not dependent on room shape."

As to their "least" supportive layout design:

For rectangular deep (Type B):

"It would limit learning only to large group more easily."
"Too many children clustered in the center throughout activity."

And for cross-shaped (Type E):

"Too cut up—loses options for layout of classroom."
"Too many corners to deal with, and too many "blind spots" for students to be out of view for supervision."
"Too many unseen corners."
"E has too many corners and flow could be a safety problem."
"Hardest to monitor."
"I did like Type E at first, maybe because it's unusual, but it would possibly be a bit exclusive (as opposed to inclusive) in design and somewhat limiting. Any of these could be workable though, depending on arrangements within."
"Too many corners—children can be out of teacher's vision."

From the one teacher in these clusters choosing fat-L (Type D):

"Hidden spots."

There are indications of two other clusters in the MDS space of Figure 13.2 (that is, Clusters 6 and 7), but these contain only five and four teachers, respectively. Their small size inhibits a compelling description here.

13.5.4 Conclusion

All settings, especially elementary classrooms, have clear patterns of conduct, norms, and expectations embedded in their behavioral agendas that tend to constrain and significantly qualify individual expression and behavioral initiatives. With respect to teaching and learning activities, Bloom (1989) places strong emphasis on the significance of a setting's context when he states that "from an ethnographic perspective, the location of learning to read and write is in the social context constructed in the classroom; or, in other words, in the classroom culture" (p. 109).

But *activity settings are structured spatially*, so that their basic spatial form is an essential and inextricable part of their context. This, in part, accounts for why activities, though obviously directed at contexts, require a variety of orientations, positions, movements, and other dynamics to enact, continue, and complete. It is in this sense, then, that the spatial layout of a setting influences the way its context becomes workable.

In this study, the fundamental inquiry was as follows: *Can the basic configuration or spatial layout of an elementary school classroom support or inhibit the ways teaching and learning activities are conducted in that setting?* Results from this investigation strongly suggest that the answer is a qualified "yes" or "it depends." The results show that it depends on the type of spatial layout and its design properties, on how both are perceived by those who use and manage activities in the classroom, and on the teaching and learning perspectives of those users.

When evaluating the ways teachers associated properties with the five spatial layout examples used in this study, it became clear that there was no universal perception of any of the five. Instead, different perceptions of the same layout emerged. Teachers generally perceived the five classroom spatial layout designs as consisting of two groups: the rectangular-shaped ones, A and B, in one group, and the T-shaped, fat-L, and cross-shaped configurations, C, D, and E, in the other. They viewed the latter group as being more flexible for innovative teaching use and characterized the rectangular layouts in the first group as those that more readily facilitate control and focus in teaching and learning activities.

A *multidimensional scaling analysis* of the teachers' rankings of their classroom spatial layout design preferences illuminated and reinforced these general impressions, but, in particular, it provided much more clarity about the finer details within these perceptual trends. It showed that teachers perceived the T-shaped and fat-L layouts, C and D, as very much alike, as they did the two rectangular-shaped ones, A and B, as well; at the same time, however, they viewed these two pairs as being very different from each other. They perceived the cross-shaped layout, E, as distinctive in itself relative to either of these pairs—although, in general, they thought it was more like the first pair of layouts than the second.

Positions of the spatial layouts in the MDS *preference space* suggested that teachers used two dimensions to discriminate among the five spatial layout designs in this study. They applied both a *traditional–nontraditional* and a *spatially simple–spatially complex* distinction to illuminate their perceptions of differences between the rectangular types and the three nonrectangular forms. This application was consistent with the ways they characterized the property makeup of each of the layouts and with their teaching and learning perspectives about the conduct of activities in the classroom.

Another unexpected finding—and one illustrating finer details—was the presence of clusters among the spatial layout preferences. Evidence clearly illustrated that there were perceptual types among the 79 teachers in the sample, for they divided into at least five and, perhaps, seven clusters in the MDS space. These clusters varied in size from very large ones containing 32 teachers to small ones containing as few as five members. In the first five of these groupings, the perceptual homogeneity of each cluster was distinctive relative to the homogeneity of the others, and was especially plausible when compared with the educational perspectives, layout design views, and descriptive comments of the teachers within it. The last two clusters—though not examined in detail due to their small size—may be indicative of still other perceptual types.

It was tempting to relate these distinct clusters and what they represent to the various characteristics of the teachers within them (see Amedeo & Dyck, 2003, Appendix 1). However, just using the data available on age, sex, teaching experience, and subject taught, no discernible trends could be detected.

With these as the apparent patterns in the information, it is useful at this point to recollect a bit and touch on some of the more prominent thoughts initially discussed to open this chapter about the presence of conceptual and methodological complexities likely to be faced by Amedeo and Dyck in their investigation and attempt to summarize what must have been some of their more noticeable effects on both the design of their study and the applicability of their results.

13.6 Discussion

The research design employed in their study is, to a considerable extent, more open-ended than structured, in the sense that there are fewer categorical and scale constraints than usually evident in the standard survey approach. This has both advantages and disadvantages; although conceptually rich, the information elicited has limitations in how susceptible it is to interpretation.

In addition, the sample itself was relatively small, and, for the most part, one of opportunity. Teachers, of course, are quite busy, so it was particularly difficult to arrange for even 79 of them to respond to the data-gathering instrument over a reasonable amount of time. Then, too, the teachers interviewed came from only four elementary schools in two districts. Under these circumstances, if this approach is to fit in anywhere, it would have to be a *case study*. Hence, logical restrictions exist on any attempts to formally attribute these results to a larger population.

Nevertheless, this approximation to a case study is a plausible beginning research format for the particular topic. At this time, a hypothesis-driven, statistical-inference design for tackling this issue is difficult, if not impossible, to construct. In addition to the enormous problem associated with attempting to delimit a population and then select an adequate probability sample to represent it, there is a more substantial reason why a formal hypothesis-driven research format is not possible at this time. The body of person–environment–behavior theory available for generating such hypotheses does not effectively entertain spatial structural conditions as one of its special cases. In this sense, the theory is incomplete. Wineman, Hillier, and Peponis (1998) explain it this way: "Incomplete in the sense that we have not done a good job of relating behaviors to structural characteristics of built space. By structural characteristics I am referring to those characteristics of space that can be quantified and compared among buildings and across building types" (p. 4). (See also Moore's, 1986, comments on this issue.)

This chapter started with the basic *assumption* that the purpose of a spatial-layout design is to facilitate and enhance the enactment, continuance, and completion of activities appropriate to the setting the design exemplifies. This assumption is based more on common sense or logic than on any persistent and universal convention designers (for example, architects) proclaim. Many designers may not see this as the purpose of design. Rapoport (1994) comments on this issue when he discusses "the need for (what) knowledge." (In that same vein, see Russell, 1994, and the discussion "Can Design Schools Survive the '90s?") What is evident from the study reported in this chapter is that teachers overwhelmingly responded quite straightforwardly to questions about the relative ability of classroom spatial layouts to facilitate activities, and they did so virtually without critical comments about the usefulness of speculating in that way. Amedeo and Dyck have a strong sense that, for teachers, spatial configuration of workplace is a significant dimension of design from the viewpoint of enhancing the enactment, continuation, and completion of activities to reach specific educational goals.

PART V
Experiences and Environments

Research on *person–environment–behavior relationships* focuses on both people's *activities* and their *experiences* as they unfold and happen in *actual surroundings*. In the case of *activities*, emphasis is on how characteristics of everyday environments might influence the behavioral processes involved. Interests about experiences, however, center more on states, emotions, or sensations felt by people transacting with environments. Experiences tend to influence how environments are understood and, in that way, exert qualifications on the enactment of activities. More research is devoted to study activities than to experiences undergone in those settings. When experiences are investigated, it is usually for the part they may play in *appraisals* of the surroundings associated with activity episodes.

Characterizing Experiences

The term *experience* is used in a variety of ways. It may refer to what one does while acquiring information, as in "one experiences it fully"; or it may be used to indicate something felt or accumulated, as in "he felt gloomy," "they have much experience," and "her experience of the place was fascinating." Sometimes "experience" is used to describe the content found in a mental state or even to one of its components. It is useful to single out distinctions like these in the use of the term because, in research on P-E-B relations, the significance of *experiences* may sometimes lie in the impacts felt from undergoing them, as in emotional episodes, and/or in their importance, in a cumulative sense, as foundations for schematic structures like cognitive maps, scene schemas, or, in general, place representations involved in knowing processes associated with the execution of activity in environments. In this part, "experience" refers to a particular reaction—as in *feeling, emoting, sensing, evaluating*—undergone by an individual provoked or aroused by either external—that is, an *environmental* and/or *spatially related* situation—or by internal information sources, or even both.

The two chapters in Part V examine two kinds of *experiences* individuals commonly undergo in daily transactions with environments: *emotions* and/or *feelings* in *everyday environments* and *aesthetic experiences* in mainly pastoral-type surroundings. These were selected for discussion here not only because they are commonly undergone but also because their potential to exert influences on the fundamental *evaluative-type appraisals* engaged in by people for functioning in environments is quite high.

Chapter 14 illustrates investigations by Amedeo and York (1984, 1988, 1990) dealing with affective experiences in ordinary environments. Its first part searches for evidence that *norm-criteria* sway or influence what is likely to be felt by people transacting with a given environment. Expectations are that *beliefs* expressed by participants about *feelings* they would *experience* in a setting should reflect such "reference points." Its second part looks for connections between affective experiences in ordinary environments and perceptions of those surroundings. Intense affective experiences, for example, are expected to interact with what gets *apprehended* of everyday environments.

Chapter 15, on the other hand, focuses on aesthetic experiences. Its interest is on the experiencing of scenic quality in pastoral-like environments. In particular, curiosity is centered on the issue of how external information from empirical circumstances of everyday surroundings might be combined with internal information in the perception of this aesthetic quality. This work, like in the previous chapter, is exploratory, though it employs a considerably larger and more representative sample of participants. Arrangements of landscapes, based on perceived differences in scenic qualities, were examined in a series of steps to estimate how external and internal information was brought together by participants to distinguish among landscapes along this scenic criterion.

The research studies discussed in this part of the book are specifically intended to suggest how research strategies may be designed and information collected under difficult contextual and methodological conditions concerning complex experience issues involved in P-E-B relationships. It will be noticed, for example, that the designs utilized in this research take full advantage of opportunities to access reflectors of covariance or commonalities at different levels of analysis. When it is not practical to test hypotheses in a formal standardized sense, these ways of proceeding can add much knowledge about issues concerning experiences in environments.

Issues That Matter in Research on Emotions

Before proceeding to examine the issues of interest in Chapter 14 on affective experiences, some basic questions should be addressed. For example, *Why is it useful to investigate affective experiences like emotions and/or feelings when studying person–environment–behavior relationships?* According to a number of writers, these experiences undergone in environmental contexts could have significant implications for how theoretical propositions commonly used as guides for describing and accounting for P-E-B relationships might be understood (see, for example, Bechtel, 1997; Golledge, 1999; Ittelson, Proshansky, Rivlin, & Winkel, 1974; Kaplan & Kaplan, 1982; Moore, 1976, 1979, 1987; Moore & Golledge, 1976; Neisser, 1976). Mandler (1985) remarks, for example:

Emotion is not only anecdotally and phenomenally part of human thought and action, there is now a burgeoning body of evidence that emotional states interact in important ways with traditional cognitive functions. For example, positive feelings determine the accessibility of mental contents in the process of decision making, serve as retrieval cues, and influence problem-solving strategies. More generally, accessibility of mental contents is determined by the mood both at the time of original encounter and at the time of retrieval. (p. 113)

When addressing the process of cognition itself in relation to emotional experiences, Blumenthal (1977) indicates:

Emotional experience is an essential aspect of the process of cognition and must be considered in any adequate description of it. . . . The emotional augmentation of experience links enduring needs and dispositions to the psychological present. It can direct the course of cognition, the retrieval of memories, the structuring of thoughts, or the formation of perceptions. (pp. 101–103)

Both writers are making it clear that *affective appraisals* and resulting *emotional incidents* possess a broad potential to exert significant influences on the nature and tone of other responses and experiences. Mandler (2002), in fact, argues for using a *constructivist* approach for understanding emotional experiences. Currently, this particular cognitive-oriented perspective is one of three principal conceptualizations (the others being the ecological and transactional) already employed in research efforts to understand P-E-B relationships, although, it should be stressed, consideration of affects is given little regard in its use. By implication, then, Mandler and Blumenthal strongly suggest that emotions be actively incorporated into research specifically concerned with such relationships. Ittelson (1973a), when discussing environmental perception, reinforces the importance of doing so when he states:

the first level of response to the environment is affective. The direct emotional impact of the situation, perhaps largely a global response to the ambiance, very generally governs the directions taken by subsequent relations with the environment. (p. 16)

Actually, the need for knowledge about affective influences extends beyond how it might fit into cognitively oriented P-E-B frameworks. Other researches engaged in person–environment studies in general, as in investigations into place attachment, place identity, sense of place, and place schemata, also require considerable knowledge about emotional experiencing because the affective dimension is thoroughly embedded in their conceptualization. Indeed, human responses to most everyday surroundings or places frequently exemplify the primacy effect of their inherent affective components. Mandler (1985), for example, states, "the indisputable observation that we frequently react affectively to events, before experiencing a more 'analytic' knowledge of the event, speaks to the primacy of affective and evaluational constructions and intentions" (p. 115).

However, if knowledge about emotional experiences is so useful in "place" and "environmental" issues, why has there generally been so little research devoted to investigating them? A response to this question reveals that there are many complexities likely to be met when investigating affective experiences, some of which seem unsolvable. To comprehend the design choices made in Chapter 14, it is worth examining the more critical of these before describing its research.

Conceptual Complexities Associated with Investigating Emotional Experiences

The way in which emotions are usually understood in the broader literature makes their incorporation into investigations emphasizing everyday environmental contexts somewhat uncertain, awkward, and complex. This is because knowledge about the *precise* nature of the experiences is inaccessible, a standard definition of *emotions* and their feeling labels is lacking, and conflict arises from competing theoretical propositions asserting opposite conceptual ends about how emotional experiences come about.

Propositions about the onset, intensity, and differences in emotions—in terms of sympathetic and central nervous systems, visceral and mental reactions, cognitive processes, and cultural issues—sometimes differ among investigators because of subscription to conceptually competing theories (for example, see Amedeo, 1993; Lyons, 1980; Mandler, 1975, 2002; Strongman, 1987).

Physiological Changes and Emotional Experiences

For example, reports about how emotions come about entertain both *physiological* and the *cognitive* levels of human functioning. Individuals frequently tell of sensing physiological changes when undergoing more intense emotional experiences like fear, rage, anxiety, and agitation. These changes, recorded or observed during emotional episodes, have been associated with adrenaline flow, blood circulation, respiration, muscular tension, gastrointestinal activity, temperature, and secretions (Goshen, 1967). One set of theorists emphasizes the importance of physiological changes for understanding both the emotional occurrence itself and differences among emotions. They argue that *emotions* are feelings of physiological changes that occurred when individuals experienced such affects, and evaluations of what one felt *followed from* physiological changes. For this view, differences in *feelings* mean differences in bodily changes.

Cannon (1927), however, questioned this contention, reasoning that the patterning of "physiological changes" during an emotion is an ineffective criterion for differentiating among the emotions, particularly because the same physiological changes often occur during emotions that are very different from one another, and even occur in nonemotional states. Schachter and Singer (1962) and Schachter and Wheeler (1962) also challenged this "physiological-changes" point of view, suspecting that significant connections might exist between evaluative-type cognitions of affective situations and the physiological changes experienced during an emotional occurrence. To evaluate that belief, experiments were devised in which actors, in the presence of individual subjects, pretended to be undergoing *emotional states* such as "anger" and "euphoria." While intensity differences had been noticed in their work with regard to some physiological aspect or another, and while certain physiological changes seemed to occur more often with some emotions than with others, no one-to-one relationship between pattern of physiological changes and specific emotion had been conclusively established. One insurmountable problem that physiological theorists have had to face is that the *same* stimulus conditions or situation can generate *different* emotions in different people. This suggests that different individuals can perceive and evaluate the same situation differently. To deal with that not-uncommon occurrence, some provision for a cognitive process in emotion was necessary.

Cognitive Processing and the Emotional Experience

Certain basic information is likely to be useful for comprehending a specific emotion. This includes the nature of the mental state that is associated with it, stimulus conditions that activate the onset of the emotion, and how the individual perceives and evaluates those conditions. According to this perspective, in other words, cognitions of situations determine *what* is felt in them. The concepts individuals use, then, to *label* their emotional reactions to surroundings, events, and others should evolve out of their evaluations of them, guided by their relevant long-term integrations to reflect their past experiences. This suggests that individuals employ an interpretative process to label their affective reactions to situations. Hence, according to this view, a person's definition of a situation and assessment of its meaning determine the nature of the affective episode the person experiences in that circumstance. The emotional experience, then, should depend on, at least, memory activity, the use of attention processes, cognitive structures, and previous experiences.

Of particular interest in the analysis of an *emotional event* in itself is the manner in which affective information in a given situation is evaluated for its meaning (see, for example, Arnold, 1970; Fiske, 1981; Lazarus, Averill, & Opton, 1970; Mandler, 1975; Peters, 1970; Shott, 1979; Strongman, 1987). In Arnold's (1970) view, the distinctive aspect of the more general evaluative process during an emotional episode is an *appraisal*. This is an assessment process that involves personal judgments about effects that objects and/or people in the perceived situation may have on "us" and "our expectations." Arnold suggests that objects, other people, and/or events as such do *not* specify an emotion. Rather, what the individual thinks of these *things* is what matters in the labeling of an emotion. In her reasoning, perception of a situation precedes an appraisal of it, and, in turn, the appraisal evaluates the perceived situation for its affective significance to the individual. Thus, all *emotions* would have *appraisals* as a base, and different types of emotions have different appraisals.

Attempts at Integrating the Physiological Emphasis with the Cognitive

Lyons (1980) extends this reasoning further. He indicates that *evaluative cognitive activity* plays an essential role in the experiencing of emotions, in that it both generates the physiological changes felt and is the means by which persons differentiate the emotions. He makes it clear that, although we can view either evaluation and atypical physiological changes as necessary components of an actual or ongoing emotional state, we need both to discuss the sufficient conditions to define an emotional state. Lyons indicates "For most emotions if not all, what emotion, if any, will well up in a person will depend on how he 'sees' the object he has apprehended or believes he has apprehended. A man is afraid because he 'sees' the object or situation as dangerous. A man is angry because he 'sees' the situation as offensive or insulting" (pp. 77–78).

Lyons (1980) also points out that if evaluations are to arouse individuals or generate emotions, they probably should involve assessments of situations that are qualitative in a negative or positive sense. In terms of the "self"—the likely reference point in any emotion—such assessments would contain approvals or disapprovals of some aspects of the situation being evaluated. This would seem necessary, since a dispassionate or indifferent evaluation probably will fail to stir the individual and more likely will be an informational one.

Difficulties with Definitions of Emotions, Feelings, and/or Affects

One problem inhibiting the use of the conceptualizing just described is the impreciseness of its relationships. As they are currently understood, these components of the theories about emotions are, at best, suggestive; they are, by and large, too opaque in their present form for converting into workable expressions needed for rigorous research. This seems traceable, in part, to existing definition difficulties associated with affects themselves.

The literature is unclear regarding the criteria for defining emotions or even affects in general. Hence, standardization of meaning across research interests is nonexistent. This lack of preciseness and clarity in meaning persists even among the definitions of specific types of emotions. Davitz (1969), for example, indicates that "a review of the psychological literature dealing with emotion provides little help in understanding what people mean when they say someone is happy or sad" (pp. 1–2). Strongman (1987) shows that little has changed, when he states, "a similar lack of precision surrounds terms which refer to specific emotions, jealousy, fear, love, anger, for example (and, particularly, anxiety)" (p. 7). More recently, Mandler (2002) points out that "emotion is one of those common language terms about which the general speaker has little doubts but about which scientists of the mind find little agreement" (p. 97). When reflecting on whether there are basic emotions from which others might follow, he states, "Basic emotions theorists cannot agree whether there are 3, 6, 12, or even more such building blocks, nor is there a consensus building; emotion theories are still procreating like rabbits" (p. 103).

Yet, there is little doubt that the emotional experience is needed for understanding other responses and even cognitive processing in general. Kleinginna and Kleinginna (1981), for example, examined *conceptual intersections* among definitions, and offered this interpretation:

> Emotion is a complex set of interactions among subjective and objective factors, mediated by neural/hormonal systems, which can (a) give rise to affective experiences such as feelings of arousal, pleasure/displeasure; (b) generate cognitive processes such as emotionally relevant perceptual effects, appraisals, labeling processes; (c) activate widespread physiological adjustments to the arousing conditions; and (d) lead to behavior that is often, but not always, expressive, goal-directed, and adaptive. (quoted from Strongman, 1987, p. 3)

While their interpretation illuminates processes said to be involved in emotions, it also exemplifies the potential difficulties that would have to be confronted by researchers when attempting to apply this sense of the emotional construct in their investigations (Plutchik, 1965).

The enormity of the undertaking needed to create a standard and/or universal definition becomes clearer when it is realized that researchers interested in emotions come from numerous and diverse interests in psychology, psychiatry, sociology, education, biology, philosophy, literature, art, and aesthetics, among other areas. Diverse interests like these strongly suggest that issues regarding affective experiences are likely to be approached with different initial assumptions and priorities about what needs to be understood and how. In addition to perpetuating multiple interpretations, vague or imprecise definitions also impose constraints on attempts to measure the characteristics of emotions. Without sure and inviolable knowledge of the quantity characteristics embedded in their essential scale, there is little reliable information available for conducting *evaluations* of emotional experiences and for making comparisons across multiple experiences of the same emotion.

It may be possible, however, to work with *broader* meaning consistencies and employ ordinal assessments of affects so that some level of reliable quantity and quality estimates may be obtainable for evaluation purposes in research on emotions. Of course, calculating means and variances of an emotion experienced by a number of individuals is currently, at best, problematic. Furthermore, an *absolute* quantity of an emotion is not discernible, nor can structural relationships governing different intensity levels be precisely determined. With these notes and practical suggestions in mind, the works that follow describe explorative attempts to examine relationships between norms, affects, and environmental attribute schemas.

CHAPTER 14

Experiences in Everyday Environments

14.1 Introduction

In the research discussed in this chapter, Amedeo and his colleagues (Amedeo & York, 1984, 1988, 1990) began by examining whether norms influence people's *affective responses* to everyday *settings*. They employ two related assumptions for their investigation: (1) *what* people feel is determined by their cognitions, not by *differences* in physiological reactions; and (2) the concepts people use to *label* their emotional reactions to surroundings, events, and others result from *cognitive appraisals*. The implication of these is that people use an interpretative process to label emotional reactions. By extension, then, this suggests that, in everyday surroundings where ordinary activity transactions occur, a person's definition of an environmental situation is likely to be influential in determining the nature of his or her affective experience. Furthermore, "if interpretation and the nature of affective experiences are so linked, then, given social-cultural influences in the assessment of meaning in general, patterns of emotional responses to environments should reflect existing emotional norms" (Amedeo & York, 1984, p. 195).

Social norms are said to be evident in the makeup of a society's environments (Hillier & Hanson, 1984) and in the "meaning" people attribute to them when appraising them (Fiske, 1981; Fiske & Taylor, 1991). Amedeo and York (1984) suggest, then, that such norms should operate directly and indirectly both in the cognitive processing used to appraise an environment and in the attributing of meaning to cues in an environment. Hence, in a given social system, this should result in:

- criteria about appropriateness, inappropriateness, and expectancies that guide individual interpretations of the definitions of the situation associated with settings;
- a constancy or uniformity among individuals in their responses to many environments; and
- a consistency in environmental response for any one individual over time.

It is suggested that, in a *pluralistic* society, responses may be both universally similar for some environments, but also more varied for others. In a traditional society, emotional responses to environments should be largely universal, well known, and common, suggesting widespread agreement in beliefs that certain *feelings* constitute appropriate *responses* to particular surroundings (see Geertz, 1959; Kemper, 1978; Shott, 1979).

14.1.1 A Search for Norm Influences in Affective Reactions to Everyday Environments

Amedeo and York (1984) initiated their investigation of norm influences on affective responses to environments by arranging to elicit subjects' beliefs about emotions they would experience if in three ordinary settings. Characteristics of the 79 individuals used in their sample are shown in Table 14.1. These were not chosen randomly, as this was not methodologically possible. Selection, instead, was based on subjects' interest in person–environment issues, ignorance of the authors' objectives, demographics, and type of environment lived in most of their lives.

Subjects were asked to view 7″ × 7″ colored-slide projections of three environments that would be known to them as *E1*, *E2*, and *E3*. These were depictions of an old city street, a social gathering, and a path in a park (a woodland setting), in that order. While contemplating each of these, subjects were asked to respond to the following request:

> "Take some time to look at this place and imagine you are in it. Using the numbers from the scale provided, indicate the degree to which each of the following feelings describes what you think you would feel if you were in this place."

Thirty-two feelings (for example, enjoyment, nervousness, boredom, anxiety, etc.) and a 7-point intensity scale ranging from 1 (lowest) through 7 (highest) were provided for subjects to register their responses to this request. The feelings used were selected because they could conceivably be experienced in various degrees in these settings (see Figures 14.1, 14.2, and 14.3) and Davitz (1969) had suggested that they received wide agreement in meaning among individuals.

Amedeo and York (1984) point out that if norm criteria govern what is felt, then beliefs expressed by participants about feelings they would experience in a given environment should reflect such reference points or social expectations. Indeed, beliefs themselves often evolve out of norms, rules, and traditions, and as such they are likely to play an important role in guiding the labeling processes involved in cognitive appraisals during emotional experiences (Green, 1972). If norm influence in emotional experiences were to be apparent in the information collected in this manner, the subjects participating in the study would be

TABLE 14.1. Characteristics of the Opportunity Sample

Sex		Place history[a]	
Male	46%	Rural area	17.7%
Female	54%	Small town	17.7%
		Medium-sized city	22.8%
Age		Large city	40.5%
17–32	40.5%	No response	1.3%
23–30	32.9%		
31–40	11.4%		
41–62	14.1%		
Marital status			
Single	69.6%		
Married	30.4%		

Note. Data from Amedeo and York (1984).
[a]Size of place lived in while growing up.

Experiences in Everyday Environments 235

FIGURE 14.1. Environment *E1*: An "old city street" scene.

FIGURE 14.2. Environment *E2*: A "social gathering" scene.

FIGURE 14.3. Environment *E3*: A "woodland setting."

expected to exhibit some *agreement* among themselves in their expressed beliefs about both the types and the intensities of the feelings they would experience. Total agreement among all participants for a specific environment would suggest that a single norm is operating, whereas multiple subsets of belief agreement might suggest the presence of multiple norm influences.

14.2 Examining Participant Responses for Evidence of Affective Norm Influences

Amedeo and York (1984) reflected on how to examine these belief responses regarding type and intensity of affective experiences to be felt in these settings. For that purpose, they suggested that *total* responses to each environment be evaluated from two ways of viewing its information.

14.2.1 Perspective 1: R-Mode Factor Analysis of a Subject–Feeling Array

For example, Amedeo and York (1984) recommended that total responses to any of the three environments be first arranged in a conventional case-by-variable matrix format in which there are N rows and n columns. The N rows refer to the 79 participants participating in the sample, and the n columns to the 32 feelings entertained in the study.

Since their subjects responded to three distinct environments, the authors have to begin their analyses, then, with three conventionally arranged arrays. For each of them, they begin their assessment of its responses by first focusing on the information inherent in its *columns*. Each column, as indicated, contains the range of intensities expressed in subjects' beliefs about the likelihood of experiencing that respective feeling if in the environment under consideration. Columns, of course, can be compared to determine the degree to which they *covary* with respect to their expressed intensity values. With that in mind, Amedeo and York (1984) correlated each column with every other to determine whether feelings fall into subsets as a result of having been rated similarly by subjects. Subsets may suggest affective categories underlying ways feelings were experienced. In an effort to estimate them and their nature, the authors reduced the variance inherent in the collection of correlation coefficients to common components by factor-analyzing them. This way of examining the initial array of subject responses for evidence of commonalities among columns is commonly referred to as an *R-mode* assessment of an initial response array's information. Its use in this case examines how feelings cluster as a consequence of intensity values assigned to them when subjects revealed their beliefs about what they would experience in a place. Clusters suggest groups of feelings having shared membership in broader affective categories. Viewing the study's response array in this way concentrates on information about *affective dimensions* embedded in subject responses to the particular environment; little, however, is revealed about similarities among subject *response protocols* for that surrounding.

14.2.2 Perspective 2: Q-Mode Factor Analysis of a Subject–Feeling Array

To obtain this latter type of information as well, Amedeo and York (1984) next focused on the rows suggested in Figure 14.4. This shift in focus involves moving from a search for feeling clusters to one looking for grouping among response protocols across all 32 feelings. To accomplish this, they correlated rows with one another to reveal the nature of

$$\begin{array}{c}f_1\ f_2\ \cdots\ f_g\ \cdots\ f_n\end{array}$$

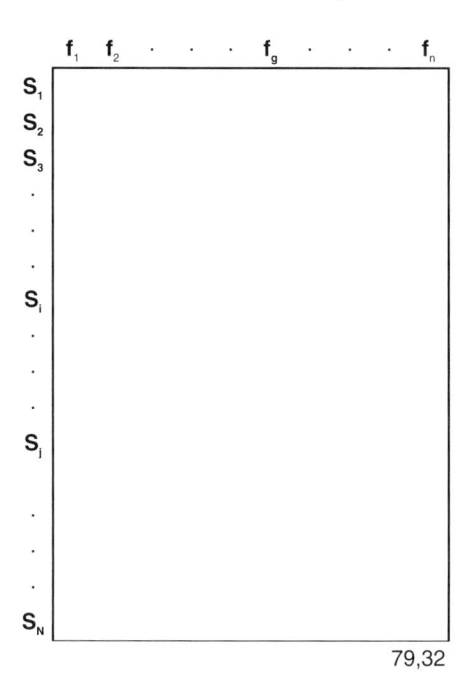

[matrix with rows $S_1, S_2, S_3, \ldots, S_i, \ldots, S_j, \ldots, S_N$]

79,32

FIGURE 14.4. Graphical example of a dataset for a given environment (where "S" refers to a subject and "f" to a feeling).

covariances in expressions about affective experiences, and then factored the coefficients to extract information about potential groupings present among subjects having similar beliefs about the feelings to be experienced in the given environment. Viewing the initial response array in this second way (that is, *Q-mode*) reduces total responses to groupings of distinctive response similarity.

14.2.3 Integrating the Q- and R-Mode Forms of Factor Information with Original Responses

These dual factor assessments of each response array were, then, interpreted for their implications about norm influences on the affective beliefs expressed by subjects. The authors reflected on three inquiries while speculating about these assessments: *who* agrees with *whom*, which *feelings* are being agreed upon, and the *collective emotional quality* of the feelings in the agreement.

14.3 Norm Influences on the Affective Responses to the City Street Scene Environment (E1)

To facilitate understanding, Amedeo and York (1984) first combined the sample's new belief scores about what would be felt in this city street with the response similarity groupings and affective dimensions that they implicated. A *partial* illustration suggesting how this was accomplished by the authors is shown in Table 14.2 (for data, see Amedeo & York, 1984).

TABLE 14.2. Subject Groups and Their Raw Scores on Feelings Characterizing Emotional Dimensions Being by Yourself in the "Old City Street" Scene

		Emotional dimensions and loadings generated by *R*-mode factor analysis																									
		DI										DII							DIII					DIV		DV	DVI
Subject groupings with similar response trends via *Q*-mode factor analysis		Contentment	Cheerfulness	Happiness	Delight	Gaiety	Elation	Friendliness	Affection	Confidence	Inspiration	Enjoyment	Love	Reverence	Serenity	Grief	Remorse	Depression	Sadness	Anger	Frustration	Hate	Fear	Nervousness	Panic	Anxiety	Boredom	Apathy	Excitement	Jealousy	Frustration	Pride	Passion
SubID	Loadng																																
Grp1	Fctr1																																
40	.91															6	7	7	7		4		6	7		6							
26	.88															4	4	4	4		4		3	3		-							
05	.83															4	3	5	6		-		-	-		3							
33	.82															5	6	7	6		-		6	7		6							
16	.82															4	5	6	6		4		6	5		5							
07	.80															4	5	5	5		4		5	4		5							
36	.79															3	4	5	4		3		4	6		4							
12	.79															4	4	6	4		4		3	4		5							
06	.75															5	4	6	6		6		4	5		5							
77	.73															6	3	6	5		6		5	4		3							
39	.71															5	3	5	5		5		6	6		5							
38	.69															-	6	6	6		6		-	4		-							
50	.67															5	4	5	6		6		4	4		3							
72	.64															4	3	5	3		3		6	4		-							
53	.60															6	4	7	6		6		-	-		6							
79	.58															4	4	5	3		5		-	-		4							
18	.57															4	3	4	4		-		4	3		3							
Grp2	Fctr2																																
19	.90	5	5	5		5		6	5	4																			5				
65	.82	6	3	5		4		4	4	5																			5				
64	.80	6	6	6		7		6	6	5																			7				
22	.79	3	3	3		3		4	5	4																			4				
73	.74	4	4	4		4		4	4	-																			3				
44	.73	5	5	5		7		7	7	3																			6				
51	.65	3	4	4		4		4	-	4																			3				
61	.56	6	7	7		3		4	4	4																			4				
54	.56	-	4	4		4		6	4	4																			3				
20	.54	5	3	3		6		4	5	3																			3				
31	.54	5	3	-		-		4	4	3																			4				
03	.54	-	3	5		3		4	-	4																			-				
46	.51	-	3	3		4		4	3	-																			3				

Note. Abridged from Amedeo and York (1984).

The response similarity groupings for the city street scene appear on the far left of this partial Table 14.2 and are exemplified by their subject member identifications and their loadings on the q-factor reflecting each grouping (see Amedeo & York, 1984, for eigenvalues and rotation details). The authors indicate that, with respect to this city street scene, 65 of the sample's 79 subjects clustered together with others of one group or another because of similarities in responses to this environment. Seventeen, for example, constituted Group 1.

14.3.1 Focusing on Salient Feelings Expressed by Subjects for the City Street Scene

Some of the responses subjects made to the study's request that they state their beliefs about the intensity of "feelings" they would experience if in the city street scene are highlighted in the central part of Table 14.2. (Intensities increase from 1 through 7.) Subjects of a particular group exhibit noticeable similarity about the specific feelings they would experience in this environment and the intensities of them. But it is also the case, at least for this environment, that the natures of response similarities differ among the groups that were extracted. Groups, in other words, are distinctive in the subset of feelings their members "agree" on. Differences like these, together with the fact itself that there are obvious grouping tendencies inherent in the total responses to this environment, strongly imply that multiple norms are operating in influencing affective responses to this place.

Amedeo and York (1984) were especially curious about the *affective nature* of these apparent norms. They noted, for example, that in responses to all three environments used in the study, subjects tended to think in terms of *coherent subsets of feelings*. Since a feeling rule or an emotional norm is likely, by its conceptual nature, to be schema-like, Amedeo and York suggested that, in most instances, people will experience environments in terms of broader affective *ambiances* rather than just in terms of particular feelings. Note from the R-mode factor analysis results the six affective dimensions and subsets of feelings they reflect at the top of Table 14.2. If these are referred to in terms of the feelings upon which most members of a given group agree, it is possible to conceptually estimate the *affective nature* of the *norms* being employed as bases for beliefs about affects to be experienced if in this city street scene.

For example, Amedeo and York (1984) point out that 17 members making up Group 1 are quite similar in their beliefs that they would experience, at relatively high intensity levels, grief, remorse, depression, sadness, frustration, fear, nervousness, and anxiety if in the city street scene (see this group in the partial Table 14.2). These affects are some of those that, because of their high loadings, were used to label affective dimensions DII and DIII when an R-mode factor analysis was performed on total responses. Hence, these authors indicate that the nature of the emotional norm influencing the responses of Group 1 suggests a combined meaning of "pessimism," "despair," "frustration," and a feeling of "apprehension." The quality of this norm is, thus, definitely negative.

Other groupings of subjects as well were present in the responses to this environment. Thirteen subjects, for example, make up a second group and 11 a third (the second is shown in Table 14.2 but none beyond that can be illustrated because of space limitations). Both of these differ from the first group in affective beliefs about this environment. The norm influencing the responses of this second group is definitely positive rather than negative in quality, as is evident from its subjects' intensity scores on the feelings constituting affective dimension 1. This suggests that the norm influencing their beliefs about affects can probably activate a pleasant state. Amedeo and York (1984) note that for the third group, only two feelings, apathy and boredom, seemed necessary to characterize their affective experience in this street setting. This suggests an indifference type of norm for this group. Six subjects constituting Group 4 (not shown in the table) also appear to be guided by a rather simple norm related to feelings like fear, nervousness, and anxiety. It, too, like that of group 1, is negative in quality and uncomfortably apprehensive (as in DIII) in nature.

14.3.2 Norm Influences on the Affective Responses to the Social Gathering Environment (E2)

The authors also evaluated the beliefs about feelings to be experienced in the social gathering environment illustrated in Figure 14.2. As in the city street scene, multiple norms appeared to be influencing subject beliefs about affects. Five affective dimensions surfaced from the authors' R-mode factoring of the total responses. The sample itself, when q-factored, divided into two large groupings and four smaller ones, each distinctive because of similarities in belief responses to this place. The 40 subjects making up the largest grouping believed they would experience feelings like cheerfulness, friendliness, happiness, and confidence if in the social gathering place. These were part of the positive collection of feelings contributing to the meaning of the first affective dimension for this environment. This suggested to the authors that the norm of straightforward *pleasantness* was influencing the common beliefs about affects for this group (see partial Table 14.3).

Pleasantness, however, is an inadequate descriptor for the norm influencing the affects expressed by the 18 subjects of the second group. The feelings members of this group believe they would experience if in this place were apathy, boredom, frustration, and nervousness as well. Apparently, subjects in this group expect they would be "bored" in this place and would certainly not care about being there; but, if their presence was, say, required, they would likely be "nervous" and "frustrated." That, according to Amedeo and York (1984), would be a plausible way to describe the underlying norm for the affects expressed by members of this second group. Notice it is negative in quality. A number of smaller groups (three to four members in each) materialized for the social gathering, but their size precludes attributing significance to them. The overall trend is nevertheless evident: multiple norms apparently govern affective responses to this environment (*E2*) as well as they did for *E1*.

14.3.3 Norms in the Affective Responses to the Woodland Setting Scene (E3)

The woodland setting, illustrated in Figure 14.3, was the third and final environment examined by Amedeo and York in their 1984 study. When compared with the previous two, this setting was obviously less built and more pastoral in appearance, and this aspect about it may have had an effect on the way the sample affectively responded to it.

Despite the appearance of distinctive grouping among the subjects for this setting, the difference among the commonalities describing each of the three prominent response groups is, in fact, a matter of degree, kind, and number of positive affects subjects believed they would experience if in this setting. In other words, all three major subject groupings are essentially governed by the influence of various versions of the most important affective dimension produced by the R-mode factoring. Sixteen positive feelings, from happiness to passion, help to define this affective dimension (see Table 4.4). Hence, the authors conclude that the guiding emotional norm is positive in quality and definitely pleasant in nature for each of the groups derived from the Q-mode factor analysis. This is a good example of an environment (clearly pastoral) for which, in a given social system, a near universal emotional norm seems likely to prevail. Some investigators would claim that this is not surprising for a surrounding like that depicted in Figure 14.2, for there is a strong conceptual orientation

TABLE 14.3. Subject Groups and Their Raw Scores on Feelings Characterizing Emotional Dimensions of Being by Yourself at a Social Gathering

Emotional dimensions and loadings generated by *R*-mode factor analysis

Subject groupings with similar response trends via *Q*-mode factor analysis

		DI										DII					DIII					DIV					DV			
SubID	Loadng	Cheerfulness	Friendliness	Happiness	Excitement	Delight	Enjoyment	Gaiety	Elation	Contentment	Confidence	Affection	Pride	Fear	Panic	Nervousness	Anxiety	Sadness	Jealousy	Passion	Reverence	Love	Serenity	Relief	Inspiration	Apathy	Remorse	Boredom	Sadness	Frustration	Depression	Hate	Grief	Anger	Depression
Grp1	**Fctr1**																																		
42	.95	5	5	6			6				6																								
35	.93	5	6	4			5				4																								
49	.90	7	7	6			6				6																								
78	.90	6	7	6			5				4																								
39	.90	5	5	5			5				5																								
28	.90	4	4	6			6				4																								
03	.90	6	6	4			5				6																								
79	.89	4	5	5			5				5																								
69	.89	5	4	4			4				4																								
18	.89	3	4	4			4				4																								
17	.89	4	5	5			5				4																								
24	.89	4	3	4			4				5																								
73	.88	5	5	6			5				-																								
14	.88	5	7	5			4				5																								
15	.87	5	5	4			5				5																								
71	.86	4	5	5			5				5																								
29	.86	5	6	5			5				4																								
29	.86	5	6	5			5				4																								
25	.85	4	5	5			4				6																								
52	.85	4	5	6			6				6																								
Grp2	**Fctr2**																																		
21	.91															3											4	4	3						
01	.88															-											5	5	4						
20	.86															5											5	6	3						
27	.82															-											6	5	5						
62	.81															3											4	5	4						
47	.81															4											3	4	3						
09	.81															3											3	3	-						
56	.79															5											4	5	4						
72	.77															3											4	5	-						
08	.76															3											5	6	4						
57	.76															3											6	6	5						
68	.75															5											4	3	-						
74	.73															3											-	4	3						
04	.64															4											3	4	4						
43	.61															5											-	4	-						
40	.57															6											5	6	5						
60	.54															3											3	4	3						
44	.42															7											7	7	7						

Note. Abridged from Amedeo and York (1984).

TABLE 14.4. Subject Groups and Their Raw Scores on Feelings Characterizing Emotional Dimensions of Being by Yourself at a Woodland Setting

Subject groupings with similar response trends via Q-mode factor analysis		\multicolumn{15}{c}{DI}	\multicolumn{5}{c}{DII}	DIII	DIV	DV
SubID	Loadng	Happiness	Cheerfulness	Delight	Enjoyment	Excitement	Friendliness	Confidence	Gaiety	Love	Pride	Elation	Contentment	Inspiration	Affection	Serenity	Passion	Reverence	Grief	Hate	Anger	Frustration	Remorse	Panic	Depression	Fear	Nervousness	Relief	Boredom	Apathy
Grp1	Fctr1																													
57	.90	7	6	7	7	5	6	7	6	7	7	6	5	7	6	7														
31	.89	7	7	7	7	7	7	7	7	7	7	7	7	7	7	7														
06	.87	5	4	4	5	5	4	5	5	5	5	5	5	5	4	5														
16	.85	6	5	7	6	6	5	5	4	6	6	6	5	5	5	6														
30	.84	7	6	5	6	6	5	6	5	6	5	6	5	7	5	7														
70	.84	7	7	7	7	7	7	6	6	6	6	7	6	7	6	7														
26	.83	5	5	6	6	4	5	5	4	6	5	4	5	4	5	6														
27	.83	6	5	6	7	5	5	6	5	6	6	4	6	6	6	6														
18	.83	7	6	7	7	6	6	6	6	6	5	6	7	5	6	5														
64	.82	7	7	7	7	7	7	7	7	7	7	7	7	7	7	7														
44	.81	7	7	6	7	7	7	5	5	6	5	7	7	6	6	7														
42	.81	7	7	7	6	6	7	6	7	7	7	7	7	7	7	7														
33	.80	7	7	7	7	4	7	5	5	7	7	7	7	7	5	7														
54	.80	5	4	4	5	4	4	5	4	4	5	4	4	4	5	5														
07	.80	5	5	5	5	5	5	5	5	5	5	5	5	5	5	5														
29	.79	5	4	5	4	3	4	4	3	3	4	4	4	4	4	4														
72	.79	5	4	5	6	3	5	4	5	5	4	5	6	6	5	5														
35	.78	6	4	6	6	4	5	5	4	5	6	4	5	5	5	5														
13	.78	7	7	6	6	5	7	7	4	7	6	5	6	6	6	7														
12	.78	7	6	7	7	5	6	7	4	6	7	5	7	7	7	7														
73	.78	4	3	4	4	3	3	3	-	4	3	4	3	4	4	-														
50	.77	6	5	6	6	5	4	6	4	5	5	5	6	4	4	7														
39	.76	6	4	6	6	4	5	5	3	4	4	5	6	4	5	7														
56	.76	6	6	6	7	6	5	7	5	5	4	4	7	5	6	7														
23	.76	6	6	6	6	6	6	6	6	6	6	6	6	6	5	6														
61	.75	5	5	4	5	4	5	4	4	4	4	4	5	5	4	4														
Grp1	Fctr2																													
21	.81	4	4		4		4	4				3																		
52	.67	7	5		6		5	5				6																		
37	.66	6	7		5		7	7				7																		
58	.67	6	5		6		6	5				4																		

Note. Abridged from Amedeo and York (1984).

throughout the person–environment research literature dealing with scenic value of places that would imply such near universality in response. (But see Chapter 15 that confronts that orientation directly.)

14.4 Overview

Amedeo and York's (1984) study on subjects' beliefs about intensities of feelings they would experience if in *E1*, *E2*, and *E3* offer a number of additional observations:

1. On one hand—at least for these three ordinary places—the responses of subjects about what they are likely to feel if in these places *by themselves* suggest that emotional-type norms are influencing the nature of their affective experiences. But, though not discussed here, in the actual request made to them, subjects were *also* asked to relate what they thought they *would feel* if in these surroundings with someone who is intimately close. In the woodland setting, this shift in social situation produced no significant change except that the results previously described became more pronounced. Such persistence in response results seems to reinforce the belief in the universality of the norm of "pleasantness" for this particular type of setting, regardless of whom one is with.

2. On the other hand, being with someone else seemed to make an important difference in how one would likely feel for the environment labeled as a social gathering. Although subjects in some groups still found this setting boring, could not care less about being in it, and would be apprehensive in it, many of their responses shifted to the "pleasant" dimension when with others. Some subjects, unenamored by the setting when alone, seemed to find it "acceptable" and even "pleasant" when there with someone else.

3. Some response shifting also took place for the city street scene (*E1*), but far less than for the social gathering (*E2*). More subjects came under the "pleasantness" dimension and fewer under other dimensions, but this effect did not erase or blur the evidence that multiple norms would be employed in responding emotionally to it. Changing the social situation of who one was with in a place had the smallest effect here.

14.4.1 Preliminary Remarks about Implications of Results

In the Amedeo and York (1984) study, *beliefs* were used as indicative of type and intensity of feeling likely to be felt by a subject if in a place. It is common knowledge, however, that people's responses and experiences do not always conform to their *beliefs*. Yet, according to Green (1972), beliefs about what is to be felt are neither entirely distinct from nor completely independent of affective experiences themselves. The results from this part of the Amedeo and York research—while certainly tentative—are, nevertheless, suggestive.

Their evaluations of raw-data affective-response arrays from two basic dimensions, across rows and down columns, uncovered distinctive commonalities from both, which, when integrated, rendered their expectations about *affective norm* influences in emotional responses to surroundings plausible. People appear to have access to emotional norms, and therefore to feeling rules in their affective responses to environments. Given a pluralistic society, for some surroundings these norms are apparently multiple and distinctive, while, for places like *E3*, they seem to be universal. It also appears that feeling rules are flexible enough so that under different social situations in environmental encounters, different norms may prevail.

But, of course, there is the question—particularly in studies emphasizing person–environment relations—about implications such results may have for more basic issues in that domain of inquiry. Can Amedeo and York's (1984) reasoning, for example, about norm influences on affective response to environments also be applied to explore the more basic issue of where *affect* itself enters into cognitively oriented conceptualizations of P-E-B relationships? To extend their reasoning, consideration should be given to exploring *affect* as an influence in the entire realm of environmental experiencing. It would seem that, if affective norms are feeling-rule schemas, then Amedeo and York's reasoning—together with their empirical results—should suggest that affect and evaluative outputs interface in the cognitive processing involved in environmental interpretation.

For example, a theme that frequently emerges from studies investigating affective experiences is that emotions result from cognitive appraisals of situations involving value components and expectations regarding them (Mandler, 2002). An interesting related question, then, is how should emotions be viewed in theoretical conceptualizations designed to describe other human issues like behavioral episodes? It would seem to be short-sighted to reason that *affects* be considered as outputs from human functioning and then not relate them to other human issues for which there are equally compelling concerns. Thus, what follows is a description of later work by Amedeo and York (1988) in which they search for relations between affective experiencing and the cognitive processing essential to engaging in activity in environments.

14.5 Affects in Cognitively Oriented P-E-B Frameworks

In their later research, Amedeo and York (1988) proposed treating relatively intense *affects* like those examined above as potentially dominant influences in what gets apprehended when people transact with their everyday environments. They contend that the significance of emotions should be found in their role as influences in central processes underlying P-E-B relationships involved in activity enactment. Their contention seems plausible when it is noted that affects like moods, emotions, and/or feelings are not manifested as actions with accompanying external impacts, but rather as *cognitive states* (see Mandler, 2002, p. 9).

14.5.1 Cognitively Oriented P-E-B Frameworks

Two theoretical perspectives—a *constructivist* and a *transactional*—are in use as cognitively oriented frameworks for organizing research questions about P-E-B relations. The two have similar "causal" orientations, although their views on what constitutes essential elements in P-E-B relations do differ (Moore, 1987). Nevertheless, both perspectives are sets of loosely integrated hypotheses and/or assumptions that collectively facilitate reasoning about fundamental inquiries like how environments are evaluated by individuals, the way in which such evaluative experiences "enter into" their behavioral episodes, and the manner by which individuals establish durable relations with environments. Both treat P-E-B events as *gestalts* and, in general, attempt to rationalize why and how actual environments constitute indispensable or essential arenas for ordinary behavior functioning. What makes these perspectives different from other theoretical orientations (for example, the ecological model; see Heft, 2001) is their fundamental assumption that activity and experience "in" an environment are quite dependent on information and its processing.

Both frameworks, then, *explicitly* incorporate a provision for perceptual–cognitive processing to support an assumption about the need to access internal and external information sources to function in environments. This provision facilitates dealing with how environmental information is acquired, synthesized, and integrated with internal sources of information in the formation of the ongoing environmental experience. The rationale here is that this experience, or the representing of coherent environmental knowledge, provides an important base for adaptive responses. Thus, by the inclusion of such processing, both perspectives emphasize the continual development of long-term cognitive integrations like environmental schemata, place images, cognitive maps, and the like, and how they function like "automatic" patterns in the organizing of sensory and other inputs into environmental experience (see Downs & Stea, 1973, 1977; Evans, 1980; Golledge & Stimson, 1997; Heft, 1981; Kaplan & Kaplan, 1982; Leff, 1978; Mandler, 1984; Moore, 1979, 1987; Moore & Golledge, 1976; Neisser, 1976; Tibbetts, 1976).

14.5.2 Affect and Cognitive Processes

The objective in the Amedeo and York (1988) study was to examine how *affects* like *emotions* and/or *feelings* might operate to alter, modify, or guide perceptual, cognitive, and behavioral outcomes in P-E-B relationships. There are many researchers in the broader, "nonenvironmental"-emphasizing disciplines who suggest that *affective experiences* acquire significance due to their potential to "control" information processing, and thereby perception and ongoing behavior. For example, Simon (1967) indicates that motivational and emotional "controls" over cognition should be included in a general theory of thinking and problem solving. Blumenthal's (1977) discussion on cognitive control specifies why such an inclusion makes sense. He points out, "The *emotional augmentation of experience* links enduring needs and dispositions to the *psychological present*. It can direct the course of cognition; the retrieval of memories, the structuring of thoughts, or the formation of perceptions" (pp. 101–102). Clark and Isen (1982) assert that there is a relationship between feeling states and social behavior and also between feeling states and evaluative thinking. Gilligan and Bower (1984) also examine how affect relates to perceptions, thoughts, and activities. Based on the results obtained in their research, Gilligan and Bower conclude:

> Emotion thus seems to be inextricably related to how we perceive and think, influencing them at every turn. Indeed, results reported throughout this chapter suggest that emotion is often a central component of cognitive processes in general. (pp. 568–569)

There is no shortage of support in the wider literature for this view that affect directly influences various phases of cognitive processing (see also Antrobus, 1970; Clark & Fiske, 1982; Geschwing, 1980; Mandler, 1975; Norman, 1980). Hence, Amedeo and York's (1988) recommendation that *affect* be investigated from the perspective of its incorporation in the structure of cognitively oriented P-E-B theoretical frameworks seems compelling, especially when it is noted that these particular frameworks—the constructivist and the transactional—are heavily involved with issues that relate to the processing of information.

14.6 Information-Processing Concerns of P-E-B Frameworks

When cognitive psychologists, social psychologists, and others argue that *affect* can "direct the course of cognition," "influence the *retrieval of memories*," "enter into *learning*," and "guide the *structuring of thoughts* or the formation of experience," then, in effect, it is asserted that *emotion* influences in decisive ways many of the subprocesses that make up information processing in general. That has significance for this discussion because such subprocesses play critical roles in the reasoning used by the *constructivist* and *transactional* frameworks when conceptualizing P-E-B relations.

Basic to the logic of these P-E-B frameworks is the idea that information "about" environments is vital to behavior and experience. Both perspectives stress that, in the fundamental process of environmental apprehension or knowing, *external information* (that is, information susceptible to being sensed by receptors) is cognitively attended to and structured under the influence of internal information to form percepts that go to make up a person's ongoing sense of his or her environment. *Internal information* for purposes of transacting with immediate surroundings is meant to refer to a capability of forming an immediate representation from a long-term integration like a place prototype, cognitive map, image, or environmental schema, all of which are constructions developed from previous experiences and patterned in long-term memory. From this sort of reasoning, it is said that the environment that is apprehended on any occasion is essentially a construction (see Heft, 1981). But the salient point is that *perception, cognition, memory*, and *learning* are *all* necessary parts of the information-processing logic of these frameworks; if that is so and if the wider literature claims are plausible, then *affect* must also be involved.

14.6.1 Conceptually Incorporating "Affect" into P-E-B Frameworks

While there is no prescription detailing how *affective experience* might be conceptually integrated into P-E-B frameworks, Clark and Isen (1982) and Gilligan and Bower (1984) provide an insight for that possibility. They propose that over time emotions "get" associated in networks with similarly toned or thematically congruent objects, events, behaviors, beliefs, roles, themes, and interpretative schemas to create the potential for the activation of distinct memory entities related to them. Clark and Isen stress similarity in tone of affect and other things that provides the bonding for association in a network, while Gilligan and Bower emphasize thematic and/or semantic bonds. Since both proposals treat affects as the central node in the associative networks, affect essentially guides recall—that is, such memory associations result in the greater accessibility of affect to the material in its networks and, through possible multiple links, material in other associative networks as well. Perhaps the most significant point of these affect-interfacing proposals for the specific focus of the Amedeo and York (1988) study is the idea that when *affect* is activated, it leads through these associations to the retrieval of internally stored related information to be brought to mind for cognitive processing with acquired external information. Gilligan and Bower (1984) put it this way: "emotional mood primes and brings into readiness peripheral categories and interpretive schemata that guides what people *attend to*, as well as how they *interpret it*" (p. 568, emphasis added).

The relevance of their reasoning for the constructivist and *transactional* frameworks should be evident. Given the purpose and significance of the environmental component in a P-E-B event, *affect* should have its most decisive influence throughout the time in a P-E-B episode in which information processing contributes to the construction of an environmental representation useful for functioning. This means that the *affective state* of a person in such an event should directly influence, in a tonal and thematic sense, what internal information is "brought forth" from memory for structuring a representation of surroundings that facilitates functioning in the ongoing P-E-B episode. Hence, if these proposals describe affect interfacing well, then congruent conceptual associations should be found between affect experienced in an environment and internal notions of such surroundings.

14.6.2 Empirical Association between Affects and Internal Information

With that expectation in mind, Amedeo and York (1988) compared results obtained in an investigation of *norm-influenced, affective responses* to *ordinary environments* with those obtained from another investigation (see also Amedeo & York, 1990) in which they searched for indications of *environmental attribute schemas,* using the *same environments and subjects* for both studies.

As described earlier, the initial research by Amedeo and York (1984) had looked for indications of emotional norms in people's beliefs about the intensities of feelings they would experience if in settings like the street scene (*E1*) and the social gathering (*E2*) scene shown in Figures 14.1 and 14.2. The results obtained from their comparing groupings of similarities in belief responses with clustering among feelings were displayed in partial form in Tables 14.2 and 14.3. Subject groupings were interpreted to reflect the influence of emotional norms, and the clusters of feelings as indicative of affective ambiances underlying these norms. Those results uncovered in their research about emotional norms were then further examined by Amedeo and York in their 1988 study for influences they might exert on information-assessment processes basic to P-E-B frameworks. It is this latter work, then, that is now being described.

Since affective norms or beliefs about what one should feel in a place are likely to be memory items and since the central curiosity in their 1988 study was with the influence of *affect* over *ongoing environmental apprehensions* in P-E-B episodes, the question Amedeo and York had to address was: *Are the thematic and tonal qualities of affective norms congruent with those of environmental attribute schemas for a particular place?* Answers to that question rest on information about the attribute schemas that subjects subscribed to when they possessed beliefs about appropriate affects to be experienced. Indications of attribute schema use were acquired by Amedeo and York in their original 1984 study of emotional norms by the use of an additional inquiry. In addition to the inquiry about beliefs about affects likely to be experienced in each of three environments, those same subjects were asked to write down "what comes to mind" while viewing wide-screen, colored projections of the three environmental settings. Their thought responses were then examined for any indications of environmental attribute categories. Hence, if n attribute categories were actually alluded to by the entire sample for, say, the city street scene environment (*E1*) in Figure 14.1, these were then used by Amedeo and York as a reference to inspect the written thoughts of each subject for determining which attribute categories were referred to and which were not. This was also done for their thought responses to the social gathering scene in Figure 14.2. In this manner, each subject's thoughts for a setting became describable as an n-length series, or an attribute protocol, of ones for mentions and zeros for nonmentions. Through the use of similarity coefficients (using the SPSS package), the authors were able to compare the *thought patterns* of any two subjects for a given environment. They then factor-analyzed the array of similarity coefficients for each environment for evidence both of grouping among subject protocols and of clustering among attributes, using the dual-perspective analytical design they suggested in their 1984 study.

14.6.3 Integrating Reflections of Affective Norms with Environmental Schemata Indicators

Norms underlying affective beliefs of subjects were compared with environmental attribute schemas devised in the way just described from their what-comes-to-mind protocols. Because of space constraints in this book, Tables 14.5 and 14.6 only summarize how these two memory items, *affective norms* and *attribute schemas*, might be associated when the environment contemplated by subjects was either a city street scene (Figure 14.1) or a social gathering scene (Figure 14.2). (See Amedeo and York, 1984 and 1988, for finer details.) The far-left column in each table contains the size of three distinct groupings of subjects from the sample, typical feelings they would experience in the respective environment and the norm characterizing their group's *affective commonality*. Consider, for example, Table 14.5.

The top of Table 14.5 contains estimates of environmental attribute scenarios devised by Amedeo and York (1988, 1990) from information in subject thought responses to the inquiry posed to them about environmental attributes. These *what-comes-to-mind thoughts* about these two settings generated five environmental attribute scenarios for each place. In their estimates of them, Amedeo and York interpreted a scenario to be a consensus that characterizes that which is common among a number of individual thought patterns and describes it by using the terms used in the thoughts that went to make it up. For example, the second scenario for the city street scene illustrates that some, but not all, subjects thought of this place as "an attractive and interesting setting" which would contain commercial and retail facilities with specialty shopping. To them, it apparently exemplifies a city mystique and is suggestive of city experiences. This scenario is positive, while three others for this city street scene were negative and one was essentially neutral.

To reiterate, then, by focusing on a sample of subjects who were asked to respond to the same environments, Amedeo and York delineated, via their designs in their 1984 and 1988 works, two *reflections of memory items*—one an affective norm, and the other an environmental attribute schemata—from two responses to these settings. The data for both investigations were collected in a single interviewing session in which beliefs about feelings were elicited first and "what-comes-to-mind" responses immediately after. It is useful to compare the results obtained in these studies in order to reflect on the plausibility of this association-in-memory assumption held by those researchers adhering to the idea of the "control" of affect over retrieval of other internal information necessary for perceptual–cognitive processing.

When results of these norm and attribute assessments were compared for the city street scene, they appeared to lend support to this association assumption between affects and cognitions. For example, for the city street scene results summarized in Table 14.5, many subjects in the first similarity grouping anticipated a rather negative *affective state* to be experienced in this setting and also characterized its attributes in ways consistent with four negative or neutral environmental scenarios (that is, 1, 3, 4, and 5). In that sense, these subjects exhibited a quality and meaning association between the affective norm governing their beliefs about the feelings they thought they would experience in this place and their attribute characterization of this environment. It should be noticed that only 6% of this grouping, for example, subscribed to the more positive second attribute scenario in Table 14.5.

Notice, however, that a second grouping exhibited a different way from the first of responding to the city street scene. Its affective norm was decidedly positive because the affects believed to be experienced in this place were positive for all its 15 subjects. Many of those subjects (approximately 47%) subscribe to the positive environmental attribute scenario (#2) as well. Like subjects in the first grouping, this group also suggests that an expected association between affects and evaluative cognitions may be plausible. The third grouping of subjects for this environment is a bit small for a detailed description, but even here there is suggestion of a quality and meaning association.

This consistency between *affective states* and *environmental scenarios* is even clearer in the subject responses to the environment social gathering scene (E2) in Figure 14.2, as illustrated in Table 14.6. Note that the first norm or feeling state is positive and consists of a combination of some rather pleasant and bright feelings. Individuals making up this group implied that this feeling state would influence the feelings they would experience if they were in this social gathering scene. For this first group, approximately 55% "subscribed" to one variation or another of a positive environmental scenario and another 15% to a neutral

TABLE 14.5. City Street Scene: Associations between Affective Norms and Environmental Scenarios

Affective norms	Environmental scenarios				
	Scenario 1 An environment of crime and violence. It is intimidating and contains prostitution and drug traffic. It is deteriorating and decaying and has high unemployment.	Scenario 2 An attractive and interesting setting. Contains commercial and retail facilities with specialty shopping. Exemplifies city mystique and past city experiments.	Scenario 3 A lifeless, unattractive, place void of activity and people. Seldom used. A dreary, depressing setting; a cold, gloomy, gray mood; decaying, run-down, and alienating.	Scenario 4 A low organizational and minimally evaluative perspective. Place is viewed in a listlike fashion. Elements are singled out, particularly features of buildings, visually prominent buildings, traffic, and lack of vegetation.	Scenario 5 Viewed as a sorrowful, depressing place, and likely to be dreary, bleak, gloomy, cold, and gray. Probably in an old or older part of town.
Group 1: *31 subjects* An air of pessimism, despair, and frustration accompanied by strong apprehension. Principal feelings: fear, sadness, nervousness, depression, and anxiety	33%	6%	6%	9%	13%
Group 2: *15 subjects* Likely to be a positive experience, definitely quite pleasant, active, or lively. Principal feelings: Happiness, delight, friendliness, contentment, inspiration, enjoyment, confidence, and excitement	6%	47%		6%	
Group 3: *11 subjects* A dull, uninteresting, indifferent experience. Principal feelings: apathy and boredom	9%	27%	18%	9%	

Note. From Amedeo and York (1988).

250 EXPERIENCES AND ENVIRONMENTS

TABLE 14.6. Social Gathering Scene: Associations between Affective Norms and Environmental Scenarios

Affective norms	Environmental scenarios				
	Scenario 1 A friendly, relaxed social setting within which conversations, eating, and drinking take place. Enjoyable setting to experience laughter and good times.	Scenario 2 No strong image. A view that is simple and straightforward; namely, the place is some sort of social function or meeting.	Scenario 3 A dull, boring office party, agitating, uncomfortable, containing social pressures.	Scenario 4 A pleasant office party or celebration.	Scenario 5 Unattractive and uninteresting; judgmental about intentions, appearances, and social values; boring and dull.
Group 1: *48 subjects* An emotional experience of some combination of the qualities associated with happiness, delight, enjoyment, excitement, cheerfulness, gaiety, contentment, and confidence	48%	15%	4%	6%	4%
Group 2: *18 subjects* Bored and apathetic	.05%	22%	28%	.05%	17%
Group 3: *13 subjects* Expected to be bored, quite nervous, and experience anxiety. May also experience friendliness and possibly enjoyment	15%	23%	15%	7%	

Note. From Amedeo and York (1988).

Sattribute rendition of this place. Approximately 8% of the subjects from this first grouping, however, expressed a negative scenario of this place, despite a positive emotional norm influencing their affects.

This association between the quality and meaning of feeling state and environmental scenarios is repeated for the remainder of the subjects. In Group 2, for example, 12 of 18 subjects in this group related neutral and/or negative "what-comes-to-mind" responses with their expected affective state of being "bored and apathetic"; in a rather small Group 3, at least 6 out of the 13 subjects displayed consistency in the quality and meaning of affects and cognitions.

14.7 Discussion

Comparing the results obtained in the Amedeo and York (1984) study on *affective norms* with those acquired from their investigation on *attribute-type environmental sche-*

mata (Amedeo & York, 1988) offers tentative but convincing support—albeit with a few exceptions—to the plausibility of the assumption asserting a tonal and semantic association between *affects* and *schematic items in memory*. In the contexts discussed in these studies, *beliefs about feelings* probably stem from *broader emotional norms,* while "what-comes-to-mind" responses likely emanate out of more *general environmental schemas*. It is commonly believed that norms and schemas—like concepts, rules, stereotypes, and so on—reflect the integrative manner in which information may be organized in long-term memory for "later" use in cognitive processing. Thus, the associations observed, being between memory items that are related because they refer to the same situation (that is, the same environment) makes the hypothesis that affect influences the organization and retrieval of other memory items for use in the construction of percepts a plausible one. In that regard, Mandler (1985) states:

> Emotion is not only anecdotally and phenomenally part of human thought and action, there is now a burgeoning body of evidence that emotional states interact in important ways with traditional cognitive functions. For example, positive feelings determine the accessibility of mental contents in the process of decision making, serve as retrieval cues, and influence problem-solving strategies. More generally, accessibility of mental contents is determined by the mood both at the time of original encounter and at the time of retrieval. (p. 113)

This is, however, about as much as can be concluded because the studies brought together by Amedeo and York to assess these associations were strictly exploratory instances of "one of a kind." Nevertheless, the results from these two studies, when compared in the manner presented here, do at least suggest that P-E-B cognitively oriented frameworks should be reexamined in terms of the role they reserve for affect. As demonstrated in the discussion of the related literature, there is considerable belief in the view that *affect* influences cognitive processing, particularly at the *attentional state* (where, incidentally, the apprehension of surroundings begins to take shape, as discussed by Mandler, 2002). Although plausible frameworks like the *contructivist* and the *transactional* are supposed to be system-like in structure and *gestalt* in conceptualization, there is often nevertheless a slip into focusing, particularly on behavior. This can be—and probably at times is—a source of mild irritation to those who believe that P-E-B events ought to be oriented around more evaluative themes like affect. The more affect is examined in terms of perceptual–cognitive processing, the more it begins to appear that what counts "initially" in an environmental encounter is how one feels. Mandler (2002) states this about emotion's significance in this regard: "Emotions and pain . . . are prima facie reactions to events and experiences of central importance to the individual. If attention needs to select anything and consciousness needs to elaborate it, it certainly would include pain and emotion" (p. 97).

The design suggested, implemented, and tested by Amedeo and York as discussed in this chapter to examine the *affective experience* and its relationship to evaluative-type counterparts is cumbersome and intensely inductive in its reasoning. Approaches to researching these issues do need to be improved, with more control and discipline in the design discussed in this chapter. But for that to happen, more needs to be known about affects themselves and the environmental schemas. Nevertheless, it has been shown that it *is* possible to devise some schema, no matter how awkward, for researching experiences in environmental contexts. Chapter 15 discusses another approach to exploring aspects of an experience equally as opaque conceptually as the one discussed in this chapter.

CHAPTER 15

Aesthetic Experiences in Environments

15.1 Introduction

This chapter describes Amedeo's (1999) attempt to examine how *external information* from everyday surroundings might be combined with *internal information* in the perceiving of scenic quality. His work offers one way to study reactions to scenic conditions in landscape-type environments and to explore whether multiple versions of *scenicness* might exist among people for the same surroundings. It uses a relatively large sample of mixed participants from Eastern and Central regions of the United States who reveal their assessments of a variety of landscapes depicted in surrogate photographs. The design employed in this study is extensive and combines Q-sort discriminations of landscapes performed by subjects to reflect their perceptions of scenic-quality differences, covariance assessments of the scenic arrangements produced by subject discriminations, commonality searches among subjects to detect distinctive sets of similarities among those arrangements, and a regressing of physical features on these landscape assessments in an attempt to isolate their potential contributions to the variation in subjects' perceived scenic quality differences. What follows first in this chapter's description of this investigation are some prominent results and views of others who also investigated scenic quality reactions to natural settings.

15.2 Information-Influencing Perceptions of Scenic Quality

Amedeo (1999) points out in his work that the *scenicness of surroundings* is a quality that has been repeatedly associated with many other issues about environments over time. It is evident, for example, that it frequently enters into discussions about the "health benefits" of natural environments, "horticultural therapeutic understanding," the importance of the "pastoral dimension" in environments for "emotional well-being," and other topics. But the nature of the *scenic-quality experience* involves considerations of *value assessments* not only from the perspective of the *person experiencing it*, but also from the viewpoint of *others* who think this *quality desirable*.

Like "emotions," *scenic quality experiences* may be more effectively understood if looked at mainly from the *experiential level*, especially since the meaning of this environmental construct is latent in nature and there exists no standard and/or universal definition for it. For that reason, it may be viewed as both a subjective reaction to, and a value-laden broader appraisal of, circumstances in surroundings. Depending on one's dispositions toward aspects of environments that are thought of as relatively "natural," it could be a rather significant experience *felt* by individuals *transacting* with such surroundings.

It is well known, however, that the notion of "scenic" is a subjectively *absorbing* one, in that it often serves as a basis for revealing or expressing value-oriented environmental preferences. As is evident in recreational and residential circumstances, it may command significant economic exchange value. Few individuals are ever dispassionate and/or objective when conscious of or contemplating the *scenicness* of surroundings. As pointed out by Nasar (1988) and Porteous (1996), reactions to this quality may have both intense *emotional* and *aesthetic* undertones. Yet, as Amedeo (1999) points out, despite many investigations by researchers from a wide variety of interest areas, answers to even the most rudimentary questions about its nature often seem inaccessible.

15.2.1 Understanding the Notion of "Scenicness"

How, then, might the notion *of scenicness* be better understood? Fenton and Reser (1988) point out that increased clarification of this construct may require linking external conditions related to *scenicness* with human propensities to "notice it." This means that the empirical view of scenic quality needs to be more conceptually integrated with its perceptual perspective. Porteous (1996) expresses similar sentiments, pointing out that there are few studies that are designed specifically to accomplish integration between these two perspectives.

In the design of his research, Amedeo (1999) attempted to establish connections between *empirical* and *perceptual* perspectives about experiencing this quality by examining some of the more central informational issues involved in understanding *scenicness* (see also Amedeo, Pitt, & Zube, 1989). He maintains that it is possible to strongly relate the empirical view of this construct with the perceptual perspective by examining how the principal information sources that are involved, both external and internal, interact and are rationalized with one another in the perceiving of scenic quality. As a necessary consequence of reasoning in that way, Amedeo approached his investigation equipped with the expectation that multiple perceptual versions of scenic quality may exist simultaneously for the same surroundings, and he maintained that, given the various ways external or empirical information can be integrated with internal information in the *recognition and assessment* of this quality, this outcome may not be uncommon. Amedeo's preliminary thoughts imply that cognition in perception plays a significant role in what is actually assessed. Since his research involves an *experience* in *everyday surroundings* that is not directly tied to the immediate information needs of activity intentions, it is useful to examine in some detail the context for his reasoning.

15.2.2 Issues Affecting the Comprehension of "Scenic Quality"

Scenic quality is frequently viewed as a "natural resource." Because of its relatively high vulnerability to degradation, it must be managed, protected, and preserved (see, for example, Elsner & Smardon, 1979; Litton, 1968; U.S. Department of the Interior, 1975; Zube, 1973). Yet there is no widespread agreement as to what this resource represents or how it is actually manifested. Rideout (1988), for example, ponders whether legislation can be formulated to conserve and/or preserve such a resource, indicating that legislation on preserv-

on preserving this quality and designating it as a natural resource is often caught up in endless debate about what it embodies and how others ordinarily view it. That assessment is informative and suggests that much remains to be resolved about this notion of scenic quality involving such basic issues as the nature of the environmental unit to which "scenic" is attributed and the way individuals apprehend this quality.

Amedeo (1999) points out that there are at least three basic issues that noticeably influence attempts to understand the notion scenic: (1) the *impreciseness* by which environmental units said to possess this quality are understood; (2) the *relatively persistent independence* of the major approaches dealing with this quality; and (3) the *significance of the ordinary attribution process* in the recognition of *scenicness*.

15.2.2.1 Impreciseness

This first issue is important because beliefs about what constitutes the nature of the unit to which *scenicness* is attributed may, in turn, influence conceptions about scenic quality itself. Segments of environments to which various degrees of *scenicness* are ascribed typically are labeled "landscapes." In much research, landscapes are treated as settings that are supposedly evident, and effort is seldom devoted to delimiting *precisely* to which segments of the wider environment they refer. The impression usually left is that landscapes are observable, coherent, distinctive, and empirically identifiable entities, and that what constitutes a particular landscape should be evident to all (for a comprehensive discussion of the *landscape* notion, see Moos, 1973; Porteous, 1996; Zube, 1973, 1976; Zube, Pitt, & Anderson, 1975). Zube (1976) states, for example, that "*landscape* refers to the combined physical attributes of the environment" (p. 90).

This suggests that combining external physical attributes is integral to the process of recognizing such a unit. The difficulty here is that there are many ways of combining a given set of physical attributes, and there exists no universal agreement about which combination or which set of attributes should constitute a given "landscape." But despite this problem, this conception of "landscape" reflects the way it is commonly viewed. Professional architects, planners, and ecologists typically refer to a "landscape" as a continuum of landform and land cover, it being *a discrete* part of the environment having some sort of continuous coherency with respect to surface cover.

This view tends to impart empirical status to the landscape unit, especially the reference to a "discrete part of the environment." Unless qualified, the definition suggests that people's renditions of landscapes more or less correspond to presumed external counterparts and leaves little room for differences among people in their conceptualization of the unit (for example, how they combine which physical attributes). Fenton and Reser (1988) point out that:

> Kreimer (1977), in his critical analysis of environmental preference methodologies, has emphasized that research in environmental preference often assumes a direct correlate between the individual's perception and construct of the environment and the "real" external environment. Such an isomorphism is, from all we know of perception and cognition, naive at best. (p. 235)

But if views like these present such reasoning difficulties, how are inquiries regarding the existence, composition, and manifestation of a *landscape* to be addressed? Cosgrove (1984) indicates that *landscape* is an imprecise and ambiguous construct. He points to a "unifying principle" that he suggests individuals use to attribute more holistic characteristics to perceived parts of surroundings. He indicates that "landscape is not merely the world we see; it is a construction, a composition of the world. Landscape is a way of seeing the world" (p. viii). He adds that "cultural landscapes can . . . be treated as manifestations of cognitive schemata, ideas held in common by the makers (and users) of these cultural landscapes" (p. viii).

Amedeo (1999) suggests further that, given the way in which landscape units actually *get recognized or known,* there seems to be little need to treat them differently from the way authors such as Cosgrove (1984), Rapoport (1982) and Fenton and Reser (1988) recommend. Better still, he suggests that landscapes be viewed just like environments in general are in the P-E-B frameworks of the *constructivists* or the *transactionalists* (see Ittelson, 1973a; Ittelson, Proshansky, Rivlin, & Winkel, 1974; Moore, 1976, 1979, 1987; Stokols, 1978; Tibbetts, 1972, 1976 ; Wapner, Cohen, & Kaplan, 1976; Wapner, Kaplan, & Cohen, 1973). Both frameworks conceptualize how individuals experience environments (that is, get to "know them") and describe how those experiences "enter into" behavioral episodes. Both reason that carrying out activity "in" environments depends on both external and internal sources of information, together with certain *mental* (that is, cognitive) processes for reconciling these two sources into immediately useful knowledge. Research indicates that individuals, in encounters with external conditions, engage in a "knowing" or perceptual–cognitive process through which they acquire, synthesize, and integrate environmental information with internal sources of knowledge to form an immediate usable contextual-arena basis for ongoing behavior. The contention is that internal knowledge in the form of environmental representations essentially directs what external information is acquired during the environmental knowing process and organizes its elaboration to render it informative (see Amedeo & York, 1990; Mandler, 1984; Neisser, 1976; Rumelhart & Ortony, 1977; Thorndyke, 1984). The noticeable difference between these two frameworks is that the "constructivist" perspective places more emphasis on the role of internal information or mental constructs in the recognition and attribution phases of the environmental knowing process, while the "transactional" viewpoint stresses the qualifying influences that ongoing transactions with surroundings have on the outcomes of environmental knowing. The differences between the two perspectives, however, are—for the most part—not conceptually contentious, and the respective emphases of each can easily be incorporated into the other's perspective (see especially Moore, 1976; Tibbetts, 1972, 1976).

The point is that the reasoning underlying these frameworks would conceptualize the process of experiencing or knowing a landscape in a manner consistent with Cosgrove's (1984) suggestion that individuals use a "guiding principle" to recognize and identify segments of environments as this or that landscape. The "guiding principle" to which Cosgrove refers probably is—as Rapoport (1990) suggests—the use of some *landscape schema* to give definition to surroundings. The relevance of Cosgrove's and Rapoport's view that the landscape notion is essentially a construct is that it is difficult to insist *solely* on empirical status for scenic quality (for example, it is a "natural resource") if the unit to which it commonly is attributed is itself a product of cognitive construing (see also Amedeo et al., 1989; Fenton & Reser, 1988).

15.2.2.2 Persistent Independence

With respect to the second basic issue referring to the *persistent independence* of perspectives, Amedeo notes that, in an attempt to comprehend the recognition of scenic quality, researchers have generally taken two main approaches. As just described, one is largely *empirically based* or "objective," while the other is *process-oriented* or "perceptual" (see, for example, Craik, 1981; Daniel & Vining 1983; Fenton & Reser, 1988; Zube, 1976):

1. The more *empirical* or *objective approach* tends to view scenic quality as something inherent in a given scene, and implies that its presence need only be identified and measured. It emphasizes measurable physical aspects of environments, which are presumed to be integral to assessments of environmental quality. The strong implication is that there are regular correspondences between such physical aspects—such as sky, land, water, and slope—and *scenicness*. The problem, however, is that empirical demonstrations of how such properties or their combinations are likely to "causally" enter into the production of *scenicness* or into the actual assessments of this quality are definitely lacking. This is not to deny that properties like these enter into *scenicness*, for that denial would be ludicrous. As an approach, however, the empirical treatment tends to seriously slight the role perception plays in determining what is actually apprehended about surroundings. In so doing, it discounts the potential significance of disparities in environmental and aesthetic experiences and, in that way, inhibits the possibility of discovering how such differences may operate in the assessment of scenic quality.

2. The *perceptual approach* to understanding the scenic experience tends to place its emphasis mainly on the processes individuals employ to know things. It treats the attribution of *scenicness* to surroundings essentially as growing out of an appraisal process during environmental perception and cognition. For example, Daniel and Boster (1976) discuss a method for estimating the scenic quality of specific scenes from individuals' perceptions and judgments of that quality. They indicate that an observer perceives scenic beauty in the landscape and assesses that perception against some internal aesthetic "standards" or "criteria" to make a judgment about the degree of *scenicness* present. This, they say, is effected through some *rule* that rationalizes the different combined effects produced by "visible landscape properties." But Amedeo and colleagues (1989) indicate that this view of scenic quality, if left unqualified, tends to deemphasize the role physical aspects play in this process, despite the fact that doing so may compromise the perspective itself, for at least one question must always be addressed in perceptual–cognitive perspectives: *What activates or evokes relevant cognitive activity and influences attention to scenicness?*

However, neither of these two perspectives ("empirical" or "objective" and "perceptual") is sufficient to describe the process by which surroundings are assessed for scenic quality. Therefore, a more integrative approach is needed. Fenton and Reser (1988) and others (Porteous, 1996; Sancar, 1985; Willard, 1980) indicate that such an approach would be

> basically an interactional perspective and hold that beauty emerges as a result of the interaction between a human experiencer . . . and the natural objects and events experienced, but that beauty is not located in, or attributable solely to, either the former or the latter. (Fenton & Reser, 1988, p. 109)

That observation makes sense. To account for the experience of scenicness, any approach must consider both perceptual–cognitive processing and those aspects of surroundings (for example, physical and other stimuli) that potentially can serve as activators of such an experience.

15.2.2.3 The Attribution Process

When addressing the third basic issue about the *attribution process*, Amedeo and colleagues (1989) suggest that it is necessary to recognize that two thoroughly interrelated fundamentals are likely to be involved in judging an environment for its scenic quality. One requires *construing* surrounding features into a coherent environmental entity, whether that entity is labeled a scene, landscape, setting, place, or something else. The other necessitates applying some "rule" or *scheme* that facilitates assigning or attributing scenic quality to such entities.

Construing is an ongoing process individuals accomplish as they gradually understand their surroundings perceptually while transacting with them. A construction or interpretation of surroundings into a coherent environmental entity—say, a "landscape"—always involves:

- The presence of feature information in surroundings
- Sensory exposure to that information
- Transactions in and with such surroundings to facilitate such exposure
- A perceptual–cognitive process for selecting and interpreting feature information and integrating it with previous experiences
- An evaluation or appraisal of the evolving construal
- A context within which this entire perceptual experience can have some rationale, purpose, or meaning.

Together, these things facilitate the construction (that is, an apprehension) of some coherent environmental image like a scene, setting, place, or landscape immediately useful at the moment (that is, fit for some intended purpose and/or activity). The characters and outcomes of such a process are highly dependent on the environmental experiences and nature of the individual constructing the image, the "demands" of the surroundings, and the manner in which the individual transacts with such environs.

The second fundamental of attributing scenic quality brings up the question of how "scenic" acquires meaning for individuals. For the general public, the construct "scenic" is certainly not a standardized concept like height, weight, or temperature, possessing like them a universal scale isomorphic to its inherent quantity property. Rather, "scenic" is more likely to be made manifest by an individual through the use of some memory-based rule of thumb or scheme that was and is continuously influenced by sociocultural aesthetic norms in its ongoing development and that is habitually used by the individual to evaluate or appraise a construed environmental entity like "landscapes" for this quality. In practice, people's current schemes about what constitutes "scenic" are likely to encompass some mixed and unknown assortment of their perspectives on other aspects of environments, including, but probably not limited to, ambiance, composition, order, continuity, usefulness, and facets less well known than these.

15.2.2.4 Overview of "Scenic Quality"

Scenic seems to be a high-level abstraction, continuously developing in the beholder, quite flexible in its application, significant in environmental preference structures, and influential in generating *emotional* and *meditational* responses to physical settings. And, if scenic is thought to reflect "beauty," then this abstraction is probably far more general than implied here, for it is evident that the notion of "beauty" extends to more than just landscapes or other environmental units. People make judgments about the beauty of many different things, including other people, art, music, compositions, objects, sounds, patterns, and so on. These judgments are probably guided by an individual's potential to evoke some aesthetic in the form of a cognitive structure or rule that is sufficiently general so as to allow the making of a wide variety of beauty judgments about people, objects, things, and surroundings. In any event, the cognitive act of discriminating among scenes for their scenic quality or beauty differences probably involves greater complexity and depth in processing than just matching each of the scenes to some ordinally calibrated standards implied by an aesthetic criterion.

For individuals, then, judgments about the scenic quality of "landscapes" are no doubt shaped by currently held notions about what constitutes scenic and by how such notions mesh with what is perceived to be "out there" in the first place. An individual's scenic notion, to be useful, is likely to be fluid, adaptable, and responsive to the environmental context. Hence, for an individual to evoke or imagine a scenic concept for use, some sort of cuing from surroundings seems necessary. This, of course, presupposes the presence of external physical information.

These, then, are essentially the thoughts offered by Amedeo (1999) when he discusses the reasoning involved in these two main perspectives: *empirical* and *perceptual*. He emphasizes the need to integrate the plausible aspects of both viewpoints into one conceptualization by taking into consideration how external and internal information sources are usually rationalized, one to the other, so as to make their individual contributions to the process of experiencing this quality evident. This chapter now turns to the research strategy he employed in his attempt to illustrate how the integration of these views might be exemplified in the empirical situation.

15.3 Assessments of Scenic Differences among Scenes

Amedeo (1999) constructed a research approach designed to entertain the question of whether it is at all plausible to expect *continuous feedback* between internal and external sources of information during the process of apprehending scenic quality.

15.3.1 The Sample and Instrument

Table 15.1 illustrates the characteristics of the 407 volunteer participants acquired for his study. To elicit their perceptions of differences in scenic quality from one setting to another, participants were presented with 56 5" × 7" color photographs of scenes taken mainly from pastoral areas in an extensive valley located in Connecticut. They included a wide variety of rolling hill–like places covered with second-growth forests, flat meadow settings, water scenes, park-like places, small-town environments, and other surroundings exhibiting various combinations of these features. Of course, color photographs are not the settings themselves, but researchers have demonstrated that they can be good substitutes for the actual physical setting when there is a concern with perception and when information is acquired mainly through the visual receptor (see Shaefer & Richards, 1976; Stewart, Middleton, Downton, & Ely, 1984). On the other hand, relating to a surrogate is not the same as relating to the actual circumstance (for example, see Hull & Stewart, 1992). But many difficulties are involved in testing for alleged differences between people's responses to a surrogate (for example, a photo) and actual circumstance (for example, an environment). Unless such differences are well known and can be defined, however, it is not possible to correct for them.

The scenes selected for his study certainly had to be sufficient in number to adequately represent those typically found throughout the extensive southern Connecticut River Valley and needed to contain enough variation among them to encourage and permit subject discriminations. The 56 photographs used were originally selected by a panel of three judges from a larger pool of over 300 photos, their selections being guided by an attempt to docu-

TABLE 15.1. Individuals Selected for the Study: Gender, Age, Places, and Groups

Gender		Age			Group size	
Male	Female	(years)	N	Group	(n)	Subjects
n = 253	n = 154	12–18	48	Amherst	26	Residents of Amherst, MA, and students at the University of Massachusetts
		19–25	126			
		26–25	96	Suffield	22	Upper-middle-income residents of Suffield, CT
		36–45	51	Engineers	30	Professional engineers from Northeast Utilities
		46–55	47	Clerical	27	Office and clerical employees of Northeast Utilities
		56–65	25	Clerical	28	
		65+	14	Hartford	11	Lower-middle-income African American residents of inner-city Hartford, CT
				Environs	27	Professional personnel of the Connecticut state office of USDA–Soil Conservation Service and the Connecticut Cooperative Extension Service
				Environs	33	Professors and graduate students in regional planning at SUNY–College of Environmental Sciences and Forestry and in forestry at the University of Massachusetts
				Endves	23	Undergraduate students in environmental design at the University of Massachusetts
				Psych	18	Undergraduate students in an introductory psychology course (high school students in Northampton and Amherst, MA)
				High school	39	Junior and senior high school students in Northampton and Amherst, MA, and throughout MD
				Kansas	20	Upper-middle-income residents of Wichita, KS
				Washington, DC	17	Members of the DuPont Circle Civic Association; predominantly upper-middle-income, entirely white residents of Washington, DC
				Boston	25	Lower-middle-income lifetime residents of the North End, an Italian community in Boston, MA
				Designer	21	Professors and graduate students in landscape architecture at SUNY–College of Environmental Sciences and Forestry
				Designer	24	Professors and graduate students in landscape architecture at the University of Massachusetts
				Nebraska	27	A mix of rural and urban middle-class individuals in blue- and white-collar occupations and in agriculture
					418	Sample
					–11	Incomplete responses
					407	Total responses

Note. From Amedeo (1999).

ment the range of landform/land cover interactions found along four transects through the rural and urban portions of the Connecticut River Valley in northern Connecticut and Massachusetts.

15.3.2 Format for Eliciting Perceptions of Scenicness

To initiate his investigation, Amedeo (1999) used a Q-sort procedure to acquire reflections of participants' perceptions (see comments on Q-sort in Block, 1961; Pitt & Zube, 1979; and, particularly, McKeown & Thomas, 1988). This is essentially a pragmatic sorting method that is designed to extract information reflecting variations in perceiving in general. It is especially useful when more subjectively involved responses—like evaluating scenes for scenicness—are of interest, because it is less structured, demanding, and intrusive than either the typical survey or the questionnaire format also used for that purpose (see Orne, 1962; Page, 1981). Amedeo's use of it specifically for eliciting perceptions of scenic value *differences* among the 56 scenes was straightforward. Each person in his sample, for example, was first asked to spread the available settings on a large table and encouraged to spend as much time as needed to view the photos and think about the available scenes before going on to the next step. Once that was accomplished, the individual was considered ready to sort the settings according to his or her perception of scenic differences among them.

Seven categories ("piles") were made available to participants as scenic-quality option positions for placement of the scenes during sorting. This number was a compromise between the belief that the use of too few categories might force subjects to overgeneralize about setting differences in scenic quality and too many might impose an unreasonable complexity to the sorting task. It should be kept in mind, however, that there are other issues as well about designing the structure of the sorting itself, which were not handled here in detail. These would include its relationship to such things as cognitive discrimination capabilities, the actual quantity characteristics of underlying metrics, and, of course, empirical versus assumed distributions of constructs. To some degree, they are clarified in discussions by McKeown and Thomas (1988) in particular and in nonmetric, multidimensional scaling in general.

15.3.2.1 Sorting Procedure

The sorting procedure adopted by Amedeo (1999) required all subjects to sort in the same manner. Previous research findings using these same photographs (Pitt & Zube, 1979; Zube et al., 1975) suggest that the average distribution derived from many sortings is likely to have a unimodal shape, with little evidence of skewing. Expectations under this likelihood are that most individuals would ordinarily perceive only a very few scenes to be exceptionally scenic or totally unscenic, but would judge somewhat greater quantities of scenes as highly scenic or highly unscenic and many as average on this quality. Each participant's sorting, then, would likely suggest a sequence of scenes consistent with some ordinal perspective of scenic quality. It may seem that the manifestation of ordinality in the responses is forced by the nature of the eliciting method itself. Though the nature of the quantity characteristics of anyone's aesthetic criterion for judging this quality certainly cannot be established conclusively, Amedeo (1999) was inclined to believe that the Q-sort procedure reinforces existing cognitive inclinations. When casually comparing places for their scenic differences, it was found that many subjects gave strong indications that they think in terms of "more than," "less than," and "the same as." Terms like "ugly" and "extremely beautiful" also were not uncommon. These are all indications that their aesthetic criterion (or rule) had at least ordinal characteristics.

The guidelines given to participants for sorting were as follows:

"Please sort the 56 photographs into seven piles according to the scenic quality of the landscapes in the photos. In pile number 1, place the three landscapes that you think have the highest scenic quality. In pile number 7, place the three landscapes that you think have the lowest scenic quality. From the remaining 50 landscapes place the seven with the highest scenic quality in pile number 2, and the seven with the lowest scenic quality in pile number 6. Note that you now have 36 landscapes remaining. From those, place the 11 with highest scenic quality in pile number 3 and the 11 with lowest scenic quality in pile number 5. Now place the remaining 14 landscapes in pile number 4.

"The number of photographs to be placed in each pile also appears on the pile identification cards on the table in front of you. You may rearrange the photographs until you are satisfied with their placement, but please make sure you place the specified number of photos in each pile."

(Note that the term "landscape" was used in these instructions for convenience.)

By working through those directions and, in the process, making personal choices as to which settings are more or less scenic than others, each participant in the sample gradually produced an arrangement of settings similar to that shown in Figure 15.1. These arrangements were of particular interest in Amedeo's (1999) research design because they could be compared with one another for their similarities and differences.

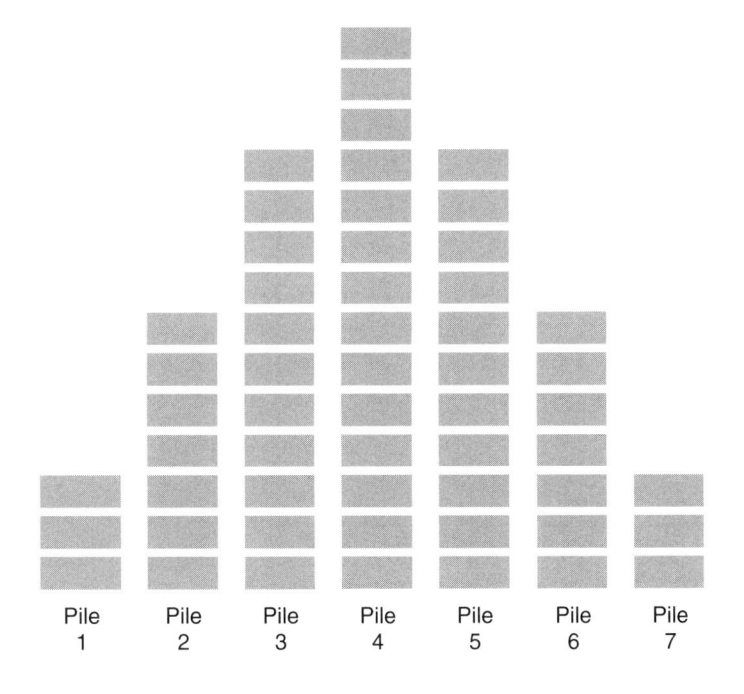

FIGURE 15.1. Completion of sorting process.

15.3.2.2 Arrangements of Settings

An arrangement is treated as the basic unit of information in Amedeo's (1999) investigation. It is an indicator that is specific to the individual producing it and reflects the way in which that individual perceives scenic quality differences among the collection of 56 scenes. Four hundred and seven people out of the sample's total (that is, 418) completed the sorting of these scenes; hence, that many arrangements were available for evaluation. If all participants perceived *scenic quality differences* among the scenes in exactly the same way, the end result would be 407 identical arrangements of scenes. If there were, instead, differences among the perceptions, they would correspond to differences among the arrangements of scenes.

In a given arrangement, the relative scenic value perceptually attributed by an individual to a specific setting is represented by the pile number the individual, in effect, assigned to the scene when following the sorting instructions. Amedeo shows how these numbers would be recorded for further evaluation in a matrix like the one graphically illustrated in Figure 15.2.

The dimensions of this matrix are suggestive of how this body of information was initially viewed by Amedeo (1999). It has 56 rows to reflect the total number of scenes that were sorted and 407 columns to mirror the number of sortings conducted by participants on those scenes. A row, then, in this array illustrates all the pile numbers assigned to that respective landscape by the individuals making up the sample to reflect their perceptions of its scenic quality, and a column displays a particular subject's scenic-quality arrangement of all landscapes in the study as a result of choices made while sorting them. Amedeo's first

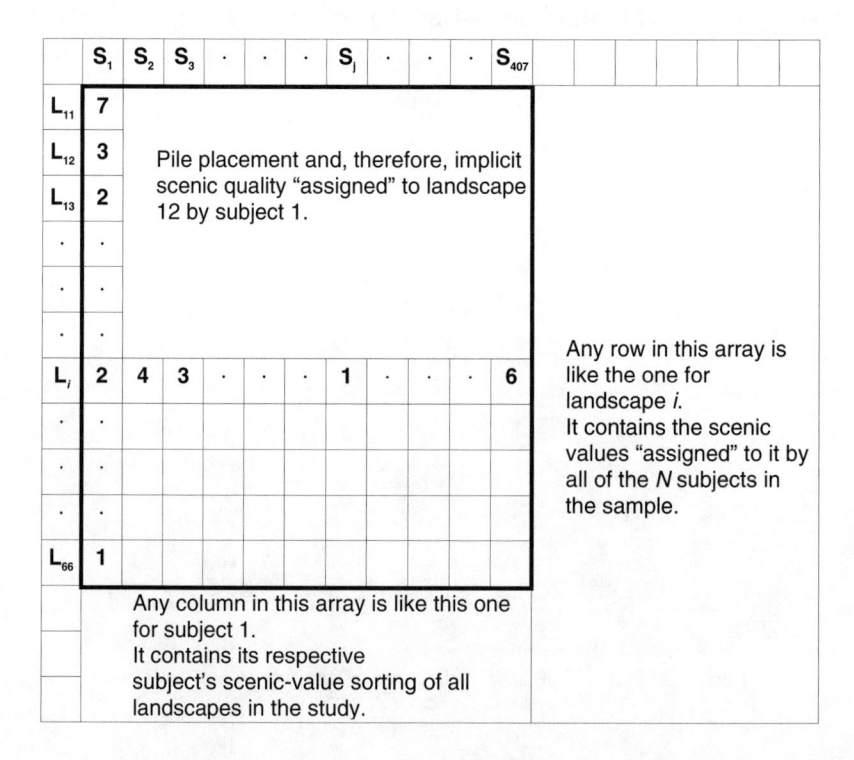

FIGURE 15.2. Subjects' arrangements of 56 landscapes according to perceived scenic quality differences. S, subject; L, landscape.

interest is how subject arrangements (or columns) compare with one another and the implications of such comparisons.

15.3.2.3 Comparing and Evaluating Arrangements

When examining this array visually, it appeared that both similarities and differences were present among the columns or arrangements in the matrix. It was also evident that "landscapes" in general were commonly assigned different scenic values by different participants. A casual inspection, of course, lacks details, so that Amedeo (1999) recommended correlations be computed between arrangements to check for the presence of similarities and differences among them. Although the property of quantity was represented as *ordinal* (seven pile positions) for the scale underlying the sorting task, the assumption employed in his study was that this property (if all possible instances of scenic quality could be observed and calibrated) can be measured by at least an interval metric. Given that assumption, a *parametric correlation procedure* was used. Searching for similarities and differences by correlating entire arrangements is more informative than a scene-by-scene comparison because the process of ordering many scenes is likely to be far more expressive of how "scenic" is generally perceived by an individual than the placement of a single setting.

When the sample size is as large as it was, far too many correlation coefficients resulted from computing one for every possible pair of scene arrangements to illustrate here. Instead, a graphic illustration like that in Figure 15.3 is provided for further discussion. From the *actual* correlations, however, it was evident that subsets were present in the sample which, for each, its individuals sorted the 56 scenes similarly. Indeed, there appeared to be multiple clustering among subjects in this matrix. This means that the sample of subjects, when examined with respect to resemblances in their arrangements of scenes, "divided" into

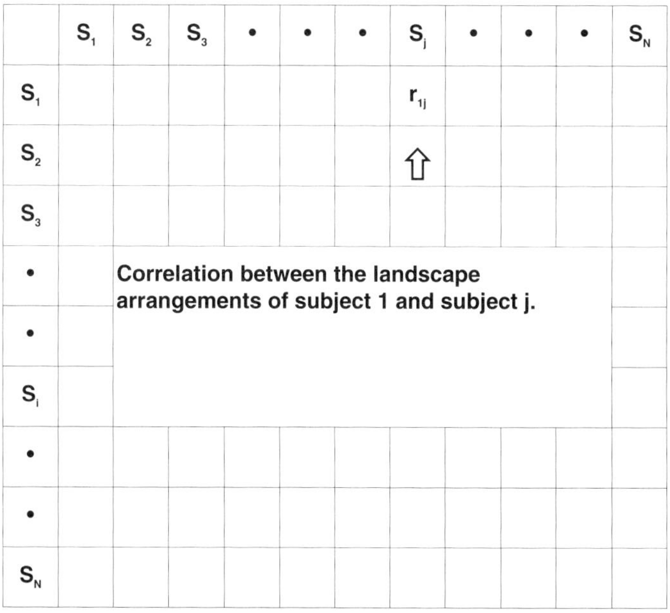

FIGURE 15.3. Nominal illustrations of correlations for all pairs of 407 landscape arrangements. r, correlation coefficient; S, subject.

groups, and that each group contained individuals who perceive similar differences in scenic quality among the 56 settings. Thus, the individuals in a particular group, if distinct from those in other groups, might be described as exhibiting a type of *perceptual commonality* among themselves, while multiple distinct groupings would suggest the presence of a variety of such commonalities.

The nature of the commonality found in Amedeo's (1999) investigation could have significant implications for ultimately deciding how scenic quality is perceived in a large sample. The immediate relevance is that it suggests the presence of common aspects among the perceptions of a group of individuals. It should be stressed, however, that what is common among individuals of one group found in a correlation matrix like that in Figure 15.3 need not be what is common among individuals of still another group in that array. To be more precise, reference should be made to a type of commonality. Although there may be a number of types of perceptual commonalities present among the 407 individuals in the sample—and that initially appeared to be suggested by the correlations—it is not possible to tell whether they are distinctive from one another by just visually examining them.

Procedures are available for describing these sources of common variance or commonalities inherent in large sets of complex information. Amedeo (1999), for example, employed an *Alpha Q*-mode form of *factor analysis* to extract out the commonalities already implied in the correlations computed between subject scene arrangements. Figure 15.4 illustrates a graphical rendering of this factoring. The Alpha Factor method was chosen because it uses a maximum likelihood procedure to estimate the factors (instead of least squares) and produces results that are proportionally consistent from one scale expression of the data to another, emphasizing the extraction of a maximum amount of common variance possible. The actual factor results were subjected to a varimax rotation before interpretations were

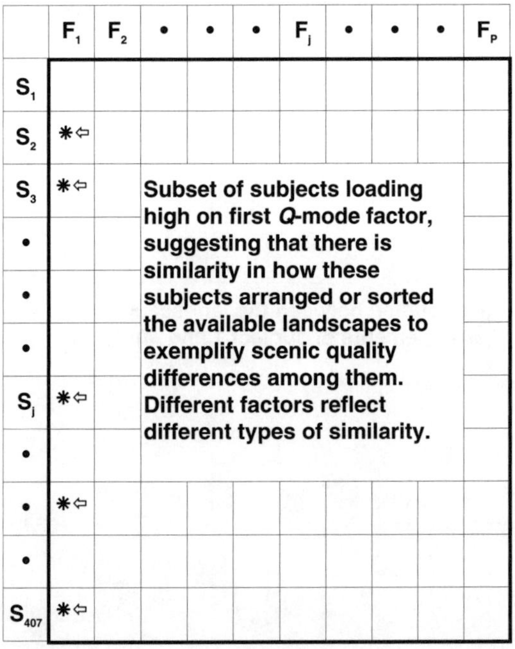

FIGURE 15.4. Nominal illustration of *Q*-mode factor matrix resulting from the alpha factor analysis procedure. S, subject; F, *Q*-mode factor.

made of the resulting loadings. The factor results produced twenty-five eigenvalues with values greater than 1. The actual "contribution" to accounting for common variance dropped off dramatically after consideration was given to the first four factors, which accounted for 68 percent of the total variance.

The choice of a Q-mode factor approach to assess the nature of similarities among subjects' perceptual arrangements of scenes greatly facilitates Amedeo's (1999) objective of attempting to integrate the empirical view of scenic quality with the perceptual conceptualization. The next step in the design exemplifies how he pursued that objective by interpreting the commonality uncovered by these q-factor indicators in terms of ways of perceiving *scenicness*.

15.4 Versions of Scenic Quality

The results Amedeo (1999) obtained from the Q-mode factoring reinforce what was already strongly suggested by the initial correlations computed between subject arrangements, namely that more than one perceptual type underlies the 407 assessments of scenes for their scenic value differences. And so it should, as the factoring adds no additional information to that which is already inherent in the correlation matrix. It only orders and clarifies it. Table 15.2, for example, illustrates the more pronounced instances of clustering of subject arrangements Amedeo (1999) found in the pattern of the actual factor analysis results. These strongly suggest that there are at least three versions of perception inherent in the collection of landscape scenic value assessments: one subscribed to by approximately 171 individuals, another by 73, and still a third by 62 individuals. Subjects were associated with the factor they loaded highest on. There were very few negative, high, or low loadings on the factors from the Q-mode analysis. (A fourth version had only 10 subjects subscribing to it and is not discussed here.)

A *version* should reflect what is perceptually common about a *group* of individual perceptions and, in that sense, should be thought of as functioning like a prototype or modal scenic value perception for that group as a whole. A significant question faced by Amedeo (1999) is whether each of the versions emerging out of the Q-mode factor analysis was distinctive enough to be considered different from the other perceptual types, or whether they are all nothing more than alternative replications of each other. If, for example, the latter were the case, this would suggest that individuals in the population perceive scenic quality in more or less the same way. Actually, that possibility seems somewhat implausible, given the factor pattern obtained in Table 15.2. Nevertheless, these three versions must be shown to be distinct from one another in order to make the claim that there exist at least three different ways of perceiving *scenicness* in this sample of 407 individuals. It is toward that task to which Amedeo (1999) next turned his attention, focusing on subjects' utilization of both empirical information from scenes themselves and on internal information in their perceptions of differences in *scenicness*.

Perceptual *versions* are different from an individual's perception. They exemplify a *type of perception* or, what is essentially equivalent, common aspects underlying the perceptions of a number of individuals. In that sense, based on such commonalities, they really suggest more prototypical renditions of scenic value perceptions. Thus, one way to assess these three apparent versions for their respective distinctiveness would be to express the modal arrangement of scenes each of them implies. For the sake of equivalency, that needs to be done in a structurally equivalent manner similar to that initially requested of individuals in the study when they sorted the scenes to reflect their perceptions of scenic differences among them.

TABLE 15.2. Subjects' Loading on Dimensions Extracted by *Q*-Mode Factor Analysis

Subject ID	Loading	Subject ID	Loading	Subject ID	Loading	Subject ID	Loading	Subject ID	Loading
Factor 1		**Factor 1**		**Factor 1**		**Factor 1**		**Factor 1**	
78	.906	297	.743	270	.686	116	.623	284	.564
388	.873	87	.739	262	.685	201	.620	355	.564
250	.862	21	.733	341	.682	112	.619	391	.563
99	.849	83	.732	343	.682	227	.617	320	.563
276	.843	57	.732	339	.680	249	.614	257	.561
14	.839	361	.730	398	.679	69	.614	291	.561
213	.836	289	.730	224	.674	280	.613	302	.560
93	.836	86	.728	215	.674	325	.612	23	.558
244	.817	314	.728	214	.673	55	.607	34	.556
210	.813	95	.728	221	.667	207	.604	359	.556
106	.811	336	.728	191	.665	290	.598	326	.556
395	.810	370	.727	264	.663	263	.596	253	.553
144	.800	287	.724	58	.660	198	.594	208	.545
334	.798	161	.723	354	.658	129	.593	16	.542
125	.797	170	.723	353	.657	72	.590	238	.541
235	.795	228	.722	261	.654	91	.589	51	.538
282	.795	131	.718	143	.652	10	.587	229	.538
260	.793	94	.716	254	.651	202	.585	313	.537
293	.792	371	.715	90	.651	312	.585	15	.537
311	.785	234	.714	348	.651	162	.584	322	.531
39	.784	82	.711	62	.649	79	.582	230	.528
Factor 2		**Factor 2**		**Factor 2**		**Factor 2**			
153	.857	37	.655	390	.598	8	.527		
266	.772	47	.653	27	.597	142	.524		
18	.771	392	.648	301	.584	400	.512		
308	.765	105	.648	327	.580	333	.502		
274	.745	328	.647	127	.574				
77	.741	80	.641	114	.569				
101	.739	141	.640	187	.568				
158	.733	49	.639	397	.567				
237	.721	36	.639	239	.561				
102	.719	278	.636	283	.558				
342	.717	223	.635	130	.554				
67	.713	117	.634	13	.553				
407	.700	33	.632	379	.553				
345	.696	199	.623	115	.549				
3	.695	303	.621	192	.549				
96	.692	338	.615	209	.547				
242	.688	405	.614	252	.544				
44	.686	40	.612	349	.543				
5	.681	258	.612	393	.542				
Factor 3		**Factor 3**		**Factor 3**		**Factor 3**		**Factor 3**	
154	.812	165	.696	182	.634	73	.567	41	.532
159	.809	135	.683	28	.624	128	.574	75	.531
318	.805	251	.679	70	.623	174	.573	32	.528
340	.791	155	.676	61	.623	332	.572	193	.522
178	.789	157	.676	167	.620	381	.570	337	.522
281	.756	175	.670	330	.619	134	.563	372	.519
52	.720	173	.665	133	.618	46	.563	48	.513
194	.718	103	.662	26	.603	389	.558	203	.513
53	.716	374	.659	89	.598	156	.556	179	.508
164	.704	383	.651	399	.591	64	.555	2	.503
181	.700	4	.641	185	.591	42	.545		
265	.699	149	.641	81	.584	111	.542		
50	.697	71	.638	279	.581	171	.536		

Note. Abridged from Amedeo (1999).

15.4.1 Arrangements of Scenes Implied by Versions of Scenic Value Perception

Versions of perception mirror common aspects of individual perceptions. In that sense, it is reasonable to expect that in practice each individual's perception is likely to contribute somewhat differently to the realization of a version. The pattern of loadings in Table 15.2 clearly illustrates this variable subscription to perceptual versions. For example, subject #78 roughly relates to (that is, technically loads on) the first factor by .906 while the next subject, #388, relates to it by .873, and so on. Amedeo (1999) points out that these variations in subject influences on the expression of a common perceptual consensus need to be considered when deriving scenic value estimates for the settings of a perceptual version. Such variations can be taken into consideration directly through the application of a factor-array procedure (see Block, 1961; MeKeown & Thomas, 1988).

To illustrate the method used to make a version explicit in terms of the common arrangement it exemplifies, Amedeo (1999) considered the group of individuals whose scene arrangements share the commonality implied by the first factor or indicator of version one in Table 15.2. To take this variable subscription into consideration, a factor-array procedure uses an expected-value approach to describe scenic quality values for the scenes underlying a perceptual version. That is to say, the procedure estimates the scenic quality value for any given setting in a perceptual version as a linear combination of weighted terms. Each term in this combination would be the product of an individual's degree of subscription to the perceptual consensus (that is, a subject's loading on the factor reflecting the version) and the individual's perception of scenic quality for the setting under consideration (that is, as indicated by the pile number the scene was assigned to in the sorting). Using this reasoning, values of scenic quality estimates for 56 scenes were calculated for each of the three perceptual versions. These scores for individuals in the sample are not reproduced here but can be obtained from Amedeo. Based on these factor-array estimates of their scenic quality value, the scenes were then Q-sorted (for example, just like individuals initially sorted their scenes) to exemplify differences among them. The resulting arrangements representing the perceptual renditions implied by each of the versions are illustrated in Figure 15.5.

These three versions, then, could be viewed as being suggestive of internal schemas influencing—to varying degrees—the sorting choices subjects in the respective groups made when arranging the scenes according to the way they perceived differences in their scenic quality. Acknowledging possibilities of sample, stimulus, and scale qualifiers surfacing later in further studies of this nature, they seem to imply, at the moment, (1) that internal information is playing a role in the perceiving of this aesthetic and (2) that the way that information is organized differs for different groups. Otherwise, the question arises, What explains the arrangements and their apparent differences shown in Figure 15.5? Amedeo (1999) points out that, given the aim of integrating the use of internal with external information in the assessment of scenic quality, it is necessary to also connect empirical circumstances (that is, selective external information) with these perceptual considerations to be able to say something relatively more explicit about the distinctiveness of the versions. He next addressed that task.

15.4.2 Information Influences in Versions of Scenic Quality Perception

The three perceptual versions depicted in Figure 15.5 certainly appear to be different, at least from visual inspection. Restating the estimations of scenic quality scores as deviations from their mean divided by their standard deviation (that is, as Z scores) and then compar-

				12			
				37			
				44			
			21	45	16		
			19	48	23		
			49	38	60		
			56	55	28		
		51	57	39	25	66	
		59	15	29	18	47	
		24	34	30	20	65	
		42	33	40	61	26	
31	46	17	43	11	64	62	
35	32	50	41	54	14	63	
52	36	27	13	58	22	53	
P_1 Most scenic	P_2	P_3	P_4	P_5	P_6	P_7 Least scenic	

Perceptual Version 1

				28			
				41			
			56	49	38		
			43	59	48		
			30	57	40		
			46	45	14		
		37	17	34	25	63	
		20	50	16	47	53	
		13	19	22	11	61	
		42	32	29	18	55	
51	33	36	27	12	58	62	
35	24	60	23	64	39	66	
52	44	31	26	15	65	54	
P_1 Most scenic	P_2	P_3	P_4	P_5	P_6	P_7 Least scenic	

Perceptual Version 2

				28			
				64			
				18			
			25	21	48		
			43	22	30		
			19	26	54		
			17	45	61		
		59	34	39	65	37	
		60	15	41	55	66	
		57	32	11	24	56	
		31	23	50	13	58	
27	33	46	29	12	14	53	
51	35	16	40	42	47	62	
52	44	36	49	38	20	63	
P_1 Most scenic	P_2	P_3	P_4	P_5	P_6	P_7 Least scenic	

Perceptual Version 3

FIGURE 15.5. Arrangements of 56 scenes according to their differences in scenicness for each of the three versions.

ing the resulting values across all three versions reinforced the appearance that there are differences among them. But are such comparisons convincing enough to conclude that the three perceptual types differ? This is an important question because if the types or versions are shown to be distinct from one another, that would strongly imply that there are, among people, notably different ways of construing scenic quality for the same surroundings. In turn, that would certainly suggest that information utilized for construing this *scenic quality perception* is processed differently by different individuals when they perceive it. And perhaps these combined points might further encourage the thought that the potential for the presence of *different cognitive aesthetic scenarios* operating in the *assessment of scenic value* is greater in societies where the possibility for multiple environmental experiential histories is greater (for example, in nontraditionally oriented social systems).

Amedeo (1999) suggests that a more effective way to evaluate the distinctiveness of the three perceptual versions may be to compare how fundamental external and internal sources of information enter into the perceiving process underlying each. That is obviously difficult to accomplish directly, especially since perceptual versions or types are reflections of what is fundamentally common about a number of perceptions, not individual perceptions themselves. Nevertheless, Amedeo points out, certain physical features of the scenes can be examined to see how they covary with the estimated scenic quality values of the settings in each of the three versions of scenic quality perceptions (see Patsfall, Feimer, Buhyoff, & Wellman, 1984). This kind of an assessment could suggest the more prominent aspects of external information use by individuals in their perceiving of this quality.

On the other hand, to obtain hints about differences in internal information use, the initial q-sortings of the individuals "subscribing" to these perceptual versions can be examined for indications of how the settings were viewed vis-à-vis one another when they were evaluated for differences in scenic quality (see, for example, Amedeo et al., 1989). If influences of both external and internal information use clearly differ for the three versions of scenic quality perception, then there can be fairly compelling grounds to begin arguing that the versions are distinctive among themselves.

Consider first Amedeo's (1999) search for possible external information use differences among the three scenic quality versions. Table 15.3 lists the kind of external information available for this purpose because it was measurable across all of the 56 scenes used in the study. With that information and the use of a stepwise regression procedure, Amedeo was able to devise, for each of the three versions of perception, two indicators of external information use: (1) the covariance of physical features with the estimated scenic values of scenes and (2) the relative importance of features in each of the versions.

Table 15.4 summarizes the results obtained from employing a *stepwise regression* procedure. Of the 28 physical features available for consideration, six were related to the scenic quality values of the first two perceptual versions, and five were associated with the values of the third perceptual type. Physical features like mean slope distribution, land use compatibility, and height contrast (that is, X_2, X_{12}, and X_{15}) seem to have had common importance as external information to many individuals, for they relate well to the estimated scenic-quality values of all three perceptual versions.

However, some physical features appear to have external information importance to only particular perceptual versions. Consider the 171 subjects subscribing to the first version. In addition to these three features just mentioned, grain contrast, absolute relative relief, and view index (that is, X_{16}, X_{20}, and X_{25}) seemed to be particularly important in the way they commonly perceived scenic quality differences among the 56 scenes (see R and R^2 in the termination step of the stepwise regression in Table 15.4). Yet, as the results in Table 15.4 show, these same external features have little significance in the other two perceptual

TABLE 15.3. Physical Features from 56 Scenes

Variable	Physical feature
X_{01}	Relative relief ratio
X_{02}	Mean slope distribution
X_{03}	Topographic texture
X_{04}	Land-use diversity
X_{05}	Naturalism index
X_{06}	Water edge density
X_{07}	Percent water area
X_{08}	Area of view
X_{09}	Land-use edge density
X_{10}	Land-use edge variety
X_{11}	Percent tree cover
X_{12}	Land-use compatibility
X_{13}	Length of view
X_{14}	Spatial definition index
X_{15}	Height contrast
X_{16}	Grain contrast
X_{17}	Spacing contrast
X_{18}	Evenness contrast
X_{19}	Naturalism contrast
X_{20}	Absolute relative relief
X_{21}	Viewer position
X_{22}	Old mean elevation
X_{23}	Ruggedness number
X_{24}	Water index multiplied
X_{25}	View index multiplied
X_{26}	Land-use edge index multiplied
X_{27}	Sky area
X_{28}	Sky perimeter

Note. From Amedeo (1999).

versions. Instead, for the 72 subjects subscribing to the second version, water edge density, spatial definition index, sky perimeter, and relative relief ratio (that is, X_6, X_{14}, X_{28}, and X_{01}) apparently are more important features in the way they conceptualize scenic value. But neither those subscribing to the first perceptual version, nor to the second, "look" at scenic quality in the way that those subjects subscribing to the third version commonly do. The external features playing a noticeable role for the latter group in their recognition and assessment of scenic quality include ruggedness number, percent water area, and naturalism index (that is, X_{23}, X_{07}, and X_{05}).

The more general indices associated with the stepwise regression analyses—particularly R and R^2—indicate that different combinations of physical features account for substantial parts of the variation in estimated scenic-quality values for each of the perceptual versions. This indicates that external information, like various physical features, must have been used differently by individuals in their assessment of scenic-quality differences among scenes. What this strongly suggests, then, is that the three perceptual types reflect distinct ways of perceiving scenic quality.

However, as Amedeo (1999) points out, distinctiveness of the perceptual versions should also be assessed from the perspective of internal information use, as both external and internal information enter into the process of perceiving scenic quality. For example, to assess *scenic-value differences* among settings, individuals must have had the preliminary capability of mentally construing a *scenic space* (so to speak) within which they could momentarily

TABLE 15.4. Relationships between Physical Features and Perceptual Versions of Scenic Quality

Regression of physical features against factor estimates of scenic-values for perception type (Version) 1

$R = .80$, $R^2 = .643$, $F = 14.13$, $p \geq .0001$

		R^2		Features specific to Type 1
X_{12}	.3956	34.04	.0001	
$X_{12} X_2$	.4822	8.52	.0052	
$X_{12} X_2 X_{16}$	.5684	9.99	.0027	Grain contrast
$X_{12} X_2 X_{16} X_{20}$	.6025	4.19	.0460	Absolute relative relief
$X_{12} X_2 X_{16} X_{20} X_{25}$	.6221	2.49	.1210	View index
$X_{12} X_2 X_{16} X_{20} X_{25} X_{15}$	.6434	2.81	.1006	

Regression of physical features against factor estimates of scenic-values for perception type (Version) 2

$R = .68$, $R^2 = .47$, $F = 6.91$, $p \geq .0001$

		R^2		Features specific to Type 2
X_2	.1721	10.81	.0018	
$X_2 X_6$	.2753	7.26	.0095	Water-edge density
$X_2 X_6 X_{14}$	.3341	4.42	.0406	Spatial definition index
$X_2 X_6 X_{14} X_{28}$	.3880	4.31	.0432	Sky perimeter
$X_2 X_6 X_{14} X_{28} X_1$	.4408	4.54	.0383	Relative relief ratio
$X_2 X_6 X_{14} X_{28} X_1 X_{15}$	.4687	2.46	.1233	

Regression of physical features against factor estimates of scenic-values for perception type (Version) 3

$R = .61$, $R^2 = .37$, $F = 5.67$, $p \geq .0003$

		R^2		Features specific to Type 3
X_{12}	.1568	9.67	.0030	
$X_{12} X_{23}$	.2275	4.67	.0354	Ruggedness number
$X_{12} X_{23} X_7$	.2980	5.02	.0295	Percent water area
$X_{12} X_{23} X_7 X_5$	.3369	2.88	.0963	Naturalism index
$X_{12} X_{23} X_7 X_5 X_2$	.3711	2.61	.1127	

Note. From Amedeo (1999).

"contemplate" any setting's scenic quality relative to any other setting's quality. A processing capability somewhat like this seems essential if a person is to fulfill a request to sort or differentiate among a collection of settings according to their scenic differences.

A potential reflector of the common traits of such construed *scenic spaces* can be obtained by factor-analyzing—via an R-mode perspective—the sorting(s) of scenes that the participants produced when they *originally* responded to the sorting guideline request described earlier. (Note that this analysis can be readily accomplished if the original response data as graphically shown in Figure 15.2 was first transposed so that rows become columns and columns become rows.) Tables 15.5a, b, and c illustrate, for each of the perceptual versions, indications of such "scenic spaces" obtained from factoring.

A visual inspection of these three tables reveals that the patterns of the scenes contributing to the description of the *factor dimensions* encompassing the *scenic spaces* are different (compare scenes and their loadings). This suggests that "scenic spaces" for the three versions differ from one another. But once again, visual comparisons frequently fail to fully detect distinctions. Factor patterns of scenes for two different spaces, for example, may appear to be different only because of the different perspective from which they were viewed. Hence,

272　EXPERIENCES AND ENVIRONMENTS

TABLE 15.5a. Rotated Factor Pattern: *R*-Mode Factor Analysis of Scene Sortings Produced by Individuals Subscribing to Perceptual Version 1

Scene ID	Factor no. 1	2	3	4	5	6	7	8	9	10
15	.73									
17	.67									
40	.49									
49	.31									
12	−.42									
38		.72								
34		.49								
54		.37								
44		−.47								
43			.78							
19			.52							
41			.39							
30			−.42							
56				.75						
24				.56						
37				.46						
58				.31						
22				−.44						
50					.73					
31					.70					
51					.34					
21						.68				
48						.66				
32						.31				
33						−.40				
26							.70			
23							−.46			
60							−.40			
57								.82		
27								.49		
62									.66	
11									.59	
39									.52	
45										.80
29										.64

Note. From Amedeo (1999).

TABLE 15.5b. Rotated Factor Pattern: *R*-Mode Factor Analysis of Scene Sortings Produced by Individuals Subscribing to Perceptual Version 2

Scene ID	Factor no. 1	2	3	4	5	6	7	8	9	10
62	.86									
66	.62									
65	.41									
63	.35									
40		.90								
15		.80								
12		−.48								
16			.84							
60			.31							
30			−.39							
42			−.66							
58				.71						
37				.63						
44				−.66						
26					.82					
25					.70					
32						.83				
50						.54				
17						.38				
19						−.37				
28							.82			
57							.52			
35								.72		
20								.56		
13								.51		
54									.90	
55									.49	
61									.39	
11										.80
41										.53
64										−.63

Note. From Amedeo (1999).

TABLE 15.5c. Rotated Factor Pattern: *R*-Mode Factor Analysis of Scene Sortings Produced by Individuals Subscribing to Perceptual Version 3

Scene ID	Factor no. 1	2	3	4	5	6	7	8	9	10
12	.87									
61	.67									
39	.48									
26	−.66									
62		.80								
63		.67								
47		.53								
56		−.52								
38			.66							
55			.52							
54			.52							
58			.42							
13			−.86							
11				.86						
27				.73						
49				.39						
33					.81					
44					.76					
25					−.43					
34						.81				
53						−.30				
30						−.34				
65						−.35				
29							.77			
31							.49			
17							.43			
19								.95		
18								.49		
40								.50		
24									.82	
32									.32	
51									-.67	
15										.89
36										.46

Note. From Amedeo (1999).

to more effectively ascertain whether the *scenic spaces* are *distinct*, Amedeo (1999) recommends that all three spaces should be inventoried to see which dimensions appear in each.

The information in Table 15.6 illustrates how that inventorying (see bottom of Table 15.6) was accomplished. If the three "scenic spaces" were similar, then a particular scene-type dimension emerging from the factor analyses should appear somewhere in all three. For example, the dimension of ECRW, a scene-type dimension whose prominent feature is rough water, has some representation as factor 1 in the scenic space associated with perceptual Version 1 and as factor 2 in the space associated with perceptual Version 2. However, it is apparently not a part of the scenic space underlying perceptual Version 3. The dimension RPBT, a scene category of rough prairie, is represented as factor 1 in the scenic space associated with Perceptual Version 3, but it is not found as a type in the scenic spaces associated with Perceptual Versions 1 and 2.

Amedeo (1999) indicates that the general point that can be made here is this: *If the three perceptual versions had the same dimensions reflecting common aspects of their subjects thinking about scenes and differences in scenic quality, they would have similar "scenic spaces."* It is clear from Table 15.6, on this point alone, that the scenic spaces for the versions are dissimilar. If the differential weights of the factors were in fact also taken into consideration, this point is further reinforced. Thus, taking into account internal information use in perceiving scenic quality differences provides yet another indication that the three perceptual versions of scenic quality uncovered from the actual perceptions of subjects are different from one another. Differences in these scenic spaces, and the differential physical features' influence in the perceptual types, make it reasonable to conclude that each of these perceptual versions reflects a distinct way of perceiving scenic quality differences among the set of 56 scenes. Among the people making up this sample of 407 individuals, then, there are at least three distinct ways of perceiving scenicness.

15.5 Discussion

To reiterate what was said earlier, Fenton and Reser (1988) put out a call for more research efforts devoted to integrating the "objective" view with the "perceptual" perspective. Porteous (1996) reinforced their call in his comprehensive work on environmental aesthetics and indicated that "a major body of substantive work in this 'interactive' or 'integrative' mode has yet to appear" (p. 143).

The purpose of Amedeo's (1999) research was to conceptually connect major facets of these two conceptual perspectives, and to do that with the aid of actual perceptual responses to scenes and by reference to indicators of both external and internal information use by individuals in the scenic attribution process.

In the process of exploring such connections, issues have surfaced that, for some, may present challenges to long-held views on such things as the recognition of landscapes, the empirical basis of *scenicness*, scenic-quality distinctiveness from other aesthetic issues, and independence of perceptual experience from external conditions. Along the way, Amedeo's (1999) work has offered some expectations about all of these issues and, given an assessment of a large number of people's evaluations of 56 scenes, has searched for indications that would, for the moment, support them. What his investigation does demonstrate is that among these 407 subjects there are at least three versions of scenic value perception for these scenes. When indications of both external and internal information use are assessed, these versions are shown to be distinctive.

276 EXPERIENCES AND ENVIRONMENTS

TABLE 15.6. Comparison of Scenic Spaces Associated with Three Versions (V_i) of Scenic Quality

Scene type	Factor no.									
	1	2	3	4	5	6	7	8	9	10
ECRW	V_1	V_2								
HEST	V_2	V_3								
RPBT	V_3									
BHWP		V_1								
FECT			V_1							
OSHP			V_2							
DHFL			V_3						V_2	
SWWW				V_1, V_2						
FSTB				V_3						
RHFL					V_3					
CWHH					V_1					
LCWI					V_2		V_1			
FHTS						V_2	V_3			
WEFS							V_2	V_3		
HPCV						V_3				
RSOS								V_2		
FPCT										V_2
HVRH										V_1
RRUL										V_3
FLBV								V_1		
VBBS									V_3	
RBCT						V_1				

Note. Scene types are as follows:

ECRW =	extensively covered by rough water		CWHH =	clam waterways in complex high hills
HEST =	highway vistas of small towns		LCWI =	large controlled waterways with industrial buildings
RPBT =	rough prairie surrounded by brush and trees		FHTS =	forested hilly terrain with streams
BHWP =	heavily brushlike, hilly, with some plains		WEFS =	wide expansive flat acenes
FECT =	flat expanses of plains with clumps of trees		HPCV =	hill with prairie covered with vegetation
			RSOS =	road or stream open to wider setting
OSHP =	ordered scene with human presence		FPCT =	flat prairies with clumps of mature trees
DHFL =	dense hills with forest land		HVRH =	high density of vegetation with rolling hills
SWWW =	scrubland with or without water		RRUL =	remote rolling upland with lakes
FSTB =	flatplains containing large streams with tree borders		FLBV =	flat lake areas bordered by vegetation
			VBBS =	dense vegetation with brush and bush and small streams
RHFL =	rolling hill farm land		RBCT =	gently rolling brushland with clumps of trees

Note. From Amedeo (1999).

But are such findings expected in a general sense, even if the issue is *scenicness*? Nisbett and Ross (1980) have this to say about that issue:

> Few, if any, stimuli are approached for the first time by the adult. Instead, they are processed through preexisting systems of schematized and abstracted knowledge—beliefs, theories, propositions, and schemata. These knowledge structures label and categorize objects and events quickly and, for the most part, accurately. They also define a set of expectations about objects and events and suggest appropriate responses to them. (p. 7)

That comment outlines the typical involvement of internal with external information in the process of how things become recognized and known or, more commonly, how they are perceived (see also Blumenthal, 1977). What they describe for the general case is certainly applicable to the perception of scenic quality in surroundings. The 407 individual discriminations among the scenes (that is, Q-sort arrangements) support beliefs expressed by others cited earlier that a scenic quality assessment of surroundings is essentially an individual construal about the visual "pleasantness" of surroundings. An individual's appraising of scenes for scenic quality differences is likely to entail a patterning of selected environmental attributes to fashion an ad-hoc visual quality theme. The theme serves as a momentary "rule of thumb" for appraising and comparing surroundings for scenic quality and its differences. The formulation of the theme itself may be colored by affective aesthetic considerations and is certainly influenced by previous environmental experiences. Hence, individuals having similar environmental experiences probably will appraise surroundings similarly for scenic quality. In societies in which a variety of environmental experience backgrounds are possible, different and distinct ways to evaluate environments for scenic quality may prevail.

It is evident from the examination of the 407 discriminations among scenes that external features of surroundings are significantly involved in the assessment of scenic quality. By their presence, external features create cuing effects, and obviously they make available content for interpretation and appraisal. Yet in an assessment process, their effects are qualified by the ways internal information interfaces with them. Attention to "scenic quality" in any given instance, for example, appears to be due jointly to both an individual's inclination at any moment to focus on construing the environment in just that way and to external stimuli in the surroundings provoking and/or activating the individual to do so. Of course, those having different environmental histories from others are likely to perceive and treat external content somewhat differently, so that distinct versions of scenic quality among individuals may result.

As to the *research design employed* in Amedeo's (1999) research, a number of interrelated steps have been taken in an attempt to demonstrate how external and internal information are "brought" together by an individual in the process of perceiving scenic quality differences among many scenes.

1. At first, a Q-sorting procedure was used to get 407 individuals to relate their perceptions of scenic quality differences among 56 scenes. For each individual, this produced an arrangement of scenes, running from most scenic to least scenic, that was expressive of perceived scenic differences among the 56 scenes. Some of these arrangements appeared similar, so that correlations were run between pairs of them all.
2. Those correlations in turn were then factor-analyzed to see if subject arrangements grouped into clusters of arrangement similarities. Four groups of subject scenic-arrangements emerged from that factor analysis, suggesting the presence of four perceptual versions of *scenicness* among the scenes.

3. A factor array procedure was then utilized to unearth the arrangements of scenes exemplifying the perceptual commonalities underlying each of the three groups (a fourth group had only 10 subscribers; hence, it was too small to include in this analysis).
4. Utilizing indicators of physical features of the 56 scenes, it was then shown by stepwise regression procedures that the different group arrangements were based on distinctive combinations of feature use. This demonstrated that the groups were distinct.
5. At that point, it was further shown through the use of an R-mode factor analysis of the initial subject Q-sorts of scenes that it was highly likely that subjects in each of the three groups possessed different scenic conceptual spaces when differentiating between scenes for assessing *scenicness*.

All of these results combined were compelling enough to label the three groups of arrangements distinctive perceptual versions of *scenicness*.

Since the observations made in the Amedeo (1999) study rely, to a considerable extent, on the information produced by 407 individuals sorting a collection of 56 scenes according to their perceptions of scenic differences among them, it is worth being a bit more critical about the procedure used here to gather such information. The use of Q-sorting for eliciting information about perceptions has some attractive features, especially for the interests of the Amedeo study. The main one is that, when compared with other methods for eliciting personal responses to complex stimuli, it imposes relatively few unrelated, peripheral demands on responders, either physically or cognitively. This is an important characteristic, as such demands can produce sources of variance that confound that which is being investigated (see demand characteristics in Orne, 1962).

In Q-sorting, individuals are given the opportunity to represent their perceptions about scenic quality differences among scenes by evaluating and ordering a relatively large variety of settings. In effect, the method provides a working definition of an individual's perception via the end product of the sorting. It should be noted that, with this procedure, a given sorting depicts the subject's evaluation of an entire set of scenes, relative to one another, not just an absolute assessment of a single one. Since it allows subjects to compare landscapes and to alter their sorting, the procedure accommodates the fluidity and contextual aspects that may be associated with the individual's moment-to-moment development of the scenic quality notion for a given set of scenes.

However, despite such advantages, as with other methods of eliciting responses from subjects, the use of sorting procedures like this one inevitably generates important research design issues as well (for example, see Block, 1961; Edwards, 1955; Frank, 1956; McKeown & Thomas, 1988; Mower, 1953). In this study questions surfaced about the number and types of settings needed for eliciting usable information on perceived landscape scenic quality differences, the number of scenic quality categories required to meet the needs of most subjects engaged in discriminating among the scenes on this dimension, and whether in general to adopt "spontaneous" sorting procedures.

15.6 Conclusion

Indications of at least three distinct perceptual versions of scenic quality in the collection of individual perceptions strongly suggest that individuals may use information differently in perceiving a scenic quality in surroundings. If that is the case, then neither the empirical nor the perceptual view can stand alone when trying to explain how scenic quality in surroundings is recognized and/or known. It also is difficult to argue for treating the environmental notion "scenic" differently than P-E-B relations in general.

When viewed from this book's purpose of enhancing the understanding of research involved with person–environment–behavior relationships as a whole, the key is the *research strategy* that was adopted by Amedeo (1999) to investigate perceptual aspects of this rather opaque aesthetic experience. The logic is found in its main features. For example:

- The study design takes advantage of opportunities to access reflectors of covariance at different levels of his analysis.
- It examines the central pattern of subject responses to the elicitation of perceived differences among the available scenes.
- It identifies the prominent features of that pattern in the form of sources of commonalities.
- It attempts to define those sources from what is generally understood in the research literature.

In other words, the design used by Amedeo (1999) accepts what circumstances are available. It is not by any means his preferred approach, as in his desire to test comprehensive hypotheses for their significance; such an approach is far from possible for investigating such experiences in everyday environments. What Amedeo emphasizes in the strategy devised for the research discussed in this chapter—and also in Chapter 14—is the constant striving to relate structural aspects of his domain (that is, arrangements) with their conceptual implications. While his research results are preliminary and suggestive, nonetheless they are useful for further investigations.

Acknowledgment

Amedeo recruited only a small part of the data analyses in this chapter. Most of the remaining information was collected by E. H. Zube and D. G. Pitt and used in much of their work on landscapes (see references to Zube's works). Amedeo is grateful for the use of their information.

PART VI
Experiences and Spaces

Part VI gives further consideration to how research investigating P-E-B relations might focus on the experiences people have of environmental settings, but the orientation of the three chapters presented is more on conducting research in large-scale operational spaces such as a city. The three chapters provide examples of a range of research designs that may be used to investigate latent constructs that relate to people's "experience of," "learning of," and/or "assessment and evaluation of" those specific spatial settings.

The three chapters use a variety of approaches, some of which are exploratory, while others seek to test explicit theories or hypotheses. The research studies discussed use a mix of secondary data analysis and the collection of primary data through surveys and experiments. A number of quantitative analytical and modeling tools are used, including factor-analytic designs and multidimensional scaling. In one instance the use of aggregation techniques to transform unit record survey–based data into aggregated spatial measures for a specific construct is demonstrated, while in another instance the focus is on testing for group differences and similarities in perceptual constructs.

Chapter 16 provides an example of the use of secondary data analysis of a social survey dataset to investigate domains of subjective quality of life (QOL) in a large-scale urban setting. In the research conducted by author Stimson and his collaborators, it is argued that the scored subjective assessments derived from the survey data, when aggregated, can be treated as indicative of the collective well-being of people living in a large-scale metropolitan region. It shows how disaggregated unit record data collected through surveys can be aggregated to measure specific aspects of QOL for particular groups in the Brisbane–South East Queensland metropolitan region in Australia. It is suggested that the characteristics of geographic space may play a significant role in creating regional variation in people's perceived QOL. Because differences are embedded in geographic spaces in terms of their environmental, economic, and social characteristics, variations in QOL might be expected as a characteristic of living in a large-scale urban area.

The approach taken in the research discussed in Chapter 16 is to analyze individual ratings of QOL domains represented by variables that were collected in a large spatially stratified probability sample survey to aggregate those ratings, and then to derive average or collective scores for subregions within a large metropolitan region to represent spatial variations in levels of well-being. With subregions as the criterion for spatial aggregation, the research experiments with the use of the ordered weighted average operator technique to measure and map aggregated subjective assessments of QOL across various life satisfaction domains. The approach to mapping of aggregated estimates of patterns of spatial variability in subjective QOL derived in this way from secondary analysis of primary survey data might have useful applications in urban and regional planning.

Chapter 17 discusses research conducted by author Golledge and his colleagues to investigate the development of the cognitive structure of a typical middle-sized city in the United States. It has long been argued that the spatial form of the city may facilitate or inhibit the development of a person's cognitive representation of that city. Four decades of research effort have been devoted to examining people's images of environments as ways to help understand human behaviors and decision making. Experimental designs and analytical methods have been developed and applied to investigate the nature of these images and how they are used, but there is still no consensus as to how cities are learned, or of what is the most probable learning format for that learning. Suggestions have included anchor point theory and hierarchical theories, and much research has been focused on the environmental learning process itself rather than on investigating the way the environment itself lends itself to or inhibits the learning process. The chapter focuses on how coherent cognitive structures emerge over time as this information about an environment develops. Experimental designs are used to investigate how cognitive configurations are obtained from relative newcomers to a city and from longer term residents to show how such configurations emerge over time and eventually stabilize. The latent spatial structures of individuals are discovered using a variety of both qualitative and quantitative methods, including multidimensional scaling.

Chapter 18 outlines the reasoning accompanying the development of a construct by describing a study in the area of environment relations for which an indicator of group conservation perspectives is sought. In the development of the social and behavioral sciences it is common to combine individual components assumed to be interrelated into single referents or indicators to build constructs (such as "self-esteem," "cognitive map," "place attachment," "personality trait," "social distance," "environmental schemas," and the like). Being integrated structures of components built to represent or reflect complex circumstances, constructs are not usually apparent or apprehended from an empirical or physical counterpart, but rather are integrations in social and behavioral context. From one perspective, these are qualities that inevitably result from their origins, but from another perspective, they are also features that facilitate larger conceptualization strategies like theorizing. When constructs are conceptually robust, general in nature, and plausible, and when they span large homogeneous domains of interest, they are often useful for theorizing about events and relationships in those realms. The chapter provides a discussion of latent constructs in a regional context to investigate a specific construct—"group conservation perspectives"—and evaluate its usefulness. It assumes that as a result of experiencing and transacting with environments repeatedly over time, people tend to develop relatively firm positions and/or views regarding the situations and relationships they repeatedly confront and respond to in their everyday existence in those surroundings, especially if they are thought to relate to their vested interests. This is not to suggest that there will be as many positions or views as there are individuals, but rather to point to the strong likelihood of multiple positions evolving in a specific region and/or environmental context.

The broader objective of the study discussed in Chapter 18 is to demonstrate why human-oriented information, when combined with the requisite physical knowledge, is an essential and necessary ingredient for shaping effective long-term environmental policy, particularly for environments in this region. In this sense, it is useful that information regarding such issues be given attention. The focus is on identifying similarities and differences in ways the various principal users of that environment think about and construe their many surroundings.

The research discussed in Chapter 18 is an example of a case format study, using a nonprobability sample of respondents selected to represent various user groups in the study region. The design of the research involves the use of a multiphased series of tasks to elicit information about views on environmental conservation issues, with respondents asked to sort a set of conservation statements in a structured survey. A series of analytic procedures are employed to extract differences and similarities among the sorting arrangements produced. The design makes use of weighting procedures to derive group conservation scores and regression procedures to see whether environmental perspectives can be used to estimate other environmental responses. The modeling conducted illustrates the reasoning used to develop a pragmatic construct for direct use in a case study regional context, and it demonstrates how this type of research design might feed into public policy.

CHAPTER 16

Deriving Metropolitanwide Spatial Patterns of Perceived Quality-of-Life Dimensions

16.1 Introduction

The characteristics of geographic space may play a significant role in creating regional variation in people's perceived *quality of life* (QOL). Because differences are embedded in geographic spaces in terms of their environmental, economic, and social characteristics, variations in QOL might be expected as a characteristic of living in a large-scale urban area. This chapter reports on a study conducted by author Stimson and his colleagues in the University of Queensland Social Research Center (Stimson, Chhetri, Akbar, & Western, 2006) in which data collected in a QOL survey in the Brisbane–South East Queensland (SEQ) region of Australia is used and subjected to secondary data analysis of individual unit record data collected in a *large-scale probability sample* to derive a *generalized spatial representation* of *domains of subjective QOL*.

In that research it is argued that the scored subjective assessments derived from survey data, when aggregated, can be treated as indicative of the collective well-being of people living in a large-scale metropolitan region. For example, disaggregated data collected through surveys can be aggregated to measure specific QOL for particular groups such as women, minorities, older people, and so on. In a similar way, aggregation can also be undertaken on a spatial basis for areas or regions. Mercer (1994) has measured QOL on

> a range of factors that make us feel good about being and staying—in a place. In other words, QOL assessments, when aggregated for areas, can indirectly reflect the spatial variation in perceived QOL. (p. 5)

However, Marans (2003) suggests that QOL in a place or a specific geographic setting is a *subjective phenomenon*, and therefore may vary according to an individual's gender, perception, cultural and ethnic background, socioeconomic status, educational level, family situation, health, disability, age, and past experiences.

The approach adopted by Stimson, Chhetri, Akbar, and Western (2006) is to analyze individual ratings of QOL items collected in a large-scale *spatially stratified probability sample survey* to aggregate those *ratings of QOL domains*, and then to derive average or collective scores for subregions within a large metropolitan region to represent spatial variations in levels of well-being. With subregions as the criterion for spatial aggregation, the research experiments with the use of a number of alternative indices that are derived using the *ordered weighted average (OWA) operator* technique to develop aggregated subregional measures of subjective QOL and to map the patterns of spatial variation in those aggregate measures of subjective QOL across the subregions of the Brisbane–SEQ metropolitan region. The mapping of such patterns of spatial variability in subjective QOL might have useful applications in urban and regional planning.

16.2 QOL: An Overview

The copious literature on QOL includes a variety of approaches, but most studies of QOL generally have focused on two levels of analysis:

- An *individual* or *micro*level, where satisfaction with life is subjectively assessed by individuals
- An *aggregated* or *macro*level, where objective indicators (such as crime rates, poverty, health, accessibility, and pollution) are used to develop a composite ranking indicating regional variations in the QOL.

There have been attempts to integrate data obtained at these two levels (Cutter, 1985; Rogerson, Findlay, & Morris, 1989), but the aggregation of individual-level QOL data collected through surveys into subregions of a city to identify spatial variability in QOL domains has not been given much attention, despite the availability of aggregation techniques to do so.

16.2.1 Defining QOL

There is, however, no standard definition of QOL. It has been said that QOL relates to the total well-being of people, including physical, mental, social, and spiritual components (Eckersley, 1998). The object of evaluation in QOL is the "life" (Veenhoven, 2000), where the focus is on assessing the life of an individual. "Well-being," "happiness," and "life satisfaction" have all been used as proxy indicators of QOL. Happiness tends to be more concerned with the psychological aspects of life and perhaps is state-centered (that is, moods, feelings, and emotions). But it is argued by Campbell, Converse, and Rogers (1976) and Marans (2003) that a "satisfaction-based measurement" of QOL is useful, as it comprises more definable properties and it implies judgmental or cognitive experiences, whereas "happiness" reflects a relatively short-term mood of elation or gaiety.

Thus, QOL is a *multilayered* and *multidimensional* concept (Marans, 2003; Marans & Rodgers, 1975; McCrea, Stimson, & Western, 2005). It is multilayered in the sense of its representation at the levels of individual, family, and community, and it is multidimensional in its reflection of various aspects of life.

16.2.2 QOL Measurement

The literature is also replete with attempts to measure QOL, although there is no widely accepted model or measure. There are many debates around how best to measure QOL or its reflection in various aspects of daily life. Traditional measures are typically "objective" and "subjective":

1. *Objective QOL* is said by Diener and Suh (1997) to reflect "objective circumstances in a given cultural or geographic unit . . . [and] are based on objective, quantitative statistics" (p. 192). For example, it incorporates health indicators, crime rates, education levels, workforce participation, and the proportion of welfare recipients in a given area as indicators of objective QOL.
2. *Subjective QOL* is said by Carley (1981) to be "based on reports from individuals on the 'meaning' of aspects of their reality, and as such represent psychological variables" (p. 31). These are assumed by Diener and Suh (1997) to be defined by "people's conscious experiences—in terms of hedonistic feelings or cognitive satisfactions" (p. 191).

Veenhoven (2000) identifies a number of interdependent categories of QOL by distinguishing "opportunities (chances) for a good quality of life" and "the good life itself as an outcome." These include:

- The livability of the environment
- The life ability of the individual
- The external utility of life
- The inner appreciation of life.

In approaches to data collection using survey research, QOL is often measured by asking subjects to "evaluate" their *level of satisfaction* with various aspects of life. Responses are typically captured using a standard response format—such as a Likert scale—that yields a numerical rating (Trauer & Mackinnon, 2001). However, aspects of QOL might not hold the same importance for everybody, and, as a result, the evaluation of the importance of each aspect or domain of QOL has sometimes been built into the questionnaire instrument used to collect data on QOL in a survey (Gill & Feinstein, 1994). When the satisfaction ratings for various life satisfaction domains are multiplied by their importance ratings and then summed, a composite score indicating the overall QOL may be generated. Such a score, with its unique weightings assigned to various life satisfaction domains, represents a *global subjective QOL measure* (Oliver, Holloway, & Carson, 1995), with lower weights being allocated to those domains that contribute little to the person's life satisfaction (Cummins, 1995). While exploring the conceptual, psychometric, and empirical issues pertaining to this approach, Trauer and Mackinnon (2001) suggest that

> satisfaction ratings already reflect a personal appraisal of the importance of the domain . . . and that the multiplicative composite of satisfaction and importance has extremely undesirable measurement properties and may be difficult to interpret. (p. 584)

In the study by Stimson, Chhetri, Akbar, and Western (2006) discussed in this chapter, a methodology is adopted that assigns weights on the basis of different scenarios to resolve some of these problems.

16.2.3 A "Domains-of-Life" Approach

In adopting a "subjective well-being approach" to the study of QOL as reported by respondents to a survey, satisfaction with life in a number of domains has been assessed by the strategies developed by researchers including Cummins (1996), Heady and Wearing (1992), and Salvatore and Muñuz Sastre (2001).

The "domains-of-life" approach appraises life as a whole on the basis of a multidimensional vector of specific appraisals in more concrete spheres of well-being (Rojas, 2004). Debates surround the number of independent domains; nevertheless, partitions based on parsimony, meaningfulness, and usefulness underpin their success (Rojas, 2004). Cummins, McCabe, Romeo, and Gullone (1994) have identified seven QOL domains: (1) material well-being, (2) health, (3) productivity, (4) intimacy, (5) safety, (6) community, and (7) emotional well-being. Van Praag, Frijters, and Ferrer-i-Carbonell (2003) have added "satisfaction with life as a whole" as an aggregate concept which, if unfolded, represents the sum of its domain components (such as health, financial situation, job, housing, leisure, and environment). In the research by Stimso, Chhetri, Akbar, and Western (2006), satisfaction with life as a whole and with its various domains is subjectively assessed in terms of perceived well-being.

16.3 Methodology

16.3.1 The Study Area

The study area for the Stimson, Chhetri, Akbar, and Western (2006) research is the Brisbane–SEQ region in Australia, a sprawling metropolitan region that has been experiencing rapid growth and socioeconomic transformation for several decades. The region is characterized by a multicentered urban structure, connecting the Queensland state capital, Brisbane, with two coastal growth corridors—south to the Gold Coast and north to the Sunshine Coast (which are tourism regions)—and with a less rapidly growing inland western corridor through Ipswich, a long-established industrial and mining city. The region's population increased from 1.8 to about 2.4 million over the decade 1991–2001, and it is forecasted to reach about 3.2 million by 2011. It is useful for planners to evaluate QOL of people occupying different residential mosaics across the urban social spaces of the region. Mapping those variations may identify areas deficient or rich in a particular domain of QOL or a combination of those domains. Studies such as this can add to the evidence base relating to the identification of factors affecting people's QOL and their adopted lifestyle and life choices in different places.

16.3.2 Data Collection

In 2003 a QOL survey in the Brisbane–SEQ region was conducted by researchers at the University of Queensland. It was a *spatially stratified probability sample survey* design using the computer-assisted telephone interviewing facility at the university to both generate the sample of household telephone numbers to obtain a minimum quota of 100 respondents in each of the designated subregions within Brisbane–SEQ and to collect data through a telephone survey mode using a standardized survey instrument with automatic coding of respondent answers to questions.

A total of 1,612 survey participants ages 18 years and older were interviewed. Data was collected on the standard socioeconomic and demographic characteristics of respondents, along with information on the location of their places of residence and work, plus a wide range of information relating to *perceived QOL across life satisfaction domains* and on the behavior of people with respect to work, recreation, and consumption. This comprehensive Brisbane–SEQ QOL survey database was used in the Stimson, Chhetri, Akbar, and Western (2006) study for secondary data analysis to address the research issues discussed previously.

16.3.3 Measurements

In the Brisbane–SEQ region QOL survey, *life satisfaction* was measured by asking survey respondents this question:
How satisfied are you with your overall quality of life?

It was measured on a 5-point Likert scale, where 1 represents "very dissatisfied" and 5 "very satisfied." Questions were asked to assess satisfaction with the following aspects of life:

1. Your employment situation.
2. The amount of money you have available to you personally.
3. Your housing.
4. The amount of time you have to do things you want to do.
5. Your relationship with your partner.
6. Your relationship with your children.
7. Your independence or freedom.

16.3.4 Aggregation Techniques

16.3.4.1 The Weighted Average Operator

The "weighted average operator" (WAO) is a commonly accepted composite index that may be derived from a set of scaled responses to survey questions. The term "composite index" can be defined as an aggregation of the indicator values that collectively convey information about the quality of some complex aspects or components of a condition (Nijkamp, Rietveld, & Voogd, 1990).

In the WAO, indicators are multiplied with their associated weights and then added together to construct the overall index. In the QOL research, weights are often assessed by asking people to assign importance scores to each item assessed in the survey. The index can be expressed as

$$U = y_1 x_1 + y_2 x_2 \ldots + y_n x_n$$

where x_n is the nth indicator and y_n is its corresponding weight.

16.3.4.2 The OWA Operator

The OWA is often used for aggregating multiple indicators to form an overall score. This is a relatively new but flexible method of aggregation. It allows the users to decide upon the types of aggregation depending on the purpose of their decision making (Filev & Yager, 1998; Mendes & Motizuki, 2001; Smith, 2000–2001; Yager, 1988, 2004). The basic formula of OWA is given as

$$F = w_1 b_1 + w_2 b_3 + \ldots + w_j b_j$$

where $b_1, b_2, \ldots, b_n$ are the positional values of the indicators, and $w_1, w_2, \ldots, w_n$ are the weights of those positional values.

OWA aggregation is a nonlinear aggregation because it uses an ordering process to aggregate the indicators' values. The values of the weights range between 0 and 1.

Yager (1988) has proposed an "OWA operator." The operator can be used to evaluate the performance of urban areas on QOL indicators (Mendes & Motizuki, 2001). The overall performance rating depends upon the criteria used to assign weights to the indicators based on their importance in the subjective assessments of subjects. There can be a situation where all indicators hold the same importance, while in other situations satisfaction with one of the indicators is all that is desired. For example, for older people health status may be a far more important domain than employment status. Therefore, their QOL is heavily dependent on health-related indicators. On the other hand, weightings might not be the same for a young, unemployed person. These combinations of situations can be adjusted through the use of "And" and "Or" operators, which combine the function that an indicator performs in the overall ranking (Yager, 1988, p. 183).

According to Yager (1988), an "OWA operator" of dimension n is a mapping function:

$$f : R^n \to R$$

which has an associated weight vector, W:

$$W = [w_1, w_2, w_3, \ldots w_n]^T$$

such that

$$w_i \varepsilon [0,1]$$

$$\sum_{i=1}^{n} w_i = 1$$

The functional value $f(a_1 \ldots a_n)$ determines the aggregated value of arguments $a_1, a_2 \ldots a_n$ in such a manner that

$$f(a_1 \ldots a_n) = \sum_{j=1}^{n} w_j b_j \quad \text{(aggregation equation)}$$

where b_j is the jth largest element of the collection of the n aggregated objects (here, indicators) $a_1, a_2 \ldots a_n$ (Filev & Yager, 1998).

A fundamental aspect of the "OWA operator" involves ordering the indicator values. If we consider ranking the indicator scores from highest to lowest, the indicator with the highest score is given the first-order weight, the indicator with the next highest score is given the second-order weight, and so on. This has the effect of weighting an indicator based on its rank in a descending order from maximum to minimum. Thus argument a_i (a particular indicator value) is not associated with a particular weight w_i but rather a weight w_i is associated with a particular ordered position i of the argument (Filev & Yager, 1998, p. 158). A known property of the "OWA operators" is that they include the *Max, Min,* and arithmetic mean operators for the appropriate selection of the vector W:

For $W = [1, 0, 0, \ldots 0]$, $f(a_1 \ldots a_n) = Max_i\, a_i$
[Optimistic OWA (OP-OWA)]

For $W = [0, 0, 0, \ldots 1]$, $f(a_1 \ldots a_n) = Min_i\, a_i$
[Pessimistic OWA (PE-OWA)]

$$\text{For } W = [1/n, 1/n, \ldots 1/n], \; f(a_1 \ldots a_n) = \frac{1}{n}\sum_{i}^{n} a_i$$
[Average OWA (AV-OWA)].

All "OWA operators" are bounded by the *Max* and *Min* operators [$Min_i \, a_i \le f(a_1 \ldots a_n) \le Max_i \, a_i$] (Filev & Yager, 1998). Recently, other types of OWA operators (that is, "Maximum entropy OWA" and "exponential OWA") have been developed (Filev & Yager, 1998; Smith, 2000–2001).

16.3.4.3 The Exponential OWA Operator and the Maximum Entropy OWA Operator

A somewhat simpler approach, which does not require the solution of a nonlinear programming problem, is the "exponential OWA operator" (EX-OWA) (Filev & Yager, 1998). This method is an alternative solution to the constrained optimization problem. OWA weights can easily be generated according to either of the following equations:

$$w_1 = \theta; \; w_2 = \theta(1-\theta); \; w_3 = \theta(1-\theta)^2; \; \ldots; \; w_{n-1} = \theta(1-\theta)^{n-2}; \; w_n = (1-\theta)^{n-1} \; [\text{EX-OWA}]$$

Here θ is a parameter of the indicators that belongs to the unit interval, $0 \le \theta \le 1$.

Yager (1988) uses the dispersion or entropy (degree of chaos) associated with a weighting vector. He used this measure to develop a procedure to generate the OWA weights that have a predefined degree of "orness," α. That is, the weights will be as even as possible (maximizing entropy), subject to yielding a given level of orness. These are called "maximum entropy OWA" (ME-OWA) weights. This approach is based on the solution of the following constrained nonlinear optimization problem (Smith, 2000–2001):

$$\text{Maximize } E(W) = -\sum_{i=1}^{n} w_i \ln w_i \; [\text{ME-OWA}]$$

subject to

$$\alpha = \frac{1}{n-1} \sum_{i=1}^{n}(n-i)w_i \; (\alpha = \text{orness}) \; w_i \, \varepsilon[0,1], \; i = 1, \ldots, n$$

16.4 Results and Analysis

The overall objective of the Stimson, Chhetri, Akbar, and Western (2006) study was to compare spatial patterns in the perceived QOL of people at a collective level as reflected in different weighting regimes. Using the 2003 Brisbane–SEQ QOL survey database, QOL has been assessed on a range of *life satisfaction domains*. The aggregation techniques discussed above are used to weight QOL indicators described on those various life satisfaction domains. This section of the chapter reports the results derived from those aggregation operators and maps and analyzes the interregional variability in QOL across the study region in association with the sociodemographic and economic characteristics of subregions within it.

16.4.1 Descriptive Statistics

Table 16.1 gives the means and standard deviations of the scores of perceived life satisfaction domains. Those aggregate descriptive statistics show the following:

TABLE 16.1. Descriptive Statistics for QOL Items

Satisfaction with...	Mean	SD
The amount of money you have available to you personally	3.12	1.20
The amount of time you have to do the things you want to	3.29	1.22
Your romantic relationships	3.77	1.27
Your employment situation	3.78	1.15
The way you spend your leisure time	3.88	0.95
Your health	3.89	0.99
Your social relationships	4.01	0.88
Your housing	4.19	0.85
Your independence or freedom	4.20	0.91
Your family life	4.24	0.91
Your friends	4.26	0.75
Living in the Brisbane–South East Queensland region	4.36	0.71
Your overall standard of living	4.07	0.80
Your life as a whole	4.24	0.73

Note. Stimson, Chhetri, Akbar, and Western (2006).

- For satisfaction with social relationships, housing, independence/freedom, family life, and friends, the means are greater than 4 on the 5-point Likert scale.
- With the overall standard of living in the Brisbane–SEQ region and life as a whole, respondents have given high satisfaction scores.
- On the other side of the spectrum, for six life satisfaction domains—satisfactions with the amount of money, the amount of free time available, romantic relationships, employment situation, leisure time, and health—the overall scores reported by the respondents are slightly lower, being between 3.1 and 3.9.

It also needs to be noted that items with relatively lower scores have high standard deviations; items with high satisfaction scores have lower standard deviations.

16.4.2 Aggregation: Results of OWA Operators

The subjective evaluations of QOL derived from survey data have no explicit spatial properties. In order to aggregate data geographically, 21 subregional areas were generated. These subregions are identified on the basis of two criteria:

- Administrative uniformity and compatibility with census geographies
- Similarity in the socioeconomic and demographic characteristics.

SEQ subregions delineated by Stimson, Roberts, Taylor, Clark, and Larnach (1997) are used for areas within the Brisbane metropolitan area, while local government areas (local councils) are adopted for the remainder of the SEQ region.

Using the "point-in-polygon function," the QOL survey data that were geocoded for every survey respondent at a street level were aggregated into a GIS database generated for the subregions. Subjective scores obtained on a number of items could be aggregated by using either a "weighted average" (WA) or an OWA. The former is a linear aggregation operator, while the latter is a nonlinear aggregation operator. In this chapter we have used

OWA because it provides a method of allocating different weights to indicators over different scenarios.

In order to aggregate data across 21 subregional areas, subjective scores on various items had to be aggregated. To illustrate the process involved, an example is given in Table 16.2 where there are 54 participants in one of the 23 subregions, Subregion 1 (R1). The scores of survey respondents living in this subregion on satisfaction with employment are aggregated and then converted into percentages. These values for different subregions are then transformed from 1 to 0 on the basis of their positional rankings. The procedure is replicated for all items in the survey. This gives us a table with all the indicators sorted on the basis of their positional values.

In order to *measure* and *compare* the performance of 21 subregions across the SEQ region study area on the *subjective QOL domains*, OWA operators were used to aggregate items derived from the survey data. Items aggregations by OWA operators were implemented using Visual Basic for Application (VBA) in the software packages MS Excel and MathCAD. The values of OWA operators vary on a scale between 1 and 0. Here a "1" means 100% satisfaction or the ideal condition of the indicators existed, and a "0" means that the indicators revealed 100% dissatisfaction.

Under the OWA operators, while considering the positional values of the QOL items and nonlinear arithmetic and/or exponential aggregation, performance of subregions on the QOL measures varies between 30 and 97% of the ideal condition, depending on the model that is considered. For instance:

1. Under the MAX-OWA operator, the average score on the QOL item is about 90% of the ideal condition.
2. In contrast, under the MIN-OWA operator, the average score on the QOL item is 39% of the ideal condition.
3. The AV-OWA reveals the trade-off among the QOL items, and the average score is about 70% of the ideal condition.
4. For the "exponential-OWA operator," the average life satisfaction score calculated is 42% of the ideal condition (while considering the low level of "orness"). This is 82% of the ideal condition (while considering the high level of "orness").
5. ME-OWA operator considers some constraints of the indicators, which means considering the desired degree of "orness" to maximize the evenness among the QOL indicators. Under this operator, the QOL score is about 60% of the ideal condition (while "orness" is low), and that situation is about 80% of the ideal condition (while "orness" is high).

TABLE 16.2. Transfer of Location-Specific QOL Survey Data into Subregions

Region	Level of satisfaction	Employment (count)	Employment (percentage)
R1 (*n* = 54)	Very dissatisfied	9	16.67%
	Dissatisfied	8	14.81%
	Neither satisfied nor dissatisfied	14	25.93%
	Satisfied	17	31.48%
	Very Satisfied	5	9.26%
		54	98.15%

Note. From Stimson, Chhetri, Akbar, and Western (2006).

16.4.3 Interregional Variability

Stimson, Chhetri, Akbar, and Western (2006) demonstrate that there are considerable differences in the degree and the pattern of interregional variability across the subregions of the Brisbane–SEQ according to which OWA operator is used. This is evident in the five maps that Stimson and colleagues produce from the application of the above five OWA operators. For reasons of space limitations, only two of those different map patterns are illustrated here, but the results derived from all five OWA operators are discussed below.

1. As shown in the map dealing with the *MAX-OWA operator*, the pattern in Figure 16.1 indicates that the areas with the highest scores are Caloundra, Noosa, Caboolture, Pine Rivers in the Sunshine Coast, and SEQ-Outer and Ipswich-Outer in the interior of the SEQ region. It has been found that subregions within the Brisbane metropolitan area and the Gold Coast have emerged to offer low QOL.

2. For the *MIN-OWA operator* scores for the item that scored lowest among all other items, a similar pattern to that of the MAX-OWA operator emerges. Caloundra, Ipswich (C), the Northern Outer, the Eastern, and the Southern Inners are found to have excellent QOL scores on the item that has minimum value, followed by the SEQ region, the Gold Coast Inner and Outer, and Pine Rivers. Most subregions in the outer Brisbane area, except the Northern Outer, are among those with low QOL scores.

3. When all QOL items are given the same weight, a clearer pattern starts to emerge in the AV-OWA operator regime. Most subregions along the coast and in the interior parts of the SEQ region have high QOL scores. It is perhaps indicative of the effects of proximity to natural areas such as creeks, beaches, and parks on the lifestyle that people choose to pursue, particularly for the baby boomer generation. Logan has low scores on MAX-, MIN-, and AV-OWA weighting regimes, while the Gold Coast Inner has scored low on the item that has the maximum satisfaction score but has performed reasonably well on the MIN- and AV-OWA weighting regimes.

4. However, much greater spatial differentiation starts to emerge for the next two weighting regimes, the "Exponential operator" and the "Maximum Entropy operator." Some of the subregions—for example, the Northern Outer and the Eastern and Southern Inners in the Brisbane metropolitan area—perform better on these two regimes. But to our surprise, the tourism area of Noosa drops its position, while Gold Coast Inner area emerges to be a winner on both of these indices. The spatial patterns in the exponential and maximum entropy are somewhat similar (correlation coefficient $r^2 = 0.72$), although they still share some similarity with MAX-, MIN-, and AVE-operators in terms of high scores for the coastal and interior subregions within the SEQ region. The pattern derived from the "Maximum Entropy operator" is shown in Figure 16.2.

The analysis carried out by Stimson, Chhetri, Akbar, and Western (2006) shows that most subregions in Brisbane City have performed relatively less well on the QOL rating, except the Western Outer suburbs. Regional and coastal subregions surprisingly have high QOL scores. These results support the findings of earlier studies (such as Andrews & Withey, 1976; Lane, 1993) that indicate that economic well-being may not necessarily result in greater satisfaction with various aspects of life. Even greater access to economic opportunities, public transport, and facilities has a minimal effect on the perception of QOL. Subregions or parts thereof across the Brisbane–SEQ study region are also identified as areas that have indicated low scores on a *social anomie scale* that has been derived from the Brisbane–SEQ region QOL survey database.

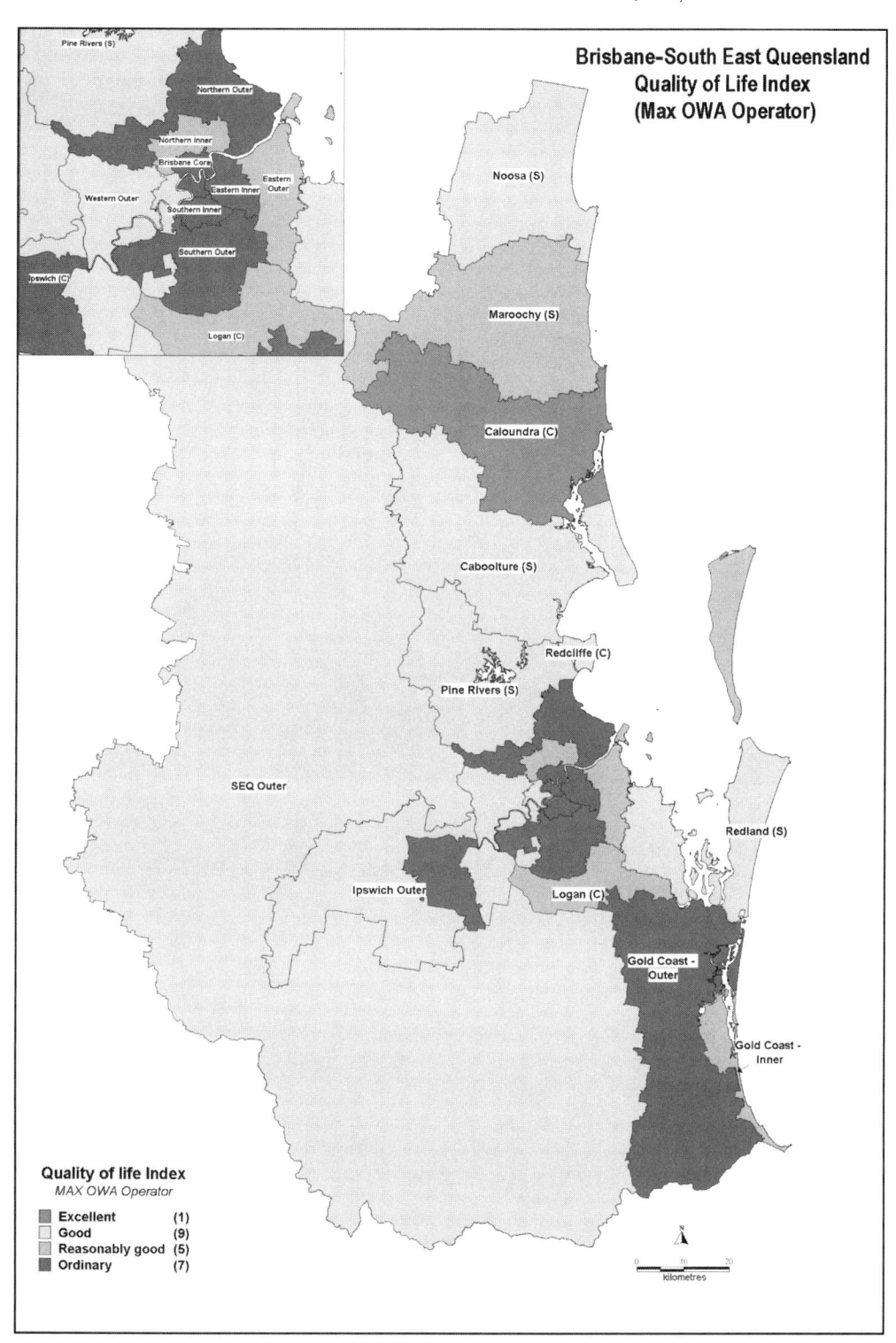

FIGURE 16.1. Variability in QOL using the MAX-OWA operator. From Stimson, Chhetri, Akbar, and Western (2006).

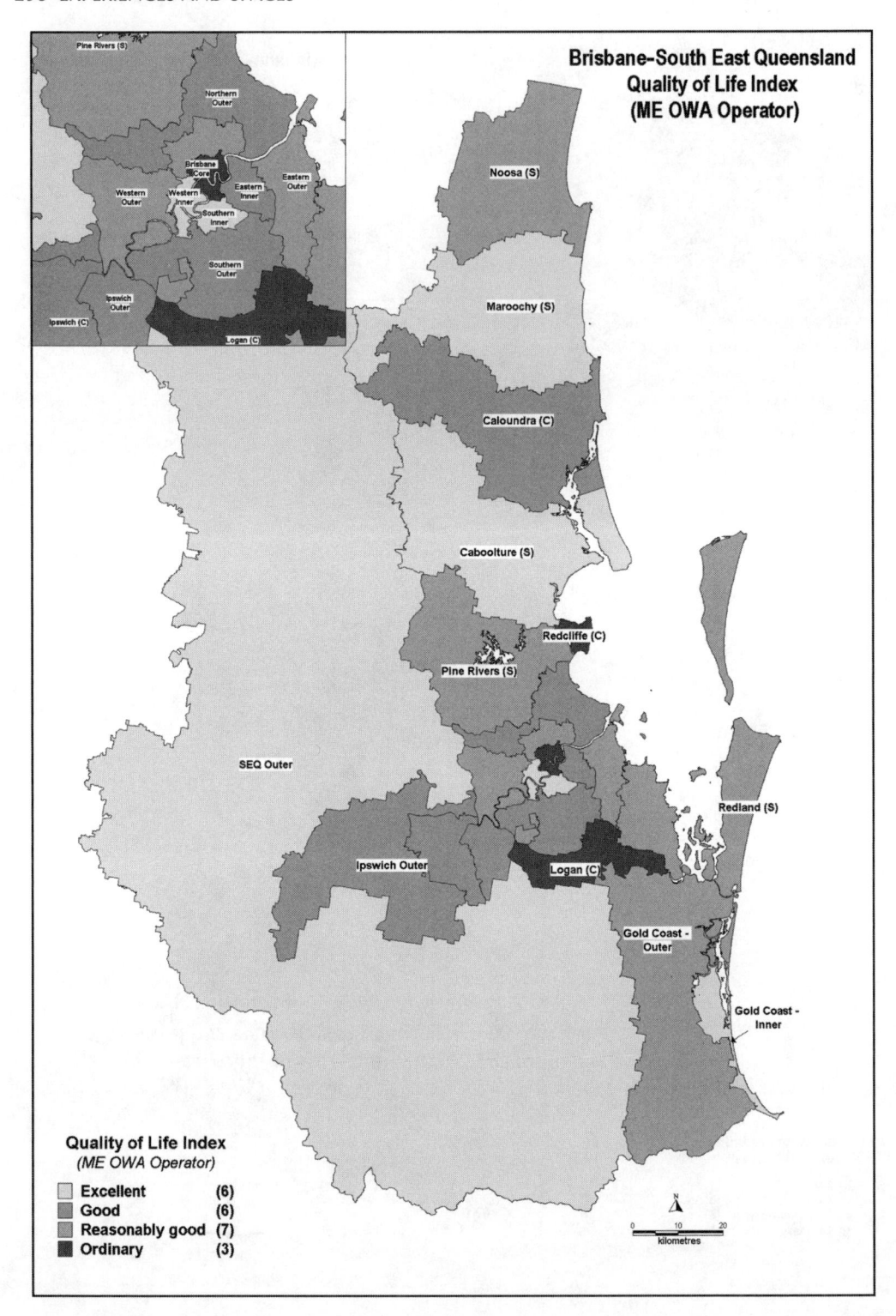

FIGURE 16.2. Variability in QOL using the ME-OWA operator. From Stimson, Chhetri, Akbar, and Western (2006).

16.5 Discussion

The study conducted by Stimson, Chhetri, Akbar, and Western (2006) uses individual unit record data from a survey of QOL in the Brisbane–SEQ region in Australia to show how the scores of survey respondents on a set of subjective QOL domains may be aggregated using the "weighted average operator" approach to derive subregional spatial patterns of subjective QOL across a large-scale metropolitan region. A variety of different OWA operator indices are derived and the resultant spatial patterns mapped and compared. It is shown that there are there are considerable differences in the regional patterns of subjective QOL across the study region depending on which of five alternative OWA operators are used. For some of the indices the patterns are similar, while for others there are great contrasts in the spatial pattern when measuring the same construct, that is, subjective QOL. Stimson and colleagues argue that the satisfaction that people report with their lives or with various aspects when explored in different weighting regimes is perhaps better understood than using a simple composite index of the various QOL domains.

However, from the exploratory analysis conducted by Stimson, Chhetri, Akbar, and Western (2006), when QOL data collected at an individual level through a survey research approach is aggregated to a "collective" subregional spatial level, and when those subjective assessments of QOL domains are converted into a single index or multiple indices, it becomes apparent that there are a number of limitations that do need to be highlighted:

1. First, the size of the sample is vital for the aggregation of data. For example, a dataset with a small-to-medium size sample or the use of geography (such as suburbs) with too many areal units can result in low frequency or counts when aggregated. The data collected for this study was from a spatially stratified sample that was designed to capture at least 100 respondents in each of the 10 regions within the SEQ region. However, this study used 21 subregions for aggregation that reduced the number of sample respondents to as few as 45 in one of the subregions.
2. Second, since the OWA operator indices used for the aggregation process simply aggregate individual survey respondent assessments on the QOL domains, the effect of an individual item on the QOL remains unknown. The items are ordered by their positional values from high to low before the index measuring the overall QOL can be constructed.
3. Third, intraregional variability in QOL within a subregion could not be explored in the indices used. Diversity measures (such as Simpson's index or a Herfindahl index) may be relatively better measures in terms of capturing intraregional variability in QOL, which the ordered weighted average indices were unable to measure.
4. Fourth, the choice of an appropriate spatial unit—for instance, a suburb or a local council area—is critical, for the analysis of the pattern may vary at different levels. This study made use of local council boundaries for areas other than the Brisbane City area, where subregions (amalgamation of suburbs) are used as units for spatial aggregation. This enabled the census geographies to be integrated and incorporated in the analysis.

Nonetheless, results of the research discussed in this chapter do suggest that subjective QOL, when measured on various aspects of life satisfaction domains, can be described in terms of three major dimensions. These include social, personal, and economic dimensions.

Overall QOL in the Brisbane–SEQ study region, as expressed by the QOL survey respondents, is exceptionally high. However, there are life satisfaction domains where satisfaction has been noted to be quite low. The survey respondents generally reported a relatively low level of satisfaction with the amount of money, available leisure time, and employment situation, and often struggle to manage their romantic relationships and health. The OWA operator technique used to aggregate the values of all of the QOL dimensions in the five different weighting regimes proved to be a useful and indeed enlightening approach to derive generalized subregional patterns of subjective QOL assessment. When the five different indices computed were mapped to display interregional variability in QOL across 21 subregions, considerable variations in patterns were evident, indicating the importance of the researcher having a clear understanding of exactly what a particular OWA operator index represents and how it is derived. All five types of aggregation used by Stimson, Chhetri, Akbar, and Western (2006) show that the average QOL score varies between 30 and 97% of the ideal condition, depending on which operator is being considered:

1. For the average-OWA, where items are equally weighted, there are trade-offs among the items, and the average score is about 70% of the ideal condition.
2. For the other weighting regimes, clear spatial differences in people's perceived QOL were revealed across the entire SEQ region. The results suggest that subregions that have more access to amenities and have connectedness to employment opportunities and activity centers in fact have low QOL scores. Contrary to this finding are those subregions that are aligned along the coast, which are situated in relatively more interior parts of the SEQ region that have performed well in all the different weighting regimes. For the mapping, the use of weighting regimes has enabled the identification of subregions—for example, Gold Coast Inner—which have low QOL scores on some items but high scores on others.
3. However, the use of different QOL indices has an apparently negligible effect on the performance of some of the subregions (as seen, for instance, in the Logan area of Brisbane–SEQ).

Thus, it seems to be important that a variety of "weighting" routines be used and outcomes compared in order to measure and evaluate the spatial variations (at a subregional level of aggregation) in perceived QOL on life satisfaction domains when transferring individual-level survey data into aggregated spatial measures of QOL. It is argued in the Stimson and colleagues study that the subjective perceptions or assessments of QOL, when investigated in different weighting regimes, has discerned myriad interpretations and meanings depending on what it is based on and that its interregional variability has been spatially expressed to reflect the levels of collective well-being of people.

16.6 Acknowledgment

The study conducted by Stimson, Chhetri, Akbar, and Western (2006) discussed in this chapter is part of a larger program of research on urban QOL funded through the Australian Research Council Discovery Scheme, Project No. DP0209146. The contribution of Prem Chhetri, D. Akbar, and John Western to that research is gratefully acknowledged. The material in this chapter comes from the paper Stimson and colleagues presented at the annual conference of the European Regional Science Association in Volos, Greece, in September 2006.

CHAPTER 17

Reflecting the Nature of Cognitive Spaces from Perceived Relations

17.1 Introduction

Researchers such as Lynch (1960) and Carr (1967) have argued that the *spatial form of the city* may facilitate or inhibit the development of a *cognitive representation* of that city. In the four decades since those pioneers suggested examining people's *images* of environments as ways to help understand human behaviors and decision making, repeated *experiments* have verified the pioneer hypotheses and they have developed more and more experimental designs and analytical methods to investigate the nature of these images and how they are used. But despite the past decades of research, there is still no consensus as to *how cities are learned*, or of what is the most probable learning format for that learning. Suggestions have included Golledge's (1976) *anchor point theory* and the *hierarchical theories* proposed by Hirtle and Jonides (1985) and McNamara (1986). Much of the research conducted has been focused on the environmental learning process itself (Montello, 1998; Siegel & White, 1975) rather than investigating the way the environment itself lends itself to or inhibits the learning process.

This chapter examines the development of research into the *cognitive structure* of a typical mid-sized city in the United States undertaken by author Golledge and his colleagues. Specifically it focuses on how coherent cognitive structures emerge over time as this information about an environment develops. The environmental setting for the research is the city of Columbus, Ohio. An experimental research design is used to elicit *cognitive configurations* from two groups of subjects—relative newcomers to the city and longer term residents—to show how such configurations emerge over time and eventually stabilize. The *latent spatial structures* of *individuals* are discovered using a variety of both *qualitative* and *quantitative* methods, including *multidimensional scaling* procedures and other multidimensional, analytical, and representational modes.

The research discussed gave particular attention to investigating the following four questions:

1. What *environmental cues* are utilized by individuals in the development of *cognitive maps* of urban environments?
2. Are the cues selected, or specific to a particular environmental structure, or are they the same regardless of how a city is physically structured?

3. Does a particular city structure facilitate the development of cognitive representations?
4. What influence does *perceived structure* have on travel behavior?

17.2 Background: The Nature of Cognitive Maps Derived from Perceived Spatial Relations

Geographers in particular have long expressed an interest in the structure of urban environments and in human movement and spatial behavior within those environments. Usually the environment is conceived as consisting of *stimuli* or *cues*, such as buildings, and *supports*, such as paths or street systems. The "stimuli" and "supports" are associated in both *sequential* and *hierarchical* fashion. Residents build *cognitive maps* based on existing environmental features by selecting and organizing those that are meaningful to them. For example, when moving through space toward a specific goal location, the individual absorbs information en route and in the vicinity of the route as well as consulting stored information about more distant cues (for example, distant landmark features). The "cues" often are used to *anchor urban images*, and include visual features such as buildings, signs, traffic lanes, traffic control systems, parks and recreation areas, and different general and specific types of land uses. These cues exist in all urban places. Their specific "relative location," "order," and "sequence," however, differ with respect to each city's particular design. At any one time, obviously, there are numerous cues present in the environment, each of which is sending out a "to-whom-it-may-concern message" to human senses. Each individual selects from these messages those cues that are relevant to his or her life activities. They endow with meaning and significance only those cues that are relevant for current or anticipated activities.

Those parts of the environment that are experienced more *regularly* yield more *meaningful cues* (for example, in relation, say, to a journey to work). Since each person lives at a different origin, a specific set of cues that are related to an individual's behavior can vary. However, as the basis for common communication about the city and its features, some cues develop an importance that goes beyond a single-user profile. These are what Lynch (1960) called *landmarks*; they provide what Golledge (1976) has called the "anchors" of a person's *cognitive map*. Among the set of landmarks that typify any given city, there will be a small number that appear on virtually everybody's cognitive map. These are the real *anchor points* that help determine how city information is internally organized and manipulated.

Given this conceptual structure, it is possible to generate sets of *hypotheses* concerning:

- The selection of environmental cues in a variety of city sizes and structures
- The relationship between the pattern of cues and city size and structure
- The relationship between human spatial behavior and the ordering of cues in a city
- The specific types of behavior that would be expected once the cognitive configuration (spatial product) that epitomizes how the city's structure has been encoded and stored in memory can be offered.

Although it takes time to build a *cognitive representation of a city*, we do not know exactly how much time this takes. Since it is rather impractical to track an individual or a group throughout his, her, or their life history to uncover the development of his, her, or their information processing and recording mechanisms for the construction of cognitive representations, we assumed first of all that a *skeletal node/path framework* initially develops and that, with *experience* of the city, additional *information* is added to this framework.

Learning about the external environment is a process by which an individual provides him- or herself with a relatively organized and systematized conception of the events and experiences of life. By systematizing the events and experiences of life into different cognitive structures, individuals are able to understand the workings of complex structures such as cities. By doing this, they are able to regularize many of their movements in the city.

17.3 The Research Approach

17.3.1 Problem Statement

Using clearly identifiable locations and features in a city (for example, distinct environmental cues), the research undertaken by Golledge and his collaborators aimed at uncovering the cognitive spatial structure of a city held by its residents and to show how, over time, this cognitive view "deviates" from or "conforms" to the objective reality of the local environment. To achieve this goal, it was necessary to have participants in the study complete a series of tests designed to elicit an externalization of spatial information that is stored in long-term memory (that is, a spatial product). In particular, the focus is on the configuration of places revealed in this spatial product.

To obtain the spatial product, people were asked to make *judgments* about phenomena existing in their environment that can be commonly identified, recognized, and used as orientation points by individuals operating in their environment. While specific cues vary from place to place and city to city, classes of cues (for example, street intersections, signs, landmarks, large buildings, parks, and so on) exist in all urban structures.

The cues used in the research are drawn from those commonly identified by local residents during a pilot study of *place awareness* in the task environment. The actual configuration of these places in the task environment is called the "objective reality of the city." For simplicity of analysis and representation, this is recorded as a two-dimensional Euclidean map.

The research was stimulated by the fact that there is still uncertainty as to how cognitive images of large-scale geographic spaces develop over time, uncertainty about how much similarity there is between cognitive and real-world physical environments, and uncertainty as to the nature of biases and distortions in the spatial products, even when revealed by multiple alternative modes of presentation or representation. While there is abundant research showing that people conceptualize real, linear, and point locational components of an area and integrate them into a knowledge base, for the purposes of the research conducted by Golledge and his colleagues, only *point*-located environmental cues are used (for example, road intersections instead of road segments).

For centuries, geographers have built maps and developed map projections from data that is essentially information associated with point location (that is, points of latitude and longitude). The goals of the research, therefore, are well established in historical precedent. Thus, the point-based cognitive configurations and the point-based environmental cue configurations can use the accumulated technical power of representation and association that has developed in order to compare maps one with another.

Consequently, the four specific goals of the research discussed here were as follows:

1. To recover the cognitive configuration of particular spatial products of an urban area from a sample of its residents.
2. To compare maps of the objective reality of a city to the recovered configurations from the residents' sample so as to show the nature of any distortions in the cognitive maps that represent their spatial knowledge base.
3. To show how increasing familiarity with the city (as length of residence increases) reduces the distortions in cognitive configurations and shows a convergence over time between cognitive and objective configurations.
4. To explore the range of methodologies and analytic procedures for investigating the spatial components and spatial relations of these recovered cognitive configurations.

17.3.2 Hypotheses

Three general hypotheses were examined in the set of experiments conducted by Golledge and his collaborators. Those are:

1. Individuals new to an area have a limited knowledge of specific locations in that area and of the relative distance between those locations.
2. The ability of an individual to accurately estimate interpoint distances in an urban environment improves over time.
3. Familiarity with the locations will increase over time.

17.3.3 Research Design

The complexity of P-E-B relations suggests that a multiple-model approach needs to be adopted with respect to examining how people *cognize, learn*, and *use* those complex urban structures we call cities.

One research design approach to investigate this issue might involve the following steps that would involve participants in an experiment to undertake specific tasks:

- *Step 1*: The first step might be to determine a set of environmental cues that are common to a considerable number of people and represent the common landmark structure of a city. This step can be accomplished by asking people to enumerate what they consider to be the important landmark features in an environment, tabulating the results, and ranking the tabulated results (Milgram & Jodelet, 1976).
- *Step 2*: The next step might be to examine how people have conceived of the city on the basis of their accumulated experience with it. A popular method is simply to ask individuals to construct sketch maps of the city including the location and labeling of city features they recall and to which they give considerable salience.
- *Step 3*: The third task may relate to the comprehension of the environment. This goal might be achieved by asking people to identify where they are on a city map or asking them to perform certain behavioral tasks (for example, pointing, describing, estimating) that require an awareness of the total environment. Sometimes this research can be undertaken in the field, but more commonly it is undertaken as a laboratory exercise that involves sketching or verbal descriptions. Another way is to present individuals with a series of slides that they are required to identify and locate on an urban map. As an alternative, still photographs, videos, or on-screen dynamic imagery can be used to elicit this information. In recent years, desktop and immersive environments have also been used.

Another possible research design might be based on human travel behavior. Individuals could be given a street map and asked to designate a travel route they would take to purchase particular goods, patronize particular services, or simply travel to specific destinations. People could also be given maps with sets of routes to a particular destination and asked to choose among those routes, presuming they will have in mind a certain route selection strategy.

Each of the above experimental designs is feasible and has been investigated at length in previous decades. The geographer has an interest in each of these methods, as well as in others that are explicitly spatial. For example, if we accept the idea that people can construct a layout or configuration of places or cues in the city and then produce a spatial product or external representation of this information in some way, then it becomes obvious that a critical part of constructing such a layout is recognition of interpoint distances, frames of reference, direction, and orientation.

Focusing just on *interpoint distances* and collecting them enables the construction of a map that shows the location of points based on the original conceptions of interpoint distances. Thus, a *configuration* of the *cognitive structure* of a city can be created from *relative distance information* using a process called "trilateration." This distance information should be most accurate if assessed between point locations representing the most familiar and commonly recognized cues or anchor points in the city. Focusing just on the estimates of distances (in metric or scale form), configurations of the layout of origin and destination points can be obtained using either the metric or nonmetric version of *multidimensional scaling* (Kruskal, Young, & Seery, 1976), which allows the construction of a cognitive representation based on interpoint distance information.

17.3.4 Collecting Information on Environmental Cues

The study conducted by Golledge and his collaborators in Columbus, Ohio, involved designing an *experiment* in which the participants complete a series of tasks as discussed below:

1. An initial study focused on collecting *information* about *environmental cues*. The procedure adopted was to ask people to compile a list of the "best known places" in the city. From this information, 84 specific cues were selected.
2. The next step was to split these cues into groups of 19. Consecutive groups of participants had a 75% overlap with the previous groups (see Figure 17.1). The instructions given to participants were to *rate* each cue for familiarity on a scale ranging from 1 to 9:
    * Participants first had to pick the place or places they "knew best" and give them a score of "9."
    * Participants then chose the location(s) they "knew least" and gave them a score of "1."
    * All other locations were to be given scores between 1 and 9, indicative of the relative amounts of knowledge or familiarity they had of the different places.

    Each of the "cue sets" consisted of a variety of "environmental cue types" (for example, landmarks, street intersections, public places, and so on).
3. Next, participants recorded the *frequency* with which they visited each place and their sources of *information* about each place (for example, personal visit, news media).
4. Finally, upon completing those tasks, each participant was then required to provide three additional new location names other than those on the list given to him or her.

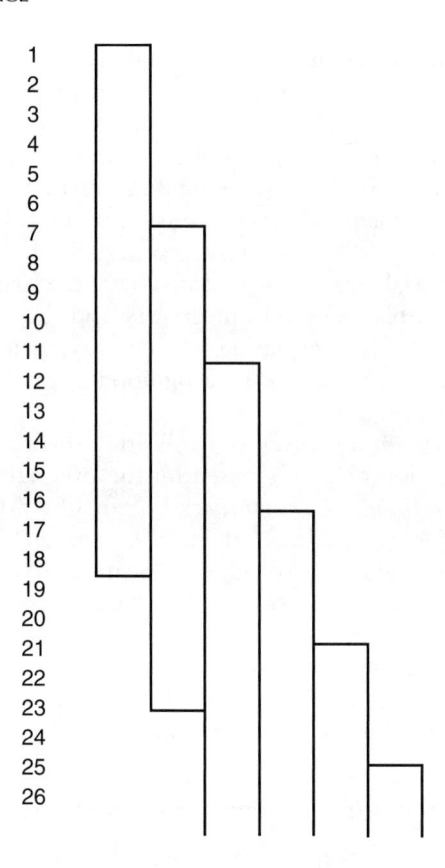

```
1
2
3
4
5
6
7
8
9
10
11
12
13
14
15
16
17
18
19
20
21
22
23
24
25
26
```

FIGURE 17.1. Cue selection procedure. From Golledge (1974, p. 117).

The three additional places obtained through the participant completing task (4) above were then added to the original list of 84, making a composite list of the cues of the city. The larger list was then reduced to the set of "cue name locations" that were given high scores (8 or 9) on a familiarity scale. A simple ratio was developed between the number of persons who gave scores of 8 or 9 on the location and the number of people exposed to that location (see Table 17.1). This was called a *familiarity ratio*. The resulting ratios were then rank-ordered. High familiarity ratios, then, indicated that most of the people exposed to the locations were familiar with them. Finally, the 24 cue locations with the highest familiarity ratios were chosen as the cue set most likely to be best known by all the participants.

Once this final cue set was decided, then a further subdivision was initiated. One of the purposes of the experiment was to collect time-oriented data concerning knowledge of the proximity to places. To minimize learning effects and pair order effects, each set was divided into three subsets, each offering a different combination of cues. However, some locations were used consistently on all trials to provide anchors for comparison procedures and to allow aggregation over the entire cue set. Pair order effects were randomized by arranging the order of cue pairs on consecutive trials. Since previous work had suggested that distances might be asymmetric (Golledge, Briggs, & Demko, 1969), a uniform bias in pair presentation on consecutive trials was maintained by ignoring pair order effects. The Latin square design was chosen for geopresentation (see Table 17.2).

TABLE 17.1. Preliminary Test: Locations in Rank Order

Locations	Familiarity ratio
1	.866
2	.810
3	.795
4	.785
5	.754
6	.741
7	.733
8	.732
9	.730
10	.674
.	
.	
.	
82	.050
83	.033
84	.033

Note. From Golledge (1977).

17.3.5 Pilot Study

The initial step was to undertake a *pilot project* to determine what the major environmental cues in the test city were and to search for those cues that were most frequently and accurately recognized. To capture this information, individuals were asked to list as many environmental cues as possible within the given time span (10 minutes). After these lists were collected, a second group of judges were asked to rate their familiarity with elements of this cue set on a five-point scale (where 1 = extremely familiar, 5 = extremely unfamiliar).

17.3.5.1 Participants

Participants in the experiment were volunteers from the local urban environment. Volunteers were solicited by advertisements in the local newspaper and were paid for participation. Most participants came from club and social groups undertaking fundraising activities. Participant structure was *stratified* to include 25 people who had been in the city for less than 6 months, 25 who had been in the city between 1 and 3 years, and 10 longer-term residents who acted as a control group. No attempt was made to balance the sex ratios because of the difficulty of recruiting the needed volunteers. Similarly, age rates of participants varied, but the bulk of the participants were between the ages of 21 and 40 years.

TABLE 17.2. Cue-Trial Allocations

	Block 1	Block 2	Block 3
Trial 1, 4, 7	*a* 1 I	*b* 2 II	*c* 3 III
Trial 2, 5, 8	*b* 2 I	*c* 3 II	*a* 1 III
Trial 3, 6, 9	*c* 3 I	*a* 1 II	*b* 2 III

Note. Subjects = *a, b, c*; cue sets = 1, 2, 3; location groups = I, II, III. From Golledge and Rayner (1982, p. 244).

17.3.5.2 Data

A number of different tasks were designed for participants to undertake. The data generated consisted of scale values derived from *paired* comparison, *stimulus* comparison, and *triadic* comparison experiments. Data from the resulting matrices were analyzed using *nonmetric multidimensional scaling* procedures (Kruskal et al., 1976), hierarchical clustering (Johnson, 1967), and a variety of *map transformation and matching* programs produced by Tobler (1965).

Data were collected using the following sets of instructions:

1. For the triadic choice experiments, participants were asked:

    "Choose from each location pair the location which is closest to the given base place."

2. For the paired comparisons experiment, participants were asked:

    "Indicate how close together each of the two paired items are with 1 corresponding to very close together and 9 corresponding to very far apart."

3. For location based on the cognitive distance experiment, participants were asked:

    "Indicate the distance of each item in the following list from item A, with 1 corresponding to very near and 9 corresponding to very far; scan the list and choose the closest pair first to establish the base and then choose the most distant pair next to establish the other end of your distance base. Allocate a 9 to this pair."

In this procedure, each cue was used as a standard in turn.

4. For the familiarity experiment, participants were asked:

    "Indicate your familiarity with items in the following list using a scale from 1 to 5, where 1 corresponds to very unfamiliar and 5 corresponds to very familiar."

5. Each participant was also required to fill out a background questionnaire, including local address, the previous two locations of residence, length of time residing at current location, length of time residing in the city, type of transportation mode generally used, demographic characteristics, travel habits and description of the route normally traveled between home and work, and nature of how each respondent measured daily travel (as in time, distance, cost, or some other procedure).

17.3.6 Cognitive Mapping

It is reasonable to assume that long-time residents of a city and/or populations acutely aware of the city as a whole (for example, taxi drivers) constitute groups who would know a city very well within the limits of their own cognitive mapping. Thus, a group of such individuals could form a *control group* that provides evidence of an asymptotic representation of a configuration of the selected location subset. It is further assumed that others of the city residents will move toward such asymptotic representations as their experience with the city increases and their levels of familiarity with significant places increases.

Once control group asymptotes have been established, it may be possible to measure the rate of learning about an environment by looking at different subsets that have been experiencing the city over different periods of time. Consequently, the participants selected for the study would include such a control group, an experimental group of newcomers to the city, and another experimental group of people who have lived in the city for some time and have experienced it enough to have an organized cognitive map of the urban area but one that does not necessarily closely match that of a control group.

17.3.6.1 Participants

Sixty participants were used in this study, broken into three groups: (1) *city newcomers* (less than 6 months residence in the city) ($n = 25$); (2) *intermediate-length residents*, or those who have lived in the city between 1 and 3 years ($n = 25$); and (3) a *control group* (those who have lived in the city more than 10 years) ($n = 10$).

17.3.6.2 Procedures

Each subgroup was further broken down into three subsets (A, B, C), which allowed for the use of a modified Latin square design in the presentation of stimuli (see previous table of sample structure):

- The 24 locations were also divided into three groups with a degree of overlap between groups (for example, Group 1 contained locations 1–9 and 22–24; Group 2 contained locations 7–18; Group 3 contained locations 16–24 and 1–3)
- Each location was allocated to one of the three cue sets with some locations being allocated to each of them.

Each subject group followed the same experimental design, given in nine trials over a 6-month time period:

1. In *trials 1, 4,* and *7*, subset A was used from cue set 1 and was given the location Group 1; participant subset B was given cue set 2 and given the location Group 2; participant subset C was given cue set 3 and location Group 3.
2. On *trials 2, 5,* and *8*, participants in subset A would get cue set 1, location Group 3; participants in subset B would get cue set 2, location Group 1; and participants in subset C would get cue set 2, location Group 2.
3. On *trials 3, 6,* and *9*, participants in subset A would get cue set 1, location Group 2; participants in subset B would get cue set 2, location Group 3; and participants in subset C would get cue set 3, location Group 1.

Using this modified Latin square design, each group would be using only one cue set on all nine trials. To prevent boredom and to minimize learning of places at each trial, they would be given the mixes of locations and one of three sets of the twenty-four locations. The overlap of cue set presentation facilitates aggregation across groups if so desired, and also facilitates the making of between-group comparisons.

The data collected from each respondent consisted of scale values of the proximities of the pairs of points. For each location group, $n(n − 1)/2$ paired comparisons were made. Specific instructions to participants in the experiment were given as follows:

> "Presented below are 66 pairs of locations. Read through the entire list and then assign a score of 1 to that pair or pairs of locations that are closest together, and a score of 9 to that pair or pairs of locations that are furthest apart. After having assigned 1's and 9's to those locations which are respectively closest together and furthest apart, go back

through the list of pairs and assign each remaining pair a number between 1 and 9. The number assigned to each pair should correspond to the relative closeness or amount of spatial separation of the members of each location pair."

17.4 Analysis and Results

Data consisted of *subjective judgments* concerning the *interpoint distances* between pairs of points. The inference from such judgments was that at least ordinal-level data could be generated from the participants' responses. It was assumed that by analyzing the responses from the paired comparison judgments, a latent spatial structure could be developed. In other words, a set of interpoint distances could be generated such that the order of these distances corresponded to the order of the original judgments. Given this set of ordered distances, it is possible to find a space of minimum dimensionality into which the points could be plotted such that the order of their interpoint distances was maintained. Techniques for doing this include *trilateration* (Tobler, as reported in Golledge & Rushton, 1972) and the use of a *nonmetric multidimensional scaling* algorithm (Kruskal & Wish, 1978).

To ensure that individual configurations, when matched with a map of objective reality, had the same orientation and the same scale, a matrix of the objective distances between the 24 sample layout locations was subjected to the same nonmetric multidimensional scaling algorithm. Configurations obtained from both the control group and the experimental groups can be compared directly to this map and locational errors can be collected. To simplify this process, configurations were produced in Euclidean two-dimensional space. Location errors for each point were calculated from the Cartesian coordinates of the locations of places in the multidimensional space (MDS) representation of the original interpoint distances using a matching program called "bidimensional regression" (Tobler, 1976).

17.4.1 Comparing the Groups Tested

17.4.1.1 The Control Group

The control group consisted of 10 long-term residents of the city. They included six males and four females. The MDS configuration obtained by simultaneously considering judgments made by the aggregate of the control group produced a significant matching. As a simple way of representing this matching, GRID, software produced by Tobler (1965), was used. This took a standard grid that could be placed over a map of objective reality, then transformed it to fit the map of subjective reality obtained from the MDS configuration. The results indicated that while some distortion was evident, the recognizable shape and structure of the grid was reasonably close to the original untransformed grid (Figure 17.2).

This grid is devoid of the actual points used in the experiment and represents a generalization or summary of the main variations found in the aggregate configuration of the control group. Grid distortions are compiled by interpolating grid lines between points of the subjective configuration. Examination of individual grids can show idiosyncratic variations such as exaggeration of short distances, elongation of the north/south extension of the main axes of the grid, or other specific and unique features.

17.4.1.2 The Newcomers

Following the modified Latin square design outlined earlier, newcomers were given a series of tasks over six time intervals requiring them to undertake the scaled paired compari-

FIGURE 17.2. Control-group grid. From Golledge and Rushton (1976, p. 109).

son procedure and familiarity ratings (additional demographic and travel data was collected but is not discussed here).

The scale values representing the data collected from newcomers was, as with the control group, analyzed initially by a nonmetric multidimensional scaling procedure (KYST; Kruskal et al., 1976). In each case, the objective configuration of the city was input as the starting configuration instead of the random configuration suggested by the authors of the KYST. Using the objective configuration as a starting configuration resulted in its modification to fit the judgments made by each newcomer and by the group as a whole. The extent to which the resulting configurations (that is, the configuration that produced the lowest badness-of-fit measure) matched the objective configuration then produced what is termed a "goodness-of-fit" measure between the two. In other words, the final output of the participant configuration showed how the starting configuration had to be warped to conform to the paired comparison scale values for each individual. The KYST nonmetric multidimensional scaling procedure is an iterative procedure that distorts a starting configuration, produces a badness-of-fit measure (called STRESS), and then modifies the starting configuration and calculates a new value of STRESS. Each iteration involves modifying the starting configuration, and each iteration ends with the calculation of a STRESS statistic. The smaller this statistic (that is, the closer it is to zero), the better the fit between the modified starting configuration and the subject data (Table 17.3).

Overall, four different starting configurations were used. The initial configuration was approximated from a Torgeson semimetric factor analysis of the dissimilarities. Two others were generated using either the Torgeson procedure or the normalized coordinates of the actual locations. The fourth starting configuration was a random configuration of points.

A *two-way analysis of variance* format was set up to determine whether or not the differences from the starting configurations were systematic and statistically significantly different. Since the underlying probability distribution of the STRESS statistics were not known at the time of the study, nonparametric statistics were used for most statistical analyses. Initially, the Friedman statistic (based on the rank sums of the STRESSes) was used. Investigating a no-difference hypothesis among the configurations produced from the four different starts yielded a confirmatory result (that is, the null hypothesis could not be rejected with a 95% confidence level). In many cases it appeared that the initial configuration affected the final results. In 86% of the 17 dissimilarity matrices examined, STRESSes varied at least marginally ($p \leq .001$) among the four final configurations derived from the scaling procedure. A two-dimensional solution produced the lowest STRESS value for 53 of the 70 trials (75.7%). Discussion of the fit between final configurations and the original objective configuration using independent bidimensional regression procedures appears later.

TABLE 17.3. Newcomer Stress Statistics over Time

Subject	T_1	T_2	T_3
N1	.047	.010	.004
N2	.066	.082	.110
N3	.082	.005	.024
N4	.128	.148	.094
N5	.108	.095	.137
N6	.042	.041	.044
N7	.027	.012	.005
N8	.028	.060	.060
N9	.038	.005	.005
N10	.093	.034	—
N11	.079	.009	.002
N12	.085	—	—
N13	.092	.067	.032
N14	.092	.056	.062
N15	.047	.029	.010
N16	.121	.057	.052
N17	.100	.119	.045
N18	.049	.067	.106
N19	.078	.004	.071
N20	.134	.084	.051
N21	.005	.061	.004
N22	.100	—	—
N23	.035	.013	.008
N24	.063	.049	.005
N25	.037	.009	.005

Note. From Golledge and Rayner (1982, p. 247).

17.4.1.3 Intermediate Group

Results obtained in comparing algorithms on data in the newcomers group were duplicated for the intermediate group. Substantial differences in STRESS values occurred depending on the starting configurations. Again it was extremely noticeable that using the actual (objective) configuration as a starting configuration proved extremely significant (Table 17.4).

17.4.2 The Analysis of Congruence

While showing some promising support for the initial hypotheses, the result of the analysis of the multidimensional scaling configurations based on the outputted STRESS values was not strong enough to justify drawing major conclusions except with respect to the newcomer group and the control group. Consequently, a further analysis was undertaken using the software CONGRU. This estimated the goodness of fit of the final MDS configuration onto a mapping of the actual locations.

The CONGRU results for the newcomers group indicated two major sources of error in the output configurations.

1. First, some specific locations were consistently mislocated and impacted the whole configuration. For example, if one cue is not familiar and is located at different parts of the maps on successive trials, it will significantly distort the overall fit and produce the type of variable results that were noticeable from the intermediate group results.

TABLE 17.4. KYST 3 STRESS Values over Time for the Intermediate Group

Subject	T_3	T_2	T_1
11	.010	.025	.051
12	.017	.010	.068
13	.017	.050	.085
14	.176	.125	.149
15	.049	.010	.010
16	.000	.010	.021
17	.018	.020	.054
18	.042	.066	.055
19	.071	.138	.101
110	.007	.036	.110
111	.050	.075	.061
112	.010	.007	.009
113	.094	.069	.128
114	.010	.010	.024
115	.010	.009	.059
116	.033	.014	.070
117	.092	.180	.163
118	.007	.012	.058
119	.067	.109	.094
120	.041	.086	.016
121	.010	.008	.056
122	.044	.042	.098
123	.031	.017	.026
Means	.039	.049	.068

Note. From Golledge and Rayner (1982, p. 248).

2. A second type of error was observed on the relative positions of places. If a few cues were consistently linked together but misplaced in the total configuration, they could also have a significant effect on the matching coefficient.

Overall, however, the congruence results supported the earlier findings in that the newcomers' configurations began the process of converging toward the objective configurations over time, while the intermediate group's configurations produced variable output over the same three time periods, and the control group's matching or congruent fit was stable over time.

17.5 Discussion

An earlier hypothesis suggested that as people learned the environment over time, their *cognitive configurations* would progress toward an *asymptote* (as represented by the configuration of a control group) (Table 17.5). In terms of the output from the MDS analysis, any decreases of the STRESS value over time would indicate that a better fit between the objective and subjective configurations occurred over time

With respect to the newcomers, it was hypothesized that environmental learning would take place and that they would begin to recognize places and more accurately evaluate interpoint distances as they became more familiar with the urban environment (that is, as length of residence increased). Using the Page statistic (a two-way analysis of variance test), a hypothesis of "no difference occurred over time" was tested and rejected with 99%

confidence ($L(3,22) = 281.5$). As shown in Table 17.3, these results indicated that over time, the individuals tested via the experimental design indicated that they could better perform the spatial relations task associated with positioning locations and estimating interpoint distances.

To evaluate whether the differences could have occurred because of the differences among the cue sets used at various times (even though there were common cues in each of the different sets), a second hypothesis was tested using a one-way nonparametric analysis of variance (a Kruskal–Wallace test). As shown in Table 17.4, the null hypothesis of no differences occurring among the groups was soundly rejected with 95% confidence. Similar data were used to examine the hypothesis of no change in STRESS values over time for the intermediate group.

A one-way analysis of variance was used to assess the significance of changes in the STRESS values over time. Here the F statistic was not significant at the $p \leq .05$ level. However, it was obvious that the data here was not normally distributed and the use of this particular test could not be justified. Thus, a nonparametric two-way analysis of variance was performed, and a Friedman statistic of 9.09 resulted. This is significant at the $p \leq .02$ level. However, here a confounding factor seemed to have occurred. Either the respondents were continuing to learn about the environment over time or they were becoming more familiar with the testing procedure and were thus able to perform the tests with greater efficiency.

Average minimum STRESS values for the group as a whole actually increased slightly over time. This presents a dilemma but might simply indicate that the initial phases of learning had occurred, that perhaps too much information had been absorbed during the early learning phase, and during the intermediate phase extraneous and less useful material was beginning to be dropped from the cognitive representation, thus producing slight increases in error that were reflected in the variable STRESS values.

The overall results from the above testing indicated that the new group clearly increased the degree of fit between "subjective" and "objective" configurations over time. The intermediate group, contrary to the proposed hypothesis, did not substantially improve over time, and in some cases actually got worse. The control group produced stable results over two time periods when they were tested, supporting the initial hypothesis that they had probably reached some type of asymptotic level of learning about the environment and had a fairly stable base of anchors and landmarks around which to build a cognitive representation.

TABLE 17.5. Control Group STRESS Values

Subject	STRESS
C1	.096
C2	.022
C3	.043
C4	.040
C5	.083
C6	.083
C7	.114
C8	.094
C9	.114
C10	.065

Note. From Golledge and Rayner (1982, p. 249).

The experiments discussed above show a logical progression from determining an appropriate dataset to advancing hypotheses, testing the hypotheses using a variety of test procedures, and analyzing the results using nonparametric and parametric statistics where appropriate. The results indicated that it was possible to recover the *latent spatial structure* of a person's *cognized spatial information base* about a city using *latent structure analysis* that was explicitly outlined in terms of the paired comparison experimental design procedure and the multidimensional scaling analysis. Graphic portrayal of the output for a control group (that is, distorted grid maps) indicated some clear ways that distortion was manifest. In some, closer distances were overestimated and longer distances underestimated (often referred to as "regression toward the mean" and reported by Couclelis, Golledge, Gale, & Tobler, 1987, as a "magnifying glass effect"). Other participants tended to distort locations by moving them closer to some cognized central location (labeled by Couclelis et al., 1987, as "the magnet effect"). A third type of distortion seemed to occur with different directional and distance distortions in different parts of the environment (labeled by Couclelis et al., 1987, as "the tectonic plate effect").

Analysis of the fit measures between subjective and objective configurations for newcomers, the intermediate group, and the control group over time indicated the following:

1. The *newcomers'* initial configurations were wildly distorted, fuzzy, and incomplete, but after the 12-week test period, their knowledge of the city structure was beginning to elaborate itself into a configurational pattern that seemed to converge toward a two-dimensional Euclidean representation of objective reality.
2. However, a similar development of the *intermediate group* was not as readily observed. Some individuals did continue to move toward some type of asymptote, while others tended to stay at approximately the same level of comprehension or indeed to do a little worse over time.
3. A *control group* maintained a relatively stable configuration over time that showed no further major modifications. Analysis of the fit between subjective and objective configurations indicated that between the newcomer group and the control group there were marked differences. The control group also differed from the intermediate group.

The results tend to suggest that cognitive representations (or cognitive maps) of a particular environment emerge over time, and tend to converge toward subjective reality. This convergence is not complete, and in no case was a 1:1 correspondence between objective reality and subject's configuration observed. This appears to suggest that although the stable framework of anchor points may be developed over time, the dynamics of the urban environment itself (that is, changes in the structure of the city), and changes in the behavior patterns of individuals over time, may result in adding new anchor points, adding new information about less important locations, or continually modifying estimates of cognized distance and direction between significant places in the city. While these experiments conducted by Golledge and his colleagues provide some insights into how environments may be learned over time, and how the process of learning might be represented graphically, it is also a reasonable conclusion that more extensive and detailed work needs to be done.

CHAPTER 18
Modeling Group Conservation Perspectives

18.1 Introduction

The purpose of this chapter is to describe how an environmental construct, labeled here as a *group conservation perspective*, might be developed or modeled for a regional context having circumstances for which it appears to have much relevance. Much of this chapter's emphasis is placed on the reasoning employed to model this construct, explain its plausibility, and describe its usefulness in this context. Douglas Amedeo and Amy Richert, joint authors of this research, found construct development to be conceptually and pragmatically useful in their much broader study of conservation perspectives in the Sandhills region of Nebraska. Their basic expectation was that conservation perspectives—certainly at the individual but also at the group level—should reflect beliefs, biases, and other such integrations involved in the ways environmental issues are perceived, construed, and evaluated.

18.2 Considering Human Perspectives in Environmental Conservation Policy

Amedeo and Richert began their modeling efforts by reflecting on questions somewhat like the following:

1. Must environmental policy turn out to be controversial?
2. Is conflict and enmity among resource users and those charged with resource-conserving environmental policy inevitable, or can some of this be anticipated prior to formulation of policy, and thus qualified to some greater degree than now?

18.2.1 Perspectives

Approaches and methodological recommendations in this field of research come from a variety of disciplines. A review by Vining and Ebreo (2002) of the theoretical approaches that have been utilized to study conservation problems suggests the focus has frequently been on "prediction" rather than on *explanation*, which would imply that an objective among researchers has been discovering the rule that forecasts how individuals will act with regard to conservation practices and using it in applications. But the Amedeo and Richert research takes a different tack, advocating greater consideration and acknowledgment of diversity among interest groups with respect to positions and viewpoints on conservation issues and the implications that that may have for environmental policy formulation. Kaplan (2000) has suggested a similar consideration.

Information about actual physical–biological relationships characterizing an environment is, without question, basic in the formulation of environmental policy. But what should be equally important, particularly during preliminary conceptualization of *policy*, is a clear and realistic estimation of the *impacts* it is likely to exert on ordinary user groups having various vested interests in its outcomes. However, when socially and/or culturally interpreted, when construed environmental information contributes to the development of meaning for user groups, this becomes an important part of the overall information base facilitating user actions, experiences, and responses. Environmental policies formulated largely on the basis of fundamental physical–biological relationships and directed mainly at hypothetical populations in some distant future may seem at times to be irrelevant, esoteric, presumptuous, and alienating to current vested-interest groups in the areas at focus.

With that in mind, an understanding of the contexts and/or settings within which environmental users engage in their activities and have their everyday experiences seems to be essential in the development of environmental policy. Comprehensive knowledge about user preferences, perceptions, beliefs, and aspirations as they relate to the environmental issues of the region under focus is needed in conjunction with and to complement other information considered vital to policy conceptualization. In other words, the need for a more inclusive and thorough consideration of the *human element* seems evident. What would be the point of establishing environmental policies if they were not fundamentally and explicitly oriented toward prominent groups currently relating in various ways to the environments in question? By "prominent groups" it is meant not just typical nonresident users of areas such as hunters, hikers, and birdwatchers—groups that frequently are the focus of policies anyway—but also other users who are often missed or given only passing consideration when long-term environmental policy is formulated. These certainly should include those who:

- Live and work in areas under consideration
- May be functionally and affectively connected to them
- Reflect aspects of their culture by their distinctive attachments to these areas
- Have their everyday experiences and conduct their daily activities in such places.

But consideration of such groups also entails a need to be attentive to the potential for diversity in ways environmental issues are construed, and this adds much complexity to the assessment of human-oriented information for policy formulation. In an attempt to form *anticipatory-type* environmental policy, it would be useful to have information on users' perceptions, beliefs, concerns, and interests about potential regulations, restrictions, and constraints to combine with requisite knowledge of the physical–biological or ecological characteristics of an environment. That would broaden the ecological perspective in environmental assessment to include, at critical stages of conceptualization, most significantly affected humans and their parts in the overall environmental system.

18.2.2 Latent Constructs

A frequent occurrence in all sorts of human-oriented research is the "opaque" or "indistinct" bases to which human responses are said to be grounded and from which they emanate. A common way to deal with such foundations is to represent them as *constructs*. Questions arise about how to express and/or model them. A variety of analytical procedures involving multivariate procedures—like factor-analytic methods, multidimensional scaling, discriminant analysis, and regression modeling—have been proposed by researchers to develop ways to represent and express the intricacies of such response contexts (for example, see the *Mental Measurements Yearbook* and the many references to "psychological testing"). But despite extensive efforts like these, there remains no standard or universal way of reasoning about the building of constructs to serve as conceptual surrogates for such indefinite bases.

18.2.3 An Example of a Latent Construct in Person–Environment Relations Research

In investigations of P-E-B relations, a "construct" from which a number of responses are believed to relate is conceptualized as *place*. Place and its derivatives actively serve as foundations to describe and account for a variety of environmental responses and/or experiences involving feelings of belonging, components in notions of self and/or identity, in emotional attachments, aging issues, and the like. Despite its intensive and extensive use by investigators, however, it is seldom sufficiently clear what the construct "place" refers to precisely.

People's notions of *places* are commonly treated as either personal reflections of social-environmental experiences (see, for example, Buttimer & Seamon, 1980; Relph, 1976; Tuan, 1974), attitudes toward personally meaningful surroundings, and/or as a "sense" of some environment having personal significance to them (for "sense" of place, see Hay, 1998; Jorgensen & Stedman, 2001). Such characterizations of place notions are inherently indefinite in their meanings and do not reflect a universal construct standard. This often makes attempts to compare place notions of the same locale somewhat problematic.

The indefinite nature of the notion "place" passes over to its important derivative constructs, particularly those that are presumed to constitute the bases for many different human responses and experiences. For example, if place was considered a part of one's self-concept, it would be plausible to assume that one would have to be emotionally and/or cognitively attached to that place, yielding the construct "place attachment." The difficulty for the purpose of research, however, is that there is no universal definition and/or measurement standard for this derivative. In efforts to define "place attachment," references are made to many things, but the resulting definitions are not necessarily equivalent. They include:

- *Feelings* of belonging to place
- *Affective* and *cognitive commitments* in terms of responsibility to community places, satisfactions with place
- *Positively experienced bonds* resulting from the development of behavioral, emotional attachments
- *Cognitive ties* between people and places, a distinctive affect in itself which is related to environmental attributes and/or culture–environmental relationships
- A *need-based relationship* between an individual and place and between group and place.

(For a discussion of these, see Altman & Low, 1992; Brown, Brown, & Werner, 1996; Giuliani, 1991; Giuliani & Feldman, 1993; Proshansky, Fabian, & Kaminoff, 1983; Shumaker & Taylor, 1983.) The inherent latent status of place, together with its indefinite definitions, is often an inhibiting reason why it is difficult to specify it precisely with confidence in highly structured data-eliciting research designs, despite what appears to be its conceptual utility for generating other environmental constructs.

How, then, are such *constructs* to be understood? In the same way that all such constructs obtain their ongoing meanings in social and behavioral sciences: hypothetical properties and their interrelationships, which seem to be suggested by ongoing research, are attributed to them, and these are then further qualified over time as more and more research results are accumulated. Conceptually indistinct constructs often present huge complexities for research activities, particularly those faced with a need to measure and define. In most cases, *latent constructs* are assumed to be *multidimensional* and to have many *interrelationships* among their supposed dimensions. They are expected to be intricately complex in structure and content. Typically there is little "evidence" from which any factual counterparts for these constructs can be "inferred," "outlined," and/or "delineated." The presence of this sort of complexity is ubiquitous in human research in general, and is especially prominent in the P-E-B relations issues discussed throughout this book.

18.3 Context for Modeling "Perspectives on Conservation"

Amedeo and Richert encountered a number of complexities when attempting to make apparent group *perspectives* about *conservation issues* in their research in the Sandhills region of Nebraska. The interest in conservation perspectives arose from the need both to account for environmental responses in general and to explain noticeable diversity in responses among typical environmental user groups in this region. The notion is always hypothetical, as no factual counterpart is available to demonstrate instances of such a concept in concrete circumstances. Nevertheless, their modeling intentionally pursued the development of this construct in order to relate it with other conceptualizations commonly a part of discussions of conservation policy.

18.3.1 Preliminaries Associated with the Development of Constructs

Conservation itself is inherently a broad concept, suggesting multiple aspects about management and preservation of environments and their resources. In the Nebraska Sandhills region, individual viewpoints about conservation are both multifaceted and multivalued. Hence, any modal indicator developed to reflect groupings of conservation perspectives would necessarily have to be a construction based on efforts to capture commonalities among individual viewpoints and positions about conservation issues.

Constructs in studies concerned with P-E-B relations research are numerous and are found to be especially useful in descriptive and explanatory scenarios. Well-known examples include "place," "scenic value," "personal space," "place identity," "place attachment," "cognitive maps and mapping," "behavior settings," "territoriality," and the like. What each of these constructs names or gives meaning to has little factual one-to-one counterpart and is therefore more conceptual than empirical in nature. Indeed, most constructs are outcomes from reasoning engaged in about the way things constituting them ought to relate rather than from observed knowledge of how they actually do.

The generalizing of inferences from logical interpretations, observations of systematic patterns in variances and covariances, and extended implications from highly developed or coherently robust conceptual systems (that is, *theories*) all contribute to the reasoning used by researchers to develop constructs. Thus, to develop a construct is to conceptually combine what are believed or assumed to be its parts. But in addition to speculating about such interrelationships to accomplish such aggregations, the activity of modeling a construct is likely to entail many concerns about scaling and/or measuring as well. Constructs that do have empirical counterparts—such as slope, wind speed, elevation, lighting, distance, location, and sound—are, in principle, fundamentally measurable because the relationships inherent in their quantity characteristics can be determined in their empirical circumstances. In effect, instruments or measuring devices incorporating structural quantity relations isomorphic to a construct can be built to assess their metric characteristics. Constructs that cannot be as readily sensed either directly or by the use of surrogate sensing mechanisms (those, for example, that are quite clearly latent and hypothetical in nature) are frequently grasped through compelling conceptual reasoning about what must be their quantity relationships if they were to reflect "this concept or that."

The purpose for constructing an indicator reflecting group conservation perspectives in the Amedeo and Richert research was to reinforce the basic contention that giving significant consideration to human factors when formulating long-term environmental policy for any region like the Sandhills is a necessity for helping to make its eventual prescriptions and regulations relevant, not only with respect to the region's purpose for environmental components, but also to the users of those components.

18.3.2 Environmental Context for the Research

The Sandhills region of Nebraska encompasses the largest sand dune area (approximately 19,300 square miles) in the Western Hemisphere. The dunes of the region are "stabilized" with natural grasses that provide land cover for cattle ranching, a primary land-use in this region ever since its extensive settlement. Although the region has always been relatively sparsely populated, the past three decades have brought significant change with respect to tourism and the presence of people from outside the Sandhills. Recent land sales attracted the attention of nonranchers, especially buyers interested in property for investment and personal use. Throughout the Great Plains of the United States, declines in agricultural populations have affected both the cultural and natural environments of many of its rural communities (Donlan, 2005; Popper & Popper, 1987). Within the Sandhills, strong trends exist leading to expectations of long-term changes in demographics, with significantly less ranching and changes in lifestyles, landscapes, and environmental perspectives.

In the late 1990s, a Sandhills Task Force intensified its assessments of the perceptions and beliefs of the region's local people about current and future conditions of the Sandhills, as well as concerns for the physical conditions and changes to them. The task force took note of the many environmental controversies surfacing on a regular basis in Nebraska, but particularly those in this large and distinctive region of Sandhills.

With task force sponsorship, Amedeo and Richert undertook an extensive assessment of how the region and its ongoing changes are perceived and thought about by inhabitants of the Sandhills region and of visitors to it. The research focused on the thoughts and perceptions about potential future changes in the region, concerns people had about types of recreation in the area, and beliefs held about conservation issues. The objective of the study was to isolate and identify differences and similarities in perceptions among groups of people that either live in the Sandhills (ranchers and commercial operators) or visit this area for a variety of recreation purposes. It is useful to note that much of the land in use in the Sandhills is owned or managed by ranchers (U.S. Census Bureau, *www.census.gov*).

18.3.3 Information for Formulating Environmental Policy

The Sandhills region of Nebraska is undergoing significant changes in how its environments and/or its many landscapes are being viewed and used. There are concerns that some of these changes may gradually exert negative impacts on the rather delicate soil–water–plant–animal balances in this region unless comprehensive, environmentally related policies are established that could neutralize their potential to do so. It is not entirely clear, however, what the informational foundations for such policy should be, particularly given this region's physical complexity, distinctive culture, tradition and/or history, variety of inhabitant and visitor users of its landscapes, its numerous wildlife and plant resources, and, most important, the way all of these mutually influence one another.

18.3.4 Human Emphasis in Environmental Policy Formulation

Concerns about threats to physical ecosystems are frequently expressed in environmental impact appraisals, which argue for optimal uses of various landscapes in regions like the Sandhills. Such uses are said to be those that will have minimal adverse impacts on existing ecological balances over the long term (for example, see Bechtel, 1997, pp. 118–119; Gauthier & Wiken, 1998; NCC, 2000; Northern Plains Conservation Network, 2004; Sampson & Knopf, 1996). They need to be identified, encouraged, and administered through an environmental framework designed to sustain a region's natural state and preserve its resource base. Arguments focusing on this kind of reasoning usually emerge out of a systematic assessment of the ways various land-uses significantly alter or adversely disturb a region's physical–biological interdependencies. Certainly not all environmental appraisals base their logic primarily on fundamental physical and/or ecological relations, but enough of them do to make this approach clearly apparent in the literature.

In some cases, optimal-use approaches tend to be narrowly focused, in that emphasis is placed mainly on ecological relationships and insufficient consideration is given to the human context within which regions usually acquire their meaning. When an optimal approach is used as a guide for environmental policy formulation, priorities typically get constructed favoring preservation of certain physical resources over others; relatively "pristine" settings are assigned greater value than, say, built or other landscape types; and "natural beauty" is designated as a primary quality to sustain in the long term (Porteous, 1996). Under this approach, the diversity in perceptions, preferences, beliefs, and aspirations of current landscape users in the region under study tend to be given at best secondary consideration in the formulation of environmental policy.

When environmental policies mandate management of activities primarily in accordance with physical and biological principles necessary to preserve a region's existing physical ecosystem relationships, they risk alienating and creating resistance among user groups. Chapin (2004) and Lomborg (2001) point to emerging trends in conservation approaches that suggest that some of the world's largest conservation organizations may be moving in that direction. Often policies having this orientation generate enmity and conflict between user groups and policymakers; see, as examples, celebrated cases in the 1990s: the spotted owl controversy and logging in the Pacific Northwest, and the denigration of the Grand Staircase Escalante National Monument in Utah in the 1990s. The state of Nebraska faces many controversies on environmental issues (for example, its two main river conflicts with neighboring states, water uses and its huge underground aquifer supply, severe drought, industrial hog-farm contaminants, among many others) that it has to confront in formulating environmental policy. What is especially notable is the relatively large number of issues faced in a short period of time, the variety of groups involved, and the many subregions that are embroiled in such issues. As would be expected, many of these disputes involve water, over which there is much controversy.

18.4 Representing Perspectives on Conservation

In the Sandhills region of Nebraska study, Amedeo and Richert set out to undertake a more human-focused assessment of the environmental issues existing in this region. One objective within the broader research agenda was to illuminate and conceptualize any modal differences that may exist in *conservation perspectives* among the *environmental user groups* in this region. It is that part of their research that is discussed here.

The study was designed as a *case format*. Amedeo and Richert adopted that format because of the challenges imposed by the physical, social, and ecological distinctiveness of this area; the costly logistics involved in sampling its vast size; the relatively low human population density; and the nature of people–environment relations in this particular region relative to the rest of Nebraska.

Alternative sampling designs—as in probability sampling—are possible. But the study region is an environmental type that is considerably remote globally from other instances of its kind, so that an attempt to treat an entire collection of them as a population and then employing a random sampling approach would be quite costly.

18.4.1 Environmental Issues and Their Potential Implications for User Groups

Environmental issues generating a variety of concerns among user groups in the Sandhills region of Nebraska included those related to ecotourism, land appropriation, depopulation, property ownership, place attachments, resource exploitation, landscape preferences, accessibility of information, land-use conflicts, and disparate environmental aspirations. Although each of these categories has distinctive characteristics of its own, they also relate with features of the others, so that the picture of what is going on environmentally in this particular region is far from elementary.

Ecotourism issues, for example, noticeably emerged to the forefront mainly from increases taking place in recreationally related activities like camping, hiking, biking, canoeing, birdwatching, hunting, fishing, and golfing in the Sandhills in the 1990s and which continue to the present. As these activities interface directly with various facets of the physical surroundings in the region, a major concern is the potential threats they may pose to the various ecologies making up the landscapes of the Sandhills. To restrict treatment of this issue to how tourist activities affect a region's physical/biological parameters may be too narrow a perspective for establishing long-term environmental policy. The Sandhills region is certainly a system of physical/biological ecologies, but those ecologies are also the bases of more complex people–environment settings. Hence, the issue of ecotourism might also be examined from how it affects the pattern of ways of doing things, traditions, history, norms, local expectations, and so on. An expanded perspective places the emphasis on a more human-oriented framework for the development of environmental policies.

Consider how this type of use might relate to different groups in the region. Many engaged in ecotourism activities come from outside this Sandhills region. In other words, the place has acquired a positive reputation externally in that regard. People who engage in tourist activities may do so not only as a recreation pursuit but also as a way of deriving a sense of personal satisfaction. For these individuals, the opportunity to transact with certain landscapes may, in itself, be an emotionally significant experience. They may certainly perceive their surroundings in a much broader, personally encompassing sense than the narrower sense of concern for physical/biological interrelationships. However, there may be important differences between the tourist group and inhabitants of this region in this regard. Inhabitants may have a strong identification not only with their immediate surroundings, but also with the larger region itself. This type of place identification may be a more belonging-type of attachment than, say, an eco-oriented one experienced by a visitor to the region. Functional and/or utilitarian issues may also be more prominent concerns for inhabitants of a region than for the tourist category of users. In that sense, people living in the area may find issues such as depopulation to be far more significant than do tourists, especially because such issues would, perhaps, portend a decline of services they depend on, an end to their type of existence, a diminishing of their subculture, and so on (see Donlan, 2005; Popper & Popper, 1987). Thus, concerns about environmental issues may be different for the inhabitant groups than for tourist groups.

It is thus reasonable to expect that, when significant distinctions exist among groups in the ways they experience regions like the Sandhills, concerns associated with those environmental issues may correspondingly differ in important ways. In addition to greater depopulation apprehensions, inhabitant groups may also have greater concerns than others about possible threats to the institution of private property, so that various types of encroachments by others may be far more important to them than to other groups. What counts as an encroachment is influenced by beliefs and interests of those perceiving such instances, so that actual physical invasions may get defined as encroachment, but so too might just the mere presence of other groups in the immediate vicinity.

Groups from outside the region—such as tourists—may believe that the region's landscapes should be developed and sustained in ways supporting their own activities and experiences in the region. For this reason, the issue of private property may be less urgent to them than it is to inhabitant groups, and therefore they may assume prerogatives for transacting with certain places that, by other perspectives, may not be theirs to assume in the first place. They may also have strong beliefs in favor of appropriating certain lands in the region to ensure long-term pursuance of their chosen activities. They may subscribe to the attitude that the landscapes in the region belong not just to the inhabitants, but to all users. Their preferences for different landscapes may thus be based on different rationales from those of inhabitant groups. They may be less functional and/or utilitarian and more affective and/or personal.

From this discussion it is obvious that different views of the region and how its landscapes should be used can lead to conflicts among users, and environmental policy ignoring the presence of diverse perspectives on the issues is likely to remain controversial for the long term and, in the process, generate resentments. It would therefore seem necessary for environmental investigations to conceptually represent such differences in viewpoints about conservation issues among the user groups of a region. Amedeo and Richert attempted to accomplish that kind of representation in their development of a construct to reflect user group perspectives on conservation issues. An illustration of their step-by-step procedure and its reasoning in their modeling of such an indicator follows.

18.5 Steps to Model Group Conservation Perspectives

18.5.1 Step 1: Acquiring Respondents for the Study

Although the Sandhills study described in this chapter is a case study, Amedeo and Richert attempted to obtain a *sample* that would reflect *at least* the variety of environmental users found in this region. Even if they had decided to look at all users in the region and treat them as *the* statistical population, an attempt to employ probability sampling instead would have been nearly impossible because of the inability to confront huge complexities like acute population density differences throughout the region, variations in exposure to different environmental issues, absence of comprehensive information about group populations, limited resources to conduct interviews at respondents' many locations, spatial and temporal constraints severely influencing accessibility to potential subjects, and occurrences of unpredictable weather and agricultural emergencies.

In the space of a year, Amedeo and Richert managed to hold *face-to-face interviews* with 127 individuals throughout the Sandhills region, of which 113 responses were found to be useable for their modeling effort. They sampled from:

- Agriculturalists engaged in ranching and farming
- Recreationalists (including canoeists, hikers, bikers, campers, hunters, anglers, and bird watchers)
- Townspeople operating fuel stations, restaurants, motels, outfitters, and retail stores.

18.5.2 Step 2: Using a Sorting Process to Obtain Subject Views on Conservation Issues

Conservation issues—particularly at the broader level of conceptualization—are found to be essentially replicated from one discussion in the research literature to another, so that there is a set of issues that appears to be generic across studies. "Ecosystem," "restoration," "renovation," "conserving," "sustaining," "redevelopment," "natural," "future generations," "resources," and the like are just a few terms that are commonly replicated in different ways from one study to the next.

Although the environmental issues in the Sandhills region would be expected to largely dictate the number and type of conservation statements selected by Amedeo and Richert for use in their sorting procedure to elicit respondents' conservation viewpoints, other issues exerted influence on both parameters as well. These included the vernacular styles used to express environmental ideas and a need to facilitate completing the sorting task requested of respondents in a reasonable period of time.

Hence, a total of 38 statements for sorting (see Table 18.1) were collected by modifying statements used in similar conservation research. The final collection, however, was influenced by guidelines that would reasonably ensure that issues specific to the study region were represented. These mandated that as far as possible the statements selected for sorting should be generic, be substantive in content, reflect conservation dimensions (for example, restoration, preservation, and management), be implied in the concept *conservation*, deal mainly with empirical issues, have relevance to habitats and/or environmental issues in the Sandhills, not be slogans, and reflect various sides of the conservation issue.

With this "conservation statement set" Amedeo and Richert asked their respondents to arrange—by using a helping panel as a guide—those 38 *general statements on conservation issues* in ways that would reflect their relative importance to them. The statements respondents used to fulfill this request were printed in large and bold formats on 3-inch by 3-inch

TABLE 18.1. The "Conservation Statements"

1. Human comfort is more important than protection of natural resources.
2. There are plenty of circumstances when individual rights exceed the greater good for the public.
3. Conservationists have overstated the need to restore rain forests.
4. Environmental laws sometimes do more harm than good.
5. Some species aren't worth saving.
6. Restoration projects that try to bring back native plant and animal species are not practical.
7. People should put human needs ahead of resource conservation.
8. Tax revenues should not be used for buying and preserving natural areas.
9. People should be concerned with only those conservation issues that occur in their local area.
10. Too much government involvement in environmental issues leads to inefficiency.
11. Local considerations should outweigh state and federal concerns when planning conservation actions.
12. The use of water resources for economic development is more important than ecological concerns.
13. It is best to use public land for multiple purposes.
14. Development that would not harm the terrain should be given serious consideration.
15. The federal government should provide financial incentives for landowners to participate in conservation programs.
16. Rural agricultural lands provide many opportunities for enhancing wildlife.
17. A problem with conservation areas is that they are not accessible to all people.
18. Wildlife managers and private landowners should cooperate to improve recreation, habitat, and management of wildlife.
19. The public should learn more about sustainable use of resources.
20. The greatest threat to wildlife is the destruction of habitat.
21. Research to discover better methods for conserving natural resources should be continued.
22. Scientific considerations should be more important than political concerns when making conservation plans.
23. Sustainable use of resources is a matter of the well-being and survival of humans.
24. It should be common national park policy to limit tourist numbers in environmentally sensitive areas even though this would decrease park revenue.
25. People should be able to buy ranch and farm land for wildlife recreation, sport, and other personal purposes.
26. Some areas, together with their plants and animals, should be set aside as preserves to study and to be enjoyed by future generations.
27. Unregulated types of land use are a major concern.
28. Population growth and nature protection contradict each other.
29. Conservation of natural areas is essential to our heritage.
30. A problem facing conservation efforts on private land is that the fate of the land is at the whim of the particular landowner.
31. Ecotourism is an opportunity not an invasion.
32. Because resources to support conservation purposes are limited, endangered species should be given a higher priority than other species.
33. Natural landscapes instill a sense of well-being and improve the quality of life.
34. It is beneficial to talk about wildlife to family and friends.
35. It is beneficial to know there are bears and wolves in North America.
36. Efforts to conserve wetlands, on both public and private land, need to be increased.
37. Protection of environment outweighs economic loss.
38. Designating an area as "natural" is a legitimate reason for taking land out of production.

324 EXPERIENCES AND SPACES

Statements most unlike my point of view				I am neutral or uncertain about these				Statements most like my point of view
Position −4	Position −3	Position −2	Position −1	Position 0	Position +1	Position +2	Position +3	Position +4
Put two statements under here	Put three statements under here	Put four statements under here	Put six statements under here	Put eight statements under here	Put six statements under here	Put four statements under here	Put three statements under here	Put two statements under here

FIGURE 18.1. Panel used for sorting.

cards, each with an identification number on its back side. This *Q-sorting* procedure followed approaches developed in other assessment and evaluation research (see Block, 1961; Maclean, Danbury, & Talbott, 1975; McKeown & Thomas, 1988; Miller, 1969; Mower, 1953). It is a useful procedure for both *eliciting* and *organizing* respondents' positions, attitudes, and other discriminating-type responses to stimuli of many different types.

To assist respondents in the sorting or arranging of these conservation statements according to their positions on such issues, a reference or helping panel, together with explicit instructions on how to sort, was given to each respondent at the time of interviewing. The panel and its accompanying instructions are reproduced in Figure 18.1 and below:

> "Here are 38 cards containing statements about conservation issues which we would like you to sort into piles showing your thinking about them. Arrange them on the table in front of you. We want you to look them over to see which statements come close to the way you think about these issues and which are unlike your views. As you look them over, you will notice that you will agree with some statements, disagree with others, and feel neither one way or another about others. To help you make your selections of statements easier, we are going to provide you with instructions about steps to take when sorting them and a panel with positions to place them on. Begin by taking a look at the panel with its position markers. Place whatever statement choices you make under the proper position marker on the table. Starting with instruction number 1, complete each instruction before going on to the next one.
>
> "Now look over the way you have distributed these 38 statements. If you feel like changing the way you placed them, go right ahead and do so. Remember that positions to the right of the 0 marker are closer to your point of view and positions to the left are more unlike your point of view about conservation. The further to the right a position is from 0, the more that position reflects your point of view about conservation. So the +4 position is closer to your point of view than any other positions. The same is true to the left of the 0 marker. The further to the left a position is from 0, the more unlike your view on conservation its statements are. So the −4 position is most unlike your point of view. Also, remember that if you move any of them around, be sure that, when you are finished, you have the same number of statements as indicated under each position."

18.5.3 Step 3: Respondents' Arrangements of Conservation Statements

When all 113 respondents completed sorting the 38 statements, their arrangements were coded by linearly transforming the panel codes they selected to avoid the use of zeros and minuses. This transformation is shown below.

Panel code	−4	−3	−2	−1	0	+1	+2	+3	+4
New code	1	2	3	4	5	6	7	8	9

A matrix (see Table 18.2 for a partial reproduction) of these arrangements constituted the *basic* informational source from which all subsequent steps in Amedeo and Richert's modeling would follow. In that matrix the rows are the subjects and the columns represent their scored responses to the 38 conservation statements. Given the guidelines used to select statements, a row in the matrix should be suggestive of the positions a respondent takes on conservation in general. This should, then, beg the question "Who thinks alike?" among the respondents about conservation in general. Likewise, any column in the matrix, by virtue of the values assigned to the specific conservation issue by all respondents when sorting, should display the

TABLE 18.2. Partial Matrix of Respondents' Arrangements

Subject	1	2	3	4	5	6	7	8	9	10	11	12	13	14	15	16	17	18	19	20	21	22	23	24	25	26	27	28	29	30	31	32	33	34	35	36	37	38
01	2	3	5	8	3	4	1	5	6	9	7	2	7	6	6	8	4	4	6	6	3	9	8	7	3	4	2	7	5	5	5	4	6	5	4	5	5	1
02	1	2	2	6	1	3	3	4	2	6	5	3	6	5	8	7	4	7	6	9	6	6	6	6	4	5	5	9	8	4	7	8	5	7	5	5	5	3
05	4	1	6	6	2	3	4	5	3	6	4	5	5	4	6	9	2	7	8	8	6	5	9	8	5	7	4	5	6	4	3	5	7	3	2	5	7	1
06	4	5	2	7	6	5	7	9	5	1	8	3	7	3	1	9	8	4	6	3	5	5	5	7	4	5	4	4	5	4	6	3	8	6	6	2	6	2
07	1	5	3	6	4	4	2	5	5	8	5	1	4	2	8	7	3	9	6	8	6	6	5	7	7	5	3	9	6	4	5	4	7	6	5	4	3	2
08	4	7	2	9	3	7	6	2	3	1	8	7	5	5	5	6	3	8	4	8	6	6	4	7	5	4	2	6	6	3	5	4	9	5	1	5	5	4
12	8	3	3	7	7	5	4	3	4	9	9	2	4	8	6	4	5	5	8	7	5	6	5	1	5	6	6	4	4	6	5	2	7	6	3	2	5	1
13	4	6	2	4	2	5	7	3	5	7	1	7	5	8	8	4	9	6	9	9	6	7	6	6	5	3	4	2	6	3	5	5	5	8	5	7	4	1
14	4	8	2	7	7	3	8	8	3	9	9	5	6	7	5	6	5	6	4	5	5	6	5	7	6	4	5	4	5	2	6	3	4	4	3	2	1	1
15	6	7	6	8	7	8	7	8	4	9	9	4	4	3	5	5	4	6	5	5	5	7	6	5	6	2	4	6	5	2	4	1	5	1	2	3	3	3
16	2	7	4	8	6	6	6	9	7	8	9	4	4	3	6	7	4	5	6	5	5	8	5	6	3	5	3	7	5	1	4	3	5	5	2	2	4	1
17	2	4	4	8	8	5	3	8	4	9	9	3	6	3	7	7	5	6	6	5	7	6	6	2	7	5	5	6	4	4	1	5	5	2	1	4	3	
18	2	4	1	7	1	4	5	5	2	5	5	6	6	7	7	4	8	6	9	5	6	8	6	7	3	5	3	6	3	9	3	8	5	4	4	4	2	
19	4	8	5	9	8	7	4	9	4	8	7	3	5	5	5	4	6	5	3	7	6	6	6	1	5	5	2	6	3	7	1	4	6	2	2	4	3	
20	3	9	2	3	6	5	8	9	4	5	8	5	7	5	7	7	6	4	6	4	8	5	5	7	5	6	4	4	4	1	5	3	3	6	6	2	1	2
21	5	4	1	1	6	6	7	8	7	9	9	5	5	6	2	5	5	6	2	8	4	4	7	6	4	4	5	3	3	5	5	3	8	7	4	3	5	2
22	4	7	6	8	5	2	7	8	3	9	8	4	7	7	9	5	2	6	5	5	5	5	6	5	3	4	3	4	4	1	5	3	6	6	1	6	4	2
23	2	6	4	6	6	5	3	8	1	7	9	1	8	5	9	7	5	8	7	6	5	6	7	5	2	5	5	4	5	3	4	6	4	4	3	4	2	3
24	2	4	5	8	3	3	5	5	4	6	7	3	8	6	5	9	6	7	7	6	7	5	9	4	5	6	4	5	5	2	3	1	6	8	4	4	1	2
25	3	9	4	8	5	5	7	7	6	7	9	6	8	4	7	5	5	8	4	6	4	3	5	3	6	3	5	5	5	2	4	2	6	6	2	1	1	4
.	.	.	.	.	.	.	.	.	.	.	.	.	.	.	.	.	.	.	.	.	.	.	.	.	.	.	.	.	.	.	.	.	.	.	.	.	.	.
91	2	4	1	3	3	8	1	4	3	5	5	2	4	4	6	6	5	8	6	9	8	6	5	7	2	7	5	3	6	5	4	5	6	7	4	9	7	5
92	2	4	1	1	3	5	4	4	4	5	3	2	5	4	9	8	3	6	4	9	6	7	5	7	5	8	8	2	6	5	7	5	5	6	3	6	7	6
94	2	2	3	5	1	2	1	3	2	4	3	3	4	4	5	8	5	6	7	7	6	8	8	5	5	6	4	5	9	4	6	6	9	7	5	5	7	6
95	1	7	2	4	1	3	2	3	4	8	4	2	4	3	6	6	3	5	8	6	5	9	7	8	7	6	9	5	7	4	5	5	5	6	4	5	6	5
96	1	4	3	5	2	4	1	3	2	8	7	2	3	4	4	6	5	5	9	5	7	6	4	6	8	3	9	7	4	6	8	5	6	5	6	6	7	
97	3	5	5	6	3	5	4	4	4	6	5	3	4	4	3	9	8	2	7	6	9	6	4	2	7	4	6	8	5	8	1	2	5	7	6	5	7	5	1
98	1	3	5	5	2	5	1	2	4	9	6	3	5	5	6	4	4	8	7	4	9	6	7	7	5	7	4	2	8	4	3	8	6	5	6	5	6	3
99	3	5	1	4	1	2	4	2	2	8	8	8	6	6	6	5	4	5	5	9	7	6	4	9	5	6	4	6	7	3	7	7	5	5	3	5	3	4
100	3	7	4	2	5	5	6	3	6	7	8	3	6	2	5	8	5	5	4	9	5	8	4	7	1	4	6	9	5	5	3	4	7	6	6	2	4	1
101	3	9	5	7	5	3	7	8	4	7	8	3	4	8	2	7	4	6	6	5	6	3	9	6	5	5	6	5	5	1	4	6	5	4	4	2	1	2
102	2	5	1	6	3	4	2	3	2	5	5	1	4	4	5	7	5	7	8	6	7	7	8	5	5	8	9	9	6	5	4	3	6	6	4	6	4	3
103	4	5	3	6	1	3	3	5	1	6	6	2	5	9	6	4	4	8	5	7	7	7	9	3	6	4	4	2	8	2	6	5	8	7	5	5	5	4
104	1	4	5	8	6	4	1	3	3	6	5	7	3	4	6	9	5	8	5	8	4	7	6	5	5	9	5	3	7	2	4	2	5	6	2	6	7	4
105	2	3	5	5	7	1	2	6	4	7	7	3	5	8	4	4	5	5	6	9	5	8	9	8	6	6	3	7	6	2	5	1	4	4	4	5	6	3
106	4	5	2	2	1	3	1	2	3	5	3	4	5	3	7	4	4	6	6	9	7	5	6	8	5	7	6	5	9	8	4	4	7	6	6	8	5	5
107	3	6	3	4	1	2	2	3	1	7	4	2	4	4	9	6	5	7	8	9	8	6	5	5	4	5	5	7	8	3	6	7	6	5	6	4	5	
108	4	3	1	4	2	3	1	3	2	4	4	3	6	6	5	9	4	8	7	6	6	7	4	6	8	8	5	6	5	2	5	5	5	5	5	7	9	7
109	6	4	2	7	5	5	4	1	5	9	6	5	7	8	4	8	4	9	7	5	6	4	4	6	6	2	3	7	8	3	5	3	5	6	3	1	5	2
110	1	4	5	6	3	2	2	6	5	4	8	3	6	7	4	4	8	6	7	9	5	6	8	3	2	7	5	1	9	6	4	5	5	7	5	5	4	3
111	1	5	5	4	5	5	4	3	3	3	5	5	4	2	4	6	6	6	6	4	2	5	6	7	7	8	9	1	4	8	7	8	6	9	7	2		
112	2	3	5	7	1	4	3	5	1	6	6	4	7	7	5	5	5	6	5	7	8	8	4	2	3	9	3	6	9	2	6	8	4	4	5	5	6	4
113	3	2	1	5	3	4	5	4	3	4	2	2	8	1	5	5	6	6	8	9	6	7	6	7	5	6	9	6	7	4	5	4	7	4	5	8	5	3

way all individuals in the sample viewed a particular issue. This should lead to the inquiry: *Are conservation issues themselves interrelated in ways suggesting higher dimensions?*

It is possible to compare arrangements (rows) between individuals in any respondent pair formed from the 113 subjects participating in the study, but doing so visually is likely to be quite tedious and impractical. For the modeling objectives of the study, what is needed is to obtain this information about differences and similarities among the positions held on conservation issues in a series of analyses that make use of these two facets of information inherent in this sorting matrix.

18.5.4 Step 4: Making Use of Information Embedded in the Array of Arrangements

It is useful to assume at the outset that some respondents will hold similar positions about many conservation issues, some will share similar views only about a limited number of the 38 issues, and some may be diametrically opposed to others with respect to their positions on many conservation issues. Related to these plausible expectations is the idea that a complete matrix of arrangements is likely to have embedded within it two major sources of covariance-type information quite useful for the process of modeling group conservation perspectives:

- One would refer to clustering among respondents that results from similarities and differences in the ways of arranging conservation statements.
- The other source of covariance also refers to clustering but, in this instance, clustering among various subsets of conservation statements.

Exactly what that second grouping type is likely to be would depend on how all of the 113 respondents in the example perceived the issues in a cluster. This is equivalent to the meanings they attributed to them. Hence, extracting information about the first source entails assessing the ways rows in the matrix of respondents' arrangements covary, while pursuing evidence for the second source involves evaluating how columns in that matrix interrelate (Table 18.2). Amedeo and Richert continue their modeling by first examining the covariance that exists among respondents arrangements (that is, the rows) of conservation statements and, then, relating it to information from the second source (that is, the columns).

18.5.5 Step 5: Similarities and Differences among Respondents' Arrangements

To access information about how individual sortings compare, correlations between arrangements of conservation statements for every two respondents in the matrix were computed. Each correlation coefficient was treated not as indicative of a causal relationship but as suggestive of the degree to which the members of a pair of respondents might covary in their sorting of the 38 conservation statements. Hence, coefficients were viewed as reflectors of standardized covariances between members of a pair of sorting arrangements. They were used to help clarify the order of the common variance inherent in this facet of the data matrix. Their appropriateness for use in this way rests on the assumption that the positions in the scale in the sorting pane—although apparently ordinal—are in fact only nine points on some more finer, at least interval, scale. The reasoning supporting this contention is that many other conservation issues could have been included for sorting. The evaluation by respondents of these additional issues with regard to correspondences to their own views could conceivably require many scale positions between the existing intervals.

The immediate purpose of these correlations was to acquire some concrete idea of the extent to which the views of any two subjects, based on what is revealed in their entire sorting of statements, correspond to one another. As the matrix containing all possible correlations is preliminary and far too large to present here, a more manageable and generalized illustration in Figure 18.2 is used for ongoing discussion.

The highlighted symbol $r_{S_1 S_6}$ in Figure 18.2 would, then, indicate the extent to which the arrangements of conservation statements for two subjects, number 1 and 6, covary. Information about similarities among 113 arrangements of the 38 conservation statements implied in these correlation coefficients is of particular interest to the modeling efforts of Amedeo and Richert. Strong similarity between two subjects, for example, would be represented by a high correlation, modest similarity by a medium-valued one, a strong difference between arrangements by a high negative correlation, and so on.

What especially matters for this study, however, is the situation in which a number of respondents, greater than two, have arrangements of statements similar to one another. That would suggest the presence of grouping and would be implicitly embedded in the correlation matrix as a cluster of respondents exhibiting a type of commonality because of similar ways in which they sorted the 38 conservation statements. There is, of course, the possibility that more than one cluster exists in a study's correlation matrix, each having its own peculiar type of arrangement commonality. Should such a possibility be present, then one *grouping* of respondents is likely to differ from another.

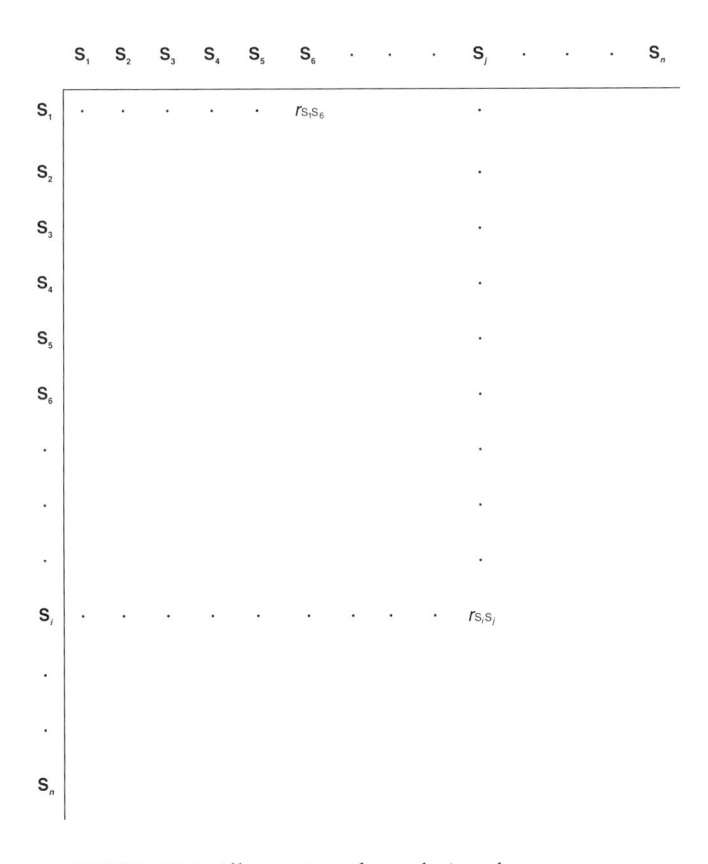

FIGURE 18.2. Illustration of correlations between sorts.

328 EXPERIENCES AND SPACES

The actual correlation matrix for the study was too large to visualize how many grouping patterns of this nature might be suggested by its coefficients, so that, to make any respondent commonality sources evident, it was factor-analyzed by the use of a principal components procedure. As shown in Table 18.3, this extracted at least three clear groupings of similarity among the 113 arrangements of conservation statements. The respondents of the sample belonging to each are listed by subject identification (see loadings on factors). The first group identified contains 36 respondents, the second 25 respondents, and the third 11 respondents. Other groups could also have been extracted from the sample by the factoring, but the belief was that such clusters would have been too small in size and too faint in the similarity that defines them to effectively discuss them here.

While it is interesting to note these respondent groupings, the more immediate question for these authors in their modeling efforts is *What is the modal or average arrangement of conservation statements characterizing the commonality exhibited by the respondents in each of these three groups?* This was the inquiry Amedeo and Richert turned to next in their ongoing process of modeling group conservation perspectives.

TABLE 18.3. Rotated Q-Mode Factor Analysis of Respondents' "Statement Arrangements"

Subject	Factor 1	Subject	Factor 2	Factor 3
89	.89152	16	.85696	
41	.86360	17	.85055	
106	.83280	70	.77150	
39	.83148	64	.74679	
120	.82337	83	.73787	
42	.82306	19	.72939	
90	.82070	48	.70849	
94	.80674	77	.69408	
125	.77897	51	.68453	
91	.77736	45	.68313	
107	.75894	74	.67651	
92	.74912	1	.67351	
113	.74447	44	.66900	
43	.74175	15	.64573	
2	.74029	23	.64072	
81	.72353	34	.63764	
121	.72019	124	.62832	
95	.71682	71	.62736	
108	.71615	14	.59417	
102	.71120	33	.58333	
40	.70270	26	.56205	
35	.70028	22	.56154	
96	.68340	54	.52448	
114	.67087	67	.52323	
117	.66921	56	.51910	
75	.64782	25		.67948
118	.63823	66		.67337
68	.63221	30		.66130
13	.61787	55		.62129
97	.60594	80		.61816
27	.58781	31		.59637
88	.58454	50		.58986
98	.56208	24		.58311
7	.55936	18		.54477
47	.52998	58		.54373
5	.52870	8		.50546

18.5.6 Step 6: Arrangements of Conservation Statements Implied in Groupings

To facilitate comprehension of the reasoning these authors employed when addressing this final question in their modeling, a preliminary example of a prototype factor is provided first in Table 18.4. The table shows, for example, how the fictitious grouping of subjects—S_3, S_7, S_{11}, S_{62}, S_{67}, S_{76}, and S_{89}—relate to the example factor in proportion to their numerical loadings on it. This means that to identify an average or modal arrangement of conservation statements implicated by the commonality among subjects constituting a grouping, differences in loadings must be taken into consideration. This is because the value of a loading reflects the relative contribution of a subject to the commonality defining the coherency of the group, and/or subjects of a particular group contribute variously to the similarity defining the distinctiveness of the group.

The actual factor results obtained (see Table 18.3) exemplify this idea that subjects loading together as a group on a particular factor share a distinctive type of commonality among themselves because of, in this case, similarity in the way they originally arranged the 38 conservation statements. The three factors in the actual results shown in Table 18.3 strongly suggest that there are at least three types of commonality present among the subjects in the sample for the study. Each contains information useful for estimating an average or modal way of sorting conservation statements for its respective group.

To see that more clearly, it is useful to momentarily refer to the fictitious information in Table 18.4 again. Subject S_3, for example, has a loading of 0.92 on that factor; when squared, the loading turns out to be 0.85. This value is typically interpreted in this manner: 85% of that subject's variance related to its sharing in defining this group's commonality is reflected by this example factor. Subject S_{62}, on the other hand, loads on this same factor to the tune of 0.76. When this is squared, only 58% of its variance from its sharing common views with others about conservation issues is reflected in this example factor. This is explained by the idea that subject S_{62} is, in many respects, like the other subjects making up the core conservation perspective distinguishing this group from other clusters, but not as strongly so as, say, subject S_3.

In general, then, this example illustrates that subjects contribute differently to the common essence of a group, and that this variation is, in each case, proportional to a subject's loading on the factor reflecting that commonality. The implication of that difference for Amedeo and Richert's modeling is that someone like subject S_3, with his or her much higher loading or approximate correlation of 0.92 with the illustration factor, then should obviously be more influential in the determination of the modal perspective implied by this factor, than, say, subject S_{89}. This sort of reasoning extends to the rest of the members of the group in the example table (Table 18.4).

In particular, of course, the focus here is on the application of this reasoning to the three *actual* factors illustrated in Table 18.3 derived for the study of the Sandhills. It is

TABLE 18.4. A Fictitious Example of a Factor

Subject	Factor 1
S_3	0.92
S_7	0.89
S_{11}	0.85
S_{62}	0.76
S_{67}	0.72
S_{76}	0.70
S_{89}	0.65

330 EXPERIENCES AND SPACES

evident from the reasoning just discussed that an estimation of the modal arrangement of conservation statements for each of these groups must, in some weighted average way, take into consideration both the individual sortings of the members in a group and the differential degrees to which these sortings contribute to the nature of their group's overall commonality.

Two items of information, then, are needed to estimate the modal sorting pattern for a group; the first is the degree of association each subject has with the factor reflecting the group's overall commonality and the second is the distinctive features of individual sorting patterns. When examining the factors derived for the study in Table 18.3 it is clear that the degree of association, as expressible in factor loadings, varies from one member of a group to another. It is also clear from the matrix in partial Table 18.2 that actual sortings for respondents, though exhibiting some similarity when in a given grouping, are not likely to be identical in the values assigned across the entire spectrum of 38 conservation statements. Hence, because these two information items interact, a *weighted average* was computed to estimate an underlying modal sorting implied by a group.

The information of the hypothetical example in Table 18.4 is again relied on here to illustrate the nature of this linear computation. Consider, for example, how the weights for this weighted average are derived using the seven example subjects in Table 18.4. In general, if r_{S_i,F_j} = loading subject i has on a factor j, then the weight for subject i is calculated as: $W_i = r_i \div (1 - r^2_i)$. For the seven subjects loading on the hypothetical factor in Table 18.4, then, the weights would then turn out to be as illustrated in Table 18.5.

It should be noticed when comparing Table 18.4 with Table 18.5 how the derived weight for a subject is greatest when the loading on the factor is greatest. This is as it should be because the higher the loading, the closer the association between what the factor reflects and the nature of the subject with respect to the issue of relevance. Since the factor is the indicator of the particular commonality characterizing what is common about the group as a whole, the subject with the largest weight reflects the meaning embedded in the commonality for the group better than any other subject having lower weights. It is clear in this example that subject 3, loading .92 on the hypothetical factor, has a calculated weight many times that of subject 89, which has the lowest loading (.65) on this factor.

The use of these weights to compute an estimate of the modal sorting pattern of conservation statements for this hypothetical example group is illustrated in Table 18.6. Notice how these seven subjects in this example, by implications of their commonality among their sortings, have in effect assigned an estimated score of 159.98 to conservation statement number 1. As is evident in Table 18.6, the computation of scores for the remaining statements continues in this way. When complete, the 38 weighted-average scores collectively reflect the *modal conservation arrangement* for this particular group. In effect, it is as if a

TABLE 18.5. Devising Weights for Computing a Weighted Average Estimate

Subject	Loading on Factor 1	Weight	Weight as a proportion of S_3
S_3	0.92	6.13	1.00
S_7	0.89	4.24	0.69
S_{11}	0.85	3.04	0.50
S_{62}	0.76	1.81	0.30
S_{67}	0.72	1.50	0.24
S_{76}	0.70	1.37	0.22
S_{89}	0.65	1.12	0.18

TABLE 18.6. Computing Weighted Conservation Statement Scores to Estimate Sorting Pattern[a] for Example Group in Table 18.5

Cons. st.	Products of weight × subject sorting scores on conservation statements[b]															Weighted conservation statement scores
	S_3		S_7		S_{11}		S_{62}		S_{67}		S_{76}		S_{89}		
	Weight	Score	Weight	Score	Weight	Score	Weight	Score	Weight	Score	Weight	Score	Weight	Score	
1	(6.13)	(9)	+ (4.24)	(8)	+ (3.04)	(9)	+ (1.81)	(8)	+ (1.50)	(7)	+ (1.37)	(7)	+ (1.12)	(8)	159.98
2															
3															
4					Ditto to estimate the weighted scores for all conservation statements										
.															
38															

[a] In general, called a "factor array."
[b] Sorting scores for these subjects are obviously fictitious for this hypothetical example.

group has sorted conservation statements based on information differentially supplied by each of its various members about some sort of shared conservation consensus.

Using the reasoning they employed in this hypothetical example, Amedeo and Richert derived the modal arrangements in that way for each of the three groups they extracted from their sample's respondents in their Sandhills research. The first three model columns in Table 18.7, for example, contain the computed weighted-average scores for all 38 statements and for each of these groups.

As such, the three columns are indicative—in absolute numerical form—of the modal arrangements for each of these respective groups. Each is reflective of the particular group's perspective on these conservation issues. However, comparing the three modal arrangements of statements—although possible—is likely to be difficult in their present form because of existing differences in internal variances in each group. What is needed for that purpose is an expression of all three arrangements using a common scaling.

To accomplish that, the weighted-average scores for the three groups were restated in the next three columns of Table 18.7 (columns 4, 5, and 6) as deviations from their respective group mean divided by their internal variance (that is, standard deviation). Amedeo and Richert, using these standardized versions of the weighted-average scores as a guide and following the same instructions used by their study's respondents, sorted the conservation statements for each group on the original panel running from a +4 to a −4 as described in the second step detailed above. Figure 18.3 shows the graphical form of the derived modal arrangements for the three groups.

A "group" in the ordinary sense is a collection of respondents. But for Amedeo and Richert's study, however, it is the group's cohesiveness that matters, and this is based on the type of commonality among the conservation positions held by its respondents on environmental issues peculiar to the Sandhills region. Hence, as is evident in Table 18.6, weighted-average scores computed for a particular group are heavily influenced by the way its individual members originally sorted statements and by the nature of the commonality prevailing among their sortings. The interaction of these two influences is taken into consideration when creating these weighted-average scores for the groups extracted in this study. In this way Amedeo and Richert jointly provide the conceptual basis for assigning the conservation statements for a particular group to the scaled sorting panel originally used by the individual subjects when they were first interviewed. Since a group's commonality, as extracted

332 EXPERIENCES AND SPACES

TABLE 18.7. Weighted Conservation Scores for the Three Groups and Their Standardized Counterparts

Cons. st.	Model 1	Model 2	Model 3	Z model 1	Z model 2	Z model 3
1	143.32	88.61	45.56	1.55081	1.52525	0.48716
2	226.51	187.6	64.56	0.7322	0.43072	0.71768
3	165.17	153.66	50.67	1.3358	0.2332	0.16312
4	246.31	259.92	70.62	0.53736	1.84542	1.10196
5	113.24	188.39	36.56	1.84681	0.44618	1.05787
6	184.47	160.05	41.67	1.14589	0.1082	0.73383
7	131.09	128.43	61.69	1.67116	0.72674	0.53568
8	185.05	243.34	57.54	1.14018	1.52109	0.27252
9	178.25	133.01	42.27	1.20709	0.63715	0.69578
10	289.08	278.38	58.22	0.11649	2.20653	0.31564
11	264.34	262.72	89.95	0.35994	1.90019	2.32772
12	133.38	104.97	58.82	1.64863	1.18566	0.35369
13	287.55	172.83	67.71	0.13155	0.1418	0.91743
14	247.50	155.93	59.64	0.52565	0.1888	0.40569
15	369.85	191.24	64.52	0.67831	0.50193	0.71514
16	463.57	216.25	70.86	1.60054	0.99116	1.11718
17	244.51	122.00	46.92	0.55508	0.85252	0.40092
18	378.10	191.26	78.25	0.75949	0.50232	1.58579
19	388.14	195.24	54.07	0.85829	0.58017	0.05248
20	556.62	182.89	71.55	2.51618	0.33859	1.16093
21	408.27	194.33	59.51	1.05637	0.56237	0.39745
22	389.53	222.46	50.97	0.87196	1.11264	0.1441
23	352.00	195.06	61.76	0.50266	0.57665	0.54012
24	367.71	194.99	45.68	0.65725	0.57528	0.47955
25	293.76	109.88	68.43	0.07044	1.08961	0.96308
26	361.85	154.04	46.78	0.59958	0.22577	0.40979
27	360.24	139.31	46.46	0.58374	0.51391	0.43009
28	285.33	168.65	50.06	0.15339	0.06003	0.20180
29	419.55	190.41	54.59	1.16737	0.48569	0.08546
30	298.48	112.58	25.22	0.02399	1.03679	1.77697
31	301.94	149.70	49.52	0.01005	0.31066	0.23604
32	305.18	111.89	27.38	0.04194	1.05029	1.63999
33	387.94	186.33	71.81	0.85632	0.40588	1.17742
34	354.39	169.24	61.57	0.52618	0.07157	0.52808
35	296.62	99.43	28.92	0.04230	1.39184	1.54234
36	425.03	88.65	32.96	1.22129	1.56359	1.28615
37	360.00	130.13	23.82	0.58138	0.69349	1.86574
38	271.03	067.29	26.12	0.29411	1.92274	1.71989

by a *Q*-mode factor analysis, is distinctive in the definition of a group itself, each group's arrangement of conservation statements in Figure 18.3 will reflect its distinctiveness.

A group's arrangement of the 38 conservation statements may, of course, be compared with those of the other two in Figure 18.3. This can readily be accomplished by combining the information in the matrix of subject scores on the 38 conservation statements—which describes the nature of the underlying conservation issue for a given numbered statement—with the information that lists some of the features about the respondents belonging to each of the three groups. If such a comparison was conducted in some detail using at least these, but other informational resources from the larger study as well, it would then be possible to comprehend some of the nuances among the group conservation perspectives implicated by the three arrangements. This, then, is the *construct* that Amedeo and Richert set out to develop in conjunction with their larger study's concern of incorporating human factors in formulating environmental policy.

Model for First Group (N = 36) Q-Factor 1

				23				
				32				
			28	31	15			
			38	30	24			
		2	11	35	26	22		
	3	8	14	25	27	19	36	
5	1	6	4	10	37	33	29	20
7	12	9	17	13	34	18	21	16
-4	-3	-2	-1	0	1	2	3	4

Model for Second Group (N = 25) Q-Factor 2

				33				
				20				
			3	13	21			
			31	34	18			
		17	27	28	15	16		
	12	30	9	6	29	19	4	
36	35	32	37	14	5	23	8	10
38	1	25	7	26	2	24	22	11
-4	-3	-2	-1	0	1	2	3	4

Model for Third Group (N = 11) Q-Factor 3

				12				
				10				
			31	8	15			
			17	29	23			
		9	26	19	7	4		
	35	6	27	22	34	25	33	
30	32	5	24	3	14	13	20	11
37	38	36	1	28	21	2	16	18
-4	-3	-2	-1	0	1	2	3	4

FIGURE 18.3. Three different perspectives on conservation issues in the Sandhills of Nebraska (distribution of conservation statement numbers).

18.6 Group Conservation Perspectives and Respondents' Preferences for Conservation Agencies

In the casual discussions conducted by Amedeo and Richert as part of their study in the Sandhills region but before formulating their overall research design for the project, it was suspected that there was a presence of pronounced group perspectives on conservation issues. Suggestions of group views not only surfaced in exchanges with others, but also were strongly evident in the mass-media coverage on environmental issues in Nebraska. Since the overall objective was to evaluate the importance of human factors for environmental policy development, the influences group perspectives might have on such things as responses to environmental changes in the region, preferences for landscape types, reactions to land-uses, attitudes toward environmental agencies, and so on, other concerns also need to be assessed.

1. The first question the researchers needed to face was how to represent group perspectives; the discussion so far has described the way they elected to do so.
2. A second question, however, dealt with how to argue for this construct's conceptual validity in the Sandhills context for which it was devised. That inquiry has not been fully confronted in the Sandhills study, but an attempt was made to address it in at least one instance.

For example, a plausible way to evaluate this construct's usefulness is to assume that a group's perspective on conservation issues constitutes a significant part of the conceptualizing utilized by its members to develop attitudes toward the nine agency types in their region charged with monitoring, regulating, and preserving environmental resources in this region. In the process of meeting the needs of their larger study, Amedeo and Richert elicited, during their extensive interviewing, some information about respondent's preferences toward such agencies in this manner:

> "If you had a great deal of money available to donate for wildlife management and habitat improvement in the Sandhills, indicate the agency listed in the table above that would be your first choice to receive your donation. Then indicate the organization you would least likely support. Please continue until each organization is ranked 1 = first choice to 9 = last choice."

Although too large to reproduce here, a matrix of the rankings by respondents of the nine agencies was produced by this question. Focusing only on the agency-preference structures expressed by respondents from these three groups discussed throughout this chapter, the question of relevance for Amedeo and Richert was as follows: *Were ranking assignments influenced by the conservation perspective underlying the group consensus to which these respondents subscribed?*

To acquire a sense of whether this was or was not the case, Amedeo and Richert factor-analyzed the initial raw data matrix of respondents' arrangements once again. This time, however, they searched by focusing on the columns of the matrix (that is, the scores of subjects on the 38 conservation statements) for indications of commonalities among the statements themselves. In all, 13 dimensions were extracted in this way. Collectively these reflected conceptual themes implicit in the conservation issues suggested by the statements themselves and the ways the statements were rated. The themes are not artifacts of this research design, but result from perspectives about conservation meanings held by respondents when they sorted the 38 conservation statements. In an effort to relate these dimensions to the distinctive conservation consensuses associated with the groups, Amedeo and Richert treated them as independent variables and assigned scores (that is, factor scores) on them to the respondents in each of the groups. In this way, it became possible to examine how well these dimensional indicators of conceptual themes originally suggested by respondent sortings could estimate respondents' preference rankings of agencies.

Taking each agency in its turn, and focusing on the respondents in one group at a time, Amedeo and Richert regressed their dimensional factor scores on (that is, using a *two-stage, least-squares, multiple regression* procedure) on the respondent rankings of the agencies. Although they could not entertain a formal hypothesis for testing because of the case nature of their sample, their conditional expectation would be consistent with the following: Since the dimensions reflect meaning about relationships among conservation issues as respondents intended that meaning through their sortings, they should exert some influence on the variance within respondent agency rankings. Table 18.8 shows the results obtained from performing these regressions.

The regression results strongly suggest that the dimensions of meaning embedded in the original sorting matrix, when qualified by focusing on group consensuses, exert considerable influence on the agency rankings executed by the respondents from each of the groups. It is likely to be the case that multiple factors influence respondents' agency preferences. But this meaning—as associated with conservation issues and as reflected by these dimensions—appears to be not only important in its influence on the variation of such preferences but also sensitive to the different commonalities distinguishing the groups from one another. Focusing specifically on the respondents in Group 1, for example, the dimensions of meaning (that is, the factors) appear to do well in accounting for the variance in the preference rankings of at least seven of the agencies, but *especially well* in accounting for the rankings of agencies f ($R^2 = 0.50$), g ($R^2 = 0.54$), and h ($R^2 = 0.46$). The actual rankings of these agencies—Nebraska Game and Parks Commission, Audubon, and Sandhills Task Force, respectively—are likely to be reflective of the group perspective underlying the consensus of Group 1.

With respect to the respondents in Group 2, it should be noted that these dimensions also do quite well in estimating the agency preference rankings of its respondents. Indeed, they account for much of the variation present in their rankings of agencies a ($R^2 = 0.81$), b ($R^2 = 0.73$), e ($R^2 = 0.62$), f ($R^2 = 0.72$), and i ($R^2 = 0.62$). These refer to the agencies Pheasants Forever, United States Fish and Wildlife Service, The Nature Conservancy, Nebraska Game and Parks Commission, and the Sandhills Task Force, respectively. Notice how the

TABLE 18.8. Dimensions Used to Estimate Respondents' Rankings of Environmental Agencies

Agency a	Agency b	Agency c	Agency d	Agency e	Agency f	Agency g	Agency h	Agency i
				Group 1 (36 subjects)				
R = .45	R = .58	R = .61	R = .58	R = .64	R = .71	R = .73	R = .68	R = .54
$R^2 = .20$	$R^2 = .33$	$R^2 = .38$	$R^2 = .33$	$R^2 = .41$	$R^2 = .50$	$R^2 = .54$	$R^2 = .46$	$R^2 = .29$
				Group 2 (25 subjects)				
R = .90	R = .85	R = .73	R = .63	R = .79	R = .85	R = .74	R = .69	R = .79
$R^2 = .81$	$R^2 = .73$	$R^2 = .53$	$R^2 = .40$	$R^2 = .62$	$R^2 = .72$	$R^2 = .56$	$R^2 = .47$	$R^2 = .62$

variations in the rankings of these agencies accounted for by these dimensions differ collectively for the two groups. This obviously reflects differences in the conservation perspectives of the two groups.

It should be noted that the rankings of Group 3 were also estimated quite well in this manner, but its small size ($n = 11$ respondents) was statistically too small to entertain its results as definitive. Hence, it was not included for consideration in Table 18.8.

18.7 Discussion

It is implausible to assume that there exist as many views about conservation issues in a region as there are individuals using its environments. A more plausible assumption is that the views or positions about such issues are shared by members in groups. In that part of their work discussed here, Amedeo and Richert maintain that knowledge of group perspectives and their influences is necessary when developing conservation policy not only because it informs policymakers about the presence of distinctive and prevalent conservation orientations, but also because it discloses influences operating in human factor issues such as:

- Responses to environmental change
- Preferences for landscape types and uses
- Attitudes toward tourists and their activities
- Beliefs about the management and use of environmental resources
- Preferences for the policies of various environmental agencies.

A problem with attempting to take group perspectives into consideration is how to represent them so that their influences on other human factor issues can be assessed. One way commonly employed in research is to develop constructs that serve as indicators. In the Amedeo and Richert study discussed here, this chapter describes how conservation perspectives might be represented through a modeling process based on applying multivariate procedures to Q-mode sortings. Individual viewpoints about conservation issues were elicited by asking respondents to sort 38 conservation statements according to the degree to which they corresponded to their own views about such issues. Respondents were assisted in doing so by nine agreement-type position placements spaced according to an assumption of normality. This structural choice directing the sorting process may, of course, be too constraining.

There are certainly alternative sorting methods that may be less structured in their position directives and in what is assumed about the ultimate shape of the prototype distribution. One example that comes to mind is to permit respondents to sort in any way they may want, thereby establishing in such a process their own relative positions to place statements on with their own underlying scaling. It is likely, however, that a different modeling procedure would, then, be required to develop group conservation perspectives. Perhaps one using a nonmetric multidimensional scaling would serve as a more plausible vehicle for searching for groupings. Actually, no one method can be recommended as best. Any procedure adapted for having respondents sort stimuli would have to be argued for compellingly and be related closely to circumstances involved in the stimuli and in the sorting. Nevertheless, 113 respondents out of the sample of 128 managed to sort conservation statements encompassing issues related to those found in the Sandhills region of Nebraska. Amedeo and Richert utilized two major sources of information to develop their construct from the array containing the arrangements produced by respondents in their sortings. One comes from its rows representing profiles of respondents and their positions about this collection of conservation issues. This facet of the array facilitated a search for clusters of similar profiles through the employment of variance-ordering properties of a Q-mode factor analysis. Three distinct groups of respondents were defined, and the arrangement of conservation statements peculiar to each group was identified with the help of factor-array procedures.

The other source of information for the construct development was in the columns or statements of this same basic array. The focus in this instance was on evaluating ways they interrelated because of how respondents construed the issues in the statements when sorting them. This facet of information provided an opportunity for Amedeo and Richert to search for resultant conceptual dimensions reflecting meaning implicated in clusters of statements. An R-mode factor analysis was employed to assess commonalities underlying column relationships, and then, once such dimensions were extracted, scores on each of them were assigned to respondents in the groups detected previously. Since each group of respondents identified was distinct in the way it thought about conservation issues, this factor-score assignment ensured that such distinctiveness qualified the meanings of dimension according to the perspective of the groups.

Amedeo and Richert illustrated one attempt to assess the validity of this construct by observing how well it estimates the preferences of respondents for the nine types of environmental agencies operating in the Sandhills. Using a *stepwise regression* procedure and treating factor scores on dimensions just described as independent variables, it appeared that their construct did quite well in estimating agency preferences. It was not possible to statistically assess the smallest of the three groups in this way because it had only 11 respondents. The validity of the constructs with respect to estimating other human factors important to these authors in the Sandhills is currently being assessed by the researchers. No reports of significance were made on the regression coefficients or multiple R^2 data when assessing the validity of this construct. This is because regression was used for its variance-ordering capabilities and, of course, no statistical hypotheses (for example, null and theory-based expectations) were offered for assessment.

The primary intention of using this study for this chapter was to provide a case study example demonstrating construct development for exploring human factor issues in conservation policy. A research design that lacks a random sample selected from a well-known population of Sandhills-type regions and one without hypotheses about these group conservation perspectives places limits on the possibility of generalizing results to that wider population. Nevertheless, the construct developed seems plausible in its narrower domain of this case study, especially since its influences on another human factor, like preferences for environmental agencies, has been demonstrated.

18.8 Acknowledgment

The research by Amedeo reported here was partially funded by the Sandhills Commission of Nebraska in 1998–1999. The contribution made by Amy Richert to the research discussed in this chapter is gratefully acknowledged.

PART VII

Planning Research
THE COMMON SENSE OF A RESEARCH PROPOSAL

This final part of the book demonstrates why it is conceptually useful and methodologically efficient, when undertaking a research project, to construct a plan or a strategy to organize and integrate the details of one's research intentions. In their research experiences, the authors have found that a clear and precise strategy outlining and interrelating the parts of a project to be absolutely essential to their investigations because it offered enormous benefits in efficiencies, focusing, and communicating with others having an interest in that research. These advantages will become abundantly evident to the reader in working through the discussion that follows in the concluding chapter.

As discussed in **Chapter 19**, a *research plan* is commonly referred to as a *research proposal* in the wider domain of social and behavioral studies. Often this has to be prepared in the context of submitting a proposal to a funding agency. The term "research proposal" is certainly suitable as all research projects start off as an intention about some idea to be explored as the research process continues. The expression *mapping* will occasionally be used interchangeably and together with the term *research proposal* in order to exemplify a proposal's usual emphases on activities of organizing, integrating, and focusing. These prominent activities, as they relate to one another, make it possible to construct an effective and useful research proposal. They collectively resemble what is literally involved in mapping itself. Like that process, the research plan not only illustrates the relative importance of each of the parts in the research strategy, but it also makes evident their overall collective implications as well. The effective research plan (or proposal)—like the effective map—may be an excellent example of a system or a gestalt, in the sense that the information it produces is often greater than the sum of the information contributed to it by its parts.

With those thoughts in mind, Chapter 19 discusses the parts or main steps involved in framing a useful research proposal, and explains the importance of communicating research outcomes and getting published.

CHAPTER 19

Mapping a Strategic Plan for Research

19.1 The Research Plan

This concluding chapter outlines the approach typically taken by an investigator in preparing a proposal to conduct research investigating an aspect of P-E-B relations. It maps out how that may be approached through a series of rational steps found over time to be quite effective for imposing conceptual and methodological coherence to the *stages of a research project* (see Table 19.1).

19.1.1 Some Issues to Consider

The steps in Table 19.1—representing as they do typical major sections of the research plan—are generic in their application, in that they are definitely *not* associated with a specific approach for conducting research. Instead they illustrate three general expectations:

1. Every research project should have a purpose describing what one would like to examine.
2. Every purpose can be related to the investigations of other researchers.
3. The execution of every purpose needs to have a way that would facilitate it.

TABLE 19.1. Steps for Preparing a Research Proposal

1. Introduction: *Aims and objectives; the broader context*
2. Purpose of the study: *Research problem specification; intent and purpose*
3. Review of relevant literature: *The research in the context of theory, method, and empirical knowledge*
4. Research design: *Research approach, methods, procedures; data sources and modes of data collection and information generation; methods of data and information analysis and modeling; information presentation and visualization, evaluation, and assessment*
5. Task responsibilities, timetable, and milestones
6. Budget and budget justification
7. Likely outcomes and contribution to knowledge; *contributions to theory, methodology, empirical knowledge*

The nature of a research proposal as described here is thus intended to imply nothing about the research approach to be employed by an investigator in examining or exploring something. It is recognized in this discussion that the choice of a useful and effective *research design* to carry out a specific investigation is often a rather complex and involved decision which, ultimately, may be dependent on many conceptual and methodological concerns (for example, see comments in the Preface to this book). Some hints at what such complexities might involve are suggested by some of the more common questions often faced by investigators. For example, consider the following:

1. Should the specifics of the environments in which human activities and experiences ordinarily occur be given explicit consideration in the investigation of human issues, or don't they matter?
2. What are some of the more *conceptual and methodological complexities* routinely faced by the social and behavioral researchers? Are any of them related to the characteristics (for example, biological, perceptual, affective, mental) of being human?
3. Under what methodological circumstances does it make sense to *test hypotheses* using *statistical-inference* reasoning? What *exactly* is known when it is ascertained that a particular research result is statistically significant?
4. How might extensive *verbal responses* from subjects be viewed and assessed for their informational content? Are verbal responses data?
5. Under what situations might *case studies* be useful in research, and what can rationally be concluded about the results they generate in research employing them?
6. What differences and implications might there be in information obtained from structured versus unstructured surveying?
7. What are the conceptual values of *constructs* in social and behavioral research? Do they predict, forecast, or explain anything? Where or what is the empirical evidence for construct existence?
8. Can a single discipline in the social and behavioral sciences provide the information necessary to conduct thorough research on a human issue?

Obviously other questions at this conceptual level can be pondered as well. For the most part, questions like these are about basic or *fundamental* issues involving ideas and methods, and reasoning about both. In that sense, their significance to research ultimately is linked to facets of *information needs in investigations.*

The relevance of these and other questions transcends peculiar epistemological concerns associated with various research design paradigms. They focus instead on features common to the construction needs of research proposals in general. They do, however, relate heavily to the persistent striving for coherence, and therefore consistency in a research plan. For that sort of an outcome, objectives like the following are pursued:

- Providing straightforward and full *description* of what is being researched while maintaining *conceptual coherence* throughout one's reasoning in one's research project.
- Continuing to *develop knowledge already accumulated* in the area being researched.
- Striving for clear and *complete disclosure* of how one is going to proceed in his or her investigation.
- Employing a *disciplined approach* in reasoning about how to deal with the issues faced in one's investigation.

With these thoughts about conceptual and methodological complexities that are likely to be met in human research and ideas about generic objectives typically pursued to meet coherency and consistency outcomes in the construction of a research proposal in mind, the discussion now turns to some potential guides or suggestions that may be found useful for the actual process of constructing a research proposal. The use of the expression "guide" is deliberate and is suggestive of a "map," a "plan," a "strategy," or a "blueprint" when referring to a *research proposal*. As it is clear from the basic issues just discussed, a research proposal should, in its major sections, *inform* the researcher and other interested parties about what it is going to be focused on, why it is going to be examined, and how the research involved will be conducted. Hence, in practice, a proposal is a plan that, in addition to its specific function of facilitating the conduct of research, is frequently made available to others too for contemplation, evaluation, and consideration. It is a proposition to investigate something that *clearly outlines and describes the strategy one intends to employ so as to thoroughly investigate a specific interest.*

19.1.2 Guides and/or Suggestions for Constructing a Research Proposal

19.1.2.1 A "Plan of Research"

The basic features associated with pursuing coherency and consistencies in the proposal are reiterated here in a more direct form to illustrate what is likely to characterize it as an effective *plan of research*, and therefore as a useful scheme for carrying out research intentions. For example, a proposal needs to have the following characteristics:

1. It must unambiguously and clearly *describe* the nature of what is going to be investigated and illustrate how that particular interest is likely to conceptually relate to a larger topical domain.
2. It must *review* and *discuss* the research conducted by others about this interest.
3. It considers how the proposed research might relate to the findings of previous research investigations.
4. It must *explain* why it is conceptually useful to conduct, in the manner being described, further research on this topic of interest.
5. It must *describe in detail* the actual steps that will be taken by the researcher to investigate this topic of interest.
6. It must provide a *list of references* that have been commented on in various ways in the proposal and which point to the published works of those who have also engaged in this or related research previously.

Frequently a research proposal is prepared for the consideration of some funding agency, research organization, interested seminar group, or evaluating committee. However, because it is a "plan" describing how to organize one's intended research goals, it is especially relevant for the researcher! In that sense, then, some research proposals are quite effective in communicating the nature of the intended research project, while others are less so, and some, unfortunately, do not communicate at all. Obviously, when constructing a proposal, it is necessary to ensure clear and unambiguous communication about what one intends to investigate and the method to be used to reach the preferred outcome, particularly from the perspective and needs of the researcher. But investigators also want those who are charged with evaluating their plan or proposal to accept it. The desired outcome preferred from external evaluators is that they have read it; find it to be "clear," "plausible," and "doable"; and, in addition, have become convinced that it serves the purpose for which the research is proposed (for example, to demonstrate that it meets the requirements of a thesis, dissertation, research project, or grant request).

It can be an enormously *excruciating experience* to engage in a major piece of research without having first constructed a proposal to guide one's efforts. Not only is it likely that a great deal of time will be wasted proceeding without a clear description of the major steps characteristically exemplified in an effective plan or proposal, but confusion and disorientation are likely to prevail throughout the research process as well. Furthermore, it is almost a certainty that both of these negative conditions will be reflected in the final research product.

19.1.2.2 A Word about an "Abstract"

Most proposals or research plans will need to include an opening *abstract*. Typically these are short—about 500 words or fewer—and usually they occur prior to the 10- to 20-page proposal itself. In many instances, abstracts are required by external evaluators. An abstract is usually a highly constrained microversion of the larger proposal. In general it can be quite useful to both the investigator and his or her interested audience.

If done well, an abstract can help external readers to acquire a quick sense of how the investigator's research project is organized. In that way, the abstract provides a basis of anticipation for the more thorough reading of the proposal itself, and thus it helps to facilitate comprehension of its ideas. The investigator also gains much from the preparation of an abstract because, in the process of constructing it, he or she finds that the abstract can function as a heuristic and/or memory activator, so to speak, for reflecting on the way the proposal's parts have been organized, for solidifying its organization in memory, and for serving as a device for focusing.

19.1.2.3 Length and Coherence of a Proposal

It may seem that the issue of the length of a proposal is mundane, yet, the potential of this feature to affect comprehension of what the proposal is attempting to communicate may be considerable. A proposal is expected to be far smaller than the completed research product (for example, a book, dissertation, thesis, or grant request) for which it was constructed to serve as a plan, guide, and/or strategy. It would seem that this recommendation would be obvious, especially since the completed proposal could not be expected to contain parts like a description of the execution of the research design, an evaluation of the analytical results that would be produced by that design, and a major discussion section. Still, it is not uncommon to find investigators inadvertently embellishing proposals with materials irrelevant and unnecessary to their central themes. An overly lengthy proposal tends to obfuscate its stream of reasoning and ideas. Even though there are no standard lengths for a proposal, there does seem to be an informal or rough "rule of thumb" about length that may be expressed as follows: Refrain from making a proposal so unnecessarily long that it strays from the central stream of reasoning crucial for the comprehension of the investigator's research intentions.

Continuing this stream of thought, a proposal should not go off on irrelevant tangents. Rather, it should focus on the intended research theme, describe what is going to be investigated, relate it to the research of others, illustrate how it is to be executed, and then should end. Coherence like this typically reduces the need for extending the proposal and increasing its length. Hence, every part or section of the proposal should relate to every other part *conceptually*, so that, as much as possible, idea coherence is evident throughout. It should always be clear, and that clarity should be directed at two sets of readers: those familiar with the research being proposed and those unfamiliar with it. If the latter comprehend what is being communicated in the proposal, it will help to increase the likelihood that the former will as well.

19.2 Elaborating on the Sections of a Research Proposal

Research proposals commonly contain a number of mutually interrelated sections of relevance to an investigation:

- An *introduction*
- Statement of the *purpose* of the proposed research investigation
- A *review of literature*
- Details of the proposed *research design*, including the proposed analytical methods
- The *task responsibilities, timetable, and milestones*
- The *budget and budget justification*
- An indication of the likely *outcomes and contributions to knowledge*.

Although extraneous material may also be present in proposals, these sections collectively and effectively reveal research intentions and guide the researcher throughout the execution of an intended investigation. The intent here is to elaborate on these sections of the research plan in order to illustrate their usual content and to exemplify their contribution to the overall conceptual orientation of the proposal.

19.2.1 An Introduction

A proposal needs to begin with an *introduction* section that lays out the conceptual background relevant for the subsequent description of the investigator's research intentions. An abrupt opening that goes directly into details of a research plan without first providing a discussion of this broader subject context within which the proposed project conceptually fits risks leaving an impression that the contemplated research topic is somehow independent of other issues in its larger domain. In the realm of social and behavioral research, that kind of distinctiveness is likely to be implausible and perhaps even impossible. If the research intent is not first related to issues in some larger conceptual domain, it will likely have much difficulty evoking the interest of readers in general and enhancing their understanding. The expression "conceptually fits" is meant to convey the idea that the topic of the respective proposal is somehow linked to ideas and issues in some broader subject context, either because knowledge about it—though critical to overall comprehension of that context—is lacking or because there are strong but potentially questionable implications regarding its nature in that domain. It is thus useful to begin the construction of a proposal with an introduction section to boost the reader's comprehension of where the intended research fits in with a larger domain of knowledge and to establish a conceptual link with the larger stream of knowledge in the broader subject context.

To enhance these objectives, it may be useful to head an introduction section of a proposal with a conceptual title so that it can serve as "natural" entrance into the broader topic covering the investigator's research intentions. To illustrate, suppose an intended research undertaking could be described by this fictitious question: *Do public spaces encourage incidents of criminal activity?* If this was an investigator's research intent, the proposal may then begin with a general discussion headed, perhaps, by a title like "Uses and Control of Public Spaces." Note how the discussion associated with this introduction relates—at least broadly—to the specific research intent of this hypothetical investigator. It is especially evident that an introductory section of this nature has much potential to conceptually lead external readers along a stream of thought to a point where the investigator of the proposal can describe his or her specific research purpose with considerable assurance that it will be immediately grasped. Obviously the issue of who uses and who controls public spaces is going to be relevant in various ways (ones that will be made clear in this introduction) to the inquiry of interest to the proposal's investigator. This is simply because his or her specific statement of interest, which is usually presented immediately after the introduction, will, in effect, continue, albeit in a more specific sense, the conceptual stream already developed in this introduction section.

Hence, through the introduction section readers and/or evaluators of this hypothetical proposal may come to learn that, although the research proposed may want to focus on a particular type of public environment, public spaces have been grouped together by others in the past to distinguish them from social and private spaces. They may also come to understand that current thinking about the relationship between public spaces and criminal activity appears to be based on the expectation that it is the "public" feature of this space type that triggers incidents of criminal activity. The introductory section may go on to discuss the extent of this expectation and to describe what it is generally meant by criminal activity, "public features," and the like in public spaces. Obviously information of this nature in the introductory section will have implications for the way the proposal's investigator will view and conduct his or her research intent.

Here is another hypothetical example that should help to exemplify the value of an introductory section in a research proposal. Imagine an investigator's research intent had expressed an interest like the following: *Will current employment in Western Europe meet its retirement funding needs by the year 2010?* An introduction section constructed to highlight where this interest might conceptually fit would probably discuss current forecasts of population declines in the countries of this area and relate them to expected category changes in the population pyramids of these countries over time. It would likely also discuss immigration policies and tax structures in each of these countries and relate them to these demographic trends. Implications these issues have on national retirement funding with regard to indices of active workers available per retired person on pension would also likely be of relevance in this introduction section.

It should be noted that when a comprehensive introductory section is provided first, the investigator's research intent almost automatically follows, by implication, from its discussion, and thus it becomes elementary for an investigator to state his or her research intent explicitly in the next section of the proposal.

An introductory section, then, should stress or give a summary-type description of the *broader context* within which the proposal's investigator is going to find his or her research focus. This context refers to this larger subject area in which the research interest is usually found. The term "larger" is relative, so that researchers will have to use their judgment about what is this broader or larger context for their intended or specific research interest. Of course, this implies that the proposal's investigator has to be thoroughly familiar with that context—but that, after all, is what is expected of someone undertaking serious research.

In any event, the introduction section needs to do the following:

1. The introduction informs interested readers and/or evaluators about basic issues prevailing in the larger subject domain within which the specific interest is found. In the process of writing this introduction, the proposal's investigator will discuss and illuminate a number of more prominent issues existing in the larger context in order to exemplify their potential connections to the specific research purpose or intention.
2. Although expected to be relevant and comprehensive, the introduction should be kept as brief as possible.

The introduction should be recognized by the proposal writer as a conceptual opportunity to effectively influence the reader's attention and reasoning about the proposed research intent. In other words, the investigator uses the issues prominent in the broader context for persuading the reader(s) to gradually focus on the inevitable plausibility of the investigator's more specific research intention. It should be noticed at this point that, though heavily implying its nature, the introduction section has not explicitly described the investigator's specific research intent. This is to be done explicitly in the next major second section of the proposal.

19.2.2 The "Purpose" of the Study: Research Problem Specification

It should be evident at this point that the opening introduction of the proposal—given the reason why it was constructed—will in effect strongly suggest or imply what the investigator's research intentions are likely to be. That in fact is partly why it is considered useful by investigators. However, it is the "purpose" section directly following the introduction that is reserved for fully and clearly revealing conceptual details of those intentions. It will specify in a detailed and clear way what the proposal writer intends to examine, evaluate, and/or assess, and spell out objectives to be pursued in that intended research.

The pragmatic title "Purpose of the Study" or "Research Problem Specification" has been used here to highlight this second section of the proposal. This is a generic heading, and although it effectively communicates in general what to expect in this second section, an investigator may find a more conceptual title to be more indicative in the particular case. The decision to use generic or topical headings throughout the construction of a proposal often rests on the nature of the expected audience. If, for example, the audience is expected to be familiar with the issues being addressed, then the decision may be to use more topical titles and subtitles. If it is thought to be unfamiliar with the issues to be addressed in the proposal, then more generic titles and subtitles may be useful to better assist the audience in tracking through the proposal. The matter may seem—on first thought—to be relatively trivial, as there are no hard and fast rules about this. Topical titles and subtitles, however, are nearly always more conceptual than generic as they focus directly on subject matter, and they do tend to assist the reader. Taking a cue from the titling discussed in the introduction section above, the topical heading "Public Spaces and Criminal Activity" might have been used instead of the more generic heading "Purpose of the Study." Of course either one will work. A topically oriented one, however, is likely to be highly suggestive. Its very presence as a clear and conceptually conspicuous subject title suggests to readers that some discussion is now going to take place in this second major section of the proposal that will focus on relating these two things (public spaces and criminal activity).

In any event, it would be helpful if the purpose section began with some general lead-in statements about the investigator's research intent. This conceptual maneuver aids in focusing readers' attention on the subject area and, if done persuasively, it leaves them anticipating a more specific description of the research purpose. After offering this general discussion, the investigator can begin the presentation of his or her specific statement of purpose in any of these illustrated ways:

"That is to say . . . "

or

"In particular, this project will examine the relationship . . . "

or

"The specific intention in this project is more focused than that; it is to investigate the influence . . . "

There are, of course, many expressions like these available for use. The point is that one is needed that facilitates moving from this general opening to statements that clearly, emphatically, and completely inform readers what the central focus is going to be!

It may seem at this point that much duplication is being produced in the proposal. The investigator's research intent, for example, was presumably already strongly hinted at in the general discussion appearing as the introduction to the proposal; indeed, it was expected that the discussion in the section was made so integrated and clear that it seems that just about anyone reading it could easily deduce what the investigator's research intent was likely to be. And now—although in a much more revealing form—it is recommended that it be presented again in the purpose section of the proposal, although of course in a more straightforward detailed form rather than as an implication. However, notice that this time the research intent is stated *explicitly* in the statement of purpose section and, in that way, it leaves nothing to inference!

Indeed, it is recommended that this explicit rendition of the research intent or purpose be expressed yet again in *different but equivalent renderings* throughout the remainder of the proposal beyond this purpose section specifically designed to contain it. This definitely leads to duplication, but it is intentional! It fosters a useful rule of thumb, so to speak, which goes something like the following: *When writing proposals, always keep readers familiar with the research purpose by restating it in different ways and at different levels (that is, general to specific) throughout.*

All statements of research "intent" or "purpose" appearing in this second major section of the proposal are expected to be distinctive, specific, and extremely clear, which is in contrast to the generalizing about it in the introduction section. This is so research aspirations will be quite clear to readers of the proposal and will communicate to them exactly what it is going to be focused on in the research, and, then, by implication what is not going to be. Thus, the specific statement in this purpose section of what will be investigated is likely to include a discussion of limits of what is to be examined in the proposed research, and hence what the investigator will *not* investigate in the research. At this point of being specific concerning the intended research, all extraneous issues are likely to be set aside for the moment so as to not confuse the intent in the overall project. Such relatively peripheral issues can, of course, be brought back into the proposal as they are needed later.

Prior to specifying and formulating a specific statement of intent in this purpose section, an investigator should attempt to assess whether the research aspired to is, in fact, achievable or doable. This amounts to thoughtfully reflecting on whether the contemplated investigation can be accomplished in a practical sense and within the context of the available or forthcoming resources. If it is concluded that such a research purpose can be carried out in the time available and under the circumstances likely to be faced, then this implies that the investigator in question has anticipated somewhat the problems, questions, and issues surrounding the topic of his or her purpose, and in particular that the researcher has some concrete or plausible ideas on how to confront and deal with them.

As a hypothetical example, suppose the research purpose proposed was stated something like this:

> "My intent is to investigate whether, as people age, their mental map of their community becomes fuzzier."

Although much elaboration is expected, ordinarily this appears to be a fairly clear purpose statement; it is interesting and potentially of wide significance. With all the usual concerns about memory functioning as people age—as in, for example, the decay of neurons, the reduced firing capacity of synapses due to changes in chemical composition, health effects on regions in the brain involved (for example, stroke), and the like—the intention seems relevant to many other issues in social and behavioral research. It is concise; it is worthy (that is, from a development of knowledge perspective) of doing; and it is certainly clear. The critical problem, however, is that it is probably not doable or achievable at this time.

There are likely to be many reasons as to why it is not, but two principal ones come to mind immediately:

1. *A mental map is a cognitive structure or a spatially oriented environmental schema.* This means that it is a hypothetical memory structure, which no one as yet knows how to replicate in some concrete way in order that its nature can be directly sensed. In other words, it is a latent construct in the sense that no one has ever observed one. People do seem to behave as if they have the capability cognitively to generate such spatial schemas; however, if such cognitive structures exist, their nature is not presently accessible.

2. *Blood flows in the brain can be traced when they are in use.* But that says little about their nature. Hence, since there is nothing currently to work with, the researcher cannot effectively examine them over time to see how they might be getting fuzzier with age. That raises another related problem of a similar nature: How does one measure the fuzziness of something that they cannot even access? Thus, though interesting, this proposed project seems to be one that is not currently doable by indirect ways.

When contemplating whether it is possible—in the practical sense—to engage in a particular research endeavor, it is useful to ask or reflect on questions similar to the following prior to committing to investigating it:

1. Can the phenomena of interest be *identified*, which is to say sensed or represented by a compelling surrogate?
2. Can *information be collected*, as from a representative sample, which will help observe that of interest?
3. Can that information be *evaluated* or *assessed* to observe trends that might be embedded in it?

If the answers are "no" to these and other necessary preliminary questions (for example, defining "fuzzier" and measuring it), then it is likely that the proposed research project is not doable or achievable. Some other research project, perhaps tangentially related to this one, has to found.

It should be evident from this discussion of a hypothetical research purpose that an investigator needs to assist and enhance the reader's comprehension of what is being proposed by engaging in much relevant elaboration of the research intent. This usually entails:

- Providing discussions of relationships likely to be investigated under the research purpose
- Describing how the intended research relates to larger bodies of knowledge
- Explaining—in a knowledge-embellishing sense—why the research being proposed has significance.

Amplification efforts like these "automatically" take the investigator into the next essential section of a proposal, namely, that which focuses on what other researchers have done on this research topic and related ones.

19.2.3 Review of the Relevant Literature

It would be quite useful at this point—both for the benefit of readers of this proposal and for the awareness of the proposal's investigator—to connect the research intentions just described in the purpose section to related research accomplished by other investigators. It is through such an assessment of the work of others that research interests in the proposal get to be viewed and thought about within a larger and, presumably, relevant subject domain of ideas within which they conceptually fit. Obviously efforts to accomplish this should be directed toward reviewing previous work that closely relates to the research issue of interest. A useful rule-of-thumb in that regard goes as follows: *The more closely related the research of others to your intended work, the higher priority that research is given for reviewing in this third section of the research proposal.* Notice how this informal "rule" neglects to recommend from which disciplines research for review is to be selected. It is highly probable in human research—particularly with regard to P-E-B issues—that investigations or relevance will come from a variety of social and behavioral areas.

Although a variety of questions are likely to be entertained in this "literature review" section of the proposal, one that is likely to have implications for all inquiries is as follows: *What research went before this proposed interest that critically relates to its issues?* The research topic described in the proposal is probably going to be examined or evaluated in ways other researchers have not pursued. But even if this is the case, it is unlikely that the proposal's investigator will be either the first or the last person to look at aspects of this topic. It may be useful, then, for the investigator to peruse past research in a *general way* at first, and then, in the process, to arrange it into groups of conceptual nearness (so to speak) to his or her specific research intent. Of course, others have also reviewed this past literature for certain periods of its development, and these reviews are often useful, as in effect they have already consolidated how this past research by a variety of authors fits together conceptually. The *conceptual development* in the relevant domain of ideas is, of course, what ultimately matters in reviewing past research work.

The strategy repeatedly found to be especially efficient and conceptually beneficial when reviewing the work of others is to focus one's reviewing efforts *directly* on how the work of others relates to the particular issue of interest as it has been described in the purpose section of the proposal. The objective in that focus would be to explore the research results they obtained in their investigations. These results, where nontrivial, should be acknowledged and summarized in the literature review section and evaluated for any implications they may have for intended research. Reviewing available literature should not only disclose what *has* been found by other researchers but also the issues that have *not* been addressed. In that way it will assist you in constructing rationalizations or justifications for entertaining the issues embedded in the purpose of one's research, a task that must be faced by every investigator proposing to undertake research.

In ongoing efforts to rationalize and/or justify why it is useful to undertake the proposed research, it may be helpful to restate the research's purpose or intent in a variety of different but equivalent ways throughout this process. Doing so tends to both:

- Highlight how the intended research will fit into the relevant literature (that is, the state of "knowledge") just reviewed
- Demonstrate why it may take on more significance as a result of that conceptual membership.

In the pragmatic sense, restating also helps to sustain a desired level of attention in the proposal's audience.

Here are some example expressions which, at certain points in the proposal, may be useful for that purpose:

"But unlike those who have spent time with the aspect just reviewed, the purpose in this investigation is to. . . . "

"Thus, it is clear from this review that this facet of the issue has not been effectively handled by other researchers. Yet, for more complete comprehension of the subject domain, it also needs to be investigated. Hence, to help fill the gap in what is known, this study will examine. . . . "

It should be especially noted in this ongoing discussion how the research purpose described in the proposal gradually gets conceptually linked to the relevant literature chosen for review. That literature has its significance because it reflects the current state of knowledge regarding the subject matter of concern in the proposed research. This linking provides still another benefit for the proposed research. On the basis of the implications and suggestions that have been coaxed out of this literature review, it now becomes possible for the proposal's investigator to begin speculating on potential outcomes or findings that may result once the proposed research is executed. This is useful information for constructing the last major section of the proposal, the contemplated research design.

19.2.4 Research Design

The heading used to title this section of the research proposal is, once again, an investigator's option. A generic one like "Research Design" may be employed, or the choice may be to use a heading more connotatively related to the subject matter slated for investigation. To illustrate, if the hypothetical example provided earlier in this chapter was the research of interest being proposed, a couple of possible headings to title this research design section might be:

Modeling Influences of Public Spaces on Criminal Activities

or

Measuring the Effects of Public Spaces on Criminal Activities.

Both function in the proposal in basically the same manner as the "Research Design" equivalent, but they carry extraneous information as well that may not be immediately inferable from the generic heading. The one using the term "modeling," for example, suggests that the research design may encompass a concern for simulation and, possibly, prediction/projection, while the other heading referring to "measuring" may exemplify a limited objective to search for quantity characteristics underlying public space effects and the magnitude relationships within these characteristics.

Although differences in headings may—on the surface—seem to be a minor matter, there is an important point embedded in that issue that was referred to in a variety of ways much earlier in this chapter. This is—in essence—the idea that the proposed research designs (that is, roughly *how* research will be carried out) will often vary according to:

- The specific topical focus selected by the researcher is consistent with what is analytically possible
- The constraints encountered because of methodological and conceptual complexities (see preface)
- The absence of critical information
- The excessive latency of construct features

among many others like the obvious one of resource availability. The recognition of this accounts for why no standard research approach has been offered or recommended in this book. Thus, when asked for an "appropriate" or "useful" approach to investigate a particular topic, the response would inevitably have to be that "it depends on the conceptual and methodological circumstances likely to be confronted" in the execution of that research.

In any event, whatever title is ultimately selected to head this research design, this section is to be treated as having the same level of importance as the proposal's introduction, purpose of the study, and review of the literature sections. In particular, its inherent reasoning should not be inconsistent with the ideas and their relationships developed within these other three sections of the proposal. Conceptual coherence among the four sections of the proposal is, in fact, the quality given considerable emphasis throughout its construction. The research design itself is intended to:

- Illustrate the steps the investigator anticipates as necessary in order to execute the intended research
- Describe how information sources needed to complete those steps will be acquired
- Discuss the features of the analysis expected to be employed to evaluate these information sources and ways they interrelate.

Obviously the methods, procedures, and approaches chosen for the study must be *closely* related to meeting the objectives—stated or implied—in the "purpose" section. Besides acting as an extremely useful plan for the investigator him- or herself, the material in the research design also affords interested readers and/or evaluators (for example, committee members, editorial boards, granting agencies, and the like) the opportunity to ascertain the overall plausibility, relevance, and appropriateness of the overall proposal. Thus, it helps them to make judgments about whether the research interests are "doable" (that is, "researchable") in their proposed form.

As is evident from the research examples discussed in the chapters in Parts III–VI, *information* is a critical ingredient for conducting any research, and it can come in a variety of forms and from various sources:

1. Some information types may be judged as relatively explicit in their current form, while others need to be explored further for their conceptual content.
2. In other instances, useful information may in fact need to be developed.
3. And in other instances surrogates, indicators, or reflectors will have to be constructed to reflect those kinds of information sets considered far too latent to reproduce directly.

Information issues like these are expected to be thoroughly addressed in the research design section.

A related concern—and one just as vital for conducting research—is the *expected connections and associations* between the things of research interest. Anticipations about these relationships and their potential variations in form—like information issues—also require considerable attention in the design section of the research proposal.

Some discussion will now be offered for additional clarification that focuses on the more salient aspects of the proposal's research design.

19.2.4.1 Information and Sampling

Discussions designed to clarify the information needs for carrying out a research project are fundamental to the research design section of the proposal. They point out in considerable detail who or what is going to be examined, over what period of time, and where they will be examined. But other issues about information are also likely to be addressed as well. For example, of considerable importance is the question *How is the information just discussed in this section going to be acquired?* Although space does not permit extensive elaboration on this issue, it is clear to many that decisions made regarding this question will often have huge implications for the research approach, which can be utilized for analyzing information, addressing measurement concerns, and generalizing potentials facilitated by the research design.

Consider, for example, the hypothetical research interest entertained earlier in this chapter. The investigator's research intention—it might be supposed—was to observe over time criminal behavior in public places with an objective of comparing that same type of behavior as it might occur in private places. The *population* of interest for this study, then, might be the collection of public places found either in the state, in a region, or even in the entire country, depending on the extent of the proposed study, among other things. If public places in the state are thought to have relatively unique properties, then the researcher may want to treat that collection of public places as a distinct population in itself. This selection may result from some additional curiosity the investigator may have about how the quality of distinctiveness influences this type of behavior along with, of course, expected impacts of public features in general. Whatever the interest, and therefore the corresponding choice of a population for collecting its information needs, the investigator is expected to thoroughly inform readers in the research design section about how the population is to be delimited and about its important characteristics like size, locations, and statistical parameters.

As previously mentioned in Chapter 6 in Part II, it is relatively rare for researchers to set out to investigate *entire* populations, particularly when interests are about human issues. Enormous size, limited resource budgets, and restricted time are the obvious main factors that effectively preclude such an undertaking. The exception here might be that rare case where the target population is, in fact, quite small and easily accessible. This then brings up the need for *sampling* from populations to secure the information needed for a proposed research project or to acquire the units from which necessary information can be extracted.

The main concern when selecting a sample from a well-known and fully understood target population is that it adequately reflects the makeup of the population in terms of content, strata, variations in distribution of occurrences, and the like. In other words, what is ultimately sought by the investigator is a representative sample achieved through a probability sampling design.

Given this fundamental objective, the obvious issues to be thoroughly discussed in the research design section include the type of sample to be selected by the investigator (for example, random, proportional, systematic), the manner in which it will be selected, whether stratification is likely to be needed to capture possible differences in the population itself, and the size of the final sample.

However, ultimate objectives aspired to in research projects may sometimes be found to be unattainable because, in the desire to pursue them, investigators find themselves faced with situations that are relatively opaque and fuzzy with respect to what is generally known about them. In other words, the existing level of knowledge about them is skimpy, undeveloped, and definitely unclear, not only with regard to the nature of relationships among things that might be of interest in research, but also with respect to what is known about those things themselves. What researchers may turn to when faced with situations like these is a search for additional knowledge about definitions, features, categories, and the like in order to better clarify them. Hence, in circumstances like these, the idea of selecting a *representative* sample is moot or somewhat out of place, especially since the information needed to delimit populations from which samples could be drawn is likely to be unavailable. Obscure situations preclude sampling from them.

Research efforts that focus on situations like these, then, are likely to emphasize *individual cases* rather than representative samples, simply because too much is yet unknown to do otherwise. In that sense, they represent efforts to get clearer understandings of the situations themselves before more complex investigations can be attempted. Nevertheless, an investigator pursuing this sort of research needs to describe in this research design section of the proposal why his or her emphasis is on cases instead of on the assessment of a representative sample from a population. In other words, the researcher will need to rationalize the use of cases as information sources. The reason this is so is that the form of information and its source are generally tied in research to the reasoning logic used to evaluate them. For example, the focus on a *case study* relative to the use of a *sampling framework* carries with it large implications about whether it is possible to generalize results obtained in one's research to some larger population. On the face of it, this should be obvious; a few cases cannot be representative of populations in general. But this does not, however, rule out the possibility of obtaining significant knowledge from the employment of case studies, especially when they are used in instances where much elementary knowledge still needs to be acquired. There are, incidentally, many circumstances of this nature in the human sciences.

But the important point here should not be lost in this discussion of what should be reported in the research design section of one's research proposal. Whatever the nature of the study employed, a focus on occurrences, incidences, or happenings—either in samples, in case studies, or any other approach—is motivated by the need for *information* to carry out research interests. To state the obvious, information or knowledge about "facts" such as properties, features, events, values, quantities, qualities, relationships, impacts, and the like is the substance upon which investigation is applied. This accounts for why there are so many issues that need to be confronted and addressed about information needs in research undertakings that range from the highly conceptual in nature to the applied. What follows are some additional remarks about *information* as a fundamental ingredient for conducting research.

19.2.4.2 Information Needed for the Proposed Research and Methods Used to Acquire It

Readers and evaluators of research proposals get informed about the subject interests of an investigator in the *statement of purpose* section of a proposal and acquire a sense of how these interests conceptually dovetail in the accumulated knowledge on this topic. For the most part, however, they cannot fully judge whether a proposed research interest is, in fact, doable until they have access to a well-spelled-out research design section of the proposal. A major part of this section is, of course, a clear discussion of how the many issues associated with information needs (that is, roughly, "data") will be handled.

Hence, aspects about information that need to be described clearly and at length in this research design section are expected to include, at least, the following:

- The sources of information to be tapped in the study
- The nature of the information types that are thought necessary to carry out the intended investigation
- The methods the investigator plans to use to collect that information.

These descriptions will reveal to readers:

- The nature of the instruments the investigator expects to employ to secure the needed information
- Their overall form as to whether they will involve direct face-to-face interviewing, telephone interviewing, mailed surveys, questionnaires, or some other method
- The internal organization of these instruments in terms of whether, for example, they are planned to be structured or nonstructured
- The nature of the inquiries, assessments, and evaluations to be made, if any.

It is quite common for investigators to propose research interests in which the information needed is likely to be derived by a systematic inference from collections of more basic data. The objective in cases like these is to construct indicators and/or reflectors for describing features of a study's domain that are relatively more conceptual than those ordinarily suggested by the basic knowledge. Procedures needed for that purpose can be directly constructed or, alternatively, use can be made of standard procedures that were designed to facilitate construction of more conceptual levels of information. The latter, for example, can be found in the methods associated with statistical analysis and modeling tools including multidimensional scaling, Q-methodology, factor-analytical methods, protocol assessments, discriminant analysis, multivariate assessments, scaling procedures in general, and varieties of regression methods.

Since the methodology and reasoning are likely to be involved in the construction of more conceptually oriented indices, clear and compelling discussions of both are needed in this research design section of the proposal to facilitate comprehension of them.

The basic data used in such derivations is often acquired from *units* like "households," "counties," "census tracts," "city blocks," "quarter sections," "acres/hectares," "states/provinces," "quadrants," "group memberships," "family member," "firms," "regions," "institutions," and the like. All units utilized for their basic data have peculiarities that may influence the way their elementary features are likely to be observed. For example, on counties in the United States, the actual data is usually an expected value or average. The assumption offered in such situations is that the variance surrounding that value is small, though this may or may not be a plausible assertion. Counties, provinces, regions, states, and so on, all come in different shapes and various sizes, and have various arrangements of their data occurrences. Obviously, a proposal's investigator needs to rationalize in the research design section of the proposal how the unit type selected for its information is to provide basic data for the construction of other more conceptual level indicators.

19.2.4.3 Assessment and Evaluation of Information for the Proposed Research

Information can be explored, examined, and judged in a number of ways, and therefore analyzed through a variety of methods designed to accomplish those appraisals. Information types, however, do vary in their basic quantity and quality characteristics, so that analytic methods selected to evaluate and relate them are normally chosen for their capabilities to handle such differences. For example, there are metric- and nonmetric-oriented analytical methods that are designed to predict, forecast, or estimate quantitative information (that is, as in parametric regression methods) or qualitative information (that is, as in multiple discriminant analysis). But, of course, this example, by the implicit assumptions it carries with it, is limited in the message it can illustrate, because information available for analysis in a research project will typically have characteristics consistent and compatible with the conceptual nature of the intended research, objectives associated with that interest, and the approach selected to explore that research interest.

Whatever the information under consideration, it should be noted that the selection of methods or procedures to process that information has, in effect, already been made—or at least strongly suggested—by the description of the research interest provided in the statement of purpose section of the proposal and referred to in subtle ways throughout the research proposal itself. Incidentally, that purpose statement has also suggested the kinds of information needed to carry out that research intent. Obviously, strong suggestions or implications like these would essentially be absent if the research intent in the proposal was originally stated vaguely or was confusing when describing what the investigator was interested in exploring. Hence, it is clear that in a proposal all sections are mutually related and that collectively they display a consistent conceptual coherence. Thus, if the investigator was consistent throughout when constructing the proposal, the analytical methods and procedures that would be needed in the research design should already be evident by implication.

Nevertheless, to avoid creating confusion and to sustain conceptual and methodological continuation of the proposal's overall plan, the methods the investigator intends to use to examine the variety of information collected need to be made quite explicit in this research design section of the proposal. Failure to do so may provoke doubt in the minds of readers and evaluators about whether the intended study will produce anything of interest to others or whether the study is even achievable (that is, "doable"). It will, in effect, appear as if the investigator has plausible ideas but no means by which their plausibility can be assessed.

Hence, in this design section, it would be useful for the investigator to address inquiries like the following when proposing analytical procedures to explore research intents:

1. What is the nature of the analysis in the study?
2. Will it be primarily descriptive, where the major focus is on classifying for the purpose of creating categories or topologies?

3. Or will the chief concern be to isolate and evaluate patterns and trends in the information?
4. Perhaps much of the analytical emphasis will be devoted to measuring things of interest and assessing the extent of associations or relationships among them.
5. It may be, instead, that the investigator aims to build process models designed to mimic the dynamics of the study situation and to simulate its observed conditions.
6. Perhaps the intent is to derive higher level conceptual dimensions from the basic information to be collected for the study areas.

The likelihood is that the planned study will entail pursuing multiple evaluative objectives—in effect, requiring a need for employing a combination of analytical procedures. Whatever the case, all of this needs to be revealed and rationalized in this research design section of the proposal. To reiterate, the procedures chosen to analyze information must be compatible with the form or forms of the available information (for example, metric, nonmetric, verbal, categorical) and aspects of it the investigator believes need to be emphasized. The latter could involve intents like illustrating the presence of simple and complex relationships, estimating significant differences among things, creating "new" dimensions, isolating clusters and/or groupings, and the like. Certainly many other emphases can be stressed as well, and even combinations of them.

Up to this point the proposal should have made it clear that the proposed research can be done well and that it can serve the knowledge interests of those who read, appraise, and evaluate it.

19.2.5 Task Responsibilities, Timetable, and Milestones

It is wise to include a section of the research proposal in which the investigator outlines to the funding agency the *responsibilities of the personnel* to be involved in the research investigation and a *timetable* for the project that sets out the *sequence of tasks* to be undertaken and that have been outlined in the earlier parts of the research design section. It is also sensible to indicate *key "milestones" and when they are planned to occur.* That might include:

- An indication of when specific aspects of the research design and analysis are to occur and what will be produced
- The establishment of websites
- When papers will be presented at conferences, reports will be produced, and publications submitted for review for intended publication
- Where primary data has been collected through a method such as a survey, what plans have been made to deposit the dataset with a recognized data archive to be available to other researchers for secondary data analysis.

19.2.6 Budget and Budget Justification

An application to a funding agency to provide financial and other support for a proposed research investigation will almost inevitably require the inclusion of a section in which the *budget* for all aspects of the project is detailed—most likely year by year. It is to be anticipated that a detailed *budget justification* will be required for the amounts asked for the various categories of budget items, including for these categories of expenditure: personnel (research staff, field staff, administrative support, programmers, and so on); equipment;

data purchase, materials, field work; maintenance and the production of reports; and travel and living expenses for field work and for giving papers at conferences.

The budget justification might need to include:

- Documentation of quotations received for items of equipment
- An explanation of why personnel need to be appointed at particular levels
- The skills needed for staff working on the project
- The specific tasks that staff working on the project will be undertaking.

It is particularly important to directly link all of the budget requests and the budget justification to the aims and objectives of the proposed investigation and to the specifics of the research design proposed for the investigation.

19.2.7 Likely Outcomes and Contributions to Knowledge

In this section of the proposal there needs to be a clear attempt to foreshadow the *likely* or *anticipated outcomes* from the research and what its contributions might potentially be to our knowledge about the topic being investigated. Thus, it might be necessary to give explicit attention to the following questions:

1. What are your expectations regarding the results from the research design and the analysis that have been outlined in the previous sections?
2. How will the investigator relate what is interpreted in the research investigation back to the body of knowledge gleaned from the literature review?
3. What will be the potential methodological contributions and/or theoretical contribution, if any, that the research will make vis-à-vis the topic being investigated?
4. Will the proposed investigation produce new insights, and what might those be?
5. Is it intended to *replicate* an existing methodology in a comparative context?
6. What will be the likely explicit empirical contributions that the investigation will make, and how might these relate to existing knowledge?

The investigator may also consider including a brief statement on the limitations of the proposed research and the approach that has been outlined, and in particular to relate that to constraints, such as time and resources available (or being sought) to undertake the work.

The proposal normally stops here! But be sure to include at the end of the proposal a reference list incorporating all the sources cited in the document and any other materials that might be required by a grant agency.

19.3 Reporting Research Findings

After an investigator has conducted the research investigations through implementation of the research design and the collection of data and its analysis, the researcher is then faced with the challenge of reporting the findings of his or her research. That in itself is an onerous and often complex task about which we do not intend to go into details here. However, there are a number of issues with which the researcher needs to be concerned, including the means of communicating research findings, different target audiences, and the challenge of publishing in academic journals.

19.3.1 Means of Communicating Research Results

There are numerous means whereby the research findings may be communicated, including through the following modes:

1. The use of text to describe, interpret, and evaluate research findings.
2. The use of tables, diagram, maps, and animations to present data collected through the implementation of the research design and the generation of information from the analysis of data.
3. Oral presentations in meetings and forums such as conferences.

19.3.2 Target Audiences

There are a variety of audiences that a researcher may need to target in communicating the results of the research investigation. That may include the following:

1. The sponsors of the research investigation, most likely a funding agency or agencies. Those will likely require the investigator to produce brief progress reports, longer regular or intermittent milestone reports, and a detailed final report. Such reports may be general or technical. Often reports will include detailed information—data and graphics—in appendices.
2. Other stakeholders—such as participant groups involved in the project and/or special interest groups—who may appreciate or require reports that are oral or specifically written in lay language.
3. Audiences from whom the investigator may wish to receive feedback, as in giving a paper at a conference or workshop. Often that will involve the preparation and presentation of a formal paper, with comments from a discussant and questions from the attendees.
4. Publication of academic journal papers and/or book chapters and/or books, the purpose of which is to feed the results of the research investigation into the national and international community of scholars in that field.
5. The oral and/or written presentation of the research findings through the press, radio (including talk-back), and electronic media. That is important so that the results of social science research enquiries are demonstrated to be relevant to society. However, dealing with the media carries both risks and benefits. It requires careful preparation and specific-form presentation of information as in the "30-second media bite" live on radio or TV. It also requires the precision writing of a report in lay language within strict word limits, such as 750 words. It is advisable for the investigator to have training to deal with the media.
6. Using the Internet through a website to post information on the research investigation to make it easily accessible to anyone.

19.3.3 Getting Published

If the investigator is intent on developing and having a career in academic research, then it is imperative for the results of research endeavors to be published in peer-reviewed journals and to get books published by an academic press. That is an onerous and often difficult task to achieve; it requires the investigator to be particularly vigilant and to conform precisely to the editorial requirements of the journal or press.

In writing a paper for a peer-reviewed journal that publishes research in P-E-B relations, it is necessary for the author(s) to ensure adherence to a particular style and format required by the journal. However, typically a paper submitted for consideration by a journal will need to incorporate sections that include the following:

- A clear statement of the research objective/question(s)
- A brief overview of the literature to which the paper seeks to contribute
- A description of the situational context of the study, the research design, the data collected, and the analytical methods used
- Discussion of research results
- Appraisal and evaluation of the research findings vis-à-vis the theoretical, modeling, and methodological issues in the field which the research investigates
- The direction for further research.

19.4 Summary

By way of a summary, here is a suggested checklist of questions that may guide the investigator in preparing the items to incorporate in a proposal for a research investigation and that are likely to need to be addressed when completing the overall proposal:

- What is the investigator planning to research?
- Why that particular topic or issue?
- Has anyone else engaged in research of that sort?
- What did they find?
- What questions remain in this domain that need further research?
- What approach will the investigator employ to pursue this research?
- Why that particular approach?
- How will the researcher investigate this topic selected for examination?
- Where will the investigator acquire information to research this topic?
- What will be done with that information to extract what it suggests or implies?
- What kinds of units will be a part of this study?
- How will those units provide the information that is needed?
- What are the preliminary expectations of this proposed research?
- What are the personnel and other resource inputs required to operationalize (and complete) the investigation, and what are the tasks and the sequence of tasks required to implement the research design?
- What is the required budget to conduct the investigation, and are the budget items justified?
- How will the outcomes of the investigation be communicated, and to what target audiences?

Notice how all of these questions relate to the same conceptual entity. This demonstrates that responses to all of them relate to responses to any of them. No response can be offered that is truly independent of what was previously said! Notice how this concluding list of relatively naive questions is actually a guide for writing the research product. If the investigator gets the proposal to answer these questions, he or she cannot miss completing the proposed research topic. In other words, the proposal has already completed the heavy thinking, so to speak, about how to investigate the topic selected for research.

19.5 Conclusion

In developing and consolidating a research career, it is most important that a researcher is an active participant in, and a contributor to, the networks of researchers in his or her field. That involves being a regular participant in professional meetings and conferences and being a contributor to the academic literature in P-E-B relations research. It is likely that over time collaborative research partnerships will develop between the researcher and other researchers in the same field and related ones. Often those may be international collaborations.

Typically the basis for developing those aspects of a successful research career will begin to be established through interaction with researchers in the department or school where the researcher undertakes his or her graduate education and training, quite likely through gaining access to the networks his or her supervisor has established. It can—and indeed we would argue must—be done. This book is, in fact, the product of that collaborative network participation to which we refer.

References

AEC/IRS. (1998). *Electoral atlas 1998*. Canberra: Australian Electoral Commission (AEC), and Parliamentary Information Service (IRS) of the Department of the Parliamentary Library.

Alker, H. R. (1969). A typology of ecological fallacies. In M. Dogan & S. Rokkan (Eds.), *Quantitative ecological analysis in the social sciences*, 69–85. Cambridge, MA: MIT Press.

Altman, I. (1975). *The environment and social behavior: Privacy, personal space, territory, and crowding*. Belmont, CA: Brooks/Cole.

Altman, I., & Low, S. M. (Eds.). (1992). *Place attachment*. New York: Plenum Press.

Amedeo, D. (1993). Emotions in person–environment–behavior episodes. In T. Garling & R. G. Golledge (Eds.), *Behavior and environment: Psychological and geographical approaches*, 83–116. New York: Elsevier.

Amedeo, D. (1999). External and internal information in versions of scenic-quality perceptions. *Journal of Architectural and Planning Research, 16*(4), 328–351.

Amedeo, D., & Dyck, J. A. (2003). Activity-enhancing arenas for designs: A case study of the classroom layout. *Journal of Architectural and Planning Research, 20*(4), 323–343.

Amedeo, D., & Golledge, R. G. (1975). *An introduction to scientific reasoning in geography*. New York: Wiley.

Amedeo, D., & Golledge, R. G. (2003). Environmental perception and behavioral geography. In G. L. Gaile & C. J. Willmott (Eds.), *Geography in America at the dawn of the 21st century*, 133–148. Oxford, UK: Oxford University Press.

Amedeo, D., Pitt, D., & Zube, E. (1989). Landscape feature classification as a determinant of perceived scenic value. *Landscape Journal: Design, Planning, and Management of the Land, 8*(1), 36–50.

Amedeo, D., & York, R. A. (1984). Grouping in affective responses to environments: Indications of emotional norm influence in person–environment relations. In D. Duerk & D. Campbell (Eds.), *EDRA 15: Proceedings*, 193–205. Washington, DC: Environmental Design Research Association.

Amedeo, D., & York, R. A. (1988). Affective states in cognitively-oriented person–environment–behavior frameworks. In D. Lawrence, R. Habe, A. Hacker, & D. Sherrod (Eds.), *EDRA 19: Proceedings,* 203–211. Oklahoma City, OK: Environmental Design Research Association.

Amedeo, D., & York, R. A. (1990). Indications of environmental schemata from thoughts about environments. *Journal of Environmental Psychology, 10*, 219–253.

Ampt, E. S., & Stimson, R. J. (1972). Mail questionnaires and the investigation of spatial behavior: The problem of respondent and non-respondent differences. *Australian Geographer, 12*, 51–54.

Andrews, F. M., & Withey, S. B. (1976). *Social indicators of well-being: Americans' perceptions of life quality*. New York: Plenum Press.

Antrobus, J. S. (Ed.). (1970). *Cognition and affect*. Boston: Little, Brown.

Arnold, M. B. (Ed.). (1970). *Feelings and emotions: The Loyola Symposium*. New York: Academic Press.
Asakura, Y., & Hato, E. (2000). *Analysis of travel behavior using positioning function of mobile communication devices* (M6 Workshop Paper). Gold Coast, Australia: IATRB 2000.
Barker, R. G. (Ed.). (1963). *The stream of behavior*. New York: Appleton-Century-Crofts.
Barker, R. G. (1968). *Ecological psychology: Concepts and methods for studying the environment of human behavior*. Stanford, CA: Stanford University Press.
Bean, C., Gow, W., & McAllister, J. (1999). *Australian election study: User's guide for the machine readable data file* (SSDA Study No. 1001, Social Science Data Archives). Canberra: Australian National University.
Bean, C., Simms, M., Bennett, S., & Wahurst, J. (1997). *The politics of retribution: The 1996 federal election*. St. Leonards, NSW, Australia: Allen & Unwin.
Beaumont, P., Gray, J., Moore, G., & Robinson, B. (1984). Orientation and wayfinding in the Tauranga Departmental Building: A focused postoccupancy evaluation. In D. Duerk & D. Campbell (Eds.), *EDRA Proceedings 15*, 77–90. Washington, DC: Environmental Design Research Association.
Bechtel, R. B. (1997). *Environment and behavior: An introduction*. Thousand Oaks, CA: Sage.
Becker, H. S. (1970). Life history and the scientific mosaic. In H. S. Becker, *Sociological work: Method and substance*, 63–73. Chicago: Aldine.
Beed, T. W., & Stimson, R. J. (Eds.). (1985). *Survey interviewing: Theory and techniques*. Sydney, Australia: Allen & Unwin.
Biderman, A. D., & Lynch, J. P. (1981). Recency bias in data in self-reported victimization. *Proceedings of the Social Statistics Section, American Statistical Association*, pp. 31–40.
Blades, M., Lippa, Y., Golledge, R. G., Jacobson, R. D., & Kitchin, R. M. (2002). The effect of spatial tasks on visually impaired peoples' wayfinding abilities. *Journal of Visual Impairment and Blindness, 96*(6), 407–419.
Block, J. (1961). *The Q-sort method in personality assessment and psychiatric research*. Springfield, IL: Thomas.
Bloom, D. (1989). Locating the learning of reading and writing in classrooms: Beyond deficit, difference, and effectiveness models. In C. Emihovich (Ed.), *Locating learning: Ethnographic perspectives on classroom research*, 87–114. Norwood, NJ: Ablex.
Blumenthal, A. L. (1977). *The process of cognition*. Englewood Cliffs, NJ: Prentice-Hall.
Bogue, D. J. (1969). *Principles of demography*. New York: Wiley.
Bonner, D. (1979). Migration in the south-east of England: An analysis of the interrelationship of housing, socio-economic status and housing demands. *Regional Studies, 13*, 345–359.
Bourdieu, P. (1984). *Distinction: A social critique of the judgement of taste*. London: Routledge & Kegan Paul.
Brabyn, L. A., & Brabyn, J. A. (1983). An evaluation of "Talking Signs" for the blind. *Human Factors, 25*(1), 49–53.
Bradburn, N. M., Sudman, S., & Associates. (1979). *Improving interviewing methods and questionnaire design: Response effects to threatening questions in survey research*. San Francisco: Jossey-Bass.
Breakwell, G. M. (1992). *Coping with threatened identities*. New York: Methuen.
Broadbent, G., Bunt, R., & Llorens, T. (Eds.). (1980). *Meaning and behavior in the built environment*. New York: Wiley.
Brown, L. A. (1968). *Diffusion dynamics: A review and revision of the quantitative theory of the spatial diffusion of innovation*. Lund, Sweden: Gleerup.
Brown, L. A., & More, E. J. (1970). The intra-urban migration process: A perspective. *Geografiska Annale, 52B*, 1–13.
Brown, P., Brown, B., & Werner, C. (1996). Privacy regulation and place attachment: Predicting attachments to a student family housing facility. *Journal of Environmental Psychology, 16*(4), 287–301.
Bryman, A. (1988). *Quantity and quality in social research*. Boston: Unwin Hyman.

Buttimer, A., & Seamon, D. (Eds.). (1980). *The human experience of place and space.* New York: St. Martin's Press.

Cadwallader, M. T. (1979) Problems in cognitive distance: Implications for cognitive mapping. *Environment and Behaviour, 11,* 559–576.

Caholun, D., Tamulonis, Y., & Verner, H. W. (1947). Interviewer bias involved in types of survey questions. *International Journal of Opinion and Attitude Research, 1,* 63–71.

Campbell, A., Converse, P. E., & Rogers, W. L. (1976). *The quality of American life: Perceptions, evaluations and satisfaction.* New York: Russell Sage Foundation.

Cannell, C. F., Fisher, G., & Bakker, T. (1965). Reporting of hospitalization in the Health Interview Survey. *Vital and Health Statistics, Series* 2(6), 1–75.

Cannell, C. F., & Fowler, F. J. (1963). *A study of the reporting of visits to doctors in the National Health Survey* (Research Report). Ann Arbor: University of Michigan Press.

Cannell, C. F., Fowler, F. J., & Marquis, K. H. (1968). The influence of interviewer and respondent psychological and behavioral variables on the reporting in household interviews. *Vital and Health Statistics, Series* 2(26), 1–65.

Cannell, C. F., Lawson, S., & Hausser, D. (1975). *A technique for evaluating interview performance.* Ann Arbor: University of Michigan Press.

Cannell, C. F., Marquis, K. H., & Laurent, A. (1977). A summary of studies in interviewing methodology, 1959–1970. *Vital and Health Statistics, Series* 2(69), 1–78.

Cannell, C. F., Miller, P., & Oksenberg, L. (1981). Research and interviewing techniques. In S. Leinhardt (Ed.), *Sociological methodology,* 389–437. San Francisco: Jossey-Bass.

Cannon, W. B. (1927). The James–Lange theory of emotion. *American Journal of Psychology, 39,* 106–124.

Canter, D. (1977). *The psychology of place.* New York: St. Martin's Press.

Cantrill, H. (1947). *Gauging public opinion.* Princeton, NJ: Princeton University Press.

Carley, M. (1981). *Social measurement and social indicators: Issues for policy and theory.* London: Allen & Unwin.

Carp, F. M. (1987). Environment and ageing. In I. Altman & D. Stokols (Eds.), *Handbook of environmental psychology* (Vol. 1, 329–360). New York: Wiley.

Carr, S. (1967). The city of the mind. In J. W. Ewald (Ed.), *Environment and man: The next fifty years,* 197–231. Bloomington: Indiana University Press.

Chapin, M. (2004, December). A challenge to conservationists. *World Watch.*

Chapman, R. L. (1977). *Roget's international thesaurus* (4th ed.). New York: Harper & Row.

Charles, C. M., Senter, G. W., & Barr, K. B. (1996). *Building classroom discipline.* White Plains, NY: Longman.

Cheetham, A. H., & Haxel, J. E. (1969). Binary (presence–absence) similarity coefficients. *Journal of Paleoentology,* 43(5), 1130–1136.

Chorley, R. J., & Haggett, P. (Eds.). (1967). *Socioeconomic models in geography.* London: University Paperbacks Methuen.

Clark, M. S., & Fiske, S. T. (Eds.). (1982). *Affect and cognition.* Hillsdale, NJ: Erlbaum.

Clark, M. S., & Isen, A. M. (1982). Towards understanding the relationship between feeling states and social behavior. In A. H. Hastorf & A. M. Isen (Eds.), *Cognitive social psychology,* 101–112. New York: Elsevier.

Clark, W. A. V. (1993). Search and choice in urban housing markets. In R. Golledge (Ed.), *Behaviour and environment: Psychological and geographical approaches,* 298–316. Amsterdam: Elsevier.

Clark, W. A. V., & Cadwallader, M. T. (1973). Locational stress and residential mobility. *Environment and Behaviour, 5,* 29–41.

Clark, W. A. V., & Hosking, P. L. (1986). *Statistical methods for geographers.* New York: Wiley.

Cohen, R. (Ed.). (1985). *The development of spatial cognition.* Hillsdale, NJ: Erlbaum.

Cohen, S. L., & Cohen, R. (1985). The role of activity in spatial cognition. In R. Cohen (Ed.), *The development of spatial cognition,* 199–223. Hillsdale, NJ: Erlbaum.

Commission for the Future. (1992, October). *Retirement villages in Australia: The future, future trends and influences to 2011.* Report to the Retirement Village Association Victoria Inc.

Committee of Inquiry. (1984, March). *Resident funded retirement villages.* Victoria, Australia: Author.

Cosgrove, D. E. (1984). *Social formation and symbolic landscape.* London: Croom Helm.

Couclelis, H., Golledge, R. G., Gale, N., & Tobler, W. (1987). Exploring the anchor-point hypothesis of spatial cognition. *Journal of Environmental Psychology, 7*(2), 99–122.

Craik, K. H. (1981). Environmental assessment and situational analysis. In D. Magnusson (Ed.), *Toward a psychology of situations: An interactional perspective,* 37–48. Hillsdale, NJ: Erlbaum.

Crandall, W., Bentzen, B. L., & Meyers, L. (1988). Talking Signs®: Remote infrared auditory signage for transit, intersections and ATMS. In *Proceedings of the California State University Northridge Conference on Technology and Disability.* Los Angeles.

Crandall, W., Bentzen, B. L., Myers, L., & Mitchell, P. (1995). *Transit accessibility improvement through Talking Signs® remote infrared signage: A demonstration and evaluation* (Easter Seals—Project ACTION No. Doc. No. 95-0050, Washington, DC, Project ACTION/NIAT). San Francisco: Smith–Kettlewell Eye Research Institute, Rehabilitation Engineering Research Center.

Cummins, R. A. (1996). The domain of life satisfaction: An attempt to order chaos. *Social Indicator Research, 38,* 303–332.

Cummins, R. A., McCabe, M. P., Romeo, Y., & Gullone, E. (1994). Comprehensive Quality of Life Scale (ComQol): Instrument development and psychometric evaluation on college staff and students. *Education Psychological Measurement, 54,* 372–382.

Cutter, S. L. (1985). *Rating places: A geographer's view on quality of life.* Washington, DC: Association of American Geographers.

Daniel, T. C., & Boster, B. S. (1976). *Measuring landscape aesthetics: The scenic beauty estimation method* (U.S. Forest Service Research Paper RM-167), 1–66.

Daniel, T. C., & Vining, J. (1983). Methodological issues in the assessment of landscape quality. In I. Altman & J. Wohlwill (Eds.), *Behavior and the natural environment,* 39–83. New York: Plenum Press.

Davis, R., & Stimson, R. (1998). Disillusionment and disenchantment at the fringe: Explaining the geography of the One Nation Party vote at the Queensland election. *People and Place, 6*(3), 69–82.

Davis, R., & Stimson, R. (2000). A GIS based model to evaluate policy impact and voter behaviour. *Regional Policy and Practice, 9*(1), 21–25.

Davitz, J. R. (1969). *The language of emotion.* New York: Academic Press.

de Vaus, D. A. (1985). *Surveys in social research, studies in society.* Sydney, Australia: Allen & Unwin.

Delmamont, S. (Ed.). (1984). *Readings on interactions in the classroom.* New York: Methuen.

Denscombe, M. (1985). *Classroom control: A sociological perspective.* London: Allen & Unwin.

Denzin, N. K. (1970). *The research act in sociology: A theoretical introduction to sociological methods.* London: Butterworths.

Denzin, N. K., & Lincoln, Y. S. (2000). *Handbook of qualitative research* (2nd ed.). Thousand Oaks, CA: Sage.

Devlin, A. S. (2001). *Mind and maze: Spatial cognition and environmental behavior.* Westport, CT: Praeger.

Devlin, A. S., & Bernstein, J. (1995). Interactive wayfinding: Use of cues by men and women. *Journal of Environmental Psychology, 15*(1), 23–38.

Diener, E., & Suh, E. (1997). Measuring quality of life: Economic, social and subjective indicators. *Social Indicators Research, 40*(1), 189–216.

Doherty, G. T. (2003). Interactive methods for activity scheduling processes. In K. G. Goulias (Ed.), *Transportation systems planning,* 7.1–7.25. Boca Raton, FL: CRC Press.

Donlan, J. (2005). Re-wilding North America. *Nature.* Retrieved from *news@nature.com*

Downs, R. M., & Stea, D. (Eds.). (1973). *Image and environment: Cognitive maps and spatial behavior.* Chicago: Aldine.

Downs, R. M., & Stea, D. (1977). *Maps in minds: Reflections on cognitive mapping.* New York: Harper & Row.
Eckersley, R. (1998). Perspectives on progress: Economic growth, quality of life and ecological sustainability. In R. Eckersley (Ed.), *Measuring progress: Is life getting better?* Collingwood, Victoria, Australia: CSIRO Publishing.
Edwards, A. L. (1955). Social desirability and Q-sorts. *Journal of Consulting Psychology, 19*(6), 462.
Eliot, J., & McFarlane-Smith, I. M. (1983). Historical background. In *An international directory of spatial tests,* 1–10. Mitchellville, MD: Nelson Publishing.
Elsner, G., & Smardon, R. C. (Technical Coordinators). (1979). Our national landscape. In *Proceedings of a Conference on Applied Technology for Analysis and Management of the Visual Resource* (USDA-Forest Service General Technical Report PSW-35). Berkeley: California Pacific Southwest Forest and Range Experiment Station.
Emihovich, C. (Ed.). (1989). *Locating learning: Ethnographic perspectives on classroom research.* Norwood, NJ: Ablex.
Evans, G. W. (1980). Environmental cognition. *Psychological Bulletin, 88,* 259–287.
Evertson, C. M., Emmer, E. T., Clements, B. S., Sanford, J. P., & Worsham, M. E. (1994). *Classroom management for elementary teachers.* Boston: Allyn & Bacon.
Fenton, M. D., & Reser, J. P. (1988). The assessment of landscape quality: An integrative approach. In J. Nasar (Ed.), *Environmental aesthetics: Theory, research, and applications.* New York: Cambridge University Press.
Fielding, A. (1992). Migration and culture. In T. Champion & A. Fielding (Eds.), *Migration processes and patterns* (Vol. 1, 201–212). London: Belhaven Press.
Filev, D., & Yager, R. R. (1998). On the issue of obtaining OWA operator weights. *Fuzzy Sets and Systems, 94,* 157–169.
Fiske, S. T. (1981). Social cognition and affect. In J. H. Harvey (Ed.), *Cognition, social behavior, and environment.* Hillsdale, NJ: Erlbaum.
Fiske, S. T., & Taylor, S. E. (1991). *Social cognition.* New York: McGraw-Hill.
Forrest, J. (1982). Social contextual and local effects in voting behaviour: The ACT Legislative Assembly elections of 1979. *Politics, 17,* 59–67.
Forrest, J. (1996). Sources of electoral support for the Australian Democrats in the House of Representatives and Senate elections of 1990 and 1993: A comparative analysis. *Australasian Journal of Political Science, 30,* 568–580.
Forrest, J., Alston, M., Medlin, C., & Amri, S. (2001). Voter behaviour in rural areas: A study of the Farrar Electoral Division in southern New South Wales at the 1998 federal election. *Australian Geographical Studies, 39,* 167–182.
Foulke, E. (1983). Spatial ability and limitations of perceptual systems. In H. L. Pick & L. P. Acredolo (Eds.), *Spatial orientation: Theory, research and application,* 125–141. New York: Plenum Press.
Fowler, H. W., Fowler, G. G., Della, F., & Thompson, D. F. (1995). *The concise Oxford dictionary of current English.* New York: Oxford University Press.
Frank, G. H. (1956). Note on the reliability of Q-sort data. *Psychological Reports, 2,* 82.
Gale, N. D. (1980). *An analysis of the distortion and fuzziness of cognitive maps by location.* Unpublished master's thesis, University of California, Santa Barbara.
Galea, L. A. M., & Kimura, D. (1993). Sex differences in route-learning. *Personality and Individual Differences, 14,* 53–65.
Gardner, I. L. (1996). Why people move to retirement villages: Home owners and non-home owners. *Australian Journal on Ageing, 13*(1), 36–40.
Garling, T., & Garvill, J. (1993). Psychological explanations of participation in everyday activities. In T. Garling & R. G. Golledge (Eds.), *Behavior and environment: Psychological and geographical approaches,* 270–297. New York: Elsevier Science.
Garling, T., & Golledge, R. G. (Eds.). (1993). *Behavior and environment: Psychological and geographical approaches.* New York: Elsevier Science.

Gauthier, D. A., & Wiken, E. (1998). The Great Plains of North America. *Parks, 8*(3), 9–20.
Geertz, H. (1959). The vocabulary of emotion: A study of Javanese socialization processes. *Psychiatry: Journal for the Study of Interpersonal Processes, 22*, 225–237.
Geschwing, N. (1980). Neurological knowledge and complex behaviors. *Journal of Cognitive Science, 4*, 185–193.
Gill, T. M., & Feinstein, A. R. (1994). A critical appraisal of the quality-of-life measurements. *Journal of the American Medical Association, 272*(8), 92–101.
Gilligan, S. G., & Bower, G. H. (1984). Cognitive consequences of emotional arousal. In C. E. Izard, J. Kagan, & R. B. Zajonc (Eds.), *Emotions, cognition, and behavior*, 568–569. New York: Cambridge University Press.
Giuliani, M. V. (1991). Towards an analysis of mental representations of attachment to the home. *Journal of Architectural and Planning Research, 8*(2), 133–146.
Giuliani, M. V., & Feldman, R. (1993). Place attachment in a developmental and cultural context. *Journal of Environmental Psychology, 13*(3), 267–274.
Glass, G., Cohen, L., Smith, M., & Filby, N. (1982). *School class size: Research and policy.* Beverly Hills, CA: Sage.
Godelier, M. (Ed.). (1982). *Les sciences de l'Homme et de la Société en France* [Social sciences in France]. Paris: Le Documentation Francais.
Golant, S. M. (1989). The residential moves, housing locations and travel behaviour of older people: Enquiries by geographers. *Urban Geography, 10*, 100–108.
Golant, S. M., Rowles, G. D., & Meyer, J. W. (1988). Ageing and the aged. In G. I. Gaile & C. J. Willmont (Eds.), *Geography in America*, 451–466. Columbus, OH: Merrill.
Golbeck, S. L. (1985). Spatial cognition as a function of environmental characteristics. In R. Cohen (Ed.), *The development of spatial cognition*, 225–255. Hillsdale, NJ: Erlbaum.
Golledge, R. G. (1974). *On determining cognitive configurations of a city: Vol. 1. Problem statement, experimental design and preliminary findings* (Final Report, NSF Grant #GS-37969). Columbus: Ohio State University.
Golledge, R. G. (1976). Methods and methodological issues in environmental cognition research. In G. T. Moore & R. G. Golledge (Eds.), *Environmental knowing*, 300–313. Stroudsburg, PA: Dowden, Hutchinson & Ross.
Golledge, R. G. (1977). Multidimensional analysis in the study of environmental behavior and environmental design. In I. Altman & J. Wohlwill (Eds.), *Human behavior and environment: Advances in theory and research* (Vol. 2, 1–42). New York: Plenum Press.
Golledge, R. G. (Ed.). (1999). *Wayfinding behavior: Cognitive mapping and other spatial processes.* Baltimore: John Hopkins University Press.
Golledge, R. G. (2004). Disability, disadvantage, and discrimination: An overview with special emphasis on blindness in the USA. In A. Bailly & L. Gibson (Eds.), *Applied geography: A world perspective*, 213–232. Dordrecht, The Netherlands: Kluwer Academic.
Golledge, R. G., Briggs, R., & Demko, D. (1969). The configuration of distances in intra-urban space. *Proceedings of the Association of American Geographers, 1*, 60–65.
Golledge, R. G., Dougherty, V., & Bell, S. (1995). Acquiring spatial knowledge: Survey versus route-based knowledge in unfamiliar environments. *Annals of the Association of American Geographers, 85*(1), 134–158.
Golledge, R. G., Gale, N., Pellegrino, J. W., & Doherty, S. (1992). Spatial knowledge acquisition by children: Route learning and relational distances. *Annals of the Association of American Geographers, 82*(2), 223–244.
Golledge, R. G., Jacobson, R. D., Kitchin, R., & Blades, M. (2000). Cognitive maps, spatial abilities, and human wayfinding. *Geographical Review of Japan, Series B: The English Journal of the Association of Japanese Geographers, 73*(2), 93–104.
Golledge, R. G., & Rayner, J. N. (Eds.). (1982). *Proximity and preference: Problems in the multidimensional analysis of large data sets.* Minneapolis: University of Minnesota Press.
Golledge, R. G., Richardson, G. D., Rayner, J. N., & Parnicky, J. J. (1983). Procedures for defining and analyzing cognitive maps of the mildly and moderately mentally retarded. In H. L. Pick & L.

P. Acredolo (Eds.), *Spatial orientation: Theory, research, and application,* 79–104. New York: Plenum Press.

Golledge, R. G., & Rushton, G. (1972). *Multidimensional scaling: Review and geographical applications* (Technical Paper No. 10). Washington, DC: AAG Commission on College Geography.

Golledge, R. G., & Rushton, G. (Eds.). (1976). *Spatial choice and spatial behavior.* Columbus: Ohio State University Press.

Golledge, R. G., & Stimson, R. (1987). *Analytical Behavioral Geography.* London: Croom Helm.

Golledge, R. G., & Stimson, R. J. (1997). *Spatial behavior: A geographic perspective.* New York: Guilford Press.

Goshen, C. (1967). A systematic classification of the phenomenology of emotions. *Psychiatric Quarterly, 41*(3), 483–495.

Green, O. H. (1972). Emotions and beliefs. *Studies in the Philosophy of Mind: American Philosophical Quarterly Monograph Series, 6,* 24–40.

Griffith, D. A. (1989). Distance calculations and errors in geographic databases. In M. Goodchild & S. Gopal (Eds.), *Accuracy of spatial databases,* 81–90. New York: Taylor & Francis.

Groves, R. M. (1987). Research on survey data quality. *Public Opinion Quarterly, 51,* s156–s172.

Groves, R. M., & Kahn, R. L. (1979). *Surveys by telephone: A national comparison with personal interviews.* New York: Academic Press.

Gump, P. V. (1987). School and classroom environments. In D. Stokols & I. Altman (Eds.), *Handbook of environmental psychology* (Vol. 1). New York: Wiley.

Guptill, S. C., & Morrison, J. L. (Eds.). (1995). *Elements of spatial data quality.* Oxford, UK: Elsevier Science.

Hägerstrand, T. (1952). *The propagation of innovation waves.* Lund, Sweden: Gleerup.

Hägerstrand, T. (1953). *Innovation diffusion as a spatial process.* Chicago: University of Chicago Press.

Hägerstrand, T. (1970). What about people in regional science? *Papers of the Regional Science Association, 24,* 7–21.

Haining, R. P. (2003). *Spatial data analysis: Theory and practice.* Cambridge, UK: Cambridge University Press.

Hakim, C. (1982). *Secondary data analysis in social sciences: A guide to data sources and methods with examples.* London: Allen & Unwin.

Halfacre, K., & Boyle, P. J. (1993). The challenge facing migration research: The case for biological approaches. *Progress in Human Geography, 32*(2), 167–182.

Hamil, J., Dufow, S. D., & Fortin, P. (1993). *Case study methods* (Qualitative Research Methods Series No. 32, A Sage University Paper). Newbury Park, CA: Sage.

Hanson, S., & Hanson, P. (1993). The geography of everyday life. In T. Garling & R. G. Golledge (Eds.), *Behavior and environment: Psychological and geographical approaches,* 249–269. New York: Elsevier Science.

Harvey, D. (1969). *Explanation in geography.* London: Arnold.

Hay, R. (1998). Sense of place in developmental context. *Journal of Environmental Psychology, 18,* 5–29.

Heady, B. W., & Wearing, A. (1992). *Understanding happiness: A theory of subjective well-being.* Melbourne, Australia: Longman Cheshire.

Heft, H. (1981). An examination of constructivist and Gibsonian approaches to environmental psychology. *Population and Environment, 4,* 227–245.

Heft, H. (2001). *Ecological psychology in context: James Gibson, Roger Barker, and the legacy of William James' radical empiricism.* Mahwah, NJ: Erlbaum.

Henkel, R. E. (1976). *Tests of significance.* Beverly Hills, CA: Sage.

Henrie, R., Aron, R., Nelson, B., & Poole, D. (1997). Gender-related knowledge variations within geography. *Sex Roles, 36,* 605–623.

Hillier, B., & Hanson, J. (1984). *The social logic of space.* New York: Cambridge University Press.

Hirtle, S. C., & Jonides, J. (1985). Evidence of hierarchies in cognitive maps. *Memory and Cognition, 13*(3), 208–217.

Huff, J. O. (1986). Geographic regularities in residential search behaviour. *Annuals Association of American Geographers, 76*, 167–182.

Huff, J. O., & Clarke, W. A. V. (1978). Cumulative stress and cumulative inertia: A behavioural model of the decision to move. *Environment and Planning A, 10*, 1101–1119.

Hull, I. V., & Stewart, W. P. (1992). Validity of photo-based scenic beauty judgments. *Journal of Environmental Psychology, 12*, 101–114.

Hunter-Zaworski, K. M., & Hron, M. (1993). *Improving bus accessibility systems for persons with sensory and cognitive impairments* (Final Report No. DOT-T-94-04). Washington, DC: Federal Transit Administration.

Hyman, H. H., with Cobb, W. J., Feldman, J. J., Hart, C. W., & Stember, C. H. (1954). *Interviewing in social research*. Chicago: University of Chicago Press.

Ittelson, W. H. (1954). Perception: A transactional approach. In W. H. Ittelson & H. Cantril (Eds.), *Perception: A transactional approach*. Garden City, NY: Doubleday.

Ittelson, W. H. (1973a). Environmental perception and contemporary perception theory. In W. H. Ittelson (Ed.), *Environment and cognition*, 1–19. New York: Seminar Press.

Ittelson, W. H. (Ed.). (1973b). *Environment and behavior*. New York: Seminar Press.

Ittelson, W. H. (Ed.). (1973c). *Environment and cognition*. New York: Seminar Press.

Ittelson, W. H., Proshansky, H. M., Rivilin, L. G., & Winkel, G. H. (1974). *An introduction to environmental psychology*. New York: Holt Rinehart & Winston.

Jacob, P. (1989). *Epistémologie: l'Ag de la Science (Epistemology: The age of science)*. Paris: Odile Jacob.

Johnson, S. C. (1967). Hierarchical clustering schemes. *Psychometrika, 32*, 241–254.

Johnston, R. R., Gregory, D., Pratt, G., & Watts, M. (2000). *The dictionary of human geography* (4th ed.). Oxford, UK: Blackwell.

Jones, R., McAllister, I., & Gow, D. (1996). *Australian election study* (Computer file, SSDA Study No. 943, Social Science Data Archives). Canberra: Australian National University.

Jorgensen, B., & Stedman, R. (2001). Sense of place as an attitude: Lakeshore owners attitudes toward their properties. *Journal of Environmental Psychology, 21*, 233–248.

Jorgensen, D. L. (1990). *Participant observation: A methodology for human studies* (Applied Social Research Methods Series, Vol. 15). Newbury Park, CA: Sage.

Kahana, E. (1982). A congruence model of person–environment interactions. In M. P. Lawton, P. G. Windely, & M. P. Byarts (Eds.), *Ageing and the environment: Theoretical approaches*, 97–112. New York: Springer.

Kalton, G. (1983). *Introduction to survey sampling*. Newbury Park, CA: Sage.

Kalton, G., & Kasprzyk, D. (1986). The treatment of missing data. *Survey Methodology, 12*, 1–12.

Kaplan, R., & Kaplan, S. (1989). *The experience of nature: A psychological perspective*. New York: Cambridge University Press.

Kaplan, S. (2000). Human nature and environmentally responsible behavior. *Journal of Social Issues, 56*(3), 491–508.

Kaplan, S., & Kaplan, R. (1982). *Cognition and environment: Functioning in an uncertain world*. New York: Praeger.

Kemper, T. D. (1978). Toward a sociology of emotions: Some problems and solutions. *American Sociologist, 13*, 30–41.

King, J., & Marans, R. W. (1979). *The physical environment and the learning process: A survey of recent research*. Ann Arbor: Survey Research Center and College of Architecture and Planning, University of Michigan.

King, L. J. (1969). *Statistical analysis in geography*. Englewood Cliffs, NJ: Prentice-Hall.

Kirk, J., & Miller, M. L. (1986). *Reliability and validity in qualitative research* (Qualitative Research Series No. 1, A Sage University Paper). Newbury Park, CA: Sage.

Kish, L. (1965). *Survey sampling*. New York: Wiley.

Kitchin, R. (1994). *CMAP (Cognitive Mapping Analysis Package): Users handbook*. Swansea: University of Wales.

Kleinginna, P. R., Jr., & Kleinginna, A. M. (1981). A categorized list of emotional definitions, with suggestions for a consensual definition. *Motivation and Emotion, 5*, 345–379.

Krueger, R. A. (1988). *Focus groups: A practical guide for applied research.* Newbury Park, CA: Sage.

Kruskal, J. B., & Wish, M. (1978). *Multidimensional scaling.* Beverly Hills, CA: Sage.

Kruskal, J. B., Young, F. W., & Seery, J. B. (1976). *How to use KYST-2, a very flexible program to do multidimensional scaling and unfolding.* Unpublished paper. Murray Hills, NJ: AT&T Bell Laboratories.

Kupiers, B. J. (1978). Modeling spatial knowledge. *Cognitive Science, 2,* 129–153.

Lane, R. E. (1993). Does money buy happiness? *Public Interest, 24,* 58.

Lavrakas, P. J. (1987). *Telephone survey methods: Sampling, selection, and supervision* (Applied Social Research Methods Series, Vol. 7). Newbury Park, CA: Sage.

Lazarus, R. S., Averill, J. R., & Opton, E. M. (1970). Toward a cognitive theory of emotion. In M. B. Arnold (Ed.), *Feelings and emotions: The Loyola Symposium,* 67–76. New York: Academic Press.

Lee, M. S., Sabetiashraf, R., Doherty, S. T., Rindt, C. R., & McNally, M. G. (2000). *Conducting an interactive survey of household weekly activities via the Internet: Preliminary results from a pilot study* (M6 Workshop Paper). Gold Coast, Australia: IATBR 2000.

Leff, H. L. (1978). *Experience, environment, and human potentials.* New York: Oxford University Press.

Legge, V. (1984). Attitude to living in a retirement village. *Australian Journal on Ageing, 3*(1), 3–7.

Legge, V. (1986). Ethnically segregated retirement accommodation: An overview of the migrant aged and a report of research in two ethnically specific villages. *Australian Journal on Ageing, 5*(4), 18–23.

Legge, V. (1987). Aged women from non-English speaking backgrounds. *Australian Journal on Ageing, 6*(2), 16–21.

Lewin, K. (1936). *Principles of topological psychology* (F. Heider & G. M. Heider, Trans.). New York: McGraw-Hill.

Lewin, K. (1951). *Field theory in social sciences; Selected theoretical papers* (E. Cartwright, Ed.). New York: Harper & Brothers.

Lewin, K. (1969). *Principles of topological psychology* (F. Heider & G. M. Heider, Trans.). New York: McGraw-Hill.

Lewis, G. J. (1982). *Human migration.* London: Croom Helm.

Litton, R. B. (1968). The assessment of scenery as a natural resource. *Scottish Geographical Magazine, 84*(3), 219–238.

Lomborg, B. (2001). *The skeptical environmentalist: Measuring the real state of the world.* New York: Cambridge University Press.

Longino, C. F. (1992). The forest and the trees: Micro-level considerations in the study of geographic mobility in old age. In A. Rogers (Ed.), *Elderly migration and population redistribution: A comparative study,* 23–24. London: Belhaven Press.

Loomis, J. M., Lippa, Y., Klatzky, R. L., & Golledge, R. G. (2002). Spatial updating of locations specified by 3-D sound and spatial language. *Journal of Experimental Psychology: Learning, Memory, and Cognition, 28*(2), 335–345.

Loomis, L., Source, P., & Tyler, P. R. (1989). A lifestyle analysis of healthy retirees and their interest in moving to a retirement village. In L. A. Partalan (Ed.), *The retirement community movement: Contemporary issues,* 19–35. New York: Haworth Press.

Lynch, K. (1960). *The image of the city.* Cambridge, MA: MIT Press.

Lyons, W. (1980). *Emotion.* London: Cambridge University Press.

Maclean, M. S., Jr., Danbury, T., & Talbott, A. D. (1975). *Analysis of Q-Sort data* (Worked Example Series, No. 1, Paper #52242). Iowa City: Iowa Center for Communication Study, School of Journalism, University of Iowa.

Magnusson, D. (Ed.). (1981). *Toward a psychology of situations: An interactive perspective.* Hillsdale, NJ: Erlbaum.

Mandler, G. (1975). *Mind and emotion.* New York: Wiley.

Mandler, G. (1985). *Cognitive psychology: An essay in cognitive science.* Hillsdale, NJ: Erlbaum.

Mandler, G. (2002). *Consciousness recovered: Psychological functions and origins of conscious thought.* Philadelphia: Benjamins.

Mandler, J. M. (1984). *Stories, scripts, and scenes: Aspects of schema theory.* Hillsdale, NJ: Erlbaum.

Manicaros, M. A., & Stimson, R. J. (1999). *Living in a retirement village: Attitudes, choices and outcomes.* Brisbane: University of Queensland Press, for the Australian Housing and Urban Research Institute.

Manne, R. (Ed.). (1998). *Two nations: The causes and effects of the rise of the one nation party in Australia.* Melbourne, Australia: Bookman Press.

Marans, R. W. (2003). Understanding environmental quality through quality of life studies: The 2001 DAS and its use of subjective and objective indicators. *Landscape and Urban Planning, 65*(1), 73–83.

Marans, R. W., Feldt, A. G., Pastalan, L. A., Hunt, M. E., & Vakalo, K. L. (Eds.). (1983). *Housing for a maturing population.* Washington, DC: Urban Land Institute.

Marans, R. W., Hunt, M. E., & Vakalo, K. L. (1984). Retirement communities. In I. Altman, L. Powell, & J. F. Wohlwill (Eds.), *Elderly people and the environment.* New York: Plenum Press.

Marans, R. W., & Rodgers, W. (1975). Toward an understanding of community satisfaction. In A. Hawley & V. Rock (Eds.), *Metropolitan America in contemporary perspective.* New York: Halsted Press.

Marston, J. R. (2002). *Towards an accessible city: Empirical measurement and modeling of access to urban opportunities for those with vision impairments using remote infrared audible signage.* Unpublished PhD thesis, University of California, Santa Barbara. Available at *www.geog.ucsb.edu/~marstonj/Dissertation_of_James_R._Marston.pdf.*

Marston, J. R., & Golledge, R. G. (1998). Improving transit access for the blind and vision impaired. *Intellimotion, 7*(2), 4, 5, 11.

Mathiowetz, N. A., & Cannell, C. (1980). Coding interviewer behavior as a method of evaluating performance. In *Proceedings of the Survey Research Methods Section, American Statistical Association, 525–528.* Ann Arbor: University of Michigan.

McCrea, R., Stimson, R., & Western, J. (2005). Testing a moderated model of satisfaction with urban living using data for Brisbane–South East Queensland, Australia. *Social Indicators Research, 72,* 121–151.

McDonald, J. (1986). Retirement villages: Segregated communities. *Australian Journal on Ageing, 5*(2), 40–46.

McKeown, B., & Thomas, D. (1988). *Q methodology* (Quantitative Applications Series: The Social Sciences No. 66). Beverly Hills, CA: Sage.

McNamara, T. P. (1986). Mental representations of spatial relations. *Cognitive Psychology, 18,* 87–121.

Mendes, J. F. G., &. Motizuki, W. S. (2001). Urban quality of life evaluation scenarios: The case of Sao Carlos in Brazil. *CTBUH Review, 1*(2), 1–11.

Mercer, C. (1994). Assessing liveability: From statistical indicators to policy benchmarks. In C. Mercer (Ed.), *Urban and regional quality of life indicators,* 3–12. Brisbane, Australia: Institute for Cultural Policy, Griffith University.

Merriam-Webster, Inc. (Ed.). (1986). *Webster's ninth new collegiate dictionary.* Springfield, MA: Author.

Michelson, W. (1979). *Environmental choice, human behaviour, and residential satisfaction.* New York: Oxford University Press.

Milgram, S., & Jodelet, D. (1976). Psychological maps of Paris. In H. M. Proshansky, W. H. Ittelson, & L. G. Rivlin (Eds.), *Environmental psychology: People and their physical settings* (2nd ed., 103–124). New York: Rinehart & Winston.

Miller, G. A. (1969). A psychological method to investigate verbal concepts. *Journal of Mathematical Psychology, 6,* 169–191.

Montello, D. R. (1988) Classroom seating location and its effect on course achievement, participation, and attitudes. *Journal of Environmental Psychology, 8*(2), 149–157.

Montello, D. R. (1993, September). Scale and multiple psychologies of space. In A. U. Frank & I. Compari (Eds.), *Spatial information theory: A theoretical basis for GIS.* Proceedings, European Conference, COSIT, Marciana Marina, Elba Island, Italy.

Montello, D. R. (1998). A new framework for understanding the acquisition of spatial knowledge in large-scale environments. In M. J. Egenhofer & R. G. Golledge (Eds.), *Spatial and temporal reasoning in geographic information systems*, 143–154. New York: Oxford University Press.

Montello, D. R., & Golledge, R. G. (1999). *Scale and detail in the cognition of geographic information.* Report of a Specialist Meeting held under the auspices of the Varenius Project, Santa Barbara, California, May 14–16, 1998.

Montello, D. R., Lovelace, K. L., Golledge, R. G., & Self, C. M. (1999). Sex-related differences and similarities in geographic and environmental spatial abilities. *Annals of the Association of American Geographers, 89*(3), 515–534.

Montello, D. R., & Pick, H. L. (1993). Integrating knowledge of vertically aligned large-scale spaces. *Environment and Behavior, 25*(4), 457–484.

Moore, D., & Glynn, T. (1984). Variation in question rate as a function of position in the classroom. *Educational Psychiatry, 4*, 232–248.

Moore, G. T. (1976). Theory and research on the development of environmental knowing. In G. T. Moore & R. G. Golledge (Eds.), *Environmental knowing*, 138–165. Stroudsburg, PA: Hutchinson & Ross.

Moore, G. T. (1979). Knowing about environmental knowing: The current state of theory and research on environmental cognition. *Environment and Behavior, 11*, 33–70.

Moore, G. T. (1986). Effects of the spatial definition of behavior settings on children's behavior: A quasi-experimental field study. *Journal of Environmental Psychology, 6*(3), 205–231.

Moore, G. T. (1987). Environment and behavior research in North America: History, developments, and unresolved issues. In D. Stokols & I. Altman (Eds.), *Handbook of environmental psychology*, 1329–1410. New York: Wiley.

Moore, G. T., & Golledge, R. G. (Eds.). (1976). *Environmental knowing: Theories, research, and methods.* Stroudsburg, PA: Dowden, Hutchinson & Ross.

Moos, R. H. (1973, August). Conceptualizations of human environments. *American Psychologist*, pp. 652–665.

Morrill, R. L. (1965). The Negro ghetto: Problems and alternatives. *Geographical Review, 55*(3), 1–23.

Morrison, D. (1969). On interpretation in discriminant analysis. *Journal of Marketing Research, 6*, 156–163.

Morrison, D., & Henkel, R. E. (1970). *The significance test controversy.* Chicago: Aldine.

Moser, C., & Kalton, G., (1971). *Survey methods in social investigation.* London: Heineman Educational Books.

Mower, O. H. (1953). Q-technique: Description, history, critique. In O. H. Mower (Ed.), *Psychotherapy: Theory and research.* New York: Ronald Press.

Nasar, J. L. (Ed.). (1988). *Environmental aesthetics: Theory, research, and application.* New York: Cambridge University Press.

NCC. (2000). *Ecoregional planning in the Northern Great Plains Steppe.* Arlington, VA: Northern Great Plains Steppe Ecoregional Planning Team, The Nature Conservancy.

Neisser, U. (1976). *Cognition and reality: Principles and implications of cognitive psychology.* San Francisco: Freeman.

Neter, J., & Waksberg, J. (1964). A study of response errors in expenditures data from household interview. *Journal of the American Statistical Association, 59*, 18–55.

Newcombe, N., Bandura, M., & Taylor, D. (1983). Sex differences in spatial ability and spatial activities. *Sex Roles, 9*(3), 377–386.

Nijkamp, P., Rietveld, P., & Voogd, H. (1990). *Multicriteria evaluation in physical planning.* Amsterdam: Elsevier Science.

Nisbett, R., & Ross, L. (1980). *Human inference: Strategies and shortcomings of social judgment.* Englewood Cliffs, NJ: Prentice-Hall.

Norman, D. A. (1980). Twelve issues for cognitive science. *Journal of Cognitive Science, 4*, 1–32.

Northern Plains Conservation Network. (2004). *Ocean of grass: A conservation assessment for the Northern Great Plains.* Retrieved from *worldwildlife.org/wildplaces/ngp/pubs/ocean_of_grass.cfm.*

Oakes, M. (1986). *Statistical inference: A commentary for the social and behavioral sciences*. New York: Wiley.

Oliver, N., Holloway, F., & Carson, J. (1995). Deconstructing quality of life. *Journal of Mental Health, 4*, 1–4.

Openshaw, S., & Taylor, P. J. (1979). A million or so correlation coefficients: Three experiments on the modifiable areal unit problem. In R. J. Bennett, N. J. Thrift, & N. Wrigley (Eds.), *Statistical applications in the spatial sciences*. London: Pion.

Orne, M. T. (1962). On the social psychology of the psychological experiment: With particular reference to demand characteristics and their implications. *American Psychologist, 17*, 776–783.

Page, M. (1981). Demand compliance in laboratory experiments. In J. T. Tedeschi (Ed.), *Impression management theory and social psychological research*, 57–82. New York: Academic Press.

Parmlee, P. A., & Lawton, M. P. (1990). The design of special environments for the aged. In J. E. Birren & K. W. Schaie (Eds.), *Handbook of the psychology of ageing* (3rd ed., 464–488). New York: Wiley.

Parsons, R., & Tassinary, L. G. (2002). Environmental psychophysiology. In R. B. Bechtel & A. Churchman (Eds.), *Handbook of environmental psychology*, 172. New York: Wiley.

Passini, A. P. (1992). *Wayfinding: People, signs, and architecture*. New York: McGraw-Hill.

Patsfall, M. R., Feimer, N. R., Buhyoff, G. J., & Wellman, J. D. (1984). The prediction of scenic beauty from landscape content and composition. *Journal of Environmental Psychology, 4*, 7–26.

Patton, M. Q. (1990). *Qualitative evaluation and research methods* (2nd ed.). Newbury Park, CA: Sage.

Payne, S. L. (1951). *The art of asking questions*. Princeton, NJ: Princeton University Press.

Peponis, J., & Wineman, J. (2002). Spatial structure of environment and behavior. In R. B. Bechtel & A. Churchman (Eds.), *Handbook of environmental psychology*, 271–287. New York: Wiley.

Peters, R. S. (1970). The education of the emotions. In M. G. Arnold (Ed.), *Feelings and emotions: The Loyola Symposium*. New York: Academic Press.

Pick, H. L., Jr., & Acredolo, L. P. (Eds.). (1983). *Spatial orientation: Theory, research, and application*. New York: Plenum Press.

Pitt, D. G., & Zube, E. H. (1979). The Q-sort method: Use in landscape assessment, research, and landscape planning. In G. Elsner & R. C. Smardon (Technical Coordinators), *Our national landscape: Proceedings of a Conference on Applied Technology for Analysis and Management of the Visual Resource*, 227–234 (USDA-Forest Service General Technical Report PSW-35). Berkeley, CA: Pacific Southwest Forest and Range Experiment Station.

Plutchik, R. (1965). What is an emotion? *Journal of Psychology, 61*, 295–303.

Popper, D. E., & Popper, F. J. (1987). The great plains from dust to dust: A daring proposal for dealing with an inevitable disaster. *Planning*, pp. 12–18.

Porteous, D. J. (1996). *Environmental aesthetics: Ideas, politics and planning*. New York: Routledge.

Pratt, J. (2000). *Piggybanking on existing surveys: A methodology for obtaining new perspectives on changing travel behavior*. Paper delivered at *IATRB 2000*, 9th International Association of Travel Behaviour Research Conference, Gold Coast, Australia.

Proshansky, H. M. (1976, April). Environmental psychology and the real world. *American Psychologist, 31*(4), 303–310.

Proshansky, H. M., Fabian, A. K., & Kaminoff, R. (1983). Place identity: Physical world socialization of the self. *Journal of Environmental Psychology, 3*(1), 57–83.

Rapoport, A. (1982). *The meaning of the built environment*. Beverly Hills, CA: Sage.

Rapoport, A. (1990). *History and precedent in environmental design*. New York: Plenum Press.

Rapoport, A. (1994). The need for (what) knowledge. In A. Seidel (Ed.), *EDRA 25, Banking on Design*, 10–15. San Antonio, TX: Environmental Design Research Association.

Regnier, V. (1987). Programming congregate housing: The preferences of upper-income elderly. In V. Regnier & J. Pynoos (Eds.), *Housing and the aged: Design directions and policy considerations*, 207–226. New York: Elsevier.

Relph, E. (1976). *Place and placelessness*. London: Pion.

Rice, S. A. (1929). Contagious bias in the interview: A methodological note. *American Journal of Sociology, 35*, 420–425.
Richardson, T., & Wolf, J. (2001). Data structures, sampling and survey issues. In D. Hensher (Ed.), *Travel behavior research: The leading edge,* 267–278. Oxford, UK: Pergamon.
Rideout, M. (1988). Scenic beauty issues in public policy making. In J. Nasar (Ed.), *Environmental aesthetics: Theory, research, and applications,* 434–448. New York: Cambridge University Press.
Ritchey, P. (1976). Explanations of migration. *Annual Review of Sociology, 2,* 363–404.
Robinson, W. S. (1950). Ecological correlations and the behavior of individuals. *American Sociological Review, 15,* 351–357.
Rogerson, R. J., Findlay, A. M., & Morris, A. S. (1989). Indicators of quality of life: Some methodological issues. *Environment and Planning A, 21*(12), 1655–1666.
Rojas, M. N. (2004). *Well-being and the complexity of poverty: A subjective well-being approach.* (Research Paper of UNU-WIDER, World Institute for Development Economics Research, 2004-2029.
Rosenthal, R. (1966). *Experimenter effects in behavioral research.* New York: Appleton.
Rosenthal, R., & Rosnow, R. L. (Eds.). (1969). *Artifact in behavioral research.* New York: Academic Press.
Roskos-Ewoldsen, B., McNamara, T. P., Shelton, A. L., & Carr, W. (1998). Mental representations of large and small spatial layouts are orientation dependent. *Journal of Experimental Psychology: Learning, Memory, and Cognition, 24*(1), 215–226.
Rowland, D. (1996). Migration of the aged. In P. Newton & M. Bell (Eds.), *Population shift: Mobility and change in Australia,* 348–363. Canberra: Australian Government Publishing Service.
Rumelhart, D. E., & Ortony, A. (1977). The representation of knowledge in memory. In R. C. Anderson, R. J. Sorio, & W. E. Montague (Eds.), *Schooling and the acquisition of knowledge,* 99–135. Hillsdale, NJ: Erlbaum.
Russell, J. S. (1994). Can design schools survive the '90's? In A. Seidel (Ed.), *EDRA 25, Banking on Design,* 15–17. San Antonio, TX: Environmental Design Research Association.
Sadalla, E. K., & Montello, D. (1989). Remembering changes in direction. *Environment and Behavior, 21,* 346–363.
Salvatore, N., & Muñuz Sastre, M. T. (2001). Appraisal of life: "Area" versus "dimension" conceptualisations. *Social Indicator Research, 53,* 229–255.
Sampson, F. B., & Knopf, F. L. (1996). *Prairie conservation: Preserving North America's most endangered ecosystem.* Washington, DC: Island Press.
Sancar, F. H. (1985). Toward theory generation in landscape aesthetics. *Landscape Journal, 4,* 116–124.
Sanoff, H. (1994). *School design.* New York: Van Nostrand Reinhold.
Saup, W. (1986). Lack of autonomy in old age homes: A stress and coping study. *Journal of Housing for the Elderly, 4,* 21–36.
Schacter, S., & Singer, J. (1962). Cognitive, social and physiological determinants of emotional state. *Psychological Review, 69,* 379–399.
Schacter, S., & Wheeler, L. (1962). Epinephrine, chlorpromazine, and amusement. *Journal of Abnormal and Social Psychology, 65,* 118–121.
Schmitz, S. (1997). Gender-related strategies in environmental development: Effects of anxiety on wayfinding in and representation of a three-dimensional maze. *Journal of Environmental Psychology, 17*(3), 215–228.
Schram, S. H. C. (1992). Testing economic theories of voter behaviour using microdata. *Applied Economics, 24*(4), 419–430.
Schuman, H., & Converse, J. (1971). The effects of black and white interviewers on black responses in 1968. *Public Opinion Quarterly, 35,* 44–68.
Schwartz, S., & Pollishuke, M. (1991). *Creating the child-centred classroom.* Katonah, NY: R. C. Owen.
Scott, M. A., & Albany, E. (1997). *Design issues in housing and assisted living for the elderly: The expertise gap.* Vancouver, BC, Canada: Gerontology Research Centre, Simon Fraser University.

Seidel, A. (Ed.). (1994). *EDRA 25, Banking on Design*. San Antonio, TX: Environmental Design Research Association.
Self, C. M., & Golledge, R. G. (1994). Sex-related differences in spatial ability: What every geography educator should know. *Journal of Geography, 93*(5), 234–243.
Self, C. M., & Golledge, R. G. (2000). Sex, gender, and cognitive mapping. In R. Ritchin & S. Freundschuh (Eds.), *Cognitive mapping: Past, present, and future* (pp. 197–220). London: Routledge.
Self, C. M., Golledge, R. G., Montello, D. R., & Lovelace, K. L. (1997). *Generational differences in the sex-typing of spatial activities* (Technical Report No. NSF Grant No. SBR9318643). Santa Barbara: University of California.
Shaefer, E. L., & Richards, T. A. (1976). A comparison of viewer reactions to outdoor scenes and photographs of those scenes. In D. Canter & T. Lee (Eds.), *Psychology and the built environment*, 71–79. Kent, UK: Architecture Press.
Sheskin, I. M. (1985). *Survey research for geographers*. Washington, DC: Association of American Geographers.
Short, J. (1978). Residential mobility. *Progress in Human Geography, 2*, 419–447.
Shott, S. (1979). Emotion and social life: A symbolic interactionist analysis. *American Journal of Sociology, 84*, 1317–1334.
Shumaker, S. A., & Taylor, R. B. (1983). Toward a clarification of people–place relationships: A model of attachment to place. In N. R. Feimer & E. S. Geller (Eds.), *Environmental psychology: Directions and perspectives*, 251–291. New York: Praeger.
Shyy, T.-K., Stimson, R. J., & Murray, A. T. (2003). An Internet GIS and spatial model to benchmark local government socio-economic performance. *Australasian Journal of Regional Studies, 9*(1), 31–47.
Siegel, A. W., & White, S. H. (1975). The development of spatial representations of large-scale environments. In H. Reese (Ed.), *Advances in child development and behavior* (Vol. 10, 10–55). New York: Academic Press.
Siegel, S. (1956). *Nonparametric statistics*. New York: McGraw-Hill.
Silverman, I., & Eals, M. (1992). Sex differences in spatial ability: Evolutionary theory and data. In J. H. Barkow, L. Cosmides, & J. Tooby (Eds.), *The adapted mind: Evolutionary psychology and the generation of culture*, 533–549. New York: Oxford University Press.
Simon, M. A. (1967). Motivational and emotional controls of cognition. *Psychological Review, 74*, 29–39.
Singleton, J., Martyn, P., & Ward, I. (1998). Did the 1998 federal election see a blue-collar revolt against Labor?: A Queensland case study. *Australian Journal of Political Science, 33*(1), 117–130.
Smith, L. M., & Keith, P. (1984). Kensington School: Unique physical features. In S. Delemont (Ed.), *Readings on interaction in the classroom*, 58–80. New York: Methuen.
Smith, P. N. (2000–2001). Numeric ordered weighted averaging operators: Possibilities for environmental project evaluation. *Journal of Environmental Systems, 28*(3), 175–191.
Smith, T. R., Pellegrino, J. W., & Golledge, R. G. (1982). Computational process modelling of spatial cognition and behavior. *Geographical Analysis, 14*(4), 305–325.
Sommer, R., & Olsen, H. (1980). The soft classroom. *Environment and Behavior, 12*(1), 3–16.
Spencer, C., Blades, M., & Morsley, K. (1989). *The child in the physical environment: The development of spatial knowledge and cognition*. New York: Wiley.
Stevens, S. S. (1957). On the psychophysical law. *Psychological Review, 6*, 153–181.
Stewart, T. R., Middleton, P., Downton, M., & Ely, D. (1984). Judgments of photographs vs. field observations in studies of perception and judgment of the visual environment. *Journal of Environmental Psychology, 4*, 283–302.
Stimson, R. J. (Ed.). (2002). *The retirement village industry in Australia: Evolution, prospects and challenges*. Brisbane: University of Queensland Press, for the Centre for Research into Sustainable Urban and Regional Futures.
Stimson, R. J., Chhetri, P., Akbar, D., & Western, J. (2006, September). Deriving spatial metropolitan wide patterns of quality of life dimensions from survey data: The case of the Brisbane–South

East Queensland region. In *Proceedings of the European Regional Science Association Conference*, Volos, Greece.

Stimson, R. J., Chhetri, P., & Shyy, T.-K. (2006, May). *Explaining patterns of support for political parties at the 2004 federal election.* Paper presented at the ARC Research Network in Spatially Integrated Social Science, 2nd National Conference, Melbourne, Australia.

Stimson, R. J., & McCrea, R. (2004). A push–pull framework for modelling the relocation of retirees to a retirement village: the Australian experience. *Environment and Planning A, 34,* 1451–1470.

Stimson, R. J., McCrea, R., & Shyy, T.-K. (2006). Spatially disaggregated modeling of voting outcomes and socio-economic characteristics at the 2001 Australian federal election. *Geographical Research, 44*(1), 242–254.

Stimson, R. J., Roberts, B., Taylor, S., Clark, L., & Larnach, A. (1997). *Monitoring South-East Queensland: Evaluating the performance of Brisbane and the South East Queensland regional economy.* Melbourne: Australian Housing and Urban Research Institute.

Stogdill, R. M. (Ed.). (1970). *The process of model-building in the behavioral sciences.* Columbus: Ohio State University Press.

Stokols, D. (1978). Environmental psychology. *Annual Review of Psychology, 29,* 253–295.

Strongman, K. T. (1973). *The psychology of emotion.* New York: Wiley.

Strongman, K. T. (1987). *The psychology of emotion* (3rd ed.). Chichester, UK: Wiley.

Sudman, S., & Bradburn, N. M. (1974). *Response effects in surveys: A review and synthesis.* Chicago: Aldine.

Sudman, S., Bradburn, N. M., Blair, E., & Stocking, C. (1977). Modest expectations: The effects of interviewers' prior expectations on response. *Sociological Methods and Research, 6,* 177–182.

Tabachnick, B. G., & Fidell, L. S. (2001). *Using multivariate statistics* (4th ed.). New York: Allyn & Bacon.

Taylor, S. (1979). Personal dispositions and human spatial behaviour. *Economic Geography, 55,* 184–195.

Thorndyke, P. W. (1984). Applications of schema theory in cognitive research. In J. R. Anderson & S. M. Kosslyn (Eds.), *Tutorials in learning and memory,* 167–191. New York: Freeman.

Thorpe, N., Law, M., & Nelson, J. (2000). *Raising transport and travel awareness through feedback from an electronic self-completion travel diary.* Paper presented at *IATRB 2000,* 9th International Association of Travel Behaviour Research Conference, Gold Coast, Australia.

Tibbetts, P. (1972). The transactional theory of human knowledge and action. *Man–Environment Systems, 2*(1), 37–59.

Tibbetts, P. (1976). Epistemology, perceptual theory, and the built environment. *Man–Environment Systems, 6,* 91–98.

Tobler, W. R. (1965). Computation of the corresponding of geographical patterns. *Papers of the Regional Science Association, 15,* 131–139.

Tobler, W. R. (1968). Geographic area and map projections. In B. J. L. Berry & D. F. Marble (Eds.), *Spatial analysis: A reader in statistical geography,* 78–90. Englewood Cliffs, NJ: Prentice-Hall.

Tobler, W. R. (1976). The geometry of mental maps. In R. G. Golledge & G. Rushton (Eds.), *Spatial choice and spatial behavior,* 69–82. Columbus: Ohio State University Press.

Tobler, W. R. (1978). Comparison of plane forms. *Geographical Analysis, 10*(2), 154–162.

Trauer, T., & Mackinnon, A. (2001). The role of importance ratings in quality of life measurement. *Quality of Life Research, 10,* 579–585.

Tuan, Y.-F. (1974). *Topophilia: A study of environmental perception, attitudes, and values.* Englewood Cliffs, NJ: Prentice Hall.

U.S. Department of the Interior. (1975). *Visual resource inventory and evaluation* (Bureau of Land Management Manual 6310). Washington, DC: U.S. Government Printing Office.

Van Praag, B. M. S., Frijters, P., & Ferrer-i-Carbonell, A. (2003). The anatomy of subjective well-being. *Journal of Economic Behaviour and Organisation, 51,* 29–49.

Veenhoven, R. (2000). The four qualities of life: Ordering concepts and measures of the good quality. *Journal of Happiness Studies, 1,* 1–39.

Veregin, H., & Hargitai, P. (1995). An evaluation matrix for geographical data quality. In S. C. Guptill & J. L. Morrison (Eds.), *Elements of spatial data quality.* Oxford, UK: Elsevier.

Vernon, M. C. (1955). The functions of schematic in perceiving. *Psychological Review, 62*, 180–191.

Vining, J., & Ebreo, A. (2002). Emerging theoretical and methodological perspectives on conservation behavior. In R. Bechtal & A. Churchman (Eds.), *Handbook of environmental psychology*. New York: Wiley.

Waller, D., Loomis, J. M., Golledge, R. G., & Beall, A. C. (2002). Place learning in humans: The role of distance and direction information. *Spatial Cognition and Computation, 2*(4), 333–354.

Walmsley, D. J. (1997). Voting patterns in recent Australian House of Representatives elections. In R. J. Johnston (Ed.), *People, places and votes: Essays on electoral geography of Australia and New Zealand*, 121–132. Armidale, Australia: University of New England.

Wapner, S., Cohen, S., & Kaplan, B. (1976). *Experiencing the environment*. New York: Plenum Press.

Wapner, S., Kaplan, B., & Cohen, S. S. (1973). An organismic–developmental perspective for understanding transactions of men and environments. *Environment and Behavior, 5*, 255–289.

Warner, K. P. (1983). Demographics and housing. In *Housing for a mature population*, 2–23. Washington, DC: Urban Land Institute.

Warner, S. L. (1965). Randomized response: A survey technique for eliminating error answer bias. *Journal of the American Statistical Association, 65*, 63–69.

Warnes, A. M. (1992). Age-related variation and temporal change in elderly migration. In A. Rogers (Ed.), *Elderly migration and population redistribution: A comparative study*, 35–55. London: Belhaven Press.

Warwick, D. P., & Lininger, C. A. (1975). *The sample survey: Theory and practice*. New York: McGraw-Hill.

Wicker, A.W. (1979). *An introduction to ecological psychology*. Monterey, CA: Brooks/Cole.

Willard, L. D. (1980). On preserving nature's aesthetic features. *Environmental Ethics, 2*, 293–310.

Wineman, J., Hillier, B., & Peponis, J. (1998). Letting buildings speak: The contributions of space syntax. *DRN Design Research News: Environmental Design Research Association, 29*(3), 4–5.

Wishart, D. (1969). *Fortran II programs for 8 methods of cluster analysis*. Lawrence: State Geological Survey, University of Kansas.

Wolcott, J. (1990). *Writing up qualitative research* (Qualitative Research Methods Series No. 2). Newbury, CA: Sage.

Wolf, J., Guensler, R., Washington, S., & Frank, L. (2000). *The use of electronic travel diaries and vehicle instrumentation packages in the year 2000 Atlanta Regional Household Travel Survey: Final test results and implementation plans*. Paper presented at IATRB 2000, 9th International Association of Travel Behaviour Research Conference, Gold Coast, Australia.

Yager, R. R. (1988). On ordered weighted averaging aggregation operators in multicriteria decision making. *IEEE Transactions on Systems, Man and Cybernetics, 18*(1), 183–190.

Yager, R. R. (2004). OWA aggregation over a continuous interval argument with applications to decision making. *IEEE Transactions on Systems, Man and Cybernetics—Part B: Cybernetic, 34*(5), 1951–1963.

Yin, R. K. (1990). *Case study research: Design and method* (Applied Social Research Methods Series 5). Newbury, CA: Sage.

Zonabend, F. (1992). The monograph in European ethnology. *Current Sociology, 4*, 49–54.

Zube, E. H. (1973). Scenery as a natural resource: Implications of public policy and problems of definition, description and evaluation. *Landscape Architecture, 63*, 370–375.

Zube, E. H. (1976). Perception of landscape and land use. In I. Altman & J. F. Wohlwill (Eds.), *Human behavior and environment: Advances in theory and research 1*, 90. New York: Plenum Press.

Zube, E. H., Pitt, D. G., & Anderson, T. W. (1975). Perception and prediction of scenic resource values in the Northeast. In E. H. Zube, J. G. Fabos, & R. O. Brush (Eds.), *Landscape assessment*, 151–167. Stroudsburg, PA: Dowden, Hutchinson, & Ross.

Index

Absolute location, 74
Abstract (concept), 19, 40, 71, 73, 117, 146
Abstraction, 49, 55, 57, 152, 155, 257
Accessibility, 157, 227, 246, 251, 286, 320, 322
Accessible environments, 159
Activities and experiences, 1–3, 9–17, 20, 24, 25, 28, 30, 36, 44–47, 52, 53, 57, 61, 79, 93, 96, 110, 118, 121, 193, 321, 342
Aesthetic experiences, 226, 256, 279
Aesthetic experiences in environments, 1, 226, 252
Affect and cognitive processes, 245
Affective, 1, 48, 227, 229, 237, 246, 315, 316, 321, 342
   affective experiences in environments, 1, 5, 78, 226–233, 236, 237, 243, 244, 246, 251, 277
   norm influences in affective experiences, 205, 236, 239, 243, 244, 247–250
   responses, 8, 109, 229, 233, 234, 237–240, 243–246, 250
Aggregation techniques, 281, 286, 289, 291
Analysis, 36, 38, 42, 45, 46, 49–53, 63, 65, 67, 81–84, 88, 126, 130, 136–139, 143, 168, 180, 195, 199, 226, 291
   activity, 1, 15, 29–35, 56, 67–69, 73, 84, 85, 88–91, 93, 94, 99, 105, 113, 124–128, 135, 137, 138, 142, 143, 164, 169, 171, 174, 180, 193, 208, 212, 229, 254, 271, 278, 279, 281, 285, 286, 288, 294, 297, 301, 310, 313, 341, 352, 355–359
   aggregated, 177
   bidimensional, 164
   of congruence, 310
   confirmatory, 97
   content, 111
   correlation, 35, 36, 188

   disaggregated, 177
   discriminant/discriminate, 125, 127, 136–141, 191, 195–197, 355, 356
   exploratory, 54
   factor, 136, 173, 180–182, 187, 236, 238–242, 264–266, 272–274, 277, 278, 309, 332, 337
   latent structure, 313
   multidimensional scaling, 211, 212, 222, 311, 313, 316
   multiple regression, 50, 125, 127, 133, 142, 335
   path, 173, 180, 181, 184
   Q-mode, 265, 328
   regression, 127
   secondary, 43, 174, 282
   univariate, 191, 195
Analysis of variance (ANOVA), 41, 163, 309, 311, 312
Areas, 9, 10, 43, 50, 51, 63, 66, 73–78, 84, 86, 88, 91, 93, 99, 103–105, 123, 130, 136, 147, 148, 159, 168, 192, 217–221, 231, 253, 258, 276, 285, 288, 290, 292–294, 297, 300, 315, 323, 350, 357
Attributes, 5, 24, 31, 32, 34, 37, 42, 43, 49–54, 60, 61, 65, 66, 88, 110, 177, 179, 180, 182, 184, 186, 189, 247, 248, 254, 277, 316
Auditory, 69, 70, 157, 158, 165, 169
Augmented
   reality, 118, 121
   systems, 121
Automated data computer systems, 105, 106

Barrier-free
   environment, 146
   movement, 159
Barriers, 146, 157, 159

379

Bias, 2, 5, 42–44, 64, 71, 72, 85, 87, 89, 92, 104–115, 151, 172, 191, 199, 301, 304, 314
Blind and visually impaired, 156, 165
Blind traveler, 158, 165, 169
Blind/blindness, 146, 156–158, 161, 163, 165, 167–169, 192, 221
  adventitious, 163
  congenital, 163
  legally, 161
Boundaries, 36, 63, 73, 75, 76, 78, 129, 297

Case study, 55, 63, 82–86, 143, 172, 204, 223, 283, 322, 337, 354
Census, 32–37, 42, 49, 51, 64, 66, 75, 101, 103–105, 129–131, 143, 174, 292, 297, 319, 355
Chance, 96, 117, 287
Choice, 3, 4, 8, 30, 36, 43, 49, 58, 76, 78, 79, 81, 87, 89, 102, 106, 108, 111, 115, 118, 123, 143, 147, 150, 155, 156, 162–165, 171–179, 190, 197, 199, 202, 203, 213, 218–221, 228, 261, 262, 265, 267, 288, 297, 306, 324, 334, 336, 342, 351, 353
City image, 119
Classification, 6, 22, 42, 44, 50, 51, 63, 66, 67, 72, 73, 75, 78, 130, 137, 199
Classroom spatial layout, 172, 202, 205–214, 218–224
Cognitive
  act/activity, 229, 256, 257
  appraisals, 233, 234, 244
  architecture, 123
  commitments, 316
  conceptualizations, 244
  configurations, 282, 299–302, 311
  difficulties, 107, 108
  discrimination, 260
  distance, 306
  environments, 301
  experiences, 286
  framework, 227, 244, 245, 251
  functions, 227, 251
  images, 118, 301
  integrations, 4, 17, 23, 245
  levels, 228
  map, 119, 123, 225, 245, 246, 282, 299, 300, 302, 307, 313, 317
  mapping, 23, 101, 306, 317
  perspective, 227, 256
  processes, 10, 48, 177, 228–230, 245, 255, 257
  processing, 8, 10, 11, 14, 22, 107, 108, 229, 230, 233, 244, 245, 246, 248, 251, 256
  psychologists, 14, 245
  representations, 282, 299–303, 312, 313
  scenarios, 269
  schemata, 255
  skills, 108
  spaces, 299
  structures, 22, 23, 229, 257, 282, 299, 301, 303, 349
  states, 244
  system, 123
  theory, 24, 83
  ties, 316
  view, 301
Complexities, 1, 3, 48, 52, 53, 109, 112, 202, 205, 227, 317, 322, 342
  conceptual, 1, 172, 202, 223, 228, 342, 343, 352
  methodological, 1, 172, 202, 223, 342, 343, 352
Compulsory registrations, 89
Computational process model (CPM), 58, 64, 116, 123, 124
Concepts, 33, 40, 42, 43, 46–51
Conducting experiments, 117, 118, 121
Configuration, 152, 153, 157, 204–222, 282, 299, 301–313
  cognitive, 282, 299–302, 311
  environmental, 24
  objective, 152, 155, 309–313
  spatial, 1, 2, 5, 10, 13, 15, 20, 76, 101, 172, 205–209, 224
  subjective, 152, 153, 155, 308, 311–313
Configurational knowledge, 144, 151
Congruence, 176, 184, 310, 311
Construct, 2, 3, 31, 116, 202, 203, 231, 253–257, 260, 281–283, 297, 314–321, 332–337, 342, 349, 352
Control group, 120, 121, 126, 144, 148–156, 161–165, 169, 305–313
Controlled settings, 64, 116, 117
Corridor, 121, 288

Data
  accuracy, 43, 92
  analysis, 27, 32, 39, 40, 45, 54, 67–70, 88, 89, 91, 125, 127, 171, 172, 180, 281, 306, 357–359
  assessment, 43
  categorical, 75
  collection, 27–36, 42–125, 148, 171, 172, 178, 180, 186, 193, 195, 223, 248, 281, 285–288, 297, 304–309, 341, 359, 360
  comprehension, 40

computer systems, 105, 106
creation, 30, 39, 41, 65
error, 43
experiential, 78
lineage, 43
manipulation, 38, 41, 67
matching, 63
matrix, 37, 38, 42, 49, 57, 60, 61, 130, 326, 334
measurement, 27, 29, 30, 31, 35, 37, 39, 76
merging, 105
missing, 44, 79, 88, 92, 122, 123
nominal, 68
patterns, 130
primary, 27, 32, 34, 43, 65–67, 87, 88, 105, 110, 113, 143, 171–174, 177, 281, 357
processed/processing, 67, 88
quality, 27, 39, 42–44, 61, 97, 106, 113
raw, 67–69, 129, 243
recording, 27–60, 92, 285, 297
reliability, 63, 95, 124
representation, 31, 41
secondary, 27, 32, 34, 43, 63–67, 127, 174, 177
secondary analysis, 32, 143, 281, 285, 288
sources, 27, 30, 32, 33, 48, 64, 66, 102, 105, 341
spatial, 35, 41–44, 64, 66, 69–71, 76, 93, 128
statistics, 40
subjective, 34
transformation, 41
type, 27, 30, 32, 33, 46, 66, 68, 118, 124
validity, 39, 93, 124
variables, 43, 47, 88, 109, 111, 128, 173, 190
Dataset, 32, 43, 54, 69, 70, 72, 78, 88, 105, 122, 125, 136, 281, 297, 313, 357
Decision process, 171, 173, 174, 178
Decision-making unit (DMU), 27, 36, 37, 40, 66, 84, 171, 174
Declarative knowledge, 123, 144, 149, 152
Deductive approach, 53–56, 85
Deficiency theory, 159
Desktop virtual display, 121
Diffusion, 6, 119
Directories, 33, 104, 127
Disability, 104, 126, 145, 158, 159, 285
Disabled, 92, 125, 126, 145–160, 169
Disabling environments, 145, 146
Disadvantage, 50, 51, 93, 117, 138, 140, 141, 145, 154, 179
Disaggregation, 27, 32, 34, 35, 49, 100, 103
Discriminant analysis, 125, 127, 136–141, 191, 195–197, 355, 356

Discrimination, 141, 145, 146, 212, 252, 258, 260, 277
Disenfranchisement, 145
Districts, 6, 33, 35, 51, 75, 101, 104, 119, 122, 124, 128, 129, 223

Ecological
 association, 36, 51, 133, 143
 balances, 319
 characteristics, 315
 concerns, 323
 correlation, 71
 data, 35
 distinctiveness, 320
 fallacy, 27, 35, 36, 143
 model, 244
 perspective, 315
 position, 8
 relationship, 83, 125, 127, 130, 142, 319
 system, 10
 validity, 116, 117
Edges, 63, 73, 75, 76, 119, 124
Egocentric
 information, 122
 locations, 73
 referencing, 74
 specification, 73
Electoral voting patterns, 129
Elementary classroom environment, 172, 202–207, 222
Emotions, 65, 68, 72, 225–234, 244–246, 251, 252, 286
Environmental, 1–48, 60, 71, 72, 76, 93, 102, 117, 121–127, 130, 136, 142, 143, 146, 149, 156–169, 197, 225, 227, 231, 233, 243–259, 269, 277, 279, 282, 283, 299, 300, 311, 314–323, 334–336
 aesthetics, 4, 46, 47, 275
 context, 24, 53, 125, 127, 162, 226, 228, 283, 318
 cues, 73, 147, 149, 154, 157, 166, 299–305
 data, 46
 information, 21, 22, 24, 46, 48, 244, 315
 issues, 227, 320–323, 331, 334
 knowing, 8, 16, 22
 policy formulation, 283, 314, 315, 318–321, 332, 334
 research, 34, 35, 46
 scenarios, 248–250
 schema, 22–24, 46, 245–251, 282, 349
 setting, 71, 118, 124–126, 144, 145, 160, 180, 247, 281
Environments as contexts and arenas, 20

382 Index

Error, 42–44, 58, 59, 72, 87, 89, 96–101,
    107–113, 152, 159, 161–165, 169, 192, 195,
    196, 308, 311, 312
  nonsampling, 44, 64, 89, 106, 107, 109, 114
  sampling, 44, 64, 88, 97–101
  total survey, 43, 44, 115
Ethics committees, 119
Exocentric specification, 72–75, 122
Experiences, 1, 65, 79–85, 93, 96, 108–110,
    118, 121, 193, 197, 225–237, 243–257,
    277, 279, 281, 285–287, 301, 315, 316,
    321, 339, 342
Experimental
  approaches, 52, 124, 160, 193
  data, 31
  design, 53, 67, 93, 101, 114, 116, 118, 119,
    144, 160, 192, 193, 282, 299, 303, 307,
    312, 313
  devices, 84
  environment, 163
  group, 126, 144, 148–156, 162, 164, 169,
    193, 307, 308
  procedures, 116, 119, 197
  research, 11, 299
  results, 117
  setting, 117, 121
  situations, 117
  studies, 114, 144
  subject, 122, 167
  tasks, 121, 201
  test, 193
Experiments, 53, 64, 80–84, 109, 115–126,
    144, 147, 148, 153–156, 160–169, 171, 172,
    191–193, 197, 201, 228, 249, 281, 282,
    286, 299, 302, 306, 313
Explanation, 3, 5, 31, 45, 46, 50, 53–55, 63, 65,
    71, 79, 82, 85, 86, 133–136, 315, 358
Exploration, 147, 168, 202, 214, 220
Exploratory analysis, 54, 297
Exponential OWA operator, 291, 293
External and internal information influences in
    perceptions of scenic quality, 267
Extrapolation, 43, 117

Face-to-face interviewing, 90, 91, 93, 113, 322,
    355
Factor analysis, 136, 173, 180–182, 187,
    236–242, 264–266, 272–274, 277, 278,
    309, 332, 337
Feelings, 5, 68, 85, 179, 226–251, 286, 287, 316
Field experiments, 118
Fieldwork, 66, 78, 86
Focus group, 86

Gender/gendering, 34, 40, 50, 100, 110, 111,
    181–185, 191, 197, 200, 201, 259, 285
Geocognitive, 117, 118
Geographic/geographical
  advantage, 184
  analysis, 53
  approach, 8
  area, 88, 99, 102, 104, 128
  association, 157
  concept, 157
  data, 69, 78
  distribution, 106, 130
  error, 72
  fact, 72
  features, 69
  inquiry, 82
  knowledge, 192–196
  modeling, 53
  patterns, 2, 129
  placement, 192
  reality, 61
  region, 174
  research, 82
  sampling, 99
  scale, 36
  setting, 285
  spaces, 117, 281, 285, 301
  tradition, 63, 82
  units, 101, 287
Geographic information systems (GIS), 31, 38,
    43, 69, 125–130, 136, 142, 292
Geospatial
  abilities, 126
  competence, 155
  context, 73
  data, 73, 74
  description, 63, 65, 73
  domain, 71, 73
  information, 77, 119
  knowledge, 192, 201
  occurrences, 75
  reference, 69
  relations, 157
  route information, 76
  scale, 126
  terms, 75
Global positioning systems (GPS), 92, 93, 106
Grid, 99, 100, 120, 121, 152, 154, 308, 309,
    313
Group/groups, 2, 10, 34, 36, 37, 47, 49–51,
    59, 65, 69, 83, 86, 88, 90–94, 99–103,
    114, 125, 126, 128, 129, 136–138, 140,
    143–156, 159–164, 167, 169, 171, 172, 174,

176, 178, 190–195, 197, 199, 200, 203, 206, 208–210, 214–219, 221, 222, 236, 238–243, 248–250, 259, 264, 267, 270, 277, 278, 281–285, 299, 300, 303–322, 326–337, 343, 350, 355, 359
  age, 50, 99
  conservation perspectives, 314, 317, 318, 334, 336, 337
  contrast, 148, 151, 152, 154
  control, 120, 121, 126, 144, 148, 149, 151–154, 156, 161–165, 169, 308–313
  disabled, 126, 146–148, 154, 156, 157, 159
  environmental user, 320
  experimental, 144, 148–156, 162, 169, 193, 308
  focus, 86
  impaired, 164
  intellectually challenged, 144, 146
  intermediate, 310–313
  newcomer, 282, 299, 307–313
  modeling, 165, 322, 326
  pointing, 161
  polling booths, 137, 138, 140, 141
  purposes, 6
  special, 144, 145
  task, 156, 161, 163
  teachers, 208–210, 217–223
Groupings, 33, 34, 50, 78, 142, 208, 210, 214, 217, 220, 236–242, 247, 248, 250, 264, 317, 327–330, 336, 357

Human
  activities, 1–5, 9, 10–31, 36, 44–53, 57, 61, 79, 93, 118, 121, 125, 127, 203, 204, 342
  experiences, 1–20, 24, 25, 28, 30, 36, 44, 45, 47, 48, 52, 53, 57, 61, 79, 118, 121, 342
Hypothesis testing, 57, 203

Immediate environments, 20–23, 146
Immersive virtual systems, 121, 122
Incomplete information, 63, 71
Indicator, 27, 30, 48, 50, 51, 117, 122, 151, 161, 166, 247, 262, 265, 267, 269, 275, 278, 282, 286–293, 317, 318, 321, 330, 335, 336, 353, 355, 356
Information-generating tool, 70
Information processing, 3, 11, 91, 107, 123, 146, 245, 246, 301
In-house interviewing, 34, 90, 91, 103
Instrument design, 64, 88, 89, 107, 109, 112, 115
Intellectually challenged, 126, 144–149, 155, 166
Intermediate group, 310–313

Internal information influences, 22, 225, 226, 246, 248, 252, 253, 255, 258, 265, 267, 269, 270, 275, 277
Interpoint distance, 196, 302, 303, 308, 311, 312
Interviewer
  behavior, 44, 107, 114, 115
  training, 93, 113–115

Judgmental sampling, 102, 250, 286

Key issues, 30, 45, 88, 116
Knowledge, 12, 22, 29–32, 57–60, 70, 72, 102, 119, 122, 123, 148, 154, 158, 161, 162, 177, 178, 202, 206, 224–231, 243, 255, 301–304, 313–317, 336, 341, 342, 345, 350–358
  accumulation, 79, 355
  acquisition, 67
  advancement, 79
  analytic, 227
  configurational, 144, 151
  contributions, 341, 358
  creating, 30
  declarative, 123, 144, 149, 152
  empirical, 341
  environmental, 22, 23, 76, 149, 245
  generation, 31
  geographic, 192–196
  geospatial, 192, 201
  integrated, 22
  internal, 22, 23, 255
  one-dimensional, 154
  perspective, 349
  physical, 283
  procedural, 123
  research, 94
  route, 195
  sequential, 150
  spatial, 8, 76, 116, 146, 192, 302
  structure, 22, 123, 149, 160, 277
  survey, 195
  types of, 21–23, 30, 31, 123, 192, 277

Laboratory
  experiments, 80, 84, 117, 118, 144, 171
  versus real-world experiments, 80, 116–118, 121, 122, 126
Landmarks, 73, 76, 113, 124, 126, 147, 149, 157, 161–163, 192, 194–196, 300–303, 312
Latent
  constructs, 253, 281, 282, 316–318, 349
  information, 119

Latent *(cont.)*
  spatial structures, 282, 299, 308, 313
  status, 317
  variables, 27, 47
Learning, 1, 5, 8, 30, 79, 121, 156, 157, 160–163, 169, 172, 192–195, 202–207, 210–222, 245, 246, 281, 282, 299, 301, 304, 306, 307, 311–313
Legally blind, 161
Levels of analysis, 94, 226, 286
Levels of measurement, 27, 40, 41, 97
Lines, 63, 73, 75, 76, 121, 308
Links, 63, 73, 75, 76, 77, 246
Lists, 33, 67, 91, 104, 149, 305

Macro scale, 4, 12, 72, 94, 146, 171, 174, 286
Mail survey, 90, 93, 111, 180, 193
Map
  board, 148, 151, 152
  learning, 194, 195
Mapping a strategic plan for research, 341
Matching data and analysis, 63, 65, 68
Measurement scales, 40, 41
Mediating/intervening variables, 17–19, 181
Memory-based environmental knowledge, 22, 23, 257
Methodological complexities, 1, 202, 223, 342, 343
Microscale, 94, 171, 172, 286
Microsimulations, 143
Migration, 6, 34, 36, 119, 171, 174–179
Mobility
  aids, 167, 168
  impaired, 156, 157, 174, 179, 181–183, 188, 189
Model
  building, 50, 58, 59, 198, 201
  of migration, 176
  quality, 60, 61
Modeling social environmental factors, 127
Models, 19, 42, 45, 53, 57–59, 77, 109, 116, 123, 125, 128, 134, 136, 164, 171, 184
  analog, 59
  behavior, 35
  complex, 58
  computational process, 58, 64, 123, 124
  conceptual, 57
  deterministic, 58
  error, 43
  logit, 128
  operational, 57
  process, 357
  regression, 133
  stochastic, 58
  table, 160
Modes for survey data collection, 29, 63, 65, 66, 79, 80, 87, 89–95, 112, 113, 341, 359
Motivational approaches, 3, 108, 112, 113, 184, 245
Multidimensional scaling, 119, 126, 172, 211, 222, 260, 281, 282, 299, 303, 306, 308–310, 313, 316, 336, 355
Multiple regression analysis, 50, 125, 127, 133, 142, 335
Multistage sampling, 99–104
Multivariate analysis, 72, 73, 125, 127, 128, 130, 133, 136, 142, 171–173, 180, 195–197, 316, 336, 355

Naive and expert description, 71–73
Narrative, 63, 86, 95
Navigation, 158, 162, 169
Nearest neighbor, 74, 119
Networks, 10, 23, 63, 73, 76, 77, 101, 147, 178, 179, 246, 361
Newcomers, 282, 299, 307–313
Nodes, 73, 75–77, 118, 124
Nonmetric MDS, 119, 211, 212
Nonsampling, 44, 64, 89, 106, 107, 109, 114, 115
Nonspatial, 15, 24, 48
Norm influences, 234, 236, 237, 240, 243, 244

Objective configuration, 152, 155, 302, 309–313
Objectivity, 38, 63, 82, 83
On-site interviews, 90
Open and closed questions, 111
Ordering of questions, 111
Other, the, 126, 145, 157
Oversampling, 105

Paired comparison, 74, 119, 306–309, 313
Path analysis, 173, 180, 181, 184
Paths, 92, 119, 124, 144, 150, 155, 300
Patterns of voter support, 125–130, 133–138, 142
Perceived
  environments, 23, 71, 75, 118, 202, 210, 213, 217–222, 226, 252, 254, 258, 262–264, 267, 269, 277–279, 288, 314, 318
  relations, 72, 197, 211, 229, 288, 291, 298–300
  spatial relations, 300
Personal guidance systems (PGS), 158

Person–environment–behavior (P-E-B), 5, 13–15, 24, 25, 176, 184, 223–227, 234, 243, 279, 316
Physiological changes, 146, 228–230
Piggybacking, 105
Pilot study, 180, 197, 199, 301, 305
Plan of research, 343, 339, 341–345
Pointing, 70, 161, 163–165, 192, 302
Points, 63, 73–77, 99–101, 111, 140, 161–165, 192, 226, 234, 269, 300, 301, 303, 307–309, 313, 326
Preferences, 42, 110, 145, 172, 178, 189, 192, 195, 201, 207, 210–216, 219, 220, 222, 223, 253, 254, 257, 315, 319–321, 334–337
Psychometric testing, 117, 153, 172, 191, 193, 195, 201
Purposive sampling, 102
Push–pull migration model, 171, 177, 178, 189, 190

Q-sorting, 269, 277, 278, 324
Qualitative
  analysis, 27, 126, 282, 299
  and quantitative approaches, 27, 52, 79, 81, 82, 93–95, 126, 201, 282, 299
  methods, 81–85, 94
Quality
  issues and secondary data, 42, 43
  of life, 1, 42, 281, 285–298, 323
  of life domains, 1, 281, 282, 285–294, 297, 298
  of life subjective, 281, 282, 285–294, 297, 298
  of Measurement, 42
  and secondary data, 43
Quantitative analysis, 126
Question
  construction, 109, 112
  wording, 110, 112
Question–answer process, 107–109, 113, 115
Questionnaire design, 44, 86, 88, 93, 106, 107, 109, 110, 112, 115, 171, 173

Random digit dialing, 91, 93, 104, 105
Real world, 14, 42, 49, 57, 58, 60, 61, 64, 80, 83, 116–118, 121, 122, 126, 150, 152, 155, 164, 192, 194, 301
Recorded observations, 39
Relational location, 74
Remote infrared auditory signage (RIAS), 159, 165–169
Research proposal, 339–346, 350, 351–357

Residential
  decisions, 171, 173–175
  location choice, 4, 36, 171, 173–175, 180
  relocation, 46, 171, 173–178
Retirees, 171, 173–190
Retirement
  community, 171, 175, 176, 187
  migration/relocation, 175
  villages, 173–190
Route knowledge, 195

Salient feelings, 239
Sample
  proportion, 97
  size, 89, 97–99, 103, 119, 219, 263
Sampling, 44, 63, 64, 89, 96, 97, 103–107, 115, 205, 320, 353, 354
  accidental, 102
  cluster, 100, 101, 103
  convenience, 102
  data sources, 102
  design, 88, 93, 96, 97, 99, 101, 115, 119, 320, 354
  distribution, 57
  error, 64, 88, 89, 97–99, 101, 106, 107, 109, 114
  expert choice, 102
  fraction, 88, 89, 97–100, 103, 180
  frame/framework, 91, 93, 97, 104, 105, 354
  geographic, 99
  haphazard, 102
  issues, 88
  judgmental, 102
  multistage, 99–101, 103
  nonprobability, 64, 80, 96, 97, 101, 102, 119
  nonrandom, 144
  primary units (PSU), 88
  probability, 63, 96, 97, 99, 101, 103, 117, 171, 173, 180, 322, 354
  procedures, 44, 117
  purposive, 102
  quota, 102
  random, 97, 99, 320
  replicated, 101
  spatial data, 64, 100
  stratification, 101
  systematic, 99, 102, 180
  two-stage/two-phase, 101
  unit, 36
Sampling-based survey, 92
Sandhills region, 314, 317–322, 329, 331–337

Scale
    macro, 4, 12, 72, 94
    micro, 94, 171, 172, 174, 286
Scenic
    quality, 47, 226, 252–258, 260–271, 275–
        l279
    versions of, 252, 253, 265–271, 275–278
Scenicness, 252–256, 260, 265, 268, 275, 277,
        278
Scheme, 4, 31, 51, 88, 143, 251, 257, 298, 343
Scientific approach, 53, 56, 78
Search, 19, 46, 54, 69, 119, 147, 169, 178, 204,
        208, 234, 236, 244, 269, 305, 337, 352,
        354
Self-completion questionnaires, 89, 90, 106,
        111, 112, 180
Self-report, 194–197
Sequencing and distancing of cues, 76, 147–
        155
Sex roles, 172, 191, 193
Sex-typing of activities, 198–201
Simulation(s), 53, 64, 80, 116, 118, 119, 122,
        123, 192, 352
Sketch, 17, 66, 76, 112, 118, 149, 155, 194, 198,
        200, 201, 302
Small samples, 117
Social
    contexts, 6, 7, 23, 52, 222
    gendering, 191, 197
Sociopolitical space, 140, 143
Sorting procedure, 260, 277, 278, 322, 324
Space
    as a dimension of environments, 9
    in human context, 1, 5–7, 10, 319
Spatial, 1, 2, 6, 11, 14, 19, 20, 22–24, 34–37,
        39, 41–43, 46–51, 53, 60, 61, 64, 66, 69,
        73, 77, 101, 104, 109, 116–118, 122, 124,
        125, 127, 130, 136, 143, 146, 151, 159,
        161, 162, 172–174, 194, 196, 197, 199,
        205, 213, 215, 220, 222, 281, 282, 285,
        297, 298, 303
    abilities, 154, 159, 172, 191, 193, 195, 197,
        200, 201
    activities, 125, 145, 171–173, 191–193,
        197–201
    aggregation/disaggregation problem, 32, 35,
        49, 103, 282, 286, 297
    analysis, 36, 43, 50, 69, 128, 142, 143
    anxiety, 195
    autocorrelation, 43
    behavior, 8, 101, 105, 117, 123, 178, 300
    boundaries, 36
    choice, 8

cognition, 8, 10, 11
competence, 156
concentration, 104, 105
concepts, 46, 73, 146
conditions, 1, 10
configuration, 1, 2, 5, 172, 205–207, 209,
    224
constraints, 322
data/databases, 35, 41–44, 46, 47, 64, 69,
    127, 128, 169
decision, 118
decision support system, 125, 127, 129
definitions, 205, 270, 271
design, 213
distribution, 69, 119
economics, 8
effects, 20
forms, 5–7. 10
friction, 6
influences, 1, 5, 17, 48
information, 11, 23, 38, 48, 69, 72, 119, 301,
    313
knowledge, 8, 76, 116, 146, 192, 302
language, 71, 73, 75, 78
layout, 23, 172, 192, 202–224
learning, 8, 192
location, 38, 72
memory capacity, 146
orientation, 4, 8, 46
patterns, 125, 127–130, 133, 134, 136, 285,
    291, 294, 297
perspective, 15, 27
prepositions, 73
product, 300–303
properties, 154, 292
relation, 23, 49, 78, 155, 159, 169, 197, 206,
    300, 302, 312
representation, 42, 60, 69, 285
research, 46, 93, 118
sampling, 100
scale, 16, 32, 34, 35, 51, 103, 127, 129, 130,
    171
schema, 349
separation, 74, 308
statistics, 68
structural effects, 7, 16, 17, 19, 22, 23, 172,
    202–205, 207, 223, 282, 299, 301, 308,
    313
terms, 5
updating, 158, 165
variables, 49, 129, 136, 143
variation, 127, 128, 130, 133, 134, 282, 285,
    286, 298

Spatialization, 69, 70, 76
Special populations, 1, 117
Standardizing interview, 113
Strategy/strategies, 32, 34, 84, 94, 119, 126, 168, 204, 205, 226, 227, 251, 258, 279, 282, 287, 303, 339, 343, 344, 350
Stratification, 99–101, 354
Structuring and scaling effects of space, 13, 15, 16
Subgroup, 10, 34, 91, 99, 100, 102, 104, 148, 156, 175, 196, 307
Survey
  mail, 90, 93, 111, 180, 193
  research, 32, 36, 43, 53, 87, 88, 90, 97, 99, 103, 106, 107, 109, 114, 115, 174, 287, 297
  total error, 43, 44, 115
Survey approaches, 34, 63, 81, 87, 95, 96, 105, 171, 178, 190, 223

Talking Signs®, 157, 158, 165, 167, 168
Target population, 36, 37, 85, 88, 89, 96, 97, 99–106, 115, 117, 353, 354
Task environment, 68, 151, 163, 169, 301
Tasks, 63, 70, 82, 87, 88, 95, 107, 117–119, 121, 144, 148, 150, 155, 156, 161, 162, 167, 168, 172, 191–197, 201, 214, 283, 302, 303, 306, 308, 357, 358, 360
Technological aids, 156
Telephone interviews, 88, 91, 93, 113, 355
Theoretical traditions, 63, 83

Theory
  construction, 54–56
  development, 54, 82, 85
Theory-grounded hypothesis testing, 57
Transforming qualitative information, 68
Travel
  mode, 165, 306
  plan, 157
Types of
  data, 27, 30, 32, 33, 38, 44, 46, 66–68, 118, 124
  measurement, 40

Verbal description, 161
Virtual
  desktop, 121
  display, 121, 169
  environments, 53, 80, 118
  experiment, 64, 116, 121
  immersive, 122
  reality, 118
  simulation, 116
  system, 118, 121
  travelers, 121
  world, 121, 122
Visual impairment, 163
Voter behavior, 1, 104, 128

Wayfinding activities, 125, 126, 150, 156, 158, 165, 169, 192
Wheelchair, 150, 157–159

About the Authors

Douglas Amedeo is Professor in the Department of Anthropology and Geography at the University of Nebraska–Lincoln. He teaches courses in behavioral approaches to geographic issues and conducts research on the importance of space in environmental settings and affective responses to environments.

Reginald G. Golledge is Professor of Geography at the University of California, Santa Barbara. He teaches courses on spatial and environmental cognition and conducts research in the areas of cognitive mapping and wayfinding, analytical behavioral geography, and spatial behavior.

Robert J. Stimson is Professor of Geographical Sciences and Planning at the University of Queensland, Australia, and Director of the Urban and Regional Analysis Research Program, University of Queensland Social Research Center. He conducts research on human spatial behavior and urban and regional analysis, development, and planning.